D

GEOGRAPHY
Student Book

Ann Bowen, Andy Day, Alan Parkinson, Victoria Ellis, Paul Hunt, Rebecca Kitchen, Claire Kyndt, Garrett Nagle, Nicola Walshe and Helen Young

Series editor: Alan Parkinson

A/AS Level for AQA

CAMBRIDGE
UNIVERSITY PRESS

University Printing House, Cambridge CB2 8BS, United Kingdom

Cambridge University Press is part of the University of Cambridge.

It furthers the University's mission by disseminating knowledge in the pursuit of
education, learning and research at the highest international levels of excellence.

www.cambridge.org
Information on this title:
www.cambridge.org/9781316606322 (Paperback)
www.cambridge.org/9781316603185 (Paperback + Cambridge Elevate enhanced edition, 2 years)
www.cambridge.org/9781316594254 (Cambridge Elevate enhanced edition, 1 year)
www.cambridge.org/9781316602386 (Cambridge Elevate enhanced edition, 2 years)
www.cambridge.org/9781316609897 (Schools Site Licence)

First published 2016

Printed in the United Kingdom by Latimer Trend

A catalogue record for this publication is available from the British Library

ISBN 978-1-316-60632-2 Paperback
ISBN 978-1-316-60318-5 Paperback + Cambridge Elevate enhanced edition, 2 years
ISBN 978-1-316-59425-4 Cambridge Elevate enhanced edition, 1 year
ISBN 978-1-316-60238-6 Cambridge Elevate enhanced edition, 2 years
ISBN 978-1-316-60989-7 Schools Site Licence

Additional resources for this publication at www.cambridge.org/education

---

Approval message from AQA

This textbook has been approved by AQA for use with our qualification. This means that we have checked that it broadly covers the specification and we are satisfied with the overall quality. Full details of our approval process can be found on our website.

We approve textbooks because we know how important it is for teachers and students to have the right resources to support their teaching and learning. Please note, however, that the publisher is ultimately responsible for the editorial control and quality of this book.

Please note that when teaching the AS and A Level Geography course (7036, 7037) course, you must refer to AQA's specification as your definitive source of information. While this book has been written to match the specification, it cannot provide complete coverage of every aspect of the course.

A wide range of other useful resources can be found on the relevant subject pages of our website: www.aqa.org.uk

Contents

Introduction

This book has been written by experienced teachers to help build your understanding and enjoyment of the geography you will meet at AS and A Level.

For ease of use, the structure of this book matches the specification. The Fieldwork chapter at the end provides advice on carrying out your geographical fieldwork investigation. The Geographical skills chapter helps you to develop your skills. 'Geography without fieldwork is like science without experiments.' We hope you have the chance to develop your fieldwork skills and also to see as much of the contents of this book out in the real world as possible. We realise you may not get to dive down to a coral reef or visit a hot desert, but you should complete several days of fieldwork as part of your course, and also take the opportunity to connect your learning when visiting locations outside of school time. The book will take you through the skills you will need, and why they are used, and also show you how to present your results accurately.

At the start of each chapter, there is a box of learning outcomes. These explain what you will learn in the chapter. The **Before you start…** section lists key concepts that you should already know. We understand that not all students will have studied GCSE Geography, so most of the knowledge here is from Key Stage 3. If you are unsure of any of the learning points, we recommend that you revisit them before going on to work through the topics in the chapter, as there may be important vocabulary that you need to recognise.

Throughout the book there are **case studies**. These are in-depth studies of a recent event that demonstrates the geographical topic that you are studying. It may be helpful to learn these case studies well so that you can use them when answering questions that ask you for examples.

There are other features throughout the book to help you build knowledge and improve your skills as you go.

Key terms

Important geographical terms are written in **orange**. You can find what they mean in the **Key terms** boxes and they are also found in the **Glossary** at the back of the book.

Investigate

Investigate boxes contain ideas for independent research projects. At A Level, there will be some topics that you may wish to investigate further, which lessons don't allow time for. We offer some pointers for websites, or people who have developed some of the key ideas further. University lecturers were involved in selecting some of the content of this new A Level, and you shouldn't be afraid to develop your knowledge independently of your teachers.

Thinking like a geographer

Thinking like a geographer boxes contain questions that invite you to critically evaluate and assess links between topics. This is one of the big differences from GCSE (which was often just asking you to describe and explain). The book introduces some topics for which there are lots of different conflicting views, and you should try to develop your own thoughts, and not be afraid to share them. Geographers have a particular way of looking at the world, and this book will develop your geographical imagination and equip you with the skills that geographers need.

Physical and human

Physical and human boxes help you to analyse links between physical and human geography. No topic will be 100% one or the other, and you should remember where people are affected by physical processes, but also how we influence physical processes through our actions.

Maths for geographers

Maths for geographers boxes contain opportunities to practice and develop your quantitative skills. There has always been some maths in geography, but these skills are more important in the new A Level course. We'll provide you with examples where you can use maths to understand a process, or be able to compare locations using statistics. This is done in a structured way, so that you can also see **why** maths is important in the examples provided.

Tip

Tip boxes provide useful information or helpful hints. Sometimes a simple tip can help you unlock a difficult problem or put you back on track.

Research point

Research points suggest opportunities for investigating topics further. As with the **Investigate** boxes, these provide ideas for taking particular topics to the next level, and perhaps helping you earn those highest grades. Some research may be done online, but there are other ways to add to your understanding.

ACTIVITY

Activities contain questions to test your understanding of topics. These will take different forms, and help prepare you for various types of questions. The activities are designed to build confidence, and make use of data, images and other stimulus materials. You may work through some of these in lessons, or outside of school time.

Assess to progress

Assess to progress boxes contain practice questions so you can test your learning in more detail. Have a go at short answer questions, or the longer essay tasks which are designed to challenge you.

Making connections

Making connections boxes identify links between different geographical topics.

The **Cambridge Elevate enhanced edition** of this Student Book allows you to annotate, highlight and add bookmarks and weblinks as you work through the materials. Videos help to demonstrate important concepts and processes, and can be watched as many times as you want. You can download worksheets to help you with completing activities. The Assess to progress tool allows you to write answers to the Assess to progress questions and submit them to your teacher for marking. Look out for the following icons in the book, which show you where you can find extra resources in the **Cambridge Elevate enhanced edition**.

Visit **Cambridge Elevate** for some useful additional information or weblinks.

Visit **Cambridge Elevate** to view a video.

Visit **Cambridge Elevate** to download a worksheet.

IMPORTANT NOTE:

AQA has not approved any Cambridge Elevate content.

Geography has never been more important, and this book will help support you as you prepare for examinations, but also go beyond the page to encourage independent research. Your study skills and mathematical understanding will improve as you use the book. Stay curious as you work through the book, and remember that your personal geographies will add depth to what you find within its pages.

Good luck with your studies – now let's get started.

Water and carbon cycles

Figure 1.1 The ocean is the most obvious store of water on the planet, but did you know that it is also the second largest store of carbon? Carbon is stored as dissolved carbon dioxide in organisms such as coral and in seafloor sediments.

By the end of this chapter you should know:

- what a natural system is and how to describe the water and carbon cycles as natural systems
- the global distribution of major stores of water
- the main factors driving changes in the magnitude of these water stores
- how drainage basins and other geographical features function as natural systems
- the global distribution of major stores of carbon
- the main factors driving changes in the magnitude of these carbon stores
- the carbon budget and the impact of the carbon cycle on the atmosphere, ocean and land.

Before you start…

You should know:

- water is continuously being recycled between the land, atmosphere, rivers, lakes, oceans and living things in a process called the water cycle
- carbon is linked to fossil fuels – these are non-renewable energy resources
- the amount of carbon dioxide in the atmosphere is increasing, and this is leading to global warming.

1.1 Water and carbon cycles as natural systems

Systems in physical geography

Rain falling, wind moving the branches of a deciduous tree, meltwater dripping from the front of a glacier or sand cascading down the front of a sand dune – they all involve energy, physical geography and a change in the environment. They are natural processes, and are all also part of a larger natural system. The systems explored in this chapter are bounded.

The systems approach is a way of exploring physical processes, by focusing on one aspect within the larger environment, sometimes simplifying it so that its operation can be understood. The simplest explorations of systems view them as a 'black box'; little is known of their workings, but the inputs and outputs can be compared. The water balance of a drainage basin would be an example of this, as it could be calculated without really understanding what was going on. To understand the system, we have to open the box, and explore the internal workings. This chapter will do that for two large scale cycles.

A natural system is therefore a portion of the larger environment chosen for analysis. There are two types, and both have a number of components.

Some systems are **open**, and have inputs and outputs as well as stores and flows through the system (transfers or flux, also called throughputs). **Closed systems** tend to be cycles, with some outputs becoming inputs, and others with no inputs or outputs. In physical geography, we are particularly concerned with natural systems and the physical processes, powered by the Sun, which lead to their continued functioning without human interference.

The cycling of both water and carbon are essential to all life, and also provide us with the basis for much of the environmental change that is explored in other chapters of this book. Systems theory is useful in helping us to make sense of processes that may be global in scale, but also operate within our local area. Water could be explored at the scale of a local drainage basin, for example, but also circulates around the global hydrological cycle. Similarly, the life and death of a tree in a garden, or the management of an allotment garden involve some of the same processes as the changing use of thousands of acres of tropical rainforest.

Throughputs within the larger system may be called sub-systems. The example of the water cycle would provide us with the drainage basin sub-system. The cycling element requires there to be stores, which will change in their volume over time, fluxes, which will operate at different rates and processes which help drive the fluxes.

The water and carbon cycles are both closed systems on a global scale. On a smaller scale, however, they include open sub-systems, such as drainage basins or the workings of a tropical rainforest. The interactions between different locations on Earth, sometimes as remote tele-connections, are sometimes hard to visualise. The interactions between the water and carbon cycles are often invisible in the same way.

1.2 The water cycle

We can think of a **drainage basin** as a complex system, which is the result of the hydrological cycle operating within a geographical area of the Earth. **Hydrology** refers to the study of water on the surface of the Earth, although water is also capable of entering the surface layer of the Earth and moving

Key terms

open system: a system that has both inputs and outputs of energy or other material, and which involves a flow or exchange of material

closed system: a system that has no inputs or outputs, but which cycles energy or resources around a closed loop

drainage basin (catchment area): the area of land that provides water to a river system

hydrology: the study of water on the surface of the Earth

Making connections

Can you find a chapter in this book where there is no connection with the natural cycling of either water or carbon to some extent?

between the surface and the troposphere (the lowest layer of the atmosphere). The systems approach means that we focus on the way that water enters and leaves the drainage basin, as well as the places it may be stored, and how it moves between those stores at different rates, and over different time scales. The combination of these provides the complexity, and also means that different rivers respond differently to similar precipitation events.

Global distribution and size of major stores of water

There is a fixed amount of water on Earth and in its atmosphere, so the whole of Earth can be thought of as a closed system. The vast majority of the Earth's water is saltwater: only 2.5% of the Earth's water is fresh, and 96.5% of the saltwater is, unsurprisingly, stored in the oceans. Of the Earth's freshwater, almost 69% is locked up in glaciers and ice caps, and 30% is stored below the ground.

This leaves just 1.2% of the original freshwater available for potential use. However, much of this is locked up in ground ice. Figure 1.2 shows the distribution of major stores of water on the Earth's surface.

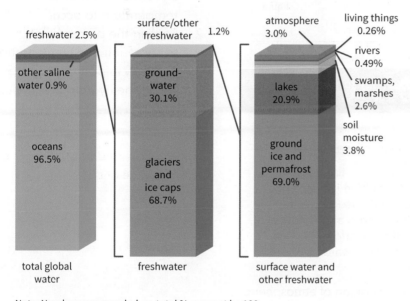

Note: Numbers are rounded, so total % may not be 100.

Figure 1.2 The major stores of water on the Earth's surface.

Water moves between these stores at different rates, and remains in storage for different periods of time. In moving from one store to another, water passes between different planetary 'spheres' or domains (also see section 1.3 The carbon cycle), including:

- the lithosphere: the rocks and soil, which may contain groundwater
- the hydrosphere: all the water on the Earth's surface including rivers, lakes, seas and oceans
- the cryosphere: the water held in the form of ice, as glaciers, ice caps and ice sheets, as well as sea ice
- the atmosphere: water held in the atmosphere as water vapour, including clouds.

Water is able to exist in three states: liquid, solid (ice) and water vapour (gas). It can move between these states by processes which require a change in temperature (Figure 1.3).

Making connections

The Sun's energy is used to drive all natural systems. This is explored further in section 6.2 Ecosystems and processes.

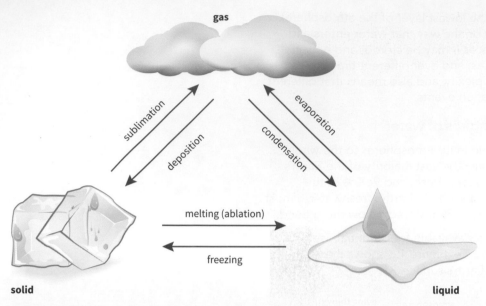

Figure 1.3 The movement of water between different physical states.

For a copy of Figure 1.3, download Worksheet 1.1 from **Cambridge Elevate**.

ACTIVITY 1.1

1   On a copy of Figure 1.3, add labels in the correct place to show the different movements of water between the states, and whether they require an increase or decrease in temperature to occur.
2   Explain the processes of evaporation and condensation, and how important they are within the hydrological cycle.

Factors driving change in the magnitude of major stores of water

The stores shown in Figure 1.2 vary temporally and spatially in the amount of water that they hold. Over time, the amount of water held in ice caps has fluctuated as global temperatures have changed. During the Ice Ages, the amount increased dramatically; at present, the Arctic sea ice is at a historical minimum. There have also been significant losses from the world's Polar ice sheets – Greenland and Antarctica. As the ice sheets decline, water is released into the oceans.

Similarly, changes in weather patterns cause the relative position of atmospheric moisture to change. Increasingly large areas of Earth are becoming affected by desertification (see Chapter 2 Hot desert systems and landscapes), with reduced soil moisture, and in some parts of the world rivers are drying up. This does not change the overall amount of water on Earth, which remains unchanged, but controls the way that is distributed globally. This may cause shortages more locally.

Rising warm air holds water vapour. As the water vapour rises, such as over relief barriers, it cools and **condenses** into clouds. These form on the windward side of a relief barrier or at the summit. Latent heat, which is used in **evaporation**, may be released at this point, slowing down the rate of cooling.

Cryospheric processes act when the temperature gets close to freezing point, or below. When water freezes, it is no longer part of the diurnal circulation. During the Ice Ages, global sea level dropped as water was 'locked away' as ice on the land. Today, some communities rely on glaciers for their water supply, but these are rapidly melting. For example, the rate of melting of Andean glaciers is threatening many cities in Peru.

A startling image created by the USGS (Figure 1.4) shows how fragile our water supply is. The blue sphere represents the amount of water relative to the size of the Earth, and of course the freshwater is a tiny fraction of that.

 Key terms

condensation: a change in state from water vapour to liquid as a result of cooling

evaporation: a change in state from liquid water to water vapour, as a result of heating

Figure 1.4 All Earth's water is contained in the blue spheres.

Drainage basins as open systems

A drainage basin or catchment area is the area of land drained by a particular river and its tributaries. Drainage basins can vary in size from a few square kilometres to millions of square kilometres, such as the area drained by the River Nile in north-east Africa. The physical boundary of a drainage basin is called a **watershed**. The watershed is marked by higher land than the surrounding area, sometimes by high mountains; from here, water is directed downslope towards the nearest river channel. Water is drained into rivers via their tributaries.

Figure 1.5 shows the different components of the drainage basin system: the inputs, outputs, stores and flows through the system. The stores are different sizes and store water for different lengths of time.

The overall balance of inputs and outputs is shown in the **water budget** or water balance equation:

$$\text{precipitation} = \text{evaporation} + \text{transpiration} + \text{river flow} \pm \text{storage}$$

The UK's water balance has a seasonal pattern in which groundwater is filled up during winter and drawn on during the warm summer months, when plants also use more water. At the end of a long dry period, there may be a water deficit. If there are several dry years in a row, river levels might be affected and crop yields could decline. Soil moisture is important in influencing other flows within the cycle. The top of the **saturated** soil is marked by the **water table**. If this is at the surface there will be higher surface runoff.

Key terms

watershed: the edge of a drainage basin

water budget: the overall balance of inputs and outputs in a drainage basin over time

saturated: all the available spaces between the soil particles are filled with water

water table: the level of the top of the saturated soil beneath the ground

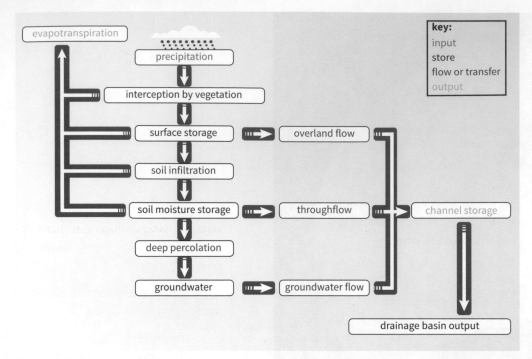

Figure 1.5 Drainage basin hydrological cycle.

Inputs

The only input for the drainage basin is **precipitation**, which is water moving from the atmosphere to the ground. Its quantity, distribution, duration and intensity will affect the pattern of flow of the river. The route that a rainfall event takes as it moves across the basin will also influence the **response** of the catchment. A storm spending a lot of time over the catchment will result in higher inputs than one that just clips the edge of it. The flowing water results in a movement of sediment.

Stores

Stores are those parts of the system where water is held in some state for a period of time. They include:

- Interception storage: water held on vegetation for a short period of time after precipitation has fallen. The amount of water held in interception storage will vary according to the time of year and the type of ground cover. A typical tree will catch water on its leaf surfaces: broadleaved trees will catch more than coniferous trees. This may then evaporate from these open surfaces without ever reaching the ground (hence the term 'interception'). Water will also fall off leaves as throughfall (stand under trees after rain has been falling and you will experience this) or stemflow (where water flows along branches and down tree trunks).
- Vegetation storage: water taken up by vegetation and absorbed into it. This will remain in the vegetation for a variable period of time, before being lost by **transpiration**.
- Soil moisture storage and soil water: water will soak into most soils at a rate that depends on the nature and structure of the soil (the **infiltration capacity**). Previous precipitation may fill up some of this storage and be held as soil water. Water held in the soil may evaporate if it is close

---

Key terms

precipitation: the movement of water from the atmosphere to the ground surface. It can take several forms, including rain, snow, sleet, hail and fog

response: the way that a river responds following the input of precipitation: some rivers rise quickly and are said to be 'flashy'; others rise and fall more slowly

transpiration: the process by which plants lose water through stomata (pores) in their leaves into the atmosphere

infiltration capacity: the rate at which water is able to pass through a soil (measured in mm/hr) – this will be high for a sandy soil; lower for a clay soil

to the surface or be taken up by vegetation, from where it is lost by transpiration. Trees take up huge quantities of water through their root systems (Figure 1.6). They also shade nearby soil, which reduces water loss.

- Surface (depression) storage: water will be stored on the surface if the ground below is impermeable. Water will naturally flow into surface depressions, such as those found on roads and in car parks, and remain there until it evaporates. This may also happen where the ground is saturated, for example in fields, forming temporary depression stores.
- Channel storage: water is temporarily stored in river channels as it passes through a drainage basin. This store will increase after rainfall, particularly if the river overtops its banks or reaches the bankfull stage.

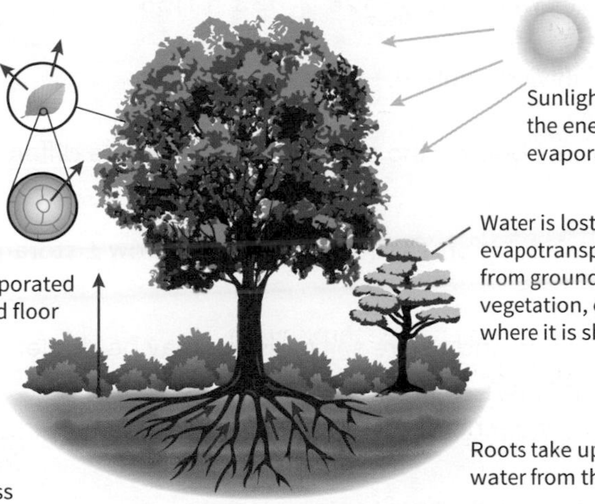

Key terms

impermeable: a surface that does not allow water to pass through it

groundwater flow: water moving through the soil

throughflow (or interflow): water moving through the rocks beneath the soil at a very slow rate

permeable: a surface that allows water to pass through it

overland flow (surface runoff): water flowing over the ground surface; this may be a result of impermeable surfaces, including frozen ground, or infiltration excess during heavy rainfall

channel flow: water held in the channel as it moves through the drainage basin. This will also act as temporary storage

evapotranspiration: the loss of water by evaporation and transpiration combined – a term sometimes used in equations representing water balance

runoff: water and sediment being moved down the river channel, and out of the catchment area

Following rainfall, water is intercepted by the forest canopy and directly evaporated back to the atmosphere

Water is lost through stomata (pores) on the surface of a leaf; when stomata are open, transpiration rates increase, especially in windy conditions

Some water is evaporated from the woodland floor

Soil dries out in summer, so less water is available; trees close their stomata to reduce transpiration loss

Sunlight provides the energy for evaporation

Water is lost by evapotranspiration from ground vegetation, even where it is sheltered

Roots take up water from the soil

Figure 1.6 How trees use water.

Flows

Water moves between stores at different rates. Any water that falls onto an **impermeable** surface will flow downhill. It then may enter artificial drainage systems or soak into the ground in processes known as **groundwater flow** and **throughflow (interflow)**. As rain starts to fall, it may also run off normally **permeable** surfaces in the form of **overland flow (surface runoff)** if the rainfall is sufficiently intense. Over time, the ground may become saturated. Water running over the surface may also wash fine particles into any gaps between soil particles and seal them.

Once water finds its way into surface water channels, it will move as **channel flow**. This tends to be quite turbulent flow, as can be seen in rivers which are seldom clear.

Outputs

Water is lost from the drainage basin back into the atmosphere as evaporation and also as transpiration from the vegetation that grows there (**evapotranspiration**). Amounts will vary depending on the climate, the soil type and geology, and the nature of the surface drainage.

Runoff may form the main output in some drainage basins, either over the surface (see overland flow) or in the river channels, which exit the drainage basin

Making connections

The movement of water through the landscape and the importance of the cryosphere are relevant to a number of topics, including Chapter 4 Glacial systems and landscapes and Chapter 11 Resource security.

as a result of infiltration excess. The area from which runoff occurs will increase during a precipitation event, as more of the drainage basin reaches saturation point. This increases the area of land that may contribute water to the channel as surface runoff. Management of drainage basins sometimes involves controlling the speed of runoff.

Maths for geographers

Table 1.1 shows data relating to the movement of water in and out of a drainage basin in north-west England over a year. It shows the pattern of precipitation (input) and evapotranspiration (output).

	J	F	M	A	M	J	J	A	S	O	N	D
precipitation (mm)	130	126	120	115	110	96	105	112	123	130	134	112
evapotranspiration (mm)	22	34	60	90	110	128	133	136	125	80	42	18

Table 1.1 Water balance values for a location in north-west England.

1 Construct a line graph for each of the two variables on the same set of axes. Use a different colour for each.
2 Using the water budget equation:

$$\text{precipitation} = \text{evaporation} + \text{transpiration} + \text{river flow} \pm \text{storage}$$

  a Identify months when there is a surplus of water available.
  b Identify months when there is a water deficit, and where soil moisture may be depleted because evapotranspiration is greater than precipitation.
  c Identify months when groundwater is being recharged.
3 Add up the total value.
  a How much water is available for river flow and storage?
  b What would be the impact on river flow of a year with above average precipitation?
  c What changes could be made to this drainage basin to reduce the amount of water available for river flow?

 For a copy of the axes for question 1, download Worksheet 1.2 from **Cambridge Elevate**.

Runoff variation and the flood hydrograph

The response of a river to a period of rainfall can be shown on a **hydrograph**. This generally shows a steady **base flow**, which may rise or fall during periods of rainfall or drought, but is usually within specific parameters based on the local geology and average monthly precipitation levels. River gauges, which measure **discharge**, are now monitored constantly and send back readings remotely. River discharge is the volume of water flowing through a river channel at any given point in a given time. The hydrograph that is produced by a particular river will reflect its response to the initial input of precipitation.

The discharge of a river (Q) is calculated using the equation:

$$Q = VA$$

where V is the velocity of the river (in metres per second) and A is the mean cross-sectional area (in metres squared). This results in a measurement of discharge in cubic metres per second (cumecs).

 Key terms

hydrograph: a graph of the water level or base flow in a river over a period of time, such as a year, and the response of the river to a precipitation event

base flow: the normal day-to-day flow of a river

discharge: water flowing through a river channel at any given point and is measured in cubic metres per second (cumecs)

A typical value for a small mountain stream would be less than 1 cumec, whereas the River Thames through London after rainfall has a flow of hundreds of cumecs.

Figure 1.7 is a flood hydrograph for a typical river and shows the response of the river to a precipitation event. Flood hydrographs are drawn over a short time period of hours or days.

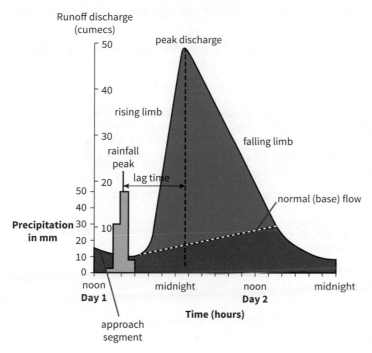

Figure 1.7 A typical flood hydrograph.

The peak rainfall time is marked on the hydrograph. You can see how the river rises a few hours after the rainfall event (**rising limb**). However, there is a time delay (the **lag time**) between peak rainfall and peak discharge as water needs to make its way to the river channel by various means. The delayed arrival from some types of flow might extend the peak of the graph (peak discharge) and therefore the lag time. The graph shows a **falling limb**, where the river is gradually returning to its normal, or base, flow. The total area under the hydrograph can be used to calculate how much water a rainfall event has contributed to the river.

The shape of the hydrograph for each river will vary depending on the nature of the rainfall that caused the discharge to increase. Intense rainfall will cause a more rapid increase than less intense rainfall.

Prolonged rainfall may take time to register, but the period of high flow might be extended. Water takes time to enter the river by different routes, and the falling limb will have a different gradient depending on the nature of these flows.

The route taken by any precipitation event may influence how river gauges respond. They are located at a few places down the course, and will not respond to rainfall that falls lower down the channel.

Factors affecting river discharge

Both physical and human factors can cause a river's discharge to vary over time (Tables 1.2 and 1.3 respectively). Although these are often local changes, some of the controlling factors may change as a result of processes of change on a

ACTIVITY 1.2

The rivers in England are monitored by the Environment Agency. All river gauges now have a weblink so that the recent flow is monitored and displayed live, with Twitter updates for each one.

Find your nearest river gauge and monitor it for the time that you are learning this topic.

1　What changes do you notice?
2　How does the river respond to any rainfall events during this time?
3　How does it compare to other gauge locations which may be further up or down the river channel? Can any aspects of the drainage basin be deduced from changes in the flow at particular gauges?

 Look on **Cambridge Elevate** to access the GaugeMap (www.cambridge.org/links/gase6001).

 Look on **Cambridge Elevate** for rivers in Wales. Go to Natural Resources Wales (www.cambrige.org/links/gase6002).

larger scale, such as the shifting of rainfall patterns over the longer term. Many desert regions, for example, have previously had a wetter climatic pattern which may have formed some of the relict landforms that are found there. These factors influence the working of the natural drainage basin system.

Geology (and soils)	Impermeable rocks (and clay soils) result in a rapid rise in discharge, whereas permeable or porous rocks may store water for a period, along with sandy soils which allow water to enter them (a high infiltration capacity).
Relief	Steep slopes cause rapid water movement in upland areas, whereas gentle slopes transfer water more slowly.
Drainage density	This refers to the average length of stream channels per square kilometre – higher values increase discharge levels more rapidly.
Vegetation	Vegetation intercepts precipitation, which may then be lost by evapotranspiration. Well-vegetated catchments delay rises in river discharge as the water is caught up on leaves or taken up by plants. In areas with deciduous trees there may also be seasonal variations in drainage as tree cover grows in spring and leaves are shed in autumn.
Antecedent soil moisture	Previous rainfall may have caused soil storage to be at, or close to, saturation, and discharge may be higher.
Precipitation type	Snow will release water once it melts, which may be weeks or months after it has fallen, and result in raised river levels after warm weather.
Precipitation intensity	Thunderstorms may provide rainfall which exceeds the infiltration capacity of the soil and lead to flash flooding. These are more common in summer than at other times of year.

Table 1.2 Physical factors affecting river discharge.

Land use	Catchment that has stopped being natural will tend to offer an impermeable surface to rainfall and speed drainage. This is particularly the case where there is additional drainage installed. This would speed up the flow of water into the river channel, and there could also be problems if the drains are blocked by storm debris.
Agriculture	Some farming practices may result in extra surface drainage. Livestock can compress the surface soil with their hooves, and loose soil may also be washed away. This not only affects water quality in the river but also potentially increases the risk of flooding. Water may also be abstracted from the river for use in irrigation during dry periods. This will be done under licence.
Construction	Some construction may restrict the channel. Water may flow faster through bridges, which may also become blocked by floating debris during high flow and form temporary debris dams. There may also be reservoirs, which hold back water, and delay its arrival into the lower channel. Any levees or raised riverbanks ultimately increase the channel capacity and may change the efficiency of the channel (its ability to transfer water). In places like Boscastle in Cornwall, which have experienced flash flooding, local river channels are often placed in larger artificial courses, and bridge levels are raised.

Table 1.3 Human factors affecting river discharge.

Tip

Although the term 'infiltration capacity' sounds like it is an amount of water that the soil can hold, it is actually a rate (measured in mm/hour).

Making connections

Flooding is a significant hazard, and the location of many cities increases their flood risk. This is explored in section 9.5 Urban drainage.

Watch a video on **Cambridge Elevate** about the effects of flooding in Tewkesbury, UK.

Changes in the water cycle over time

All drainage basins will undergo natural variations over time, which will influence the water cycle. These vary in scale and also through the year. There will be seasonal changes.

Storm events will occur during the year. Some individual storms may be significant enough to result in major changes, such as the record rainfall that fell in parts of Cumbria in December 2015. Water may also be abstracted at certain times of year for irrigation, which may result in a lowering of the water levels. If oxygen levels in the river drop as a result, fish are threatened. For this reason, abstraction of water on a large scale requires a license.

Catchments are also subject to change as a result of human activities which influence the way they are managed and used. Management of the river for water supply, construction along its course and the seasonal changes in weather and vegetation cover will also influence the way that water moves through the drainage basin.

Typical changes

Typical changes which might be observed include:

- the removal of vegetation, such as deforestation (removal of trees) for construction
- impermeable surfaces such as concrete and tarmac replacing permeable ones as houses and roads are built as a result of urbanisation (Figure 1.8)
- changing land-use practices by farmers, such as drainage, or changes in cropping.

Each of these changes would change the balance of transfers between the different stores, and the overall water balance at the end of each year. This may affect the availability of soil moisture and the flow in river channels. The water cycle will continue, but the relative importance of certain stores, and the rate of movement through the cycle, will also vary.

Figure 1.8 House construction changes the drainage basin's response to rainfall.

ACTIVITY 1.3

1 Use Ordnance Survey maps of different ages to explore the changes that have taken place in a selected 5 km stretch of river. Produce an annotated map or sketch map to show the changes that you identify.

Tip

Access Ordnance Survey maps of different ages to explore the changes that have taken place in your local area, *particularly on the urban–rural fringe of settlements, where the rate of change has often been fastest.* These can be accessed online if you do not have paper copies.

1.3 The carbon cycle

Carbon is the fourth most common element in the universe and its chemical properties mean it is essential to all life on Earth. The Earth's carbon cycle is, like water, a closed system (in that only insignificant volumes of carbon are added to, or lost from, the Earth) but consisting of key sub-systems within. These operate as open systems, exchanging and transferring carbon between them and, in doing so, affect conditions for all life on Earth. They are characterised by inputs, flows (flux), stores (reservoirs) and outputs operating between the upper atmosphere and the lower reaches of the Earth's crust. Carbon compounds are not only the basis for all life, but in changing forms and volumes they alter the conditions for how environments (and species) develop. Varying amounts of carbon in the atmosphere, the oceans and in rocks alter the climate, the shell-building capacity of life in the seas and the rate of erosion of a continent's surface. The geography of the living, and many non-living, features of the planet at any one period in the Earth's history is largely a response to the state of carbon in its various sub-systems.

Global distribution and size of major stores of carbon

Carbon compounds may take a range of chemical forms: as a gas (carbon dioxide, methane), as a liquid (calcium bicarbonate, carbonic acid) and as a solid (carbonate rocks). Its distribution is classified in six key zonations, or spheres, of the planet.

These six zonations are:

- The atmosphere: carbon dioxide (CO_2) makes up only 0.04% of the Earth's atmosphere but it is the key component, along with sunlight and water, of photosynthesis in plants. It also reacts readily with water droplets to form carbonic acid, resulting in rain that is naturally acidic. Methane is a compound of carbon and hydrogen (CH_4) and is produced by biological processes.
- The biosphere: this is the living fabric that comprises plants and animals. Carbon is extracted from the atmosphere and oceans and builds **organic** (living) structures which, when they reach the end of their life cycle, return it to the atmosphere or ocean as carbon dioxide and other gases, or decompose into the soil or ocean bed as carbon compounds.
- The cryosphere: the tundra regions contain vast stores of organic carbon within and just above the permafrost layer. Vegetation, growing under warmer conditions, has been locked into a cold state of reduced decomposition. It contains approximately 2.5 times the amount of carbon currently in the atmosphere.
- The pedosphere: the soil layer that represents the skin of the Earth is composed of millions of organisms as well as weathered rock. Carbon is present in gaseous, liquid and solid form in both organic as well as **non-organic** (non-living) soil structure.
- The lithosphere: the rock of the Earth's crust is by far the largest store of carbon (Figure 1.9). It is locked into solid form in carbon-based rocks such as dolomite, limestone and chalk, and is concentrated in stocks of fossilised organic remains (oil, gas and coal) and in organic-rich rocks where it is more dispersed (oil and gas shales). Carbon rocks are gradually shifting location due to the movement of the Earth's tectonic plates.
- The hydrosphere: covering 71% of the Earth's surface, the oceans contain the second largest quantity of carbon in both organic and non-organic forms. Much is dissolved carbon dioxide absorbed from the atmosphere, some is in organisms such as plankton, corals and shells, and much is in seafloor sediments containing both methane (CH_4) and carbon dioxide (CO_2).

Key terms

organic: matter derived from living things; both plant and animal residues

non-organic: compounds that derive from non-living matter

Figure 1.9 Chalk cliffs of the English Channel represent a store of fossilised calcium carbonate in an exposed section of the lithosphere.

Table 1.4 shows the global carbon reservoirs. It indicates that the world's oceans and rocks contain by far the largest proportions of carbon, particularly the latter. The category **sedimentary rocks** includes carbon locked into solid lithology, diffuse remains of organic life and concentrations of the same which, due to local geology, have concentrated into coal seams, oil and gas reserves and sediments that are accumulating on ocean floors at the earliest stage of a **lithification** process (Figure 1.10).

Major store		Gigatons carbon (GtC)	Gigatons carbon (sub group)
sedimentary rocks		51×10^6	
	limestone		40×10^6
	organic carbon		10×10^6
	fossil fuels		4.7×10^3
	marine sediments		2.5×10^3
world oceans		39×10^3	
	carbonate ions		37×10^3
	bicarbonate ions		1.3×10^3
	dissolved CO_2		0.7×10^3
soils		1.6×10^3	
permafrost		0.9×10^3	
atmospheric CO_2		0.76×10^3	
living biomass		0.6×10^3	

Table 1.4 Global carbon reservoirs.

 Key terms

sedimentary rocks: rocks resulting from heat and pressure compressing and consolidating depositional material; they most often form on seafloors (e.g. limestone, chalk and shale)

lithification: the process by which sediments become compressed into solid rock (lithology) due to pressure (e.g. mud into shale, calcium carbonate into chalk and limestone)

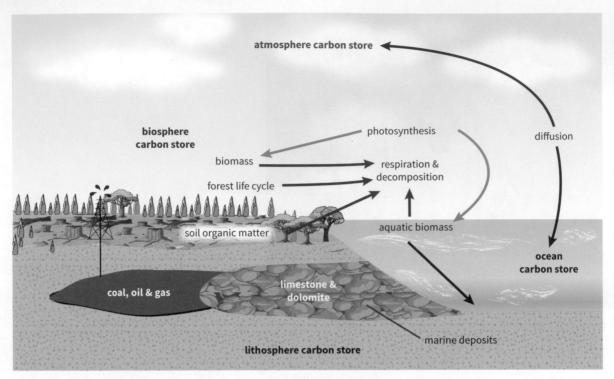

Figure 1.10 Carbon stores.

Maths for geographers

Study Table 1.4

1   The sedimentary rocks group is measured in units to the power of
    six (10^6), as are the sub-groups 'limestone' and 'organic carbon'.
    Convert these values to the power of three (10^3) to match the rest of
    the table.
2   What proportion of the total global carbon reservoirs does the combined
    group 'sedimentary rocks and world oceans' constitute?
3   Construct a pie chart to represent the Earth's carbon reservoirs.

Factors driving change in the magnitude of major stores of carbon

Carbon stores represent a natural reservoir of carbon before it is transferred into
another chemical or physical environment. Each store can be both a **carbon
source** and a **carbon sink**:

*   Carbon sources (natural and human) release more carbon than they absorb.
*   Carbon sinks absorb more carbon than they release.

The size of the Earth's carbon stores fluctuates as a result of a number of
processes in all spheres of the planet. Some change rapidly as a result of
relatively fast input and output flows (**fast carbon cycles**), while others show
long-term stability as they are subject to transfers over a timescale measured in
millions of years (**slow carbon cycles**).

With its chemical flexibility, carbon takes many forms and goes through
many processes or flows and transfers. The systems involved represent carbon
sub-cycles and they take place within and at the interface between the
dominant spheres of the planet.

Key terms

carbon source: a store in which
the release of carbon occurs at a
faster rate than it is absorbed

carbon sink: a store in which the
absorption of carbon occurs at a
faster rate than it is released

fast carbon cycle: relatively rapid
transfers of carbon compounds
over years, decades and centuries

slow carbon cycle: transfers
of carbon compounds over
extensive timescales (possibly
millions of years)

Cycle duration

There are four major cycles of carbon that operate over different timescales:

- The fast organic carbon cycle operates from months to centuries and mainly involves the transfers of organic carbon via living things – plants and animals – between the atmosphere, soil and biosphere.
- The fast non-organic carbon cycle involves **ocean–atmosphere exchange** of carbon dioxide depending upon the relative conditions of both.
- The slow organic cycle takes hundreds of millions of years and involves the long-term sequestration of the remains of marine creatures and terrestrial forests as fossil deposits of oil, gas and coal.
- The slow non-organic cycle, taking place over a similar timescale, involves the transfer of carbon from the atmosphere to the hydrosphere and then to sedimentary stores of carbon-rich rocks in the lithosphere, which are recycled via tectonic movements and subsequent volcanic activity back into the atmosphere.

Factors in fast carbon cycles

Figure 1.11 shows that the fast carbon cycle includes **terrestrial** as well as **marine** processes. The organic components of the system include photosynthesis, respiration, decomposition, digestion and excretion. Other natural phenomena such as volcanic eruptions and wildfires can also have pronounced short-term effects on the amount of atmospheric carbon dioxide.

Key terms

ocean–atmosphere exchange: the ability of the ocean to both absorb CO_2 from, and release it to, the atmosphere, depending on ocean and atmospheric conditions

terrestrial: applying to the land rather than air or water

marine: applying to seas and oceans

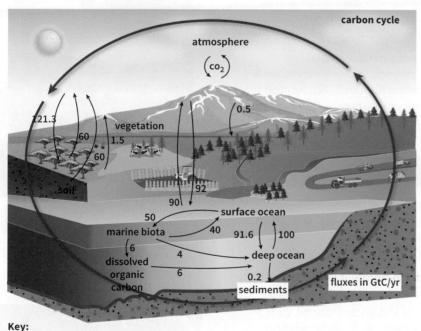

Key:
GtC/yr = gigatonnes of carbon per year
(1 gigatonne = 10^9 metric tonnes, which is the mass of one cubic kilometre of water
1 GtC corresponds to ~3.67 Gt CO_2)

Figure 1.11 The fast carbon cycle.

Photosynthesis: the process by which plants draw in carbon dioxide to create essential sugars via the action of sunlight, is one of the most significant influences on the amount of atmospheric carbon dioxide.

$$6CO_2 + 6H_2O \xrightarrow{\text{sunlight}} C_6H_{12}O_6 + 6O_2 + \text{energy}$$

$$\text{carbon dioxide} + \text{water} \xrightarrow{\text{sunlight}} \text{glucose} + \text{oxygen} + \text{energy}$$

The growth of vast forests absorbs carbon dioxide annually, but the forests release it at a slower rate as vegetation dies and decomposes, meaning these forests represent a carbon sink.

Respiration and digestion: are two other processes in the biosphere that affect the magnitude of carbon stores on Earth. All animals, whether marine or terrestrial, release carbon in the form of carbon dioxide (from respiration) and methane (from digestion). Approximately half of the carbon dioxide absorbed by terrestial plants via photosynthesis is returned to the atmosphere as a result of plant respiration. Animal respiration adds to this release. Organic compounds combine with oxygen during respiration, releasing carbon dioxide and water in the process.

$$C_6H_{12}O_6 + 6O_2 \longrightarrow 6CO_2 + 6H_2O + energy$$

$$glucose + oxygen \longrightarrow carbon\ dioxide + water + energy$$

Decomposition: is another process by which CO_2 is returned to the atmosphere. Approximately 50% of the CO_2 absorbed by photosynthesis is released in plant respiration. The remainder is contained in plant structures, most of which is released later when plants, or their parts, die. This process is known as decomposition or microbial respiration. The decomposing plants release carbon dioxide where oxygen is available to them, and methane in anaerobic conditions.

$$C_6H_{12}O_6 \longrightarrow 3CO_2 + 3CH_4$$

$$organic\ compounds \longrightarrow carbon\ dioxide + methane$$

The remaining carbon is retained in the soil as humus – organic material that supplies carbon compounds to the roots of growing plants and is recycled as part of their growth process, together with plant remains.

Combustion: wildfires and persistent smouldering of peat accumulations contribute to a more rapid release of carbon compounds into the atmosphere than would take place under microbial decomposition (Figure 1.12). Ignited by lightning or volcanic eruptions, naturally occurring combustion of dry vegetation rapidly converts solid carbon-rich material into gaseous carbon dioxide.

Thinking like a geographer

Geographers need to consider changes to systems over different timescales. Why is burning biomass in power stations considered 'carbon neutral' when burning coal – which is fossilised biomass – is not?

Factors in slow carbon cycles

The storage of carbon over geological timescales is known as (natural) **carbon sequestration**. This refers to the operation of long-term sinks accumulating substantial stores of carbon that are not released back into the global carbon system for millions of years.

Tip

The term 'carbon sequestration' should be classified as 'natural' to distinguish the process in slow carbon cycle stores from the current human (or artificial) procedure of deliberately burying carbon dioxide in the depleted strata of exhausted oil and gas reserves – also known as carbon capture and storage (CCS).

Making connections

Examine further the delicate relationship between living organisms and their environment in section 6.1 Ecosystems and sustainability.

Figure 1.12 Tundra combustion releasing gaseous CO_2 from peat accumulations.

Key term

carbon sequestration: the removal of carbon from active cycles by natural or artificial transfer and burial in a long-term store

Making connections

Read about some of the schemes for carbon sequestration being implemented by energy companies to reduce carbon emissions in section 11.2 Natural resource issues.

For activities on carbon cycles, download Worksheets 1.3 and 1.4 from **Cambridge Elevate**.

Carbon sequestration (natural): is a range of processes by which carbon dioxide is removed from the atmosphere and oceans to be held in solid or liquid form in a long-term store. A slow transfer of carbon takes place in oceans as organic matter falls to the ocean floor, accumulates and forms carbon-rich strata that lithifies (turns to rock).

Burial and compaction: decomposed plants and animals that lived millions of years ago have been buried. Over time, these layers of organic matter have been greatly compressed to form today's carbon-rich oil, coal and gas hydrocarbons.

Chemical weathering: when atmospheric CO_2 is dissolved within precipitation, the solution is slightly acidic and reacts with certain unstable rocks, releasing potassium, sodium, magnesium and calcium ions that eventually find their way to the ocean. Here, the calcium ions combine with bicarbonate ions to form calcium bicarbonate, which is absorbed by corals, plankton and shell-building creatures. These organisms convert it into secretions of solid calcium carbonate which eventually end up on the ocean floor where, over millions of years, layers of shells and skeletal remains are compressed to form rocks such as limestone and dolomite. This is another form of carbon sequestration.

Long-term changes to the carbon cycle

The highest concentration of carbon dioxide in the atmosphere occurred 500 million years ago with 7000 parts per million (ppm). In the last 2 million years (part of the Quaternary Ice Age), the amount has reduced to as low as 180 ppm. For extensive periods of time, however, carbon dioxide has operated within a negative feedback loop: a rise in inputs has an impact on outputs which serve to dampen down the next cycle of inputs. As atmospheric carbon has risen, it has stimulated growth in vegetation, which has absorbed more carbon dioxide and regulated the atmospheric levels. Several key factors interact to regulate change over the long term.

Global temperatures:

- Lower temperatures restrict plant growth, reducing CO_2 release from vegetation.
- A colder ocean increases its capacity to absorb CO_2 from the atmosphere.
- Cooler oceans restrict marine biology reducing CO_2 absorption for photosynthesis.
- Changing ocean temperatures may impede the flow of currents bringing nutrients to the surface to feed marine biology.
- **Methane hydrates** are more likely to form on the ocean floor of colder seas trapping carbon.

The Earth goes through periods of relatively stable climate when carbon cycles are in a state of **dynamic equilibrium** and relative balance has been achieved between the various stores. But these eras can be interrupted by an alteration of conditions that introduce a change in inputs, outputs or transfers. Since the last interglacial began, around 20 000 years ago, there has been a positive **feedback loop** with rising global temperatures reflected in rising levels of CO_2 to around 300 ppm by the start of the Industrial Revolution in the 19th century (Figure 1.13). The average interglacial carbon dioxide content is 280 ppm.

Tip

Be able to distinguish between positive and negative feedback loops/cycles. A 'positive feedback loop' is when an increase in inputs results in a change in outputs that produce a further increase in inputs. The change becomes self-sustaining. In releasing fossil-fuel carbon into the atmosphere human activity is increasing ocean temperature which is then less able to absorb CO_2; tundra regions are melting releasing stored carbon, and polar ice melts increasing solar radiation absorption. All increase air temperatures yet further which continue to magnify the effects.

Key terms

methane hydrates: crystalline structures within sediment deposits of continental shelves and polar seas consisting of methane locked within an ice framework

dynamic equilibrium: relative stability in a cycle when key components have reached a state of balance. A change in a component can induce change in the rest of system so that equilibrium is lost

feedback loop: where an output may become an input into another part of the same system, instigating a further change in the output

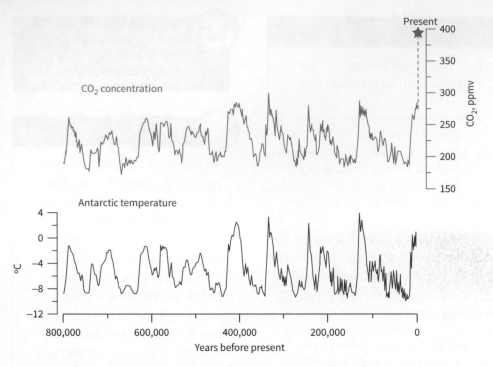

Figure 1.13 Graph of CO_2 concentration and Antarctic temperature.

Asteroid impact: the impact of the asteroid event 65 million years ago, which extinguished vast swathes of life on land and in the sea, is believed to have released large quantities of carbon. The vaporisation of carbonate rocks on impact created large amounts of carbon dioxide, but even more carbon monoxide. It also released huge amounts of organic carbon in the subsequent combustion of vegetation in the impact vicinity.

Carbon cycle exchange imbalance: the transfer of carbon dioxide from the atmosphere and surface geology to the ocean and back is not in equilibrium, but has a small yet consistent bias in favour of ocean absorption and burial. This is thought to be due to volcanic activity slowing down over time, reducing the rate of carbon recycling.

Short-term changes to the carbon cycle

Natural events

- Climatic events: drought, floods and other climate factors that increase or decrease vegetation affect the biological store of carbon.
- Disease and predators: insect damage is ravaging much of the coniferous woodland of Canada. The loss of vast forests due to the pine bark beetle is damaging this particular carbon store.
- Natural hazards: wildfires and volcanic activity release significant amounts of carbon. The combustion of vegetation and the loss of photosynthesising capacity result in higher CO_2 levels in years of frequent wildfire incidence. Sporadic eruption events add to carbon levels via direct emission.
- Ocean conditions: if the upwelling of nutrient-bearing cold currents from ocean depths increases, surface plankton growth is stimulated, increasing their rate of CO_2 absorption (Figure 1.14).

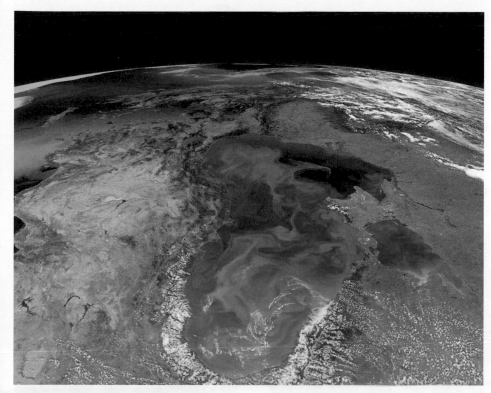

Figure 1.14 An algal bloom of plankton in the Black Sea.

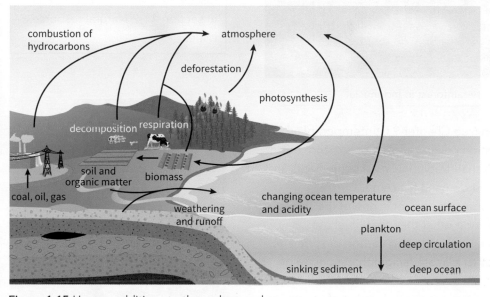

Figure 1.15 Human additions to the carbon cycle.

Research point

Research carbon offset schemes. What do they invest in and how do they operate? Are they able to make a significant difference or are they examples of 'greenwashing'?

Human impact

Besides the natural processes at work bringing about changes in the magnitude of the planet's carbon stores, there are **anthropogenic** (human) processes that also affect it (Figure 1.15).

Key human influences on carbon cycles include:

Key term

anthropogenic: impacts as a consequence of human activity

- Deforestation: the destruction of forests for timber, agricultural land, hydroelectric power generation and mineral exploitation removes a natural carbon store, reduces soil carbon content and closes down photosynthesis.

- Afforestation: the planting of new forests and reforestation (regrowth of forest after an alternative land use) may increase absorption of carbon dioxide. This is one form of **carbon offsetting** scheme.
- Agriculture: intensive use of artificial fertilisers and other farm chemicals can lead to soils becoming sterile with the loss of their organic content. The increasing global demand for beef, pig products and dairy produce is causing a rise in animal digestive gas emissions, particularly from cattle.
- Plantations: oil-palm and rubber plantations are much poorer carbon sinks than primary rainforest and the peatlands they replace (Figure 1.16).

Key term

carbon offsetting: a deliberate scheme to reduce atmospheric CO_2 through absorption (tree planting) or reduced emissions (moving to green energy use)

Making connections

Read more on how human population growth is exerting pressure on natural environments in meeting the demand for more food in section 10.2 Environment and population.

Making connections

Read more on how fossil fuels are discovered, exploited and used in section 11.2 Natural resource issues.

Figure 1.16 Oil palm plantation replacing primary rainforest in Indonesia.

- Land-use change: growing urbanisation (see Chapter 9 Contemporary urban environments) not only reduces vegetation coverage as cities expand, but urban structures consume more energy than traditional rural settlements and urban construction materials increase the demand for cement.
- Cement production: processing limestone into cement is one of the largest single sources of man-made carbon dioxide other than fossil fuel use. Calcium carbonate is heated to produce lime, releasing carbon dioxide as a major by-product. The fuel needed to reach the high processing temperatures adds to the release of CO_2.
- Burning of vegetation: both the deliberate and accidental burning of vegetation releases stored carbon in smoke and reduces future capacity to absorb atmospheric CO_2. The practice of clearing forests for agriculture by burning and careless actions of tourists and residents in drought-prone rural areas can result in wildfires that lead to the combustion of large areas of biomass.
- Fossil fuel extraction and use: the largest single contribution to atmospheric carbon dioxide is the burning of fossil fuels (coal, oil and gas). This effectively takes the slow carbon cycle store that took millions of years to sequester and releases it into the fast cycle in quantities far higher than natural cycles can process, resulting in an atmospheric build-up of CO_2 (Figure 1.17).

Figure 1.17 Oil well 'gushers' release the stored hydrocarbons of millions of years' accumulation to be combusted in a few decades.

Feedback effects of human impact on carbon cycles

Extracting and then releasing vast quantities of stored carbon in the combustion of hydrocarbons has some of the most serious implications for mankind's impact on the planet. Since the Industrial Revolution, fossil fuel dependency has been releasing increasing quantities of carbon dioxide from a long-term store into the fast carbon cycle. Some impacts may intensify through feedback loops.

Increasing atmospheric CO_2: carbon dioxide as a proportion of the atmosphere is now at 400 ppm, and higher than at any stage in the last 800 000 years, possibly in the last 20 million years. Having been relatively stable between 3000 BCE and 1800 AD, it has increased rapidly in roughly 200 years from 280 ppm to the present level, and is set to increase further.

ACTIVITY 1.4

1 Justify each of these views:
   a There is a causal correlation in which rising atmospheric CO_2 is resulting in higher global temperatures.
   b There is a causal correlation in which higher global temperature is resulting in rising levels of atmospheric CO_2.
   c There is a correlation between atmospheric CO_2 and global temperatures, but it is not necessarily causal in nature.
2 Which view do you most agree with? Why and on what evidence?

Global temperature increase: carbon dioxide is a key **greenhouse gas** and methane even more so. Whilst shortwave solar radiation passes through the atmosphere, the Earth's surface reflects longwave radiation that is readily absorbed by carbon dioxide and methane, retaining heat close to the Earth's surface rather than releasing it to space. There is a strong correlation between increasing CO_2 levels and the rise in global temperatures (Figure 1.18), which may result in a positive feedback loop of temperature rise.

* Warming oceans: as temperatures increase, the melting of Arctic sea ice reduces **albedo**, converting a highly reflective surface of ice to a darker ocean surface. The most rapid increase in temperature is being experienced in Arctic regions, possibly because seas are warming due to the greater absorption of solar radiation (Figure 1.19). This then leads to faster melting of ice cover in succeeding seasons.
* Release of methane: as air and sea temperatures in the Arctic rise, the melting of tundra permafrost has the capacity to release substantial quantities of methane. For example, methane is produced as a result of decomposition of sphagnum moss in anaerobic conditions. While methane is relatively short-lived in the atmosphere compared to carbon dioxide (approximately nine years versus over 100), it is 23 times more effective as a greenhouse gas.

Climate change: rising global temperature affects climate components such as wind patterns, pressure systems and rainfall regimes, as well as rates of ice melt. Some areas are likely to see an increase in drought, others more floods. Tropical storms are likely to be more intense as ocean temperatures increase. Higher temperatures and increasing CO_2 may, in the medium term, stimulate faster growth of biomass, moderating the increase in atmospheric carbon dioxide. But this effect is thought to level off with further CO_2 rise.

Making connections

Read about the connection between atmospheric carbon, climate change and increasing desertification in section 2.4 Desertification.

Key terms

greenhouse gas: a gas that absorbs infrared radiation and contributes to the warming of the atmosphere, such as methane and carbon dioxide

albedo: the reflectivity of surfaces that redirects shortwave solar radiation back into space with limited heat absorption; ice sheets and sea ice have a high albedo

Investigate

Some argue that climate change may bring benefits to people in some regions. Which regions and what benefits? Who is likely to experience negative consequences and what are they? List the criteria you would use in weighing up the potential gains versus the losses.

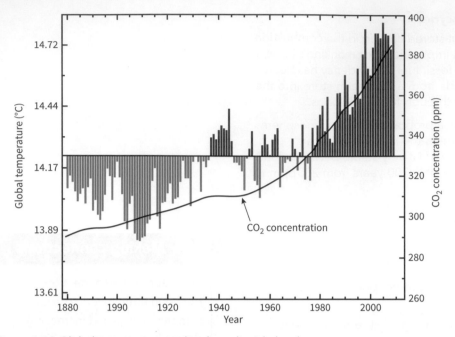

Figure 1.18 Global temperature and carbon dioxide levels.

Figure 1.19 Declining surface cover of sea ice at the poles increases solar radiation absorption.

Warming oceans: ocean temperatures are rising as they absorb heat from the atmosphere. This reduces their ability to absorb CO_2 from the atmosphere. A change in ocean currents and reduced upwelling of colder waters may reduce surface plankton, which might accelerate the effect by absorbing less CO_2 in photosynthesis.

Ocean acidification: oceans are a major sink for human-released CO_2. It is thought that between 30 and 40% of the carbon dioxide generated by human activity has been absorbed by rivers, lakes and seas. As in the atmosphere, reaction with water results in carbonic acid. These molecules can break down and inhibit **marine calcification** processes (Figure 1.20). As a result, plankton is weaker, coral is bleached and the shells of molluscs are thinner. This is considered to be as great a threat to planetary biological systems as the rise in atmospheric temperatures.

Making connections

Read more on how carbon levels in the atmosphere are related to historic sea level changes in section 3.4 Coastal landscape development.

Key term

marine calcification: the uptake of soluble carbon compounds by marine creatures and conversion into solid carbonate compounds

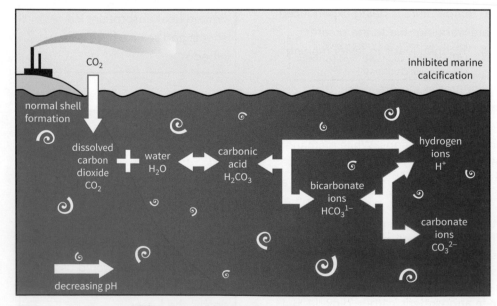

Figure 1.20 Ocean acidification and shell deformities.

Physical and human

What are the difficulties in accurately estimating the impact of human activity on atmospheric carbon dioxide levels (sometimes referred to as 'enhanced' greenhouse gas emissions) compared with natural levels?

Three key carbon sub-cycles operate and interact to regulate global temperature, climate, biomes and ocean conditions. They are:

* the atmospheric carbon cycle
* the ocean carbon cycle
* the terrestrial carbon cycle.

The carbon budget and the impact of the carbon cycle upon the atmosphere

The **carbon budget** is the net change between inputs from a carbon source and outputs to a carbon sink. Before anthropogenic (human) intervention, these were exchanges in the natural world.

Natural carbon sources

Natural carbon sources are found on both land and sea and include organic and non-organic processes that release carbon dioxide and provide an input into the atmospheric carbon cycle (Figure 1.21).

Key terms

carbon budget: the surplus or deficit of carbon once carbon output is subtracted from carbon input

flux: a flow of a gas, liquid or solid matter resulting in a transfer between two locations

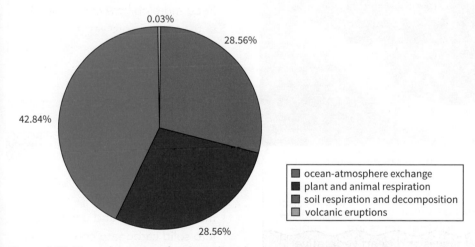

Figure 1.21 Natural sources of carbon dioxide.

Ocean–atmosphere exchange: ocean outgassing represents the largest source of carbon dioxide into the atmosphere. Dissolved CO_2 in seawater is released, particularly from the surface of warm, tropical waters, into the atmosphere. Oceans absorb carbon dioxide from the atmosphere as well as release it in a relationship known as the ocean–atmosphere exchange. As carbon moves from one store to another, it is said to be in **flux**.

Volcanic activity: surface and submarine volcanoes release a small but significant amount of carbon dioxide along with other carbon compounds.

For information on respiration and decomposition, see the earlier section on Factors in fast carbon cycles.

Carbon sinks

Whether a carbon sink becomes a carbon store depends on the relative rates of input and output by the sink. If significant amounts of carbon accumulate and the rate of release is slow, the sink is also a store.

One of the main terrestrial carbon sinks is tropical forest, which absorbs carbon dioxide from the atmosphere (Figure 1.22). Other carbon sinks include:

Tundra: the tundra biome supports a slow-growing ecology in which plants, such as sphagnum moss, extract carbon dioxide from the atmosphere during growth. However, in the cold, acid and anaerobic conditions of the bogs, the plants decompose at an even slower rate. Carbon is consequently stored in thick layers of peat. The world's largest continuous landmasses occur in northern tundra regions, giving rise to extensive carbon sinks in this form. Should temperatures in these regions rise, as they seem to be doing, the potential for sizeable carbon release in the form of methane is a key concern as decomposition starts to extend over more of the year.

Making connections

Read more on periglacial environments and tundra conditions in section 4.1 Glaciers as natural systems.

Figure 1.22 The Amazon Basin is one of the major carbon sinks of the planet.

Soil: the soil is one of the largest carbon sinks depending on the prevailing conditions. Plants release surplus carbon through their roots into a stable form of soil carbon known as humus. Animal faeces and dead vegetative material in the form of leaves, stems and roots may be slow to decompose if conditions are too acidic or anaerobic, and accumulate a store of carbon in the soil.

Ocean–atmosphere feedback: in higher latitudes especially, oceans absorb gaseous carbon dioxide directly from the atmosphere, where it dissolves into surface waters. The interrelationships between atmosphere and ocean result in self-regulating feedback cycles operating over decades and centuries. More atmospheric carbon dioxide can result in increased ocean absorption, which can in turn result in increased biological activity. This may return some carbon to the atmosphere, but store a proportion in the deeper ocean. As a result, the atmosphere may cool, reduce terrestrial plant growth and diminish the sourcing of carbon dioxide to the atmosphere.

The carbon budget and the impact of the carbon cycle upon oceans

Ocean–atmosphere gas exchange

There are complex cycles operating between the atmosphere and oceans, which can lead to mutual carbon dioxide exchange between the two.

- Solubility cycle: carbon dioxide will diffuse from the atmosphere into the ocean surface and vice versa depending on the relative concentrations. Cooler waters can aborb more CO_2 than warmer water, while warm water and saturated concentrations will release carbon dioxide to the atmosphere.
- Biological cycle: photosynthesis by **phytoplankton** follows the same chemical process as for terrestrial plants but, in this case, the absorption of carbon dioxide is from the sea (Figures 1.23 and 1.24). In turn, these plankton are consumed by **zooplankton** which release carbon dioxide as part of their digestion process. This contributes to a **carbon pump**, transferring carbon from the surface waters to the deeper ocean in the form of faecal matter and the sinking of their dead organic structures to form carbon-rich marine deposits on the ocean floor. In another constituent to this pump, marine creatures form skeletal and shell materials from soluble calcium bicarbonate sourced from river discharge into coastal seas. Their conversion of it into calcium carbonate causes a further accumulation of carbon compounds on the seafloor as they die and sink to the bottom.

Key terms

phytoplankton: the 'plant' form of plankton using sunlight in surface waters to photosynthesize carbon dioxide into sugars

zooplankton: the 'animal' form of plankton that can be found at a range of depths and feeds on phytoplankton and its remains

carbon pump: a natural energy force resulting in a carbon flux; both gravity and descending cold currents transfer plankton remains from ocean surfaces to seafloors in the ocean pump

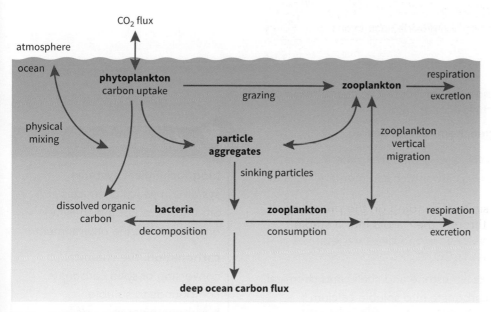

Figure 1.23 The marine carbon cycle.

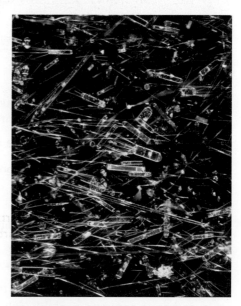

Figure 1.24 Plankton are the basis of the entire marine food chain.

The carbon budget and the impact of the carbon cycle upon the land

Vegetation and soils are closely linked within the terrestrial carbon cycle, particularly the fast carbon cycle. They are both sources of carbon dioxide to the atmospheric cycle, and vegetation is a key absorber of atmospheric CO_2.

Fast carbon cycle

The seasonal growth and dormancy of vegetation creates a fluctuating rate of CO_2 absorption by plants from the atmosphere. In the Northern Hemisphere, where landmass coverage is significantly larger, there is a large increase in the rate of CO_2 uptake by vegetation in the spring and summer months (Figure 1.25). The smaller landmasses of the Southern Hemisphere are unable to compensate for winter dormancy in the north with the summer uptake of their plant chemistry. Consequently, there is an annual fluctuation in global atmospheric CO_2 coinciding with summer (trough) and winter (peak) in the Northern Hemisphere.

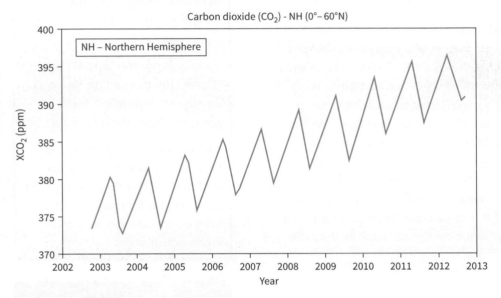

Figure 1.25 Graph of annual global atmospheric carbon dioxide fluctuations.

Slow carbon cycles

The recycling of carbon in various compounds over millions of years is a result of organic and non-organic sequences interacting (Figure 1.26).

The long-term carbon cycle involves a **biogeochemical** interaction:

- Tectonic and seismic activity at constructive and destructive plate margins creates uplift of thrust mountains, exposing carbon-rich sedimentary rocks to surface weathering and erosion.
- Atmospheric carbon dioxide readily reacts with water droplets in clouds to produce carbonic acid.

$$CO_2 + H_2O \rightarrow H_2CO_3$$

- Acid rain falls on calcium carbonate rocks (limestone and chalk) and chemical weathering converts insoluble calcium carbonate into soluble calcium bicarbonate (Figure 1.27), which flows as surface and groundwater to the sea in a process known as **carbonation**.

$$CaCO_3 + H_2CO_3 \rightarrow Ca(HCO_3)_2$$

- Calcium bicarbonate breaks down into component ions in the sea where marine creatures such as coral and plankton extract biogenic calcium carbonate from the ocean to create body and shell material in a process of marine calcification. Upon death, skeletal and shell remains fall to the ocean bed and accumulate as thick deposits rich in calcium carbonate.

 Key terms

biogeochemical systems: systems in which chemicals are transferred between living organisms and the environment

carbonation: the chemical conversion of solid carbonate compounds to soluble bicarbonate compounds

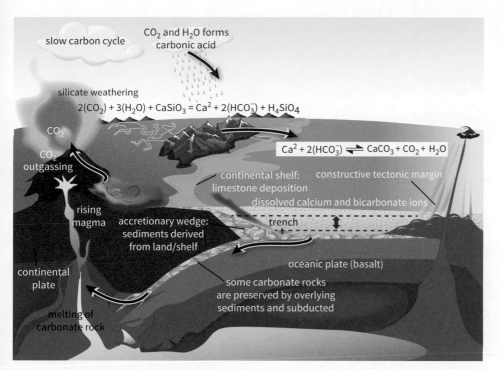

Figure 1.26 The long-term carbon cycle.

Figure 1.27 Solid calcium carbonate has been dissolved by carbonic acid on this weathered cathedral gargoyle.

- Over millions of years of heat and pressure, sedimentary rocks develop beneath the ocean floor. As part of an ocean tectonic plate they move slowly, driven by convection currents in the mantle.
- At subduction zones, sedimentary rocks are taken down into the mantle where they melt. Carbon is then ejected as CO_2 back into the atmosphere at surface volcanoes. (Marine volcanoes release carbon dioxide into the oceans.)

Hydrocarbon sequestration

The burying of organic remains of marine creatures or swamp vegetation is a sub-cycle of the long-term carbon cycle. This carbon-rich matter is sealed into buried reservoirs of organic material to become **hydrocarbons** (Figure 1.28).

- Over time, vegetative concentrations that accumulate in anaerobic conditions may become compacted into coal beds. Many of the world's coalfields were formed during the Carboniferous period, 360–290 million years ago.
- Marine remains decompose in sedimentary layers on the ocean floor, releasing their carbon content to form oil- and gas-rich rocks. These fluid and gaseous hydrocarbons seep slowly to the surface through permeable rocks, but if the overlying layer is impermeable, they become trapped to form organic-rich sedimentary rocks.
- Under anaerobic conditions, organic material reaching the seafloor decomposes and may be stabilised as methane hydrate deposits – methane molecules caged within ice molecules. These occur on continental shelves and Arctic sea floors around the globe. Some estimates suggest there is as much potential energy locked in methane hydrate sediments as in the world's coal, gas and oil reserves combined.

Making connections

Discover more about how crustal plates move and the tectonic forces that drive the slow carbon cycle in section 5.1 The concept of hazard in a geographical context.

Key term

hydrocarbon: a wide range of chemical compounds based on carbon and hydrogen

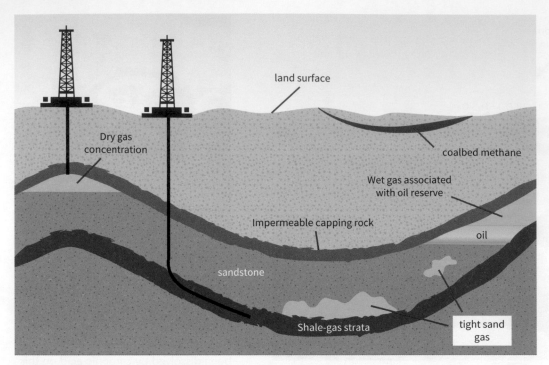

Figure 1.28 Sources of natural gas.

- Where the geology has an impermeable capping layer and is folded into an anticline so that trapped hydrocarbons migrate towards and accumulate in the highest point, oil and gas reserves sequester past atmospheric carbon deep underground so long as they are not released for human energy use. It is these concentrations that form exploitable oil and gas fields. The carbon they contain has been re-introduced into atmospheric carbon systems on a large scale over the last hundred years when burnt as fossil fuels.

Making connections

- Read more on how countries are attempting to reduce their reliance on fossil fuels in their energy mix in section 11.1 Resource development.
- Read more about the impact of urban areas in generating carbon emissions and attempts to develop more sustainable cities in section 9.7 Sustainable urban development.

Attempts to reduce anthropogenic carbon emissions

The WWF (World Wide Fund for Nature) defines the carbon budget as 'a tolerable quantity of greenhouse gas emissions that can be emitted in total over a specified time'. The budget needs to be in line with what is scientifically required to keep global warming and thus climate change 'tolerable'. Many of the world's governments are now committed to actions designed to limit further increases in carbon emissions to between 450 and 550 ppm. The intention is to restrict projected global temperature increase to less than 2% (from pre-industrial levels) by 2100. It was announced in November 2015 that a 1% increase in average global temperature had been recorded for the first time.

Effective action on carbon emissions requires a collective international agenda; action by individual countries occurs but is bound by tighter commitment when part of negotiated agreements between nations. This currently occurs at a range of scales.

The global framework

The UN (United Nations) is the key driver for global action on carbon emissions. Whilst it can broker negotiations and agreements and organise conferences, it has limited power to enforce member nations to adhere to actions they have signed up to. This, however, is changing as effective action on climate change is recognised as becoming more critical. Key developments have been:

1988: the establishment of the IPCC (Intergovernmental Panel on Climate Change) by the UN. An independent panel of scientists and climate experts is set up to monitor, analyse and summarise reports on aspects of climate change to advise the UN on policy.

1992: the first coordination of national policy towards carbon emissions was through the UNFCCC treaty (United Nations Framework Convention on Climate Change) in 1992 as a UN response to the 'Earth Summit' in Rio de Janeiro of that year. The general term of the agreement was to stabilise levels of human-induced greenhouse gas levels in the atmosphere in order to prevent significant climate change. But this had no binding national limits on emissions or mechanisms for managing enforcement. Subsequent treaties and protocols have aimed to tighten up this initial agreement of principle.

1997 Kyoto Protocol: this set binding national targets for developed countries to reduce greenhouse gas emissions. It also established the concept of trading carbon emissions between member countries. Not all developed nations signed up, some subsequently withdraw, and others recognised their target but declined to make it legally enforceable.

2010 Cancun (Mexico) Agreement: this meeting identified a maximum average global temperature rise of 2 °C on pre-industrial levels as the target for managing global greenhouse gas emissions. It also established the 'Green Fund' to assist developing countries develop low-carbon energy initiatives.

2012 Doha conference: this meeting identified growing concern that the stated and acutal actions of countries were unlikely to be sufficient to meet the 2 °C increase and that higher average global temperature could be anticipated without further, more regulated, agreements.

2015 Paris conference: this was the first attempt to establish tough, binding greenhouse gas emission targets on all member states of the UN across the world. Member countries agreed to report every five years on their efforts to reduce greenhouse gas emissions and to aim for a target of no more than a 1.5 °C increase in global average temperature on pre-industrial levels.

Making connections

There is more information on how global frameworks operate in section 7.1 Globalisation.

ACTIVITY 1.5

1   Read about the outcomes of the 2015 Paris UNFCCC (United Nations Framework Convention on Climate Change) – also known as COP 21 (21st meeting of the Conference of the Parties signed up to the UNFCCC).

2   In your opinion, were the objectives of the meeting fully met, and are there effective measures in place to monitor and enforce national reductions in greenhouse gases to meet the 2 °C target and 1.5 °C aspiration?

Look on **Cambridge Elevate** to read about Cop 21 Paris on the UNFCCC website (www.cambridge.org/ links/gase6003).

National frameworks

Organisational frameworks also cover **trading blocs** such as the EU (European Union) and specific agreements between two or more countries.

Regional commitments: the 28 members of the EU operate the EU ETS (European Union Emissions Trading System), which is the biggest international system for trading greenhouse gas allocations. Using a 'cap and trade' format, individual industries/companies are allocated a capped emission allowance per year (which declines over time). They are fined if they emit over their cap, but are incentivised to reduce their carbon emissions by being permitted to sell under-used emission allocations on the carbon trading market.

Bilateral commitments: in 2014 the world's two largest greenhouse gas emitting nations, China and the USA, signed a secretly negotiated agreement to limit their emissions. China agreed to cap its carbon emissions by 2030, and the USA agreed to reduce carbon emissions by an average of 27% by 2025 on 2005 baseline emissions.

Measures national governments take to achieve their greenhouse emission reduction targets include:

- committing to national carbon emission target agreements
- national industry/company carbon emission caps and enforcement frameworks
- investment in sustainable, renewable energy options
- providing subsidies to encourage private energy generating companies to develop sustainable options
- renewing interest in nuclear energy options
- de-investment from hydrocarbon energy sources
- promoting energy-efficiency schemes
- promoting carbon offsetting schemes
- encouraging artificial carbon sequestration (CO_2 burial) via planning arrangements and subsidies (Figure 1.29).

Key term

trading bloc: a group of countries who agree a range of measures to facilitate trade between themselves

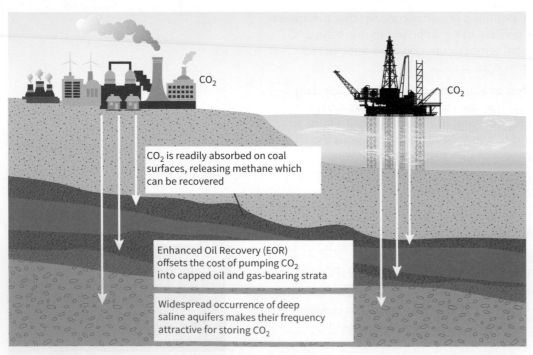

CO_2 is readily absorbed on coal surfaces, releasing methane which can be recovered

Enhanced Oil Recovery (EOR) offsets the cost of pumping CO_2 into capped oil and gas-bearing strata

Widespread occurrence of deep saline aquifers makes their frequency attractive for storing CO_2

Figure 1.29 Carbon sequestration/burial.

Making connections

To find out more about attempts to reduce carbon emissions to prevent critical climate change, read section 11.7 Resources futures: water, energy and ore minerals.

Making connections

Read more about water security in section 11.3 Water security.

1.4 Water, carbon, climate and life on Earth

The cycling of water and carbon are central to the continued health of life on Earth, with which they are intimately connected. There are challenges in maintaining these cycles, and the consequences of changes within them will impact on climate change, water security and flooding – all significant global issues today. The level of water availability influences the ecosystem that develops within an area.

The key role of the carbon and water stores and cycles in supporting life on Earth

The world's climate is influenced by the level of particular gases within it. These include gases which are responsible for maintaining a temperature which enables natural processes and systems to continue, and to retain sufficient heat to sustain life. Carbon cycling is involved here, as gases move between the atmosphere and the ground surface, influenced by human activities. One concern is that particular gases, generally called 'greenhouse gases', are increasing in their volume, and the number of parts per million (ppm) of some of them is reaching levels which we may not have seen before. Efforts are being made to reach international agreements to reduce the emissions of carbon dioxide and similar gases. Almost all carbon released into the atmosphere is the result of land-use change. Large-scale forest fires in Indonesia which generated smog over large areas of Southeast Asia in 2014 and 2015 are a recent manifestation of the stress that these cycles are being placed under.

The relationship between the water and carbon cycles in the atmosphere

Water and carbon interact with each other in different ways, most directly in running water (where rivers transport carbon into the oceans). The release of carbon into the atmosphere may lead to warming temperatures.

Air temperature affects its ability to absorb moisture, and this potentially changes the larger climatic pattern. One way this occurs is in the development of a phenomenon called El Niño. This is a warming of the oceans and results in a reversal of the normal circulation of winds within the atmosphere over a large area. The consequence is a shift in the normal pattern of rainfall (the Walker circulation), which can be catastrophic for local ecosystems. The reversal of the normal wind pattern brings drought instead of the expected seasonal rains, and large parts of Northern Australia suffer water shortages and increased risk of bushfires.

In addition to storing and releasing water, plants and trees are also important as carbon sinks. Trees lock in carbon as they grow (a process called sequestration). The tropical rainforests partly generate the rain they receive each day. If the trees are removed, often by burning, not only is the carbon within them released into the atmosphere, but their role in cycling water is also disrupted and local precipitation levels drop dramatically (see 1.5 Case study: Amazon rainforest).

One area of concern relates to the permafrost, which is found in cold environments (see Chapter 6). A warming in polar regions may accelerate the release of carbon and other gases which have been locked in the permafrost for centuries.

1.5 Amazon rainforest

Tropical rainforests cover just 6% of the Earth's surface and yet they account for between 30 and 50% of global photosynthesis (Figure 1.30). Yet their capacity to recycle both moisture and the world's increasing carbon dioxide emissions is beginning to appear in doubt as human activity alters their extent and dominant processes. The impact of human intervention on the Amazon Basin of South America is being closely-studied.

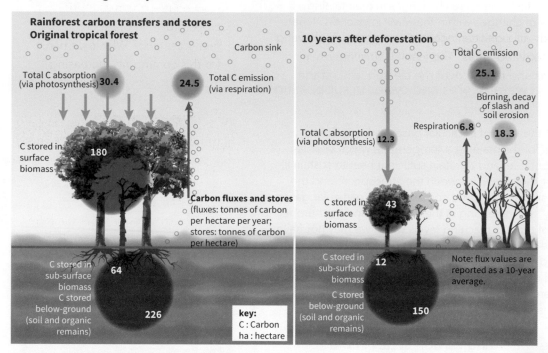

Figure 1.30 The tropical rainforest carbon cycle.

Maths for geographers

Study Figure 1.30.

1   Calculate the total carbon store 'Before' deforestation and 'After'. What is the difference?
2   Calculate the net flux changes (absorption minus emissions both 'Before' and 'After'). What is the difference?
3   Which component of either store or flux shows the largest proportional change between the two phases of rainforest cover? What are the wider implications of this change?

Amazon rainforest cycle changes

It is estimated the Amazon Basin has lost 17% of its primary rainforest in the last 50 years, largely due to clearance for cattle ranching (80%). This is most marked in the east and south-east parts of the basin (Brazil) and in the north-western arc (Colombia and Ecuador). The Amazon Basin produces roughly one-third of

ACTIVITY 1.6

1   List the likely groups with an interest in changing current rainforest to a different use in southern Brazil. Which claim has the strongest case?
2   Consider the impact of rainforest destruction by distinguishing between the effects on the hydrological and the carbon cycle in terms of scale.
3   "The countries of Europe have removed their forests in the pursuit of development. The countries of the Amazon basin should be permitted to do the same." To what extent do you agree?

its own precipitation in the recycling of evapotranspiration; the other two-thirds arriving as moisture-laden air from the Atlantic Ocean. As land is cleared of primary forest, the consequences of human intervention are affecting both the hydrological and carbon cycles of the region.

- Reduced evapotranspiration from cleared areas means the air is less moist, resulting in a reduction in cloud cover. More solar radiation is reflected by cleared land (than the darker forest canopy) and temperatures increase.
- Greater radiation reflectivity and increased ascension of warm air reduces the influence of the dominant low-pressure system over the Amazon Basin that draws in moisture-laden air from the Atlantic, leading to less precipitation.
- 'Vegetation breezes' occur over cleared land as air above crop/ranch land warms faster, rises more quickly and creates localised low pressure, drawing in moist air from surrounding forested areas. The result is an increase in cloud coverage, thunderstorms and rainfall over the cleared land, at the expense of forested areas.
- River discharge increases on a watershed scale as a result of deforestation, as increased surface flow discharges into local river systems.
- River discharge decreases on a continental basin scale as decreasing precipitation leads to a reduction in river discharge.
- Particles resulting from the deliberate burning of forest to clear for agriculture, or in the production of charcoal, increases the density of airborne aerosols around which water vapour condenses. As a result, smaller droplets occur in clouds which are too small to precipitate, resulting in less local rain.
- Selective logging of mahogany and ipe often damages neighbouring trees, leading to open gaps in the forest which are more exposed to sunlight and winds. They subsequently dry quickly and lead to more frequent wildfires. The forest scrub that replaces primary forest stores 40% less carbon.
- When burned for land clearance, between 30 to 60% of the carbon in tropical rainforests is immediately released to the atmosphere. The size of the Brazilian Amazon rainforest has been decreasing at an average rate of 0.3% per year since 2000.

In a typical year, the Amazon rainforest absorbs 2.2 billion tons of CO_2, while emitting 1.9 billion tons through decomposition and organism respiration. This makes it a major carbon sink. However, the capacity of the Amazon rainforest to absorb carbon is declining. In the 1990s, it drew down over 2 billion tons of CO_2 per year; by 2015, this had declined to just 1 billion. This is less than the total carbon dioxide emitted by Latin American countries each year, so the Amazon Basin no longer represents a continental carbon sink.

The reasons for the decline are thought to relate to substantial tree death within the Amazon Basin. It has been assumed that increased atmospheric carbon dioxide levels would stimulate biomass growth (carbon fertilisation) and regulate the emission rise. However, it appears that while rainforest plants do grow faster, they die sooner. This increased metabolic stress has been compounded by recurrent drought, unusually high temperatures, continued illegal logging and conversion to agriculture (Figure 1.31). It appears the rainforest is under stress from both direct human activity and climate change arising from indirect action in releasing stored hydrocarbons in such massive quantities.

 Research point

What are the principal uses for soya bean – one of the principal crops grown in Brazil on cleared rainforest land? Why is demand for this commodity increasing?

 Investigate

What are the key pressures responsible for rainforest loss other than conversion to soya-bean cultivation? Are all the world's rainforest regions affected by them equally, or is there regional variation?

Figure 1.31 Amazon rainforest being cleared for agriculture by burning.

1.6 The Tweed river catchment

UK rivers vary in length, from the River Severn at over 200 miles long to the River Bain in North Yorkshire, which is less than three miles long. Every river has certain characteristics, but also a unique 'fingerprint' which is made up of its long profile, course and flow pattern through the year (known as its **regime**).

The River Tweed

The River Tweed, which flows in the Border region of Scotland and northern England, has historical as well as geographical importance. It rises in the Lowther Hills and flows for almost 160 km to the east (Figure 1.32, Table 1.5). The River Tweed is a dynamic system and varies from fast flowing boulder-strewn streams to a meandering channel with a sandy bed.

Key term

regime: the pattern of flow of a river, influenced by its catchment characteristics and the climate

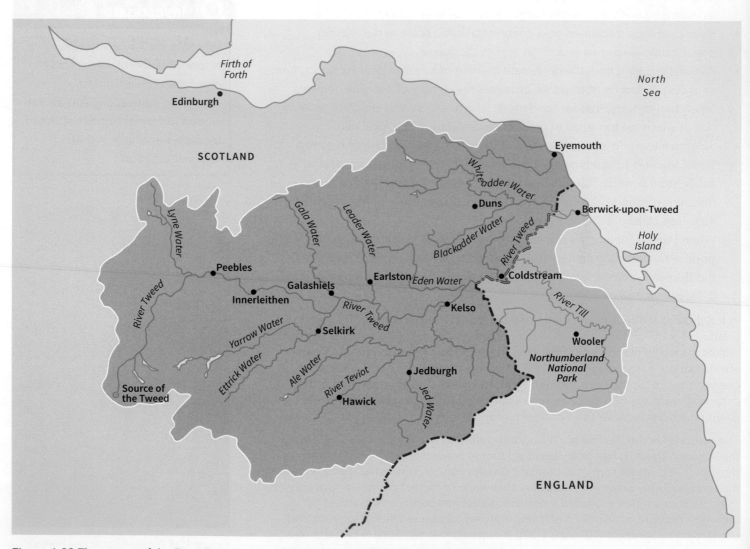

Figure 1.32 The course of the River Tweed and its tributaries, in Scotland and northern England.

length	156 km (97 miles)
source	Tweed's Well, in the Lowther Hills
catchment area	approximately 5000 km² – the second largest in Scotland
tributaries	these include the Whiteadder and Gala Waters, and the River Till
key locations within the river's catchment	Berwick-upon-Tweed (mouth), Hawick, Selkirk, Galashiels and Kelso; most of the local population live in small rural communities
industries	fishing, agriculture (around 80% of the catchment is used for agriculture, including hill sheep and beef farming), tourism and recreation
forestry	after the Second World War the Forestry Commission planted many large-scale conifer plantations in the catchment
water supply	a series of river works and reservoirs are used to supply water to two of the main water companies and cities such as Edinburgh
habitat	various fish and aquatic mammals including otters, **riparian** and wetland environments, plus birds

Table 1.5 The River Tweed at a glance.

Figure 1.33 Salmon fishing at Coldstream on the River Tweed.

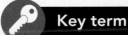

Key term

riparian: habitats associated with the land alongside flowing water

Industry

One of the main industries linked with the River Tweed is salmon fishing (Figure 1.33); trout fishing is also popular. This attracts tourists from across the UK and overseas, who pay for the privilege of catching a wild fish. The industry is estimated to be worth around £18 million to the local economy, and supports around 500 local jobs in an area where there are limited employment options.

The River Tweed Commission is charged with keeping fish stocked in the river, and flow levels need to be maintained so that this industry is not affected. There is also the Tweed Forum, which has a management role. Farmers are asked to take care with chemicals such as nitrate fertilisers and sheep-dip chemicals to avoid the risk of runoff or accidental spillage.

There are plans to increase tourist activity along the river, linked with the adoption of a number of codes of conduct. These help avoid conflict between groups such as canoeists and anglers. Walking and cycling trails are promoted, along with places to watch ospreys and salmon.

Berwick-upon-Tweed

The town of Berwick-upon-Tweed lies at the mouth of the River Tweed (Figure 1.34), where it flows into the North Sea. By this point, the river is flowing quickly and carrying plenty of sediment in its water. Where the river discharges into the North Sea, the output from the drainage basin cycle is complete.

The River Tweed flooded in 2008, and around 10% of properties in the catchment are considered to be at risk from river flooding. Efforts have been made to reduce the river's susceptibility to flooding. This has involved protecting wetlands (which act as flood storage), planting trees in the uplands (to increase interception storage) and reinstating meanders (to slow flow). It is also planned to leave boulders and woody debris in smaller streams, but clear it from larger channels to increase channel capacity.

Figure 1.34 The mouth of the River Tweed at Berwick-upon-Tweed.

ACTIVITY 1.7

The rivers in Scotland are monitored by the Scottish Environment Protection Agency (SEPA). Many rivers now who have gauges placed along them.

1   Identify the current flow along the River Tweed using the SEPA Water Level Data, and monitor it for a few weeks. Explore gauges along the river.

 Look on **Cambridge Elevate** to access SEPA Water Level Data from the SEPA website (www.cambridge.org/ links/gase6004).

 Look on **Cambridge Elevate** for more information on the River Tweed from the following websites:

- the Tweed Forum Catchment Management Plan provides a useful description of flood management measures (www.cambridge.org/links/gase6005)
- the River Tweed Commission provides information about the protection and improvement of salmon and freshwater fisheries (www.cambridge.org/links/gase6006)
- the British Geological Survey (BGS) mySoil app may be useful for assessing soil type and geology in the area (www.cambridge.org/links/gase6007).

ACTIVITY 1.8

1   The Tweed Forum Catchment Management Plan includes a number of strategic aims. Some are listed below.
    i   Maintain and enhance water quality
    ii   Ensure water is available for abstraction while protecting the needs of the natural environment
    iii   Maintain habitats, including riparian and wetlands
    iv   Adopt a catchment-based approach to flood management
    v   Promote the sustainable development of river-related tourism
    Can you make a connection between these aims and the way the drainage basin might affect the river's response to rainfall?

2   Some stakeholder groups are listed below.
    i   Northumbrian & Scottish Water
    ii   Forestry Commission
    iii   National Farmers Union
    iv   Association of Salmon Fishery boards
          a   Which aspects of the river's catchment and water cycle might each stakeholder group be interested in, and why?
          b   Why would the flow level of the river be of specific interest to them?

3   Suggest how land use in the River Tweed catchment might influence its response to rainfall events.

✓ Assess to progress

1   Explain the role of storage in the water balance of a drainage basin.   **3 MARKS [AS LEVEL]**

2   Describe the characteristics you would expect of a drainage basin that produced a 'flashy' river.   **3 MARKS [AS LEVEL]**

3   Explain how a drainage basin could be adapted by humans so that it was less likely to flood after a period of heavy rainfall.   **6 MARKS [A LEVEL]**

4   With reference to a river you have studied, outline the way that the river channel itself is managed so that human impact is kept to a minimum.   **6 MARKS [A LEVEL]**

5   Explain the sources of carbon in the oceanic carbon cycle.   **6 MARKS [AS LEVEL]**

6   Examine why the atmospheric level of carbon compounds is increasing when there is a finite amount of carbon on the planet.   **20 MARKS [AS LEVEL]**

7   Distinguish between the fast carbon cycle and the slow carbon cycle.   **6 MARKS [A LEVEL]**

8   Assess the extent to which rising global temperatures may result in a positive feedback cycle of yet higher carbon content in the atmosphere.   **20 MARKS [A LEVEL]**

Hot desert systems and landscapes

By the end of this chapter you should know:

- the processes and conditions that create hot desert environments
- the global distribution of hot desert environments
- what part wind and water play in forming hot desert environments
- how different geomorphological processes act in the desert
- the causes of desertification, and its impact on humans, ecosystems and landscapes
- the predicted impact of climate change on hot desert environments
- desert landforms are assemblages of landforms of different scale and formation.

Figure 2.1 The Sahara desert is the largest hot desert in the world. The desert covers 3.6 million square miles in North Africa, extending into Algeria, Chad, Egypt, Libya, Mali, Mauritania, Morocco, Niger, Western Sahara, Sudan and Tunisia.

 Key terms

geomorphology: the study of processes that change the shape of the Earth; they include weathering and erosion, and may result from the action of waves, glaciers and rivers

ecosystem: a complex set of relationships among the living resources, habitat and flora and fauna in an area

biodiversity: the variety of species of flora and fauna that are found within an area, and which influence the productivity of an ecosystem

Before you start…

You should know:

- deserts are shaped by **geomorphological** processes
- deserts are part of a larger **ecosystem** which has a range of different components
- desert **biodiversity** is significantly less than other ecosystems you may be familiar with, but there are interesting relationships between abiotic (non-living) and biotic (living) factors in these landscapes – which are not just sand and camels!

2.1 Deserts as natural systems

Deserts, as with all ecosystems, can be thought of as natural systems. A natural system is a portion of the world that is focused on for analysis, rather than the wider world that is the 'environment', which is made up of multiple systems.

Systems concepts and their application to the development of desert landscapes

Natural systems can be open or closed. Each system is the result of processes involving flows and stores of energy, water or **sediment** (inputs and outputs).

Deserts are open systems as they involve the transfer of sediment into and out of them as a result of movement by the wind. Desert sediments are carried by atmospheric circulation, as well as by local winds, and water also moves through them. Many systems are in a state of dynamic equilibrium: the flows through them adjust to remain in balance. Where energy or water is lost, there may be losses from the system, which results in negative feedback. For example, desertification can result in desiccation of the surface so that dust is lifted into the atmosphere. The local warming that can result may destabilise the local atmosphere and cause negative feedback (speeding the rate of uplift). The Saharan dust has a cooling effect when it is carried beyond the desert, even as far as the UK.

Water losses in the desert may also be accelerated by the removal of vegetation which leads to less water retention. Some areas of deserts may also receive new volumes of sediment as a result of positive feedback.

Inputs

Inputs into desert systems include:

- insolation (incoming solar radiation): **insolation** provides the greatest source of energy for these systems, and also acts on the landscape to drive the geomorphological systems that are driven by heat
- precipitation: inputs are low, as a result of the aridity of hot desert environments. Water that falls on the ground usually takes several routes back to the atmosphere. In the hot desert, this often happens very quickly as a result of evaporation, and doesn't follow the routes that it might do in other environments
- sediment: the breakdown of rocks by weathering creates further sediments over time.

Outputs

Outputs from desert systems include:

- long wave re-radiation from the desert surface
- water: this is lost through evapotranspiration and runoff
- winds: they tend to blow away from these regions, which may result in the loss of any available moisture
- groundwater movement: a small amount of groundwater movement may occur after heavy rainfall, which may result in water being lost from the system for some time as it goes down into artesian storage
- sediment: this can be lost from an area as a result of erosion or movement by wind and water.

Sediment

Sediment is transported into and out of desert systems by the wind. Weathering and erosion act on the rocks within deserts to create new sediment over time. Each desert will have a series of sediment cells, which are often self-contained, but there will also be a flow of sediment due to the prevailing winds. This results in changes to the local sediment budget, resulting in sand accumulation in some areas as sand dunes, or the loss of sand as depressions.

The global distribution of mid- and low-latitude deserts and their margins

Figure 2.2 shows the location and global distribution of hot desert areas. See how this compares with Figure 2.3, which shows annual precipitation across the globe.

Key terms

sediment: fine particles of soil or weathered rock, which can form regolith (a thin layer of loose rock and dust) or soil when mixed with organic material and water over a long period of time

insolation: incoming solar radiation received at a point on the Earth's surface; values are high in hot desert regions due to the lack of cloud cover

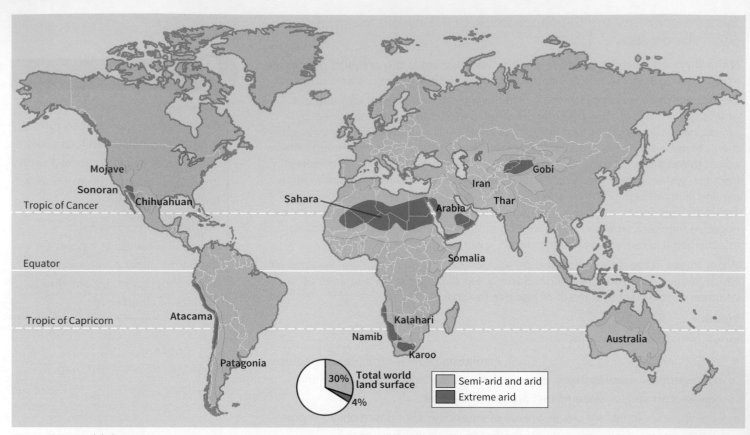

Figure 2.2 World deserts.

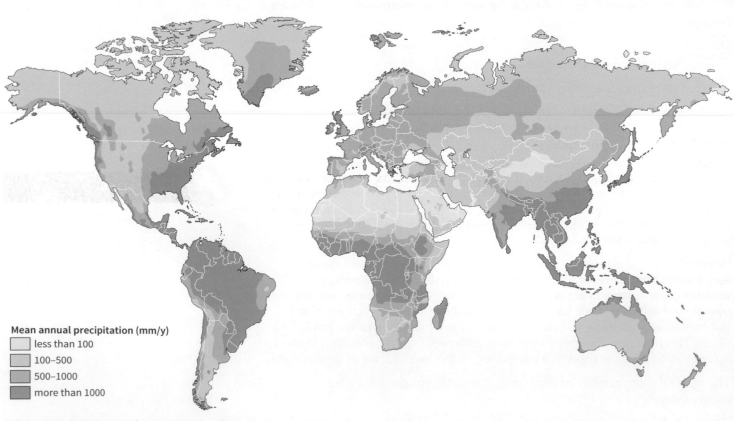

Figure 2.3 Global annual precipitation 1950–2000.

Table 2.1 shows some of the major hot deserts of the world and their locations. The largest hot desert in the world is the Sahara.

Name	Location
Sahara	North Africa
Libyan (part of the Sahara)	Libya, Egypt
Nubian (part of the Sahara)	Sudan
Arabian	Egypt
Rub' Al Khali (the Empty Quarter)	Saudi Arabia
Kalahari	South Africa, Botswana
Great Sandy	Australia
Gibson	Australia
Taklamakan	China
Thar	India, Pakistan
Atacama	Chile
Mojave	USA
Danakil	Ethiopia, Djibouti
Namib	South Africa, Namibia, Angola
Colorado (part of the Sonoran)	USA
Painted	USA
Negev	Palestine, Israel

Table 2.1 A selection of major hot deserts of the world.

Characteristics of hot desert environments and their margins

Deserts, or arid areas, are usually defined as 'those areas that have less than 250 mm of precipitation in a year', with semi-arid areas or desert margins receiving up to 500 mm.

Thus the first and most obvious characteristic of these regions of the world is a very dry climate. Low amounts of precipitation and high levels of evaporation result in limited soil moisture.

Desert soils

Desert soils (also known as **aridisols**) contain little biomass and are therefore not fertile. Thin soils are found beneath the sand in many deserts, some of which are low in organic matter and may be called **regolith**. Organic matter comes from the growth and subsequent death of plants, so it is slow to build up but may be present as a **relict feature** from earlier vegetation which grew before the area became a desert.

Desert soils are also lacking in moisture, particularly near the surface where they are dried out by evaporation. Water may move to the surface by capillary action and then evaporate. The soils are likely to have high levels of salt.

Water which has fallen in the past may be present in the bedrock. In some cases, this is exploited by being pumped up. The danger with using fossil water from these artesian sources is that the present climate means there is little chance of it being replenished.

Desert vegetation and animals

Flora and fauna found in desert areas have evolved over long periods to cope with the high temperatures and lack of water. Plants have a harder task to survive

Key terms

aridisols: desert soils; they are often lacking in organic material, and can also be baked hard on the surface by the heat, forming a duricrust

regolith: a layer of loose rock and dust, usually thin, that sits on bedrock

relict feature: a feature in the landscape, which was formed under previous climatic conditions

than animals. They cannot move away from the sun and wind, while desert animals can become nocturnal (active at night), burrow into the sand or hide under rocks to avoid the most extreme heat.

Vegetation found in hot deserts and their margins tends to have particular characteristics:

- A reduced biomass (smaller and slower growing). Desert plants are long-lived. One way to survive is by slowing down their internal metabolism, so that they grow very slowly. The total biomass is far less than other ecosystems.
- Lower biodiversity than other ecosystems.
- Specific adaptations to drought and salt. These drought-tolerant (**xerophytic**) plants are able to adapt to dry conditions. Some plants also acquire an ability to tolerate salt (**halophytic**), as this is sometimes present at high levels due to the evaporation of moisture close to the surface. Many plants cannot tolerate salt.
- Limited nutrient cycling. As there are few leaves to shed and no water to help the process, the extensive cycling of nutrients, which is so important to ecosystems such as tropical rainforests, fails to take place in arid environments.

Some plants are capable of storing water in their stems or leaves, or have roots that are adapted to exploiting water stored at depth or closer to the surface. Succulents are plants which can store water within their fleshy stems. They include a range of cacti, of differing shapes depending on the relative aridity of their surroundings. Cacti also grow very slowly. The iconic saguaro cactus (Figure 2.4), which grows in the southern deserts of Arizona and Colorado in the USA, can grow over 10 m high and live for 100 years.

The thorns which many hot desert plants are covered with not only reduce water loss, but also produce a still layer of air close to the plants which helps to moderate temperatures. Small scattered yuccas and occasional Joshua trees may stand above the surrounding shrubs where there are patches of moisture available. Creosote bushes can spread across an area, each bush sending up a series of small, flexible stems, with the roots sucking droplets of moisture from underground. Mesquite trees have small leaves and taproots which drill down as far as 50 m to find underground water. These are known as **phreatophytes** as they seek out water held below the water table.

Other plants become **ephemeral**. Their seeds can lie dormant in the ground, waiting for months or even years for the arrival of rains, which allow them to germinate.

Trees are rare in the desert, although there was the famous tree of Ténéré in Niger (Figure 2.5), which was once the loneliest tree in the world. It was surrounded by miles of empty desert, but despite this it was still unlucky enough to be hit by several lorries.

The tree was the remnant of a forest, which is a reminder that deserts have not always been the same as they are now. They have resulted from long-term climate patterns and associated geomorphological processes. The presence of vegetation changes the nature of the processes which act in desert areas. Some desert areas experience short-term changes as a result of vegetation flowering after rainfall.

There is no abrupt transition from arid and semi-arid. In reality, there is a transition zone between the two. Once more than 250 mm of rainfall arrives annually, the vegetation starts to respond to the availability of extra moisture and changes as a result. Grasses and small bushes will start to appear, and these will then transition to trees if there is further precipitation.

Figure 2.4 The saguaro cactus, Arizona, USA.

 Key terms

xerophytic: characteristic of plants which can cope with low levels of water availability and high temperatures

halophytic: characteristic of plants which have adopted strategies to increase their tolerance to salt, including excretion of salt on the surface of leaves

phreatophytes: plants which have long taproots so that they can exploit water lying in the phreatic zone (below the water table) that other plants can't reach

ephemeral: referring to a plant which flowers occasionally, when the conditions are right, and not every year

Figure 2.5 The tree of Ténéré in Niger, an acacia.

Desert animals

Animals that live in hot deserts need to:

- keep their body temperature as low as possible
- withstand the low temperatures that occur at night
- retain as much water as possible.

This results in a range of behavioural adaptations, alongside **morphological** adaptations.

Behavioural adaptations may include:

- living in burrows during the day – a strategy used by reptiles
- nocturnal movement – results in adaptations to sight and hearing to operate in darkness and to avoid predators
- reducing contact with hot sand (e.g. the sidewinder snake and other reptiles move in such a way that they don't overheat)
- migration away from the region during the hottest part of the year – some bird species do this.

Morphological adaptations may include:

- long legs to create a distance between the animal's body and the high ground temperatures
- light-coloured skin to reflect heat
- large pads on feet to avoid sinking into the sand and to facilitate movement in loose sand
- tolerance to dehydration (a physiological adaptation)
- humps, as in camels (Figure 2.6), to store fat for long periods while in environments with little food.

The aridity index

The degree of dryness of the climate at a particular location is useful to know for studying arid environments.

 Key term

morphological: relating to the form or structure of an animal or plant

Figure 2.6 The camel – adapted to life in the desert.

The **aridity index** takes into account a range of climatic factors, including the amount of precipitation that reaches the ground surface and the rate of potential evapotranspiration. Data about aridity can also include an estimation of the humidity of the air. The aridity index developed by the United Nations Environment Programme (UNEP) is frequently used.

Human settlement and hot deserts

As many as one billion people live in hot desert regions. However, the total size of these regions means they are very sparsely populated. Population is concentrated in more favourable locations such as along rivers (e.g. the Nile) or other watercourses, or in areas where artesian water is available.

The causes of aridity

Most deserts and their margins are found in areas where a number of factors combine to create the necessary climatic conditions. The main factors that cause a lack of precipitation in desert areas include:

High pressure

Most hot deserts occur in a band, a few degrees either side of 30 degrees north and south of the equator, although the boundary is variable as a result of local landscape and climate conditions.

Global circulation of the atmosphere is responsible for warm air rising along a belt close to the equator. This rising air forms one part of a circulation called the **Hadley cell** (Figure 2.7). At high altitudes, the air flows towards the poles until it meets air moving in the opposite direction from the mid-latitudes, where it descends around 30° north and south of the equator.

The descending air 'dries out' as it warms during the descent. As a result, condensation and cloud formation are unlikely to occur.

The descending air also causes relatively high atmospheric pressure in desert areas. Consequently, any wind will move away from these areas rather than into them, so winds carrying moisture do not blow into desert regions. Although deserts are open systems, the outputs therefore tend to outweigh the inputs.

Low precipitation levels are therefore inevitable, resulting in a low biomass, and a reduction in the rate of physical weathering processes, caused by the high temperatures and low moisture levels.

Continentality

Many desert areas occur near the centre of continents. This is aided by a factor called **continentality**. Continentality refers to the proximity of an area to the ocean. Oceans have a moderating influence on local atmospheric conditions because of their high heat capacity and rates of evaporation. Areas further from the ocean tend to experience more extremes of temperature because they are not moderated by the sea, which means they can be hotter and colder than coastal areas.

Rain shadow

Deserts can also occur close to mountain ranges. Air is forced to rise over the mountains and warms as it descends in their lee. Arid areas may therefore form on the downwind side of these relief barriers, in the **rain shadow**. Some deserts such as the Thar in Asia is a result of a combination of factors and is particularly dry. The Atacama Desert lies in the rain shadow of the Andes. The city of Arica, in Chile, is on the edge of the Atacama and is recorded as the driest city on Earth, with an average annual rainfall of less than 1 mm per year.

Key terms

aridity index: an index which determines the aridity of a region, based on the actual precipitation that falls, combined with water losses through evapotranspiration

Hadley cell: a tropical atmospheric circulation pattern in which air rises at or near the equator, flows toward the poles, returns to the Earth's surface in the subtropics and flows back towards the equator

continentality: the effect of distance from the sea on the aridity of the air in a region; this tends to create a more extreme climate with higher temperatures in summer

rain shadow: the dry area on the lee side of a mountain or mountain range, away from the (rain-bearing) wind

Figure 2.7 Atmospheric circulation: the Hadley cell.

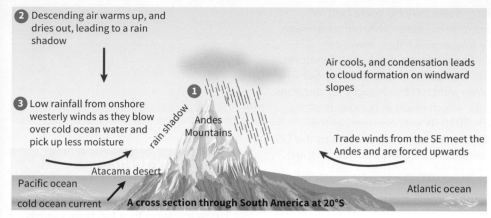

2 Descending air warms up, and dries out, leading to a rain shadow

3 Low rainfall from onshore westerly winds as they blow over cold ocean water and pick up less moisture

rain shadow

Andes Mountains

1

Air cools, and condensation leads to cloud formation on windward slopes

Trade winds from the SE meet the Andes and are forced upwards

Atacama desert

Pacific ocean

cold ocean current

A cross section through South America at 20°S

Atlantic ocean

Figure 2.8 Rain shadow and cold ocean currents, and their impact on deserts.

Cold ocean currents

Cold ocean currents such as the Humboldt Current of the southeast Pacific Ocean influence the air above them, chilling the winds so they are unable to pick up moisture. As the onshore winds move inland, they warm up and dry out further as a result. Cold ocean currents influence the deserts in South America, and coastal locations along the Chilean coast are drier than they might otherwise be (Figure 2.8).

These upswellings of cold water are also the reason why deserts are often found on the western sides of continents like Africa and South America.

2.2 Systems and processes

Desert systems involve the use of energy to drive the processes that shape them. The main energy source in hot deserts is insolation (incoming solar radiation), which also provides the problems.

Sources of energy in hot desert environments

Energy provided by insolation lies behind all desert processes, whether by affecting the rocks directly or creating winds which move sediment.

Temperature

Hot deserts are characterised by high temperatures, but they also exhibit large variations in temperature. The mean temperature is generally between 20 and 30°C. There may also be some seasonal variation as well as the **diurnal** differences between day and night-time temperatures.

Dry desert air fails to retain the day's heat (there are no clouds to reduce night-time losses due to radiation). The loss of this heat by radiation from the surface of the ground means that the diurnal range can be very large. Imagine daytime temperatures exceeding 40 or 50°C alternating with night time temperatures close to freezing. The diurnal range is reduced closer to the sea, in deserts such as the Atacama, but can be greater in inland locations such as Death Valley in Arizona. This places greater pressure on any living thing, including the human population.

The temperature declines towards the desert margins, as does the diurnal range.

Precipitation

The lack of cloud in desert areas means that the levels of incoming solar radiation reaching the desert surface are high, causing the ground surface to heat up dramatically during the day. This in turn warms the air immediately above it. In other environments, this would normally result in convectional rainfall, but as the air is so dry in deserts this rarely occurs.

ACTIVITY 2.3

1 Carry out an image search: what appears when you search for 'hot deserts'? Images usually feature a sandy landscape, often with camels or cacti, but how true is this of the world's deserts?

a Produce a description of hot desert landscapes based on your image search results.

b Amend the description to make it more accurate. Include elements that are missing from your image search results.

c How much variety is there in hot desert landscapes in different parts of the world?

Key term

diurnal: daily; a pattern that occurs every day

For a number of activities exploring the characteristics of hot desert environments, download Worksheet 2.1 from **Cambridge Elevate**.

Precipitation levels are low in the desert. In fact, there may be years between rainfall in some locations. As with temperature, there is some variability between deserts, and also temporally. Due to normally low annual totals, there can sometimes be large annual variations in rainfall caused by a single intense storm event. Marginal areas, close to deserts, are susceptible to drought. Many Sub-Saharan African nations, for example, have been affected by drought for decades. By contrast, there can be intense rainfall events, which result in hundreds of millimetres of rain in just a few hours. In March 2015, floods occurred in the Atacama Desert after seven years of rain fell in just 12 hours. According to the US Geological Survey, more people die by drowning in the desert than die of thirst.

The position of the intertropical convergence zone (ITCZ) moves through the year, leading to some seasonal rainfall variation in those marginal areas closest to the equator.

Not all the precipitation that falls is effective. In Death Valley, for example, clouds sometimes form but the raindrops evaporate before they reach the ground, creating features called **virga** below the clouds (Figure 2.9).

Key term

virga: wisps, streaks or shafts of precipitation that fall from clouds but evaporate before they reach the ground

Figure 2.9 Virga clouds over the desert, Nevada, USA.

The amount of effective precipitation (that which is available for plants to make use of) is low for several reasons:

* rainfall tends to arrive as intense storms, which result in high surface runoff as the desert surface can be baked hard or fine particles can block access for groundwater
* desert soils lack organic material which means the water drains through them quickly and isn't retained for later use
* evaporation rates are very high, so water will be lost very quickly back into the atmosphere
* rainfall may occur when vegetation is dormant, or not in flower
* storms are very localised, so there may be very high rainfall totals in one area and nothing just a few kilometres away

Some coastal deserts benefit from fog, which can form at certain times of the year when the air is sufficiently humid. Its formation is associated with cold ocean currents. Fog can add significantly to precipitation totals, contributing between

50 to 300 mm per year. Parts of the Namib Desert (Figure 2.10) are often shrouded in fog, as are the Sonoran, Madagascar and Somali-Chalbi deserts.

Sediment sources, cells and budgets

Deserts store huge amounts of sediment, some of which moves within geographical areas inside the desert boundary (cells). Some moves beyond the area, expanding the desert over time. Deserts with a negative sediment budget will lose material. There are occasions, for example, when Saharan sand is carried away from the area by the atmospheric pressure patterns in the high atmosphere. These sands can reach the UK, and be seen deposited on parked cars after rainfall (Figure 2.11).

Sediment is produced by the breakdown of rocks, and varies in size as a result, which affects the way that it is moved around. The accumulation of sediment into temporary landforms is one significant aspect of desert landform creation and may reduce the rate of loss from an area. Climate is an important controlling factor in sediment production.

Geomorphological processes

Geomorphological processes act on the surface of the Earth to change its shape. In desert areas, some of the processes are specific to arid areas and others are processes which will also be active in all parts of the world. They include the slow process of weathering, more rapid mass movement and the sequence of erosion, transportation and deposition. Desert regions change more than many people appreciate, and are geomorphologically active despite their appearance.

Distinctively arid geomorphological processes

Geomorphological processes are almost as active in hot deserts as in other landscapes. However, as water is required to enable or control the rate of weathering that occurs, they do not occur in the same way. These processes operate constantly, but the changes they produce are often subtle.

Desert surfaces tend to be made from stone and sand, but there are processes acting on them which will constantly sort and regrade this material over time.

Weathering

Rocks are broken down by weathering *in situ*. There are usually three main types: physical, chemical and biological. Due to the lack of water, chemical processes are limited and the majority of processes are mechanical, which means that weathering is usually confined to the surface.

Weathering is selective and depends on exposure to the sun or to the occasional moisture that may come from dew, fog or rain. Some rocks are more susceptible to weathering or weather at different rates.

Physical weathering

Block disintegration is the breakdown of large rocks into smaller rocks. This is followed by **granular disintegration**, which is the breakdown of rocks into fine particles, mostly sand grains.

Thermal expansion and fracture

This is caused by extreme diurnal temperatures, which heat up the rock to temperatures as much as double the air temperature. Heating and cooling cause the rock to expand and then contract by a very small amount. The minerals that make up the rock also expand and contract. As these are not responding identically to the heat, internal stresses build up which may lead to cracks forming.

Figure 2.10 Fog from the sea at Sossusvlei in the Namib Desert.

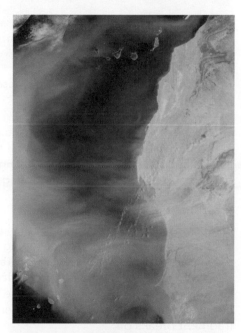

Figure 2.11 A satellite photo showing Saharan dust blowing northward off the coast of Spain and Portugal.

 Key terms

block disintegration: the breakdown of large rocks into smaller ones of varying sizes through the expansion of small cracks in the rock

granular disintegration: the breakdown of rocks into fine particles, the most common being sand

Figure 2.12 Weathering of rocks in the desert, Nevada, USA.

Thermal expansion and fracture occurs on the surface of rocks and can result in the cracked surface peeling off, as if the rock was laminated. This is known as **exfoliation** (or onion-skin weathering). The products of exfoliation lie on the ground next to the weathered rock (Figure 2.12).

Frost shattering

Frost shattering is less important than other forms of weathering but can contribute to the others by weakening rocks, particularly sections close to the surface. This occurs when any water that may be present freezes overnight as the temperature drops. Ice has a greater volume than water so puts pressure on weaknesses in the rock. When the ice thaws as the Sun rises, the water penetrates deeper and the process repeats until rock fragment breaks off.

This process is more likely to occur in deserts that experience a greater diurnal temperature variation, such as the Gobi desert.

Chemical weathering

This is the breakdown of rocks as a result of chemical reactions. Chemical weathering happens less in deserts than in other environments, but there may be **oxidation** (when ferric minerals in rocks react with oxygen and 'rust') or **hydration** (when minerals absorb water and swell, causing pressure to build up inside the rock). Both of these processes will occur when dew or mist is present.

Salt weathering

Salt weathering can occur in areas where rain has fallen or as a result of salts from groundwater that have been drawn up to the surface by evaporation. The high temperature leads to salt crystals forming on the surface of the rock and within any small gaps. These salt crystals exert pressure on the rock as they grow.

Salt weathering also occurs in coastal salt flats, called **sabkhas** (Figure 2.13), and where there are **endorheic drainage basins**.

Biological weathering

Biological weathering is rare in the desert due to an absence of decomposition of organic material. Plant roots may contribute to the fracturing of rocks in their search for water.

 Key terms

exfoliation: a type of weathering which leads to the surface of rocks breaking down (also known as onion-skin weathering)

oxidation: the reaction of a substance with oxygen; in the case of rocks containing iron, it forms iron oxide which is rust-coloured

hydration: in geology, when water molecules combine with a mineral leading to a change in structure and a swelling of the rock

sabkhas: flat areas, often between a desert and an ocean, with crusts of salt and other minerals resulting from evaporation

endorheic drainage basins: drainage basins that do not have an outlet to the ocean; the rivers usually flow into an inland lake or sea

Figure 2.13 A sabkha near the Tunisian coast.

Controls on weathering

The geology of deserts is important. Rocks in the desert are broken down by weathering to smaller particles. For many rock types, the smallest particle size they can reach is that of sand grains. They are unable to be broken down further, so accumulate as piles of sand close to where they were existing as parent rock. Sand grains vary in their coarseness, or grade. Partially broken down material forms regolith, the thin layer of loose rock and dust covering the ground surface in some desert regions.

Sand in the desert is constantly moving due to the wind, and migrates over time. The sheer volume is evidence of erosion taking place over millennia, and sand that moves on needs to be replaced by freshly formed sediment. The sand accumulates and is shaped by the wind to create a range of landforms.

Studies in the Namib Desert suggests that the sand is originally from the Orange River in South Africa, and can take up to a million years to cross the desert. This confirms that many desert areas are very old. The landforms found in them are also ancient, having taken a very long time to develop.

The role of wind

Aeolian processes are one of two main forces which shape the desert landscape, along with the action of running water. The wind blows unimpeded by barriers. Some deserts, such as the Thar, have mountainous uplands but many have a subdued relief.

Winds blow out from desert areas. There are times when the air is still, but these are rare. For many desert peoples, wind is a constant companion. Desert winds can be seasonal, but when they do blow, they are uninterrupted by vegetation or other barriers, and can reach hurricane force.

Many desert winds are named. Some have been adopted by car manufacturers for particular models, such as the Sirocco, Bora or Harmattan. Where do these three winds blow?

There can also be localised winds, caused by the sunbaked earth heating the air directly above it, leading to rising columns of air which spin due to the Earth's rotation, taking fine sediment with them. These features are known as dust devils, or willy willies (Figure 2.14).

The wind both transports and erodes rock particles, and shapes sediment into features. Some may be temporary, including small dunes, but others, such as natural arches, take thousands of years to form.

Erosion, transportation and deposition by the wind

Wind erosion is particularly important in desert areas. The lack of vegetation to bind the surface and slow down the wind means deserts suffer more wind erosion than other environments. This places stress on flora and fauna, although some have adaptations to better cope with it.

Sand particles are carried by the wind in a number of ways (Figure 2.15):

- Suspension: sand is physically carried aloft by the wind. It only happens when the wind is blowing particularly strongly, and is short-lived.
- Saltation: the movement of grains in a series of jumps along the ground, often just a few millimetres above the surface. It appears as a steady stream of sand grains swirling above the surface, and involves only smaller grain sizes. As a saltated grain lands back on the surface, it may impact with other sand grains and provide the extra impetus for them to move.

Making connections

One of the processes that moves sand through desert landscapes and sculpts it into dunes is also found on beaches, as covered in 3.2 Coastal systems: Inputs. Sand is the result of weathering and the effects of this can also be seen at the coast.

Key term

aeolian processes: the action of the wind on the landscape, involving the movement of fine sediment, which can be used to erode the landscape and eventually be deposited in a new form or location

Figure 2.14 A dust devil in Namibia.

To explore some of these desert processes further, download Worksheet 2.2 from **Cambridge Elevate**.

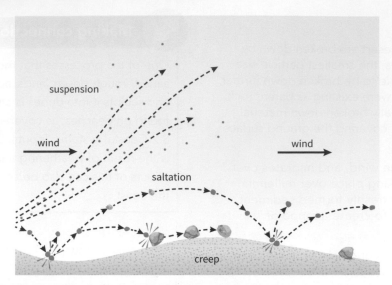

Figure 2.15 The movement of sand grains by the wind in the desert.

- Surface creep: the movement of sand over the surface as the wind rolls large grains along, or they bump into each other.
  The sediment carried by the wind is capable of erosion, which takes two main forms:
- Abrasion: small particles are scraped against rocks and abrade them. The analogy of sandpaper is appropriate here: cars driving through desert sandstorms have been known to lose their painted surface, or have their windscreens etched. Visibility is reduced to a minimum by airborne sand.
- Deflation: fine, loose particles are removed by the wind. This can result in small-scale features or may cover hundreds of square miles, depending on the scale and duration of the winds involved.

Sometimes the wind is generated by localised events, such as a **haboob** – a desert storm which can arise quickly and threaten human activity. The Arizona Department of Public Safety and other interested parties run a campaign called 'Pull Aside, Stay Alive', which teaches drivers how to drive safely when these storms hit.

The wind acts on particles it *can* move, and they in turn act on those it *cannot* move. The desert is used against itself. The abrasive action of sand grains being blown against rocks wears them away in a similar process to the sandblasting used to clean buildings by removing the dirty outermost layer of the stone it is built from.

Sediment is deposited in areas where the wind speed drops, as a result of topography. Dune systems may change shape as winds eddy around them. Sediment may be picked up and dropped many times in its journey across desert regions.

Thinking like a geographer

Geographers need to think critically about ideas like sustainability. Is it possible for people to live in desert areas without leading to unsustainable use of water and other resources? Is this sort of development desirable in the long term?

It may be that our future energy needs will be met by giant solar power plants located in desert regions. What physical and human factors will need to be taken into consideration when siting and managing such facilities?

Key term

haboob: a desert storm, with wind-blown sand, which can build up quickly and last for a relatively short time but can create hazardous conditions for human activity

Research point

Visit the 'Pull Aside, Stay Alive' website to find out more.

Research point

How do people who live in deserts act to reduce the impact of the climate on everyday actions? Visit the Geography All the Way website to see a MapJournal geographer Richard Allaway produced to describe the Drâa Valley in Morocco. Interrogate this resource, and use it as a model to create your own case study of a desert region that you have studied.

Sources of water

Water is not something one associates with drylands, but water has always played, and continues to play, a vital role in the development of many desert landforms. Spatial and temporal patterns of water availability control many of the processes described in this chapter, and water is the second main erosive force in the desert, alongside wind.

There are three main sources of water:

- **Exogenous** water arrives in the area from other places. For example, the River Nile rises in Ethiopia but runs into the Sahel region.
- **Endorheic** water is within a closed system, which involves rivers that do not flow to the sea – they usually flow into an inland lake or sea. Artesian water is drawn up from groundwater stores, depending on geology. Oases are localised features, where the geology enables water to rise to the surface.
- **Ephemeral** water occurs as a result of torrential rainfall and is short lived. This results in sudden flash flooding and is part of the mechanism for the creation of features such as wadis and arroyos.

The importance of rivers such as the Nile can be seen by looking at Figure 2.16, a map showing the population density of Egypt. Where there is water, farming is possible, and so water means life.

Investigate

Desert landscapes are notoriously difficult to map because they shift around and have few landmarks. What particular features do you think may be mapped using GIS in desert regions?

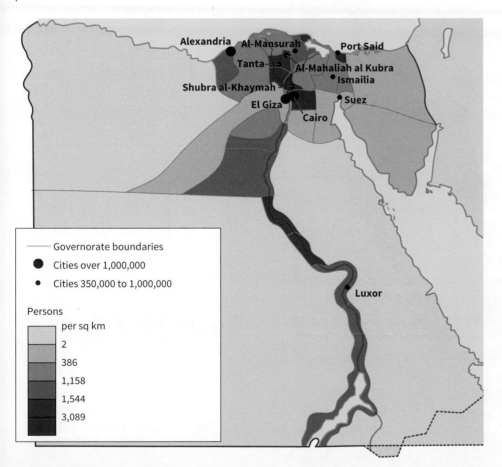

Figure 2.16 Population density in Egypt.

Map legend:
- Governorate boundaries
- ● Cities over 1,000,000
- • Cities 350,000 to 1,000,000

Persons per sq km
- 2
- 386
- 1,158
- 1,544
- 3,089

City labels: Alexandria, Al-Mansurah, Port Said, Tanta, Al-Mahaliah al Kubra, Ismailia, Shubra al-Khaymah, El Giza, Suez, Cairo, Luxor

Look on **Cambridge Elevate** for more information on how people who live in deserts act to reduce the impact of the climate on everyday actions, for example:

- Pull Aside, Stay Alive (www.cambridge.org/links/gase6008).
- Geography All the Way (www.cambridge.org/links/gase6009).

To help you explore the StoryMap of the Drâa Valley, download Worksheet 2.3 from **Cambridge Elevate**.

Flash flooding in the desert

Flash flooding is a large, but short-term increase in the discharge of a river channel. Flash floods are particularly associated with deserts, as any rainfall tends to fall in intense events, and the surface is often baked dry which leads to rapid runoff.

On 25 and 26 March 2015, heavy rains which had been forecast, affected the northern coastal region of Chile called Atacama (Figure 2.17). In one of the driest regions in the world, seven years worth of rain fell in just 12 hours, following days of high temperatures. It was the most extreme event for decades.

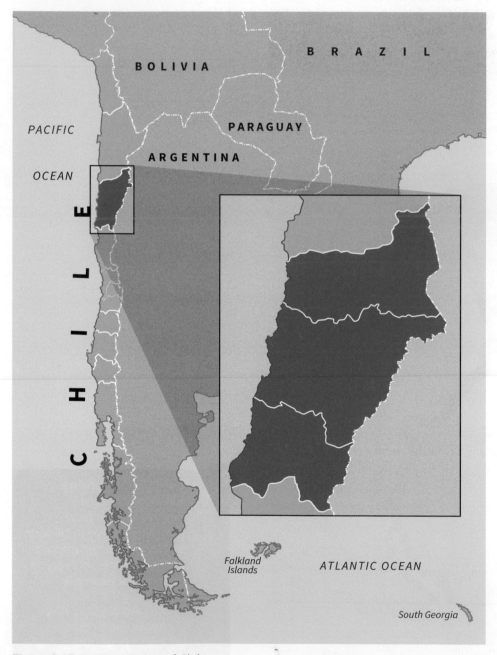

Figure 2.17 Atacama region of Chile.

Figure 2.18 Using a security line to cross a river in Copiapo, flooded by the overflowing of the Copiapo River.

Following the intense rainfall, local rivers such as the Copiapo swelled as water was funneled down from the Andes. Many local communities are located close to these watercourses, as they are the main water supply to this arid region. The floods caused significant damage to the areas as a result, and a state of emergency was declared (Figure 2.18).

Impacts of the flash floods:

- Bridges were cut through by swollen rivers, and cars and other vehicles were carried for miles downstream.
- The city of Copiapo was badly affected, as were other riverside towns – communities were divided, and communications severed.
- Over 6000 people were affected in some way by the floods.
- Mudslides were triggered by the heavy rain, and affected roads and property.
- Hundreds of homes were damaged or destroyed, and livestock and crops were killed or damaged in rural areas.
- Copper mines run by state-owned company Codelco had to be closed, as supply roads were blocked, resulting in a worldwide increase in copper prices.
- Infrastructure, such as electricity and water supplies, were disrupted to around 40000 people and residents risked electrocution from downed power lines
- Residents had to be rescued from the roof of their homes by helicopter.

The International Federation of Red Cross societies (IFRC) were mobilised and provided support to the affected areas in the short term. The government also provided millions of dollars to support the communities affected. The military were drafted in to support local people, and provide temporary shelter.

It is difficult to provide suitable measures to protect against such events, as they are short term, localised and impossible to predict. Settlements will locate near to any available water which, for a few short hours may turn from life-saver into a real risk to life.

Sheet flooding in the desert

Water flowing in rivers or along a defined route is called stream flow, but there can also be **sheet flooding**, where water flows evenly across the land surface after heavy rain. The ground is usually impermeable as it is baked hard by the Sun, and has little vegetation to break it up to allow water to infiltrate. This baking plus an accumulation of salts near the surface leads to the formation of a hard surface layer called a **duricrust**. Water runs over this surface at speed, and may then be funnelled into channels to amplify flooding there.

Key terms

sheet flooding: flooding where water flows evenly over the surface after heavy rainfall rather than running along a channel

duricrust: the hard-baked surface that forms on desert soils

Tip

The events that lead to flash flooding happen very rarely, and don't make the news as often as those that affect urban areas. They occur for similar reasons, and it would be useful to compare events that happen in deserts with those in cities.

2.3 Arid landscape development

Arid landscapes share some characteristics with other landscapes, but also contain some features that are not found elsewhere because of the abundance of sediment and the absence of vegetation cover.

Origin and development of landforms of mid- and low-latitude deserts

Desert landscapes occur in several major settings, including:

- desert uplands: geology controls relief, so these are high landscapes with bedrock often exposed at the surface
- desert piedmonts: separated from uplands by a break of gradient, these areas receive sediment from the uplands
- stony deserts: consisting of stony plains and plateaus covered by stone pavement
- desert lake basins: often salty and flat, sometimes filling with water after intense rainfall
- sand deserts: materials created by wind action removing material from flood plains and lake basins and characterised by dune systems.

Desert landforms are more visible than in other environments because of the lack of vegetation or surface material. Their absence also speeds up certain surface processes, allowing them to be more active. Desert landforms can be classified according to their creation.

Bahadas

Where water flows over the land surface, even if only for a short period, it carries sediment with it. As water moves away from the channel onto flatter ground, it spreads out. This causes it to lose energy, and sediment is deposited to form a small alluvial fan.

A bahada is an alluvial plain which forms as a result of the lateral growth of several smaller alluvial fans. As the water flows out from the mountains, several fans may join together to form a larger fan, which slopes down towards the surrounding plains.

Deflation hollows

Deflation hollows, or depressions, can range in size from small features on individual dune systems to very large depressions where weaker rock has been hollowed out. They are the result of wind removing sediment from an area, sometimes because it is funnelled along a particular route, or because the sediment is finer than the surrounding material.

Desert pavement

Extensive areas of flat, stony surfaces known as desert pavements or 'reg' (Figure 2.19) and large boulders are also left exposed by the removal of sand by the wind.

Erg

An erg is a sand sea – a large expanse of dunes, which can stretch for hundreds of square kilometres. These are found in the most arid areas of the world. They are called sand seas because the dunes look (and in a way act) like very slowly moving ocean waves, as sediment moves through them. Erg Chebbi, which extends from Algeria into Morocco, is a popular place for tourists to visit to experience desert conditions (Figure 2.20).

Hamada

Hamada are barren, rocky desert landscapes with hard surfaces and very little sand due to deflation (Figure 2.21). The finest particles have been stripped away by the winds, leaving only the largest rock pieces behind. They are similar to desert pavement.

Ventifacts

Not all desert landforms shaped by wind are dramatic. The wind will also act on stones to shape and orientate them according to where they lie in relation to wind direction.

Yardangs

Yardangs are narrow, streamlined ridges, usually several times longer than they are wide, although they can be discontinuous. As wind blows over a region, it exposes the more resistant areas by removing the softer materials. The prevailing wind direction means that these more resistant areas eventually stand out to form ridges, or yardangs.

Figure 2.19 Desert pavement in the Mojave Desert, Nevada.

Figure 2.20 Erg Chebbi, Morocco.

Figure 2.21 Hamada du Draa, Morocco.

Figure 2.22 Goblin Valley, Utah, has thousands of rock pillars or hoodoos, locally known as 'goblins'.

Zeugen

Zeugen are mushroom-shaped rocks, created by the abrasive action of wind-blown sand around their base. They form more readily where rocks have horizontal strata of varying resistance.

Rock pillars

Rock pillars, or cap rocks, also called hoodoos in the United States, are formed when pillars of rock are not eroded at the same rate. The top part of the pillar may be eroded less, as sand-laden winds swirl around the base. The cap then protects the lower part from some of the worst of the weather. This produces a pillar topped by a large cap stone (Figure 2.22).

Sand dunes

Only around 20% of deserts are covered by sand dunes, although they are the feature many people most associate with deserts. Dunes take different forms depending on the nature of the sand they are made from and the wind direction(s) in the areas where they form (Figure 2.23). Individual dunes can

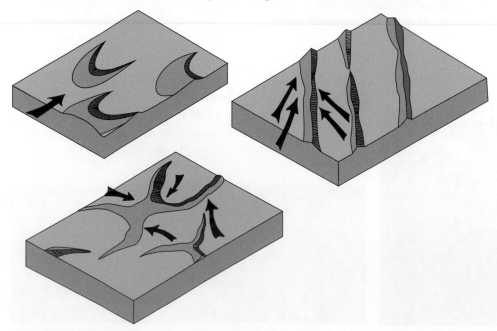

Figure 2.23 The formation of barchan, seif and star dunes.

 Research point

Research the way that dune migration has threatened a number of settlements in hot desert areas. These include the old sets used in the *Star Wars* movies.

extend up to hundreds of metres high and several hundred more in length. Their size depends on the availability of sand, so they are often found in areas where there are (or were) major rivers.

Table 2.2 shows some of the types of sand dunes.

Dune type	Description	Processes
Barchan	Crescent shaped, and perpendicular to the prevailing wind direction	Driven by winds, and tend to be the smallest of all the dune forms. Many join up to form ridges called aklé dunes. Often isolated, and form in areas with limited sand.
Seif	Straighter than barchans, and running parallel to the wind	As winds move over the sand surface, they can create vortices which shape the sand.
Star dunes	Form in the shape of a star	Created by wind from several different directions. Extend over 300 m high in the Namib Desert.

Table 2.2 Types of sand dunes.

Dunes change shape over time. They also migrate. Sand is pushed up the downwind slope and then falls down the leeward side.

Wadis

Wadis (also known as arroyos) are formed by the intermittent flow of water, rather than a permanent river valley or gully. Wadis are often dry all year round, except after heavy rain. The channeling of water into deep gullies concentrates the erosive power, carving out steep sided, deep gullies. This can be very dangerous to anyone caught out by the sudden downpours.

The entrance to the famous treasury at Petra (Al Khazneh) is through a split in the rock, called the siq, which leads to Wadi Musa. The building is carved into the rock, and has been a World Heritage site for over 30 years.

Playas

Playas are large flat expanses where water used to sit, perhaps as remnants of endorheic lakes. They are often high in salt, due to evaporation, and may even have a crust of salt on the surface. 'Playa' is Spanish for beach. The term is used in the US in particular; they are called sabkhas in some other regions (see Figure 2.13). Playas are used for salt harvesting.

Racetrack Playa, in Death Valley, USA, is famous for its 'sailing stones', which move along the surface leaving a track behind them (Figure 2.24). Playas are also used for high-speed record attempts, as being so flat, they are ideal for racing vehicles.

Inselbergs

Inselbergs are also known as 'island mountains' and are remnants of previous mountains, rising out of the flat surrounding plains, and often representing the most resistant core of mountains that have otherwise been worn down over centuries. Sugar Loaf Mountain in Rio de Janeiro, Brazil, is an example.

In Monument Valley, USA, the larger features are called mesas, often flat-topped pinnacles. Smaller versions of these are called buttes (Figure 2.25). They are iconic features, and attract climbers and thrill-seekers.

Tip

These landforms don't exist in isolation. They combine to create a range of different landforms. Make use of images of deserts to practise your landscape interpretation skills. Can you identify specific landforms on photos and explain how each was formed? What processes are evident in the photographs which could help explain the formation of these landforms?

Figure 2.24 Racetrack Playa, Death Valley, USA, showing its famous 'sailing stones'.

Figure 2.25 Mesas and buttes in Monument Valley, USA.

Pediments

A pediment is a gently sloping area which has a rock surface and is sometimes covered with gravel deposits. They can result from the retreat of hillslopes by weathering, so that material is deposited at the change of gradient. They can also be associated with river flood plains.

The relationship between process, time, landforms and landscapes in mid- and low-latitude desert settings

At the end of the last Ice Age, many desert areas looked much as they do today, assemblages of landforms which had developed over long periods of time, resulting from the breakdown of rocks by geomorphological processes. However, others have changed drastically over the last 10000 years. The Nile Delta has long been a place where humans concentrated, but research suggests that around 10000 years ago, monsoon rains temporarily transformed the desert either side of the river Nile into habitable land. Archaeologists have carbon-dated human and animal remains, and suggested the desert turned into a savannah-type environment. Rock art depicts people swimming in pools, and domesticating sheep and goats. This is a reminder that both short term and long term processes work together in desert areas, and when we look at an image of a desert, we are looking at the underlying structure, which has taken millennia to develop, overlaid by shorter term accumulations of sediment which make up the present-day landforms, such as sand dunes, or incised wadis caused by recent rainfall. Somewhere between 7000 and 5000 years ago, retreating monsoon rains caused the return of the dry period, and the desiccation of the land south of the Nile delta.

Other evidence of previous climates include large areas of screes, which are a sign that the temperature may have once been colder, and large dune systems which have become stable, suggesting that wind speeds were once greater and there was a greater supply of sediment, which would have made them more mobile in the past.

Present-day features are evidence that geomorphological processes have always shaped these regions. The action of humans is less significant in hot desert areas than other ecosystems, which means that the physical processes are more visible. All hot desert landscapes have evolved over long periods, with short term processes still being active, and producing variations which are usually identifiable.

 Research point

What evidence of past climates remains in desert regions? In other landscapes, the signs may be more obvious, such as ancient woodlands, or the course of ancient rivers.

2.4 Desertification

Desertification is defined by the United Nations Environment Programme (UNEP) as a process which involves the 'persistent degradation of dryland ecosystems, such that it threatens the livelihoods of vulnerable populations'. It results from unsustainable practices which use scarce resources. It occurs where changing climate and difficult weather conditions meet extreme poverty. Droughts and famines threaten people's livelihoods. As people give up on their farmland, the land becomes prone to erosion. Land degradation causes people to leave their farmland, to move to the cities, and the deserts to grow. Even ecosystems such as tropical rainforests are not immune from the threat of desertification.

The changing extent and distribution of hot deserts over time

Deserts are growing. Estimates of the total land area covered by deserts varies according to the source you read, but what they all show is that increasing areas of land are being degraded by processes that involve people.

Marginal lands

Deserts do not 'end' in a straight line. There is a zone along which they blend into semi-arid landscapes. There is a growing threat of desertification in these marginal areas. Land management practices can hold back the encroaching sands, or they can speed up the removal of vegetation and lower the water table.

Efforts to overcome the loss of production often lead to land being farmed using methods that speed up its degradation, as the balance of moisture in the ground has to be carefully protected using specific methods of ploughing and cultivation. Surface soil turned over by a plough will dry out on exposure to air, thereby losing some precious groundwater.

The causes of desertification

Climatic variations

Climate change may be a cause of desertification. Although this is disputed, there is evidence of disruption to weather patterns and temperatures which are regularly above long-term averages.

Human impact

Poverty leads to soils being damaged by unsustainable practices. In an attempt to increase production, human populations extract groundwater for irrigation or domestic use, and graze animals. The hooves of livestock degrade the surface, making it more prone to erosion. Animals may also overgraze any existing vegetation, which protects the land surface and reduces erosion.

Deforestation

The main source of energy for more than a billion people is fuelwood. This comes from vegetation, ideally sourced close to home to reduce the effort needed to transport it. This results in degraded zones close to villages, where all available fuelwood has been used. Trees are not given the chance to grow – once they reach a size where they can be useful, they are removed and burned.

In communities that develop tourism, there is further demand for fuelwood as tourists have higher expectations than locals in terms of hot water, heating and other amenities.

Key term

desertification: land degradation in arid and semi-arid areas due to climatic variations and human activities, which threatens the livelihoods of vulnerable populations

Look on **Cambridge Elevate** to find out more about the future of deserts from the UNEP report website (www.cambridge.org/links/gase6010).

Population pressures

Population growth increases the demand for food, which may lead to farmers taking less care over soil management in the longer term, for short-term gain. A feedback loop develops as a result of these processes. As desert is formed, carbon from soil is released into the atmosphere which potentially speeds up global warming still further.

Impact of desertification on ecosystems, landscapes and populations

Desertification affects ecosystems by removing the stability of the surface cover and reducing the availability of moisture. Landscapes lose biodiversity, trees are stripped out for fuel and weathering processes alter. Population density is reduced as people leave the area looking for alternative employment.

Community involvement can help reduce these impacts. People may have to share land and resources. Education is also important, and this is increasingly coming from sources such as text messages which provide guidance and information to farmers at low cost.

Predicted climate change and its impacts

Climate change could result in a different pattern of rainfall, resulting in crop failure or flooding if rain arrives in one season. Deserts could also become less arid if the trend is for more rainfall, which was suggested by some recent reports, although there is some argument over the precise location of these impacts.

Populations living in the desert have proved their resilience by continuing to live in such an extreme environment. Due to climate change, the resilience of these populations will be tested further in the future.

Water management is important, as water-table lowering is an issue. Use of water in some areas has become unsustainable. Previously, water-use was more in balance with the number of people. Once again, however, tourism and other land uses in these areas have created a problem, and water budgets are no longer in balance.

To further explore the implications of desertification for humans, and the way that they are managing it, download Worksheet 2.4 from **Cambridge Elevate**.

Look on **Cambridge Elevate** to explore relative humidity around the world. Go to the Earth Null School tool and click on the map to see it expressed as a percentage figure bottom right. How does humidity vary across desert regions? (www.cambridge.org/links/gase6011).

Maths for geographers

The aridity index measures the degree of dryness of the climate at a particular location. It takes into account a range of climatic factors, including the amount of precipitation that reaches the ground surface and the rate of potential evapotranspiration.

Data about aridity can also include an estimation of the humidity of the air.

Investigate

What methods are being used to slow down the process of desertification in marginal areas? Evaluate their effectiveness.

Maths for geographers

Is there a link between population density in desert areas, and threats to invertebrate animal species that live there? Investigate the potential link by calculating Spearman's rank correlation coefficient for the data shown below, for a number of desert locations around the world.

The equation is as follows:

$$r_s = 1 - \frac{6 \sum d^2}{n(n^2 - 1)}$$

1   Rank the locations in Table 2.3 with the highest values as 1, down to 10.
    Add up the sums of the differences squared.
    Calculate the final value using the equation.
    n = 11 in this case
    If the value is close to 1, there is a strong positive correlation. Close to 0 means that there is little correlation between the two factors.

2   Discuss the results and the possible reasons for them. What other factors could be taken into account.

Desert location	Threatened animal species	Rank	Population density (km²)	Rank	*d*	*d²*
Namib	8		1.2			
Thar	10		102.5			
Mojave	12		17.7			
Atacama	6		5.9			
Arabian peninsula	11		35.2			
Sonoran	16		44.2			
Central Asia	20		4.5			
Gibson	6		0.0			
Indus	5		200.2			
Baja California	5		6.9			
Skeleton coast	5		3.2			
					Sum	

Table 2.3 Population density in desert areas and threats to invertebrate animal species.

2.5 Namib Sand Sea

The Namib Sand Sea region has been given World Heritage status as a landscape of significant importance. It covers large parts of Namibia, extending into Angola and South Africa, and is part of the larger Namib-Karoo-Kaokoveld region. In one of the local languages, its name – Nama – means 'vast' or 'place where there is nothing', and it is one of the oldest deserts in the world.

The area is home to some of the world's tallest dunes (Figure 2.26), and has temperatures that can rise up to 60 °C. Local conservation programmes aim to protect the desert's unique biodiversity. Some ecotourism is allowed. The region stretches for around 1900 km along the Atlantic coast, and is virtually uninhabited. The coastal fringe is known as the 'Skeleton Coast'. This is a National Park, and entry is restricted to preserve the fragile environment.

In the past, there was some industrial activity, with minerals and diamonds being mined. There was also some concern over possible damage to the desert landscape caused by filming of a new *Mad Max* movie in 2013. The tyre tracks of vehicles cut through surface algae and the crust on top of the soil, leaving scars which may persist for years.

Desertification has acted on this area and Namibia is facing a battle against desertification, as it tries to feed its growing population. Half the population lives in the central plateau region and the land is being placed under increasing pressure. The country's cattle population is said to be above the land's natural carrying capacity, which in the past has led to desertification in other regions. Water scarcity, the linking of social status with cattle ownership and the need for sustainable agricultural practices are all areas that need developing. The area around the Kunene river is being targeted for particular support.

The Kunene region is one of the areas worst affected by the process of desertification. A reduction in migration in the Opuwo district means that animals are constantly grazing the same areas, which don't get a chance to recover. There is overgrazing and trampling of soil as a result. Trees are cut, and overuse of water lowers the water table. Rates of soil erosion increase. This results in valuable top soil, including alluvial soils, being washed into the nearby Atlantic Ocean following rainfall.

Environmentalists are working in the area to educate people to the dangers. Special indabas (meetings) have been held with community leaders. They are recommending rotational grazing, so that grass is retained. There are also efforts being made to repair damaged areas by tackling gully formation. Owners of large herds of cattle are being asked to avoid communal grazing areas and establish their own areas. The EU has also been involved by providing N$100 million to fund projects aimed at adapting to and mitigating the impacts of climate change in Namibia.

 Now that you know about desert landforms and how they are created, why not try 'building your own desert'. Download some ideas for how to do this in Worksheet 2.5 on **Cambridge Elevate**.

Figure 2.26 Namib dunes, Namibia.

 Research point

A number of sporting events take place in hot desert areas. The landscape provides a challenge, but may also be damaged in turn by the events. The famous Paris–Dakar Rally no longer takes place in the Sahara desert because of its impact, and has been moved to South America (now known as the Dakar Rally).

Explore **one** of the following events:

a   the Paris–Dakar Rally

b   the Marathon des Sables

c   the Namib Desert Challenge

Produce a guide for competitors on the fragile environment they will be passing through, and how they might minimise their impact on it.

2.6 Holkham Estate, Norfolk

Although there are no hot desert environments within the UK, some of the processes that occur in deserts may be found in sand dunes.

The website for the Holkham Estate, Norfolk, notes:

> In some parts of the world deserts stretch for miles and are a pitiless wilderness of parched days, cold nights and storm-blown sand mountains. With a temperate British climate it is hard to believe that such severe conditions can apply here, but in miniature, this is exactly what happens to coastal sand dunes.

There are many sand dunes around the coast of Britain. They are usually found in areas where there is a sandy shoreline, with plentiful sediment, often where the geology of the area is not particularly resistant, or is low-lying. When the tide goes out, particularly on coasts with a shallow offshore gradient, the beach is wide, and dries out between high tides. Onshore winds blow sand towards the vegetation, trapping it to build up a dune network. Holkham beach and the dunes behind (Figure 2.27) frequently feature on lists of the best beaches in the world. Dunes tend to form in exposed locations, because the wind is important in their formation.

Norfolk's coastal dunes are managed as they form part of the sea defence along this low-lying section of coastline. Holkham is a National Nature Reserve (NNR). Holkham dunes were planted with pine woods as part of the Holkham estate management, and boardwalks are provided to guide visitors along particular routes. Fences are temporarily placed around areas which have eroded, to allow marram grass to grow back, and for dunes to stabilise. The pine woods are also removed where they have overtaken the dunes, as they are not a native part of the ecosystem. Some sections of the beach also have salt-tolerant saltmarsh plants.

The dunes are part of a Site of Special Scientific Interest (SSSI) and also lie within an Area of Outstanding Natural Beauty (AONB). Dune slacks (the area between dunes)

Figure 2.27 Sand dunes, Wells-next-the-Sea, Norfolk.

are also being managed to ensure damp habitats survive for additional species such as toads. Users of the dunes include birdwatchers, dog walkers, horse riders, ramblers and many school groups studying the dune systems. Thousands of pink-footed geese visit the area during the winter months.

Sand is moved by the wind by saltation and surface creep, and this creates a well-established dune system.

1. Follow a transect from the strand line to the back of the grey dune near the pinewoods.

2. Use ranging poles and clinometers to calculate the gradient of each section of the dune system, and measure the distance between each break of slope, so that you can reconstruct the shape of the dunes at a later date. Mark on the position of any dune slacks.

3. Use quadrats to sample relative abundance of the different plant species you can identify using a sand dune vegetation key.

4. Within each quadrat, make a visual survey of the species present.

5. Calculate the relative abundance of each species using the ACFOR scale: whether each species is Abundant, Common, Frequent, Occasional or Rare. Give a number to each of these values – abundant being 5 and rare being 1 – as this is useful when you come to graph your data.

6. Estimate percentage cover – the percentage of the quadrat covered by each species. Make your estimations to the nearest 5% or 10%.

7. Sample several abiotic factors along your transect. These could include: light intensity, soil pH, soil water, humus content of soil, temperature and wind speed at intervals along your transect and record where these values were measured along the final transect.

Figure 2.28 Fieldwork instructions for a trip to Holkham Dunes.

Tip

Field data could be collected in coastal dune systems on the coast of the UK, which experience some of the aeolian processes associated with mid- and low-latitude desert environments. In particular, study the movement of sand by saltation and the accumulation of dunes around vegetation, some of which has been planted for management purposes.

ACTIVITY 2.4

1. Study the information in Figure 2.28, which has been provided to students who are embarking on a fieldtrip to Holkham Dunes.
2. What aspects of the sand dunes were measured as part of the fieldwork?
3. Why is the vegetation coverage and its diversity important in the formation of dunes?
4. What do you think the typical findings would be from the measurements taken of the abiotic factors listed in the instructions?
5. Suggest how the data collected on this fieldtrip could be presented.

Assess to progress

1 Explain how ocean currents can be a cause
of aridity.
`4 MARKS [A LEVEL]`

2 Summarise the ways that people use hot desert
landscapes and the impact these have on the
environment.
`6 MARKS [A LEVEL]`

3 Describe the vegetation shown in Figure 2.4.
How has it adapted to the desert climate?
`6 MARKS [A LEVEL]`

4 Critically assess methods being used to slow
down the process of desertification.
`6 MARKS [A LEVEL]`

5 Outline the causes of flash flooding in hot desert
regions, and the landforms that occur as a
consequence.
`6 MARKS [A LEVEL]`

6 Discuss the view that the Namib Desert can be used
sustainably if managed carefully.
`20 MARKS [A LEVEL]`

Coastal systems and landscapes

Figure 3.1 The storm of February 2014 caused an estimated £1.5m of damage to Aberystwyth's seafront. Could an alternative approach to coastal management have reduced the impact of the storm?

By the end of the chapter you should know:

- how coastal systems operate to create a dynamic environment
- the key processes operating at the shore and in the sea, and how they impact upon the coast
- how coastal landscapes change over time and the factors affecting their development
- long- and short-term changes to the coastal environment that are responses to both natural processes and human influence
- how people modify coastal environments both intentionally and unintentionally
- strategies in managing coastal zones for sustainable outcomes
- how coastal environments may change in the near-future and consequent human responses.

Before you start...

You should know:

- the difference between coastal processes and coastal features
- coastlines are zones of erosion, transportation and deposition of material
- people have a range of strategies to reduce rates of coastal erosion, but these can have unforeseen consequences on other parts of the coastline

- human influence at the coast can have both positive and negative consequences
- a significant proportion of the world's population lives on or near the coast and is likely to be affected by future changes to global sea level.

3.1 Coasts as natural systems

The coast is the dynamic interface where sea and land meet (Figure 3.2).

A systems approach defines the components that interact in the coastal zone, their relationship to each other and their place within a sequence. At its simplest, a coastal system consists of:

INPUTS → PROCESSES → OUTPUTS

A systems approach helps explain variations and change in the general pattern of a geographical phenomenon. It also helps us predict possible consequences of natural processes or proposed human interventions – and judge whether they are desirable or not.

This perspective allows an understanding of how the elements that bring about change and stability at the coast interact with each other. A **coastal system** is an open one, receiving inputs of energy and sediment from elsewhere, involving transfers and flows and resulting in outputs of energy and sediment from the system. Recognising the links and roles in how they interact helps us understand why some coastlines are changing rapidly, while others appear relatively unchanging. This also helps us understand how deliberate human interventions at the coast may affect the way the system operates to bring about a range of consequences. Without understanding the system fully, we may intervene, and end up with undesirable consequences that we hadn't anticipated.

The usual trajectory for coastal systems is to move through a phase of dynamic equilibrium in which a balance between inputs and outputs is eventually achieved and relative stability exists within the system. If inputs change due to some external factor the internal **equilibrium** is disturbed, affecting processes,

Look on **Cambridge Elevate** to read an article from the *Western Morning News* about how 'We must learn to adapt over threat to our coastline' (www.cambridge.org/links/gase6012).

Key terms

coastal system: a series of linked elements affecting the coastal zone through which energy and material circulate

equilibrium: a state of balance between outputs and inputs

Figure 3.2 A coastal landscape is a dynamic environment.

stores and outputs until a new equilibrium is achieved. Components of the landscape, or landscape features, are altered in the transition through processes of erosion, weathering, mass movement and deposition. The rate at which change takes place is dependent upon the size of energy and material budgets (surplus or deficit) and the nature of the environmental controls within which they operate: climate, rock type and rock structure.

The main system elements are:

- inputs: introductions of sediment (from land and offshore sea), and energy (wind, wave, tides, currents)
- stores: repositories of sediment that may be added to or removed from
- flows: transfers of energy and sediment from one location to another
- outputs: sediment and energy losses to the system.

These operate upon the coastal attributes that prevail along particular stretches of coastline:

- Processes: marine, terrestrial, atmospheric and biological mechanisms that move material between stores. Different processes may operate in contrasting environments.
- Controls: the given of the coastal environment - climate, geology, rock structure, sea level. They can be subject to change, as in climate variation and sea level change over time.
- Landscape components: physical features of erosion and deposition that are shaped by systems but may also contribute to inputs and receive outputs. Features such as beaches may also function as sediment stores.

Coastal systems can be seen operating at various scales. An individual beach may be considered a material store and subject to inputs and outputs (Figure 3.3). The beach will extend (height, length and/or width) if inputs exceed outputs, giving a positive **sediment budget**. It becomes smaller if outputs exceed inputs (negative sediment budget) and remain a similar size if they are in balance (balanced sediment budget). The state becomes one of dynamic equilibrium as material may still be added and removed, but within a net balance.

By considering a beach from a systems perspective, we can quantify the main stores and flows and begin to understand how the different elements of the system relate to each other.

At a larger scale, systems operate on more extensive sections of coastline known as **sediment (littoral) cells** (Figure 3.42). These tend to be tens or even hundreds of kilometres in length, bounded by major headlands at either end. They represent sections of coast in which sediment is largely recycled, maintaining a state of relative balance and are, as such, **closed sediment systems**. Similar to a single beach, if a key energy input changes, the system alters in response transporting the sediment around within the system. Particular sediment stores may change in volume, as material is removed from one area and deposited elsewhere.

The value of this perspective is, taking the beach in Figure 3.2, if it has a positive sediment budget, then somewhere in the wider littoral cell might be

Key terms

sediment budget: the net sum value between quantities of input and output of sediment in a system. Excess is a positive budget, deficit is a negative budget and no overall difference is a neutral budget

sediment (littoral) cell: a section of coastline in which sediment is recycled but not added to or lost

closed sediment system: a coastal system that receives no additional sediment inputs and has no losses of sediment to areas external to the system

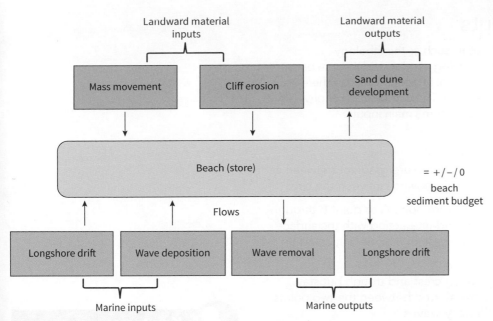

Figure 3.3 A simple beach system indicating inputs, flows, stores, outputs and sediment budget.

experiencing a sediment loss for the overall balance to remain the same. Alternatively, a beach with a negative sediment budget means more sediment is ending up elsewhere. Charting the volumes, direction, rate and impact of these changes can help indicate the connections within the system.

In reality there may be a slight loss of sediment to outputs beyond the system. Under very high energy conditions sediment may leak into neighbouring littoral cells through unusually strong waves and currents, be lost to deeper sea areas offshore, or see a transfer of sediment to stores beyond the active coastal zone, such as upper beaches, coastal dunes and mudflats. When sediment is permanently lost to the system, the destinations are known as **sediment sinks**.

Systems may enter phases of feedback cycle whereby a change in inputs leads to a change in the outputs, which may alter the overall budget to result in a change in the size of a store. Most frequently this takes the form of a **negative feedback cycle** in which the impetus for change in the system is dampened down. This has the effect of limiting the change and returning it to a more stable situation. An example might be cliff erosion that results in considerable slumping. Reducing further cliff retreat until the slumped material can be removed by wave action. Less frequent is a **positive feedback cycle** in which the change continues to amplify its initial impact. This may occur as a spit extends across a river estuary, reducing river velocity further with increased friction, leading to increased spit-head material accumulating and yet further river velocity reduction.

The degree of **dynamism** is reflected in whether a particular coastal system is in equilibrium. That is, whether the inputs, transfers and outputs are in balance and subject to relatively little change, or whether a state of imbalance has been introduced between the elements and more rapid change is taking place.

 Key terms

sediment sink: when sediment is lost to the system by transfer to a location beyond further access. Different to a 'sediment store' where additions and removal of sediment are possible

negative feedback cycle (loop): where changes within the system slow down or reduce the causes of further disruption, dampening down the impetus for change

positive feedback cycle (loop): where the effect of change is to amplify the original causes so that additional further change occurs

dynamism: the degree of change taking place within a system in terms of scale and/or rate

3.2 Coastal systems: Inputs

Inputs operate upon legacy physical control factors such as the lithology (characteristics of the rock), the structure of the geology and the tidal range between high and low tides. Inputs are transferred into the coastal zone from elsewhere, such as energy flows in the form of wind and wave energy. The combination of physical material and energy transfers constitute a coastal system's main inputs.

The energy of water and wind

Wind is a transfer of energy via the atmosphere. A pressure gradient between an area of high pressure and low pressure results in air moving between the two.

Waves can be thought of as a transfer of energy from point A to point B through a liquid. The input of that energy is usually the wind interacting with the surface of the sea or large body of water (although in the case of a tsunami it could be seabed movement due to a seismic shift).

Water particles move in a circular motion between crest and trough but stay largely in situ (Figure 3.4). It is *energy* that is transferred between the two points. Waves in the open ocean are known as **oscillatory waves**.

Key terms

oscillatory wave: a wave in open sea with full circular motion of particles

translatory wave: a breaking wave in which the circular motion is broken by basal friction

fetch: the length of ocean over which winds blow from a consistent direction

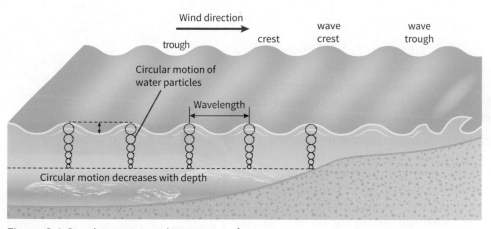

Figure 3.4 Circular motion within a series of waves.

This motion changes when a wave encounters shallow water. The lower circular motion encounters friction with the seabed and slows down while the upper motion continues with the original velocity. This results in waves crashing onto the shore. These are known as **translatory waves** (they translate their energy into actual forward motion).

Wind and wave variables

Wave energy shows itself in wave frequency or wave period (how many waves per minute), wave height (amplitude), wave length (from one crest to the next crest), wave velocity (forward motion from the wave peak) and wave steepness (angle of downward trajectory). The characteristics of waves often depend on the wind variables that drive them.

Fetch: the distance the wind has been blowing over a body of water. The longer the fetch, the greater the energy the waves absorb.

Variability of wind direction: winds that consistently blow from the same direction are known as prevailing winds and generate more high-energy waves than conditions where the wind direction is constantly shifting.

Pressure gradients: a high-pressure system over the North Atlantic will generate low wave energy, but a passing depression of very low pressure will generate stronger winds and more high-energy waves.

Storm surges: if an intense area of very low pressure resides over the ocean, the reduced air pressure allows the sea surface to rise higher than in surrounding areas of higher pressure (where the sea level is more depressed by descending air). This creates a pressure wave that may encounter the coast as a storm surge of higher water.

The characteristics of waves

Waves breaking at the coast can build up beaches or remove material (and make it available for transport and deposition elsewhere), depending on their characteristics (Figure 3.5).

Key terms

storm surge: sea level raised to an abnormal height beyond the usual tidal range as a result of particular short-term weather conditions

swash: the forward movement of a breaking translatory wave as it surges up the shore

backwash: the return flow of water due to gravity as the energy of the swash subsides

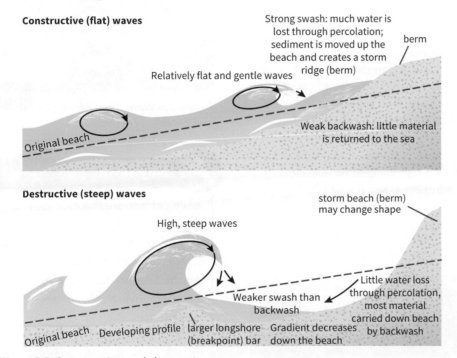

Figure 3.5 Constructive and destructive waves.

Constructive waves

These waves have the net effect of adding to beach deposition. Over reasonably short timescales, their **swash** pushes more material from offshore up the beach than the **backwash** removes.

- They are low in both height and frequency with most of their energy being expended in forward movement up the beach rather than steeper crashing down onto the beach.
- With an extensive swash there is a large surface area of sand/shingle for the water to percolate into, so the backwash contains a much reduced proportion of the original wave and can do less beach removal.
- The following swash is less impeded in its movement up the beach by the reduced backwash.
- At low tide, there is a net gain of material lower down the beach which, as the tide rises, is transferred to the upper beach with each further-advancing swash.

Destructive waves

These waves are steep in height, short in frequency and high in energy. As they crash down they destabilise and loosen existing beach material. Here the net effect is removal of beach material along the affected shoreline.

- As energy has gone into a more vertical impact the swash is relatively short-lived, but the backwash is strong and forceful in taking material down the beach.
- What swash there may be from one wave has to overcome the strong backwash of the preceding wave and so makes little progress up the beach.
- Subsequent waves are frequent and, with a falling tide, remove unconsolidated beach material seawards. A rising tide has the effect of loosening material incrementally further up the beach.

Wave refraction

Around a headland, waves have a tendency to 'bend' and have a higher frequency on the promontory (convergent waves). There is an increase in erosive power. This is because waves approaching the headland encounter shallower water sooner, while their constituent part in the bay is still in deeper water. Friction with the sea floor slows the headland-approaching waves and causes their frequency to increase. In bays the reverse occurs, with wave lines splaying out (divergent), being less frequent, having less energy and producing a more constructive impact (Figure 3.6).

Wave refraction is a key process in the formation of caves and particularly arches. Refracted waves cause the lateral sides of a headland to have direct wave action, as well as the promontory head facing open sea (Figure 3.7).

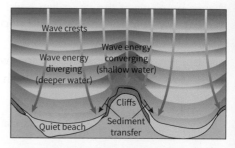

Figure 3.6 Wave refraction around a headland.

Key term

wave refraction: the changes in wave orientation and frequency as they encounter a non-uniform coastline; waves may be refracted (bent) towards a feature (convergence) or away (divergence) as water depth varies

Figure 3.7 Lateral erosion of a headland due to wave refraction.

Tides

A regular and consistent input of energy into an open coast system is a result of tides with, approximately, two high and two low tides each day. Tides are caused by the effect of gravity from the Moon and – less powerfully – the Sun acting upon the rotating Earth. Ocean surfaces lift where the Earth's gravity is slightly neutralised.

- One ocean bulge is experienced on the side of the Earth facing the Moon, with a corresponding one on the opposite side of the Earth at the same time. Between them the sea is lower, creating low-tide conditions (Figure 3.8).
- The time it takes for the Earth to spin between the two bulges is approximately 12 hours 25 minutes, so a low tide is experienced about 6 hours 12 minutes after a high tide.
- This effect is greatest when the Moon and the Sun are in line with the Earth, intensifying each other's gravitational effect, giving spring tides. This happens at Full Moon and New Moon.
- Seven days after a spring tide the Moon is at right angles to the Earth and Sun and the gravitational effects are diluted. High tides are not so high, and low tides are not so low. The **tidal range** (difference in metres between the maximum daily high tide and low tide) is much reduced, giving neap tides.
- The tidal range is greatest where an ocean is funnelled into a constricted channel and the water volume is forced to rise as it is contained. The highest tidal range in the world is in the Bay of Fundy, Nova Scotia, Canada, at 16.3 m.

The significance of tides in coastal systems extends to both physical and human contexts:

- the larger the tidal range, the more extensive the **intertidal zone** subject to erosional and depositional processes
- the smaller the tidal range, the more consistently a part of the coastline will be subject to prevailing destructive or constructive wave action
- the significant flow of sea into and then, a few hours later, out of a coastal section can generate strong currents that influence the direction and scale of coastal sediment movement
- increased flood-risk to coastal communities often occurs when a low-pressure system coincides with a high tide; the combined effect of a high tide rising yet further due to the low air pressure can lead to a storm surge that can overwhelm coastal flood defences
- the energy potential of dependable rises and falls in sea level are exploited in tidal power-generators. Swansea Bay, Wales, has a major scheme in development to generate renewable energy from the twice-daily rise and fall of the coastal waters.

High- to low-energy coastlines

High-energy coastlines experience consistently strong waves. They are likely to see winds approaching from a consistent onshore direction (prevailing winds) with a long fetch. Combine that with periodic low-pressure systems and a large tidal range, and the inputs of energy into the system will come from a range of sources.

High-energy coastlines are associated with significant erosion and substantial transportation of eroded material within the system. There is a net transfer of material from coastline to sea.

Low-energy coasts exist where waves are less powerful, air pressure gradients less extreme and tidal currents are relatively gentle. They are more likely to be associated with material being deposited.

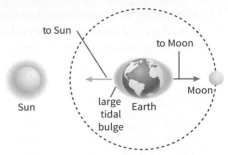

Spring tide: Sun and Moon aligned with Earth

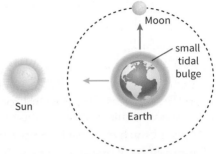

Neap tide: Sun and Moon at right angle to Earth

Figure 3.8 Variations in tides.

Key terms

tidal range: the vertical difference in height of sea level between high and low tide; it varies with the monthly lunar cycle and is at its maximum with spring tide conditions

intertidal zone: the shoreline between the highest and lowest spring tides; it is where the predominant wave activity occurs so is subject to most marine erosion, transfer and deposition

high-energy coast: a coastline subject to maximum inputs; it is likely to be dynamic

low-energy coast: a coastline that has key inputs, transfers and outputs in balance and is more likely to be in a state of stable equilibrium

Coastlines can vary seasonally between high- and low-energy conditions. Months of winter storms can make for a high-energy coastline. The same coast in summer may become a low-energy environment.

Physical material inputs

Inorganic matter

Besides energy, another key input into a coastal system is physical material. The forms this may take are as particles in suspension, sediment, sand and gravel, pebbles, boulders and cliff debris. The key sources of this input are:

- River discharge: sediment and fine material brought to an estuary and entering the sea.
- Ocean currents: these may transport material thousands of miles and upwelling currents may bring material to surface waters from significant depths.
- Seabed disturbance: severe storms can destabilise material on the sea floor and move it towards a coast.
- Cliff and shore disintegration: the transfer of material as cliffs erode and upper beach material is removed into the active zone of coasts provides an input of solid material that can be transported.

Organic matter

The coast is a living environment that provides a habitat for flora (plants) and fauna (animals). These can colonise an area of seabed from elsewhere if conditions become hospitable (such as kelp, or coral), or can decline if conditions deteriorate. Species can invade an area of coast and compete to the detriment of another species (e.g. crown-of-thorns starfish devastate some coral reefs). Many species of fish are migratory and make a regular passage through a region of coast while others inhabit localised feeding grounds all year round.

Biota is not only part of the natural coastal system in its own right but can contribute to biological weathering of the shore zone, as well as reducing erosion in the form of living shorelines.

3.3 Coastal geomorphology: Processes

Process is the 'how and why' of change; the mechanisms operating upon the inputs that result in particular outputs.

Weathering

Coastal weathering is the disintegration of rock as it loses its integrity or coherence. The rock mass stays largely the same, but its structure is increasingly fragmented. Because coastal weathering is not dependent on the sea, it often takes the form of **subaerial weathering**.

The coastal zone involves weathering due to subaerial and marine processes. The processes take place via physical changes in rock (mechanical weathering), changes in mineral structure (chemical weathering) and the action of plant and animal organisms (biological weathering).

Thinking like a geographer

Geographers need to consider potential changes within a system and consider 'scale' in terms of both area and time. Are mechanical weathering processes likely to operate equally all year round on coasts, or will there be a seasonal variation in each of them?

Research point

Consult tide tables for a selection of coastal regions. Identify spring and neap tide phases from the high- and low-tide heights. What is the tidal range at spring and neap tide conditions?

Physical and human

Large tidal ranges have considerable potential for energy generation. But what *problems* do changing daily tide times and variable monthly tidal ranges, as spring and neap tides alternate, cause for human activity?

For an activity on coastal inputs, processes and outputs, download Worksheet 3.1 from **Cambridge Elevate**.

Key terms

biota: the distinctive animal and plant life of a particular habitat or environmental zone

subaerial weathering: involves processes at the base of the atmosphere that cause solid rock to lose integrity, internal coherence and to fragment

Mechanical (physical) weathering

Internal pressures are exerted on rock as a result of changes in the physical structure within its mass. This occurs due to:

- Wetting and drying: rock in the intertidal zone (and some above, within wave and spray reach) may alternate between being wet and being dry. Some rocks, such as shale, expand when they are wet and contract when they are dry, and this can contribute to tiny fissures developing and the rock fragmenting.
- Exfoliation: dry rock in the sunshine may absorb considerable heat, then be cooled rapidly by contact with the much colder sea. Repeated expansion and contraction may lead to the outer layers of rock fracturing.
- Crystallisation: the high salt content of seawater can lead to the growth of salt crystals within rock under drier conditions. These can exert pressure within small joints and, over time, cause the rock to lose integrity.
- Freeze–thaw activity: rainwater penetrates joints in exposed rock and if night temperatures drop below freezing, the resulting conversion to ice expands and exerts pressure within the rock, enlarging the fissure (Figure 3.9).

Chemical weathering

Both rain and seawater contain chemicals that can increase the reactivity of minerals within coastal rocks. As mineral compounds undergo chemical reaction, they can alter the rock structure.

- Carbonation: coastlines composed of chalk or limestone may be dissolved by acidic rainwater or seawater. The rain/sea absorbs carbon dioxide from the atmosphere, creating a weak carbonic acid. This can convert solid calcium carbonate to soluble calcium bicarbonate and the rock dissolves.
- Oxidation: rocks containing iron (ferrous) compounds experience oxidation of the iron into a ferric state (or 'rusting') when oxygen and water are readily available from air or sea. This can lead to disintegration.

Biological weathering

Living organisms can contribute to the **weathering** of coastal rocks through the activity of both plants and animals which can disrupt the existing structure of rocks.

- The roots of surface plants on cliff tops can create and expand tiny fissures. Subsurface seaweed such as bladderwrack attached to rocks can weaken and detach them as it sways in the currents of storm conditions.
- Surface animals such as sand martins and puffins may excavate nesting burrows in cliff faces. Subsurface marine creatures such as the piddock drill holes in rock and limpets create a home indentation on their base rock to which they return after grazing.

Mass movement

This is the movement of consolidated material (solid rock) or unconsolidated material (clay and soil) due to gravity (Figure 3.10). It is a common feature of coastlines with higher relief. Wave action in the intertidal zone at the base of a cliff undercuts the cliff face via a **wave-cut notch**, resulting in material above becoming unsupported and more likely to collapse. Forms of mass movement include (rapid to slower):

- Rockfall: arch roofs, stacks and cliff faces collapse as a weakness becomes unsupportable.

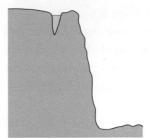

Rainwater enters a joint

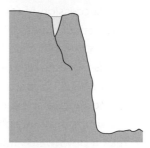

The temperature falls below 0°C. The water freezes and expands, enlarging the joint

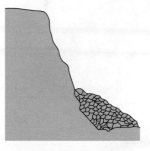

Eventually after repeated freeze-thaw cycles, the loosened rock breaks off

Figure 3.9 Freeze–thaw action: a form of mechanical weathering.

 Key terms

weathering: the disintegration of rock in situ

wave-cut notch: a horizontal indentation at the base of cliffs where wave action is most focused and erosional processes are concentrated; it results in the undercutting of cliffs

- Landslides: a significant section of the cliff becomes detached and slides down. They usually affect less consolidated geology, such as boulder clay or weathered shales and sandstones.
- Runoff: when sheet flow of intense rain or snowmelt occurs on an impermeable clifftop surface it may flow over, transporting fine material onto the cliff face.
- Mudflows: fine particles of mud flow down the face of cliffs, often heavily saturated by persistent rainfall which adds to its bulk and makes it a more liquid consistency.
- Slumping: a succession of rotational landslips in which the cliff face collapses in distinct stages. Heavy rain may lubricate a curved slip plane and undercutting at the cliff base by wave action results in a slippage of material down towards the beach. It often occurs on cliffs composed of glacial deposits (Figure 3.11).
- Soil creep: the gradual movement downhill of individual particles due to gravity. Raindrops or wave splash may dislodge a particle, and it is most likely to take a downwards trajectory due to the influence of gravity.

Figure 3.11 A caravan site on a cliff edge showing evidence of slumping.

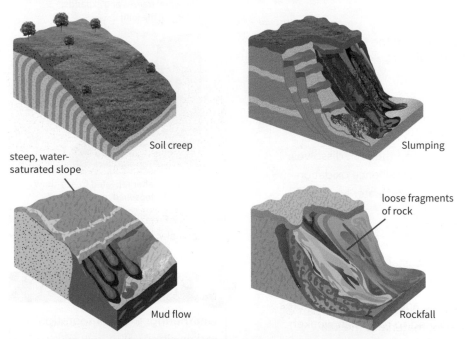

Figure 3.10 Different forms of mass movement.

 Maths for geographers

Glacial till is slumping along a rapidly eroding line of cliff. Measurements were taken along the top of the cliff to record the loss of land (in cm) over 12 months. Calculate the interquartile range (IQR) of the data set (see Chapter 12 Fieldwork).

146	97	102	136	158	142	127	114	108	92

83	61	77	35	22	24	56	73	99

Figure 3.12 Corrasion/abrasion chip marks on a cliff face.

Coastal erosion

Erosion is the breakdown and subsequent removal and transportation of material. It is usually caused by the direct action of the sea on the shore (Figure 3.13).

- Hydraulic action: when waves break against a rock face with joints facing the wave, air inside the joints is highly compressed. This leads to wedging, as the compressed air forces fractures further apart. As the wave recedes, the air expands with a forceful release of pressure. The changing pressure inside the joints' water content leads to **cavitation** – the violent effervescence of air bubbles coming out of solution as the pressure drops (like opening a bottle of carbonated drink). The resultant shockwaves can enlarge rock fractures and fragment the cliff.
- Corrasion/abrasion: the launching of rock fragments and pebbles against cliffs by waves during high-energy sea conditions can break off pieces of solid cliff and weaken rock structure.
- Quarrying: destructive waves in storm conditions can plunge heavy hydraulic pressure on cliff faces. The vibration of the cliff structure can dislodge bits of rock to the point of undercutting the base of cliffs.
- Corrosion/solution: some rock, such as chalk and limestone, is readily soluble and dissolved rock is removed in solution rather than disintegrating into fine particles.
- Attrition: this is the smoothing and reducing of angular rock fragments into pebbles, shingle and – eventually – sand particles. This occurs due to friction as particles are rolled over each other by the continuous action of waves and currents.

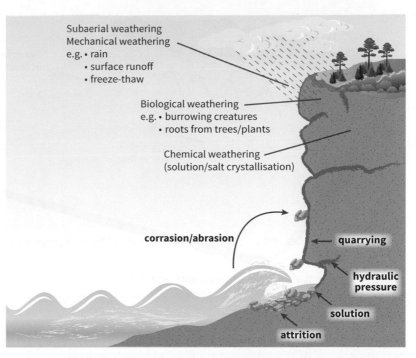

Figure 3.13 Erosion and weathering processes.

Transportation of eroded material

While the wind can move dry, unconsolidated beach material from one part of the shoreline to another, the dominant transporter of material is the sea.

- Waves move material up and down beaches when approaching the coast directly. Swash transports material up the beach; backwash removes it down the beach.
- Longshore drift (littoral movement): when the wind direction is oblique to the shore, swash rushes up the beach consistent with the wind direction. The shelving angle of the beach, however, means the backwash scours material back to the sea at right angles to the shore. The next wave approaches obliquely and the effect of this is to move material in a zigzag fashion along the shore over a period of hours (Figure 3.14).
- Offshore currents: some, such as rip currents, move material out to sea at right angles to the shoreline. As they weaken some distance from the shore, the material they have carried is deposited to form sand banks in their eddies. Other currents re-shape depositional landforms.

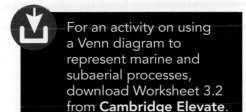

For an activity on using a Venn diagram to represent marine and subaerial processes, download Worksheet 3.2 from **Cambridge Elevate**.

 Key terms

erosion: the degradation of rock and its removal to expose a fresh rock face

cavitation: the opening up of cavities within cliffs as a result of stresses imposed by the breaking of waves due to pressure variations as waves crash into and then recede from joints

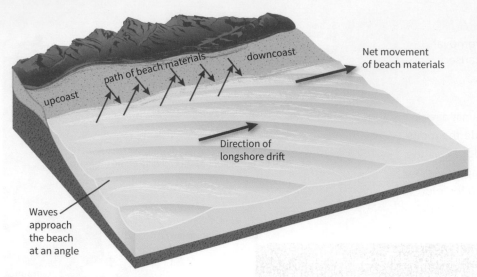

Figure 3.14 Longshore drift.

Look on **Cambridge Elevate** to read more about the coastal marine environment in 'An introduction to the coastal geomorphology of Great Britain' (www.cambridge.org/links/gase6013).

The methods by which material is transported depends largely on its size, weight and the energy of the transporting flow. Methods include:

- In solution: dissolved material – particularly calcium-based (chalk and limestone) – will not be visibly moving and yet it is in transit from one area and may be deposited in another as marine creatures extract calcium from seawater and use it to construct shells or corals.
- In suspension: very small particles are kept in motion by even quite light currents and turbulence.
- Saltation: shingle and pebbles may be bounced along the seabed under higher-energy wave and current conditions; the added buoyancy of being submerged in seawater means they travel in a series of hops.
- Traction: larger rocks may be dragged and sometimes rolled along the seabed, usually in high-energy (storm) conditions.

Figure 3.15 Wooden groynes intercept material transported by longshore drift making beaches wider and higher.

Deposition of transported material

Once the energy flow that is moving material declines, then deposition is likely to occur (Figure 3.15). This may be on the seabed, as extensions to existing coastal features, on the shore or along estuaries. Energy flows may decline due to:

- the energy source altering, such as a current weakening or prevailing winds becoming more variable in direction or lighter in strength, or at the point of tidal change – the peak of high/low tide
- discontinuity in flow: turbulence between opposing currents can result in deposition – such as at the end of a spit – where the colliding flow of two currents causes both to slow; turbulence may be seen at the surface but this may be accompanied by deposition below
- increased friction: the more energy required to overcome friction with the seabed or shoreline features, the less material can be transported, resulting in deposition of the largest and heaviest particles
- increased load: a sudden discharge of material from a river, landslip or beach will mean the energy of the system is not sufficient to transport the additional load, so deposition of some of the material in transit will occur.

ACTIVITY 3.1

1 Draw up a table to compare key inputs, processes and outputs for high-energy coasts with low-energy coasts. What are the most significant differences, and what similarities occur?

Tip

Make sure that you are clear about the distinction between 'coastal feature' and 'coastal process'; they refer to different aspects of the coastal environment.

3.4 Coastal landscape development

If coastal processes are the 'how and why' of what is taking place in a coastal system, coastal features are the components upon which they operate and alter. They can be classified as features of erosion or features of deposition.

Features of coastal erosion

Headlands and bays

Headlands are most likely to develop where varying geology is aligned at right angles to the coast – termed a discordant coast. If the alternation lies parallel to the coast (concordant coast), then a series of cliffs and coves may develop depending on whether the more resistant rock forms the cliff line (Figure 3.16).

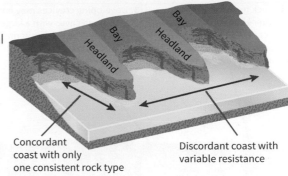

Concordant coast with only one consistent rock type

Discordant coast with variable resistance

Figure 3.16 Discordant and concordant coasts.

 Watch a video on **Cambridge Elevate** about coastal erosion on the Jurassic coast in England.

Cliff line and wave-cut platform

As cliffs of solid rock recede over time from their original shore position they may leave a basal shelf, uncovered at low tide and submerged at high tide. This wave-cut platform represents the base of the cliff that lies below the dominant intertidal zone erosion processes (Figure 3.17). As the cliff line retreats, the wave-cut platform becomes wider and has an increasing frictional effect on advancing waves.

A negative feedback loop develops in the erosional system, as wave energy dissipates the wider the wave-cut platform. Erosive power at the base of the cliff declines and the rate of cliff retreat slows. A change in inputs, such as sea-level rise, can induce a system response and result in more rapid cliff erosion once again.

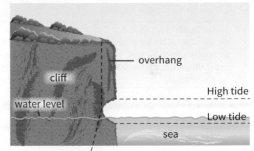

overhang
cliff
water level
High tide
Low tide
sea
Wave-cut notch

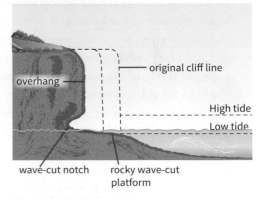

original cliff line
overhang
High tide
Low tide
wave-cut notch   rocky wave-cut platform

Figure 3.17 Cliff retreat.

Maths for geographers

You wish to calculate the height of a cliff. Study Figure 3.18. You are standing 22.6 m from the foot of the cliff and measure an angle of 36° to the cliff top using a clinometer. Your eye-height is 1.7 m above the beach. What is the height of the cliff?

Use the formula: $X = D \times \tan(\text{angle}) + H$

$$X = 22.6 \times \tan 36 + 1.7$$

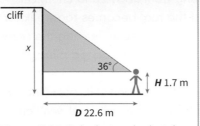

cliff
x
36°
H 1.7 m
D 22.6 m

Figure 3.18 Calculating the height of a cliff.

Caves, blow holes, arches, stacks and stumps

A succession of features can develop on a headland where the geology is hard enough to provide some resistance and support (Figure 3.19). Where the rock is more jointed, fractured or weakened by earth movements, the agents of erosion and weathering can wear it away more rapidly. Joints enlarge into small caves, which become larger caves over time.

- **Cave to blow hole:** where caves face directly towards oncoming waves, the full hydraulic force of the wave is experienced towards the rear of the cave. Over time, this can enlarge joints in the cave roof and weaken the overlying rock to the extent that localised roof collapse occurs and a blow hole represents the exposed cave roof.

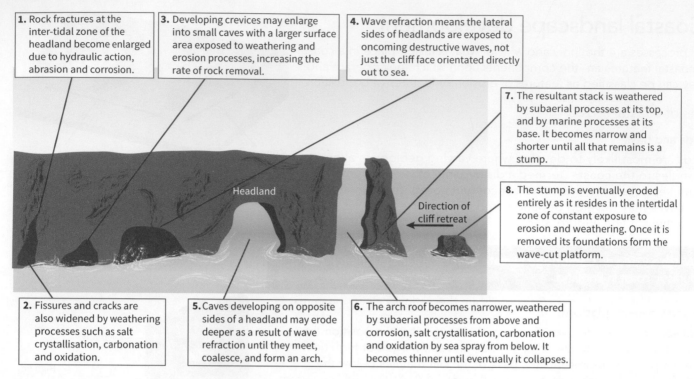

1. Rock fractures at the inter-tidal zone of the headland become enlarged due to hydraulic action, abrasion and corrosion.

3. Developing crevices may enlarge into small caves with a larger surface area exposed to weathering and erosion processes, increasing the rate of rock removal.

4. Wave refraction means the lateral sides of headlands are exposed to oncoming destructive waves, not just the cliff face orientated directly out to sea.

7. The resultant stack is weathered by subaerial processes at its top, and by marine processes at its base. It becomes narrow and shorter until all that remains is a stump.

8. The stump is eventually eroded entirely as it resides in the intertidal zone of constant exposure to erosion and weathering. Once it is removed its foundations form the wave-cut platform.

Headland

Direction of cliff retreat

2. Fissures and cracks are also widened by weathering processes such as salt crystallisation, carbonation and oxidation.

5. Caves developing on opposite sides of a headland may erode deeper as a result of wave refraction until they meet, coalesce, and form an arch.

6. The arch roof becomes narrower, weathered by subaerial processes from above and corrosion, salt crystallisation, carbonation and oxidation by sea spray from below. It becomes thinner until eventually it collapses.

Figure 3.19 Cave to stump development.

- Cave to arch: where caves develop along the sides of a headland, they can be enlarged by hydraulic action and other processes to erode through to the opposite side of the headland or through a curtain of more resistant rock. Sometimes two or more caves coalesce.
- Arch to stack: while the arch walls may be further eroded by marine erosion, the roof – extending increasingly above wave height – is more likely to be subject to subaerial weathering from above and chemical action due to wave splash from below. If the roof becomes too weak for the sides to provide sufficient support, it may collapse, leaving the seaward wall unattached to the headland and standing as an isolated pillar of rock – or a stack (Figure 3.20).
- Stack to stump: a stack in the intertidal zone will be eroded at its base (and slightly above) by marine erosion and at its summit be subject to subaerial weathering. It is reduced in both height and width, collapsing in successive stages until it becomes a much smaller remnant of the original stack. This is a stump, which is eventually worn away completely to the level of the wave-cut platform.

Figure 3.20 A stack and wave cut-notch.

Investigate

Look up images of arches and stacks on the internet. Try to establish the type of rock that forms the coastline in these locations. Why are some types of rock more likely to result in the development of arches and stacks than others?

Features of coastal deposition

A sediment (littoral) cell is defined as a section of coast that operates as a closed sediment system with material transferred within it and compartmentalised by major headlands. Sediment is transported from inputs (cliffs, dunes, rivers, offshore beds) by the available energy (winds, waves, tides, currents) to stores (beaches, spits, offshore bars, mudflats, and shallow water deposits), which may accumulate or decline according to the local sediment budget. The direction of movement can be on-/off-shore or along the shore (littoral movement).

Most depositional features are stores of sediment cell material unless fixed in sinks. The rate of addition to, or loss from, these stores depends on the amount of sediment available and the level and consistency of energy to transfer material.

Material may be lost to the sediment cell if it contributes to a feature that puts it beyond future accessibility. These sediment sinks may take the form of stabilised inland dune systems, offshore sea floor ravines and, under very high-energy conditions, out of the sediment cell altogether to neighbouring cells or into deep offshore water. So while sediment cells are theoretically closed systems, there is leakage both in and out at times.

Understanding the concept of sediment cells is important to seeing depositional features as elements within the wider system operating at the coast. Their form and characteristics depend upon the inputs of material and energy operating and the transfer processes at work.

Beaches

Beaches can be thought of as a store of eroded material along the shoreline. Sometimes they represent net accumulation, other times they experience net loss depending on the nature of the tides and whether waves are destructive or constructive. Beaches accumulate material from marine deposition, wind-blown material from upwind beaches and from mass movement if there are cliffs behind.

- Beach characteristics: beach material can range from mud, fine to coarse sand, shingle and pebbles with rock fragments to boulders deposited during storm conditions, eroded out of glacial deposits or the result of rock falls. Beach gradient depends on the size of material contributing to the beach (courser leads to steeper), whether a phase of deposition or removal is occurring and the rate of beach store change.
- Beach features: at the top of the beach there may be a storm beach of larger material deposited by high-energy waves at high tide during storm conditions. This may be beyond the influence of usual high tides – even spring high tides. There may be a series of beach terraces, known as berms, which represent the positional change as each high tide maximum occurs at a slightly lower position on the beach during the spring to neap tide weekly cycle. Beach cusps are arcs of coarser beach material in the horns with finer material in the bay. It is not clear how they form but once they have, they are self-sustaining as approaching swash is funnelled by the two horns towards the centre of the embayment where their combined backwash is then strongest. At the low-water mark, there may be ridges of finer material running parallel to the shore deposited by backwash, separated by deeper channel runnels where water finds a route back to sea as the tide falls (Figure 3.21).

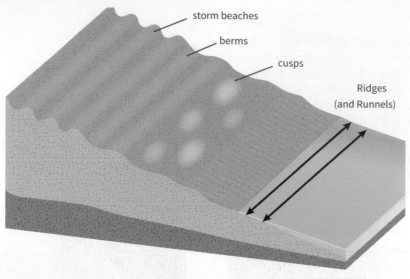

Figure 3.21 Beach features.

Research point

Select a range of images of coastal landscapes with similar features of erosion and/or deposition. Describe the variations in the features and suggest what element of the physical control factors, inputs and processes at each location contribute to each distinctive coastal landscape.

Investigate

Study OS maps of a section of coast. Aim to identify beaches and other depositional features, their composition and structure and look for map evidence of the processes that may be forming them.

Physical and human

To what extent are beaches an entirely natural phenomenon, or can human activity influence their development?

Spits, bars and tombolos

Spits, bars and tombolos are all features resulting from deposition of beach material constantly fed by longshore drift (Figure 3.22).

The particular shape and form of each feature gives the type of classification.

Spit: a long narrow beach of sand or shingle with one end attached to the shore and the other extending into the sea or estuary (Figure 3.23). A spit forms where

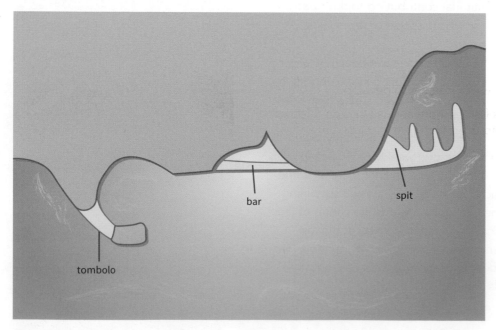

Figure 3.22 A tombolo, bar and spit.

Figure 3.23 A spit at Sidney Island, British Columbia, Canada.

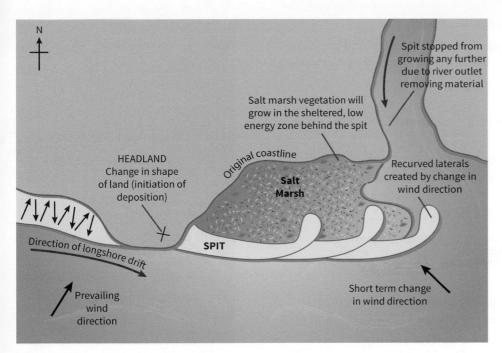

Figure 3.24 A compound spit.

To annotate a diagram of a chalk headland, download Worksheet 3.3 from **Cambridge Elevate**.

Figure 3.25 A bar at Slapton Ley.

there is a break in the direction of a coastline along a length with strong and consistent longshore drift. Movement of beach material extends out from the shore to a point where turbulence with another current causes sediment-carrying currents to slow and material to be deposited. Spit development may be considered a positive feedback cycle in that the longer the spit, the further the distance (and the greater the channel friction) a river experiences. Consequently, velocity is lost and more sediment is deposited on the landward side of the spit and its tip. The spit extends in length over time and its tip may become recurved as it is shaped by the prevailing wind, currents and wave refraction. If a substantial recurve of the end of the spit occurs, it is equivalent to the break in direction of a coast, and the prevailing longshore-drift current may cause new deposition consistent with its general direction of flow. After a period of deposition, this may also become recurved. A spit showing evidence of a series of sequential growth and recurvature is known as a compound spit (Figure 3.24).

Bar: this is where a spit extends across a bay and rejoins the coast on the opposite shore, completely confining saltwater behind it in a lagoon (Figure 3.25). The absence of a second intervening current allows this feature to develop.

Tombolo: in some instances, a spit extends from a shore and reaches an offshore island, joining the previously isolated land to the main shore by means of a shingle/sand beach (Figure 3.26).

In all three cases, the flow of currents behind the feature are slowed and deposition is more likely to take place on the landward side, leading to mudflats, saltmarsh and new habitat-formation.

Barrier islands

These are a series of depositional islands running parallel to the shore but detached from it. The cause of their formation is unclear but they are more likely to occur in a coastal zone of limited tidal range with a gentle gradient to the offshore shelf, high-wave energy and a plentiful supply of depositional material. A longer stretch of deposition is known as an offshore bar, and barrier islands may be due to erosional wave activity along certain sections of an extensive bar dividing it into separate sections (Figure 3.27).

Figure 3.26 A tombolo, joining Portland to the mainland near Weymouth.

Sand dunes

Immediately behind an active beach zone sand dunes may develop from wind-blown sand until fixed in location by vegetation. They are most likely to develop where:

- beaches are largely sandy
- there is a large tidal zone, exposing considerable beach between low and high tide as source material
- the beach gradient is shallow, so low tide reveals a large body of beach and there is a significant store of sand to dry out and be moved
- there are persistent onshore winds to both dry the sand and move particles by saltation to the inland zone beyond the beach.

The formation of dunes goes through a sequence of stages (Figure 3.28):

- Embryo dunes develop where wind speeds slow and sand is deposited beyond the beach.
- Drought- and salt-tolerant plants (e.g. prickly saltwort and tough grasses, such as marram) begin to colonise the sand. This starts to stabilise the dune as well as accumulate more sand by decreasing wind velocity.
- Foredunes develop with higher sand accumulations. As more vegetation grows, dies, decomposes and adds organic matter to the dune, it creates an environment for additional plant colonisation.
- Other species of grass develop with more surface root systems and flowering plants find conditions survivable as salt content reduces. The dune surface is further fixed and a humus layer changes the dune colour from yellow to grey.
- Dunes inland become fixed with a considerable vegetative matting. This is still a fragile surface and can be easily damaged by funnelled high-velocity winds or footpath erosion. This can result in a blowout, where exposed loose sand is excavated by the wind and the dune structure deteriorates.
- Dune slacks may develop in between substantial dunes. These are depressions with higher moisture content as the water table comes close to, or cuts, the surface. Reeds, rushes and small shrubs may take advantage of the damper, milder, more sheltered microclimate.
- A dune heath may develop inland from the dune system. Drought-tolerant larger shrubs such as gorse, broom and sea-buckthorn colonise the zone beyond active sand accumulation. They help further modify soil pH, humus content and moisture-retentiveness.

Figure 3.27 Barrier islands at North Captiva Island to Captiva Island, Florida, USA.

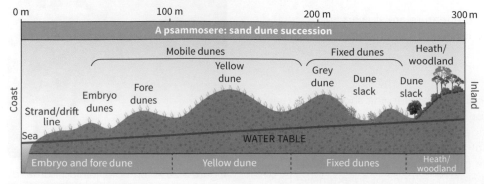

Figure 3.28 Cross section of a dune.

- A climatic **climax vegetation** of birch, pine and other conifers may eventually develop where conditions are suitable. A plant succession that represents the environmental evolution of a habitat from initial sand dune to pine woodland is called a psammosere.

Saltmarsh and estuarine deposits

In areas of sheltered water – behind spits and bars and along the banks of river estuaries where tidal currents are slower – deposition of finer sediments occurs. As mud, silt and fine sand settles, the depth of saline water reduces to a point where salt-tolerant (halophytic) plants can become established and can exist with twice-daily submersion at high tide and exposure at low tide.

Pioneer plants are early colonisers of shallow water and include eelgrass (after prolonged submergence) and, where exposure time increases, spartina (or cordgrass). The dense stems and roots of these plants further reduce the speed of tidal flow, and increased deposition takes place once they have become established. As the plants die, collapse and decompose they further raise the level of the submerged shore.

Increasingly, mudflats are transformed into saltmarsh as sediment accumulates. The intertidal shore is submerged for shorter periods and exposed for longer until it is only the highest spring tides that cover the vegetation. Colourful flowering plants such as sea thrift, sea lavender and marsh samphire become established and develop a denser coverage of vegetation

Some higher saltmarsh meadows are reclaimed by farmers for grazing sheep, but where human intervention doesn't occur a climatic climax vegetation of alder, ash and oak may develop on British coasts. The fully completed plant succession (Figure 3.29) from muddy shore to vegetation climax in a saltwater environment is known as a halosere.

Key term

climax vegetation: the dominant mix of vegetation species that characterise an environment within a particular climate region given sufficient time for conditions to suit colonisation and attain stability

Physical and human

In what ways may human activity impede the full development of a halosere succession?

ACTIVITY 3.2

1   Classify the major coastal landform features according to whether they are formed due to:
    a   predominantly subaerial processes
    b   predominantly erosional processes
    c   predominantly marine processes
    d   a significant contribution by all of the above.

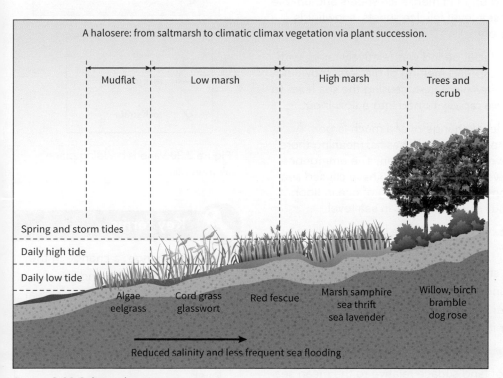

Figure 3.29 Saltmarsh succession.

Coastal components

The same coastal features in different locations may have formed by similar processes, but it is the totality of features, along with the nature of the rock that contribute to a coastal landscape. Rock lithology can have a significant effect on the form and characteristics of the features that develop over time.

Rock hardness: some rocks are more resistant than others due to their chemical composition and hardness. Granite erodes far more slowly and is more angular than an equivalent mass of chalk.

Rock structure: some rocks are naturally more jointed and fractured. Others can be more massive, with significant solid blocks between major joints and bedding planes such as carboniferous limestone. However, even these can be more fractured in places as a result of localised earth movements, faulting and folding.

Structural alignment: sedimentary rocks often occur in distinct layers or bedding. The angle of orientation of bedding where it is exposed at the coast can influence the rate of erosion and shape of cliff (Figure 3.30).

Changes in relative levels of sea and shore

The intertidal zone between high and low tide is not fixed: the land may be ascending or sinking; sea level may be rising or falling; in some cases – both.

Eustatic change

Eustatic change is the change of sea level relative to the land (Figure 3.31). The fluid nature of oceans means the change is global in scale. Global sea level can be thought of as a system that depends on relative rates of input (river system discharge, ice melt and rainfall) and output, in the form of ocean evaporation and tectonic subduction (see the carbon cycle in Chapter 1). Substantive changes in sea level arise as a result of variation in the balance of these key components.

At the height of the last major ice advance, global sea levels were considerably lower as evaporation continued to remove water from the world's oceans. In the higher latitudes, so much water was locked up in immense ice sheets and unable to replenish the oceans via river flow that sea level fell. Ice sheets, snowfields and glaciers may be considered a water store.

The transition to the current warmer interglacial period was relatively rapid, with global temperatures rising swiftly. The widespread melting of glaciers, snowfields and ice sheets resulted in immense meltwater discharge, causing the sea level to rise to near current levels. A long-term store rapidly turned into a flow input.

Tectonic activity can result in eustatic sea level change over a much larger timescale by increasing and decreasing the size of ocean basins, meaning there is a larger (or smaller) area to contain a given volume of ocean. The emergence of the mid-Atlantic ridge of subterranean volcanoes is likely to have caused sea level rise of several hundred metres. In contrast, the spreading of ocean floors through tectonic plate divergence can result in eustatic falls in sea level.

Current and future eustatic rise as a result of climate change is thought to be occurring due to two effects:

- rapid melting of previously stable ice sheets and glaciers, releasing vast amounts of freshwater into the surrounding oceans
- thermal expansion of warmer seawater – the same given mass of ocean occupies a greater volume the higher its temperature.

Isostatic change

Isostatic change is the change in height of land surface relative to the mean sea level (Figure 3.31). It operates at a more localised scale than eustatic change.

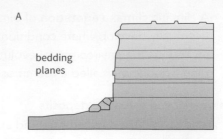

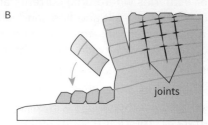

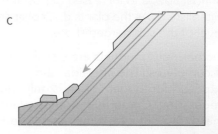

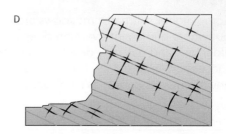

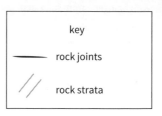

key	
——	rock joints
//	rock strata

Figure 3.30 Various bedding plane alignments.

Key terms

eustatic change: a change in the relative level of land and sea due to rises and falls in the global seal level

isostatic change: the rise or fall of land in relation to a given sea level

Possible causes of sea-level change

Sea level changes over geological time scales. There are four stages to this process.

1. Warming of the oceans leads to thermal expansion

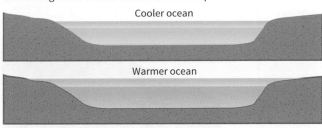

Cooler ocean

Warmer ocean

The impact of this ranges from a few centimetres to several metres. The surface warms much faster than the deeper water, which may need thousands of years to be affected.

2. Oceanic water locked up in ice sheets during glacial periods

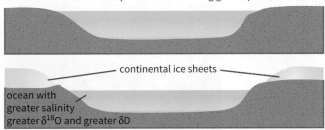

continental ice sheets

ocean with greater salinity greater $\delta^{18}O$ and greater δD

Can lower sea level by hundreds of metres, but occurs slowly as ice sheets grow. As ice melts, sea level rises again. This changes the actual amount of water in the oceans.

Volume of water in the oceans changes
Volume of the ocean basins changes

3. Sea floor spreading

Newer ocean crust may take up some of the volume previously occupied by the sea. Tectonic spreading from a mid-ocean ridge may raise sea level.

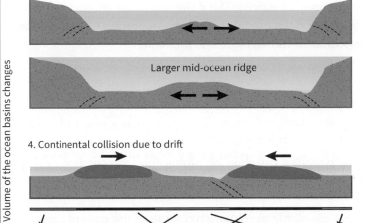

Larger mid-ocean ridge

4. Continental collision due to drift

new ocean area

Sea level changes over tens of millions of years because the total amount of continental area is reduced, and oceanic area increases. The changes in continental position happen incredibly slowly.

Figure 3.31 Eustatic and isostatic change.

The sheer weight of ice sheets can have the effect of lowering the land's surface by depressing the crust into the viscous mantle. When ice sheets melt, the land can 'bounce' back up, a process known as isostatic recovery.

Postglacial isostatic readjustment takes place in two phases: an initial rapid rise as the continental crust resumes its buoyancy upon the mantle, and then a longer more incremental rise as viscous mantle that had been forced away from beneath the depressed crust slowly flows back. Britain is still rising from the effects of the last ice advance, but there is a tilt to the isostatic recovery that sees the north west of Scotland emerging most rapidly (having been subject to the heaviest weight of ice) while the south east of England is submerging due to a geological axis.

Tectonic activity can result in uplift of land particularly at plate margins. This can be a few metres as a result of one seismic event, or whole mountain ranges, as in the Andes of South America, the summits of which contain fossilised marine creatures. Alternatively, seismic activity can result in downthrust leading to the submergence of previously dry coasts. Some coastal sections of north-east Japan dropped up to 0.84 m following the devastating Tōhoku earthquake of March 2011.

Look on **Cambridge Elevate** to read an article from *The Huffington Post* about eustatic and isostatic change in 'Coastal flooding more frequent in US due to sea level rise and sinking land' (www.cambridge.org/links/gase6014).

Making connections

Refer to section 4.1 Glaciers as natural systems, to see the extent of the earth subject to post-glacial isostatic readjustment and whether it is likely to continue to experience it as global temperatures rise.

Tip

Eustatic and isostatic changes in relative sea level may operate independently or alongside each other. Consequently, not all coastlines will experience a uniform impact of current rising sea levels. Eustatic rise together with isostatic recovery at the same rate may mean relative sea level remains unchanged along some coastlines.

Thinking like a geographer

Geographers need to think about how processes interact. It is generally accepted that rising sea levels are likely to lead to increased rates of erosion along many coastlines. But if there is more erosion, what is likely to happen to the additional material that has been eroded? What are the implications for depositional forms, rates and locations?

Features of emergent coastlines

Emergent coastline features can emerge as a result of eustatic fall in sea level or isostatic rise – or a combination of both.

Raised beaches: beaches left higher than the current shoreline represent a fall in sea level relative to the land. Vegetation may have subsequently colonised the former beach.

Relict cliffs: cliff lines that are higher than the current active wave action of the sea indicate a past higher sea level relative to the land. In addition, wave-cut (marine) platforms and headland features such as caves, arches, stacks and stumps are left higher than the current sea level (Figure 3.32).

Figure 3.32 Raised cliff, caves and arch on the west coast of Scotland.

Features of submergent coastlines

Submergent coastline features develop as a result of eustatic sea level rise or isostatic descent.

Rias: these are flooded river estuaries with valley sides emerging from the water (Figure 3.33). They occur when the flood plain of a river close to the coast is submerged by a relative rise in sea level.

Dalmatian coast: the pattern of offshore islands along the western coast of Croatia and Albania has given its name to a series of longitudinal island ridges parallel to the coastline (Figure 3.34). It arises when sea level rise leaves the dividing hills of previously parallel river systems as long islands.

Fjords: these are a glacial form of ria where glaciers have eroded deep U-shaped troughs. Subsequent sea level rise floods them, leaving deep, relatively straight inlets with near-vertical cliffs arising out of the sea either side (Figure 3.35). They are often shallower at their mouths and deepest some distance inland where a number of separate glaciers combined to overdeepen the glacial valley floor with their accumulated erosive power. They are common on the western coast of Norway, New Zealand and Chile – areas which demonstrate substantial glacial activity next to a current coastline.

Figure 3.33 A ria in Salcombe, Devon, UK.

Figure 3.34 The Dalmatian coast of Croatia in the eastern Mediterranean Sea.

Process, time, landforms and landscapes in coastal environments

The physical landscape at the coast is more than an assemblage of individual landforms, features and dominant processes. It is attractive to consider coastlines as predominantly 'erosional' or 'depositional' depending on the net sediment budget, but the reality is more complex. A coastal landscape is an accumulation of processes and resultant features that may have been different under past conditions but form the present landscape upon which contemporary processes operate. Changes over time (temporal scale) as well as different regions interacting at the coast (spatial scale) provide a variety of contexts that the current coastal systems are responding to, and acting upon. They also operate at different rates, from the hourly shifts in tidal shoreline, to the geological eras of continental movement.

Figure 3.35 A fjord in New Zealand.

Think of a particular coastal landscape as a multiple set of layers, representing different sequences over time and space and operating according to different clocks. There may be relict coastal features that were formed largely by past processes, but that contemporary processes are altering and upon which current features are being imposed. Similarly, processes and systems are operating at a range of scales from the small sand ripples on a beach to the erosion of a continental interior and the input of much of that resulting sediment at a point on the coast. There is also a temporal scale of rapid, short duration changes through to extremely slow, long duration events.

The unifying element in these various contexts is that there are sequences of change with identifiable components. In effect, the sequences all definemechanisms that can be disaggregated to interpret a particular coastal landscape and chart its evolution. The sequences operate in various contexts that defines how they inter-relate (Table 3.1). A coastline may have a range of headland features at different stages of development but that all follow the same sequence eventually (process sequence). Those same stacks and arches along a sandstone cliff line may be accompanied by bays with wide sandy beaches, whereas the similar features on a chalk cliff line would have far smaller beaches of larger material size (causal sequence). A stretch of coastline may have far more depositional features than the limited coastal erosion would suggest, due to the input of large amounts of sediment from an inland river system entering the coast giving links between a major river system and a coastal system (spatial sequence). Many coasts have relict features that were formed under previous conditions and different systems to the ones that operate now, or have processes currently operating that commenced in different periods and will operate at different rates (temporal sequence).

Sequence concept	Inter-relation of elements	Illustrative form	Landscape evidence
Process sequence	Developmental	Cave→arch→stack	Multiple landform stages evident along a coastal stretch: joints, caves, arches, stacks, stumps, wave-cut platform
Causal sequence	Consequential	Cliff erosion→beach deposition	Chalk cliffs with narrow chalk pebble beaches (chalk is soluble); sandstone cliffs with extensive sandy beaches
Spatial sequence	Area zonation	Large interior river system (erosional zone) discharging into coastal delta (depositional zone)	Coast featuring more depositional features than accounted for by purely coastline sediment inputs: Louisiana coast where the Mississippi River enters Gulf of Mexico: delta, offshore bars, mudflats
Temporal sequence	Simultaneous	Multiple contemporaneous processes of different duration (see Valentin's classification)	Rapidly rising sea level as a result of climate change on a slower emerging coastline from isostatic recovery resulting in relative sea level maintenance
	Successive	Superimposed coastal landscape processes and features over time	Erosional features developing into cliff line of a relict raised beach

Table 3.1 Multiple sequences operate at the coast to create distinctive coastal landscapes.

The fact that a number of processes at a range of temporal scales may be operating simultaneously at the coast was recognised by Valentin (1952) in his classification of coasts. His model operates on two axes: erosional/depositional coasts and emerging/submerging coastlines. The classification recognises that coasts may be erosional and emerging, as well as depositional and emerging (Figure 3.36), with current rapid processes operating in conjunction with long term, much slower processes simultaneously. In combination, these can magnify the effect, or neutralise each other.

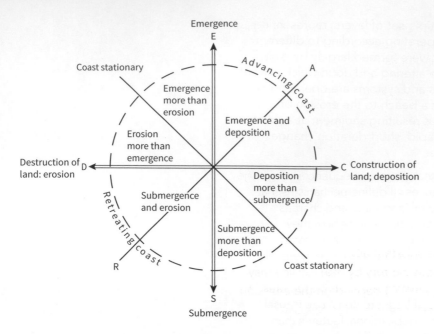

Figure 3.36 Valentin's classification of coastal contexts.

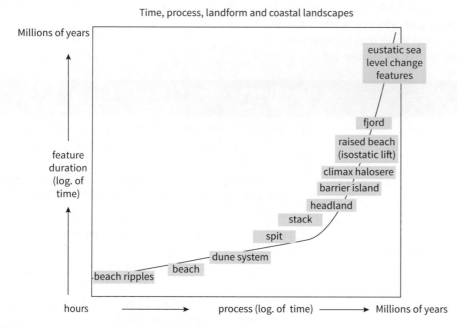

Figure 3.37 Coastal features may accumulate over time to create landscapes with a complex temporal sequence.

In addition, the rate at which change takes place in coastal features can influence a coastal landscape. Some coastlines are relatively stable in their landscape where the system is largely in equilibrium and features are evolving over long development periods, while others are subject to more rapid change where their distinguishing features are created and removed according to much shorter time frames (Figure 3.37). However, it is more common that coastal landscapes are derived from an assemblage of rapidly-changing, short-duration features, medium term and long-term ones in combination. Current systems may be responsible for the more recent features, but they are likely to be modifying the relict ones.

Following the last glacial maximum, about 20000 years ago, it is estimated the sea level has risen by 125 m. The most rapid increase took place at the onset of the present interglacial, with a 10 m rise in just 500 years averaging 20 mm per

 Making connections

Refer to section 1.3 The carbon cycle and section 3.4 Coastal landscape development, Outputs examining how historic and contemporary changes in the atmospheric carbon dioxide level correlates with sea-level change.

year during this period, indicating that temperatures rose very rapidly before the rate of warming slowed. Since then the rate of sea level rise has fluctuated, but has always been higher and this is likely to continue into the future.

- Over the last 3000 years it is estimated that sea level has been relatively stable until the mid-19th century when increase started again. The rate has increased from a 6 cm rise during the 19th century to 19 cm (averaging 1.7 mm per year) during the 20th century.

- The current rate of sea level rise is around 3.2 mm per year, the largest proportion of which is estimated to be due to thermal expansion of seawater, but with significant contributions from glacier and ice-field melt. The part played by the melting of the Greenland and the West Antarctic ice-sheets is smaller at present but is set to become the dominant process in sea-level rise if global temperatures increase substantially.

- Estimates of future rates of sea level rise in this century by the Intergovernmental Panel on Climate Change (IPCC) depend on the emission forecasts and the likely rates of global heating. Low-emission forecasts suggest sea level may increase by a further 0.44 m by 2100, with a worst-case scenario suggesting a rise of almost 1 m could be anticipated.

- Beyond 2100, it is expected that sea level will rise over the following centuries by a further 4–6 m based on anticipated rises in global temperatures of 1–4 °C above the 1990–2000 global average (Figure 3.38). This is likely to arise largely from continued melting of the Greenland and West Antarctic ice sheets.

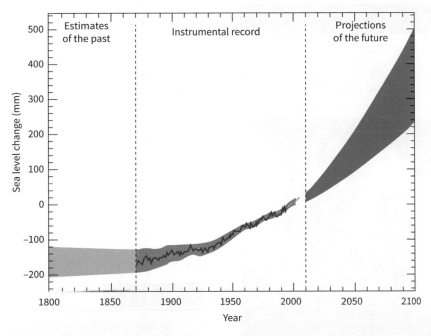

Figure 3.38 Anticipated sea level rise.

 Thinking like a geographer

Geographers need to be able to evaluate evidence. Would you advise that a national government invests its available finances in coastal 'adaptation' to rising sea levels or 'mitigation' – in reducing the causes of sea level rise (Figure 3.39)?

Figure 3.39 Road collapse at a cliff edge.

Anticipated impacts of continuing sea level rise include:

- inundation of low-lying coastal land, both temporarily from storm surges and permanently from higher seas (e.g. in Northern Europe, Figure 3.40); it is estimated a 440mm sea level rise will permanently flood 11% of Bangladesh
- increased river flooding inland due to slower discharge because of reduced long-profile gradient
- saltwater contamination of coastal freshwater sources and agricultural land as it permeates groundwater-holding rocks inland
- loss of productive coastal, delta and river flood plain agriculture
- increased costs for flood-protection measures (**coastal adaptation strategies** and **coastal mitigation strategies**) for coastal cities
- higher rates of insurance for loss of industry, transport and infrastructure at the coast
- loss of coastal habitats
- submergence of atolls and low-lying islands such as the Maldives
- greater migration away from coastal areas.

Given that many of the world's major urban areas are coastal (New York, London, Mumbai, Shanghai, Tokyo) and 44% of the world's total population live within 100km of the coast, the economic, social, environmental and demographic impacts of higher sea levels will have considerable political implications for national governments, global organisations and international cooperation.

Physical and human

Examine the principle of gradually transferring coastal populations inland onto higher ground as a more reliable response than investing in unproven coastal protection systems or attempting to eradicate the causes of sea-level rise.

Key terms

coastal adaptation strategies: investment in measures to negate the impacts of sea level rise

coastal mitigation strategies: investment in measures to reduce the factors responsible for sea level rise

Investigate

Use a GIS mapping process to locate, name and represent the total population size of the world's cities of over five million inhabitants that are at risk of coastal flooding resulting from anticipated sea-level rise of 1m.

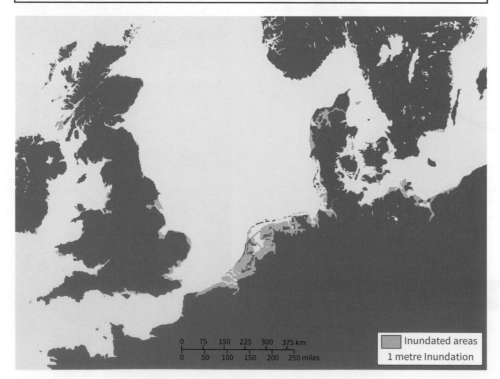

| | 0 | 75 | 150 | 225 | 300 | 375 km |
| 0 | 50 | 100 | 150 | 200 | 250 miles |

Inundated areas
1 metre Inundation

Figure 3.40 Areas of Northern Europe likely to be inundated by a 1 metre rise in sea level.

ACTIVITY 3.3

1 List the negative impacts of anticipated global sea level rise. Code your points as economic, social, environmental or political. Classify them as *early* and *later* impacts and then rank them in order of seriousness. Justify your decisions.

3.5 Managing the coastline profile

Human intervention in natural processes at the coast is most often designed to:

- manage the shape and profile characteristics of the coastline
- reduce rates of coastal erosion
- limit the likelihood of coastal flooding.

Not only is it uneconomic to protect the whole coastline from the effects of coastal erosion, it is undesirable from an environmental perspective and, if we view the coast as a system, what is eroded from one part of the coast provides the material that protects another part.

In England and Wales the Environment Agency is responsible for funding coastal protection (Figure 3.41). The agency's criteria for identifying which sections of coast to protect include:

- how many households (particularly deprived households) are at risk
- the likely impacts on agricultural land and farming practices
- the likely impacts on environment, wildlife and habitats
- whether erosion is affecting local infrastructure and transport
- the cost of construction of management schemes and on going maintenance.

Sediment cells

The coast of England and Wales has been divided into 11 sediment cells (also called littoral cells). Figure 3.42 shows these cells.

Figure 3.41 The storm of February 2014 caused an estimated £1.5m of damage to Aberystwyth's seafront. Could an alternative approach to coastal management have reduced the impact of the storm?

Look on **Cambridge Elevate** to see a list of Shoreline management plans from the Environment Agency. Select and read some of the plans. (www. cambridge.org/links/gase6015).

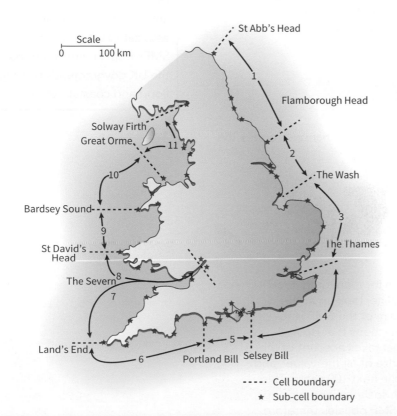

Figure 3.42 The 11 sediment cells into which the coastline of England and Wales is divided.

Sediment cells are sections of coast that form the basis of planning zones around a national or state coast. They can be considered to have an **equilibrium budget**: where a state of balance has been achieved between energy and sediment in terms of erosion, removal, transport, storage and deposition. There is little overall change over a fixed period.

Sediment can be transported. Its **source** is where it originates from; where it is deposited is either a **store** (available for future retrieval) or a **sink** (beyond future access). Sediment can originate from and be deposited at a specific coastal location (**point source** or **store**) or from an extended zone of coast (**line source** or **store**).

	Example
Point source	river discharging into the sea
Line source	length of cliff and beach being eroded
Point store	deposition on a sand bank
Line store	deposition along estuarine mudflats

The relative balance between erosion and deposition in any one sub-cell is known as the sediment budget. This is the net consequence resulting from input of sediment and its deposition. At any one time some material is likely to be in a state of transportation (flux).

Shoreline equilibrium

Coasts can be undergoing significant change (**dynamic**) or be in a state of balance with relatively little change (equilibrium). The components responsible for the degree of change are:

- the supply of physical material available
- the intensity of energy in normal operation
- the key processes in operation
- changes in sea level
- the consistency of shoreline geology.

A feedback loop occurs when outputs (in material or energy changes) modify the inputs or processes such that subsequent outputs are altered.

Table 3.2 shows the different coastal states.

Shoreline management plans

Around the coast of England and Wales there are 22 individual Shoreline Management Plans (SMPs) operating and covering the 11 sediment cells identified.

> "A **Shoreline Management Plan** (SMP) is a plan for managing flood and erosion risk for a particular stretch of shoreline, looking at the immediate, medium and long term. The main aim of the SMP is to develop a sustainable management approach (actions that do not cause problems elsewhere) for the shoreline that takes account of the key issues and achieves the best possible balance of all the values and features that occur around the shoreline over the next 100 years. This needs to recognise the strong relationship with social, economic and environmental activities around the shoreline. SMP policies therefore have to be realistic."

Source: East Riding of Yorkshire council's SMP non-technical summary document

Key terms

equilibrium budget: the sediment inputs and outputs are in equilibrium

source: contributes sediment

store: sediment deposition that may be added to or taken from

sink: site of sediment deposition beyond future potential access

point source/store: a specific coastal location where sediment is removed from (source) or deposited (store)

line source/store: an extended zone of coastal where sediment is removed from (source) or deposited (store)

dynamic: a state of constant change

Shoreline Management Plans (SMPs): documents describing and addressing the risks associated with coastal evolution; SMPs form an important part of the UK government's strategy for flood and coastal defence

Coastal state	Definition	Example
Steady state equilibrium	The shoreline doesn't deviate from the long-term average. All input and output components have achieved a state of balance.	Beaches remain relatively unaltered (other than regular tidal adjustments); shorelines and cliffs become stabilised and no longer accumulate or retreat.
Metastable equilibrium	Balance exists for most of the time, but episodic abrupt events shift the steady state to a new equilibrium, which then reverts to the steady state average.	Tropical storms bring immense new energy to a shoreline and can dramatically alter beaches, offshore bars and cliffs, before they readjust to average conditions.
Dynamic equilibrium	Gradual adjustment to a new state as one or more components shows long-term change.	Rejuvenated cliff erosion occurs on a previously stable cliff as sea level rise takes place, until a new equilibrium is achieved.
Negative feedback loop	The outputs slow down or dampen the inputs or processes that are responsible for them. Promotes self-regulation in a system.	Boulder clay cliff slumping causes substantial material to cover the base of the cliff, reducing further cliff erosion until it is removed (Figure 3.43)
Positive feedback loop	Less frequent than negative loops. When the output is amplified, it leads to a greater input which further increases the output.	A slowly retreating cliff exposes fractured limestone that is more easily eroded, and the rock fragments provide more material for abrasion that further increases the rate of cliff retreat.

Table 3.2 The various states that a shoreline can pass through.

Look on **Cambridge Elevate** to read an article from the *Cornish Guardian* about how 'The Cornish coastline has made a remarkable recovery from the devastating storms of 2014' (www.cambridge.org/links/gase6016).

For an activity on coastal management, download Worksheet 3.4 from **Cambridge Elevate**.

Figure 3.43 Cliff slumping gives rise to a negative feedback loop that delays further erosion of the cliffs at Holderness.

The four strategic options available in managing the coast are:

- Hold the Line: put in place measures to stop further coastal retreat due to erosion
- Advance the Line: extend the coastline further from the existing shore with new defences seaward
- Managed re-alignment: (managed retreat) construct defences further inland sacrificing identified land to the sea
- No Active Intervention: put no management schemes in place and allow natural processes to continue

The possible future impact of sea level rise is taken into account with specific phases of timed intervention. The Environment Agency issues plans for coastal management covering 2010–2030, up to 2065 and up to 2100.

Each sediment cell is subdivided further into distinct sub-cells in which different coastal processes prevail, or where conditions in the cell are different at different places: for example, sections of hard resistant cliffs vs. softer glacial deposits.

This classification helps avoid making the situation worse elsewhere when protecting one section of coast by unintentionally depriving a neighbouring section of essential coastal material.

Thinking like a geographer

Geographers need to consider events from different viewpoints. How would you explain the benefits of coastal erosion to a disgruntled farmer whose land is being lost?

Investigate

On the Environment Agency website, find shoreline management plans for different sediment cells around the coast of England and Wales. What factors encourage the decision to 'Hold the Line'?

3.6 Reducing the rate of coastal erosion

A variety of engineering methods are available to protect the coast from erosion.

Hard engineering

Some strategies are intended to intercept and impede natural marine and coastal processes so that they are less likely to produce undesirable consequences. They are referred to as **hard engineering** methods (Table 3.3).

Key term

hard engineering: strategies that are designed to intercept and impede natural marine and coastal processes so that they are less likely to produce undesirable consequences

Hard engineering techniques	Operation	Advantages	Disadvantages
Revetments	A form of wooden or rock beach fence that allows waves through but reduces their power.	Can be implemented swiftly. Relatively cheap in the short term.	Unattractive and might reduce beach access. Require regular maintenance and repair.
Gabions	Open wire cages filled with rocks placed at the foot of soft cliffs to absorb wave force.	Can be implemented swiftly. Relatively cheap.	Looks unnatural. Can house rodents in gaps between rocks. Deteriorate over time.
Groynes	Wooden or boulder structures extending at right angles from a beach. Accumulate material from longshore drift to build up beach width and height.	Traditional technique used at resorts since Victorian times. Increased beach area benefits tourism.	Traditionally built from unsustainable hardwood sources. Down-coast beaches robbed of sediment, increasing their rate of erosion.
Concrete tetrapods	Moulded concrete multi-pronged forms placed in interlocking concentrations along a shoreline.	Can be created onsite using standard moulds, which reduces transport costs. Long-lasting, requiring little maintenance.	Can restrict shoreline access. Can be hazardous to coastal vessels. Unattractive.
Rock armour (rip-rap)	Large boulders of highly resistant rock (often granite, gneiss or schists) placed at the foot of cliffs.	Effective at absorbing wave energy. Long-lasting, requiring little maintenance. More natural looking than tetrapods.	Can restrict shoreline access. May be hazardous to people climbing on them. High transport costs.

Hard engineering techniques	Operation	Advantages	Disadvantages
Offshore reefs / breakwaters	Man-made islands, bars or reefs just offshore to cause waves to break and provide calmer water between them and shore.	Arguably the least 'hard' technique in that it is relocating a natural process to offshore. Islands may form additional habitats.	May need regular replenishment if material is eroded swiftly. Construction material may contaminate local waters.
Sea wall	Thick concrete or rock encasement of shore front. May have recurved top to assist deflection of waves back to sea.	Standard frontage of seaside resorts for many decades. Effective and long-lasting.	Expensive construction costs. Maintenance required to prevent fracturing and undercutting beneath foundation.

Table 3.3 Hard engineering coastal protection methods.

Soft engineering

Soft engineering techniques work with natural processes, altering and redirecting them to bring about a desired influence. These often require continuous intervention, distributing the costs over time into the future.

3.7 Managing increasing coastal flood risk

The likelihood of more frequent and severe flooding at the coast is increasing around the world due to one or more of these factors:

- higher storm surges as a result of more intense low-pressure systems. The flooding of New York by Hurricane Sandy in 2012 is thought to have led to 48 fatalities and cost over $18 billion in damage.
- rising sea levels as a result of climate change
- estuarine flooding due to high river discharge, high tides and storm surges coinciding
- tsunami risk as densities of populations living on coasts increase globally.

Precautions that can offer protection against current and future coastal flooding impacts are costly. The implications are serious for many developing countries that have major coastal cities that are growing as urbanisation rates continue to climb, but lack access to funds to implement major coastal engineering. In a recent study of cities vulnerable to the effects of climate change, nine of the top ten identified as 'at extreme risk' are in Asia, topped by Dhaka, Manila and Bangkok. While Manila, in the Philippines, is preparing a largescale 50-year plan for coastal barriers and reclaimed land, other cities such as Mumbai face claims of increasing flood risk by permitting removal of energy-absorbing mangrove wetlands in order to build the new Navi Mumbai airport.

Hard engineering

Hard engineering strategies to reduce flood risk include:

- flood barrage: sophisticated engineering constructions across estuaries that contain sluices to permit passage of tidal water but close when unusually high tides, storm surges or flood tides are forecast.

Look on **Cambridge Elevate** to find out about the cost of coastal defences in 'Cost estimation for coastal protection' from the Flood and Coastal Erosion Risk Management and Research Development Programme (www.cambridge.org/links/gase6017).

Key term

soft engineering: low-incursion, sustainable coastal protection strategies that work with nature to manage the coast

Research point

Find out the responses to the Indian Ocean tsunami of Boxing Day 2004 that resulted in the deaths of over 220 000 people. What has been put in place to reduce the impact of future tsunami events?

Soft engineering techniques	Operation	Advantages	Disadvantages
Beach nourishment	Moving sand/shingle from areas of accumulation to zones of denudation. This may mean offshore dredging to rebuild beaches (Figure 3.44) or trucking longitudinally from an area of longshore drift deposition to an area up-coast of beach net loss.	Less visually and environmentally intrusive long term. Can be undertaken at key points throughout the year when the impact on wildlife breeding or tourist activity is at a minimum. Low specific-point cost.	Has to be maintained continually. Visually and environmentally intrusive when being carried out. Relative costs increase the longer the beach nourishment takes.
Beach re-profiling	Adjusting the gradient of the beach to maximise frictional impact on approaching waves. Usually takes place after winter storms and in autumn.	(as above)	(as above)
Dune regeneration	Stabilising, extending or creating sand-dunes through replanting of vegetation, managing footpath erosion or restricting grazing. Provides a barrier between shore and inland.	Maintains a natural environment/habitat. Relatively low cost.	Takes time for slow-growing dune vegetation to become established and develop a succession. Tourists and locals may ignore footpath restrictions (no enforcement).
Living shoreline barriers	Creating mudflats (via managed retreat), encouraging surface and submerged vegetation (mangroves) and stimulating marine crustaceans (oyster beds) to absorb wave energy.	Increases/improves a natural environment. Encourages species diversity. Relatively low cost.	Takes time to establish. May be sensitive to pollution contamination. May not adjust to rising sea levels or warmer seas.

Table 3.4 Examples of soft engineering coastal protection methods.

Look on **Cambridge Elevate** to read about the disappearance of sandy shorelines in 'Scientists foresee losses as cities fight beach erosion' from Climate Central (www.cambridge.org/links/6018).

Figure 3.44 A dredger transferring material ashore for beach nourishment, using the 'rainbow' method, so called because the jet of sand is arc-shaped like a rainbow.

- closure dams: may take the form of coastal 'levees' in North America and 'dykes' in the Netherlands. These solidly constructed physical barriers can sometimes be found 'advancing the line' in reclamation projects.
- sea wall: a 3–4 m high concrete sea wall protects much of Canvey Island on the Thames estuary (Figure 3.45).

Figure 3.45 A high sea wall protects Canvey Island from flooding by the Thames.

Soft engineering

Lower cost sustainable strategies to reduce coastal flooding involve releasing the pressure of flood water onto land that has been identified for temporary inundation.

Coastal realignment: rather than avoiding all flooding, the concept behind managed retreat is to permit flooding on land with low economic and environmental value in order to absorb flood water and protect nearby low-lying coastal areas with a resident population and other recognised value (Figure 3.46).

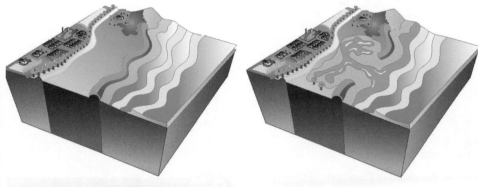

Prior to realignment
Coast defences present
Little intertidal habitat

Managed to realignment
Coastal defences breached
Creation of intertidal habiat

Figure 3.46 An example of managed retreat on the Essex coast, where a flood protection embankment has been deliberately breached to permit flood waters to inundate marginal land, creating an intertidal habitat and giving some protection to the populated zone behind it.

 Look on **Cambridge Elevate** to read about Wallasea Island and the history of its flood defences in 'The Wallasea Island site visit' (www. cambridge.org/links/ gase6019).

3.8 Integrated Coastal Zone Management (ICZM)

The idea behind **ICZM** is to consider the coastal zone – landward as well as seaward – as a sophisticated set of systems that meet and become integrated at the coast (Figures 3.47 and 3.48). It takes into account, for example, runoff of fertiliser and pesticide residues from farmers' fields into waterways that discharge into the sea and affect marine organisms. The intention is to manage all the components to permit the best sustainable future in the short and long term for the natural coast and the human users of it.

 Key term

Integrated Coastal Zone Management (ICZM): a process for the management of the coast using an integrated approach to achieve sustainability

Key features of ICZMs:

- Monitoring, measuring and recording what is taking place at the coast
- Involving all interested parties
- Reflecting local characteristics and adapting to local needs
- Being holistic – taking the wide and deep view of what is occurring
- Planning collaboratively with all stake-holders
- Working with natural processes
- Being sustainable
- Taking a long-term perspective
- Involving continuous decision-making in the light of new information and emerging priorities

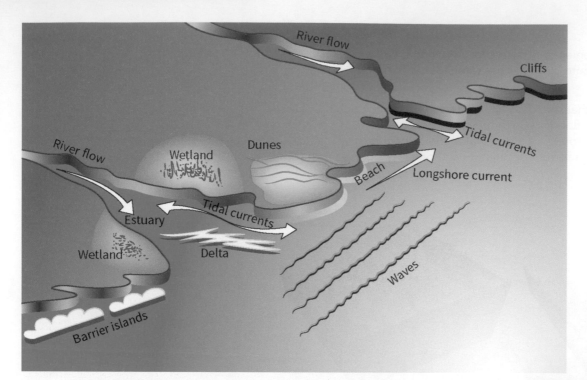

Figure 3.47 An example of a natural coastal system on the shore of Denmark, showing its processes and features.

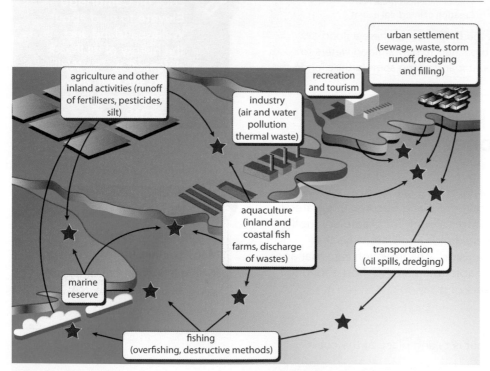

Figure 3.48 Examples of user functions along a stretch of coastline, and possible conflicts between them.

Coasts will inevitably face increasing pressures in the future – from the effects of climate change, human population pressure and resource demands. A sustainable and holistic approach to coasts depends upon an understanding of the systems operating, and comprehensive management through ICZMs.

Look on **Cambridge Elevate** to read more about 'Integrated Coastal Zone Management' in Australia from the Australian Government (www.cambridge.org/links/gase6020).

Look on **Cambridge Elevate** to read about the threat to Asia's coastal cities from flooding in 'Danger to cities by the sea' from Yale Global Online (www.cambridge.org/links/gase6021).

ACTIVITY 3.4

1   Compare ICZMs for different coastal zones around the world. Draw up a table identifying similarities and differences. Do they have more in common, or more that distinguishes them? How are they managed and what enforcement procedures are in place? Evaluate their effectiveness.

3.9 The Holderness coast

The Holderness coast in the UK is bounded by the chalk headland of Flamborough Head to the north and the long finger or spit extending into the Humber estuary, known as Spurn Point, to the south (Figures 3.49 and 3.50). Table 3.5 shows the key features and processes of this dynamic coastline.

Tip

Be prepared to describe and explain contrasting coastal landscapes in Britain.

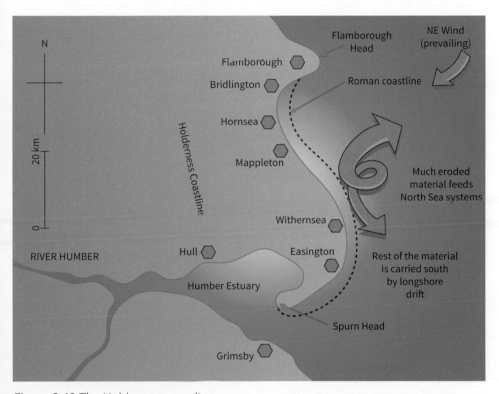

Figure 3.49 The Holderness coastline.

Figure 3.50 Rock armour at Withernsea: an example of a hard engineering coastal management solution.

Coastal management on the Holderness coast

The vulnerable Holderness plain is a relic of melting glacial ice leaving a residue of easily-eroded boulder clay. The coast has retreated over 3 km since Roman times. The SMP for this section of the sediment cell looks to protect key settlements (Bridlington, Hornsea, Withernsea), important coastal roads (Mappleton) and a strategic gas pipeline landfall and gas processing facility (Easington). A mix of coastal protection methods operate to Hold the Line at these locations (Figure 3.51).

Maths for geographers

The Holderness coastline 1 km north of Mappleton is eroding at 1.2 m per year, while 1 km south of the defences it is eroding at 2.7 m per year. Calculate how much more the coastline has retreated to the S. than the N. after 20, 50 and 100 years.

Use a GIS source to draw on the predicted coastline as an overlay on a scaled aerial image of this area.

Figure 3.51 Beach sediment at the tip of Spurn Head spit.

Location	Features	Processes	Key issues
Flamborough Head	Chalk Headland Caves Arches Stack Stump Wave-cut platform	Corrasion/abrasion Corrosion/solution Hydraulic action Attrition Subaerial freeze-thaw Subaerial solution Dominant process: erosion	Rock falls Tourist cliff accidents Ships hitting rocks
Bridlington Bay	Boulder clay Bay Beaches Cliff slump Wave-cut notch Constructive waves Destructive waves Prevailing NE waves	Coastal retreat Slumping Rotational slip Beach accumulation Beach reduction Dominant process: erosion and longshore drift	Rapid cliff erosion Loss of farmland Loss of key facilities Transport disruption Decisions about coastal protection
Spurn Point	Spit Recurved head Nature reserve Migration route Pilot/Lifeboat station	River/sea current convergence Deposition Spit extension Erosion of spit neck Cyclical spit development Dominant process: Longshore drift and deposition	Full erosion of spit neck Isolation of spit head Relocation of crews Dredging Humber channel Impact of sea level rise

Table 3.5 Key features and processes along the Holderness coast.

Elsewhere the policy is No Active Intervention; a controversial decision on Europe's fastest eroding coastline that has considerable implication for many arable farmers, caravan site owners and rural coastal settlements. The material eroded from this coast is, however, essential to the formation of Spurn Point.

Spurn is a key feature protecting a deep water channel into the Humber estuary – essential for the 20% of UK shipping imports that come into Britain through Humber ports. The Victorian practice of attempting to fix Spurn in position through the use of wooden groynes has been abandoned. The current policy is to allow the spit to migrate westwards naturally, through a process of wash-over whereby sand is washed across the spit to be deposited in calmer waters on the western side. However, rising sea levels and storm surges threaten to destabilise this policy by permanently breaching the neck of the spit.

 Look on **Cambridge Elevate** to read an article from the *Guardian* about the increasing rate of coastal erosion in 'Yorkshire is disappearing up to three times as fast as last year' (www.cambridge.org/links/gase6022).

 For an activity on The Holderness coast, download Worksheet 3.5 from **Cambridge Elevate**.

3.10 Bangladesh coastal challenges

One of the most densely populated coastlines in Asia occurs in Bangladesh (Figure 3.52). With over 730 km of coast and numerous coastal islands, the region is home to over 50 million people – approximately a third of the entire population of the country. Many settlements are rural fishing or farming communities with significant ports where natural harbours offer trade, processing and manufacturing opportunities. The coastline is characterised by three main zones:

- the eastern coast of rapidly rising folded hills emerging from the Bay of Bengal
- the central region where major world rivers, the Ganges and Brahmaputra, enter the Bay of Bengal and deposit huge quantities of silt
- the western coast is a low-lying coastal plain deeply scoured by channels with a habitat of dense mangrove forest.

Research point

Locate a map showing population distribution in Bangladesh. Compare this with Figure 3.53 showing land height. Draw up an impact assessment list if coastal protection measures are ineffective.

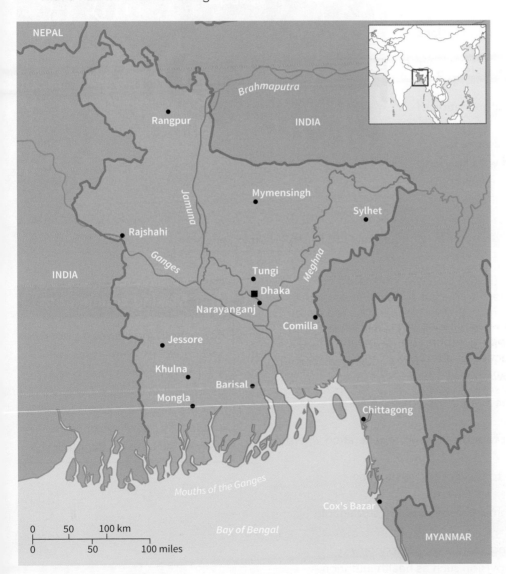

Figure 3.52 Map of Bangladesh.

One of the most distinctive features of all three regions is the amount of low-lying land, much of which is less than 5 m above sea level and significant areas less than 1 m above current sea level (Figure 3.53). This accounts for the frequent deaths during seasonal cyclones which can see storm surges well above that height. The most disastrous was the 1970 Bhola cyclone, killing over 300 000 people with a 10.6 m storm surge. In 1991, a tropical storm surge of between 5–8 m caused the deaths of a further 150 000 Bangladeshi.

The main challenges facing the population of the coastal regions come from a combination of physical factors, human land-use pressure and the implications of climate change, and include:

- a high risk of flooding and devastation from cyclone storm surges
- tidal surges and river flooding
- coastal erosion
- siltation of channels
- contamination of groundwater with saline intrusions and arsenic compounds
- pollution and contamination of coastal waters by cities, industry and fish-farming
- destruction of mangrove forest and deforestation of coastal hills
- a 1 m rise in sea level will cause major issues for farming by increasing soil salinity and will likely lead to large-scale migration of population away from the coastal islands and plains as agricultural yields decline.

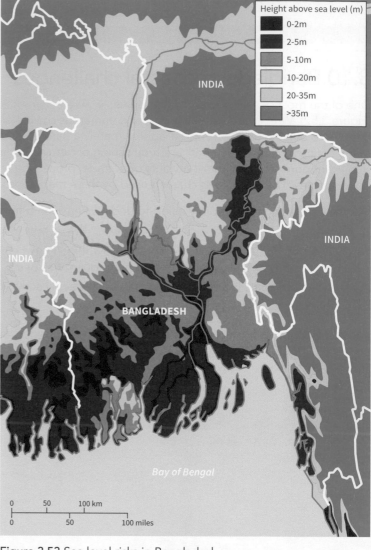

Figure 3.53 Sea level risks in Bangladesh.

Bangladesh ICZM

An Integrated Coastal Zone Management (ICZM) plan was introduced in 2005 to enable coastal people in Bangladesh to pursue sustainable economic development in a safe and secure environment that would lead to a reduction in poverty. It integrated key proposals with the Millennium Development Goals of the UN. The Priority Investment Program (PIP) was drawn up to focus available funds on the perceived essential needs of the Bangladesh coastal zone. Investment has been targeted at the following areas:

- measures to protect and safeguard the population against natural hazards
- protection of the natural environment together with its regeneration where it had suffered deterioration
- management of freshwater resources to protect and sustain their provision
- improving rural livelihoods and economic prospects along sustainable paths
- development of the tourism and fishing sectors of the economy
- improving infrastructure and social provision such as health, nutrition, sanitation and education.

Making connections

Read about the causes, features and impact of storm in section 5.1 The concept of hazard in a geographical context. Consider why the frequency, intensity and impact of tropical cyclones are likely to increase for Bangladesh.

Key developments

Over 2000 cyclone storm surge shelters (Figure 3.54) have been constructed, serving 27% of the coastal population at risk of flood hazard. These multiple-storey constructions are intended to serve each village as a social centre when not functioning as a storm refuge, being used as schools and community centres. In addition, it has been recognised that saving the livestock of farmers is essential if they are to maintain their livelihood immediately after a flood event and so nearly 1500 raised mounds (killas) are in the process of construction for the protection of farm animals. Some argue that this is not nearly enough for the scale of need.

Figure 3.54 A storm refuge in Bangladesh.

Nearly 5000 km of embankment, in the form of 123 barrier dams (Figure 3.55) have been raised as part of the Coastal Embankment Project to protect vulnerable farmland from inundation by saline flood water. However, this has been controversial in consequence as they have reduced the flow of tidal waters, increased sediment deposition, raised the channel bed of distributaries and increased the waterlogging of adjacent farmland. This has caused deterioration of farmland, forestry and fisheries such that people have had to abandon ancestral homes.

Mangrove – a semi-marine tropical species of tree that grows in shallow water with roots that rise above the surface – has been recognised as a key constituent in absorbing cyclone wave energy along storm-prone coasts. In the last few decades, over 148 000 hectares of mangrove afforestation has been promoted by the Forest Department along on- and offshore coastlines of the central region of Bangladesh (Figure 3.56). As part of this initiative, the Coastal Green Belt policy planted vegetation along 9000 km of rail, road and coastal embankments and island foreshores. Not always successful, it was found that inadequate knowledge of suitable species and local habitat conditions meant that much planting was hit and miss in its survival. It is seen as essential that this strategy is central to the ICZM plan in integrating national funds, technical expertise and data analysis with local people's knowledge and assistance in the replanting process.

Figure 3.55 A barrier dam in Bangladesh.

Figure 3.56 Mangrove afforestation at a young stage.

ACTIVITY 3.5

1   To what extent are the improvement strategies in Bangladesh helping to address the Priority Investment Program areas of need?
2   Evaluate the improvement strategies and comment on the extent to which they support Millennium Development Goals.
3   Bangladesh is one of the most vulnerable countries to sea level rise as a consequence of climate change. Should nations that produce the most carbon dioxide have to compensate countries like Bangladesh to help fund coastal protection plans? Discuss.

For an activity on Bangladesh's coastal challenges, download Worksheet 3.6 from **Cambridge Elevate**.

Assess to progress

1   Discuss the relative advantages and disadvantages of using soft engineering coastal protection methods.   `9 MARKS [AS LEVEL]`

2   Which three coastal processes would you argue have the biggest impact on the evolution of the Holderness coast?   `9 MARKS [AS LEVEL]`

3   To what extent is human activity contributing to the developing profile of the Holderness coast?   `9 MARKS [AS LEVEL]`

4   Explain why the coastal landscape of one section of coast may be very different to that of another section 150 miles away despite the coastline consisting of similar rock type.   `9 MARKS [AS LEVEL]`

5   For a feature of either coastal deposition or coastal erosion, explain its formation using the concept of the coastal system.   `6 MARKS [A LEVEL]`

6   'Subaerial processes are far more important in creating distinctive coastal landforms than marine processes.' To what extent do you agree with this statement?   `20 MARKS [AS LEVEL]`

7   To what extent can coastal management schemes be considered both effective and sustainable?   `20 MARKS [A LEVEL]`

Look on **Cambridge Elevate** for more information on coastal flooding and management from the following websites:

- Shoreline Management Plans (England and Wales) (www.cambridge.org/links/gase6023).
- An article from *The Huffington Post* that finds 'Coastal flooding more frequent in the US due to sea level rise and sinking land' (www.cambridge.org/links/gase6024).

4

Glacial systems and landscapes

Figure 4.1 The Drang-Drung glacier in the Kargil district of Jammu and Kashmir in India. Erosion by the glacier has led to the landforms that you can see.

By the end of this chapter you should know:
- the physical characteristics of cold environments and their past and present distribution
- glacial processes and the landforms associated with them
- human occupation and subsequent development of cold environments
- a case study of a glaciated environment at a local scale, to illustrate processes and landscapes
- a case study of a glaciated environment from beyond the UK, to illustrate the challenges and opportunities for human occupation and development.

Before you start…

You should know:
- the main features of a glacier
- the location of the world's cold environments
- an understanding of the characteristics of an Ice Age
- the processes of erosion and deposition.

4.1 Glaciers as natural systems

Glaciers can be studied as natural systems. Geographers use a systems approach to develop a greater understanding of interconnecting relationships between the wider environment and local landforms. Most systems share a set of common characteristics:

- a structure defined by its parts and processes
- generalisations based on reality
- inputs and outputs of material or energy
- a flow and transfer of energy
- an exchange of energy or matter beyond the boundary of the system itself to the surrounding environment.

Within the boundary of a system such as a glacial system, three properties exist:

- Elements: such as water, snow and ice, the substances that form the system.
- Attributes: the characteristics of the elements, which can be studied, measured and recorded, such as the temperature of the ice or the colour of the ice.
- Relationships: how the elements and the attributes interact, based on cause and effect.

Natural systems can be open or closed. Each system is the result of processes involving inputs and outputs of matter (in this case water and ice) flows and stores of energy.

Glaciers as systems

Glaciers operate as systems with inputs, flows/transfers and outputs, as shown in Figure 4.2. In a perfectly balanced system, inputs and outputs would be equal. The size or mass of the system would therefore remain constant. If a glacier system were in a perfectly balanced system, the mass of the glacier would not change. However, glaciers do not achieve a perfectly balanced system and remain unbalanced. As a result, they shrink and grow with changes to the inputs and outputs.

Making connections

Open and closed systems are explored in Section 1.1 Water and carbon cycles as natural systems.

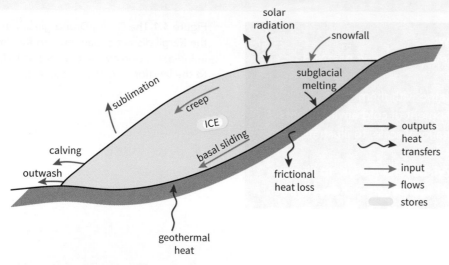

Figure 4.2 The glacier system.

Within the overall glacial system there are also smaller systems. The formation of glacial ice operates within a system, as does the energy transfers of the glacier.

Consider one of the inputs to a glacier system, the input of snow. This input can also be studied as a separate system. The inputs to the system are snowflakes. Energy is transferred through the process of melting, evaporation and compaction. The output of the system is eventually glacial ice.

Snows fall on to the surface of the glacier, with each snowflake containing 80–95% air and a density of 50–200 kg/m³. Over time, this snow becomes **névé** through the process of melting, evaporation and compaction. The density of névé is 400–500 kg/m³, while it now contains only 40–50% air. If this layer of névé survives the summer melting season, more compaction by further snowfall changes the

Key term

névé: granular snow consisting of low-density ice crystals; also called firn névé until it becomes firn, with only 20–30% air and a density of 600–700 kg/m³. Each year, another layer of firn is added to the glacier and it takes a further 25–100 years before the firn ice changes to become glacier ice, with a density of 750–850 kg/m³ and an air content of only 10–20%.

The glacier energy balance

Energy enters the glacial system through solar radiation and downward infrared radiation. Most of the solar radiation is reflected in the process known as albedo, while the remaining radiation is absorbed. The rate of albedo is affected by levels of precipitation and ablation – fresh snow is more reflective than old snow.

A glacier receives energy from both solar radiation and downward infrared radiation. Energy can also be received at the surface by **sensible heat** if the glacier surface is colder than the surrounding air temperature.

Glaciers exchange energy through the process of melting. Glacier energy balances often have small or sometimes negative net radiation. Any energy surplus is used to melt the snow and ice. The energy balance of a glacier is shown in Figure 4.3.

Making connections

To fully understand the energy budget of a glacier, it is important to understand the energy system of the atmosphere. See Chapter 1 Water and carbon cycles.

Key term

sensible heat: the amount of heat energy that occurs when an object is heated; when heat is removed from an object and its temperature falls, the heat removed is also called sensible heat

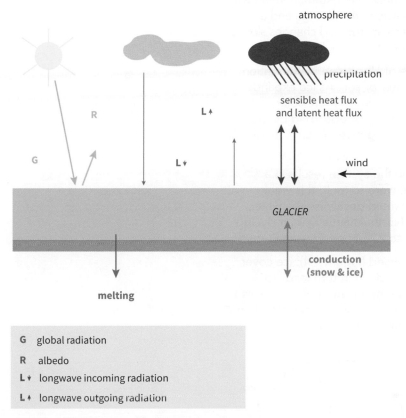

Figure 4.3 The energy balance of a glacier.

In some cases, if a glacier surface is too cold it will not be able to eliminate all the heat transferred and so will warm, until such point that the energy losses balanced and the system becomes balanced.

In the tropics, glaciers are often warmer on the surface than the surrounding air during the day because of the amount of solar radiation received. Therefore, melting on the surface of the glacier occurs even if the air temperature is below 0°C, as is commonly witnessed on Mt Kilimanjaro.

There is another process by which energy is transferred away from the glacier: heat rises from its surface and is transferred to the surrounding environment.

There are two forms of heat rising from the surface: sensible heat and latent heat. Sensible heat takes heat out of the surface of the glacier – if it is cooler than the surface and, conversely, if it is warmer than the surface. Latent heat carries away mass and as well as energy due to ice losing energy as it is converted to water vapour in the process of **sublimation**.

It takes 8.5 times more energy to turn a kilogram of ice into water vapour by the process of sublimation than it does to convert a kilogram of ice into water. Therefore, an excess of energy on the surface of the glacier can cause a large amount of surface meltwater.

Meltwater from a glacier can have an important effect on the ice temperature deep within the glacier. If meltwater from the surface percolates into the glacier and undergoes refreezing, latent heat is released. This will, in turn, warm the surrounding layers of the glacier.

Positive and negative feedback

By adopting a systems approach, complex systems such as glaciated landscapes can be subdivided into a number of interrelated parts. Any changes such as those through a process can lead to wholescale changes within the system. Sometimes these changes can accelerate as the system itself reacts to the change and a positive feedback loop begins. Sometimes the reverse is true and changes slow or are counteracted by the system, producing a negative feedback loop.

An example of a positive feedback loop is the role of albedo on ice formation. Ice has a higher albedo than that of vegetation, water or soil. As ice expands over an area, an increase in albedo occurs, leading in turn to more solar radiation being reflected back to space. As less radiation is absorbed by the surface, temperatures decrease, promoting further ice growth. In turn, this leads to greater albedo and the cycle is repeated.

A negative feedback loop occurs when a change in the system results in a reduction in the system. If the Greenland ice sheet were to melt, this would cause freshwater to enter the North Atlantic. This would desalinise the water, making it less dense. In turn, this could affect the North Atlantic Drift, reducing its effect and causing temperatures to drop by up to 2 °C in north-west Europe.

When ice begins to melt, this feedback can be reversed (Figure 4.4): ice cover recedes, albedo reduces, surface temperatures rise, which in turn leads to further ice melting, decreasing albedo even further. The location of the ice also plays an important role in the feedback. Sea ice, for example, melts faster than continental ice sheets, thus reacting quicker to changes in albedo.

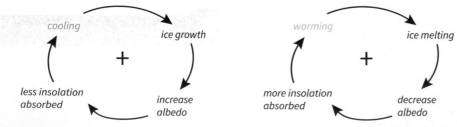

Figure 4.4 Ice – albedo positive feedback.

Dynamic equilibrium

The glacier system consists of inputs, stores, flows and outputs. Rates of **accumulation** and **ablation** are rarely equal but, if they were, the glacier snout would remain constant and the glacier would be in a state of equilibrium. However, this is not a static equilibrium, but a dynamic equilibrium.

Key terms

sublimation: the transition of ice to water vapour without a liquid stage

accumulation: the addition of snow or ice in a glacier

ablation: the natural removal of snow or ice in a glacier

The glacier is still undergoing flows. Ice still moves under gravity flowing downhill, with the new ice forming in the **accumulation zone** eventually being lost in the **ablation zone** through melting or sublimation. Therefore, this situation is said to be a dynamic equilibrium. At the firn line, for example, where accumulation and ablation rates are equal, the glacier will still be moving, transporting sediment down the valley.

Landforms and landscapes

Landforms are used to describe the configuration of the surface of the land and provide the stage into which a landscape is set. As a result, they determine the geographical character of the surface. Glacial landforms such as pyramidal peaks, arêtes, outwash plains and drumlins help us to define the landscapes around us.

'Landscape' is the term used to describe the complex materials and landforms that make up the environment around us. Different systems – such as glacial, water, climate and soil – all operate within the landscape.

Glaciers are effective at eroding the landscape. The amount of material that an alpine glacier system erodes from a mountain valley is significantly greater than a river could erode in the same area. Worldwide, however, because ice covers only 10% of the surface of the Earth, the amount eroded is lower in comparison to rivers. However, when looking at how landforms and landscapes are shaped, it is important to understand the interconnected relationships that exist.

For example, the rate of erosion caused by weathering reduces in times of ice advance because precipitation falls as snow and not water. The snow forms ice. In turn, this leads to a greater rate of erosion by the glacier as glacial troughs are carved into the landscape. Sedimentary rates on the sea floor reveal that much more sediment is deposited during glacial periods compared to warmer periods. Glacial erosion in some areas is most rapid in the early stages of an Ice Age on account of the larger quantities of weathered bedrock and pre-glacial sediment available.

However, to fully understand the landscape, it is important to recognise the interaction of different systems at work over different time scales. The Sierra Nevada mountain range in North America is marked by a series of glacial troughs. Glacial erosional processes formed these landforms and erosion rates were high during this period. However, the presence of glaciers also helped to promote rates of erosion and weathering after the glacier retreated. As temperatures warmed and the glacier retreated, the exposed landscape of loosened and crushed rock meant that subsequent rivers could more easily transport the material out to the seabed, thus increasing the rates of erosion and weathering.

The landscape itself also defines the type of landform that a glacier creates. When alpine glaciers extend, they follow the path of alpine stream systems. As the glacier system extends down the previous drainage system of the stream, the valleys are filled with ice. As the valley is often narrow and deep (caused by river erosion), the ice is confined and a greater erosional stress is occurs on the valley sides. Loose material present on the valley sides before glaciation is therefore removed by the glacier as it moves down the valley. The glacier then begins to erode the valley floor, eventually creating the classic U-shaped glacial trough. When studying the landscape, the shape of a valley can therefore be a good indicator of ice extent.

Glaciers therefore offer a clear example of using a system approach. Glaciers themselves form part of a larger environmental system and changes within those environmental systems are reflected in changes within the glacial system. Glaciers also have clear inputs such as snowfall and outputs such as meltwater. Differences between these inputs and outputs determine how a glacier behaves. Glacial processes such as erosion and deposition will, in turn, transform the landscape.

Key terms

accumulation zone: the area of net gain in a glacier or ice mass

ablation zone: the area of net loss in a glacier or ice mass

Making connections

To learn more about drainage basin systems, read about the water cycle in section 1.2 The water cycle.

4.2 The nature and distribution of cold environments

Paleoclimatic evidence suggests that the climate of the Earth has been in a state of dynamic change. Evidence from ice core samples, sea sediments and tree rings provide an opportunity to study the climate of the past. The data gathered from such sources suggests that most of the Earth's past has seen global temperatures in the region of 8–15°C warmer than at present.

However, there have also been colder periods during the last billion years, with the last one starting approximately 2 million years before present (BP), known as the **Pleistocene era**.

During the Pleistocene era, the distribution of cold environments was very different to the pattern today, as shown in Figure 4.7. Large ice sheets were present over the continents of North America, Europe and Asia. The distribution and advance of ice during this time illustrates how different systems interact. As global temperatures started to decrease, a positive feedback loop was created leading to a dramatic change in the environment.

A small temperature increase in the polar regions of just 1–2°C delays the summer melting of the sea ice. As a result, the albedo in the region is higher for longer, which results in reduced heating at the surface and ice occurring for longer periods. In turn, the albedo increases once more. The cycle is therefore self-perpetuating.

During this period, the glaciers of North America began in the higher **altitudes** of the Rocky Mountains, while also advancing in high **latitude** regions of Greenland and Canada. The ice then expanded following the topography of the surrounding landscape. At its peak, ice cover in North America at this time extended to 40° latitude.

Similar patterns of glacial advance also existed in Europe and Asia, although the ice sheets only extended south as far as 450°N. At this time, 30% of the Earth's land surface was covered in ice.

Currently approximately 10% of the Earth's land surface is covered by ice, whereas sea ice covers about 7% of the Earth's surface and about 12% of the world's oceans, as shown in Figure 4.7. Antarctica accounts for 85% of ice cover, whereas Greenland accounts for 10%. The remaining 5% is located in mountainous regions across the globe and in tundra areas in parts of Russia and Canada. Ice takes different forms in these different locations, leading to a range of different characteristic features.

The physical characteristics of cold environments

For a region to be classified as a cold environment, the temperature for a significant period of the year must be close to or below freezing. In mountainous regions such as the Alps or the Rockies, cold winters are experienced, whereas in the more extreme environments of Antarctica year-round temperatures often fail to rise above 0°C and can fall as low as –60°C.

There are four main types of cold environment: polar, alpine, glacial and periglacial. Their present-day distribution is illustrated in Figure 4.7.

Polar environments are the most extreme of the four cold environments. During the winter months, temperatures drop to below –50°C. Figure 4.5 shows such a polar environment: Antarctica. Although snow seems to dominate the landscape, the amount of precipitation is very low. Polar regions are characterised by large expanses of sea ice.

Alpine environments (Figure 4.6) are located in mountainous regions such as the Alps and the Rockies. Winters are cold and heavy snow is common.

Key terms

Paleoclimatic: climatic conditions in the geological past reconstructed from a direct or indirect data source

Pleistocene era: the first epoch of the Quaternary period

altitude: the height of land in relation to sea level

latitude: the distance north or south of the equator, often measured in degrees and minutes

Figure 4.6 Alpine regions experience cold winters and mild summers.

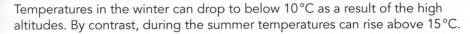

Figure 4.5 Despite its appearance, Antarctica receives very little precipitation.

Temperatures in the winter can drop to below 10 °C as a result of the high altitudes. By contrast, during the summer temperatures can rise above 15 °C.

Glacial environments are associated with the world's active glacial systems, in mountainous regions where ice is the main transport process. Heavy snowfall in winter provides the input of ice for glaciers in the longer term. During the summer months, warmer weather promotes meltwater under the glacier.

Periglacial environments are found on the edge of glacial and polar regions, in parts of Canada, Russia and Greenland. They are characterised by the presence of **permafrost**. Summers are brief and temperatures only rise high enough to be able to influence the very top surface layer of the soils.

The distribution of these four environments is affected by altitude and latitude.

Climate, ocean currents, soils and vegetation

Climate

Cold environments have unique climates that are as a result of a number of factors. The climates of both the Arctic region and Antarctica are affected by high latitude. Sunlight in high latitudes hits the surface at a lower angle compared to lower latitudes. This results in the energy being spread over a much larger area. In Antarctica, south of the Antarctic circle during the southern winter, the Sun does not rise above the horizon. Between 21 September and 21 March, sunlight is continuously present, while during the rest of the year it remains in darkness. Even in the southern winter, heat is lost from the surface. This, together with the fact that the air over Antarctica is very dry, leads to little retention of the heat that is lost from the surface.

In the southern summer months, a relatively high amount of sunlight reaches the surface. This is due to the long day length and the thin atmosphere. However, little heating occurs as albedo is high, reflecting much of the sunlight back into the atmosphere. The effect of the landscape on surface temperatures is most keenly felt in the East Antarctic Plateau region. The high elevation, combined with high levels of albedo, result in very little differences in surface temperature in summer compared to winter.

Key term

permafrost: areas of permanently frozen ground

Antarctica remains colder than the Arctic region. Both regions have high latitudes and seasonal day length, but it is the effect of the landscape that results in Antarctica being much colder. Looking at a globe, it is clear that the Arctic is surrounded by landmasses (Russia, Canada and Greenland), but Antarctica is a landmass surrounded by Ocean (the Southern Ocean). The sea has a different heat capacity to land. Oceans are slower to heat up and slower to cool down than land. Therefore, it would be expected that Antarctica would be the cooler region. However, it is also important to understand the role that elevation plays in changing the climate of the two regions.

The Arctic sea ice has a low elevation compared to Antarctica's ice sheet, which is on top of the large continental landmass. This difference in elevation is important, as temperature reduces with altitude. This occurs due to the decrease in air pressure. This is why Antarctica has lower average temperatures than the Arctic region, and shows the importance a landscape has on the landforms present in the area.

Ocean currents

The effect of albedo, elevation and low angle sunlight results in an energy deficit at the polar regions, but these areas are not getting colder and colder. The Earth's climate system transfers energy from low to high latitudes. This is achieved through wind systems and ocean currents.

In the northern hemisphere, the North Atlantic Ocean has a strong north–south circulation. This takes warmer water from the tropics to higher latitudes, the North Atlantic Drift current and the Gulf Stream moving this warmer water northwards. These two small systems are themselves part of a much larger ocean circulation system, the **thermohaline system**, which also includes the deeper ocean currents bringing colder water south. The thermohaline circulation heats the North Atlantic and northern Europe, extending to the Greenland and Norwegian Seas. The atmosphere above these warmer surface currents brings warm, moist air to the higher latitude landmasses, often resulting in precipitation.

The ocean circulation of the Antarctic Ocean is very different. Here, the currents run east–west. This moves the cold water around Antarctica, which in turn acts as an effective barrier to the warmer waters. The Southern Ocean is known for its rough seas, which are caused by the temperature difference between the cold Antarctic air and the milder maritime air masses from the mid latitudes creating storms moving south-east.

Soils

Soil is the result of interactions between different large-scale systems: the atmosphere, biosphere and geosphere (rocks and sediments). Soil is defined as any lose material at the surface of the Earth capable of supporting life. Soil itself is a system. Energy and matter are the inputs to the system and are stored in the soil for a period of time. They are then released as outputs at varying rates. The difference between the inputs and outputs determines whether the soil is gaining or losing organic matter, minerals, chemicals or water, for example.

Soil can be seen as a geomorphic system, in the same way that glaciers are: both systems involve the erosion, transport and deposition of material, shaping the land around them. The soil system begins with soil being eroded in the mountains and hills by rivers and glaciers, while groundwater promotes chemical erosion of minerals. Eventually, the soil is deposited on the continental shelves of the oceans. Before the development of agriculture 12 000 years ago, this soil geomorphic system transported about 9 billion tons of sediment (mineral particles) to the sea each year. This was balanced by the input of crustal rock and ash from volcanic eruptions. With the rise of agriculture, the system has become

Key term

thermohaline system: part of the ocean circulation, caused by differences in water density; differences in density occur due to water temperature and salinity

out of balance and soil is being lost faster than it is replaced. This has been caused by the clearing of land for farming and grazing, resulting in higher rates of runoff.

Soil consists of a complex mixture of organic material, minerals and chemicals, sediments and water. In the pores of the soil, soil air is present, which has a higher concentration of carbon dioxide than present in the atmosphere. However, the most important element of soil is the organisms that live within it.

When soil is studied in a vertical section, several roughly horizontal layers can be identified. These layers have different colours, physical structures and chemical characteristics from the underlying bedrock. These horizontal layers are called soil horizons and are assigned letters to distinguish them (Table 4.1). Several other layers can also be recognised, such as I where **ice lenses** and ice wedges are present and F denoting frozen ground.

Making connections

Learn more about the role of surface runoff in section 1.2 The water cycle.

Key term

ice lenses: formed when moisture, diffused within soil or rock, accumulates

Horizon	Characteristics
O	The topmost organic horizon, containing the remains of plants.
A	Topsoil. A dark horizon containing a mixture of organic and mineral. This layer contains the most nutrients and chemical and biological processes.
B	Much less organic material than the A horizon. Brown or red colours originate from iron oxides, whereas grey tones result from chemical reactions in low oxygen conditions.
C	The lowest mineral layer.
R (bedrock)	Solid rock.

Table 4.1 The characteristics of soil horizons.

Soil-forming processes in cold environments

The weathering of parent material provides plants with the chemicals and minerals they require to grow. In cold environments, chemical and biological weathering is limited, but physical weathering of the rocks can be very high at times due to the freeze–thaw cycle. Cryohydration also occurs in very cold environments. This is where induvial mineral particles in the soil are split as a result of the freezing and contraction of water on the surface of the mineral particle. This has the effect of producing fine-grained (silt-sized) particles in the soils.

Frost heave plays an important role in the formation of soil in the northern hemisphere polar regions. In soils that are subjected to frost heave, water moves from warm to cold areas because the ice molecules have a lower energy state than liquid water. Ice lenses develop and increase in size, resulting in an upward movement of the ground. If permafrost or an impermeable rock layer lies beneath the soil, tremendous pressure can build up, resulting in dramatic structural change to take place. Frost heave causes fine particles to be separated from larger materials and stones within the soil can become orientated in a uniform direction.

Cold environments have well defined soil and vegetation characteristics. In the polar regions, the landscape is mostly tundra. Tundra landscapes are dominated by lichens, mosses, dwarf shrubs and grasses. These landscapes have a short growing season and cold annual temperatures. Permafrost is also present, which restricts vegetation growth further. During the summer months, the ground undergoes freeze–thaw cycles. Despite being a harsh environment, tundra soils support many different species, although not as numerous as soils in more temperate climates.

The McMurdo Dry Valley in Antarctica illustrates the extremes of these environments. The region has a very low precipitation rate of less than 100 mm per year and an average temperature of –20 °C. This extreme environment limits the availability of water to periods when the soil temperatures are above 0 °C, which are between 25 and 75 days a year. As a result, the landscape is dominated by soils that are very low in nutrients and very dry.

Thermal characteristics in cold soil

In areas of permafrost, the soil temperatures are low. The topsoil can be as low as –30 °C during the winter and not get above 10 °C in the summer months. Such low temperatures reduce the rates of chemical erosion and weathering, as well as reducing biological activity. The temperature gradient in the soil allows for the formation of ice lenses and the movement of water. This promotes features such as pingos to form.

Vegetation

There is a considerable difference between vegetation types in the Arctic compared to Antarctica. In Arctic regions, there are over 1700 different species of plants living in the tundra, compared to just over 500 different types of mosses and lichens found in Antarctica.

Arctic vegetation

The tundra environment is home to many different flowering plants, dwarf shrubs, grasses and lichens. These plants have a shallow root system because of the thin nature of the active layer of the permafrost, which prevents larger plants such as trees from growing in the region. Small plants dominate the tundra landscape, typically being only a few centimetres tall, growing close together and close to the ground. The Arctic willow is a dwarf shrub that provides food for the caribou. The caribou also feed on cottongrass and particularly lichens in the winter, which grow in mats on the ground and on rocks and include the reindeer lichen or caribou moss found across the Arctic.

Antarctic vegetation

There are only two species of grasses found in Antarctica: Antarctic hair grass and Antarctic pearlwort. These are found where the temperatures are milder and precipitation rates are higher on the west coast of the Antarctic peninsula. There are over 300 different types of mosses found in Antarctica and 150 different species of lichen. The lichens in particular can withstand very cold temperatures, which is why this plant dominates both the Antarctic and Arctic.

Adapting to the cold environment

The vegetation found in these cold environments has adapted in order to survive the harsh conditions. The plants are small and have a shallow root system, with small leaves to reduce the amount of water lost through transpiration. Plants also grow in clumps close together. This limits the effect of the cold weather and the damage caused by wind-blown snow. Vegetation in these areas has also adapted to the very short growing season. Many plants in the Arctic are able to grow under a layer a snow and are able to photosynthesise in extremely cold temperatures. The short polar summers are used to quickly develop and produce flowers and seeds, whereas some plants such as the Arctic poppy are cup-shaped to direct the Sun's rays. Further adaptations include the reproduction asexually through the root system, while many plants are perennials, reducing the need for seed growth.

Making connections

To learn more about the landscapes in permafrost areas, see the section on glaciated landscape development in section 4.3 Systems, processes and landscapes.

The global distribution of past and present cold environments

The current global distribution of cold environments is concentrated in high-latitude and high-altitude areas, as shown in Figure 4.7. The largest areas of snow and ice occur in the polar regions, dominated by the ice sheets of Antarctica and Greenland. Most of the world's highest mountain ranges – including the Alps, the Himalayas, the Andes and the Rockies – also support glaciers and icefields.

Periglacial regions are located in subarctic Canada, Siberia and Alaska. Although there is a lack of glaciers and ice sheets in periglacial environments, it is still cold enough for permafrost to persist.

The present global distribution is a relatively new one, as the Earth's climate oscillates through a cycle of ice advance every 200–250 million years. The most recent advance occurred in the Pleistocene epoch of the Quaternary period, which began 2.5 million years before the present and ended 11 700 years ago (Figure 4.8). Over the last 2 million years, there have been fluctuations in the mean global temperatures, giving rise to cold periods known as **glacial periods** and warm periods known as **interglacial periods**. Ice core measurements have confirmed that in the last 1 million years the Earth has experienced eight glacial periods separated by eight interglacial periods.

For an activity on the distribution of cold environments, download Worksheet 4.1 from **Cambridge Elevate**.

Key terms

glacial period: a time period when ice masses develop and advance into lower altitudes; they are characterised by a sustained decline in temperature and the formation of continental ice sheets

interglacial period: a time period when ice cover retreats to the polar regions; we are currently experiencing an interglacial period

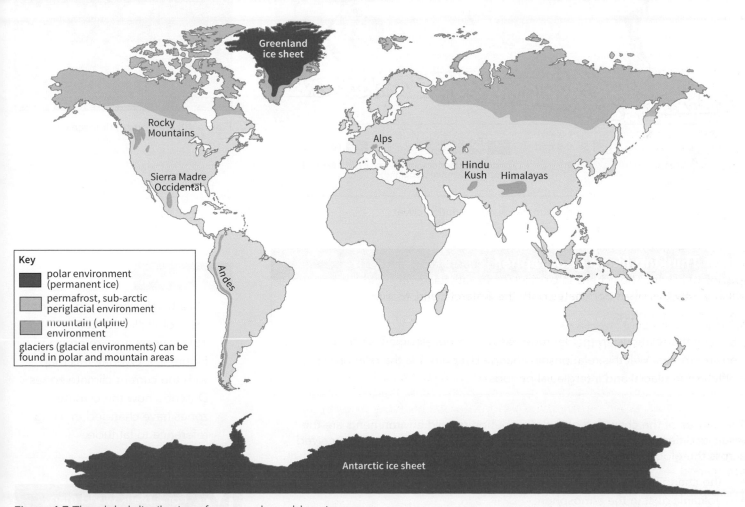

Key
- polar environment (permanent ice)
- permafrost, sub-arctic periglacial environment
- mountain (alpine) environment

glaciers (glacial environments) can be found in polar and mountain areas

Greenland ice sheet

Rocky Mountains

Sierra Madre Occidental

Andes

Alps

Hindu Kush

Himalayas

Antarctic ice sheet

Figure 4.7 The global distribution of present-day cold environments.

During glacial periods, ice cover extended to over 30% of the Earth's surface, compared with 10% today. Proximity to ice changed climatic regions, with areas such as southern England experiencing a tundra environment. Some 18 000 years ago, most of the northern hemisphere was affected by advancing ice and reducing temperatures (Figure 4.9). Glaciers retreated from the UK at the end of the last Ice Age just 10 000 years ago, and their impact can still be seen through studying the erosional and depositional landforms created as a result of their retreat such as glacial valleys in Wales, ribbon lakes in the Lake District and eskers in East Anglia.

Era	Period: Millions of years ago (mya)
Cenozoic	Quaternary (1.8 mya–present)
	Tertiary (65–1.8 mya)
Mesozoic	Cretaceous (146–65 mya)
	Jurassic (200–146 mya)
	Triassic (251–200 mya)
Paleozoic	Permian (299–251 mya)
	Carboniferous (359–299 mya)
	Devonian (416–359 mya)
	Silurian (444–416 mya)
	Ordovician (488–444 mya)
	Cambrian (542–488 mya)
Precambrian (4570–542 mya)	

Figure 4.8 Geological timescales.

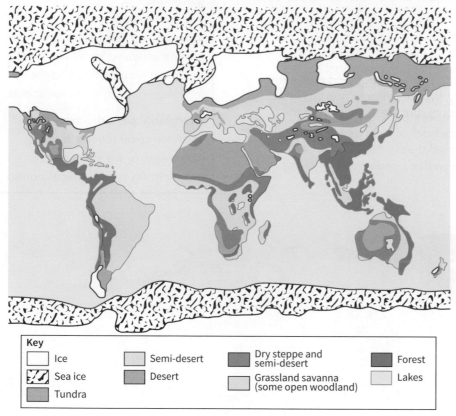

Key
- Ice
- Sea ice
- Tundra
- Semi-desert
- Desert
- Dry steppe and semi-desert
- Grassland savanna (some open woodland)
- Forest
- Lakes

Figure 4.9 18 000 years ago: world climates and vegetation cover.

Thinking like a geographer

A key aspect of thinking like a geographer is the ability to recognise and explore relationships.

Explain the relationship that latitude has on the development of cold environments. Will this relationship change over time? Is the relationship different in glacial and interglacial periods?

The causes of the changing global distribution of cold environments are the result of different factors contributing to the levels of solar radiation received across the globe. These factors include:

- the changing position of the Earth's orbit and tilt
- volcanic dust in the atmosphere
- variations in ocean currents
- storage levels of carbon dioxide in the oceans.

ACTIVITY 4.1

1   On a blank world map, annotate the global climate zones 18 000 years ago, referring to Figure 4.9. Overlay this map with the current climate zones. Describe how the climate zones have changed, making reference to latitude.

For a blank world map, download Worksheet 4.2 from **Cambridge Elevate**.

4.3 Systems, processes and landscapes

Glacial systems including glacial budgets

Glaciers can be seen as an open system, with inputs, processes and outputs.

The main inputs to a glacier system are snow and, to a lesser extent, avalanches. Snow falls on the accumulation zone of a glacier, where inputs exceed outputs, and becomes compacted as further snow falls. Eventually, the low-density ice crystals (called firn or névé) that form from snow are transformed into high-density clear glacier ice.

Glacial processes include plucking and abrasion, as well as ablation and accumulation. These processes help to form the erosional and depositional landforms discussed later in this chapter.

Outputs from a glacier system include sublimation, evaporation and meltwater, as well as sediment from the surrounding valley. Where these outputs or losses from the glacier system are greater than the inputs, the area is known as the ablation zone. The zone on the glacier where inputs and outputs are equal is known as the firn (or equilibrium) line. These zones are shown in Figure 4.10.

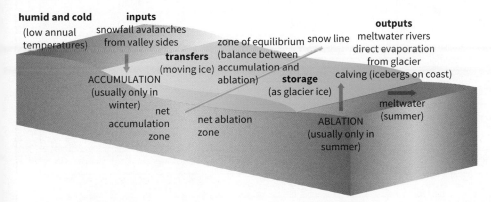

Figure 4.10 The glacier as a system, illustrating inputs and outputs.

Ablation and accumulation

The effects of ablation and accumulation combine to give a glacier a budget, also known as the mass balance of a glacier. During a year, the mass balance of a glacier varies. In the summer months, ablation reaches a maximum as higher temperatures promote the melting of glacier ice. In the winter months, melting is reduced and inputs dominate, resulting in greater accumulation than ablation. Over the course of several years, if ablation is greater than accumulation then the snout of the glacier retreats, whereas greater levels of accumulation over ablation cause an advance in the glacier. The rate of ablation and accumulation can also give an indication of the long-term changes in climate. Alpine glaciers in particular are seen as a reliable indicator of climate change. Photographs of glaciers such as the McCall glacier in Alaska taken between 1958 and 2015 clearly show a glacier in retreat and this has been linked to climate change.

Several factors combine to develop glaciers in the accumulation zone:

- More precipitation, in the form of snow, is found in high-altitude areas.
- Snow, particularly new snow, reflects sunlight, therefore absorbing less heat and in turn melting more slowly.
- Higher winds in higher altitude areas result in snow being blown into hollows, promoting the build-up of snow and subsequently ice.
- Lower temperatures result in lower rates of sublimation.

 Making connections

Glaciers have a system of inputs, outputs and flows. How does this compare to a river system? See section 1.2 The water cycle.

Maths for geographers

The Norwegian Water Resources and Energy Directorate has extensive mass balance data for a number of glaciers in Norway. The data in Table 4.2 has been collected from the Storbreen glacier, which is situated in the Jotunheimen mountain complex in central southern Norway.

Date	Winter balance (metres of water equivalent)	Summer balance (metres of water equivalent)	Net balance (metres of water equivalent)
1990	2.59	−1.34	1.25
1991	1.26	−1.41	−0.15
1992	1.61	−1.53	0.08
1993	1.81	−1.05	0.76
1994	1.52	−1.76	−0.24
1995	1.77	−1.92	−0.15
1996	0.82	−1.84	−1.02
1997	1.75	−2.78	−1.03
1998	1.54	−1.34	0.20
1999	1.66	−1.92	−0.26
2000	2.03	−1.50	
2001	1.04	−1.32	
2002	1.09	−2.87	
2003	1.11	−2.68	
2004	1.00	−1.59	
2005	1.83	−1.89	
2006	0.86	−3.01	
2007	1.35	−1.74	
2008	1.99	−1.88	
2009	1.60	−1.82	
2010	0.79	−2.55	
2011	0.99	−2.34	
2012	1.63	−1.86	
2013	1.31	−2.46	
2014	1.57	−2.75	

Table 4.2 Mass balance data for the Storbreen glacier, 1990–2014.

1   Calculate the net balance for the years 2000 to 2014.
2   Show the net balance of the glacier in the form of a bar graph.
   a   Draw a horizontal line to represent a 0 net balance. Time runs along this line from 1990 to 2014.
   b   Draw bars above the horizontal line to represent a year with a positive net balance, shaded in blue. For years with a negative net balance, draw bars below the line and shade them in red.
3   a   Using your net balance graph, describe how the glacier has changed from 1990 to 2014.
   b   Can this change be connected to climate change?

Warm- and cold-based glaciers

Glaciers can be classified as either cold-based or warm-based glaciers. This classification is governed by the temperature of the ice within the glacier.

Cold-based glaciers occur where the glacier ice has become frozen to the bedrock. This is particularly true of glaciers located in Antarctica and Greenland. As the ice is frozen to the bedrock, very little ice movement occurs.

In a warm-based glacier, the ice is warmer at the base, allowing meltwater to be present. This is typical of glaciers located in more temperate regions such as the Alps and Alaska. In warm-based glaciers, movement of between 20 and 200 m a year can be expected.

Ice movement within a glacier varies depending on whether the glacier is cold- or warm-based. In cold-based glaciers, internal deformation dominates, whereas in warm-based glaciers basal sliding and internal deformation are present (Figure 4.11):

- **Internal deformation** occurs when individual ice crystals slide past each other. The force of gravity pulls the ice crystals downhill and they become deformed along parallel planes, orienting themselves with the direction of flow of the glacier. This can lead to the formation of **crevasses** at the surface and within the glacier itself.
- **Basal sliding** occurs only in warm-based glaciers, as meltwater is a key factor in promoting ice movement. When ice at the base of a glacier comes into contact with an obstacle, pressure between the ice and the obstacle increases. This increase in pressure leads to pressure melting, producing meltwater. This is governed by the **pressure melting point**. The melting ice can now flow around the obstacle and, once passed, will refreeze as the pressure reduces.

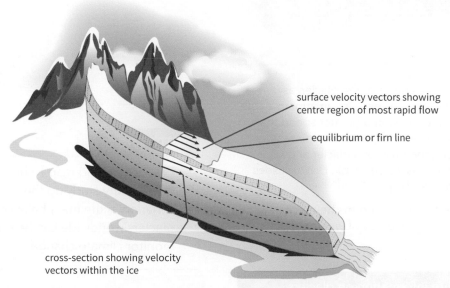

surface velocity vectors showing centre region of most rapid flow

equilibrium or firn line

cross-section showing velocity vectors within the ice

Figure 4.11 Internal flow and basal sliding.

The rate of movement within a glacier is determined by a number of factors:

- gravity
- meltwater
- ice temperature
- ice mass
- the nature of the bedrock, particularly its permeability.

Look on **Cambridge Elevate** to obtain further mass balance data for a glacier situated in northern Norway from CyroClim. Does it share the same pattern as the Storbreen glacier? What landscape and climatic factors might be affecting the glacier? (www.cambridge.org/links/gase6025).

Key terms

internal deformation: small-scale movement and deformation of ice crystals because of the effect of gravity and ice mass

crevasses: a deep fissure or fracture in the glacier

basal sliding: large-scale movement of ice as a result of subglacial meltwater

pressure melting point: the temperature at which ice under pressure melts; this can occur at temperatures below freezing

Ice masses do not move downhill until they reach a critical mass. Glaciers with a thickness of around 60 m will begin to move downhill. The force of gravity affects the speed at which the glacier moves down a valley. Steep gradient glaciers move faster compared with those forming above a gentle gradient and as a result will be generally thinner. Changes in the gradient of a valley result in corresponding changes in the velocity of the glacier. In the steep sections, as the ice flow increases in velocity, the ice becomes thinner, often forming numerous crevasses and **seracs**. The glacier flow at this point is known as **extensional flow**. If the gradient of the valley decreases, ice flow slows, causing a build-up of ice and making the glacier thicker. The ice closes any crevasses at this point. This is known as **compressional flow**. In between extensional and compressional flow, the glacier moves in a rotational direction, eroding the base of the valley as it does so (Figure 4.12).

Key terms

seracs: steep faults on the surface of a glacier

extensional flow: ice is moving faster in front than the ice behind, resulting in the development of crevasses

compressional flow: ice in front is moving slower than the ice behind, so a build-up of ice occurs

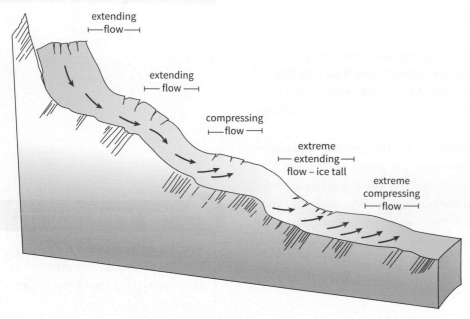

Figure 4.12 The effects of gradient on glacier flow.

Glacier ice at the margins moves slower than in the centre of the glacier, as friction with the valley sides reduces speed. Glaciers moving over an impermeable bedrock, such as metamorphic granite and basalt, move at a greater speed than a similar sized glacier travelling over a permeable bedrock, such as sedimentary sandstone and conglomerates. Melting between the base of a glacier and impermeable rock encourages basal sliding, whereas a permeable bedrock sees meltwater infiltrate, minimising its effect on basal sliding.

The movement of a glacier results in several different landforms being created. The formation of these landforms is linked to the processes of weathering, erosion and deposition.

ACTIVITY 4.2

1   Produce a mind map to help explain why studying the variation in the mass balance of glaciers worldwide can help to monitor climate change.

 Look on **Cambridge Elevate** for more information on glaciers worldwide from the following websites:
*   Global Glacier Changes (www.cambridge.org/links/gase6026)
*   National Snow and Ice Data Center (www.cambridge.org/links/gase6027)
*   British Geological Society (www.cambridge.org/links/gase6028)
*   A time lapse video from *The Telegraph* (www.cambridge.org/links/gase6029)
*   US Geological Survey (www.cambridge.org/links/gase6030).

Geomorphological processes

Weathering is the breakdown of rock in its original position. In cold environments, frost shattering dominates (Figure 4.13). Frost shattering is a physical weathering process. The process occurs when water infiltrates into rocks, through bedding planes and pores. When the temperature drops below 0°C, the water becomes ice and its volume increases by approximately 10%. This increase in volume causes pressure to build and weakens the rock. As the temperature rises, the ice melts, water enters the resulting crack and the process begins again. Over time, pieces of rock break away and often fall on to the glacier. This weathered rock is sharp-edged and angular. When transported by the glacier, the angular nature of this material can promote further erosion at the base of the glacier.

Figure 4.13 Frost shattering.

Glaciated landscape development

Glaciated landscapes are a function of geological processes working over long time spans. For example, the Norwegian landscape has been formed by a number of geological events. The most ancient landscape in Norway can be traced to a process involving the break-up of the North Atlantic, but most landforms in Norway are as a result of the Quaternary glaciations or periglacial processes.

Figure 4.14 shows the time it takes for different glacial landforms to develop from one day (friction cracks) to the longest, fjords, which take around 10 million years to develop fully.

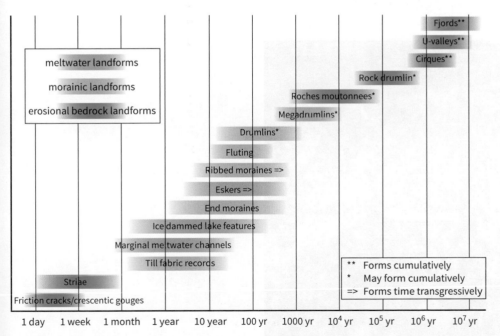

Figure 4.14 Glacial erosional and depositional landforms, and the time required for their formation.

Large glacial troughs and fjords dominate the Norwegian landscape, particularly on the coastal regions. Further inland, where the presence of glaciers are not as evident, the landscape has more pre-Quaternary features, with little periglacial influence. The glaciers of the Quaternary redistributed the rock and sediment, now providing valuable resources for the aggregate industry as well as agriculture. The isostatic depression of the Norwegian landmass has resulted in the deposition of large areas of thick, fine-grained **glaciomarine sediments**, which are potentially unstable.

In a typical Norwegian alpine landscape such as the Lyngen Alps, there are a variety of landforms of different ages in close proximity to each other. The youngest landforms are often late glacial and consist of moraines and meltwater channels, along with fluvial landforms such as deltas and alluvial plains. At the coast, due to isostatic rebound, wave-cut beaches and raised beaches occur. Close by, glacial landforms are present, including eskers and drumlins, while all of the landforms themselves can occur in glacial troughs or fjords carved during the last glaciation. It is therefore important to study the wider geographical landscape when investigating glacial landforms so that they can be fully understood in the correct context.

Erosional processes

There are three main processes by which a glacier erodes and, as a result, shapes the landscape: abrasion, plucking and rotational movement.

Abrasion

Abrasion occurs as a result of the weathered angular rock discussed above. Rock fragments become embedded into the glacier and grind over the bedrock and valley sides. This eventually wears away the valley's floor and sides. Over time, larger rocks may carve striations into the bedrock surface, as shown in Figure 4.15. These are scratches or elongated grooves orientated in the direction that the glacier is moving. Rocks within the glacier eventually break down to become **rock flour**. This fine material smoothes the bedrock to leave a polished and smooth surface.

Key terms

glaciomarine sediments: inorganic and organic material deposited in a marine setting by a combination of glacier- and marine-related processes

rock flour: very fine rock particles caused when rocks are ground down by glacial erosion

Figure 4.15 Striations on a surface of basalt bedrock.

Plucking

Plucking occurs as a result of the pressure melting point and obstacles in the path of the glacier. The combination of melting and refreezing can create landforms known as roche moutonnées (see also the Erosional landforms section).

Rotational movement

Rotational movement causes the bedrock to be scoured. This process is most effective in warming environments where the temperature fluctuates above and below freezing point. This promotes freeze–thaw weathering at the base of the glacier, further increasing the scouring process.

Erosional landforms

Corries

Corries (also known as cwms or cirques) are depressions or hollowed-shaped areas on the mountainside. The characteristic features of a corrie are a steep back wall, which due to the process of frost shattering will have a **scree** base, and a rock basin (Figure 4.16). In the UK, corries are found on slopes with a north-west or east/south-east facing aspect. This corresponds with low ablation rates and high snow accumulation rates. Sometimes a small lake is present, which is called a **tarn**.

Figure 4.16 Cwm Idwal, Snowdonia, Wales, illustrating the main features of a corrie.

Corries are formed as deepening snow hollows out the bedrock base due to a process of **nivation**. Further snowfall results in greater ice mass, which in turn leads to the ice rotating as it begins to flow downhill. Abrasion and plucking promote the development of a steep back wall. Water flowing down the **bergschrund** encourages further freeze–thaw action, creating a much larger corrie in the process. At the front of the corrie, pressure is reduced and as a result erosion rates are also reduced. This leads to the development of a rock lip, where erosion rates are reduced. Deposition of material as **moraine** can lead to the rock lip building up further.

Key terms

scree: a mass of small loose stones covering a slope

tarn: a small mountain lake

nivation: the erosion of the ground and sides of a hollow as a result of continued freezing and thawing

bergschrund: a crevasse that forms where a moving glacier ice separates from the back wall of a corrie or stagnant ice above the crevasse

moraine: rocks and sediments carried and then deposited by the glacier

---

ACTIVITY 4.3

1   Draw a labelled sketch to show the features of a corrie.

Arêtes and pyramidal peaks

If two neighbouring corries erode back towards each other, the ridge between the two becomes increasingly narrow. Eventually, a knife edge ridge is formed, which is known as an arête. The sides of an arête are often very steep-sided due to the erosion of the corrie glacier.

If three or more cirques erode towards each other, the ridge becomes isolated and forms a pyramid-shaped peak such as the Matterhorn, located in the Alps on the border of Italy and Switzerland.

Glacial troughs

As a glacier travels down a valley, the erosion caused creates a U-shaped valley. Freeze–thaw weathering on the sides of the valley weakens the rock, as does plucking as the ice freezes to the sides and tears pieces away as it moves – these provide the tools for abrasion. As a result of these processes and the solid mass of ice, the interlocking spurs of the former river valley are bulldozed out of the way to create the steep sides of the glacial trough. These are steep-sided and flat-bottomed valleys, and are only evident once the glacier has retreated or completely melted. Unlike rivers in upland areas, a glacier is dominated by both lateral and vertical erosion, resulting in a more steep-sided and flat-floored valley, which results from the dominant process of vertical river erosion. Glacial troughs are generally straight and any interlocking spurs that are present will be cut through, leaving behind truncated spurs. This can result in the formation of hanging valleys, with waterfalls often present (Figure 4.17). The top of these is marked by a break in the slope marking the depth of the ice. Above this level are former tributary valleys, also occupied by ice during glaciation. However, the depth of ice here was less and so there was less erosive power. These valleys were not deepened to the extent of the main valley. As a result, when the ice has gone, they end abruptly. The previous, gentle end of the valley is cut off by the truncated spurs of the main valley and they are left 'hanging' at this point.

If a glacial trough were formed below the lower sea level, then once sea levels rise after the glacial period ends, the trough will become flooded to form a fjord, such as those found in Norway.

ACTIVITY 4.4

1   Draw a sequence of diagrams to help explain the formation of a pyramidal peak.

To develop your field-sketching skills, download Worksheet 4.3 from **Cambridge Elevate**.

Ribbon lakes

Extensional flow within the glacier can result in an increase in erosion of the bedrock. In these locations, where the bedrock has been carved out to a greater

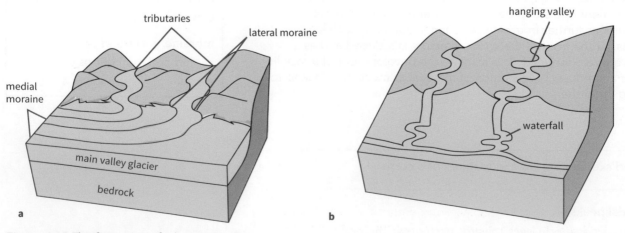

Figure 4.17 The formation of a hanging valley.

Figure 4.18 Lake Windermere in the Lake District an example of a ribbon lake.

Figure 4.19 A roche moutonnée.

extent than the surrounding bedrock, a long, deep and narrow depression is created. When the glacier retreats, this depression can be filled with meltwater, creating a lake known as a ribbon lake. These lakes only occur in post-glacial periods. In the UK, ribbon lakes occur in the Lake District, such as Lake Windermere (Figure 4.18).

Roche moutonnées

This French term can be translated directly into English as sheepback/fleecy rock. These are rock formations created by the passing of a glacier, resulting in asymmetric erosion on the stoss (upstream) and lee (downstream) sides of the rock. The melting of ice upstream of an obstacle such as a large rocky outcrop because of increased pressure results in a smooth eroded surface on the upstream or stoss side of the rock. As the pressure reduces, refreezing occurs downstream of the obstacle. As the glacier continues to move downstream, the ice pulls away the rock it has frozen to. This leaves a jagged surface on the downstream side, or lee side, of the rock due to plucking (Figure 4.19).

Depositional landforms

As the glacier moves across the landscape, several landforms are created. This section explores how these landforms are created in more detail.

Drumlins

Drumlins are oval-shaped hills, composed mainly of glacial till and aligned in the direction of ice flow. The word 'drumlin' is derived from the Gaelic word for rounded hill. A drumlin is typically a few kilometres in length and up to 50m in height. They are found in former glaciated landscapes such as Canada, Sweden, Scotland and Ireland. Drumlins can be classified as subglacial bedforms together with related landforms such as flutes, as they occur within major end moraine systems.

Drumlins generally have a classic streamlined, smooth shape (Figure 4.20). When present in the landscape, they tend to occur in fields, known as swarms, numbering between 10 and 1000. When viewed together, the swarm of drumlins shares a similar morphology and long axis orientation and are closely packed together. The shape is elongated with a typical ratio of 2:1 to 7:1. The highest, blunt end of the drumlin is known as the stoss end and points upstream of the glacier direction. The gently sloping tail end, known as the lee, points downstream. There are variations in drumlin shape, with some resembling barchan dunes from above. The role of the landscape

Physical and human

How has the development of the tourism industry around Lake Windermere been influenced by the features of the ribbon lake?

Look on **Cambridge Elevate** for more information from swisseduc on how glaciers shape the landscape from the following websites:

- Shaping the landscape (www.cambridge.org/links/gase6031)
- Stereo photos (www.cambridge.org/links/gase6032).

is also important in the formation of drumlin swarms. In the central lowlands of Scotland, for example, drumlins align with the direction of flow of the last ice sheet as expected. However, the ice sheet took this direction because of the local topography, which meant that successive ice sheets followed the same path.

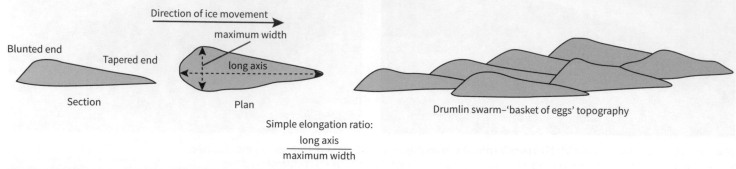

Figure 4.20 The streamlined appearance of a drumlin.

In some areas, drumlin fields have been found to occur on the edge of the ice margins, suggesting that they are formed as the ice retreats. Some drumlin fields have been found to occur above former drumlin fields with different orientations, suggesting that older landforms can sometimes be preserved beneath glaciers.

The sedimentation of a drumlin reveals a complex array of sediment types and structures, making it even more difficult to agree a theory on formation. Some drumlins have been found to have a rock core surrounded by poorly sorted till, ranging from silts and sands to gravel and boulders. However, some drumlins do not share this sedimentation pattern; they have sorted material, suggesting a fluvial origin. As a result of the different nature of the sediment within drumlins, different theories of their formation have been proposed, dominated by either deposition or erosion as the main agent.

Drumlin formation remains a controversial topic, as the glacier bed remains an inaccessible area to study.

Theory 1: Deforming bed model

In this theory, the sediments of the bed deform because of the overlying weight of the ice. Some of the deforming till layer at the bed is stronger than others and deforms less, while the weaker till deforms and become more mobile. The strength of the till has been associated with grain size. Coarse-grained sediments remain strong compared to finer-grained sediments.

A layer of till with different-sized material will therefore have variable strength. In turn, this results in some areas of the till being able to flow and become shaped by the movement of the ice, while other areas do not and form the stronger cores of the drumlin.

Theory 2: Erosion and deposition by meltwater floods

The second theory of drumlin development focuses on the role of meltwater floods at the base of a glacier. These floods are large scale, regional floods that are 10 000 to 100 000 km wide and are powerful enough to separate the glacier from the bedrock. The floods erode large drumlin-shaped cavities in the base of the ice. These voids are then infilled with sediment as the flood recedes and the ice becomes once again connected to the bedrock. As the glacier continues to move, the sediment till within the cavity is shaped.

Erratics

Another landform created by deposition are erratics. These range in size, but are often associated with large boulders that a glacier has deposited. Erratics are *ex situ*, meaning that they do not belong in the landscape they are deposited in. It is common for erratics to have travelled hundreds of kilometres within a glacier before being finally deposited. As a result of these large distances, erratics often have a different rock type to the surrounding geology.

Erratics transported by glaciers provide an important method for reconstructing directions of glacier flows in conjunction with landscape features such as drumlins and moraines. They can be used to determine the path of past glacier movement by tracing the rock to the parent bedrock, confirming the direction of the glacier. For example, in the Cairngorms the distribution of erratics has helped to understand the different ice advances in the area. In the northern Cairngorms there are a significant number of metamorphic erratics, reaching a maximum elevation of 800 m. This suggests that they were carried by the late re-advance originating from Strathspey. Further metamorphic erratics on the northern slopes of Ben Avon have been used to define a phase of ice movement that occurred in the late Devensian. At this time, glacier ice was able to flow south-east across the present An Lurg ridge. Cairngorm granite erratics have also been used to indicate the glacier flow from the cairngorm. Such erratics have been found on the northern slopes of the mountain range, as well as in Morven to the east of the Cairngorms.

Moraines

Moraines are landforms created by the deposition of material carried by the glacier. There are different types of moraine (Figure 4.21), depending on where the material was deposited.

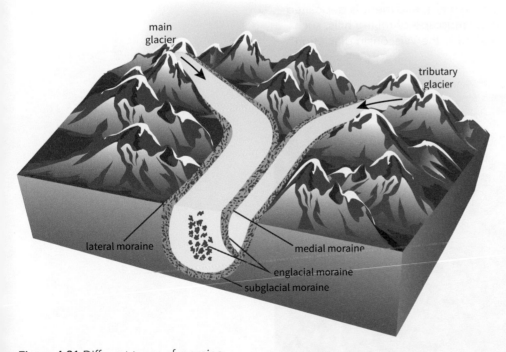

Figure 4.21 Different types of moraine.

- Lateral moraine: these landforms consist of the frost-shattered materials from the valley walls that have fallen on to the glacier surface. The material is transported on the edge of the glacier. Once the glacier has melted, the material forms long embankments of material along the sides of the valley.

- Medial moraine: when a smaller tributary glacier joins a larger glacier, two lateral moraines join to form a medial moraine, which occurs in the centre of the glacier surface.

- Englacial moraine: this material is transported within the ice, having been buried over the years by snowfall. It is deposited during ablation and may then be reshaped by meltwater.

- Terminal moraine: this material signifies the maximum extent of the glacier and often occurs across the valley floor in a high mound, not usually higher than 20 m. These moraines are often crescent-shaped, which corresponds with the snout of the glacier. The greater the development of the terminal moraine, the longer the glacier snout was fixed in that location. Where the depositing mass is an ice sheet, ridges can extend for many kilometres. Subsequent meltwater can destroy terminal moraines.

- Recessional moraine: these mounds of material mark the retreat of a glacier. Each recessional moraine indicates a period of retreat. These may be removed by future advances.

- Push moraine: these moraines may develop due to climate change. If the climate deteriorates enough for the glacier to advance, already deposited moraine will be pushed into a mound. Within push moraines, stones are orientated in a more vertical position than in other moraines.

Till plains

Till plains are formed when a large sheet of ice becomes detached from the main section of the glacier. As the detached ice melts, sediment is deposited in irregular heaps giving rise to a post-glacial landscape of rolling hills, such as those in northern Ohio which were deposited in the Wisconsin glaciation (Figure 4.22).

Figure 4.22 Till plains in northern Ohio.

ACTIVITY 4.5

1 Obtain two photographs of landforms resulting from glacial deposition. Annotate the photographs to explain how the landforms were created.

 Maths for geographers

During a recent field trip, students collected data on the orientation of material within a moraine (known as **clasts**). The results are shown in Table 4.3.

 Key term

clasts: rock fragments resulting from the breakdown of larger rocks

Orientation (degrees)	Number of clasts with orientation
360–009	4
010–029	12
030–049	14
050–069	8
070–089	7
090–109	0
110–129	0
130–149	3
150–169	6
170–189	4
190–209	12
210–229	14
230–249	8
250–269	7
270–289	0
290–309	0
310–329	0
330–349	0

Table 4.3 Data on the orientation of material within a moraine.

1 Using the data, produce a rose diagram to illustrate the general orientation of the material.
2 Suggest the direction in which the glacier may have been moving.
3 Which methods and equipment might the students have used to collect this data?
4 What would the students have needed to consider in relation to assessing the risks involved and the reliability of the data?

 To help you with this activity, download Worksheet 4.4 from **Cambridge Elevate**.

Glacial transportation and deposition

Transportation

Glaciers transport material (known as till or moraine) on, in and below the ice. The position of material being transported by the ice can be defined using these terms:

- Supraglacial: material located on the surface of the glacier, either at the sides of the glacier or in the middle (as medial moraine).
- Englacial: material located in the main body of the glacier and covered from subsequent snowfall.
- Subglacial: material located under the glacier and transported by subglacial meltwater channels in warm-based glaciers.

Deposition

Glacial deposits (Figure 4.23) are known as drift geology to make the distinction between the glacial materials and the surrounding underlying geology of the area.

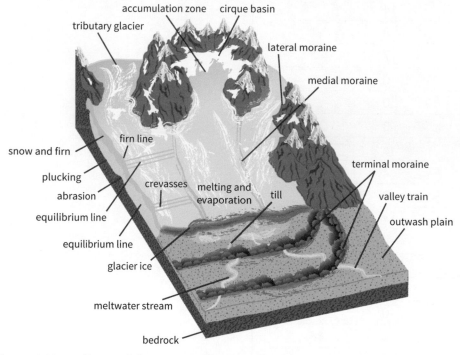

Figure 4.23 Landforms of deposition created by a glacier.

When a glacier deposits material, the material will be either unsorted or sorted.

- If the material is directly deposited by the ice, it is known as till and is a mixture of different sized sediment, largely unsorted in nature. The composition of the till is governed by the geology of the area through which the glacier has moved. The transportation of the material by ice means that there is little smoothing of material. Rocks retain their angular features and often become aligned in the direction of glacier flow.
- If the material is deposited by meltwater streams, it is known as fluvioglacial material. This is usually sorted, with larger material deposited by the snout of the glacier and finer material deposited further away.

Deposition is also encouraged where ice becomes overloaded with sediment at the base or as a glacier retreats.

The location of till deposits and the orientation of the material can offer an insight into how far, when and from where the ice advanced through the landscape. Till deposits in north Norfolk, for example, suggest that the glacier that deposited the material advanced from southern Norway because this is where the deposited material originates from.

Fluvioglacial processes

The term 'fluvial' refers to flowing water. When studying fluvioglacial processes, the focus is therefore on processes caused by glacial meltwater. Water can move through the glacial system in a number of ways:

- supraglacial channels: on the surface of the glacier
- englacial channels: channels of meltwater flowing within the glacier
- subglacial channels: meltwater channels under the ice.

Meltwater streams on a glacier have dynamic and variable discharge as well as sediment load. Discharge varies in relation to the seasons. In the summer months, discharge from meltwater streams is high, whereas in the winter discharge decreases and for some glaciers ceases. Discharge is also affected on a daily basis as the glacier responds to the daily maximum and minimum temperatures.

Meltwater streams cause erosion in a similar way to erosion by rivers, namely abrasion, hydraulic action, attrition and corrosion, although the subglacial meltwater tends to be under a greater pressure so erosion rates are higher than comparable supraglacial flows.

Fluvioglacial landforms

Just as a river channel creates landforms of erosion or deposition, so do the meltwater streams of glaciers. Fluvioglacial landforms are created by the erosional and depositional power of meltwater streams in front of a glacier. The meltwater streams stratify the glacial till sediments into layers, sorting them into size and eroding the sediment so they become rounder. The fluvioglacial landscape is a dynamic and changing one because of the changing nature of the meltwater streams. Discharge and sediment load can be highly variable throughout the year. In the summer months meltwater discharge is high, whereas in the winter months discharge ceases if temperatures do not rise above the pressure melting point. Meltwater streams can also have a daily change, with the greatest discharge occurring after the highest temperature for that particular day.

Kames

Kames occur along the front of a melting ice sheet. They are irregular and undulating mounds of generally unsorted material of sand and gravel. Three different types of kame can be identified:

- kame terraces
- kame deltas
- crevasse kames or 'pudding-bowl' kames.

Kame terraces are the most extensive type of kame landform. They occur as a result of the infilling of a marginal glacial lake or stream. Kame terrace material is generally better sorted than other kames. In a post-glacial environment, kame terraces can be identified as a ridge on the side of a valley.

Kame deltas are smaller features than kame terraces. They form mound-shaped hills on the valley floor as a meltwater stream enters a marginal lake. The sediments of a kame delta share the same characteristics as a river delta.

Crevasse kames occur as meltwater streams enter the glacier through surface crevasses. Material is deposited on the valley floor under the glacier, forming a small hummock or 'pudding-bowl' feature.

Associated with kames are kettle holes. During deglaciation, ice sheets and glaciers break up, leaving blocks of 'dead-ice' among the fluvioglacial deposits. As these ice blocks melt, they form kettle holes, which are depressions surrounded by the fluvioglacial deposits. Water filling the kettle holes can lead to the formation of lakes called kettle lakes.

 Investigate

Investigate how these different forms of esker formed and where they can be found.

Eskers

Eskers often dominate the surrounding landscape and are formed within former ice margins, as defined by the surrounding moraine systems. They are generally aligned parallel to the glacial ice flow, therefore oriented down the valley as opposed to moraines which are aligned across the valley floor. Eskers are formed as a result of the meltwater streams flowing subglacially. They can be divided into two basic types, related to the position of the formation of the landform:

• Eskers forming at the same time as a subglacial tunnel system extending into the ice sheet.

• Eskers that are formed over time, in repeated subglacial tunnel systems at the edge of a retreating glacier or ice sheet.

If an esker formed as the same time as the subglacial tunnel system, this could indicate a rapid formation due to higher levels of meltwater during the winter months or the presence of water at the glacier margin, maintaining water within the subglacial tunnels. In this case, the ice would melt around the esker rather than a slower systematic retreat.

Eskers are long ridges of sand and gravel and can be up to 30 m high and several kilometres in length. They are sinuous in nature, following the path of the original meltwater channel. They are formed by deposition of the subglacial river as it travels through the glacier. The sediments are sorted as would be expected from a fluvioglacial deposit. As with a river, deposition occurs when the velocity of the subglacial stream reduces.

In a post-glacial landscape, eskers often appear as a set of discontinuous hills, as subsequent post-glacial rivers and meltwater erodes the material away. They also form up-slope indicating that, at that point, the water under the glacier was moving under pressure. It is therefore important to consider the role of present-day erosional processes and landforms such as rivers when investigating the path of eskers. Some eskers can also be formed in englacial channels. These sediments are then lowered to the valley floor when the glacier melts, leading to a more discontinuous appearance.

There are three distinct esker forms:

- sharp-crested eskers
- multi-crested eskers
- broad-crested eskers.

Outwash plains

One of the most extensive fluvioglacial landforms created by both erosion and deposition is the outwash plain or **sandur** (Figure 4.24). Outwash plains can be located in front of the snout of the glacier, in areas glaciated by ice sheets and then remodelled by meltwater. During the summer months, when ablation is the dominant process, glaciers are retreating and meltwater streams deposit gravels, sands and clays. As the meltwater streams exit the glacier at the snout, it loses energy as it is no longer under hydrostatic pressure. Material is therefore deposited. Larger material is deposited nearest the snout and can often form an alluvial fan. If several fans merge, an outwash plain is formed. The finer material is generally found further from the snout of the glacier, whereas the coarser material such as gravel and sand are nearer the snout.

Iceland and Alaska offer the most extensive outwash plains today, where braided meltwater streams meander across the valley floor. Braided streams develop due to the highly variable discharge of the meltwater, causing the meltwater channel to spilt into smaller channels. These meltwater streams may be milky in colour because of the rock flour carried in suspension. Lateral erosion of the meltwater streams promotes an often flat layered landscape.

Key term

sandur: a glacial meltwater outwash plain

 Watch a video on **Cambridge Elevate** to learn more about the fluvioglacial landforms being created by the Sólheimajökull glacier.

Figure 4.24 Skeiðarársandur in south-east Iceland, 1000 km² in area, is the world's largest active outwash plain.

4.4 Snowdonia, Wales, a glaciated environment

Snowdonia is an example of a glaciated upland area. The Ice Age that covered the area in the Devenisan epoch saw the development of arêtes, cirques, roches mountonnées and glacial troughs.

There have been many glaciations affecting Wales in the past, although the most recent advance of ice occurred in the Devensian epoch. During this time, glaciers extended from the mountains of Snowdonia, travelling northwards towards the Irish Sea.

Pentir, in north-west Wales, is located to the north of the Snowdonia mountains and has many lowland glacial features. A drumlin field surrounds Pentir (Figure 4.25) and is oriented in a north-east to south-west orientation, giving an insight into the direction that the ice was flowing during the last Ice Age.

Figure 4.25 The drumlin field around Pentir, Wales.

Thinking like a geographer

GIS mapping can be used to investigate which areas around the Migneint area would have been classified as nunataks. Create a map of the area showing an ice thickness of 1400 m to discover which areas remain untouched by ice sheet erosion. Do these places exhibit a lack of glacial erosion today?

Depositional landforms are also found in the area. The Pentir esker is 5 m in height and approximately 400 m in length and is composed of sands and gravels.

Glaciated plateau

In Snowdonia, the ice sheet was probably centred on the Migneint area. The ice sheet was at its greatest extent around 18 000 years ago. It is estimated that the Merioneth and Snowdonia ice cap was over 1000 m in depth at its maximum extent, covering many of the highest peaks in the area. Areas above the ice sheet and therefore not affected by glacial erosion are known as nunataks. The landscape seen today is a direct result of this ice sheet advance. The major passes within Snowdonia were created as the ice sheet formed glacial breaches. Glacial breaches occur when the glaciers cut through the existing watershed boundaries after repeated abrasion and plucking. In the Migneint area today, the ice sheet has been replaced with marshy depressions and peat deposits that filled irregular-shaped lakes.

Glacial troughs

To the north and south-east of Snowdon are several glacial troughs dominate the landscape. The Nant Ffrancon valley was carved by a glacier moving north-west. The valley was straightened, deepened and widened by the glacier as it moved towards Anglesey. Within the valley, there is evidence of several corries, a ribbon lake including Llyn Peris and Llyn Gwynant and a post-glacial valley.

Ribbon lakes

A ribbon lake was formed as the valley floor was filled from meltwater from the retreating ice, filling the depression created by glacial erosion. Sediments were deposited within the lake, creating the flat floor present today, which the Afon Ogwen flows through. The river is too small to have eroded the valley and as such is known as a misfit stream. Waterfalls are present in the current landscape and illustrate the power of the glacier as it truncated the interlocking spurs of the original valley to leave the hanging valleys seen today. Cwm Amarch is a typical hanging valley, starting on the southern side of Cadair Idris. The valley river flows into the Tal y Llyn valley, a drop of 315m.

Arêtes

Snowdon has a series of well-developed arêtes, including Crib Goch (Figure 4.26) and Bwlch, both of which radiate out from the central peak of Snowdon. Crib Goch translated from Welsh means 'Red Ridge' and it is very popular with tourists and mountaineering groups. Although the ice and glaciers that formed the arête are no longer present, the impact on the landscape is still very clear. Now it is frost action and rivers that erode the landscape, along with the thousands of tourists who visit every year.

Figure 4.26 Crib Goch, a typical knife-edge arête.

Ecosystems influenced by the glacial landscape

As the glaciers retreated in Snowdonia region, lichen and mosses dominated. Alpine plants were soon to follow, establishing themselves in the crag slopes that were the result of plucking. As the climate began to warm, the alpine plants withdrew to higher slopes, while the oak woodland ecosystem became dominant. The evidence of such a woodland ecosystem can be seen in the peat deposits such as those found in Cwm Idwal.

Much of the landscape today has been modified by human activity. The stone walls that dominate the area were a practical solution to the wild animals that threated livestock, the glacial deposition of stones and till material providing the material for the tone dry walls. In the 16th century, woodland accounted for 65% of the landscape whereas now this figure is less than 3%, illustrating that it is in a continuous cycle of change.

The challenges of living in the area

Transport around Snowdonia has been difficult because of its mountainous terrain. It was not until 1830 that the A5 was completed, serving as a postal route from London to Holyhead. This brought tourists to the area for the first time. Many of the roads built follow the landscape rather than cut through it, contrasting with the road network in southern Norway, which often cuts through valley sides due to the deep fjords present.

Thinking like a geographer

Being able to understand changes of time and making connections are important aspects of thinking like a geographer. Can you explain why Snowdon has well defined arêtes but it does not have a fully developed pyramidal peak like the Matterhorn?

ACTIVITY 4.6

Obtain a copy of a 1:25 000 Ordnance Survey map centred on the Cwm Idwal area (Explorer OL17). Cwm Idwal is within the Nant Ffrancon valley.

1   Look carefully at the contours of the region. How do these contours help to identify the glaciated landforms?
2   On the map, identify and highlight the following landforms:
    * a ribbon lake
    * a corrie
    * a glaciated trough.
3   Draw a transect line across the glaciated trough from SH 655 619 to SH 627 607. Using this transect, draw a cross-section of the glaciated trough. Identify on the cross-section the A5, the Afon (River) Ogwen and the A road.
4   To what extent is there evidence that the area centred on Cwm Idwal has been affected by glaciation?

For an activity on glaciation in Snowdonia, Wales, download Worksheet 4.5 from **Cambridge Elevate**.

Look on **Cambridge Elevate** for more information on Welsh glaciation from the British Geological Society (www.cambridge.org/links/gase6033).

Fieldwork opportunities: investigating glacial deposition

Snowdonia offers an excellent opportunity to collect fieldwork data focusing on glacial deposition. There are several considerations to take into account when undertaking work in the field.

Site suitability

When undertaking till fabric analysis, select a site that has been exposed. Newer exposures are better as older ones may have been affected by soil creep. Ideal locations would include river cliffs on meanders when water levels make it safe to access the site.

Data collection

There are several different sets of data that could be collected in the field. To undertake an analysis of till, an investigation into stone orientation can be undertaken. A sample of between 50 and 100 pebbles will provide a suitable sample size. Decide the longest axis for each pebble, without displacing from the sediment section. Measure the orientation using a compass. The angle of dip or rise for each pebble can also be recorded using a clinometer. A rose diagram can be drawn to investigate the possible direction of glacial movement.

Statistical analysis

If two sets of data have been collected, the Chi-square test (X^2) can be used to compare both sets of data:

$$x^2 = \Sigma \frac{(O - E)^2}{E}$$

where:

Σ = the sum of; O = observed value; E = expected value.

This example explains how to use the Chi-square test to test the null hypothesis that ice flow did not affect the orientation of clasts in the deposited till.

Start by sorting the data for each site into four 45° intervals. These are the observed values. Now calculate the expected values. In this example, if ice flow did not have any effect on orientation it would be expected to find an equal number of stones in each 45° interval. If 50 pebbles were collected, the value of E is 12.5.

Calculate the degrees of freedom, which is the number of intervals minus 1. In this example, the degrees of freedom is 3 as there are 4 intervals.

Choose a significance level such as 1% (this means that chance should only account for the results in up to 1% of occasions during which the field test is carried out.)

Compare the result with the critical value, found in a table of critical values of Chi-square distribution. If the calculated value is greater than the critical value in the table, the null hypothesis must be rejected and ice flow *did* affect pebble orientation.

For a step-by-step Maths for geographers activity based on this example, download Worksheet 4.6 from **Cambridge Elevate**.

Periglacial processes

Periglacial areas are those areas that have a cold climate and the presence of permafrost. Around one-quarter of the world's surface can be said to be periglacial, including areas of Greenland, Russia and Canada, as well as parts of mountainous areas such as the Alps.

Permafrost

Permafrost is permanently frozen ground, which is one of the most important characteristics of a periglacial environment. As temperatures in periglacial areas rarely reach above 0 °C, the ground is permanently frozen, often to a depth of 100 m. It is this frozen layer of soil that is known as permafrost.

As temperature is a defining factor in the development of permafrost, colder temperatures deepen the permafrost layer while warmer temperatures decrease it, as shown in Figure 4.27.

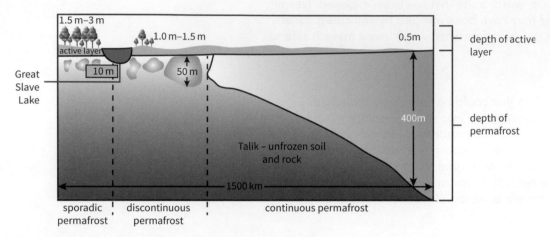

Figure 4.27 The effect of temperature on permafrost depth.

Permafrost can be classified into three distinct types: continuous permafrost, discontinuous permafrost and sporadic permafrost. Continuous permafrost occurs in the coldest parts of the world, often reaching depths of 400 m, while in the coldest parts of Canada the depth can reach 700 m. Discontinuous permafrost occurs as the environment becomes warmer, resulting in the development of lakes and rivers. The soil temperatures around these features is higher than the surrounding areas, melting the permafrost and therefore becoming discontinuous. As shown in Figure 4.27, the average depth of the discontinuous layer is between 20 and 30 m. Sporadic permafrost occurs in isolated areas as the temperatures are warmer, hovering at around 0 °C.

Permafrost will change from continuous to discontinuous to sporadic to none the further southwards (in the northern hemisphere) or the further northwards (in the southern hemisphere) you travel. Unfrozen material in the permafrost zone is known as talik.

The top few centimetres of the permafrost is known as the active layer. During the summer months, this active layer may melt temporarily if temperatures rise above 0 °C. As temperatures drop again in the winter, the active layer refreezes.

ACTIVITY 4.7

1   On a blank map of the world, label the periglacial areas. What characteristics do the locations of the periglacial regions share?

For a blank world map, download Worksheet 4.7 from **Cambridge Elevate**.

Investigate

Investigate the solutions that have been developed to allow settlements to be built in permafrost regions, which minimise the environmental impacts.

Periglacial landforms and mass movement processes

Patterned ground

Frost heave occurs as a result of freezing soil and water below the surface. When the soil freezes, fine-grained materials expand. This is an uneven process due to the presence of ice crystals and results in small domes of uplifted soil forming. If stones are present in the soil, this promotes the creation of patterned ground (Figure 4.28). The stones decrease in temperature faster than the surrounding soil. As a result, any moisture under the stones is frozen and turns to ice. The increase in volume results in the stones being pushed upwards. If the ground undergoes repeated freezing and thawing, stones are moved upward through the soil profile. The stones are sorted as they are exposed on the surface of the small dome. The larger and heavier stones roll down the hill farther than the smaller stones. If the dome gradient is less than 6° the stones form a polygon shape, whereas a steeper slope results in the heavier stones moving greater distances and producing stone stripes.

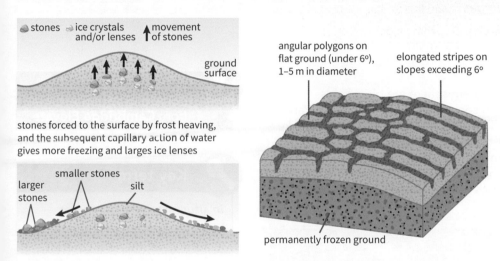

Figure 4.28 The formation of patterned ground.

Ice wedges

Ice wedges are formed where cracks in the permafrost are present. During the summer months water enters the cracks as meltwater flows over them. In the winter, the water freezes in the cracks to form ice wedges. Over several seasons, the size of the ice wedge increases, growing up to 1 to 3 m in depth.

Pingos

Pingos are created in a similar way to patterned ground, as the freezing water in the upper layers of the discontinuous permafrost soil causes the sediments to rise and create a dome shape (Figure 4.29). Pingos vary in size but are generally less than 100 m high, although they can be up to 600 m in diameter. They are commonly found in sandy soils and those formed in the way described above are called open-system pingos.

In low-lying areas of permafrost, a different type of pingo is formed, known as a closed-system or Mackenzie pingo (after the Mackenzie delta region in Canada where over 1000 are present). In areas where small lakes are present, groundwater can be trapped by the permafrost below and the freezing water in the lake above. The groundwater freezes and expands. Over several seasons, the centre of the lake rises to form a pingo surrounded by the remaining lake. If the core of the pingo collapses, a small lake can subsequently be formed as it fills with water.

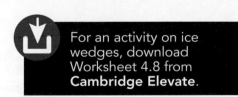

For an activity on ice wedges, download Worksheet 4.8 from **Cambridge Elevate**.

a. Open-system type

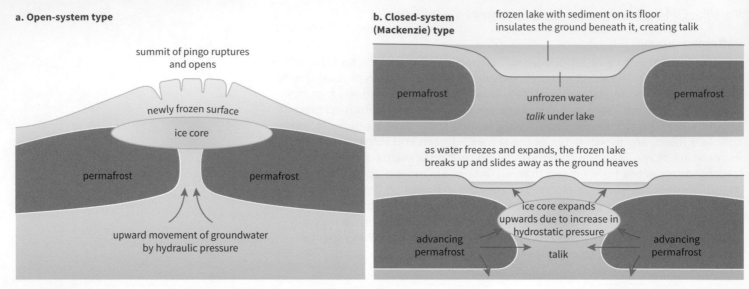

summit of pingo ruptures
and opens

newly frozen surface

ice core

permafrost

permafrost

upward movement of groundwater
by hydraulic pressure

**b. Closed-system
(Mackenzie) type**

frozen lake with sediment on its floor
insulates the ground beneath it, creating talik

permafrost

unfrozen water

talik under lake

permafrost

as water freezes and expands, the frozen lake
breaks up and slides away as the ground heaves

ice core expands
upwards due to increase in
hydrostatic pressure

advancing
permafrost

talik

advancing
permafrost

Figure 4.29 The formation of open-system and closed-system pingos.

Blockfields

A landscape feature common in the northern hemisphere are blockfields
(Figure 4.30). Examples of blockfields can be seen in Snowdonia National Park
in Wales, on the summits of the Glyder and Carneddau mountain ranges. Unlike
solifluction lobes which are created by mass movement, blockfields develop as
a result of freeze–thaw weathering and form *in situ*. The freeze–thaw weathering
breaks up the top layer of rock, leaving behind an assortment of angular jagged
boulders. Blockfields only form on landscapes with a surface angle of less than
25° and are typically 1 m in depth.

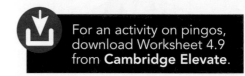

For an activity on pingos,
download Worksheet 4.9
from **Cambridge Elevate**.

🔑 **Key term**

in situ: material that has not
been transported during or after
its formation; this is in contrast
to *ex situ*, where material has
been moved by transportation
processes and deposited a
distance from its original location

Figure 4.30 A blockfield landscape in Snowdonia, Wales.

Solifluction

Solifluction is the downslope movement of rock and soil as a result of the force
of gravity on the melting active layer in the summer months. If the active layer of
the permafrost is situated in steep slopes then, over time, as it melts in spring,

the force of gravity slumps the material downhill forming solifluction lobes. The lobes move between 5 cm and 1 m a year, with the tongue-shaped end reaching up to 50 m in width.

Terracettes

Another feature formed by soil creep are terracettes. These are found on slopes of about 5° and are small 20–50 cm steps on the hillside. They are present in the active layer of the permafrost.

Thermokarst

Thermokarst is a landscape that has resulted from the melting of the active layer of the permafrost. The parts of the surface subside, giving rise to a hummocky landscape with lake-filled hollows. The size of the features within a thermokarst landscape varies depending on the depth of the active layer. A regional thermokarst landscape suggests an overall warming of the local climate, whereas more localised thermokarst development could be attributed to human activity in the permafrost layer such as the construction of buildings.

4.5 Human occupation and the development of cold environments

This section explores how humans have learnt to live in and adapt to cold environments and the impact this has had, while also studying recent developments such as the search for oil and gas, which have led to more pressure on these areas.

Human impacts on cold environments

Although polar and periglacial environments are harsh, humans have managed to live there in a sustainable way. There are currently 1.3 million people living in the polar Arctic and tundra environments, existing in balance with the environment and having done so for thousands of years. This balance with the environment has been achieved by leading a subsistence way of life, hunting and herding. This is important as cold environments such as the Arctic and tundra are environmentally fragile.

Environmental fragility

Cold environments are becoming more environmentally fragile. In Alaska for example, some regions have seen an increase in surface temperature of 1.5 °C. This change affects the depth of the active layer of permafrost and leads to significant changes in the landscape. A change of 1.5 °C leads to an increase in the thermokarst, which may release large volumes of carbon dioxide stored in the frozen peat permafrost. Recent studies have shown that the summer melting season is lasting longer each year, resulting in a shrinking permafrost. As more permafrost melts releasing more carbon dioxide, this could in turn raise local surface temperatures, promoting further melting.

The short growing season and long dark days in winter also affect the fragility of cold environments as the mosses and lichens take years to recover if they are overgrazed or destroyed by human activity.

The impact of climate change

The Porcupine caribou herd illustrates the fine balance that exists between climate and animals in cold environments. Between the 1970s and 1989, the caribou herd gradually increased from 100 000 to approximately 160 000.

Porcupine caribou migrate across the north-eastern area of Alaska and into Canada (Figure 4.31), crossing the Porcupine River in spring as the herd moves

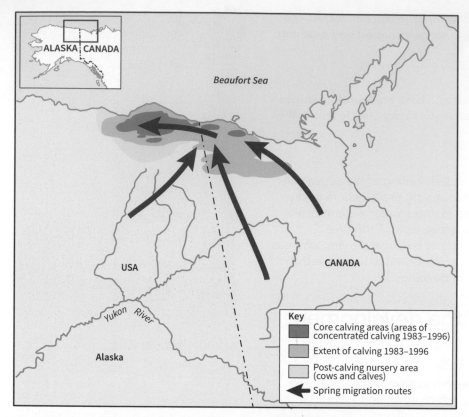

Figure 4.31 The Porcupine caribou migration route across the tundra.

northwards towards their calving grounds on the north coast of the Yukon, within the Arctic National Wildlife Refuge (ANWR) area and the **1002 area**.

Due to increased snowfall at the wintering grounds and shorter summers, the caribou are not always able to graze well. This has led to a decrease in the condition of the females in the herd, resulting in a lower birth rate for calves.

Cold environments as human habitats

Cold environments offer habitats for humans to inhabit, although the conditions are harsh and a fine balance is needed for humans to be successful in these areas. The tundra area of the Yukon in Canada is one such location that humans have adapted to. The area is dominated by low relief, peat bogs and spruce woodland on the hills. Tundra vegetation covers most of the slopes.

This is a very fragile environment and one where the Vuntut Gwitchin community have learnt to live in a fine balance between nature, animals and humans. The community, which lives in the North Yukon, were originally nomadic, following the caribou herds as they migrated across the Yukon as well as collecting berries and fruit.

The community uses the caribou for food and hides for their clothing and tents. The bones of the caribou are also used to make soups, as well as tools such as spears. Although the community no longer uses traditional methods to catch the caribou, using snowmobiles and rifles they ensure that they only take what they need and do not over-kill. A number of caribou are killed during the migration season and the meat dried to last several months. This ensures that the caribou can breed in sufficient numbers for the herd to continue the following year and once again supply the community. In this way, the community is living in balance with its harsh environment.

Key term

1002 area: a 6070 km² coastal plain area lying between the Brooks Range and the Beaufort Range; it is the only area of the ANWR that does not have protected wilderness status

Research point

Research the migration of the Porcupine caribou. Produce a report that explains what drives their migration and how the results of climate change might affect their migration patterns in the future.

For an activity on the Vuntut Gwitchin community, download Worksheet 4.10 from **Cambridge Elevate**.

Research point

The Nenets are an indigenous community living in Russia. Research how their community and way of life compares to the Vuntut Gwitchin community. Do they face similar challenges?

The Vuntut Gwitchin community has adapted to life in the tundra in other ways as well. Hunting and fishing of a seasonal nature provides some income. By understanding the seasons and the onset of the thawing season in particular, the community can hunt muskrat. These small animals build their homes on the ice. The muskrat can provide meat, but their main use is the provision of fur, which is used for trading with other communities.

Varying impacts of human activity on fragile cold environments over time

The impact of the Vuntut Gwitchin community on the tundra environment is limited, as the people are aware that they are part of the complex and fragile ecosystem in which they live. However, larger-scale human activity can have a much larger impact on the tundra if not managed carefully.

Oil and gas exploration

Oil and gas exploitation in Alaska has the potential to have major environmental consequences for the region if not managed correctly. Pressure groups such as Greenpeace demonstrate against transnational corporations such as Shell and BP drilling for oil and gas in the Arctic and highlighting the possible environmental impacts of such activities. Demonstrations can often be controversial in their methods (Figure 4.32).

Oil exploitation in Alaska is centred on Prudhoe Bay. The Prudhoe Bay oilfield is situated on Alaska's North Slope – a northern region in Alaska. It is the largest oilfield in the USA, covering an area of 86 418 ha. When it was first discovered, it was estimated that it held approximately 25 billion barrels of oil. BP, which operates the oilfield, believes that 2 billion barrels remain.

The oilfield has not been without its problems. In 2006 there was a major oil spill which remained undetected for five days. During this time, it is estimated that just over 1 million litres of oil spilled over an area measuring 7700 m². BP was fined $20 million. The impact on the tundra was considered to have been limited because the oil spill occurred in the winter months when the active layer was frozen. Most of the oil spill was vacuumed and the remaining snow and oil mix was melted and cleaned. Crews were then sent to scrape the oil from the tundra surface. If the oil spill had occurred in the spring, the migrating caribou could have been affected. Not only would this have caused major issues for the caribou herd, but also for the Vuntut Gwitchin community, who rely on the caribou as a vital food source.

It is not only oil spills that can affect cold environments. With greater oil and gas exploration in cold environments in recent years, there has been a growth in the construction of roads, pipelines and settlements for workers. For example, the building of the Trans-Alaska Pipeline System (TAPS) (Figure 4.33) created a number of social, economic and environmental impacts, including:

- the growth of boomtowns
- the economic well-being of Alaska
- an increase in tourist numbers.

Before being built, many local Alaskans felt that the Trans-Alaska pipeline would bring benefits. However, its construction led to a number of unforeseen consequences. Boomtowns were created as the pipeline progressed. Small towns were flooded with construction workers not familiar with the local Alaskan customs. With the population boom came increases in crime rates and the overstretching of local infrastructure. The boomtown effect was keenly felt in Fairbanks. Economic changes included an increase in sales in the local McDonald's restaurant, which became number two for sales in the world during this time. Houses prices rose as

Look on **Cambridge Elevate** for more information on the Vuntut Gwitchin community from the following websites:

- Yukon Community Profiles (www.cambridge.org/links/gase6034)
- Government of the Vuntut Gwitchin First Nation (www.cambridge.org/links/gase6035)
- Old Crow – Yukon (www.cambridge.org/links/gase6036)
- First Nations Community Profiles (www.cambridge.org/links/gase6037).

Figure 4.32 Greenpeace activists outside Shell Centre in central London, protesting over Shell's presence in the Arctic.

Tip

The exploration for oil and gas in Alaska is a constantly changing situation. Ensure that you visit the websites and read the press releases for the major oil exploration transnational corporations (TNCs) to keep up to date.

Figure 4.33 The Trans-Alaska Pipeline raised above ground to allow caribou to migrate.

construction workers could afford higher prices, forcing many local people out of the housing market.

However, the pipeline also brought economic prosperity to the region. Before it was built, Alaska was one of the highest taxed states in the USA at 14.5%. However, after the pipeline started operating, personal incomes rose and the state become almost tax-free. Tourist numbers to Alaska have increased as a result of the pipeline. This unexpected impact has led to pipeline tourist trips and several films based around the pipeline, such as *On Deadly Ground*.

In 2015 the operators of the pipeline reduced output to 500 000 barrels a day. Estimates suggest that the pipeline will be operational until 2075. Once closed, Alaskan law states that the pipeline must be removed and the landscape returned to its natural state.

Alternative futures

The 1002 area within the ANWR are estimated to contain large amounts of oil and gas deposits. However, it is also one of the key calving areas for the caribou. Different groups are in favour of the development:

- the Alaskan people
- the oil industry
- local Alaskan Congress members.

These groups argue that exploiting the region would bring economic benefits to the area while ensuring that the USA becomes less reliant on overseas oil and gas production and therefore improving national security.

However, opposition groups counter these arguments by suggesting that there is only a 50% chance of finding oil in the region and that, even if oil and gas were discovered, it would be equivalent only to the total US demand for 90 days. Environmental concerns are also raised focusing on the impact on the caribou herds and their migration paths and calving grounds. President Obama entered the debate in January 2015 when he proposed that 5 million hectares of the ANWR should be classified as wilderness. This would mean an end to drilling in the area and protect the 1002 area from future development. This added political weight to the opposition groups' arguments.

Making connections

Alaska is not the only cold environment under threat from development. See section 4.6 Case Study: Southern Norway, a glaciated environment.

Look on **Cambridge Elevate** for more information on Shell's and BP's plans for the future in the Arctic from the following websites:

- Shell (www. cambridge.org/links/ gase6038/)
- BP (www.cambridge. org/links/gase6039).

4.6 Southern Norway, a glaciated environment

Norway offers an excellent case study to see how glaciated environments can be developed by humans. Norway was covered with ice in the last Ice Age and today still has over 2600 km² of land covered by ice, representing 1% of the total surface area of the country. The largest ice cap in Norway is the Jostedalsbreen ice cap, which covers 487 km² and is the largest continuous ice mass in continental Europe. Glaciers in Norway are concentrated in two areas (Figure 4.34):

- the mountainous regions of southern Norway – Jostedalsbreen, Hardangerjøkulen and Folgefonni
- northern Norway – Nordland.

Norway's glaciated landscape has provided opportunities and challenges as Norway has developed. This case study focuses on southern Norway and the Hordaland region. This region was a barren ice tundra around 20 000 years ago and, as the climate warmed, flora and fauna began to thrive and shape the landscape that is present today.

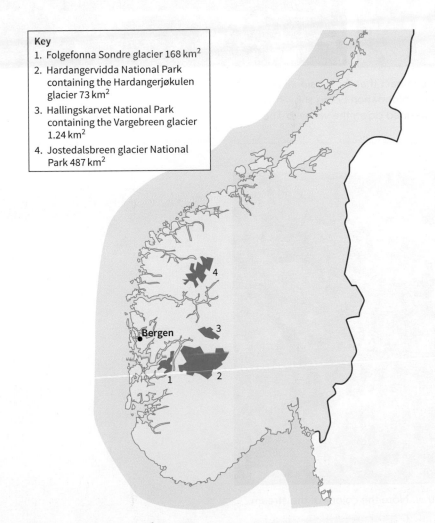

Key

1. Folgefonna Sondre glacier 168 km²
2. Hardangervidda National Park containing the Hardangerjøkulen glacier 73 km²
3. Hallingskarvet National Park containing the Vargebreen glacier 1.24 km²
4. Jostedalsbreen glacier National Park 487 km²

Figure 4.34 Glaciated regions of Norway.

Tourism

The glaciated landscape of Norway has provided many opportunities. The Bondhus glacier has provided tourists with a focal point for centuries and many of the first tourists from the UK would have arrived in Norway and visited the Bondhus glacier. As a result of this long-standing tourist attraction, evidence from images from the last 100 years used in postcards can be used to estimate the impact of climate change on the glacier (Figure 4.35). Walking tours to the foot of the glacier now provide local employment (Figure 4.36).

Figure 4.35 The retreating Bondhus glacier. Note the impact that the erosional power of the glacier has had on the mountain walls. **a** Tourist information board showing a postcard from c. 1890. Note how far the glacier extended down the valley. **b** The Bondhus glacier in 2011.

Figure 4.36 Tourists following the Bondhus glacier trail. Note the colour of the stream. This is caused by the rock flour from the glacier.

The flooded fjords also offer opportunities for tourism, transport and fishing. The Flåm to Gudvangen Fjord trip is a popular tourist fjord route. 'Flåm' means a small meadow surrounded by steep mountains, which perfectly describes the geography of the area. The fjord route attracts tourists from around the world, with cruise ships offering an app to provide tourists with a commentary on the local landscapes that are passed on the journey. The journey is perfect for experiencing the flooded glaciated valley, kame terraces and hanging valleys (Figure 4.37).

Physical and human

The Flåm railway is a popular tourist attraction in Norway. How has the glaciated landscape that the Flåm railway travels through contributed to its popularity?

Figure 4.37 Glaciated landscapes along the fjord route. **a** A hanging valley and waterfall. **b** Evidence of a moraine terrace, now used for agriculture. **c** A fjord – a flooded glaciated valley.

Fishing

Salmon farms can be found within fjords (Figure 4.38). The deep, clean fjord water offers excellent conditions to farm salmon, reducing the need for chemicals and providing space for the salmon to live. This increases the health of the fish.

Figure 4.38 Salmon farming in a fjord.

Energy

The glaciated landscape of Norway has produced perfect conditions for the development of hydroelectric power (HEP). Steep, narrow valleys can be dammed and height differences allow HEP plants to generate energy. High rainfall and snowmelt in the spring provides reliable water supplies.

One of the largest HEP stations in Europe is located in Norway. The Sima power plant is located near Eidfjord on a branch of the Hardangerfjord and has four main reservoirs. The turbines are located 700 m inside the mountain at Simadalen. The main generator hall is 200 m long, 20 m wide and 40 m high.

To learn more about the importance of HEP, download Worksheet 4.11 from **Cambridge Elevate.**

Challenges

One of the challenges of living in Norway is road building. The presence of fjords means that roads often have to be built around them, so journey times from one settlement to another are extended. Tunnels have had to be built to reduce journey times between towns. These tunnels are often very long and provide different routes, so roundabouts have even been built deep inside the tunnels (Figure 4.39).

Figure 4.39 A roundabout inside a fjord tunnel.

Improved transport has been a challenge in the fjord regions. Although they are beautiful and a tourist attraction, for road planners they pose challenges. Fjord crossings are technically difficult and involve either the construction of suspension bridges or tunnels cut into the sides of the valleys. As a result, the ferry system in Norway is a common sight that is defined as part of the road network. Ferry services have traditionally been used to cross fjords, but this increases journey times.

The Hardanger Bridge has one of the longest suspension bridge spans in the world, at 1380 m, and crosses the Hardangerfjord (Figure 4.40). The bridge replaced the ferry connection between Bruravik and Brimnes. Constructing the bridge was a challenge: it cost $3.89 billion and took four years to complete. The fjord landscape meant that a 2.4 km long tunnel was also required on the northern side of the bridge. The construction of the bridge has made long-distance travel and transport ferry-free, providing quicker and easier journeys both towards the north-south and east-west of Norway.

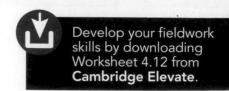

Develop your fieldwork skills by downloading Worksheet 4.12 from **Cambridge Elevate.**

Figure 4.40 The Hardanger Bridge in south-west Norway has one of the longest suspension bridge spans in the world.

Environmental concerns

Norway's glacial environment is also subject to development from local and international businesses. There has been much debate in the town of Glomfjord over the use of the local glacier for exporting ice cubes. This example highlights the issues that countries in cold environments face. Are the natural resources used and developed to provide local employment or should the natural landscape be protected from development?

ACTIVITY 4.8

1   Read the article 'A Norwegian company's plan to make ice cubes out of glaciers unsettles some' from the *Guardian*. As a class, debate the advantages and disadvantages of the ice cube business. Consider these questions:

   a   Is it a sustainable venture?
   b   Is this business plan good for the local area?
   c   What would be the environmental concerns over this project?
   d   Would this project still be a concern if the glacier was not retreating? Why?

2   Produce a mind map to summarise how the glaciated landscape of Norway has influenced and shaped how people live.

Look on **Cambridge Elevate** to read the full article from the *Guardian* newspaper (www. cambridge.org/links/ gase6040).

Look on **Cambridge Elevate** for more information on how glacial processes have shaped Norway's transport and tourism networks.
   •   Visit Norway - Flåm (www.cambridge.org/links/gase6041).
   •   Visit Norway - Hardangerfjord (www.cambridge.org/links/gase6042).
   •   Discover Geography (www.cambridge.org/links/gase6043).

Assess to progress

1   What is meant by sublimation?   `1 MARK [AS LEVEL]`
    A   The melting of glacier ice due to increasing temperatures.
    B   The transition of ice to water vapour without a liquid stage.
    C   The natural removal of snow or ice in a glacier.
    D   The balance between accumulation and ablation.

2   Distinguish between discontinuous and sporadic
    permafrost.   `3 MARKS [AS LEVEL]`

3   Analyse the links between climate, process and
    landform which lead to growth of discontinuous
    permafrost.   `9 MARKS [AS LEVEL]`

4   Assess the challenges associated with oil extraction
    in cold environments and evaluate measures to
    overcome these challenges.   `20 MARKS [AS LEVEL]`

5   Explain the development of cold based glaciers.   `4 MARKS [A LEVEL]`

6   Figure 4.41 shows the Franz Josef glacier in New Zealand.

Figure 4.41 The Franz Josef glacier in New Zealand.

    With reference to Figure 4.41, interpret the
    evidence that suggests this glacier is changing.   `6 MARKS [AS/A LEVEL]`

7   'Glaciers respond quickly to changes in climate and
    as such can be used to gauge the impact of global
    climate change.'
    To what extent do you agree with this view?   `20 MARKS [A LEVEL]`

Hazards

By the end of this chapter you should know:

- the nature, forms and potential impacts of natural hazards
- hazard perception and its economic and cultural determinants
- characteristic human responses to hazards and their relationship to hazard incidence
- plate tectonic theory
- the nature of vulcanicity and its causes
- the nature of seismicity and its causes
- the nature of tropical storms and their causes
- the nature of wildfires and their causes
- the spatial distribution, randomness, magnitude, frequency, regularity and predictability of tropical storm events
- the impacts and responses to volcanic, seismic, storm and wildfire events.

Figure 5.1 On 25 April 2015, a 7.8 magnitude earthquake struck Nepal's capital city Kathmandu and its surrounding areas. The resulting destruction from the earthquake and its aftershocks killed over 9000 people and injured nearly twice as many. Nearly half a million people were displaced.

Before you start…

You should know:

- the global distribution of tectonic hazards and tropical storms
- the physical processes occurring at each of the three types of plate boundary (constructive, destructive and conservative)
- the physical conditions required for tropical storms to occur
- the reasons why people live in areas susceptible to hazards
- how monitoring, protection, prediction and planning can reduce the risks from hazards

- contrasting case studies that describe the hazard, the impacts and how people have responded to the hazard in locations with different characteristics.

5.1 The concept of hazard in a geographical context

A hazard is a threat which has the potential to cause injury, loss of life, damage to property, **socio-economic disruption** or **environmental degradation**. A hazard can be caused either by natural processes (e.g. volcanoes and avalanches) or by humans (e.g. contamination of groundwater supplies). The focus of this chapter is on natural processes, specifically volcanoes, earthquakes and tropical storms, which pose a threat to humans.

The interaction between people and the environment is crucial in the definition of a hazard. For example, Mount Belinda on Montagu Island, one of the South Sandwich Islands in the far southern Atlantic Ocean (Figure 5.2), posed no threat to people or property when it erupted for the first time in recorded history in October 2001.

Mount Belinda's **effusive**, **basaltic eruption** and isolated location on the uninhabited Montagu Island meant that it was not a hazard. Contrast this with the eruption of Stromboli, located on the Aeolian Islands off the north coast of Sicily (Figure 5.3), which also occurred in October 2001.

Here, the **stratovolcano** ejected large blocks of lava 40 cm in diameter. A group of tourists were pummelled by the ash and lava bombs and one person was killed, making this a hazard event.

Key terms

socio-economic disruption: disruption to social (lifestyle) or economic (money or jobs) aspects of society

environmental degradation: the deterioration of the natural environment

effusive eruption: an eruption where lava flows on the ground rather than being expelled in an explosive manner

basaltic eruption: a gentle (effusive) eruption, which is characterised by fluid lava and is relatively predictable

stratovolcano: a steep-sided volcano made up of alternate layers of lava and ash

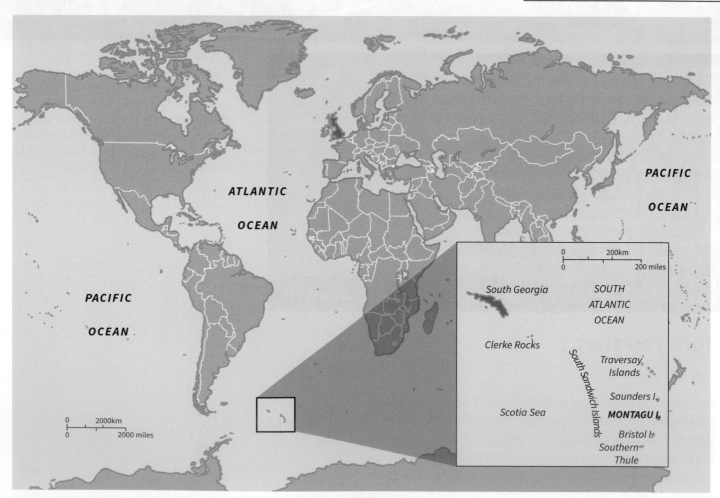

Figure 5.2 The location of Montagu Island in the South Atlantic Ocean.

Figure 5.3 The location of Stromboli in the Tyrrhenian Sea.

The definition of a disaster is slightly more challenging. It can be defined simply as the realisation of the hazard. However, it can also be defined as a major hazard event that causes widespread disruption. The United Nations (UN) is more specific and records a hazard event as a disaster if one or more of these criteria are met:

- a report of ten or more people killed
- a report of 100 or more people affected
- a declaration of a state of emergency by the relevant government
- a request by the national government for international assistance.

Based on the UN definition, the eruption of Stromboli in October 2001 was a hazard but not a disaster.

Making connections

Volcanic activity has an important role to play in the carbon cycle. How do you think that volcanic activity leads to natural variation in the carbon cycle? See section 1.3 The carbon cycle.

Investigate

Investigate the evidence linking fracking to increased earthquake activity. Do you think that fracking should be allowed in the UK? Why do you think this?

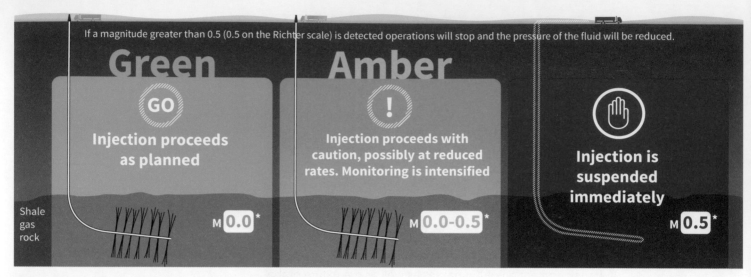

Figure 5.4 A traffic-light monitoring system for fracking in the UK.

The nature, forms and potential impacts of natural hazards

Hazards are highly variable in terms of their nature, magnitude, frequency, geographical location and scale of impact. It can therefore be useful to classify events according to these criteria. For example, hazards can be classified according to their nature. Typically, natural hazards are tectonic, geomorphological, atmospheric or biological. While this seems a relatively straightforward way of classifying hazards, divisions between categories can become blurred. For example, many earthquakes (tectonic) trigger landslides (geomorphological) and fires (biological), and so their impacts may be inextricably linked.

Also, while the majority of natural hazards are entirely natural in origin, some may not be. For example, there is some evidence to suggest that hydraulic fracturing or 'fracking' – where water, sand and chemicals are injected under high pressure into rocks to release shale gas – has the potential to cause small earthquake events (Figure 5.4). The process is therefore highly controversial given the possibility for it to increase the hazard risk.

Hazards can also be classified in terms of their magnitude (size in terms of the amount of energy released) and their frequency (how quickly they reoccur). Generally, there is an inverse relationship between these two variables: the smaller the magnitude the more frequent the event and vice versa. While generally high-magnitude events tend to have a greater impact on people and therefore can be considered more of a hazard, the relationship is not as straightforward in reality. Human factors such as the density of population and the level of development of the affected region or country are closely linked to the impacts of hazards.

Hazard perception and economic and cultural determinants

People tend to respond to a hazard in ways that are consistent with their **perception** of the risk. It is therefore important for inhabitants of hazardous areas to have an accurate perception of the hazard as this can minimise damage and aid survival. The most effective way of ensuring accurate hazard perception is through experience and education. However, because many hazards are infrequent – they may occur only once in a human lifetime – education is the most reliable way to gain information about natural hazards and to inform local populations how to react during emergencies.

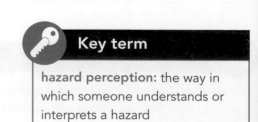

Key term

hazard perception: the way in which someone understands or interprets a hazard

Hazard perception therefore depends upon both the formal and informal education that the local community receives. Cultural and economic factors, as well as age and gender, are likely to influence this. There are three general approaches to hazard perception:

- Acceptance: this includes fatalistic tendencies, where people may believe that hazards are part of life or 'acts of God'.
- Domination: this perspective suggests that hazards are predictable and that they can be better understood by scientific research.
- Adaption: this perspective takes the view that hazards are influenced by natural and human events, and their magnitude and frequency can be estimated based on experience.

Characteristic human responses to hazards

People respond to hazards in order to reduce risk. The nature of their response is likely to be influenced by their perception of the hazard as well as the nature of the hazard itself, the technology available and the infrastructure of the government.

There are three general ways in which people respond to hazards:

- They may try to prevent or modify the event. **Prevention** is currently seen as unrealistic. Spraying water jets on advancing flows of lava has been successful but requires very slow-flowing lava and huge reserves of water. However, engineered solutions such as flood defence schemes can more reliably protect people and structures from the full extent of the hazard (see Chapter 3 Coastal management).
- They may attempt to modify their vulnerability. This can be done through **prediction** and warning, community preparedness and land-use planning.
- The loss resulting from the hazard can be modified. Aid is one method of achieving this and can be provided for relief, rehabilitation and reconstruction. In many higher-income countries (HICs), insurance is also used as a strategy for sharing the loss.

The Park model of human response to hazards

The **Park response model** (also known as the disaster-response curve) illustrates the changing quality of life through different phases of a disaster from Stage 1 (pre-disaster) through to Stage 5 (reconstruction). At each stage humans respond to the hazard through prevention, protection or preparation and modification. Figure 5.5 shows the Park model.

Stage 1 occurs before the hazard event where quality of life is at 'normal' levels and people work to prepare by educating the local population about what to do should a disaster strike, stockpiling supplies or putting medical teams on standby. Stage 2 occurs simultaneously with the hazard event. The quality of life of the local population dramatically deteriorates and people respond with methods of protection such as erecting barricades and evacuation. In the hours and days after the hazard the relief effort occurs (Stage 3). Search, care and rescue teams work to reduce and eventually reverse the decline in quality of life. This is followed by Stage 4, the rehabilitation phase, where people attempt to return the quality of life to normal levels. This may include providing food and water supplies or shelter for those who are deprived of these basic human needs. Finally, in the longer term, reconstruction takes place where property and infrastructure are rebuilt and crops are replanted (Stage 5). This stage offers the opportunity to learn from past mistakes in order to respond more effectively to future hazards and to improve the quality of life for the local population.

Key terms

prevention: the action of stopping something from happening

prediction: suggesting what might happen in the future

Park response model: a model to show the changing quality of life through different phases of a disaster

A Disaster Response Curve (after Park 1991)

Figure 5.5 The Park model of human response to hazards.

Lines for different hazard events can be shown to highlight the steepness of drop in quality of life, the duration of the decline and the speed and nature of recovery. One criticism is that, as it is a model, it is generalised and does not account for differences in development or other considerations regarding hazard impact and recovery. However, it does allow for the trajectories of different events to be compared and highlights the significance of emergency relief and rehabilitation in the aftermath of natural hazards.

The Hazard Management Cycle

The **Hazard Management Cycle** (Figure 5.6) highlights the attempts of governments, businesses and other stakeholders to reduce the losses from the hazard, to provide rapid assistance to victims and to achieve a rapid and effective recovery. In other words, it attempts to minimise the drop and speed the recovery in quality of life shown in the Park model. Appropriate actions

> **Key term**
>
> Hazard Management Cycle: a cycle showing phases of response, recovery, mitigation and preparedness in the management of a hazard

Response – Efforts to minimise the hazards created by a disaster. For example, search and rescue and providing emergency relief

Preparedness – Planning how to respond. For example, creating preparedness plans, engaging in emergency exercises and training and putting warning systems in place

Recovery – Returning the community to normal. For example, providing temporary housing, grants and medical care

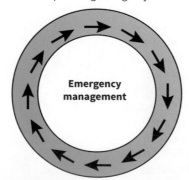

Emergency management

Mitigation – Minimising the effects of the disaster. For example, building codes and zoning, vulnerability analyses and public education

Figure 5.6 The Hazard Management Cycle.

can result in greater preparedness, more effective warnings and the likelihood of reduced vulnerability should the hazard strike again. Whilst Figure 5.6 suggests a fairly straightforward cycle, in reality the four phases do not occur in isolation nor necessarily in this order. More often they overlap with their length being determined by both the severity of the hazard and the area's level of development.

5.2 Plate tectonics

The Earth's structure and internal energy sources

The Earth is thought to have been formed about 4.6 billion years ago as a result of collisions between clouds of dust and gas. Meteorite collisions, radioactive decay and planetary compression caused temperatures in this newly formed planet to increase until they reached 2000°C, the melting point of iron. This formed the Earth's core and slowly, as the planet started to cool, layers began to form as the heavier, metallic materials sunk and the lighter, rocky materials rose to the surface (Figure 5.7).

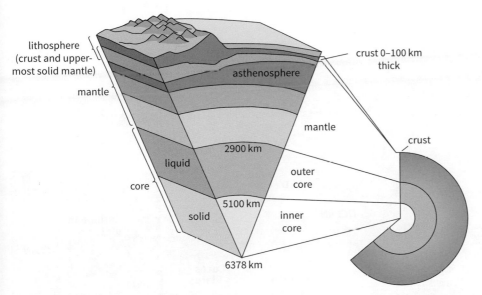

Figure 5.7 The Earth cutaway from core to crust.

Starting from the centre of the Earth and radiating outwards, these layers are the:

- inner core: the inner core has a radius of 1200 km and temperatures which are thought to be in excess of 6000°C. It is mainly composed of iron and nickel and is a solid, dense ball of metal
- outer core: the inner core is so hot that it causes the outer core, which is also composed of iron and nickel, to melt and become liquid. The outer core has a radius of 2200 km and reaches temperatures of between 4000 and 5000°C. The outer core moves around the inner core and this creates the Earth's magnetic field
- mantle: at 2900 km the mantle is the thickest layer of the Earth and makes up 84% of its volume. It is made up of silicates of iron and magnesium, sulphides and oxides of silica and magnesium and is 3000°C on average although

ACTIVITY 5.1

1 Research an example of a hazard and create an illustrated fact file. How would you classify this hazard in terms of its nature, magnitude and frequency?

159

temperatures are hotter closer to the core. The bottom part of the mantle, extending from approximately 100km to 700km below the Earth's surface, is the asthenosphere. Heat from the core keeps the asthenosphere malleable and generates convection currents pushing magma upwards and through volcanic vents to create new crust. The lithosphere, which lies on top of the asthenosphere, is composed of the solid, upper part of the mantle and the crust

- crust: the Earth's outermost layer is called the crust and is composed of two different types; oceanic and continental. Oceanic crust is typically found beneath the world's oceans and is formed at spreading centres on oceanic ridges which occur at constructive plate boundaries. It is typically composed of basalt and gabbro and approximately 6km thick. In contrast, continental crust is, at 35km, thicker, older and less dense than oceanic crust. Mainly composed of granite, it is structurally more complex than oceanic crust and is generally formed at subduction zones.

The theory of plate tectonics

The rigid lithosphere is cracked into large sections called plates (Figure 5.8). These plates move laterally at a rate of between 0 and 100mm per year and the theory which describes this movement is known as plate tectonics.

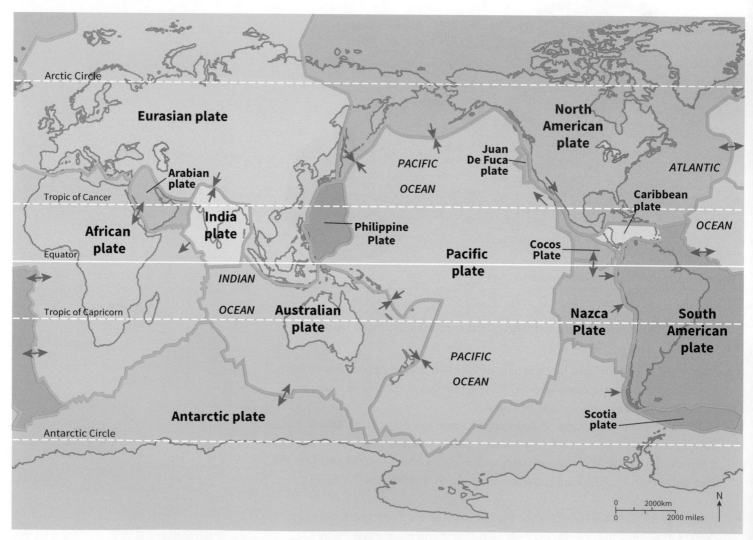

Figure 5.8 Plate tectonics as mapped in the second half of the 20th century.

The edge of the plates are known as plate boundaries and their movement relative to their neighbouring plates describes the type of boundary, destructive, constructive, conservative or collisional, as well as their associated landforms.

Whilst scientists are agreed that the plates move they continue to debate the mechanisms which drive this movement. Until recently, the dominant theory suggested that heat from the core was transferred to the Earth's surface via large convection currents in the asthenosphere. The heated magma spreads out underneath the lithospheric plates and begins to cool which cause them to become denser and start to sink downwards. However, many scientists do not believe that convection explains the massive forces needed to move the plates. Instead, they have suggested two alternative hypotheses; ridge push and slab pull (Figure 5.9).

Ridge push, which can be more accurately named gravitational sliding, occurs at mid-ocean ridges which are associated with constructive plate boundaries. The magma which rises to the surface at mid-ocean ridges is very hot and heats the surrounding rocks. These expand and become elevated above the sea floor forming a slope. As new rock is formed it cools and becomes denser. Gravity then causes it to slide down the slope, away from the mid-ocean ridge. This results in seafloor spreading, where new oceanic crust is formed through volcanic activity causing the tectonic plates to move apart from each other. Computer models have been used by scientists to show that this movement down the slope could drive plate movement. However, it is likely to be more significant where there is no slab pull acting on the plate (for example on the margins of the Antarctic plate).

Slab pull has emerged as the more dominant theory over the last decade for explaining the movement of the plates. At a destructive plate boundary, the subducting oceanic plate (which is usually composed of basalt) is denser than the surrounding material. As the plate begins to sink into the mantle it pulls the rest of the plate behind it.

Types of plate margin and their associated landforms

There are four main types of plate margin – constructive, collisional, destructive and conservative – which are illustrated in Figure 5.21. At constructive boundaries the plates are moving apart and new crust is created. In the oceans this produces mid-ocean ridge systems such as the mid-Atlantic ridge. The mid-Atlantic ridge occurs where the North American and Eurasian plates are moving away from

Research point

Research the evidence that exists to support the theory of plate tectonics.

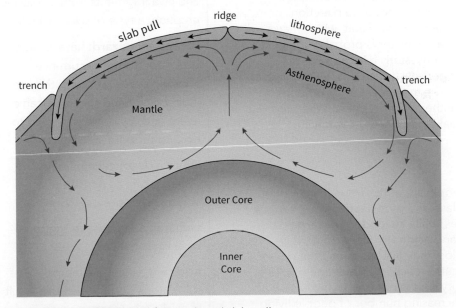

Figure 5.9 The mechanisms ridge push and slab pull.

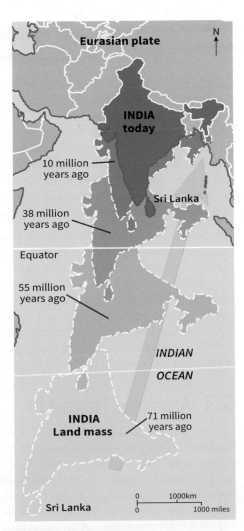

Figure 5.10 The movement northwards of the Indian subcontinent.

each other and rises to between 2–3 km above the ocean floor. Where plates diverge within a continent then rift valleys such as the East African rift valley are formed. Here the continental crust becomes stretched and thins. This process is occurring in northern Ethiopia as the Arabian plate moves away from the African plate forming the Red Sea and the Gulf of Aden. Further south, the African plate is also rifting to form two new plates; the Nubian and Somalian plates. In the future, these will continue to move apart until the crust between them becomes thinner, drops below sea level and starts to create its own mid-ocean ridge.

Collisional and destructive plate margins are both examples of convergence, i.e. the plates are moving towards each other. However, their behaviour depends upon the composition of the plates and whether they are made from oceanic or continental crust. Where continental crust meets continental crust this is known as a collisional boundary and perhaps the best example can be seen where the Indian plate has collided with the Eurasian plate to form the Himalayas. 225 million years ago, India was a large island off the coast of Australia. It moved 6400 km northwards at a speed of 9 to 16 cm per year and, between 40 and 20 million years ago, collided with Asia. As the continents collided neither could subduct as continental crust has a low density and is therefore buoyant. This caused the crust to buckle and thicken forming the young fold mountains we know as the Himalayas (Figure 5.10).

Where oceanic crust meets continental crust at a destructive plate boundary, then the denser oceanic crust subducts at an angle under the continental crust. For example, the Nazca plate (oceanic crust) is moving eastwards and subducting under the South American plate (continental crust). This forms the Atacama trench, a deep, v-shaped sea trench which is located approximately 160 km off the coast of Peru and which is 8065 m deep, 5900 km long and 64 km wide.

Islands arcs, long chains of volcanic islands, are typically formed where oceanic crust meets oceanic crust at a convergent plate boundary. As one oceanic plate begins to subduct under the other so it reaches a depth where it begins to melt. This hot magma can leak out of cracks in the crust as a series of volcanoes to form an island arc. Examples of island arcs include the Japanese islands and the Aleutian Islands of Alaska. Magma plumes, an upwelling of abnormally hot rock within the mantle, can also form island arcs through hotspot activity. The plate passes over the magma plume and weaknesses in the crust allow it to escape onto the surface as an active volcano (see Figure 5.17).

The final type of plate boundary is known as a conservative or transform plate boundary. Here, the plates rub past each other, either in opposite directions or in the same direction but at different speeds. The San Andreas Fault, which marks the junction between the North American and Pacific plates is probably the best known example. Both plates are moving in a north-westerly direction but the Pacific plate is moving at between 7 and 11 cm per year, which is faster than the 2.3 cm movement of the North American plate. The movement is not smooth and friction can lock the lithospheric plates together for many years. When the pressure is released then shallow focus earthquakes are the usual result.

5.3 Volcanic hazards

Current estimates suggest that 500 million people are at risk from volcanic hazards worldwide. **Primary hazards** include lava and **pyroclastic flows**, **tephra**, **nuées ardentes**, ash fallout and volcanic gases, while **secondary hazards** include **lahars**, volcanic landslides, **tsunamis** and **acid rain**. Since 1500, it is estimated that globally 200 000 people have lost their lives as a result of one or more of these hazards. In the 20th century, deaths reached an average of 845 per year – far more than in any previous century. This is not due to increased levels of vulcanism, but is instead due to an increasing number of people living on or near the slopes of active volcanoes.

Key terms

primary hazard: hazards that are directly related to the volcano and its eruption (e.g. lava flows, ash falls and gas clouds)

pyroclastic flow: a mixture of hot rock, lava, ash and gases arising from a volcanic eruption that moves at a rapid speed along the ground

tephra: rock fragments ejected during volcanic eruptions

nuée ardente: a dense, rapidly moving cloud of hot gases, ashes and lava fragments from a volcanic eruption; a type of pyroclastic flow

secondary hazard: hazards that occur due to the occurrence of another, primary hazard; they are indirectly related to the volcanic event and, by definition, tend to occur after primary hazards

lahar: a destructive mudflow which occurs as a result of a volcanic eruption

tsunami: a large wave triggered by seismic activity

acid rain: volcanoes erupt sulphurous gases which can result in acidic rainwater

Maths for geographers

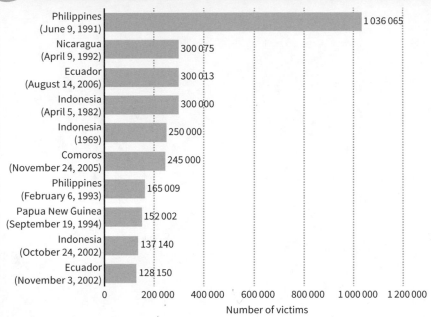

Figure 5.11 The number of people affected by the world's major volcanic eruptions in the last fifty years.

Refer to Figure 5.11

1 Calculate the mean number of people affected per event.
2 Is this a useful way of presenting and analysing the data? Explain why.

Physical and human

It is estimated that 4.7 million people have been affected by volcanoes between 1900 and 2009.

The nature of vulcanicity and its underlying causes

Volcanic hazards are largely dependent upon the position of the plate boundaries; 95% of all volcanic eruptions are associated with plate margins, although 5% are **intraplate** (Figure 5.12).

The nature of volcanic hazards depends upon the type of eruption.

Hawaiian eruptions are effusive and produce basalt lavas which have relatively high temperatures of between 1100 and 1250 °C. Basalt lavas also have a low silica content (less than 52%), which means that the lava is fluid and can flow long distances of over 20 km at speeds of 50 km/h (Figure 5.13).

In contrast, Plinian eruptions are much more explosive and produce andesitic or rhyolitic lavas. These lavas have lower temperatures (600–1000 °C) and a higher silica content (in rhyolites, typically over 69%) than basaltic lavas. This means that the lava is more viscous, flows more slowly and builds up in the vent of the volcano until it is suddenly released in an unpredictable and explosive eruption. Lava flows tend to be more of a threat to property than to human life. However, when large quantities of lava are released at once, they can be incredibly dangerous.

Key term

intraplate: in the middle of a plate, away from the plate margins

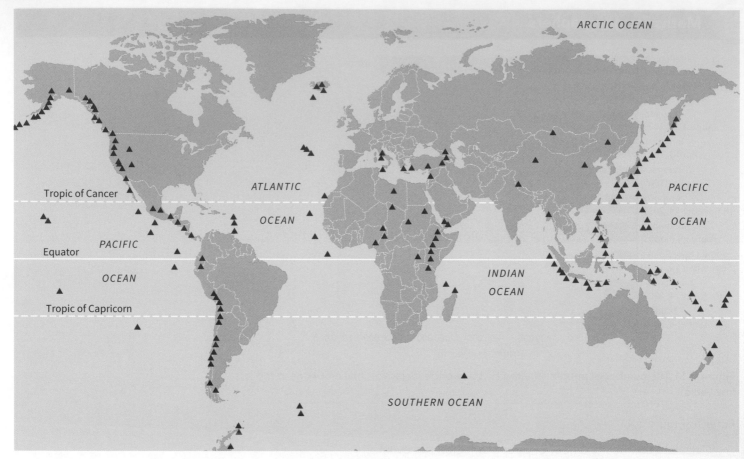

Figure 5.12 The global distribution of volcanoes.

Pyroclastic flows are a dangerous mixture of hot rock, lava, ash and gases (Figure 5.14). The most dangerous pyroclastic flows are those that erupt sideways. This occurs where the summit crater is blocked and the magma and gases explode through a weakness in the volcano's flank. They can move at speeds of 200 m/s and typically have temperatures of between 350 and 1000 °C. Pyroclastic flows are more common in eruptions with andesitic or rhyolitic lava which tend to occur at **subduction zones**.

Nuée ardente means 'glowing cloud' and was initially named from the pyroclastic flows seen at the eruption of Mount Pelée in the Caribbean in 1902. They contain more dense material than most pyroclastic flows and therefore do not travel as far; 50 km from their source is common.

Tephra are rock fragments that are ejected during volcanic eruptions. The largest fragments (over 1 m in diameter) tend to fall close to the volcano, while smaller particles (ash of less than 2 mm) are carried by the wind and travel greater distances both laterally and vertically (Figure 5.15).

Larger fragments can clearly cause injury or death to people, but ash can also be very disruptive. It can cover a wide area, often thousands of kilometres, but predicting its range is often difficult as the strength and direction of the prevailing wind can vary. Ash is highly abrasive and can cause breathing problems, disrupt machinery and clog filters. It can also obstruct sunlight, reducing visibility and temperatures. Almost 20 million tonnes of ash erupted from Mount Pinatubo in the Philippines in 1991, causing global cooling of 0.5 °C between 1991 and 1993.

Figure 5.13 A basalt lava flow, Hawaii.

Key term

subduction zones: zones where thin, dense oceanic crust is forced beneath thicker, less dense continental crust at a destructive plate boundary

Figure 5.14 Pyroclastic flow from the eruption of the Soufrière Hills, Montserrat.

Figure 5.15 Tephra at Hverfjall volcano, Iceland.

Figure 5.16 Lahars covering the slopes of Tungurahua volcano, Ecuador.

When ash and other volcanic material are mixed with water, they can cause fast-flowing mudflows or lahars. These flow at speeds of up to 60 km/h and are highly erosive (Figure 5.16). The lahars created from the eruption of Nevada del Ruiz in 1985 engulfed the town of Armero in Colombia, killing over 20 000 people.

The frequency and predictability of volcanic hazards

The frequency of volcanic eruptions depends largely upon their type. Kilauea, on the island of Hawaii, is an active **shield volcano** which has erupted basaltic lava continuously since 1983. In contrast, many volcanoes that erupt rhyolitic lava erupt very infrequently. The Yellowstone **caldera** has erupted three times in the last 2.1 million years, with an interval of between 600 000 and 800 000 years between each. Generally, basaltic lava is erupted from volcanoes at constructive plate boundaries and **hotspots** (Figure 5.17), while volcanoes at destructive plate boundaries tend to erupt more viscous, andesitic or rhyolitic lava.

Key terms

shield volcano: a volcano with gently sloping sides, characteristic of fluid, basaltic lava

caldera: a large volcanic crater, often formed following a highly explosive eruption where the summit of the volcano is removed

hotspots: sites where mantle plumes rise up through areas of thin crust, causing volcanic activity in areas away from plate boundaries

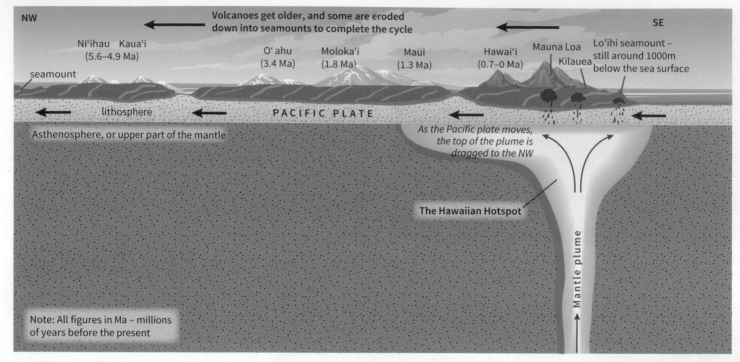

Figure 5.17 The formation of hotspot volcanoes.

To begin to accurately predict an eruption, vulcanologists (geologists who specialise in volcanic eruptions) need to know a volcano's eruption history and to be currently monitoring it. They then need to interpret the data. Even with this information, it is impossible to predict the exact size, nature and timing of an eruption.

Vulcanologists can measure local seismic activity and **ground deformation** using tiltmeters as the magma starts to move and bulge beneath the volcano (Figure 5.18). Changes in the concentration of carbon dioxide (CO_2) and sulphur dioxide (SO_2) can also signal an imminent eruption. The United States Geological Survey (USGS) successfully 'predicted' the 1991 eruption of Mount Pinatubo, in the Philippines, after noticing that SO_2 levels around the volcano increased dramatically from 500 to 16 500 tonnes per day as the magma rose to the surface of the chamber.

Key term

ground deformation: the change in shape of the ground before or after a volcanic eruption; often it is due to the movement of magma below the surface

To find out more about how volcanoes are monitored, download Worksheet 5.1 from **Cambridge Elevate**.

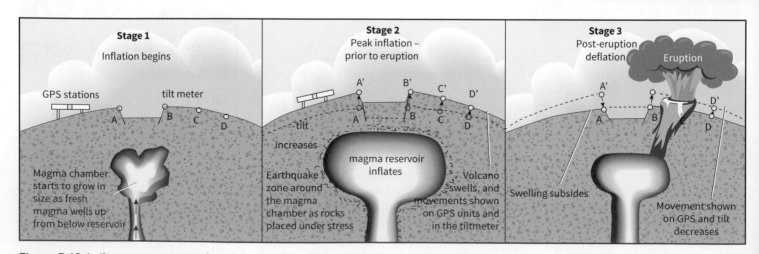

Figure 5.18 A tiltmeter measuring the ground deformation of a volcano.

Impacts of volcanic hazards and short- and long-term responses

Primary impacts

The primary impacts are those that occur immediately following a volcanic eruption. Lava and pyroclastic flows can destroy roads and cause buildings to collapse. Crops can also be damaged and water supplies contaminated by ash fall. People can be injured or killed by tephra, lava flows, pyroclastic flows or increased levels of CO_2, which cause suffocation.

Secondary impacts

The secondary impacts are those that occur in the days and weeks that follow the eruption. Lahars often occur when volcanic material mixes with water from rainfall or snowmelt. These fast-flowing rivers of mud can kill and injure people. They can cause further destruction to roads and buildings, making it difficult for emergency services to reach people in need, and lead to businesses being destroyed, causing high levels of unemployment. People can experience psychological problems if they lose their homes or lose relatives and friends in the eruption, and there may be a shortage of food, particularly if the area is dependent upon agriculture. Environmental impacts could include fires caused by lava flows and pyroclastic flows, which can then spread out of control, and acid rain as a result of SO_2 being released into the atmosphere.

In the eruption of Mount Pinatubo in the Philippines in 1991, for example, 847 people lost their lives; 300 died as a result of buildings collapsing and 100 due to lahars. Other social effects included the evacuation of 58 000 people from a 30 km radius around the volcano and 1.2 million people who lost their homes and had to move to shanty towns around Manila. In addition, over 650 000 people lost their jobs which affected the economy of the area. The Aeta people were particularly vulnerable to the impacts of the eruption. They practised slash-and-burn agriculture on the slopes of the volcano and their farmland was destroyed by falling ash and pumice. Some people who refused to be evacuated were killed by the eruption. Those who agreed to be evacuated struggled to adapt to the conditions in the evacuation camps. Their previously isolated lifestyle meant that they were susceptible to disease, such as measles. Malnutrition due to an unfamiliar diet also added to the death toll.

Short-term responses

The responses to volcanic eruptions depend upon the magnitude of the eruption as well as the vulnerability of the local population. Short-term responses are likely to involve the evacuation of people at risk from further eruptions and the deploying of emergency services to provide first-response treatment. Sometimes the short-term response is domestic. However, if the country is particularly vulnerable, then often international help is offered.

Long-term responses

Longer-term responses involve risk management to reduce the impacts of the volcanic hazards through **preparedness**, **mitigation**, prevention and **adaption**. If the volcano is monitored effectively, then it is likely that vulcanologists will be able to better predict future eruptions. Hazard maps can be created and evacuation strategies put into place if necessary. Alert systems, shelters and evacuation camps can be constructed for the local population, and emergency food and water supplies can be stored.

Investigate

Investigate the relationship between the different types of lava and their hazards and potential impacts. Create a fact file to organise the information.

Key terms

preparedness: the state of readiness for a volcanic eruption

mitigation: the action of reducing the severity or seriousness of a volcanic eruption

adaption: the action of changing or adapting behaviour in order to reduce the severity of a volcanic eruption

Physical and human

The number of people at risk from volcanic hazards is increasing due to localised population growth and people choosing to live in the vicinity of a dormant volcano which they believe will not erupt during their lifetime. What are some of the natural advantages of living near volcanoes which might encourage people to risk their lives?

167

5.4 Mount Ontake, Japan

Mount Ontake volcano is located on the main island of Honshu, Japan, approximately 200 km west of Tokyo.

The volcano is a sacred mountain and, at 3067 m, the second highest in Japan. It is therefore popular with tourists, hikers and climbers. Until 1979, it was thought to be dormant. Then, it underwent a series of minor eruptions; similar eruptions occurred in 1991 and 2007. On 27 September 2014, Mount Ontake erupted without warning. Despite being a monitored volcano, the minor earthquakes which usually signal an impending eruption were not detected. The weather was also pleasant and over 250 tourists were on the flanks of the volcano at the time.

The nature of vulcanicity

The islands of Japan lie at the junction of four major plates – the Pacific, Philippine, Eurasian and North American. The subduction of the Pacific plate under the North American and Philippine plate, and the subduction of the Philippine plate beneath the Eurasian plate has formed a series of trenches and volcanic island arcs. Indeed, there are over 100 active volcanoes (10% of the global total) on the Japanese islands; the majority of which are stratovolcanoes.

The eruption was **phreatic**, meaning that water seeped into the volcano and became superheated by the magma. This then ejected hot ash, rocks and steam; phreatic eruptions do not involve the eruption of magma from within the volcano. The eruption was not particularly explosive – it had a **Volcano Explosivity Index (VEI)** of 3 – but the proximity of the hot ash to the hikers made it a deadly threat.

Hikers are encouraged to register with tourism officials so that there is a record of who is hiking at any one time. However, only between 10 and 20% of hikers actually do this, and so it was difficult for the authorities to know how many people were likely to have been affected by the eruption (Figure 5.19).

 Key terms

phreatic: steam-driven explosions which occur when water beneath the ground is superheated by magma

Volcanic Explosivity Index (VEI): an index that measures the explosivity of volcanic eruptions; volcanoes with a VEI of 0–1 are effusive, while Plinian eruptions tend to have a VEI of between 4 and 6; there have been 42 eruptions of VEI 8 or above in the last 36 million years, including the eruption of Yellowstone in 640 000 BCE

Figure 5.19 Searchers looking for hikers after the eruption of Mount Ontake, Honshu, Japan.

The response to the eruption

Over 1100 firefighters and police took part in the rescue effort. At the end of the day, 40 people were reported to be injured. Some of them had cuts, bruises and broken bones, while others reported lung damage. These injuries were a result of tephra which were ejected into the atmosphere at speeds of over 300 km/h. On 29 September, rescuers had to abandon their search as the levels of poisonous hydrogen sulphide being emitted by the volcano were becoming too dangerous. Efforts were further interrupted by Typhoon Phanfone, which affected the region on 5 and 6 October. A month after the eruption, the death toll stood at 57 with six others still missing. The search for the missing was resumed on 29 July 2015, with a search party of 220 people. The delay of ten months between the eruption and the resumption of the search was due to the volcano's continued activity. The activity had reduced, but the rescue team still had to build four shelters to withstand small projectiles.

Most of the victims of the eruption were between 30 and 59, while three were children and five were over 60. Of the people who died, 31 were found near the summit where they had been resting or having lunch. The others were found on a trail at a slightly lower elevation. Over half of those killed had taken photographs of the eruption on their smartphones and were still holding them when they were found.

The volcano was being monitored extensively and should have resulted in the prediction of an impending eruption. However, volcanologists have highlighted that this was a fairly small eruption and this, combined with its phreatic nature, made it virtually impossible to predict. There were also no visible signs that an eruption was about to occur, such as changes to the mountain surface or earth movements. Coupled with this, whilst some seismologists detected an increased amount of seismic activity in the region, they were unprepared for the devastation caused by the eruption.

5.5 Seismic hazards

The United States Geological Survey (USGS) estimates that several million earthquakes occur each year. However, the vast majority of them are either too small to be felt or occur in remote locations. Approximately 15 earthquakes a year are of magnitude 7–7.9 and around 130 between 6 and 6.9.

Some of the most seismically active regions of the world (Figure 5.20) coincide with densely populated areas. Cities such as Islamabad, Istanbul and Lima are increasingly at risk. Given that poorly constructed housing is also common in these cities, it is unsurprising that, on average, 63 000 people die each year from seismic hazards.

The nature of seismicity and its underlying causes

The movement of tectonic plates causes pressure to build up in the Earth's crust. When the pressure is released, a series of tremors known as earthquakes occur. Consequently, the global distribution of earthquakes is closely related to the location of plate boundaries (Figure 5.21).

- At constructive plate boundaries, shallow focus earthquakes occur as a result of tensional forces in the crust. Often these earthquakes occur at mid-ocean ridges and therefore pose little hazard to people.
- Shallow focus earthquakes also occur at collisional plate boundaries where **continental crust** is pushing against continental crust to form fold mountain belts, and at conservative margins where two sections of Earth's crust move laterally.

ACTIVITY 5.2

1 Create a mind map to organise the case study of Mount Ontake, Japan. You may want to do further research to ensure your case study is up to date.
2 Sketch what the Park response model curve would look like for the Mount Ontake eruption. Annotate your curve to explain its shape.

 Making connections

The number of people at risk of being affected by earthquake hazards is increasing year on year as a result of rapid urbanisation. Why do you think that people choose to live in earthquake prone areas? See section 9.1 Urbanisation.

 Key term

continental crust: the Earth's crust which is found under the continents (although the fit is not exact); it is relatively thick (10–70 km) and not as dense as oceanic crust

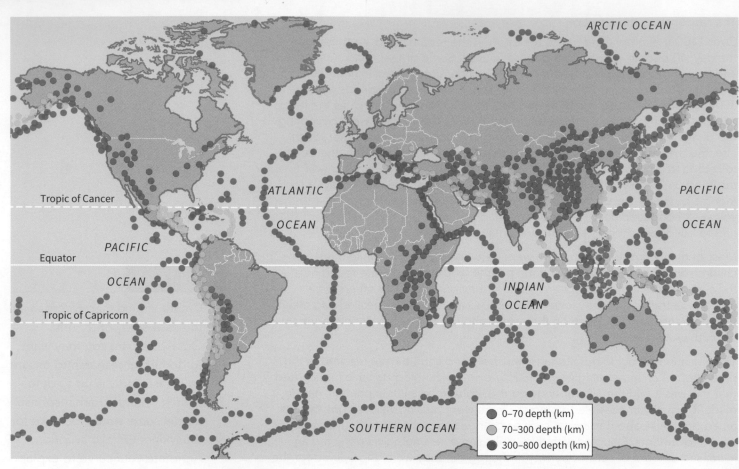

Figure 5.20 The global distribution of earthquakes.

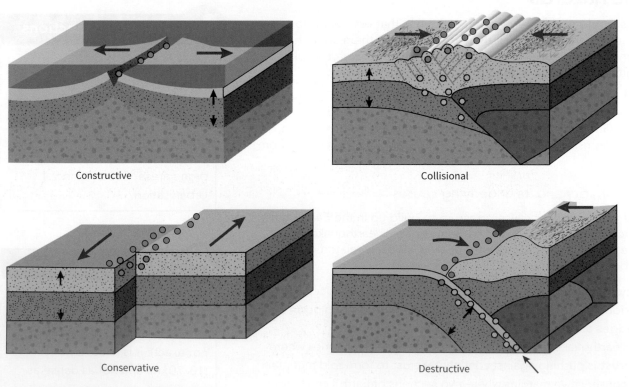

Figure 5.21 The tectonic plate boundaries.

- Earthquakes that occur at destructive plate boundaries tend to have deeper foci. They occur in a narrow zone known as the **Benioff zone**. Here, there are compressional forces as the **oceanic crust** subducts underneath the continental crust.

While about 90% of all earthquakes occur at plate boundaries, approximately 10% are intraplate. The UK experiences minor earthquake activity on a fairly regular basis despite sitting in the middle of the Eurasian Plate, many hundreds of kilometres away from a plate boundary. It is estimated that the UK experiences between 20 and 30 earthquakes each year, which are strong enough to be felt by people, and hundreds of smaller tremors are recorded by the British Geological Survey (BGS) using **seismometers** (Figure 5.22).

Key terms

Benioff zone: the zone where earthquakes tend to occur as the oceanic crust is being subducted underneath the continental crust at a destructive plate boundary

oceanic crust: the crust which is found under the oceans (although the fit is not exact); it is relatively thin (5–7 km) and more dense than continental crust

seismometer: an instrument that measures the seismic waves generated by an earthquake

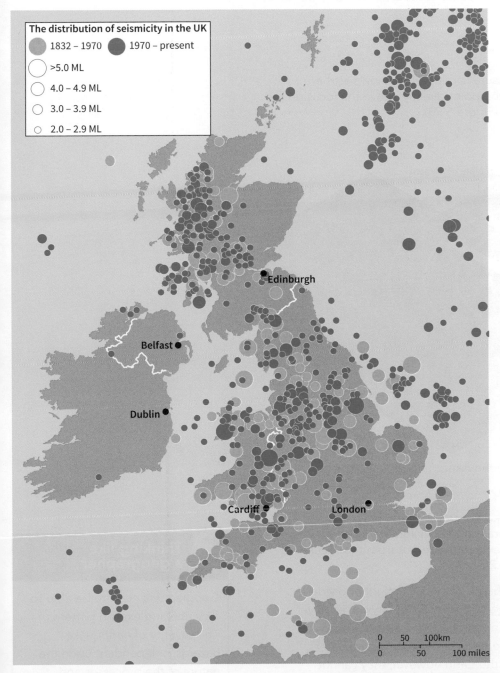

Figure 5.22 The distribution of seismicity in the UK, 1832–1970 (yellow) and 1970–present (blue).

Investigate

Investigate the extent of the earthquake hazard in the UK. The British Geological Survey website is a good place to start.

The cause of UK earthquakes is not fully understood. There are, however, a series of hairline fractures that crisscross the mainland. One theory is that these fractures are being locally compressed by either the movement of the Earth's tectonic plates or the uplift that continues to occur following the melting of the ice sheets that covered the north of the UK during the last ice age.

Thinking like a geographer

Geographers need to assess evidence and form carefully-considered judgements. Could you describe the UK as being at risk from an earthquake hazard? Why do you think this?

Earthquake hazards

Primary hazards

The point inside the crust where the pressure is released is known as the earthquake focus (or hypocentre), while the point directly above the focus on the Earth's surface is known as the epicentre (Figure 5.23).

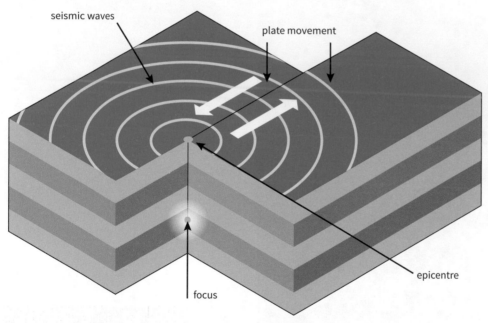

Figure 5.23 The focus and epicentre of an earthquake.

Shallow-focus earthquakes occur a few kilometres into the crust whereas deep-focus earthquakes can occur several hundred kilometres down. Seismic waves, which are also known as shockwaves, radiate out from the focus and can be divided into two types (Figure 5.24):

- Body waves: they travel through the Earth. They can be further divided into Primary or P waves and Secondary or S waves. Primary waves travel through both solids and liquids at a speed of about 5.5 km/s. These are the faster of the two and therefore are detected first by seismometers. Secondary waves also travel through the Earth however, they cannot travel through liquids. They are slower than Primary waves and travel at a speed of 3 km/s.

Thinking like a geographer

Geographers need to be able to describe and explain patterns. The severity of earthquake hazards is dependent upon the nature of the processes and location.

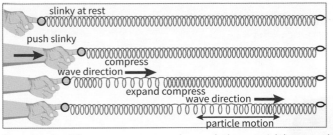

A compression (P) wave compresses and expands the material they pass through.

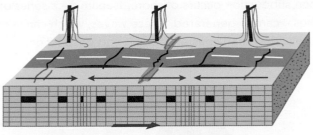

Rocks move back and forth and cause the ground to break up.

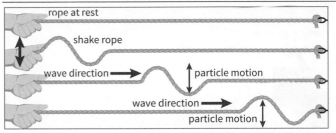

Transverse (S) waves cause material to shake at right angles to direction of wave motion. The greater the displacement the greater the amplitude of the wave.

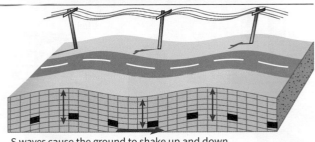

S waves cause the ground to shake up and down.

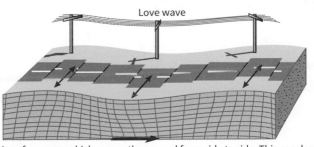

A surface wave which moves the ground from side to side. This can damage infrastructure and buildings.

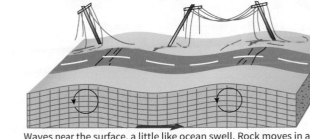

Waves near the surface, a little like ocean swell. Rock moves in an ellipse as the wave passes and breaks up the surface.

Figure 5.24 The different types of seismic waves.

- Surface waves: travel along the Earth's surface. Surface waves can also be further divided into Love and Rayleigh waves. Love waves shake the ground at right angles to the direction of movement, while Rayleigh waves have a rolling motion.

The underlying geology of the area can affect the way in which surface waves travel. For example, **unconsolidated sediment** can cause the seismic waves to be amplified. During an earthquake event, it is the surface waves that are the greatest hazard as they tend to cause the most damage to buildings, which may collapse and injure or kill their occupants.

Secondary hazards

Secondary hazards may occur after the initial earthquake and include liquefaction, landslides and tsunamis.

- Liquefaction occurs in unconsolidated sediments that are saturated with water. The sediments act as a liquid when the ground begins to shake, which can cause the subsidence of building foundations or the destruction of utility pipes (Figure 5.25).
- Landslides and avalanches can occur on even fairly gentle slopes as a result of the ground shaking. Falling rocks can destroy buildings and injure people and can also block roads, hindering the efforts of the emergency services.

> **Key term**
>
> **unconsolidated sediment:** loosely arranged particles of sediment that are not joined together

173

- When subduction occurs offshore, tsunamis – a series of large waves – can be generated. These waves, which can reach 10 metres high, cause widespread coastal flooding and destruction.

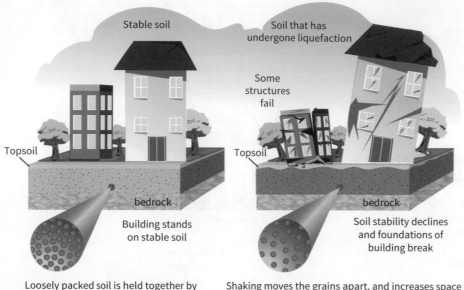

Figure 5.25 Soil liquefaction.

Impacts of seismic hazards and short- and long-term responses

The impact of earthquake events depends upon the magnitude of the earthquake and the vulnerability of the population.

Measuring earthquakes

The Richter scale was first used to determine the magnitude of earthquakes in 1934. It used a formula based upon the amplitude of the largest recorded seismic wave and the distance between the earthquake focus and the seismometer. However, while the Richter scale is useful for measuring small-scale earthquakes, it is less accurate when measuring large events. Today, the Moment Magnitude scale (M_w) is used globally. It measures the total moment release of the earthquake, where moment is a product of the distance the fault has moved and the force required to move it. For most earthquakes, the Moment Magnitude scale is roughly equivalent to the Richter scale, although for events greater than magnitude 8 it is significantly more accurate.

Another method of measuring earthquakes is the Modified Mercalli Intensity scale (MMI), which uses the observations of people to determine the amount of damage caused by the event. The 12-point scale describes the impacts of the earthquake event and ranges from I – where the earthquake is not felt – through to XII – where damage is total and objects are thrown into the air.

Short-term impacts

There is a saying that 'earthquakes don't kill people, buildings do'. Around three-quarters of all deaths during an earthquake are caused by collapsing buildings. In many cases, rapid urbanisation has increased the earthquake risk. Low cost, poorly built housing is a particular hazard, and so people living in slums are disproportionately vulnerable.

Earthquakes may also destroy infrastructure, including roads, which then may hinder the rescue effort. Water pipes may also burst, contaminating or disrupting the water supply which can cause disease to spread. After the 2010 Haiti earthquake, water supplies and sewage treatment were inadequate and 738 979 cases of cholera were reported. This resulted in 421 410 hospitalisations and 8927 deaths. The problem can be exacerbated by the increase in refugee camps following the collapse of buildings and the need for people to be rehoused.

Long-term impacts

Long-term impacts of seismic hazards include infrastructure problems and associated disruptions to supply lines and the economy. It is estimated that Haiti's economy fell by 5.1% following the earthquake. In addition, two thirds of the population, who were predominantly working in the agricultural and industrial sectors, were left unemployed.

Maths for geographers

We can investigate the relationship between the magnitude of an earthquake and the number of fatalities by carrying out Spearman's rank correlation; Chapter 13 Geographical skills and techniques contains more guidance about how to approach this.

1. Use the information in Table 5.1 to work out whether or not there is a statistical relationship between the two variables.

Earthquake	Magnitude	Number of fatalities
Nepal, 2015	7.8	9018
Nicaragua, 2014	6.1	2
Chile, 2014	7.7	0
Pakistan, 2013	7.7	825
Alaska, 2013	7.5	0
Visayas, 2012	6.7	51
Eastern Turkey, 2011	7.1	604
India/Nepal, 2011	6.9	111
Spain, 2011	5.1	9
New Zealand, 2011	6.1	185
Sumatra, 2010	7.7	408
China, 2010	6.9	2698
Haiti, 2010	7.0	160 000
Samoa, 2009	8.1	189

Table 5.1 The magnitude of earthquakes and their associated fatalities.

For help to complete the Spearman's rank correlation, download Worksheet 5.2 from **Cambridge Elevate**.

Social impacts

Following the Kashmir earthquake in October 2005, 3 million people were made homeless and had to survive the harsh Himalayan winter. As part of the aid, 15 000 tents were provided, however, these were not sufficient to protect people from hypothermia.

Economic impacts

Economic impacts include the loss of jobs resulting from damage to communication and infrastructure and the risk of looting. Following the 2010 Haiti earthquake, violent looting broke out on the streets of the capital, Port-au-Prince, which was exacerbated by the collapse of the city's main prison, allowing 4000 convicts to escape. In the longer term, the cost of rebuilding earthquake-hit areas can be expensive. The 2011 Japanese earthquake is suggested to be the costliest in history with the World Bank estimating the damage to be $235 billion. However, this does not include economic losses from power outages and so the Japanese government put the estimate at closer to $309 billion.

Prediction, prevention and preparation

Earthquakes are currently impossible to predict or prevent. Preparation is therefore the main way in which their effects can be managed. Preparing people who live in earthquake zones for an event is important and many regions carry out regular earthquake drills. In Japan and the USA, schools hold drills once a month, sometimes in earthquake simulation structures, and students are taught to '*drop* to their knees, *cover* their heads *and hold* onto their desks' (Figure 5.26).

When an earthquake does occur, the emergency response is vital and often is met both domestically and internationally. For example, following the 2010 Haiti earthquake, national governments, international organisations and **non-governmental organisations (NGOs)** supported the Haitian government by providing military and disaster relief personnel, field hospitals and emergency facilities.

Given that the collapse of buildings is the greatest risk to human life, designing and engineering buildings that are life-safe is important in the long term. For low cost, informal housing, simply strengthening the corners using wooden buttresses can prevent collapse. However, more sophisticated engineering solutions have been put in place in high-risk earthquake zones in Japan and the USA. Skyscrapers have been built on ball bearings, springs and padded cylinders which act like shock absorbers.

Key term

non-governmental organisation (NGO): an organisation that is not part of a government or for-profit businesses; charities, such as Oxfam, are good examples of NGOs

Research point

Research some of the ways in which buildings can be made earthquake proof. You could design an earthquake-proof building and annotate it to explain its features.

Figure 5.26 Earthquake drill in California.

5.6 Nepal, 2015

Nepal lies on the collisional plate boundary where the continental Indian Plate is pushing into the continental Eurasian Plate at a rate of 45 mm/y.

At 11.56 (Nepal Standard Time) on 25 April 2015, part of the Indian Plate shifted 3 m to the south resulting in a magnitude 7.8 earthquake. The epicentre was 80 km northwest of the capital, Kathmandu (Figure 5.27), and the focus was relatively shallow, at 15 km, meaning that the seismic shockwaves were magnified. After the main quake, there were 329 aftershocks with magnitudes higher than 4, including a 7.3 magnitude quake on 12 May 2015. It is thought that only part of the Main Thrust Fault, where the two plates collide, ruptured or 'unzipped' during the event, meaning that the western part of the fault is still susceptible to another significant quake in the not too distant future.

A severe earthquake affecting Nepal had long been predicted by experts who had used computer models and simulations to calculate the risk. However, experts could not predict when the earthquake would take place and this, coupled with the rapid urban growth of Kathmandu, meant that its inhabitants were increasingly vulnerable to the hazard.

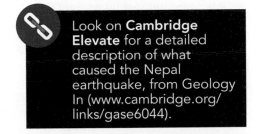

Look on **Cambridge Elevate** for a detailed description of what caused the Nepal earthquake, from Geology In (www.cambridge.org/links/gase6044).

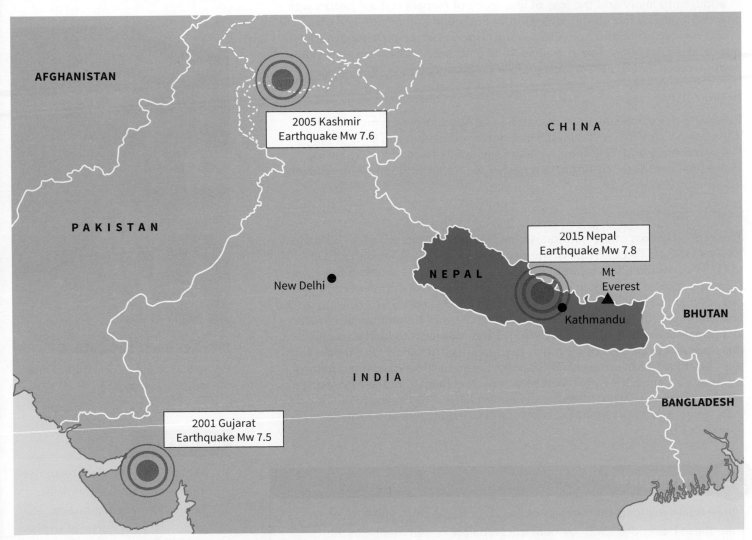

Figure 5.27 The location of the epicentre of the 2015 Nepal earthquake.

Social impacts

Over 9000 people lost their lives on 25 April 2015, and a further 218 lost their lives on 12 May. Twice as many were injured and 450000 people were displaced. The majority of those affected were in Nepal, although people in India, China and Bangladesh were also injured and there were some fatalities. In Nepal, the worst hit areas were Sindhupalchok, where over 2000 died, and Kathmandu, where 180 buildings were destroyed and fatalities reached 1000. People in rural Nepal escaped relatively unscathed as they were outdoors working during the event and so were not trapped by falling buildings or debris. However, the Tibeto-Burman people, who are considered a lower caste within Nepalese society, were hardest hit as they tend to live on the higher slopes and these were harder to access after the quake.

The initial ground-shaking triggered a series of avalanches throughout the Himalayas. Nineteen people were killed on Mount Everest and 329 reported missing following an avalanche in the Langtang valley, which is a popular trekking route. Of these, 52 bodies were subsequently found. The avalanche was estimated to be between 2 and 3km wide and destroyed a number of villages, including Chyamki and Mundu.

In addition to injury and the loss of life, much of Nepal's cultural history was also damaged by the earthquake. Durbar Square in Kathmandu is a UNESCO World Heritage Site and home to several pagodas which collapsed in the quake. The Dharahara Tower, built in 1832 (and rebuilt following a previous earthquake in 1934), also collapsed, killing 180 people.

Relief effort

Following the earthquake, Operation Sankat Mochan (which means 'Operation Crisis Relief' in Nepali) was deployed. It involved 90% of the Nepalese Army and 17000 members of the police force in three phases: immediate response, co-ordinating rescue and relief, and follow-up recovery operations (Figure 5.28).

Economic impacts

The economic cost of the earthquake has been estimated at around 35% of Nepal's GDP. As Nepal is one of the poorest countries in Asia, with a GDP of US$19.6 billion (2014 figures), it was unlikely to be able to afford the reconstruction effort without outside help. The Asian Development Bank (ADB) provided a US$3 million grant for initial relief efforts and US$200 million for the first phase of rebuilding. The UK Disasters Emergency Committee also made an appeal for aid and raised £83 million, which was used to fund a range of development projects. For example, Tearfund have provided 58000 people in the Tistung area (where over 90% of homes were destroyed) with temporary shelters, strengthened with iron sheets to protect them from the monsoon rains, which arrived several months after the earthquakes. They also donated food (rice, lentils and salt), tarpaulins, blankets, cooking utensils and hygiene kits (Figure 5.29).

Figure 5.28 Relief work in the aftermath of the Nepal earthquake.

Investigate

Investigate the long-term effects of the 2015 Nepal earthquake. How are these being dealt with by both the Nepalese government and the international community?

ACTIVITY 5.3

1   Sketch what the Park response model curve would look like for the Nepal earthquake. Annotate your curve to explain its shape.

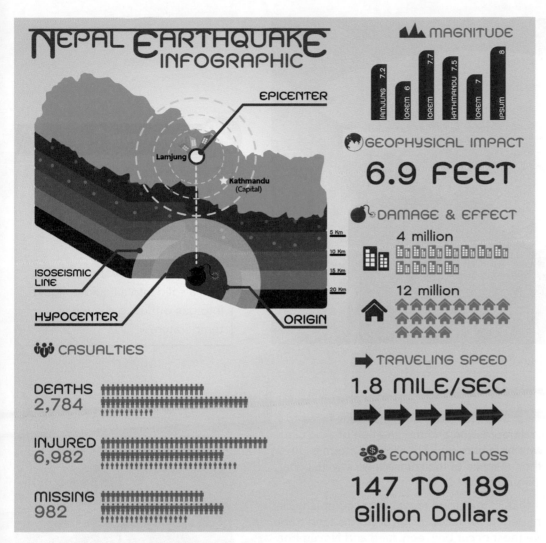

Figure 5.29 The effects of the Nepal earthquake.

5.7 Tropical storm hazards

There are on average 45 storm events every year, which originate in tropical latitudes. The region which experiences the most tropical storms is Eastern Asia (33% of the total), although other notable regions include the East Pacific (17%), West Australia (13%) and the Caribbean (11%). Tropical storms are known by different names, which are dependent upon where they originate. For example, typhoon is the term used in Asia, while hurricane is used for storms in the Atlantic and Northeast Pacific, and cyclone is the term used in the South Pacific and Indian Ocean. Over the last 200 years, tropical storms have been responsible for around 1.9 million deaths – an estimated 10000 per year – most of which have occurred in coastal areas.

The nature of tropical storms and their underlying causes

Tropical storms are an essential element in the transfer of heat between the equator and the poles. Most originate in the intertropical convergence zone (ITCZ) at latitudes of between 5 and 25° north and south of the equator. However, specific conditions are required for tropical storms to form. These include warm, deep oceans with temperatures of 27 °C to a depth of at least

Watch the video on **Cambridge Elevate** about the formation of tropical storms.

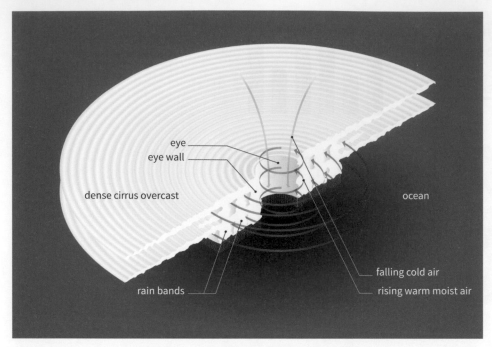

Figure 5.30 The structure of a tropical storm.

70 metres, the increased importance at these latitudes of the **Coriolis force** to accelerate the spinning of the original depression and the creation of a circular pattern of winds, and unstable air with high humidity. The tropical storm is driven by energy from **latent heat**, while the presence of moisture allows low frictional drag with the surface of the ocean (Figure 5.30).

Where these two factors decrease – that is, the storm moves into cooler latitudes or passes over land – then the storm begins to decay. Tropical storms tend to be seasonal. In the northern hemisphere most occur between June and November (with the peak occurring in September), while in the southern hemisphere the season runs from November to April.

Primary hazards

Hazards resulting from tropical storms include high winds, heavy rainfall and storm surges. These can result in coastal and river flooding and in landslides. The intensity of a tropical storm is measured using the Saffir-Simpson scale, which is based on the speed of the highest winds. The scale ranges from category 1 – a tropical storm with winds of between 119 and 153 km/h up to category 5 – a tropical storm with winds over 249 km/h. Strong winds can destroy buildings and roads and turn cars and other objects into flying projectiles.

Heavy rainfall, while being a hazard in itself, can also result in secondary hazards such as flooding and landslides. Totals of 100 mm of rainfall a day are not uncommon, although Hurricane Amelia (1978) holds the record in the USA for the wettest hurricane with 1200 mm of rainfall, of which 110 mm fell in one day. Flooding can damage houses, and standing water combined with warm temperatures can become a breeding ground for mosquitoes and associated diseases such as malaria.

Storm surges account for approximately 90% of tropical storm deaths (Figure 5.31). Waves over 5 metres high (over 10 metres if the surge coincides with high tide) can devastate coastal communities by destroying buildings and roads and contaminating agricultural land with salt from the influx of seawater. Communities

Figure 5.31 A storm surge off the coast of Florida during Hurricane Dennis.

For an activity on managing a tropical storm hazard, download Worksheet 5.3 from **Cambridge Elevate.**

can be protected from surges by maintaining coastal wetlands or mudflats, which absorb the water and energy produced during a storm surge. These can act as a natural barrier protecting homes and businesses from flooding and wind damage.

Prediction

Improvements in weather models and forecasting have made the prediction of tropical storms more reliable and accurate in recent years. In the USA, the National Hurricane Centre and Joint Typhoon Warning System provide coverage of the Atlantic and Pacific oceans respectively. They use geostationary and polar orbiting satellites to provide them with data about storm structure, rain, wind speed and direction. They also run numerical models through supercomputers on a daily basis to enable the prediction of the likely tropical storm track.

Impacts of tropical storms and short- and long-term responses

Social impacts

Tropical storms bring widespread flooding which can cause death and injury. However, many people continue to suffer the social effects many days, weeks or even months after the event. As a result of sewers being flushed out with floodwater, people may catch waterborne diseases such as cholera. Properties are likely to be severely damaged and people may become homeless, which can break up communities if the area is not restored. There may also be looting of both domestic and commercial properties, which can lead to the loss of possessions and people may lose their jobs if the area in which they work has been particularly badly affected. If insurance premiums rise, some people may not be able to afford them and will therefore not be fully protected against future storms. All of these impacts are likely to cause stress and trauma for those affected.

Economic impacts

Economically, there are the obvious costs of repairing any damage caused and the fact that while affected businesses are closed their earnings and profits will be lost. Hurricane Katrina currently stands as the most expensive Atlantic hurricane, costing the United States $125 billion. However, there may be other economic impacts which are individual to the local area. For example, crops may be damaged and exports lost, or oil prices may increase because of difficulties with oil extraction and transportation.

Environmental impacts

As many of the affected areas are coastal, storms can result in sensitive ecosystems being damaged and plant and animal habitats lost. For example, sea fish are often killed because of **silting** while freshwater fish may be killed during a storm surge. Other environmental impacts such as flooding and mudslides can lead to communication and infrastructure being destroyed which can hamper the rescue effort.

Ways to reduce the impacts of a tropical storm include communicating warnings and evacuating people who are likely to be affected. It is also possible to reduce the effects of storm surges by building flood defence schemes along vulnerable coastlines.

Key term

silting: where grains of sand or silt accumulate

5.8 Superstorm Sandy, 2012

Nature and characteristics

Hurricane Sandy (also known as Superstorm Sandy) is the second most expensive and, at 1800 km in diameter, the largest hurricane in US history. It originated in the Caribbean Sea on 22 October 2012 and made landfall in

Jamaica two days later. After landfall it lost energy and as it started to track to the northeast it was temporarily downgraded to a tropical storm. However, by 28 October it had re-intensified to a category 2 hurricane. It hit the eastern seaboard of the USA in the early hours of 29 October with winds of 185 km/h.

Sandy was not a particularly strong hurricane and yet several of its characteristics were unusual. Firstly, as it moved northwards, the dimensions of the storm grew – it reached 1700 km in diameter – and this resulted in a larger area being affected by the winds Secondly, a *blocking high* in the jet stream, forced the hurricane to make a sharp turn to the west which resulted in its collision with the New Jersey coast. However, perhaps the most significant factor was the timing of its landfall. The collision with the coast occurred at the same time as high tide and the moon was full which resulted in a higher than normal spring tide. These unusual circumstances resulted in a storm surge which was an additional 3 metres higher than it would normally have been.

Impacts

The impacts of Superstorm Sandy were felt throughout the Caribbean and a total of 24 US states were also affected. The number of fatalities reached 233, of whom 158 were in the USA (71 were a direct result of the hurricane and 87 an indirect result). Of these deaths, 49 occurred in the state of New York which was particularly badly affected. More than 2 million people in the state were without power due to flooding and trees having fallen on power lines (Figure 5.32). The East River overflowed its banks and this, combined with a water surge of 4.2 m in Battery Park, resulted in subway tunnels becoming flooded and 10 billion tonnes of partially treated sewage being released. Other states, including Florida and North Carolina, saw airports and roads closed and schools shut for several days. The total cost of the damage was estimated at US$65 billion, making Sandy the second most expensive hurricane in US history after Katrina.

Responses

Much of the relief effort was domestic and involved telethons and concerts to raise money for those affected. Disney and ABC held a 'Day of Giving' during which US$17 million was raised for the American Red Cross, and a concert featuring

Figure 5.32 A house in New York damaged by Superstorm Sandy.

 Look on **Cambridge Elevate** to read more about Hurricane Sandy in the *Guardian* newspaper (www.cambridge.org/links/gase6045).

artists such as Bon Jovi, Eric Clapton and Kanye West was held in Madison Square Garden. The US government also passed a relief bill for US$48 billion for the states affected by Superstorm Sandy. However, over 18 months after the event, most of the funding had not been spent and 30 000 residents in the states of New York and New Jersey remained displaced and unable to return to their homes.

In the aftermath of Sandy there have been plans suggested to protect coastal areas from future flooding events. One idea is to build a string of artificial islands off the coast of New Jersey and New York state which would bear the brunt of future storm surges, thus protecting the mainland. However, many groups oppose such a plan. The US Fish and Wildlife service are concerned that coastal habitats will be altered and there are others who believe that strengthening dunes along the existing coastline is a cheaper option than the US$12 billion which the construction of the islands would cost.

5.9 Typhoon Haiyan, 2013

Typhoon Haiyan (also known locally as Typhoon Yolanda) was one of the strongest tropical storms ever recorded, and the deadliest in Philippine modern history. It originated as a low-pressure system several hundred kilometres southeast of the Federated States of Micronesia on 2 November 2013 and then moved westwards.

Warnings were issued in the Visayas islands and police officers and military personnel were deployed in preparation.

The typhoon hit landfall in the Philippines on 7 November, by which time one minute sustained wind speeds of 315 km/h had been recorded. In addition to the strong winds, heavy rain fell – 281.9 mm was recorded at Surigao City in a 12-hour period. Despite the strong winds and heavy rain, it was the accompanying storm surge with waves of 5.2 m which caused the most devastation and loss of life.

People living in the Philippines are used to typhoon events and yet they underestimated the strength of Haiyan. Any one of the hazards – high winds, heavy rainfall or storm surge – occurring in isolation would have resulted in destruction, but the combination of all three was particularly deadly. Many people stayed in their homes rather than evacuating and the 544 000 who did evacuate were caught in evacuation shelters which became death traps due to severe flooding. Furthermore, many of the emergency response teams who would have coordinated and supported the relief effort were victims themselves.

Impacts

In the Philippines, 6300 fatalities were confirmed – 5877 in the Eastern Visayas – and over 22 000 people were reported missing. The low-lying areas in Tacloban City were particularly badly hit with many buildings destroyed, trees blown down and cars piled up. Tacloban airport was also flooded, which slowed the relief effort. While international aid was flown into local airports, much of it stayed there as roads remained closed.

Responses

The UN released US$25 million in emergency funds and also issued an appeal for US$300 million. Twenty-five humanitarian groups including international response teams and NGOs operated in the region, and the Philippines Red Cross delivered basic food aid including rice, canned food, sugar and cooking oil (Figure 5.33). However, despite a coordinated response there was criticism that many of the victims struggled to access aid and £1 million worth of food packs were wasted due to improper storage.

Research point

Research what has happened in the aftermath of Superstorm Sandy up to the present. The websites of newspapers such as the *Guardian* and *The Times* are good places to start.

Figure 5.33 Relief aid being organised and distributed following Typhoon Haiyan.

Research point

Read the article 'The impact of climate change on natural disasters'. Design an A4 poster to explain what is likely to happen in the future.

A June 2015 report published in *Nature Climate Change* suggested that both Superstorm Sandy and Typhoon Haiyan were made more devastating than they otherwise would have been by human-induced climate change. The report suggests that, in the case of Superstorm Sandy, human-induced sea level rise added to the storm surge which flooded subway tunnels in New York and caused tens of billions of dollars of damage. The report also suggests that increased sea temperatures and ocean heating increased the strength of Typhoon Haiyan, which made the impacts worse. Future storms may therefore be exacerbated by the rapid sea level rise predicted in such reports.

Look on **Cambridge Elevate** for the article 'The impact of climate change on natural disasters' from the Earth Observatory (www.cambridge.org/links/gase6046).

ACTIVITY 5.4

1   Construct a table to compare the impacts of and responses to Superstorm Sandy and Typhoon Haiyan. You could use the headings shown in Table 5.2 or create your own.

	Superstorm Sandy	Typhoon Haiyan
Social impacts		
Political impacts		
Environmental impacts		
Economic impacts		
Short-term responses		
Long-term responses		
International responses		

Table 5.2 Impacts of and responses to Superstorm Sandy and Typhoon Haiyan.

2   Sketch what the Park response model curve would look like for both Superstorm Sandy and Typhoon Haiyan. Annotate your curves to explain their shape.

5.10 Fires in nature

The nature of wildfires and the conditions which favour them

Fire occurs when oxygen combines with carbon, hydrogen and other organic materials in a rapid chemical reaction. Controlled fires are of benefit to humans, providing warmth and being used for cooking and clearing land for agriculture. For example, communities engaging in shifting cultivation, a subsistence form of agriculture commonly used in the tropical rainforest, use slash and burn to quickly remove forested areas and to prepare the land for future crops. However, if the fire is uncontrolled it becomes hazardous and is termed a wildfire (Figure 5.34).

It is the natural conditions of the environment, particularly the type of vegetation, climate and topography, which encourage the fire to develop in intensity and determine its characteristics. Wildfires can be classified into three different types; surface fires, ground fires and crown fires.

Figure 5.34 A wildfire burns at New South Wales, Australia.

- Surface fires are the most common and burn along the forest floor burning leaf litter and fallen branches. Whilst they typically burn at around 900°C, they cool quickly and are relatively easy to control.
- Ground fires burn organic matter in the soil, such as peat, and spread slowly, smouldering at fairly low temperatures (around 540°C) for long periods of time.
- Crown fires burn through the top layer of foliage known as the canopy. Loose bark can allow fire to spread up the trunks of trees and into the crown and once the foliage in this layer has combusted it can generate temperatures in excess of 1100°C. Crown fires affect the whole of the forest and are the most intense and often the most difficult to contain.

Naturally wildfires are most likely to occur in those climates which allow vegetation to dry out and become susceptible to burning. However, once these conditions have been satisfied the nature of the fire is hugely dependent upon wind speed and direction and humidity. The most intense fires occur in dry, windy conditions with low humidity. The wind fans the flames and also serves to drive the flaming front (front edge of the fire) forward. The rate of this movement increases as wind velocity increases. However, if wind speeds are very strong then the movement of the flaming front can be so rapid that it prevents a **convection column** from forming. Humidity is also important as it determines the amount of moisture content in the air. Where there is above 15% relative humidity the risk of wildfire hazard is low but, below 7% the risk is much higher. Relative humidity varies during the day and is lowest in the early afternoon explaining the increased incidence of wildfires at this time of day.

In addition to vegetation and weather, topography is the third factor affecting the nature of wildfires. Wildfires travel faster uphill than they do downhill and typically the steeper the slope the faster they travel. This is due to the fact that fires travel in the direction of the ambient wind which tends to flow uphill. Also, because the heat and smoke rise this means that the fire can pre-heat the vegetation allowing it to combust more easily.

The causes of fires

In reality, wildfires are examples of quasi-natural hazards as, whilst they can be started by natural occurrences such as lightning, volcanic eruptions and sparks

 Key term

convection column: a vertical, rising column of smoke, ashes and particulates caused by a fire

from rock falls, they can also be started by human agency. In the United States it is estimated that around 90% of wildfires are caused by humans leaving campfires unattended, discarding lit cigarettes, lighting agricultural fires or arson. The remaining 10% of wildfires have natural causes, the most common of which is lightning.

Lightning can be divided into two types; hot and cold lightning. Cold lightning has an intense electrical current but has a short duration; whilst hot lightning has a lower voltage but tends to occur for a longer period of time. It is the particularly long lasting forms of hot lightning which cause wildfires. However, the sources of wildfires are not always clear and can be multiple. For example, the fires which raged in Australia in 2009 which covered around 4000 km² and killed 173 people, were caused by lightning, a downed power line and arson.

The impacts of wildfires

Wildfires can have significant and negative environmental impacts, particularly if they are intense or frequent (Figure 5.35). For example, natural ecosystem cycles can be disrupted if native plant species are eradicated. These may be replaced with either fire-resistant species or other invasive plant species which tend to be highly flammable. This therefore perpetuates the cycle creating an enhanced risk of fire in the future which has the potential to remove even more native species. Coupled with this, wildfires produce a large volume of ash and destroy soil structures and plant nutrients which further reduces the biodiversity of the affected area. The removal of vegetation also reduces rainfall interception rates and this, in turn, can lead to flash flooding and soil erosion. Finally, on a global scale, wildfires release particulates, toxic gases and carbon dioxide into the atmosphere, which can result in temporary shifts in climate and an exacerbation of the greenhouse effect.

However, wildfires also provide a number of benefits to the environment. For example, they can quickly remove dead or decaying material on the forest floor, harmful insects or diseased plants. This clearance increases sunlight and the release of nutrients into the soil which, in turn encourages new plant growth. There are also some species of plant which cannot reproduce without fire. The Douglas fir, sequoia and ponderosa pine (Figure 5.36) all require fire to aid seed

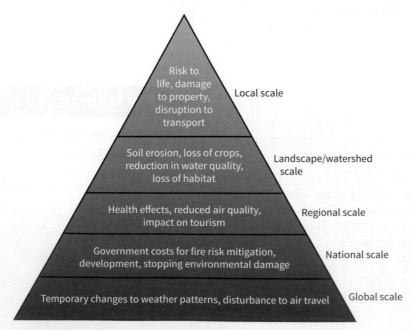

Figure 5.35 The negative impacts of wildfire.

germination. Research in the Everglades National Park, USA suggested that 33 species of tree depend upon fire for their long-term survival.

Wildfires tend to occur in rural areas with small, remote populations being at the greatest risk. However, population growth on the fringes of urban and forest areas in North America and rural depopulation and the abandonment of traditional agriculture around the Mediterranean has led to larger areas and greater numbers of people being at risk. The economic impacts of wildfires can vary dramatically between events. The destruction of property and infrastructure causes some of the greatest direct economic losses. However, indirect losses resulting from pollution leading to problems with human health, contamination of water sources or the increase in flood events or soil erosion can also be significant.

There does not appear to be a direct relationship between human population and economic losses as whilst wildfires may affect more people in densely populated areas, this does not necessarily mean that they suffer greater economic loss, particularly in LEDCs.

Figure 5.36 The ponderosa pine.

Continent	No. of events	People killed	Total people affected	Economic costs ($)
Africa	25	272	21 672	440 000 000
America	118	234	1 229 175	25 228 900 000
Asia	50	748	3 188 257	11 892 500 000
Europe	89	462	1 295 562	12 618 811 000
Oceania	21	224	74 320	2 120 869 000
Total	303	1940	5 808 986	52 301 080 000

Table 5.3 A summary of human and economic losses caused by wildfire from 1984 to 2013 (source: EM-DAT 2013).

Whilst arguably the greatest impacts of wildfires are on property and vegetation, they can also adversely affect human health. The smoke from wildfires is composed of carbon dioxide and water vapour, although other particulates are also present. It is these particulates which have a diameter of less than 2.5 micrometres in diameter which pose the greatest threat as they can enter the respiratory tract, become deposited in the lungs and, ultimately, enter the bloodstream. This can then cause bronchitis and exacerbate asthma and, in extreme cases, lead to pneumonia.

Managing wildfires

In many countries where wildfires are a potential hazard, the approach to management has been to attempt to prevent the spread of fire in the first place. For example, where burning is used as a vegetation management method, it is undertaken in suitable weather conditions and the burn is highly controlled; it removes the litter but does not damage the trees. A Global Early Warning System for Wildland Fires (Global EWS) has also been developed in order to mitigate the fire hazard. It provides 1–7-day forecasts using satellite technology to help those assessing the fire hazard in their decision-making processes.

However, should a fire become uncontrolled there are a variety of response mechanisms which can be put in place. In the USA, the Federal Emergency Management Agency (FEMA) suggest that individuals, on discovery of a wildfire call the emergency services. They should then attempt to protect their property by filling containers with water, turning on the lights so the house is visible through the smoke and placing a ladder against the side of the house, before evacuating.

Once the emergency services – fire, police and medical services – arrive, an assessment is made in terms of the immediate needs. For example, individuals may require temporary evacuation and accommodation, or there may be a need for search and rescue teams or to focus on the distribution of resources.

Methods for fighting fires include spraying the fire with water or chemicals from either the ground or from the air (Figure 3.37) in order to reduce their heat, creating firebreaks by removing areas of vegetation to reduce fuel supply and beating the flames in an attempt to reduce the oxygen availability. However, this type of emergency response effort is often dangerous and very expensive. In 2011, a wildfire devastated over 31 000 acres of North Carolina, USA. Fire crews were drafted from both local and national centres – some from as far afield as Alaska – in an attempt to control the fire. However, despite over 200 individuals being involved in the response effort, the fire burnt for over three months and cost an estimated $3.5 million to fight.

In the period following a wildfire, provision is required to support the local community and repair the infrastructure and also to assess the damage to vegetation. The strategies that are then put in place are dependent upon these assessments. Those owning the land are encouraged to map the damage and report statistics to a central body which collates this information. They are also encouraged to reduce the risk of landslides and soil erosion by placing straw wattles (mats of straw) which intercept and absorb rainfall and hold soil in place.

Communities which are susceptible to wildfires have developed building codes so that structures that need to be rebuilt are more effectively adapted to withstanding wildfires in the future. These include:

- considering site layout so that incombustible material, in the form of driveways and patios act as a barrier
- installing fire-resistant roofing material
- installing roll-down metal fire doors and window shutters
- installing sprinkler systems.

Figure 5.37 A helicopter dropping water on a wildfire.

Californian wildfires, 2015

In 2015 more than 11 million acres – an area the size of Denmark – was devastated by wildfire in the western United States. The number of individual recorded fires was over 51 000. However, this was a relatively small total compared to recent years. Over 84 000 fires were recorded in 2006 and between 1960 and 1980 the number of fires regularly exceeded 100 000. However, despite the greater number of individual fires, the total acreage burned never exceeded 5.5 million acres. It therefore appears that there has been a rise in recent years of mega-fires, which can be attributed to the increase in populations close to forests, fire-management practices and the trend towards hot, dry seasons.

One of the most significant fires in the 2015 California season was the Rough fire which burned over 151 000 acres of land in the Sierra National Forest, Fresno County. The fire was caused by a lightning strike at the end of July and continued to burn until the beginning of November. At its peak in September, 3741 firefighters were involved in fighting the fire and 345 fire engines, 19 helicopters and 45 bulldozers were used in the emergency response. Despite the size and intensity of the fire, the impacts were minimised due to an effective management approach. 2500 people were evacuated from camps around Lake Hume and over 3 million gallons of water from surrounding lakes were used to saturate the ground. Mules were also used on the northern flank of the fire to support rescue crews. Teams of five mules were lead into the forest with nearly 70 kg of equipment to restock the fire crews and remove refuse and other items. Despite this, four buildings were destroyed, 10 people were injured and the economic impact was estimated to be in excess of $100 million.

5.11 Multi-hazardous environments

The impact of a hazard event can be devastating. The *Climate Change and Environmental Risk Atlas*, which compares risk data for 198 countries, has identified 32 countries that are at 'extreme risk' from hazards. These hazard hotspots occur in areas at risk from multiple hazards. As urbanisation occurs, particularly in countries that are developing, the potential for hazards to turn into disasters is increased (Figure 5.38).

A common characteristics of **disaster hotspot** countries is that at least 65% of their working population and 28% of their economy is reliant upon agriculture. At present, the country most at risk is Bangladesh, followed by Sierra Leone, South Sudan, Nigeria and Chad. Haiti is in sixth place.

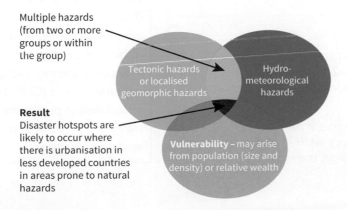

Multiple hazards (from two or more groups or within the group)

Result
Disaster hotspots are likely to occur where there is urbanisation in less developed countries in areas prone to natural hazards

Tectonic hazards or localised geomorphic hazards

Hydro-meteorological hazards

Vulnerability – may arise from population (size and density) or relative wealth

Figure 5.38 Disaster hotspots.

ACTIVITY 5.5

1   Describe the distribution of wildfires shown on the map on **Cambridge Elevate**.

Go to **Cambridge Elevate** to see a map of wildfires in California in August 2015, from KIBS/KBOV Radio (www.cambridge. org/links/gase6047).

Key term

disaster hotspot: a location which is at risk of experiencing two or more hazards; Haiti is a good example of a disaster hotspot as it is vulnerable to both tropical storms and earthquakes

For an activity on disaster hotspots, download Worksheet 5.4 from **Cambridge Elevate**.

5.12 Haiti, a multi-hazardous environment

Haiti is a Caribbean country with an estimated population (2015) of 9.9 million, 10% of whom live in the capital city, Port-au-Prince. The country occupies the western part of Hispaniola island, shared with the Dominican Republic to the east (Figure 5.39).

Figure 5.39 The location of Haiti.

Haiti ranks 168 out of 187 countries in the 2014 **Human Development Index (HDI)** with a value of 0.471. Life expectancy at birth is 62.17 years and the country's GDP per capita is US$1200, making Haiti the least developed country in the western hemisphere (Table 5.4).

Haiti's location in the middle of the Caribbean basin makes it particularly exposed to multiple hazards. The World Bank estimates that 96% of the country's population is at risk of mortality from two or more hazards, the most common of which are tropical storms and earthquakes.

Key term

Human Development Index (HDI): a composite index combining life expectancy at birth, mean and expected years of schooling and gross national income (GNI) per capita (calculated at purchasing power parity or PPP US$) to measure and rank countries

Development indicator	Haiti	Norway	Niger	South Korea
GDP per capita (US$)	1200	53300	800	30000
Life expectancy at birth (years)	62.17	80.20	53.40	79.05
Total fertility rate (per woman)	3.07	1.77	7.60	1.23
Literacy rate (%)	51.2	100	28.7	97.9

Table 5.4 Haiti's level of development compared with Norway, Niger and South Korea.

The nature of Haiti's hazards – social, economic and environmental risks

Haiti's location makes it vulnerable to hurricane damage. The Atlantic hurricane season runs from June to November with an average of 12 storms per season, half of which strengthen to become hurricanes. Hurricane Jeanne hit Haiti in 2004, killing over 3000 people, most of whom lived in Gonaives, the country's fourth largest city; Hurricane Flora killed over 8000 in 1963.

Arguably, Haiti's most devastating hurricane season to date was in 2008 when four storms – Fay, Gustav, Hanna and Ike – made the country vulnerable to strong winds, flooding, landslides and coastal surges. Nearly 800 people were killed, 310 people were reported missing and 593 people were injured. In addition, 22702 homes were destroyed and a further 84625 were damaged. Once the floodwaters had receded, millions of cubic metres of mud remained which took nearly three years to clean up. Around 70% of Haiti's crops were destroyed, leading to severe malnutrition and the deaths of dozens of children in the months following the storms. In total, 800000 Haitians were affected (8% of the population) and the damage was estimated to be in excess of $1 billion, over 5% of the country's US$17 billion GDP.

Since 1851, only six category 3 or higher storms have hit Haiti. It therefore seems that the country suffers disproportionately from flooding hazards. This is largely due to the vulnerability of the population rather than the magnitude of the natural disasters themselves. The severe poverty experienced in the country means that the cost of oil is too expensive and so Haitians depend upon charcoal for 85% of their fuel needs. This has resulted in large swathes of forest being cut down, leaving **denuded mountains**. In 1980, Haiti still had 25% of its forests; by 2004, this had reduced to 1.4%. The lack of trees, whose roots bind the soil together, increases the landslide hazard following severe rainfall, and it is this which is thought to have contributed to the increased death toll in 2008.

Haiti is located on the conservative plate boundary where the Caribbean Plate is moving eastwards against the North American Plate at a rate of 20mm/y (Figure 5.40). As a consequence, pressure builds up along the fault over the course of many years. When the plates eventually slip, pressure is released, triggering earthquakes and associated tsunamis.

The most recent and most devastating earthquake occurred on 12 January 2010. The epicentre of the initial magnitude 7 quake was near the town of Léogâne, 25km west of the capital, Port-au-Prince, although a further 52 aftershocks with magnitudes of 4.5 or above were recorded between the 12 and 24 January.

The damage was particularly focused on Port-au-Prince where most of the major infrastructure, including hospitals, transport and communication systems, were destroyed (Figure 5.41).

Nearly 25% of Haiti's civil servants were killed, meaning that the coordination of the rescue effort was difficult. Over 3.5 million people were affected by the

Key term

denuded mountains: mountains that have been stripped of their vegetation cover

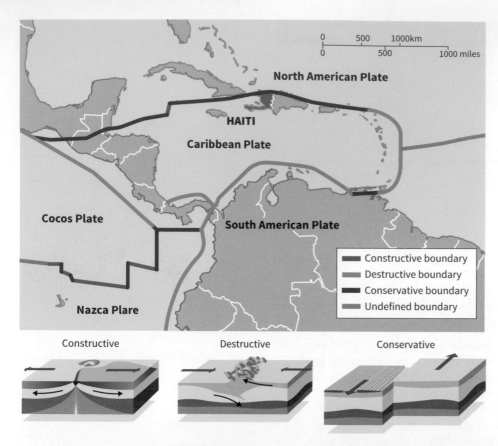

Constructive   Destructive   Conservative

Figure 5.40 Haiti's location in relation to plate boundaries.

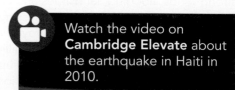

Watch the video on **Cambridge Elevate** about the earthquake in Haiti in 2010.

Figure 5.41 Damaged buildings in the Haiti capital, Port-au-Prince.

quake, with 220 000 fatalities and over 300 000 people injured, many as a result of poorly built houses collapsing on top of their occupants. In total, 188 383 houses were badly damaged, of which 105 000 were destroyed, creating 19 million tonnes of rubble and debris.

This devastation led to 1.5 million people being made homeless and having to relocate to emergency camps. The temporary nature and location of these camps, however, meant that 100 000 occupants were at critical risk from storms and flooding. A severe outbreak of cholera occurred nine months after the earthquake, in October 2010, killing a further 8927 people.

Resilience, adaptation, mitigation and management

Following the 2010 earthquake, several agencies worked together to provide relief for the people of Haiti. Many countries pledged search-and-rescue teams, and the neighbouring Dominican Republic was the first to send water, food and heavy lifting machinery. Médecins Sans Frontières (MSF) provided 28 640 tents, 2800 rolls of plastic sheeting and 85 000 emergency supply kits to people living near the epicentre. They also set up makeshift hospital tents to provide emergency surgery, saving an estimated 20 000 lives per day.

Mobile-phone technology was used to coordinate the relief effort. A group of companies, including CrowdFlower and Samasource, set up a text-message hotline which was supported by the US Department of State and advertised by Haitian radio stations. People in Port-au-Prince could send an SMS message to a toll free number to ask for help and these messages were then routed to emergency crews. **Crowdsourcing** also allowed the collection of information from people on the ground so that real-time maps could be produced to support the humanitarian response.

In terms of rehabilitation, the Disasters Emergency Committee (DEC) put out an appeal which raised £107 million. This money allowed the water supply to be improved for 340 000 people which, in turn, curbed the increase in cholera deaths (Figure 5.42). Drugs were given to five cholera treatment centres and, as a consequence, 18 000 people were treated for the disease. In addition to direct medical care, improved shelter was provided for 34 000 people, and tools and seeds were given to 23 000 farmers.

Planning and preparation was also improved with 116 000 people receiving information about preparing for future disasters, and 60 000 women were given literacy classes to help them support themselves and their families.

The Haitian people are vulnerable because they live in a multi-hazardous environment; there is little they can do to prevent hazardous events from occurring. However, the fact that Haiti is one of the poorest countries in the world increases their vulnerability – many of the buildings were not designed to withstand hazardous events and a lack of formal education means that the dominant perception of the hazard is acceptance.

Conclusion

The natural hazards that affect Haiti are an important reminder that it is the most vulnerable who tend to be the most affected in terms of injury and death. However, it is often the countries with a well-developed infrastructure that have most to lose economically. It is important to minimise the risk through monitoring and preparation and for governments to plan effectively for hazard events.

In terms of future change, volcanic and seismic events are unlikely to increase in either frequency or magnitude. However, the number of people exposed to the hazard risk is likely to increase with population growth and urbanisation, particularly in poorer countries of the world. Research into the effect of climate change upon the frequency and magnitude of tropical storm hazards is in its infancy. It is, however, likely that an increase in ocean temperatures will make storms more intense, thus making coastal populations more vulnerable.

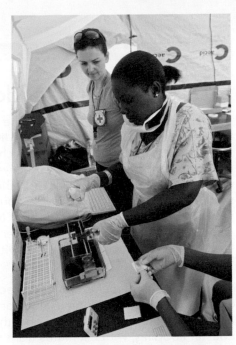

Figure 5.42 A health worker conducting tests in a makeshift tent laboratory in Port-au-Prince, Haiti.

 Key term

crowdsourcing: a way of obtaining information by enlisting the services of a number of people usually through the internet or mobile-phone technology

5.13 The UK, a hazardous environment

It is perhaps difficult to conceive of the UK as particularly hazardous. Sitting in the middle of the Eurasian Plate, the UK is many hundreds of kilometres away from its nearest subduction zone, which is located south of Greece. Even the nearest plate boundary, the constructive Mid-Atlantic Ridge, is too distant to constitute an earthquake hazard and the earthquakes it does generate are too small to trigger a tsunami. Tropical storms are also not considered hazardous to the UK. Situated between 50° and 58° N, the UK is a significant distance from the warm, tropical seas that produce the energy required for storm generation. Yet, the UK is a hazardous setting, albeit with hazards of magnitudes significantly less than those seen in Haiti.

Perhaps the greatest hazard that affects the UK is flooding – 1.7 million homes and 130 000 commercial properties are at risk of flooding in England alone. As a group of island nations, the UK is particularly susceptible to coastal flooding, with estimates from the Royal Institute of British Architects suggesting that 1.5% of the UK population is at risk. The section on coastal management in Chapter 3 Coastal systems and landscapes discusses in detail measures that are taken to reduce the risk of flooding in vulnerable coastal areas.

Coastal areas are not the only parts of the UK at risk. Many inland areas are vulnerable to flooding, usually as a result of unusually high levels of rainfall. The winter of 2013–14 was the wettest on record. Prolonged heavy rain caused local rivers to overflow and flood parts of the Somerset Levels so severely that they remained under water for months. One of the flattest areas in the UK, the Levels are an area of coastal plain and wetland in central Somerset, in the southwest of England, about 70 000 ha in extent, drained by the rivers Axe, Brue and Parrett. They consist mainly of agricultural land (principally dairy farming with some arable agriculture) with some wetland that provides an important habitat for birds and wetland plants, and some peatlands.

The use of the Levels for farming has been made possible by drainage measures such as ditches on farm fields that drain to the rivers, and periodic dredging of the rivers so that they do not become silted up. During the 2013–14 flooding, farmers were bitterly critical of the Environment Agency – the organisation responsible for this dredging – saying that it was not being carried out often enough and the major drainage rivers were badly silted up. The Agency argued that the Levels have long been subject to periodic flooding and so have good measures in place to tackle it. However, the prolonged nature of this flood and the depth of the water were of such a scale that the community could not cope.

People were trapped in their homes, unable to leave because of high and rising water. Approximately 600 homes were actually flooded. Some villages were cut off from the outside world entirely. Power supplies were cut off in several locations. Local businesses such as shops and pubs could not open, which meant they lost considerable revenue. Major as well as minor roads in the area were impassable (Figure 5.43), and local people reported increased levels of crime such as theft. Things were not helped by the fact that it continued to rain throughout much of the period, hampering flood relief efforts and adding to the swollen rivers.

Figure 5.43 A flooded road during the 2013–14 floods in England.

The response to the 2013–14 floods

In response to the situation, rescue boats were sent to collect people who were stuck in their homes, police numbers were increased and the Royal Marines were sent in to help with measures such as laying sandbags. In February 2014, the Environment Agency installed 13 giant pumps imported from Holland to remove water from the Levels, some parts of which had by then been covered with water for almost two months.

In March 2014, the Minister for the Environment announced a 20-year plan, 'The Somerset Levels and Moors Flood Action Plan', to better protect the Levels from devastating floods. Some of the actions included:

- dredging sections of the rivers Parrett and Tone as soon as possible
- making some temporary flood defences and pumping sites permanent
- helping local partners take more responsibility for water management on the Levels through a new Somerset rivers board
- supporting farmers to manage flood risk better
- ensuring new developments meet the highest standards for water and drainage.

The government allocated £10 million to help pay for these measures.

In addition to coastal and fluvial flooding, around 2 million people in the UK are at risk from pluvial flooding. This is flooding caused by extremely heavy downpours of rain which saturate urban drainage systems, meaning that excess water cannot be absorbed. The number of people in the UK at risk of pluvial flooding is likely to increase by 1.2 million by 2050 as a result of both climate change and population change. Interestingly, it is population change which is likely to have the greatest impact, being three times more likely than climate change to put people at risk. In addition, it is low-income residents who are more at risk given that pluvial flooding tends to concentrate in low-lying areas around town centres – areas dominated by terraced housing and flats.

Thinking like a geographer

Geographers need to be able to apply new information to their existing knowledge and consider the implications. To what extent can technology mitigate the impact of hazard events?

ACTIVITY 5.6

1   Throughout the chapter there are references to various hazards. Locate these on a world map and annotate the map to include four or five facts about each hazard event.

Physical and human

In the context of natural hazards, are physical or human factors more important in determining the impacts? Explain your answer.

For a blank world map, download Worksheet 5.5 from **Cambridge Elevate**.

Assess to progress

1   In the context of natural hazards, what is meant by
     the term 'perception'?   **1 MARK [A LEVEL]**

   A   This is where people local to the hazard believe that
       death is imminent as a result of factors beyond their control.

   B   This is the way in which someone understands or interprets a
       hazard. People tend to respond to hazards depending on their
       understanding and interpretation.

   C   This is the formal and informal education which people receive
       about hazards.

   D   This is the view that hazards are influenced by natural and human
       events, and their magnitude and frequency can be estimated based
       on experience.

2   Figure 5.44 shows the eruption of Cotopaxi in Ecuador
     on 14 August 2015. Examine the potential impact
     of the ash cloud.   **9 MARKS [AS LEVEL]**

Figure 5.44 The eruption of Cotopaxi, Ecuador on 14 August 2015.

3   Discuss how well the hazards associated with tropical
     storms can be managed.   **20 MARKS [A LEVEL]**

Tip

In question 2, think about the location of the volcano when trying to examine the impacts. What is Ecuador like in terms of its level of development? Are the impacts here likely to be similar or different to eruptions elsewhere in the world?

In question 3, you could consider how the management of hazards is likely to change over space and time. For example, you could consider how different countries manage tropical storm hazards and how tropical storm management may change in the future as a result of climate change.

Look on **Cambridge Elevate** for more information on natural hazards from the following websites:

- BBC Earth has information, links and videos to explain and illustrate ten different natural hazards (www. cambridge.org/links/ gase6048)

- the USGS has a homepage with links to a number of webpages detailing a variety of, mainly geomorphic, hazards (www.cambridge.org/ links/gase6049)

- Incorporated Research Institutions for Seismology (IRIS) has a number of factsheets explaining different aspects of seismic hazard (www. cambridge.org/links/ gase6050).

Ecosystems under stress

Figure 6.1 The illegal burning of tropical rainforests in Indonesia is causing the loss of the ecosystem and life threatening haze in towns and cities.

By the end of this chapter you should know:

- what biodiversity is and how and why it is changing
- how ecosystems work and how and why they may change over time
- the distribution and characteristics of two biomes
- the nature of a local ecosystem, the impact of change and management strategies
- about case studies of ecosystems at local and regional scales to illustrate how changes may lead to sustainable development.

Before you start...

You should know:

- biodiversity is crucial to planet Earth to sustain life
- human activity may cause a decline in biodiversity and the destruction of ecosystems
- different management techniques may ensure the sustainable development of ecosystems and biomes.

6.1 Ecosystems and sustainability

In the Amazon rainforest, a single tree can provide a home for up to 2000 species of birds, insects, fungi, **epiphytes** and microorganisms. This is the biodiversity or biological diversity for that single tree – the variety of plants and animals in an ecosystem.

 Key term

epiphytes: plants such as lianas that grow on other plants, using them to reach the sunlight or as a source of nutrients

Globally there are over 375000 known species of plants that produce flowers and 15000 known species of mammals and birds. There are thousands of small organisms or microorganisms that scientists have yet to identify.

Over time, there have been some catastrophic reductions in global biodiversity as a result of natural causes including continental drift, Ice Ages and the resulting climate change, but in recent years biodiversity has declined significantly. This is mostly as a result of human activity such as changing land uses, population growth, pollution, overexploitation and invasive species.

- More land has been converted for crop growing and grazing since 1950 and reservoir storage has increased at least four times.
- Farming practices have changed and there has been a rise in **monoculture**.
- Desertification as a result of farming and irrigation has increased.
- About 50% of mangrove swamps and 20% of coral reefs have been lost.
- Large areas of rainforest have disappeared because of illegal logging and slash and burn practices.
- Increasing numbers of animals and plants are on the endangered species list, e.g. the decline of red squirrels and puffins in the UK.
- Significant amounts of land have been lost to urbanisation and industrialisation including mines and quarries.
- Pollution and the impact of acid rain (Figure 6.2) have also been significant, particularly in Europe.

Key term

monoculture: the repeated growth of a single crop, often with the aid of large quantities of artificial fertilisers and irrigation

Figure 6.2 Extensive areas of forest have been destroyed by acid rain.

In recent years large areas of trees, especially coniferous trees, in north-west Europe have turned yellow, suffered die-back and died. This is a result of acid rain, precipitation polluted by oxides of sulphur and nitrogen (Table 6.1). The main sources of the pollutants are the burning of fossil fuels due to growing industrialisation and car ownership; increased use of electricity and major volcanic eruptions that release large quantities of sulphur into the atmosphere.

Acid rain is an international problem. Norway, for example, produces very little acid rain but 92% of sulphur deposition in the country comes from other countries, mostly Britain. There have been many international conferences and

Research point

Monsanto Company is an American multinational agrochemical and agricultural biotechnology corporation with its headquarters in Missouri, USA. It is a leading producer of genetically engineered (GE) seed and Roundup, a glyphosate-based herbicide. It attracts considerable controversy over some of its activities. Investigate the arguments for and against the use of genetically engineered seeds.

Country	Forest area (km²)	Extent of damage (km²)
Austria	375 400	9 600
Sweden	265 000	10 600
Finland	194 000	67 900
France	150 750	2 796
Germany	102 230	41 740
Poland	86 770	22 730
Norway	83 330	4 100
Italy	63 630	3 180
Hungary	16 700	1 837
Switzerland	12 000	4 320
Belgium	6 160	1 100
Netherlands	3 090	1 548
Luxembourg	820	423

Table 6.1 Damage to forests in Europe by acid rain.

EU directives and most countries have made progress in reducing emissions to reduce acid rain and climate change. This should reduce the loss of trees as a result and prevent further reductions in biodiversity.

ACTIVITY 6.1

1 What is acid rain? Explain its impact on forests.
2 Explain why acid rain is an international problem.

Maths for geographers

1 Using the data in Table 6.1, calculate the percentage of forest that has been damaged in each country.
2 On an outline map of Europe, draw a choropleth (shading) map to show the percentage of forest damaged in the countries shown in Table 6.1. See the Cartographic skills section of Chapter 13, Geographical skills and techniques for more about choropleth maps.
3 Describe and explain the pattern shown on your map.

Research point

Select a country in the EU and summarise its response to the need to reduce emissions of greenhouse gases. Research the outcomes of the December 2015 climate change conference held in Paris.

Making connections

Acid rain occurs when atmospheric pollutants, mostly produced by human activity, combine with rainfall. How does this happen? See the information on the water cycle in section 11.3 Water security.

For an outline map of Europe, download Worksheet 6.1 from **Cambridge Elevate**.

In some cases, a single action may lead to an increase in the destruction of habitat. For example, road construction in the Amazon rainforest is thought to have significant feedback effect (Figure 6.3).

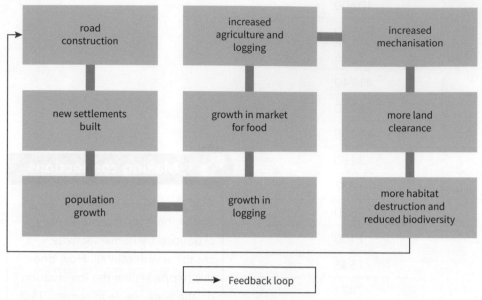

Figure 6.3 The feedback effect of road construction.

On a global scale, biodiversity is declining in all biomes but it can vary within and between different ecosystems (Figure 6.4). Initially, the most rapid rates of decline in biodiversity were within the developed countries but today the greatest losses are in the developing world. Areas with the most rapid losses since the 1990s are the Amazon basin and South East Asia (deforestation and expansion of farmland); the drylands of Asia (where farmland has been overused) and Bangladesh, the Indus valley, parts of the Middle East and East Africa. These are often called **biodiversity hotspots** – the tropical regions that may contain over half of the world's terrestrial species. It is thought that there were about 16 million hectares of tropical rainforest habitat originally, of which only 9 million hectares remain today. Today 160 000 km² are deforested each year.

Key term

biodiversity hotspots: biogeographic regions with significant reservoirs of biodiversity that are under threat from humans

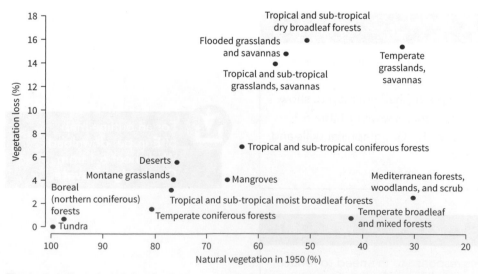

Figure 6.4 The relationship between native habitat loss by 1950 and additional losses since 1950.

ACTIVITY 6.2

Study Figure 6.4.

1 Describe the pattern of natural vegetation in 1950.
2 Suggest reasons why the boreal forests and tundra retained almost 100% of their natural vegetation in 1950.
3 What does Figure 6.4 show about the loss of natural vegetation before and after 1950? Suggest reasons for this pattern.

The impacts of declining biodiversity

In today's world, most habitats are destroyed as a result of human activities using the natural resources for farming, industry and urbanisation. These human activities bring advantages, but they also result in disadvantages because of the reduced biodiversity. Reducing biodiversity leads to many consequences, both physical and human.

Physical consequences

When vegetation is removed and replaced with bare ground or less species-rich plants, the **biomass** is reduced and more species of plants and animals may be threatened with extinction. Logging often increases the flood risk in India and Bangladesh and the threat of avalanches and mud slides may also be increased. Loss of vegetation leads to the reduced production of oxygen but increased carbon dioxide from burning of vegetation, contributing to global warming. There will be increased soil erosion from bare ground as a result of wind and overland flow and reduced soil fertility through increased **leaching** and lower inputs of organic matter.

Human consequences

Clearing land for human activity often increases resources from mining, logging or agriculture. However, the land cleared for agriculture often leads to monoculture, which encourages diseases that may destroy the crop and reduce food supplies. Local people may be moved away from their homes and land to make way for developments, which may cause increased hunger and poverty. Resources may be lost that are valuable in drug manufacture and there are fewer natural forests to counteract industrial pollution. Some problems such as acid rain are international; others are a product of globalisation that require political solutions, such as US companies clearing land in South America for agriculture. Both are difficult and expensive to resolve.

Ecosystems and their importance for human populations

Reductions in biodiversity mean that the world's ecosystems are being damaged. Ecosystems are vital for the health of human populations, but they need to be managed carefully in order to accommodate future population growth and economic development. People and human activities are an integral part of ecosystems and their activities can harm an ecosystem and, at worst, result in its total destruction. For centuries, people – especially those in the developed world – have damaged and destroyed ecosystems with little knowledge or thought about the long-term impacts, for example cutting down trees for farmland, burning fossil fuels or increasing urbanisation. Today there are similar pressures in the developing world.

 Key terms

biomass: the total amount of living matter in an ecosystem; it is highest in tropical rainforests

leaching: the loss of soluble nutrients from the soil by the movement of water

 Tip

Remember that if you are asked to write about the impact of something, include both advantages and disadvantages.

 Thinking like a geographer

To what extent should the developing world be allowed to alter or destroy its ecosystems in the name of progress?

There is now much greater knowledge and understanding about the workings of ecosystems, their importance and the benefits of maintaining the richest biodiversity possible. Therefore, human populations are taking a much greater interest in and practical steps towards maintaining and developing ecosystems to ensure future sustainability. This will ensure the conservation and preservation of a rich and diverse plant and animal life in healthy ecosystems rather than their gradual destruction and the extinction of more plant and animal species.

There have been a number of International Conventions such as Rio in 1992, Rio+20 in 2012 and Conventions on Biological Diversity, the most recent being in 2010 in Nagoya, Japan. The European Commission has also published directives for members to promote habitats and wildlife. In some countries, including the UK, Biodiversity Action Plans (BAPs) and Biodiversity Frameworks have been published. Research has led to detailed mapping of landscapes that have been denuded and counts of threatened plants, animals and birds. The article *Puffins and turtle doves in serious decline across Europe* provides information about the demise of puffins reported in 2015, but they are not alone in being under threat. In the UK, BAPs cover habitats, land and marine animals and birds. A new BAP published in 2007 identified 1149 species and 65 habitats needing conservation and greater protection including hedgehogs, otters and red squirrels.

A variety of initiatives are in place to encourage the recovery and sustainability of ecosystems and to encourage the maintenance of biodiversity. In the UK, *Biodiversity 2020: A strategy for England's wildlife and ecosystem services* summarises the plans to meet international and EU targets. Some of the initiatives include:

- laws protecting wildlife
- funding projects by other groups and charities
- expansion of National Parks
- creation of Sites of Special Scientific Interest (SSSIs)
- new Nature Improvement Areas (NIAs)
- new Marine Protected Areas (MPAs)
- better education in schools and children learning outdoors
- the Big Wildlife Garden scheme
- agri-environmental schemes
- expansion of woodland and their sustainable management
- river basin planning and flood and erosion management.

Making connections

MPAs are just one strategy to attempt to preserve global biodiversity. What are they and how do they work? You can find out more about MPAs in section 7.7 The global commons.

Investigate

Many local authorities, universities and other groups have their own BAP. Investigate a plan of your choice. What are the main aims of the plan and how does the organisation hope to achieve them?

For more questions on biodiversity, download Worksheet 6.2 from **Cambridge Elevate.**

Puffins and turtle doves in serious decline across Europe

By Christian Nordqvist

Puffins and turtle doves are in serious decline across Europe, as are several other bird species, according to a new report announced by Bird Life International on behalf of the International Union for Conservation of Nature.

There are now eight bird species in the UK considered to be facing the risk of extinction.

More information on this year's changes

Atlantic Puffin: also known as the common puffin *(Fratercula arctica)*, it still has a global population in excess of one million. However, breeding failures in some important colonies over the past few years have been worryingly high. There has been a severe decline in the number of young puffins being recruited into the breeding population. In the Faroe Islands, Norway and Iceland, which hold 80% of the European population, numbers have fallen considerably. Fair Isle and the Shetland Islands in the UK have seen populations plummet. However, it is doing well in other parts of the country.

Turtle Dove: Streptopelia turtur used to be a familiar visitor across Europe,

Figure 6.5 The Atlantic puffin breeds in Norway, Greenland, Iceland, Newfoundland and several North Atlantic islands, and as far south as Maine in the west and the British Isles in the east.

including the south-east of England. Since the turn of the century, populations across the continent have declined by over 30%. Its status has deteriorated from Least Concern to Vulnerable. Experts from the RSPB and BirdLife International partners are currently trying to find out why numbers are falling in the UK and the rest of Europe. The turtle dove population has fallen by more than 90% in Britain since the 1970s

ACTIVITY 6.3

Read the news article on puffins and turtle doves.

1 Explain why there is a concern over the reduction of puffins.
2 Why do you think populations of puffins are declining in some areas but not in others?
3 To what extent would you agree that the demise of the puffin and turtle dove are a mini version of the state of the world's biodiversity?

Look on **Cambridge Elevate** for more information on global diversity from the following websites:

- A Government policy paper on biodiversity (www.cambridge.org/links/gase6051)
- A Biodiversity implementation plan from Defra (www.cambridge.org/links/gase6052)
- Joint Nature Conservation Committee Biodiversity news from Defra (www.cambridge.org/links/gase6053)
- Institute of Oxford Assessing Ecological Value of Landscapes Beyond Protected Areas (LEFT) (www.cambridge.org/links/gase6054).

6.2 Ecosystems and processes

Studying an ecosystem is a useful way of looking at the interaction of plants, animals (including people), soil and climate in an area (Figure 6.6). An ecosystem is a natural unit in which **biotic** and **abiotic** components interact with each other to produce a stable system that is in equilibrium, that is, in balance with little change. This balance is maintained by the flow of energy and cycling of nutrients through the ecosystem. Biotic components are the living organisms, animals, people, microorganisms, trees and other plants, whereas the abiotic components are the inorganic or non-living elements such as the soil, climate, relief and drainage.

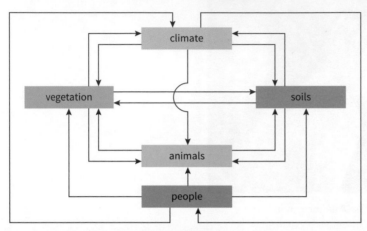

Figure 6.6 The structure and flows of an ecosystem.

Most ecosystems are named after the most recognisable feature – the vegetation – for example tropical rainforest, coniferous forest or desert. Ecosystems can also be studied at different scales from an individual tree, pond or hedgerow to the scale of a biome – the global or large-scale ecosystems such as the tropical rainforest.

In an ecosystem there are two organic elements: the biomass and the dead organic matter. The biomass is the total amount of living matter including the organic matter above ground (stems, leaves and animals) and that found below ground (roots, microorganisms and burrowing animals). The largest biomass is found in the tropical rainforests where it measures 4500 g per square metre. One of the smallest is in the **tundra** where the mosses and lichens generate a biomass of only 60 g per square metre. Dead organic matter includes the soil **humus** and the **litter layer**, the dead organic matter of twigs and leaves at the soil surface.

Energy flows, trophic levels, food chains and food webs

The main source of energy for all ecosystems is the Sun. Green plants photosynthesise using energy from the Sun. They are the only plants to do this and therefore they are called **primary producers**. The energy produced is used by the plants for growth and plant processes such as root uptake of water.

Animals that eat plants are called herbivores or primary consumers. They also use the energy for growth and life processes such as breathing, movement and keeping warm. Other animals may eat the primary consumers and these are carnivores or secondary consumers. Other carnivores may then eat the secondary consumers. This process is called a **food chain** and each level in the food chain is called a **trophic level** (Figure 6.7).

At each level, 90% of the energy is lost through heat, dead organic matter and other life processes, so only 10% of the energy is available for the next trophic level. This means that few food chains have more than four or five trophic levels because only 10% of the energy survives across each level. As a result, any producer or consumer can support only a small number of organisms above it in the food chain.

Key terms

biotic: the living components of an ecosystem (e.g. the plants, animals, people and soil microorganisms)

abiotic: the non-living or physical components of an ecosystem (e.g. the climate, soil and drainage)

tundra: the word means 'barren land'; located in arctic or alpine regions where no trees grow because of severe environmental conditions

humus: the dead organic matter incorporated into the soil

litter layer: the layer of dead organic matter lying on the soil

primary producers: mostly the green plants that are able to produce nutrients or biomass using chemicals in the presence of sunlight

food chain: energy transfer in the form of food from plants to herbivores to carnivores

trophic level: the level at which energy, in the form of food, is transferred from one group to another (e.g. from plants to herbivores in a food chain, sometimes called a feeding level)

Thinking like a geographer

Study Figure 6.7 and think about why a pyramid is a good form of presentation. Why are vegetarians/herbivores considered to be the most efficient consumers?

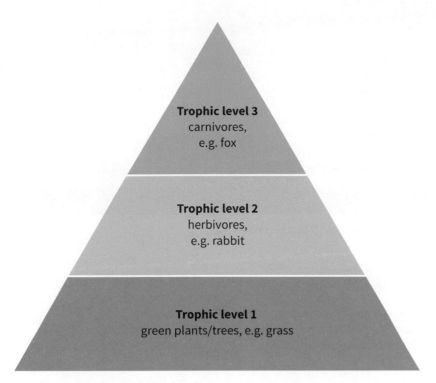

Figure 6.7 Food chains and trophic levels.

In reality, food chains are too simple a representation of ecosystems – consider just how many primary consumers feed on grass. It is more realistic to use a **food web** (Figure 6.8) that can show the complexity of food chains in an ecosystem or a pyramid that groups the producers and consumers into trophic levels (Figures 6.9 and 6.10).

Key term

food web: a series of interconnected food chains showing how energy is transferred in an ecosystem

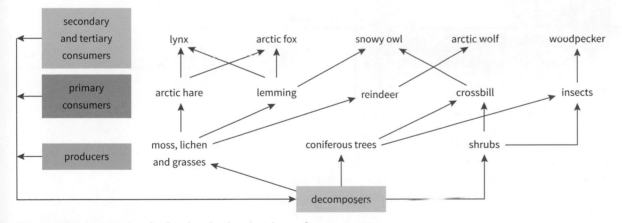

Figure 6.8 An example of a food web: the deciduous forest ecosystem.

ACTIVITY 6.4

1 Define the terms 'biomass', 'ecosystem', 'food web' and 'trophic level'.
2 Explain why green plants are called primary producers.
3 Why are there rarely more than four or five trophic levels in a food chain?
4 Using Figure 6.8, explain why a food web is a better representation than a food chain for a deciduous woodland.

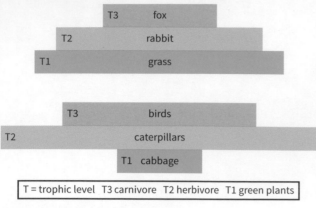

Figure 6.9 Pyramid of number.

Figure 6.10 Pyramid of biomass.

Systems concepts in ecosystems

An ecosystem is an open system with inputs, outputs, stores and transfers (Figure 6.11). When the inputs and outputs are balanced, the ecosystem is in equilibrium. If one element changes, it upsets the balance and affects other parts of the ecosystem.

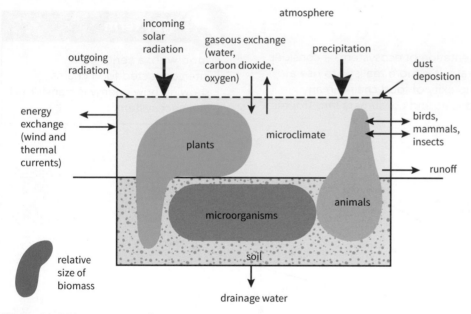

Figure 6.11 The structure of an ecosystem.

ACTIVITY 6.5

1   Study Figure 6.11. For each label, decide whether it represents an input, an output, a store or a transfer.
2   What does the diagram suggest about the location and size of the stores of nutrients in an ecosystem?

Biomass and net primary production

Productivity is the rate at which energy is absorbed or fixed by green plants. Gross primary production (GPP) is the total amount of energy that is used and absorbed for life processes and for growth. **Net primary production (NPP)** is

Key term

net primary production (NPP): the growth rate of vegetation in an ecosystem, usually measured by the increase in biomass in a year; high in rainforests and low in deserts

the element that is used for growth only. It is therefore the growth rate of the vegetation measured by the increase in biomass over a year, for example tonnes per hectare per year (Table 6.2).

Ecosystem	Mean net primary production ($g/m^2/year$)	Annual total net primary production (10^9 tonnes)
tropical rainforest	2200	47.4
deciduous forest	1200	7.0
tropical grassland	900	12.0
temperate grassland	600	7.2
coniferous forest	800	7.8
tundra and alpine	140	1.3
hot desert	90	1.3

Table 6.2 Net primary production in selected ecosystems.

Where there is ample light, carbon dioxide, water, nutrients and high temperatures – as in tropical rainforests – productivity is high. Where one or more of these factors is lacking or in poor supply – as in tundra or desert environments – productivity is low (Figure 6.12).

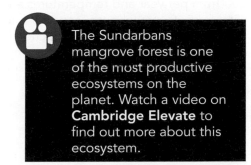

The Sundarbans mangrove forest is one of the most productive ecosystems on the planet. Watch a video on **Cambridge Elevate** to find out more about this ecosystem.

Tropical rainforest

- High productivity.
- Abundant heat, light and moisture.
- Huge range of plants and trees in several layers.
- Vast quantities of nutrients rapidly cycled.

The arctic ecosystem

- Low productivity.
- Rarefied atmosphere, low amounts of CO_2.
- Cold temperatures hinder plant growth.
- Water mostly frozen, so unavailable.
- Sparse vegetation; small, low growing and little organic matter and nutrients.

Figure 6.12 High and low productivity ecosystems.

The oceans cover about 70% of the Earth's surface but only generate about 33% of the total net primary productivity. The land surface generates the other 67%, the forests contributing the greatest proportion at 46%. The tropical rainforests are particularly important, contributing 27% of the total.

Figure 6.13 shows the global distribution of net primary production. High productivity areas are dominated by the tropical rainforests in Central and South America including the Amazon Basin, parts of Indo-Malaysia and the north coast of Australia, and parts of West Africa including the Congo Basin. These are the humid tropics – areas of tropical rainforest where rainfall exceeds 2000 mm per year and temperatures are uniformly high at over 27 °C. The climate gives 'greenhouse' conditions ideal for all-year-round and rapid growth of vegetation. Net primary production reaches 2200 g/m²/year – the highest of any natural ecosystem – which is why there are global concerns over the destruction of forest environments, especially those in the rainforests.

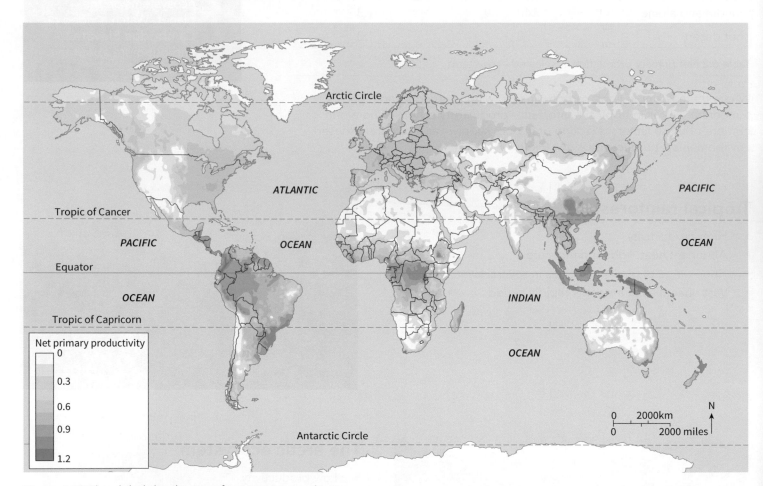

Figure 6.13 The global distribution of net primary production.

Areas with low net production are the Arctic and alpine tundra areas and the hot deserts. Here, climates are severe: either too hot or too cold and dry. In all of these areas, moisture is unavailable to plants for a large part of the year and soils tend to be thin, infertile and low in organic matter. The vegetation tends to be sparse and low growing with few trees and the biodiversity is low with typically fewer than 100 species of plants, often in a single layer. Nutrient levels are low and cycling of nutrients slow. There is little storage of nutrients, the biomass is small and growth is slow. Very little litter reaches the ground during the year and decomposition is slow, so few nutrients are added to the soil. Net primary productivity is therefore very low.

The impact of human activity has in general been to reduce productivity. For example, pastureland has only about one-third of the productivity of forested land. Cropland may reduce productivity by as much as 75%. Therefore, the clearance of forests for farmland reduces productivity.

However, human activity can attempt to increase productivity by breeding high yielding varieties of crops and animals, increasing inputs of fertilisers and pesticides, using intensive farming techniques such as double cropping, irrigation and shortening food chains. The most efficient trophic level is the second level – that of the herbivore or, in human terms, vegetarians. Many more people can be fed from a field of wheat or rice than on the animals grazed on the same area of land.

Succession, climax vegetation and seres

The vegetation in an area may change over time in a process called **succession**. Where the process begins on areas of bare rock or where there has been no previous soil formation, it is called **primary succession**. Sometimes there may be a change within an environment with some existing vegetation such as a change in the climate, drainage or soil. This change may cause the vegetation to change and this process is called **secondary succession**.

Eventually, plant succession comes to an end when no further changes in the vegetation take place. The vegetation is then in equilibrium with its environment and this is called the **climatic climax vegetation**. This status is maintained until further environmental changes take place in the ecosystem.

The climatic climax vegetation is the most complex vegetation the environment can support where the **dominants** are the tallest trees or plants that can grow. In deciduous woodlands the dominants are the tall trees such as oak or beech – often up to 30 metres tall – whereas in hot deserts the dominants may be the low growing xerophytic plans often only a few centimetres above the ground level.

On the global scale there tends to be specific vegetation zones that approximate the world climate zones. These global vegetation zones are called biomes. In a biome, the dominant plants can be recognised, such as oak trees in deciduous woodlands or lichens in the tundra. In reality, the pattern of vegetation is more complex because of the many small-scale variations in climate, rock type, relief and drainage in areas.

All vegetation types that exist but are not the climatic climax vegetation are called **sub-climax vegetation** types. In a sub-climax vegetation, the plant succession is interrupted and the climatic climax vegetation is not achieved. This is a result of **arresting factors** such as:

- natural events such as volcanic eruptions, hurricanes or fires caused by lightning
- human activity such as burning, clearing land for farming, dam building, urban and industrial developments
- local variations in soils, relief and drainage as in upland areas, lakes and sand dunes.

These arresting factors cause other vegetation types to become dominant, often for long periods of time. This is the sub-climax vegetation. If it is a consequence of human activity, it is called a **plagioclimax community**.

Plant succession goes through a series of stages such as from mosses to grasses to small shrubs to trees. Each of these stages is called a **seral stage** and the plant communities that are in succession but not at the climatic climax vegetation are called **seral communities**. The whole succession is called a sere and there are two main types:

Physical and human

Compare Figure 6.13 with a map of population density and distribution in an atlas or on the internet.

1. In small groups, discuss the patterns shown on both maps. Is there any correlation between NPP and population density and distribution?
2. Suggest reasons for any patterns.
3. What are the implications for global biodiversity of the patterns?

Key terms

succession: the stages vegetation goes through from colonising a bare surface to reaching the climatic climax vegetation

primary succession: succession from a bare rock surface where there has been no previous soil formation or vegetation, such as bare rock, a volcanic eruption, a mudslide or a sand dune

secondary succession: succession where there is some pre-existing soil and vegetation

climatic climax vegetation: this is the final point in a succession when no further changes will take place; the vegetation is in equilibrium with the environment

dominants: the tallest plants/ trees that will grow in an environment (e.g. oak trees in deciduous forests)

sub-climax vegetation: the vegetation that results when arresting factors interfere and stop the succession towards the climatic climax vegetation

- **Priseres** or primary succession on new inorganic surfaces where there has not been any soil formation or vegetation; Figure 6.14 shows a classification of priseres.
- **Subseres** or secondary succession on sites where there has been some previous soil formation and vegetation but where the climatic climax vegetation or a succession has been interrupted by arresting factors.

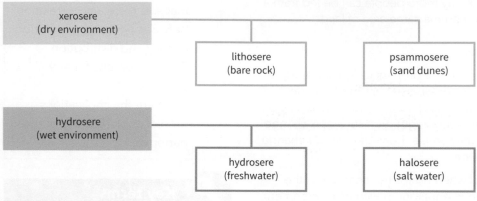

Figure 6.14 Classification of priseres.

Making connections

A psammosere is the plant succession that takes place in an area of sand dunes. What does this succession look like and how and why does it take place? See section 3.4 Coastal landscape development.

Primary succession

Primary succession begins in areas where there has been no soil formation or pre-existing vegetation – a **lithosere** (Figure 6.15). Examples are rare in the world as most land surfaces have had time for soil and vegetation to develop. The most common sites where primary succession can be found are bare rock surfaces exposed by quarrying, on material left after mudflows and landslides, and on new land created by lava flows from volcanic eruptions.

The first plants to colonise a surface are called **pioneers**. These are usually lichens and mosses that do not require any soil to survive but break down the rock into particles of sand, silt and clay. As the mosses and lichens die, they add dead organic matter or humus to the minerals and so start the process of soil formation. As time progresses, the soil becomes deeper and richer until eventually grasses and herbs germinate and grow, the seeds having been transported in by water, birds, the wind or animals. The grasses and herbs eventually become dominant and shade out the mosses and lichens. The process of soil formation continues and the grasses and herbs may then be replaced by seedlings and shrubs and eventually young trees will dominate. Faster-growing tree species dominate first, later to be replaced by slower-growing dominants that form the climatic climax vegetation.

Key terms

arresting factors: natural or human events that interfere with succession, leading to the establishment of a sub-climax vegetation

plagioclimax community: a sub-climax community formed as a result of human activity in an area

seral stage: each stage in a succession with a different type of vegetation is called a seral stage

seral community: plants that occur together in a seral stage such as the lichens or the shrubs

prisere: primary succession on a bare inorganic surface where there has not been any soil formation or vegetation

subsere: secondary succession on a surface where there has been prior soil formation and vegetation

lithosere: plant succession on a dry, bare rock surface

pioneers: the first vegetation to colonise in a prisere; usually mosses and lichens

Trend of succession in lithosere				
Pioneer community	Seral communities			Climax community
1	2	3	4	5
Lichens stage	Moss stage	Herb stage	Shrub stage	Forest
General trend of succession →				

Figure 6.15 The seral stages in a lithosere from a bare rock surface to tropical rainforest.

A lithosere: Surtsey, a volcanic island close to Iceland

Surtsey (Figure 6.16) was created following a volcanic eruption that reached the surface of the sea in November 1963 and ended in June 1967. The island reached its maximum size of 2.7 km² in 1967. Since then, wave erosion has reduced the island to just 1.4 km². The maximum elevation in 2007 was 155 m above sea level. The island currently loses about 1 ha of land each year, but it is not likely to disappear totally as parts of the island are covered in hard lava flows that are resistant to erosion.

The island has been intensively studied by botanists and biologists because of its uniqueness as a lithosere ready for colonisation by plants and animals. Table 6.3 shows the succession that has occurred on Surtsey and Figure 6.17 shows the island in 1999.

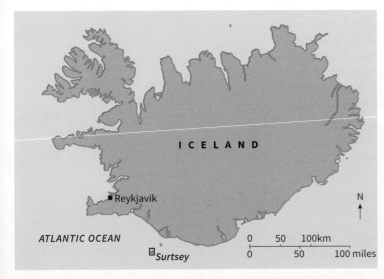

Figure 6.16 The location of Surtsey, off the south coast of Iceland.

Figure 6.17 Surtsey in 1999.

Download Worksheet 6.3 from **Cambridge Elevate** to see how a fieldwork study can be based on vegetation and soils.

Date	Plant life	Birds	Other life
1964			First insects seen – flying insects
Spring 1965	First vascular plant		
1967 eruptions ended	Mosses detected	First bird life seen	Insects increased over time and provided food supply for birds
1970	Lichens found on lava	First birds nesting – fulmar and guillemot	
1984		Gull colony established	
1985	Extensive coverage by mosses and lichens 20 species of plants observed over time but only 10 established in the infertile sandy soils	Birds used plants for nesting material but also spread seeds and fertilised the soil with guano (the excrement of sea birds and bats)	
1993			First earthworm found, probably brought over by a bird
1998	First bush found, a willow		Slugs found
2004		First evidence of nesting puffins	
2008	69 species of plants had been found of which 30 had established (compared with 490 species on mainland Iceland)	12 species found regularly	
2009		Golden plover nesting	

Table 6.3 Succession on Surtsey.

Secondary succession

Secondary successions begin in areas where there has been some soil formation and pre-existing vegetation that has been modified or destroyed. In many areas of the world, arresting factors have removed or prevented the climatic climax vegetation from being achieved. If the arresting factor is relaxed or removed, succession can recommence. This is called secondary succession or a subsere and the vegetation passes through a series of well-defined stages or seres just as in primary succession.

There are few parts of the world where people have not had an impact on vegetation. Human activity usually has a retrogressive effect on the vegetation, making it less complex and reducing biodiversity, such as when forests are replaced with grassland for grazing. Where the arresting factor is a result of human activity and is relaxed, the succession is called a plagiosere.

Examples of secondary succession include the following:

- Renewal of a forest after a fire: seeds, roots and the soil remain, so gradually the plants and trees begin to grow again, eventually returning to the original ecosystem.

- Secondary forest growth after logging: a large amount of trees are chopped down by loggers. Over time, trees grow back and the area returns to something like its original state.
- Regrowth of vegetation after a flood affecting farmland: after the waters recede, vegetation can regrow in the soil. Eventually a secondary succession can occur and the vegetation that had previously grown there can regrow.
- Regrowth of plants after attack by pests: when the pest overpopulation is resolved, the plants return to thrive in the soil in which they had previously lived.

Secondary succession is usually much quicker than primary succession because there is an existing seed bank of suitable plants in the soil and roots, and tree stumps and other plant material can regenerate quite quickly. There is also pre-existing soil which is suitable for growth.

Mineral nutrient cycling

The plants and animals in ecosystems require nutrients such as calcium, phosphorus and nitrogen. These nutrients or chemical elements are circulated within the ecosystem. These transfers in an ecosystem are best summarised in a model of **mineral nutrient cycling** (Figure 6.18).

Key term

mineral nutrient cycling: the movement of nutrients from the soil to the biomass to the litter in an ecosystem

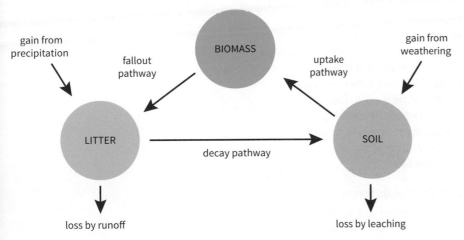

Figure 6.18 A model of mineral nutrient cycling.

Tip

The model represents the storage and flows of *nutrients* in the ecosystem, not the size of the biomass, soil and litter.

The model has three circles representing the amount of nutrients stored in the ecosystem in the biomass, soil and litter. The biomass is the living plants and animals. Some of the biomass is above the ground surface, such as the tree trunks and canopy and the land animals, but some is below ground, such as the roots, burrowing animals and microorganisms. The soil is a non-living or abiotic component where nutrients are held in the dead organic matter or humus in the

213

soil. The litter is the dead organic matter that lies on the soil surface. Typically, deciduous trees shed their leaves, building up a layer of litter on the soil surface. This gradually decomposes over time and may become incorporated into the soil by the activity of earthworms and other burrowing animals.

Between each of the stores – the biomass, soil and litter – the arrows indicate the flows of nutrients. Between the biomass and soil stores there is the uptake (or growth) pathway. This indicates the uptake of nutrients such as nitrogen, potassium and phosphorus from the soil into the vegetation. Another chemical element circulated within an ecosystem is carbon.

 Making connections

A key nutrient to be cycled in an ecosystem is carbon. How is carbon cycled in the natural environment? See Chapter 1 Water and carbon cycles.

The fallout pathway represents the addition of nutrients to the litter as a result of the death of plants and animals. When the litter is decomposed to form humus and the nutrients are returned to the soil, this is the decay pathway.

Nutrient storage may change over time. Nutrient cycling is an open system as nutrients may be added or lost from the ecosystem, for example losses from runoff and leaching and gains from precipitation, lightning, wind-blown leaves and weathering. Animals, birds and insects may also move into and out of different ecosystems, transferring nutrients.

Human activity may also have an impact on the nutrients in ecosystems. People may add nutrients through organic fertilisers such as dung and manure, inorganic fertilisers (manufactured compounds of nitrogen, phosphorus and potassium) and by planting trees and other plants. However, most human activities have a negative impact on ecosystems, resulting in the loss of nutrients. Examples include deforestation resulting in soil erosion, farming practices causing overgrazing and overcultivation, wood shortages leading to the use of crop stalks and manure as fuel that could otherwise be used as fertiliser on the land, and harvesting which removes nutrients from the ecosystem.

Mineral nutrient cycling in the tropic rainforest and deciduous forest

In Figure 6.19, the size of the circles represents the amount of nutrients stored in the biomass, litter or soil and the width of the arrows shows the nutrient flow as a percentage of the nutrients stored in each circle.

In tropical rainforests, very little litter collects on the forest floor because it is rapidly decomposed in the hot, wet climate. The tropical soils also contain few nutrients. There are high rates of weathering and of leaching, which means that soils are deep

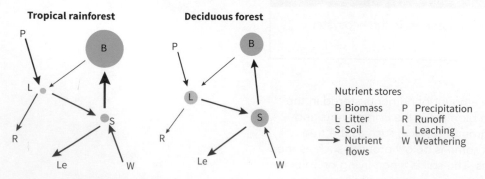

Figure 6.19 Nutrient cycling in the tropical rainforest and the deciduous forest.

but lacking in nutrients. As a result, the vast amount of nutrients in the rainforest, often over 90%, are held in the forest biomass. The nutrient circulation is rapid as a result of the hot, wet climate which makes growth and decay rapid. In the tropical rainforest, three to four times more nutrients are returned to the soil in a year than in deciduous forests, where the short **growing season** restricts both growth and decay. In deciduous forests the distribution of nutrients is relatively even between the biomass, soil and litter. The soil and litter are well supplied compared with the tropical rainforest, although the generally smaller trees and fewer layers of vegetation mean the nutrient store in the biomass is smaller.

Key term

growing season: the length of time in a year when the temperature is above about 5 °C to allow plant growth; the rainforest growing season is all year, but it is only a couple of months in the tundra

Making connections

Weathering is the disintegration of rocks in situ. How does this happen in different climates and environments? See section 4.3 Systems, processes and landscapes.

Complete Worksheet 6.4 from **Cambridge Elevate** to check your understanding of nutrient cycling.

Terrestrial ecosystems

Terrestrial ecosystems are those found on land as opposed to marine ecosystems associated with oceans and seas. The major global biomes (see 6.3 Biomes) are a product of the interactions between climate, vegetation, soil and topography in an area. A global map of vegetation types suggests that the UK should have a vegetation cover of deciduous woodland with some coniferous woodland to the north and west. However, there are a number of different natural ecosystems in the UK, as shown on Figure 6.20. This shows what the natural vegetation would have been like without 3000 years of human activity.

The landscape in Figure 6.20 shows a variety of ecosystems such as deciduous forests, coniferous forests, heaths, moorlands and wetlands. This is a result of variations in climate, relief, soils and drainage and the impact of a long history of human activity.

Temperate deciduous forest

In the UK, deciduous woodland is the climatic climax vegetation for large areas of the country. Most deciduous woodlands have four layers of vegetation (see Figure 6.49). The canopy is the tall deciduous trees, 30–40 m high, such as oak or ash. Below the tall trees is a sub-canopy composed of young tree saplings ready to take advantage of any clearing created by a fallen tree. Below this is the shrub layer with a variety of vegetation such as bramble, ivy and hazel, and where the light allows there will be a ground or field layer of grasses, bracken and plants like bluebells that flower in spring before the canopy grows. The upper layer of trees is called the canopy and levels of light penetration through the canopy impact on what vegetation can grow below. Sycamore trees, for example, have large leaves that allow little light to penetrate and therefore there is often little vegetation below. Oak and ash trees have smaller leaves and allow a greater amount of light to penetrate, so there is often a rich shrub layer and ground vegetation in woodlands where these species dominate.

Ecosystem change

Factors that lead to change in an ecosystem are known as 'drivers' and they may be direct or indirect. A direct driver influences the ecosystem itself, whereas an

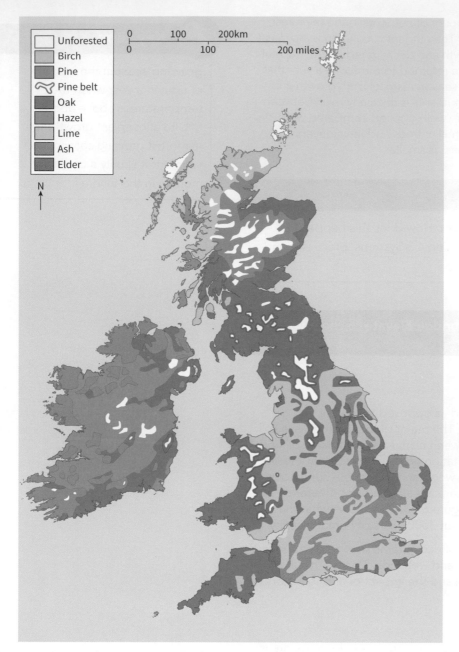

Figure 6.20 Natural ecosystems in the UK.

indirect driver operates by changing one or more direct drivers. Table 6.4 shows some examples of drivers in ecosystems.

Direct drivers	Indirect drivers
changing land use/cover	population change
fishing and hunting	change in economic activity
climate change	sociopolitical factors
invasive species, pests and diseases	cultural factors
pollution	technological changes

Table 6.4 Drivers in ecosystems.

Direct drivers

In terrestrial ecosystems the most important direct driver is changing land use, in particular the conversion of land to cropland and the logging of forests. Only biomes relatively unsuited to growing crops such as deserts, boreal forests and tundra have remained largely unchanged by human action.

In freshwater ecosystems the main direct drivers are dam building (see 6.13 Three Gorges Dam), invasive species and pollution.

Eutrophication

Excessive amounts of nitrogen may cause eutrophication and can threaten biodiversity in different ecosystems. Eutrophication shows that excessive fertiliser is being lost from farmland or there is excessive sewage or manure entering water courses. Eutrophication causes:

- high nitrate concentrations in drinking water, leading to the excessive growth of algae and causing algal blooms
- increased costs of water treatment
- depletion of dissolved oxygen
- reductions in harvestable fish and shellfish
- decrease in aesthetic value of the water body
- decreased biodiversity.

Algal blooms reduce the sunlight for organisms on river and lake beds. Dissolved oxygen increases during the day, but is greatly reduced after dark. These changing conditions and increased nitrogen may allow new species such as the common carp, which is adapted to living in eutrophic areas, to invade. If the level of dissolved oxygen falls too far, fish and other marine animals may die.

Climate change

In 2014, the Inter-Agency Climate Change Forum published a paper called *Biodiversity and Climate Change in the UK*. It states that climate change is a reality and describes:

- an increase in land temperature of 1 °C since 1980
- an increase in sea surface temperature of 0.7 °C since 1980
- a sea level rise of 10 cm since 1990
- eight out of ten of the warmest years on record since 1990
- an increase in annual precipitation – greatest in winter, with possible summer decrease.

Some scientists claim that climate change in the past century has already had an impact on ecosystems. They point to changes in species distributions, the timing of reproduction or migration and an increase in the frequency of pest and disease outbreaks, especially in forested systems (see the Ash dieback section in this chapter.)

Continuing climate change is expected to have an impact on ecosystems and biodiversity. The distribution and abundance of plants and animals changes along with the timing of seasonal events such as breeding and migration, both of which are getting earlier. Habitats and ecosystems will change as drainage and soil moisture change. There is increased decomposition in bogs and a northward shift in animals, birds, vegetation and agricultural practices. Some of the possible positive and negative effects of climate change are shown in Table 6.5.

Indirect drivers

The global population has doubled in the past 40 years, reaching 6 billion in 2000, and about half the people in the world now live in urban areas.

Positive effects	Negative effects
Growing new crops, especially in the south and east – Figure 6.21 shows a vineyard in Kent	Risk of deoxygenation of freshwater in summers if they are hotter and drier
Higher growth rate in forests – increased biomass	Drier summers will lower the water table, drying out upland soils and clay soils and leading to more erosion; already affects 35% of blanket bog in Scotland
Northward shift in farming types, increasing productivity in some areas	General decline in mountain (e.g. and sedges)
Increased potential for tourism and recreation	Declines in some species (e.g. ring ouzel)
	Earlier breeding and migration often means the food supplies they rely on are not available, leading to decline in populations
	Increased spread of invasive species (e.g. Chinese mitten crab)

Table 6.5 Possible positive and negative effects of climate change in the UK.

Figure 6.21 Biddenden Vineyard in Kent, established 1969.

Global economic activity has also increased nearly sevenfold between 1950 and 2000. As a result, the demand for many ecosystem products grows but the type of products in demand changes. For example, in terms of food the importance of staples (such as rice, wheat and potatoes) declines and diets include more fat, meat, fish, fruit and vegetables. This leads to changes in land use, with more urban, industrial and agricultural land and increased logging of timber for fuel.

Sociopolitical and cultural drivers influence ecosystem management and the use of ecosystem products. There has been a rise in elected democracies, which has helped give power to local communities, especially women. Different cultures also value different ecosystem products and have different attitudes to conservation practices.

 Making connections

Global population growth has been rapid but how and why has population growth changed over time? See Chapter 10 Population and the environment.

The development of science and technology has important implications for ecological systems, which may be positive or negative. Much of the increase in agricultural output over the past 40 years has come from an increase in yields rather than an expansion of farmed areas. For example, in developing countries wheat yields rose 208%, rice yields rose 109% and maize yields rose 157% in the past 40 years.

Ash dieback – the impact of pests and diseases

In recent years large numbers of elm trees have been lost due to Dutch Elm disease and since 2010 ash trees are being killed by Chalara, a fungus which causes leaf loss and lesions in the ash trees. This is often called ash dieback. The ash trees become so weak that they are often attacked by other pests and diseases, especially the honey fungus.

Incidences in Britain

The first signs of ash dieback were found in 2012 in a tree nursery in Buckinghamshire and later in both Norfolk and Suffolk. Since then, further cases have been identified especially in Eastern Scotland and in South-East England (Figure 6.22).

Implications of outbreaks

Ash dieback has killed many ash trees in Europe, especially young saplings, and the impact may be similar in the UK (Figure 6.23).

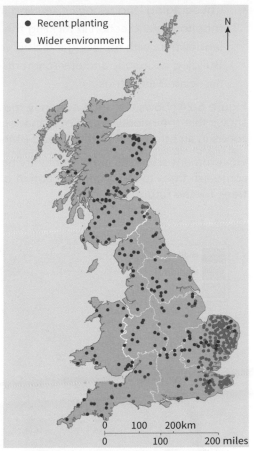

Figure 6.22 Outbreaks of ash dieback in recently planted sites and the wider environment, 2014.

Figure 6.23 Ash dieback.

Management

Department for Environment, Food and Rural Affairs (Defra) has a Chalara Management Plan in place, which sets out action around four key objectives:

* Reducing the rate of spread of the disease.
* Developing resistance to the disease in the native ash tree population.

- Encouraging landowner, citizen and industry engagement in surveillance, monitoring and action in tackling the problem. Funding is available to help landowners with replacing infected young ash trees.
- Building economic and environmental resilience in woodlands and associated industries.

Figure 6.24 shows the areas currently most at risk from ash dieback. Figure 6.25 shows that the priority areas for management lie just beyond the most at-risk zones in an effort to stop the spread of the fungus further.

Government scientists are currently trying to identify the genes which enable some ash trees to resist the infection in order to use these to breed new ash trees for the future.

Figure 6.24 Areas of Britain most at risk from ash dieback, 2013.

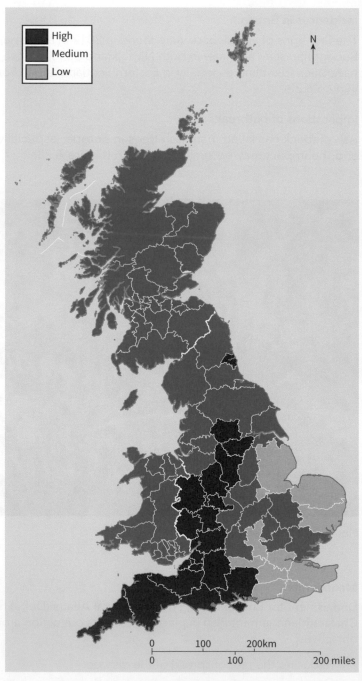

Figure 6.25 Priority areas for management of ash dieback, 2017.

ACTIVITY 6.6

1 How and why is Chalara threatening Britain's ash trees?
2 Why is it important to implement a management plan to try to maintain ash trees in Britain?
3 Explain the significance of the high priority area shown on Figure 6.25.

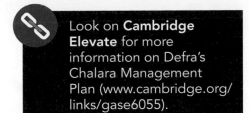

Look on **Cambridge Elevate** for more information on Defra's Chalara Management Plan (www.cambridge.org/links/gase6055).

6.3 Biomes

Biomes are large-scale or global ecosystems. A world map of biomes (Figure 6.26) tends to be a map of the world vegetation zones. These major global ecosystems are also closely linked to the world maps showing the distribution of **zonal soils** (Figure 6.27) and climate (Figure 6.28).

Climate has a strong influence on soil type and similar climatic areas tend to have similar zonal soils. In turn areas with similar soils and climate tend also to have similar vegetation types. Climate is usually the main controlling factor in the location and distribution of different types of vegetation. A study of Figures 6.26, 6.27 and 6.28 shows that areas with a humid tropical climate largely have **latosol soils** and tropical rainforest vegetation. Similarly, areas with an arid tropical or hot desert climate have desert soils and desert vegetation. Figure 6.29 shows the temperature and precipitation associated with different world biomes.

Key terms

zonal soils: the global soil types

latosol soils: the typical soil type below tropical rainforest; it has a very deep, red colour because of iron and aluminium in A horizon

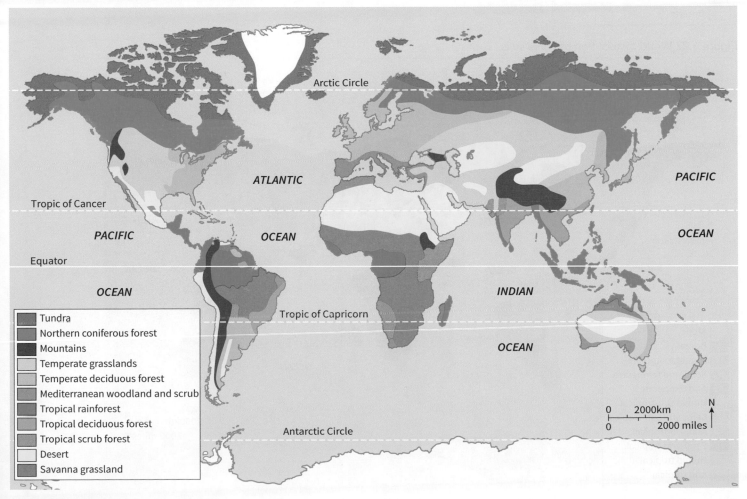

Tundra
Northern coniferous forest
Mountains
Temperate grasslands
Temperate deciduous forest
Mediterranean woodland and scrub
Tropical rainforest
Tropical deciduous forest
Tropical scrub forest
Desert
Savanna grassland

Figure 6.26 World distribution of biomes.

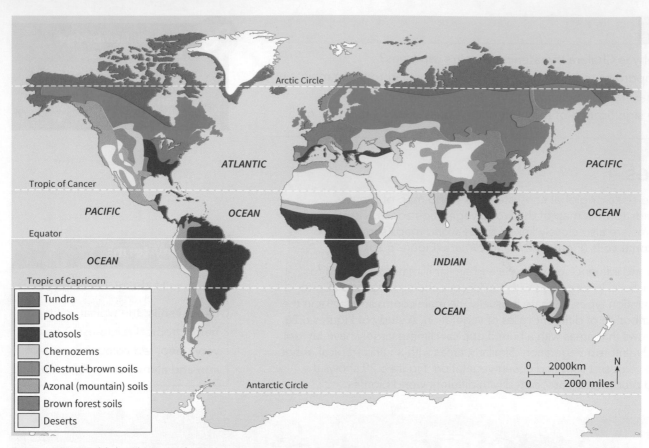

Figure 6.27 World distribution of zonal soils.

Legend:
- Tundra
- Podsols
- Latosols
- Chernozems
- Chestnut-brown soils
- Azonal (mountain) soils
- Brown forest soils
- Deserts

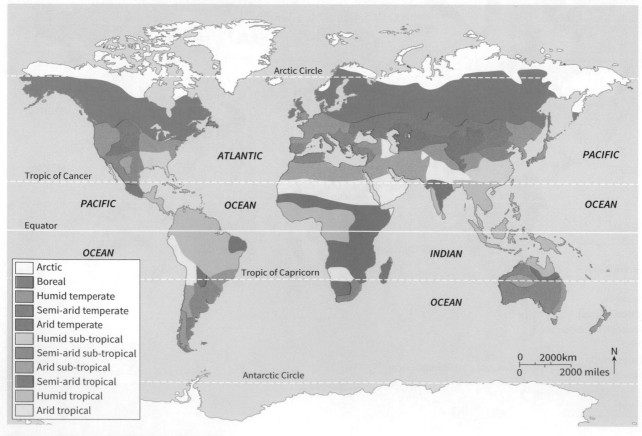

Figure 6.28 World distribution of climate.

Legend:
- Arctic
- Boreal
- Humid temperate
- Semi-arid temperate
- Arid temperate
- Humid sub-tropical
- Semi-arid sub-tropical
- Arid sub-tropical
- Semi-arid tropical
- Humid tropical
- Arid tropical

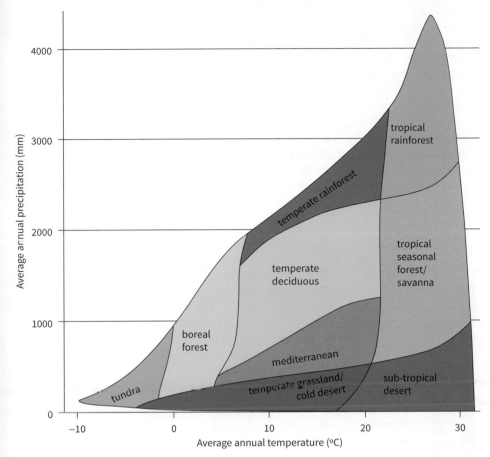

Figure 6.29 Temperature and precipitation associated with different world biomes.

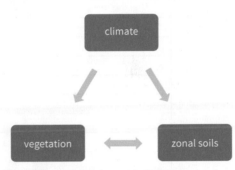

Figure 6.30 The relationship between climate, soils and vegetation.

Figure 6.30 shows how climate, soils and vegetation interact. Climate is the dominant factor, with its influence on both soils and vegetation. It determines the temperatures in regions and the precipitation, which in turn affects rates of evapotranspiration in plants. Different **fauna** (animals) and **flora** (plants) can tolerate different temperature ranges and amounts of precipitation, so the climate has a direct impact on the fauna and flora in an area.

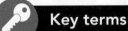

Key terms

fauna: the animal life in an ecosystem

flora: the plants and trees in an ecosystem

ACTIVITY 6.7

1 Using Figures 6.26, 6.27 and 6.28, fill in a table like the one below. Select eight biomes from Figure 6.26 to complete the table.

Biome	Climate	Vegetation	Soil type	Locations

2 To what extent is there a link between the world distributions of soils, vegetation and climate?

Savanna grasslands

Savanna grasslands are areas with predominantly grass or up to 50% tree cover with grasses. They are located in a broad band either side of the equator between the Tropics of Cancer and Capricorn (Figure 6.26) mainly in Africa, South America and Northern Australia.

Climate

The climate is always hot and there is a long dry season (Figure 6.31), which may be the cause of limited tree growth. However, rainfall totals may vary between 500 mm to over 2000 mm per year and hence some areas of savanna may be a plagioclimax vegetation as a result of the removal of trees by felling, fire or grazing animals.

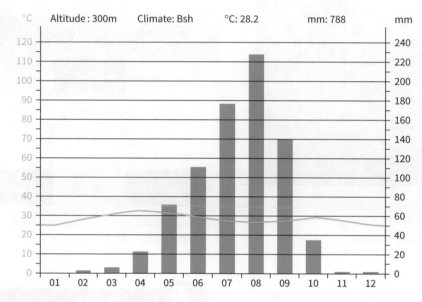

Figure 6.31 Climate graph for Burkino Faso.

Soils and soil moisture budget

The characteristic soils of savanna areas are similar to those of the tropical rainforests, the red, iron rich latosols (see Tropical rainforest, a high productivity biome). However, the lower rainfall totals and long dry season reduces the weathering and leaching processes, meaning soils are richer in silica and organic matter than in the tropical rainforests. In the long dry season there is an upward movement of water through the soil profile and evaporation at the surface may lead to the deposition of salts on the soil surface (salinisation) creating duricrusts. These may prohibit plant growth.

Vegetation structure and types

Tropical savannas generally have just one or two layers of vegetation, which are either all grasslands or grassland interspersed with trees that do not form a continuous canopy. Most savanna vegetation has drought resistant features. There are many different types of grasses and some may grow up to 3.5 metres in height (elephant grasses). Most die back in the dry season. Trees are also xerophytic or drought resistant, such as acacias and the baobab tree.

Savanna vegetation is well adapted to the drought and is called xerophytic. The trees and plants often have long tap roots to reach water sources deep

 Key term

salinisation: the process whereby land becomes increasingly salty, ultimately becoming desertified

below the surface. Leaves are often small and limited in number to reduce moisture loss by evaporation. In the dry season many plants and trees lose their leaves to conserve water. Figure 6.32 shows a baobab tree with its large trunk for water storage. The bark is thick to reduce evapotranspiration and to protect against fire.

Productivity

Tropical savanna covers about 21% of the Earth's land surface and mean net primary production is about 900 g/m² per year, less than half of that of the tropical rainforests but higher than temperate grasslands and coniferous woodlands. The productivity varies spatially depending upon the vegetation cover and the length of the dry season.

Fauna and its adaptations

The dominant animals in the savanna are the large grazing animals such as the zebra, giraffe, antelope, elephant and wildebeest. The greatest variety are found in the African savanna lands. Burrowing rodents are also characteristic of savanna, as well as the large carnivores such as lions and hyenas who are the natural predators of the grazing animals (Figure 6.33).

Figure 6.32 A baobab tree.

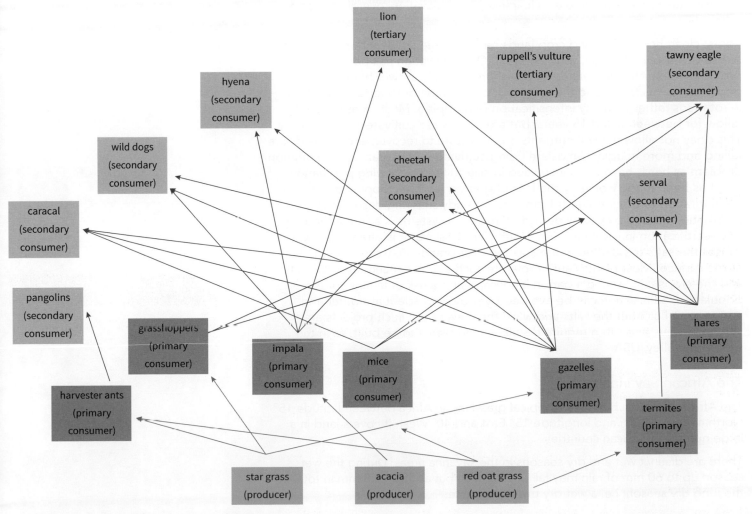

Figure 6.33 A food web for the savanna biome.

The animals of the Savanna have undergone many unique adaptations. The African wild dog is fast with long legs to chase its prey. They also have good eyesight and strong teeth for hunting. The giraffes are well adapted too, being able to go for long periods without water and having long necks to reach vegetation at higher levels and to watch for predators.

Human activity and its impact upon the biome

The traditional users of the savanna are the nomadic pastoralists, who herd their cattle to find pastures where rain has fallen and who cultivate only small patches of land. The land has low productivity and this is the most effective use of the savanna which is very easily damaged if population numbers increase leading to over population, over grazing, over cultivation and widespread wood cutting. The ecosystem is delicately balanced and easily becomes unsustainable and unusable in a process called desertification.

Desertification is a process that begins with a loss of vegetation cover as a result of either human activity or a period of drought. The reduced vegetation cover means that less organic matter is incorporated in to the soil, so less moisture and nutrients are retained and the soil surface is also open to erosion by wind and water. The bare surface is also baked hard by the sun to form a crust that may be impermeable to water. Over time the African savannas have been worst hit by desertification, with reports from the Sahel as long ago as the 1970s. Desertification can result from periods of drought but human activity is also a major cause as a result of forest clearance, overcultivation, overgrazing and salinisation.

Forest clearance for fuel and crop lands removes tree cover and exposes the soil to damage by the sun, wind and rain. Overcultivation has been a particular problem in the African savanna lands, where the only answer to growing populations was to expand the area under cultivation or to reduce the fallow in rotations rather than any intensification of cropping. Most areas were left fallow for between 8 and 15 years, but are now being cultivated more quickly. This does not allow the soil nutrients and moisture to recover, and so yields are falling and more marginal lands are being cultivated. Overgrazing is a common problem as herds have been increased in size to feed a growing population. This has been made worse by the loss of grazing land to cropping and by the migration of other nomads from areas already suffering desertification. Salinisation caused by poorly designed irrigation systems is also contributing to desertification in savanna areas. Insufficient freshwater is often used, which causes the salts to build up in the soil and evaporation may cause a salt crust at the surface. Most plants cannot tolerate such a high concentration of salts and the crops fail, leaving a barren landscape and a risk of famine for the population. Salinisation can be avoided by providing adequate water and drainage to flush out the salts and wash them away, but such projects are very expensive and often require desalinisation plants to be built, as in the Colorado Valley, USA.

The African Savanna biome

The African Savanna biome is a tropical grassland in Africa between latitude 15° North and 30° South and longitude 15° East and 40° West. It covers land in a large number of African countries.

There are distinct wet and dry seasons in the savanna areas. During the wet season up to 60 mm of rain may fall each month but as little as 8 mm in total in the long dry season; i.e. a wet dry tropical climate.

The savanna regions are mostly grassland dotted with trees, which may form up to 50% of the ground cover (Figure 6.34). There are many different types of grasses, such as Bermuda grass and elephant grass, and trees, such as the baobab, the acacia and the candelabra tree. Savanna lands support large numbers of animals and birds including many large plant-eating mammals. Animals include lions, wildcats, rhinos, antelopes, zebra, elephants and giraffes.

Figure 6.34 The African Savanna.

The plants and animals are very well adapted to the environment. Some animals choose to migrate to other areas when it becomes too hot or too dry, others burrow into the ground. Others are very fast to catch and kill their prey.

Human activity has been important in savanna regions. In recent years increased human populations have led to overgrazing and over cultivation which has turned savanna areas into desert. Fires, both natural and artificial, also destroy the land although some species like the baobab are fire resistant. The use of fuel wood for fires has also caused the loss of trees and led to desertification. Poaching has damaged the animal life, along with hunting for ivory, safari shoots and hot air balloons, which frighten away the animals.

Some efforts have been made to preserve and conserve the savanna environment, including controlled burning, national parks and nature reserves. South Africa has a biosphere reserve and the Serengeti has several conservation areas and a National Park, which is now a world heritage site.

ACTIVITY 6.8

1   Explain why the savanna biome is such a fragile ecosystem.
2   How should countries like Burkino Faso respond to threats to the ecosystem?
3   To what extent should the traditional way of life be preserved?

Tropical rainforest, a high productivity biome

Location

The tropical rainforests of the world are mostly located between 10° north and south of the equator, including:

- parts of Central and South America, including the Amazon Basin
- parts of West Africa, including the Congo Basin
- parts of Indo-Malaysia and the north coast of Australia.

Climate

Figure 6.35 shows a climate graph for Manaus in the Amazon Basin in Brazil.

The climate in tropical rainforests is that of the humid tropics: hot and wet all year. Temperatures in the tropical rainforests are hot all year round, with a mean monthly temperature of 27 °C and an annual temperature range of only about 4 °C. Annual rainfall totals are often in excess of 2000 mm, relatively evenly distributed throughout the year. In some areas there may be a short drier season of 1–2 months. The humidity is often over 80% and the combination of heat and wet generates 'greenhouse' conditions ideal for rapid growth of vegetation. The growing season is all year round.

Soils and soil moisture budget

The tall trees and dense vegetation cover suggest that the soils are rich and fertile. However, this is not the case. The soils are varied but mostly infertile latosols rich in iron and aluminium, which gives them their characteristic red colour. They are a product of intense weathering and leaching, and high acidity. The latosols contain little organic matter because of rapid decomposition and uptake by plants, as well as strong leaching.

The soils are often very deep (up to 30 m), as intense weathering has continued for thousands of years. The horizons are often difficult to see because of rapid and intense leaching in the tropical downpours (Figure 6.36). The minerals in the soil are broken down and soluble minerals are washed downwards, leaving the iron and aluminium behind and giving the soil its red colour (Figure 6.37). The year-round growing season gives a continuous input of leaf litter as the trees do not shed their leaves all together. The decomposition and nutrient cycling is rapid, so the litter store is small.

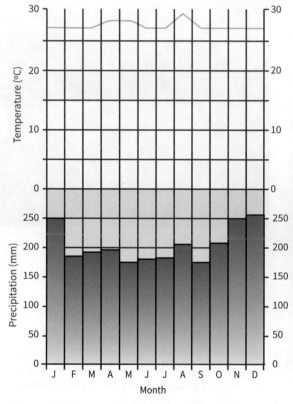

Figure 6.35 Climate graph for Manaus, Brazil.

Vegetation structure and types

The soil moisture budget is high in tropical rainforests because the amount of precipitation exceeds that lost by leaching or evapotranspiration. Therefore, water supply is abundant and not a limiting factor for vegetation growth.

The tropical rainforests are the richest and most productive biome in the world. They cover less than 5% of the world's surface, but are home to up to 80% of terrestrial plants and animals. No single species of tree dominates the forests and there are no large stands (clusters) of a single species. A single hectare of tropical rainforest may contain over 200 species of plants. The forest has an evergreen appearance, but the trees are broad-leaved deciduous and they lose their leaves throughout the year, which is why the forests look permanently green. Species are mostly hardwoods such as mahogany, teak and rosewood, as well as rubber trees, wild banana and cacao (the raw material for cocoa).

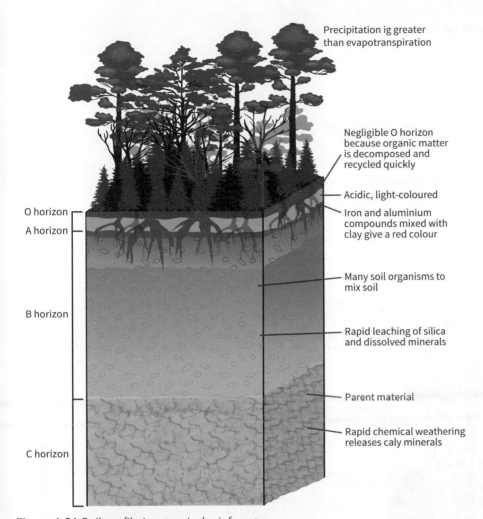

Precipitation ig greater than evapotranspiration

Negligible O horizon because organic matter is decomposed and recycled quickly

Acidic, light-coloured

Iron and aluminium compounds mixed with clay give a red colour

Many soil organisms to mix soil

Rapid leaching of silica and dissolved minerals

Parent material

Rapid chemical weathering releases caly minerals

O horizon
A horizon
B horizon
C horizon

Figure 6.36 Soil profile in a tropical rainforest.

Figure 6.37 Latosol soil.

The tropical rainforest is stratified and five layers can often be recognised, as shown in Figure 6.38:

- Emergent trees, often up to 45 m tall, stick out above the canopy to ensure efficient photosynthesis.
- Below the emergents lies the canopy layer at 15–30 m.
- At 10–20 m grows the understory, including young trees ready to take advantage of any clearing that emerges.
- Under 10 m is a shrub layer with ferns.
- A ground layer may be present if sufficient light penetrates. There may also be parasitic plants that feed on the dead organic matter on the forest floor.

Crossing these layers are the epiphytes such as lianas, orchids, ferns and creepers, which climb up the taller trees to reach the sunlight.

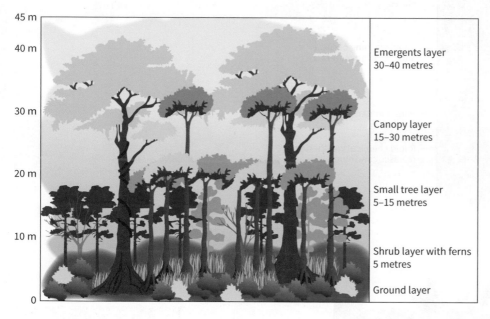

Figure 6.38 The structure of the tropical rainforest.

Adaptations of the vegetation

Trees have slender trunks and thin, smooth bark to maximise water loss and because there is no need to protect from frost. The trees grow tall to reach the light for maximum photosynthesis, so they have few branches and shallow roots to make maximum use of moisture and nutrients in the surface of the soil. **Buttress roots** allow massive uptake of water and nutrients, as well as providing some support (Figure 6.39).

Fruits and flowers appear on tree trunks, using energy in new growth (this is called **cauliflory**). Leaves are grown and cast off continuously, reflecting the all-year-round growing season and giving the forest an evergreen appearance, although the trees are broad leaved and deciduous. Large, leathery and shiny leaves may develop **drip tips** to shed water rapidly. This encourages transpiration and reduces rotting. There is little development of a shrub or ground layer because of lack of light. The vegetation grows rapidly to compete for sunlight and leaves are able to twist to maximise sunlight for photosynthesis.

 Key terms

buttress roots: very large roots of trees in the tropical rainforests, which allow the rapid and massive uptake of water and nutrients by the tree; they may also have a support function

cauliflory: the production of flowers and fruits from the trunks of tropical trees

drip tips: the pointed ends of the leaves on many tropical rainforest trees to encourage the shedding of water in order to avoid blocking stomata and the development of bacteria and fungus

Figure 6.39 Giant buttress roots in the rainforest.

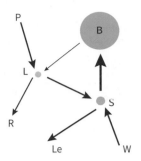

Nutrient stores

B Biomass P Precipitation
L Litter R Runoff
S Soil L Leaching
→ Nutrient W Weathering
flows

Figure 6.40 Nutrient cycling in the tropical rainforest.

Nutrient cycling

Figure 6.40 shows nutrient cycling for the tropical rainforest.

The nutrient cycling diagram for the tropical rainforest shows the huge store of nutrients in the biomass, reflecting the massive trees and the complex layering of the vegetation. The litter and soil stores are relatively small because of the rapid decomposition of the litter and then its rapid uptake by the roots from the soil. Therefore, the cycling of the relatively small nutrient stock in the tropical rainforest is rapid, continuous and almost leak-free due to the constant high temperatures and rainfall. At any time most of nutrients are held in the vegetation and therefore this is a major impact of deforestation in tropical rainforests. Losses from leaching and runoff can be significant in the wet climate.

Water is a major component of tropical rainforests and carbon is a key nutrient.

Productivity

Net primary productivity is 2200 g/m²/year, the highest of any natural ecosystem.

Fauna and its adaptations

The tropical rainforest supports about 30 species of animals per hectare and about 40 000 species of insect. Overall, it is thought to be home to over 20% of the world's birds, 90% of all primates and 50 million species of invertebrates. The animals tend to favour different ecological niches or layers within the tropical rainforest, so that many animals live only in very limited areas.

Most the animals are **arboreal** and live in the canopy layer. The winds in the emergent layer make it largely empty except for birds of prey. The ground has few residents, although tapirs in Brazil and tigers in Malaysia are exceptions. Figure 6.41 shows a possible food web for the rainforest.

Human activity and its impacts on the biome

The traditional inhabitants of the rainforests, such as Amerindians in the Amazon Basin, are well adapted to life in the tropical rainforest. They live by hunting and gathering, fishing and shifting cultivation. Their way of life is in harmony with the

Tip

In a nutrient cycling diagram, remember the circles and arrows are proportional to the stores and flows of nutrients in each ecosystem, not the size of the trees, litter or soil.

Making connections

Refresh your knowledge of the cycling of water and carbon by looking again at Chapter 1. See section 1.1 Water and carbon cycles as natural systems.

Key term

arboreal: relating to trees and usually an animal's habitat

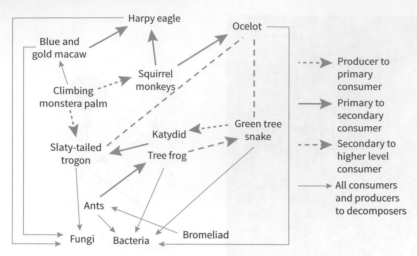

Figure 6.41 A food web for a rainforest system.

environment and sustainable as long as population numbers and density remain low. In recent years, population growth and the development of the rainforest has seen large areas deforested with negative impacts on the ecosystem. The greatest tropical rainforest clearances are caused by logging forests, not only for the timber itself but also to create land for ranching or agriculture, mining, road building, dam building and settlements. In some cases, governments have given incentives to foreign firms to invest and develop tropical rainforest areas. Deforestation in the rainforests is also a result of the intensification of shifting cultivation. As populations increase and the land available for the local people is reduced, they are forced to clear land for agriculture more quickly before the nutrients have been restored fully. The nutrient decline means that the tropical rainforest cannot regenerate and land becomes deforested. Increased populations also causes increased collection of wood for fuel, which removes vegetation. The deforestation removes most of the nutrients from the tropical rainforest, leaving behind relatively infertile latosols exposed to heavy rain which results in leaching and soil erosion.

The tropical rainforests are one of the most threatened ecosystems on Earth. They used to cover 14% of the land surface, but now it is only 6%. At the current rate of deforestation, they could disappear in 40 years with a massive impact on global biodiversity. Not only will individual species disappear, but more significant is the loss of ecosystem functions which are critical for human life, such as oxygen production, cycling of water and nutrients and climatic controls. The destruction of the tropical rainforests has been a global cause of concern for several decades because of the severe implications for biodiversity, climate and sustainability.

Thinking like a geographer

To what extent are the impacts on biodiversity and sustainability of developments in the tropical rainforests potentially more damaging than in the tropical savannas?

The impact of deforestation may lead to the loss of up to 50% of all plant, animal and microorganism species. Ponds in the tropical rainforest may hold more fish species than live in all of Europe's rivers and a 10 h plot may have 700 species of tree, more than in all of North America.

There may be the loss of some species not yet even identified, along with 50 000 other tree species every year. The traditional inhabitants lose their land and way of life.

Forests, and especially tropical rainforests, are the source and maintenance of life on Earth. Tropical rainforests provide 20% of the world's oxygen, they are an important carbon sink and their loss will increase global warming. There would be increased leaching and runoff because of less transpiration and interception and the storage of freshwater will be threatened. One-quarter of modern drugs – such as rosy periwinkle (or Madagascar periwinkle), effective in treating childhood leukaemia – come from tropical rainforests and these may be lost. Some 80% of the world's foodstuffs, such as avocados, rice, yams, chocolate, sugar cane and nuts, as well as rubber, also come from tropical rainforests.

Madagascar

Madagascar (Figure 6.42), situated in the Indian Ocean, is the fourth largest island in the world and a biodiversity hotspot. As a result of continental drift Madagascar, like the Galapagos Islands, has been isolated from other countries for thousands of years. As a result, 90% of the plants and animals are found nowhere else on Earth, i.e. they are endemic. Lemurs are one of the island's endemic species (Figure 6.43).

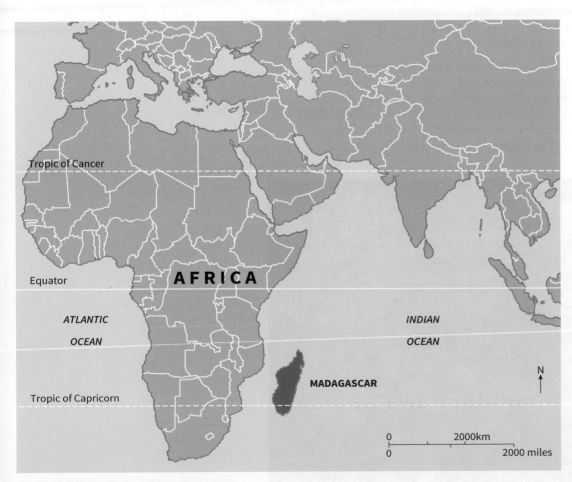

Figure 6.42 The location of Madagascar.

Figure 6.43 Madagascan lemurs.

Threats to biodiversity

Activities that damage the ecosystems on Madagascar threaten the unique flora and fauna, for example the Madagascar periwinkle is unique to Madagascar and is used to treat Hodgkin's disease and leukaemia.

In Madagascar traditional land uses, such as slash-and-burn farming and collecting fuelwood, have caused significant loss of tropical rainforest (Figure 6.44). These activities have caused air pollution, the loss of forest and the extinction of animals such as the pygmy hippopotamus. Forest fires have added to this. Madagascar today only has about 10% of its original forested area. However, not all of the forest loss is a result of traditional

Figure 6.44 Rainforest in Madagascar.

activities. In recent years, forest has been cleared to make way for cattle grazing, coffee growing, charcoal production and the legal logging of some valuable hardwoods. It is thought that all of the island's forests outside of the protected areas will have been cleared by 2025.

In 1986 the RTZ Corporation began to explore for ilmenite, a chemical that is used as a whitener in paint and toothpaste. Deposits were found in the forested areas where endemic plant and animal species were located. The Madagascan government and the World Bank were in favour of the RTZ project mainly because of the economic gains. The government would own 20% of the shares and the income could help reduce the country's debt. In August 2005 the decision to mine was made. Undoubtedly, mining will contribute further to the loss of biodiversity in Madagascar.

Protecting biodiversity

In 1997 the Masoala National Park was created with the aims of protecting several threatened animal species including the aye-aye and the lemur, creating corridors of vegetation to allow the safe migration of animals, educating the local people and protecting coastal coral reefs.

In 2003 'the Durban Vision' was announced, with the aim of trebling the island's protected areas to over 60000 km² (Figure 6.45). Since 2011 areas protected include five strict nature reserves, 21 wildlife reserves and 21 National Parks.

ACTIVITY 6.9

1   Create a table to compare and contrast savanna grassland and tropical rainforest biomes. You could use the following table as a model.

Feature	Savanna grassland biome	Tropical rainforest biome
Climate		
Soils		
Soil water budget		
Vegetation structure		
Vegetation adaptations		
Fauna and adaptations		
Productivity		
Nutrient cycling		
Human impacts		
Effect on biodiversity and sustainability		
Techniques of conservation and preservation		

2   Imagine you are a delegate attending an annual biodiversity conference. Prepare a five-minute report to present to the conference, justifying the need to preserve the biodiversity of Madagascar and suggesting actions that should be taken on both a global and national scale.

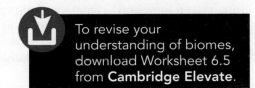
To revise your understanding of biomes, download Worksheet 6.5 from **Cambridge Elevate**.

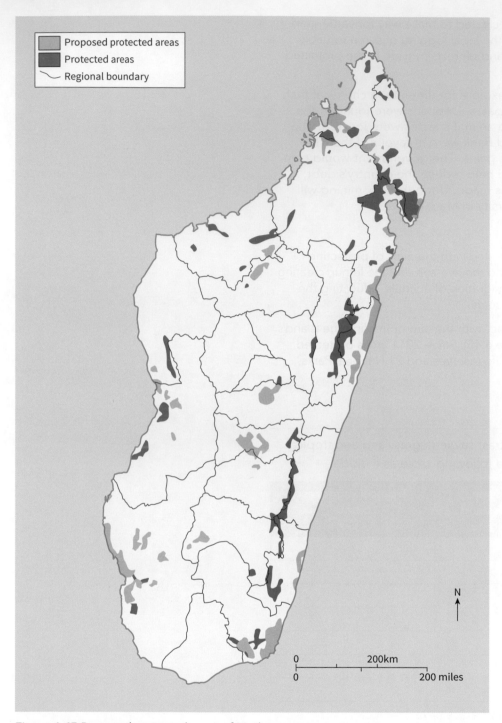

Figure 6.45 Proposed protected areas of Madagascar.

6.4 Ecosystems in the British Isles over time

Succession and climatic climax

Britain has a temperate climate and the vegetation is temperate deciduous forest. However, this is a generalisation as human activity has removed large areas of the natural vegetation and in other areas, variations in relief, soils and climate have meant the climatic climax vegetation cannot be achieved.

Mountainous areas such as the Lake District, Scottish Highlands and Snowdonia have steep relief and high altitude giving rise to a colder, wetter climate and thin, acid soils. As the altitude increases, the deciduous woodland is replaced by coniferous woodland and then on the summits tundra vegetation and bare rock. In other upland areas there are large expanses of heather moorland or heathland.

In some lowland areas with sandy, infertile soils such as the Brecklands in south-east England there heathland or areas of sand dunes where marram grass grows. In other places, there are areas of marshland and bog where alder and willow grow.

In some areas primary succession towards the climatic climax can be seen, such as in **hydroseres** and lithoseres. Examples and also example of secondary succession may also be seen.

> 🔑 **Key term**
>
> **hydrosere:** plant succession in a freshwater environment

Primary succession: a hydrosere on a small loch in Scotland

Ponds and lakes often demonstrate the characteristics of a hydrosere, an example of a prisere. This is the primary succession from a freshwater surface with floating plants to the climatic climax vegetation. In Figure 6.46 the hydrosere of a small loch in Scotland is shown and there are six seral stages identified by the growth of different plant species.

Stage 1 The floating plants grow and dead material decomposes to form organic mud, a layer in which other plants can then grow.

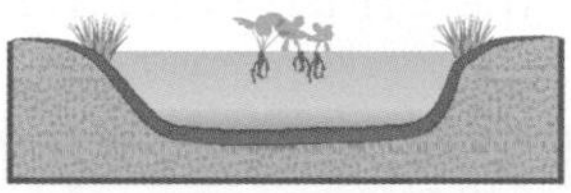

Stage 2 Plants such as sedges grow in the organic mud. They too add organic material and trap sediments, increasing the 'soil' depth and nutrient content. Gradually, the area of open water is reduced.

Stage 3 Areas with the deepest soils begin to dry out, allowing bog vegetation to grow.

Stage 4 Further drying out allows soil to develop and the bog gives way to grasses.

Stage 5 The process continues and grasses give way to heathland with heather, gorse, small bushes and trees. This is called Carr vegetation.

Stage 6 Eventually the climax vegetation of deciduous woodland may be reached with oak, birch and beech trees.

Figure 6.46 A hydrosere.

Primary succession: a lithosere

Lithoseres are rare in the British Isles as most areas have pre-existing soil formation and vegetation cover. The limited examples in the UK are mostly found on quarry faces where new rock is exposed, an example being Holme Park quarry (Figure 6.47).

Home Park quarry

Holme Park quarry in Cumbria is a limestone quarry (Figure 6.48) and has been in use for over 50 years. The quarry has areas of limestone pavement and one forms an island in the centre. The management team, county council and members of the community have worked hard to restore areas within the quarry.

Access for the community and visitors was increased, allowing people to learn about the nature and geology that the quarry and surrounding area have to offer.

Figure 6.47 Home Park quarry will be used until 2021, then returned to nature.

Figure 6.48 A limestone section of the quarry.

The characteristics of the climatic climax in the British Isles: the temperate deciduous woodland biome

In the UK, deciduous trees shed their leaves in autumn to conserve moisture and nutrients and avoid damage to the tree by snow and ice accumulation. This adds an annual layer of litter to the soil surface, which decomposes and is mixed into the soil by the actions of earthworms, so the soil fertility is high (Figure 6.49).

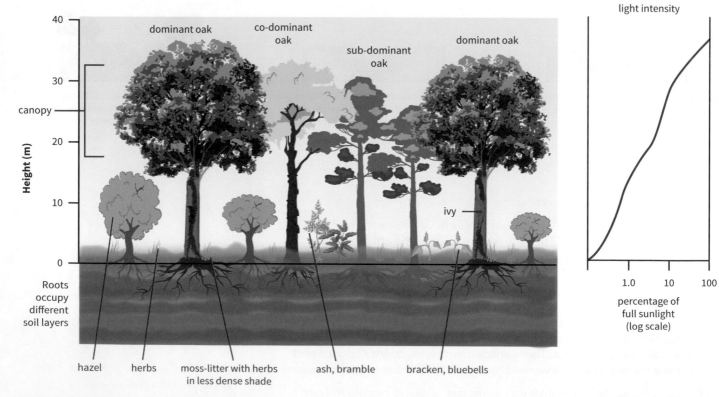

Figure 6.49 The structure of a deciduous woodland.

The net primary productivity is also high at 1.2 kg/m²/year on account of the relatively high summer temperatures and long hours of daylight. The biomass is also quite high at 35 kg/m² because of the large number of trees in the ecosystem.

The most common tree species in British woodlands are oak, lime, elm, beech, chestnut, ash and maple but there are also areas with rowan, birch, willow and alder. These variations result from differences in local climate, soils and relief. Birch and rowan prefer areas where soils are more acid, whereas maple tends to dominate where soils are alkaline. Oak tends to be tolerant of a range of soil types. Elm and lime prefer clay soils, whereas willow and alder can tolerate more waterlogged soils.

The climate in deciduous forests is temperate maritime climate, typical of lowland areas in the UK. This is mild and wet, as shown in Figure 6.50. Rainfall totals tend to be between 500 and 1500 mm per year, often with a slight winter maximum. Most of the rainfall in the UK falls as a result of fronts in depressions arriving from the west. Precipitation is mostly in the form of rainfall and is usually greater than evapotranspiration, generating a surplus of moisture available to be held in soil, rivers and lakes. Temperatures are usually above freezing in the winter, averaging about 5 °C because of the warm current called the North Atlantic Drift along the west coast. Summers tend to be cool on average, between 15 and 20 °C, with temperatures decreasing northwards. It is therefore a climate with few extremes.

Soils in deciduous forests – brown earth soils

The soils in deciduous woodlands are typically **brown earth soils** (Figure 6.50), with good fertility and drainage. They are a response to the geology and climate in an area. They have a rich litter layer that lies above a reddish-brown **soil horizon**, often over 30 cm deep. Below this lies a paler, mineral-rich B horizon that is partly weathered. The layers tend to merge into each other because of the large amount of earthworm activity that mixes the soil and also because there is limited leaching of minerals. The low amount of leaching also means the soils are rarely acid, with a pH of 6.0 to 6.5.

Figure 6.51 shows a nutrient cycling diagram for deciduous forest. The largest store of nutrients is in the biomass, a result of the tall trees and dense vegetation. The second largest store is in the soil because of the weathering, which adds nutrients from the bedrock and decomposition of the rich litter layer. This is rapidly mixed into the soil by the action of earthworms. Leaching can be quite high, but it is offset by the high rates of decomposition of the litter.

Deciduous woodland is not the dominant vegetation in all areas of the UK. Even in areas where it does represent the climatic climax vegetation, different arresting factors mean it is no longer present. There are areas of semi-natural vegetation in Britain, mostly in harsher environments where plant communities only have a small number of species, such as the uplands alpine vegetation, heather moorlands and heathlands. In these areas it is often the physical environment that is the arresting factor such as a harsh climate, infertile soils or the presence of waterlogging.

Changes in climate, soil, relief or drainage often give rise to the zonation of vegetation. Figure 6.52 shows a typical zonation of vegetation in the Scottish Highlands. As the altitude increases, temperatures decrease but cloud cover, wind speeds and precipitation increase. Soils change from brown earths to **podsols** to alpine soils and, ultimately, the upper slopes are bare rock and scree. The soils are increasingly less fertile, thinner and more acid as the altitude

Key terms

brown earth soils: the relatively fertile soils found beneath deciduous woodlands

soil horizon: the different layers in a soil, usually a layer of litter at the surface, then horizons A, B and C, then the bedrock or parent material

Key term

podsol: a relatively infertile and acid soil mostly found below coniferous forests

Typical mean monthly temperatures in a deciduous forest area in the UK

Brown earth soil

Brown earth soil profile

litter layer
humus layer
O horizon
A horizon
B horizon
C horizon
bedrock

surface litter decomposes to give a mull humus with a neutral pH

rich brown horizon well mixed by earthworms and other microorganisms

transition to B horizon is blurred because of earthworm activity; weakly illuviated

Figure 6.50 The climate and brown earth soils typical of a deciduous forest in the UK.

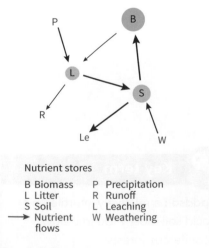

Nutrient stores

B Biomass   P Precipitation
L Litter   R Runoff
S Soil   L Leaching
→ Nutrient   W Weathering
  flows

Figure 6.51 Nutrient cycling in deciduous woodland.

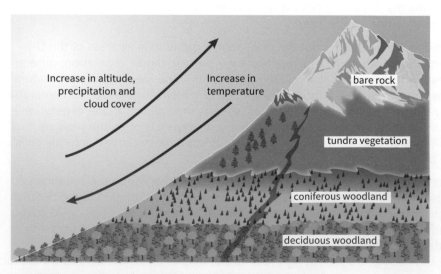

Increase in altitude, precipitation and cloud cover

Increase in temperature

bare rock

tundra vegetation

coniferous woodland

deciduous woodland

Figure 6.52 The zonation of vegetation in the Scottish Highlands.

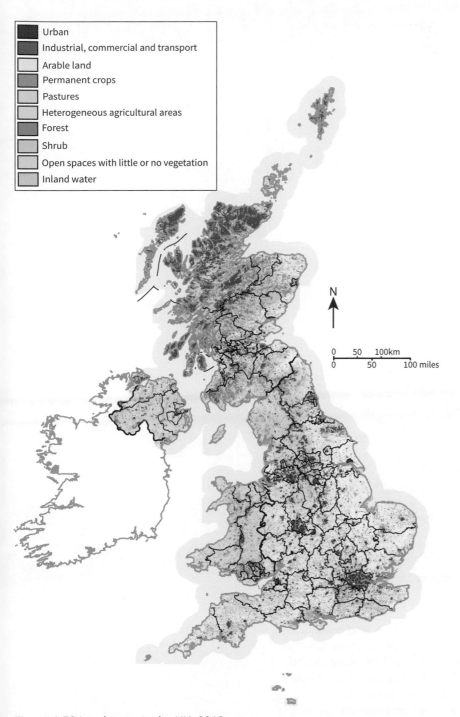

Legend:
- Urban
- Industrial, commercial and transport
- Arable land
- Permanent crops
- Pastures
- Heterogeneous agricultural areas
- Forest
- Shrub
- Open spaces with little or no vegetation
- Inland water

N

0   50   100km
0   50   100 miles

Figure 6.53 Land cover in the UK, 2012.

increases. The capacity of the environment to support vegetation declines with increasing altitude and the vegetation has to be increasingly adapted to the harsher conditions.

Figure 6.53 shows the current land cover in the UK. It is the most recent publication as part of a European Union monitoring project under the Copernicus Programme. It was published by the University of Leicester and reflects land cover in 2012. Figure 6.54 shows where changes have occurred in areas over 5 ha between 2006 and 2012. The most dominant land cover type is agricultural land, followed by forest and semi-natural vegetation. Artificial surfaces, mostly urban areas, cover 8% of the country.

Areas of change
Administrative regions

Figure 6.54 Areas of over 5 ha in which changes have occurred between 2006 and 2012.

Between 2006 and 2012, 1% of the total area showed a change in land cover, a total of 225 200 ha. Most changes occurred in Scotland and Wales, where there has been extensive clear-cutting of coniferous forests. Only about 50% will be replanted, so overall the forested land area is reduced. A further 3000 ha of conifers have been cleared for industrial development, especially for the creation of wind farms in Scotland, and 7000 ha of forest and 1000 ha of wetlands for urbanisation. Quarrying caused 3000 ha of arable land and 2000 ha of grazing land to be lost, but 2000 ha of mineral extraction land were converted back to pasture land.

The effects of human activity on succession: the heather moorland plagioclimax

Upland heathland (heather moorland)

Almost all of the world's heather moorland is found in the northern and western uplands of the UK. The climate, geology, relief, soil and human activities all combine to give rise to the heather moorlands.

In upland areas, plant growth is limited by cold temperatures, high levels of precipitation, strong winds and more limited sunshine because of increased cloud cover. Soils are thin and often lack nutrients as the parent rocks, such as granite, are resistant to erosion and composed of acidic minerals. They weather slowly and high rates of leaching can wash away any nutrients.

Many heather moorlands were once forested, but about 5000 years ago the forests began to disappear. Early Neolithic people started using the trees for animal fodder, fuel and building materials, and cleared areas for grazing. Gradually, the trees were replaced with heather and grasses and grazing animals prevented the growth of new seedlings. At the same time, the climate became wetter and the soils more acidic and infertile due to increased leaching. In many areas, soils became waterlogged, the dead plant material could not decompose in the anaerobic conditions and thick layers of peat developed. Heather moorland is therefore a plagioclimax vegetation – a result of human activity. Figure 6.55 shows a food web for an upland moorland.

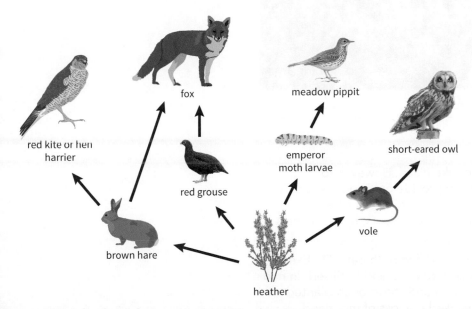

Figure 6.55 A food web for an upland moorland environment.

Red grouse

No other bird in the world makes such extensive use of heather as the red grouse (Figure 6.56). They eat the heather; shelter, nest and rear their young in it; and typically do not move far from their home heath in their entire lifetime. Heather is their main source of food. Patchwork patterns on grouse moors show where controlled burning has been carried out to promote heather growth for grouse food and cover. Regular burning of the moors encourages new shoots to grow – an important food supply for grouse chicks. If heather moorland is threatened, so is the population of red grouse.

Over the years, the numbers of grouse have steadily declined because of a 30% loss of heather between 1950 and 1980, largely due to conversion to forestry; increased winter grazing by sheep; an increase in grouse predators such as hen harriers, foxes and crows; and diseases such as a nematode worm that causes strongylosis.

Ecological development and change

Moorlands left unmanaged and cleared of any grazing animals such as deer, sheep and rabbits would gradually become covered in bracken and scrub and then birch and oak woodland would develop, i.e. a secondary succession

Figure 6.56 Red grouse grazing in heather moorland.

towards the climatic climax vegetation would take place. However, for centuries the moorlands have been managed to provide grazing for sheep, cattle and ponies and food for red grouse. They are also popular areas for walking and tourism, as well as the home for some rare plants, birds, animals and insects.

Many moorland areas are subject to a number of different threats. On Exmoor in the 1970s, some moorland areas were fenced, drained and fertilised. In mid Wales, afforestation has occurred where the moorlands have been planted with coniferous plantations. Recreation has caused the loss of moorland vegetation and soil erosion, especially in National Parks and on long-distance footpaths such as the Pennine Way. Some moorlands that are not managed by burning or grazing may be overtaken by grasses and bracken. However, there are many areas of moorland that are being actively managed to preserve them and their fauna and bracken is often sprayed or cut to stop its spread. Landowners, National Park authorities and organisations such as Natural England and the Royal Society for the Protection of Birds (RSPB) are all active to ensure the moorland ecosystem survives. In other areas, such as Kielder Water in Northumberland, moorlands have been flooded to create reservoirs for water supply.

Helicopters have been used to transport paving slabs to repair sections of the Pennine Way. The numbers of sheep and ponies are being managed to control overgrazing. Controlling the numbers of ponies on Dartmoor and Exmoor is a particular problem.

Haytor, Dartmoor National Park

National Park authorities have a duty to manage both the ecosystems and the people who wish to visit and enjoy them. Haytor is a popular tourist attraction in Dartmoor. It lies at a height of 450 m and receives over 1500 mm of rainfall each year. The soils are thin, stony and acidic, with waterlogging in some areas. The area is covered in heather moorland, with some patches of grass and bracken.

 Investigate

Investigate the management of ponies in the moorlands of Dartmoor and Exmoor.

On a busy day there may be over 250 cars and 1000 people at any one time. As shown in Figure 6.57, management by the Dartmoor National Park Authority helps to maintain the area's ecosystems and manage visitor numbers.

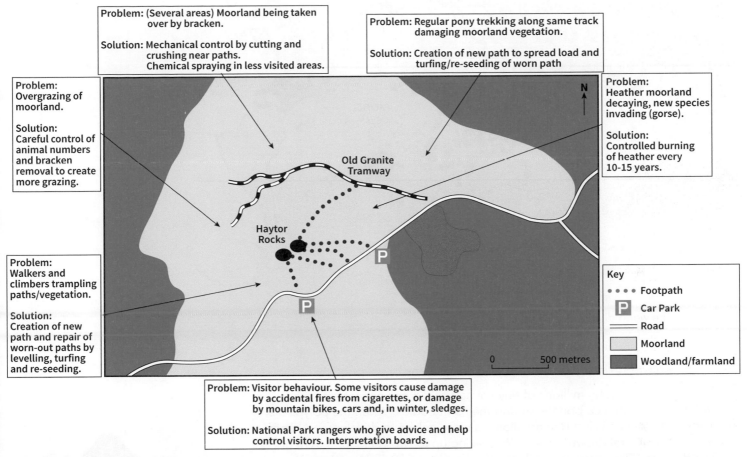

Problem: (Several areas) Moorland being taken over by bracken.

Solution: Mechanical control by cutting and crushing near paths.
Chemical spraying in less visited areas.

Problem: Regular pony trekking along same track damaging moorland vegetation.

Solution: Creation of new path to spread load and turfing/re-seeding of worn path

Problem: Overgrazing of moorland.

Solution: Careful control of animal numbers and bracken removal to create more grazing.

Problem: Heather moorland decaying, new species invading (gorse).

Solution: Controlled burning of heather every 10-15 years.

Problem: Walkers and climbers trampling paths/vegetation.

Solution: Creation of new path and repair of worn-out paths by levelling, turfing and re-seeding.

Problem: Visitor behaviour. Some visitors cause damage by accidental fires from cigarettes, or damage by mountain bikes, cars and, in winter, sledges.

Solution: National Park rangers who give advice and help control visitors. Interpretation boards.

Old Granite Tramway

Haytor Rocks

Key
• • • • Footpath
P Car Park
═══ Road
⬜ Moorland
⬛ Woodland/farmland

0   500 metres

Figure 6.57 Problems and management solutions at Haytor National Park.

ACTIVITY 6.10

1   Describe the different trophic levels in a moorland ecosystem.
2   How have moorland ecosystems been managed over time and what would happen if management practices were relaxed?
3   Why is it important to protect moorland ecosystems and what strategies may be successful?

For more questions on upland moorlands, download Worksheet 6.6 from **Cambridge Elevate**.

6.5 Marine ecosystems

The distribution of coral reef ecosystems

Coral reefs are located in warm, tropical waters where sea temperatures are typically 25–29°C. The seas are clear and shallow. Figure 6.58 shows the world distribution of coral reefs. Coral reefs are limited in their geographic distribution to 30° north or south of the equator mostly in the Indian and Pacific Oceans. The reefs in the Bahamas at 32 degrees north of the equator are an exception because of the warm water currents they receive from the Gulf of Mexico.

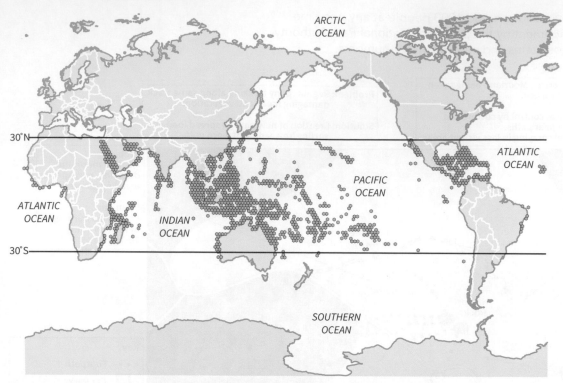

Figure 6.58 The world distribution of coral reefs.

The main characteristics of coral reef ecosystems

Coral reefs are formed by millions of tiny animals called polyps that create an exoskeleton of calcium carbonate around their soft bodies. When the polyps die the calcium carbonate is left behind allowing more polyps to develop and hence the coral grows. Coral growth is very slow, taking up to two years for 2.5 cm of coral to develop. The complex coral structures create an intricate pattern of cracks and crevices which provide an array of habitats for other species such as anemones, sponges, molluscs and fish. The polyps have a symbiotic relationship with small algae called zooxanthellae. The algae supplement the polyps' food intake and photosynthesise using sunlight, while the polyps provide the algae with a secure habitat and nutrients such as phosphorus and nitrogen.

There are three main types of coral reef:

- Fringing reefs that grow in shallow offshore waters and separated from the coast by a narrow and shallow stretch of sea.
- Barrier reefs separated from the coast by a lagoon. These are often large and continuous reefs parallel to the shore.
- Atolls, circular or horseshoe shaped reefs formed round a central lagoon often found in deeper water.

The basic coral reef classification scheme described above was first proposed by Charles Darwin (Figure 6.59), and is still widely used today.

Darwin explored coral reefs in the Pacific and Indian Oceans. He classified reefs into three main types, which he saw as stages in the geological evolution:

- Stage 1: Fringing reefs develop along the coastlines of newly formed islands.
- Stage 2: The islands begin to sink into the sea but at a slow enough rate for the growth of the coral to keep pace and so form a barrier reef some distance from the coast.

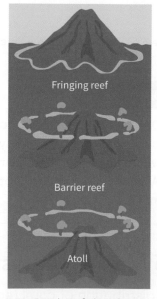

Figure 6.59 Coral reef classification scheme.

- Stage 3: The island continues to sink until it is submerged below the sea surface leaving a coral atoll, a ring of coral with a central lagoon; e.g. Bikini atoll.

In the early 1950s Darwin's theory was accepted, although other processes may also result in coral formation in other areas.

The environmental conditions associated with reef development

Coral reefs only develop in highly specific environmental conditions. Ideally the water temperature is between 25 and 29°C and the salinity about 36 ppm (parts per million). There is generally an absence of wave action, so the waters are relatively calm and with low turbidity. Shallow waters encourage coral development so that sunlight can reach the algae to allow photosynthesis to take place.

The Red Sea Coral Reefs

The Red Sea lies between Africa and Asia; a body of salt water connected to the Indian Ocean in the south by the Gulf of Aden and the Gulf of Aqaba and Suez to the north (Figure 6.60). Coral reefs are common in the Red Sea but best developed off the coasts of Saudi Arabia, Egypt and the Sudan.

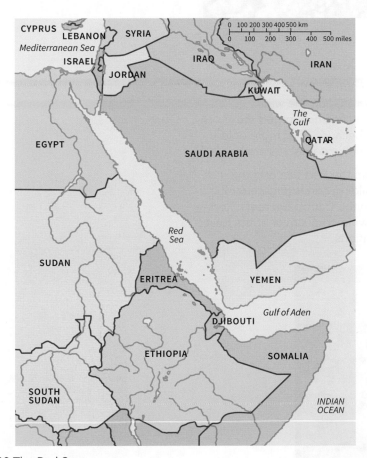

Figure 6.60 The Red Sea.

The Red Sea coastal reef complex extends along some 2000 km (1240 miles) of shoreline and the fringing reefs are over 5000 years old. Most of the reefs grow directly from the shoreline but there are also numerous offshore reefs and atoll like rings of coral.

The Red Sea is part of the East African rift valley and hence there have been many tectonic events throughout history which have resulted in the formation of the Red Sea coral reefs (Figure 6.61).

247

Figure 6.61 Red Sea coral reef.

Factors in the health and survival of reefs: natural factors

Coral reefs are second only to the tropical rainforests in terms of their productivity and biodiversity. The natural conditions in the Red Sea including the water temperature, low acidity, high salinity and algal blooms have encouraged the growth of coral reefs. The Red Sea region is distinctive because of its more or less enclosed nature. There is very little exchange of water with external sea areas.

About 300 hard coral species have been recorded from the Red Sea and the Egyptian coast supports about 200 species of reef building corals (Figure 6.62). This represents about four times as many species as in the Caribbean reefs. Red Sea coral reefs are generally healthy with up to 85% living coral cover at the best sites and over 50% live coral cover at many other locations.

Figure 6.62 A fringing reef rims the shore of Egypt's Ras Mohammed National Park.

Human activity and impact on coral reefs in the Red Sea

Many Red Sea coral reefs situated near urban centres and other developed parts of the coast have been heavily damaged or lost due to population growth and coastal development which has led to a decline in water quality.

Films by Jacques Cousteau in the 1960s encouraged tourism to develop along the coast of the Red Sea. Scuba diving and snorkelling on the reefs with their clear water and plentiful marine life became popular. Today Eilat, Aqaba and Sham-el-Sheikh are all very popular destinations.

The growth of tourism has led to a huge increase in hotels and other developments in coastal areas. In the Gulf of Aqaba hotel numbers increased from five in 1989 to 141 in 2006 with room numbers mushrooming from 565 to more than 48 000. To cope with the increase in tourism and associated developments desalination plants have been built to provide freshwater. However, the plants have caused an increase in the discharge of chemicals in to the sea, in particular chlorine and copper. The growth of tourism and consequent increase in hotels and other developments has led to an increase in sewage runoff causing pollution and the loss of coral reefs and the associated fauna and flora.

The development of coastal petrochemical and fertiliser industries, e.g. Aqaba in Jordan, have increased pollution in the Gulf of Aqaba damaging the reefs and the population. Industrial growth has led to the laying of electricity and telecommunications cables on the seabed that have cut through the coral reefs. Aqaba has increased its container port trade and the ships often have to anchor offshore. The anchors fracture the coral and the illegal practice of flushing the sludge from their oil tanks pollutes the waters. There has been a dramatic fall in fish numbers and the reef flora as a result.

In some reef areas, the growth in diving tourism has resulted in reef damage from boat anchors and scuba divers. In Sham-el-Sheikh dive boat numbers have increased from 23 in 1989 to 350 in 2006. Studies suggest that continued dive tourism expansion at some of the more popular tourist destinations would be ill-advised and will lead to serious reef degradation.

There are few natural beaches along the Red Sea coasts, so developers have created artificial beaches on rocky shores. However, this leads to the transportation of sand along the shores increasing sedimentation and turbidity which impact negatively upon the reefs.

There has been an increase in fishing and recent surveys report an overfishing of sharks, prized for their fins, and also of invertebrates such as sea cucumbers. Reports suggest that overfishing is a major threat to 55% of coral reefs. Some of the damage is also caused by dynamite fishing.

Growing human activity in the Red Sea area has led to a loss of biodiversity. The deterioration in the coral reefs disturbs the coastal ecosystem often causing the coral to die and the loss of associated plants and animals, including fish. However, the development of tourism has been promoted in order to increase tourism revenue and generate economic growth and employment opportunities.

Thinking like a geographer

Evaluate the costs and benefits of tourism development on the shores of the Red Sea. Is there a workable solution to satisfy the economic and the environmental arguments?

Future prospects for coral reefs

A growing number of marine protected areas (MPAs) have been established in the Red Sea to help alleviate some of the problems. Ras Mohammed National Park was established by Egypt in 1983 and includes miles of healthy fringing reefs. The Red Sea Marine Peace Park in the Gulf of Aqaba was founded in 1994 by the governments of Jordan and Israel to preserve and protect the area's coral reefs. A 7 km stretch of coast is protected. Jordan has also sponsored the Gulf of Aqaba Environmental Action Plan to develop strategies to protect the environment. Sewage treatment works have been built at Aqaba to reduce pollution. New underwater attractions have been built to reduce the tourism pressure on the more accessible and natural coral reefs. A derelict cargo ship, the Cedar Pride and several army vehicles have been sunk to create new attractions for diving.

Research Point

To investigate further into the threats to the Red sea visit the UNEP as a starting point.

6.6 Local ecosystems

Ecosystems may be studied at three scales:

- biomes: global or large-scale ecosystems such as the tropical rainforest or tundra
- meso-scale ecosystems: such as large lakes or forests
- small- or microscale ecosystems: such as sand dunes, hedgerows, ponds, single trees or heathlands.

A small-scale ecosystem: lowland heathland

There are two main types of heathland in Britain:

- lowland heathland: mostly in southern England, such as in Breckland in mid-Norfolk and on the Suffolk coast, the New Forest and parts of Devon and Dorset
- upland heathland or heather moorland: mostly found in the north and west of Britain, such as the Pennines and Lake District, Scottish and Welsh uplands.

Heathlands are limited by soil and climatic factors. Heathlands develop on soils with low fertility, i.e. those lacking in nutrients. Some heathlands are natural, such as those on lowland sands and gravels including sandy coastal areas. Others result from human activity such as deforestation, overgrazing and the impact of fire. These are plagioclimax communities because their formation is a result of human activity.

Heathlands are dominated by heather vegetation normally below 1 m in height. Other species that may grow alongside the heather are cotton grass, bilberry, gorse and broom. The vegetation is well adapted to the physical conditions. Heather is evergreen so can begin growth as soon as the temperature rises, which is useful when the growing season is short. The heather plants grow together, forming a thick, bushy carpet, sometimes up to half a metre tall. This helps the plant to withstand strong winds. The plants also have tiny, narrow leaves that stop them from losing too much water (reduces evapotranspiration), which is vital in windy environments, and shallow roots make best use of nutrients in the thin soils.

Lowland heathland

Lowland heathland is located where rainfall is between 600 and 1000 mm per year and relatively evenly distributed, and where soils are sandy, leached and infertile. As a result, heathland tends to be quite dispersed and patchy in Britain. This makes it vulnerable to development for housing and industry and to grazing, fires and the encroachment of other vegetation such as scrub and bracken.

Over the past 200 years large areas of lowland heathland have disappeared, including 85% of Breckland's heaths, 75% of Surrey's heaths and 80% of Dorset's heaths (Table 6.6).

The loss and increasing patchiness of Dorset's heathlands are largely a result of human activity. Most has been ploughed up to grow cereals or conifers, or for urban and industrial uses. In some areas heathlands are threatened by more competitive species such as bracken, birch and pine. These are invading the heathlands and recommencing secondary succession because some environmental controls have been removed. Sheep grazing has been stopped, rabbit populations have declined as a result of Myxomatosis and the use of burning has been regulated. This secondary succession may ultimately lead to the re-establishment of the climax vegetation.

Year	Heathland (000s hectares)
1750	39.6
1811	30.4
1896	22.7
1934	18.2
1960	10.0
1978	5.8
1992	5.6

Table 6.6 The decline of Dorset's heathland.

Maths for geographers

1 Draw a suitable graph to show the decline of Dorset's heathlands from the data in Table 6.6.
2 Describe and suggest reasons for the trend shown in the table.

The Dorset Heathlands

The Dorset Heathlands are located to the west of the Hampshire Basin and lie close to Bournemouth and Poole. Over time large areas of the heathland have disappeared. About 75% was lost in the 20th century to agriculture, forestry and other developments. Today only about 150 patches of heathland remain. However, they are all very similar with large areas of both dry and wet heath. The heaths are a small-scale ecosystem with a unique fauna and flora. The areas are also important for birdlife, including merlins, nightjars, the Dartford warbler, woodlarks and hen harriers.

Heathlands have different amounts of water in their soils giving rise to dry heaths and wet heaths. These different heathlands support different fauna and flora. For example, the sandy soils of dry heaths have ling and bell heather (Figure 6.63), sand wasps and sand lizards. The sandy soils mean that nutrients are easily washed out of the soils. Wet heaths tend to be waterlogged and lacking in oxygen. There is very little decomposition of dead organic matter and peat soils develop which supports cross leaved heather, insectivorous plants, such as the sundew, the bog brush cricket and raft spider.

The heathlands have few species of plants, but some are unique to the heathland areas. Many survive well on the nutrient-poor, acidic soils such as gorse with its spiky foliage and yellow flowers. Grasses are also an important plant found in heathlands.

The heathland is a plagioclimax community, which means that it depends on human intervention for its survival. In Dorset the heathlands were developed by Neolithic farmers and then maintained by people grazing their livestock, cutting gorse for firewood and heather turfs for fuel. When agricultural use ended, the heathlands were neglected and invaded by scrub as the secondary succession recommences.

The significance of the Dorset Heathlands has encouraged the local council to include it as part of a strategic plan for the area and also for the Royal Society for Protection of Birds (RSPB) to carry out a special project in the area.

Figure 6.63 Dorset heathland showing bell heather and grasses.

The Dorset Heathland project

The Dorset Heathland project aims to:

- increase area of heathland by 560 ha
- monitor results of management on bird numbers
- offer habitat management services to local landowners
- raise awareness of heathland within local community.

The RSPB project involves staff working with landowners to remove invasive scrub species (e.g. rhododendron, pine and birch and rejuvenate heather and gorse). This is done during the winter so that nesting birds are not disturbed. Areas of former heathland that would be 'corridors' between larger blocks of heath are also prioritised.

The initial aim to increase the area of good heathland by 560 ha was reached in 1996 and by 2006 about 1300 ha of heathland management was in place. The Dorset Heathland Project was successful.

 Look on **Cambridge Elevate** for more information on the project, from the Dorset Heathlands Planning Framework document (www.cambridge.org/links/gase6056)

6.7 The Three Gorges Dam, a region experiencing ecological change

The Three Gorges Dam is the world's largest producer of hydroelectricity. It is located on the Yangtze River in China (see Figure 6.64). It generates 9% of China's electricity. Emissions of carbon dioxide, dust and other greenhouse gases from coal burning have declined and 31 million tonnes of coal have been saved from burning in power stations.

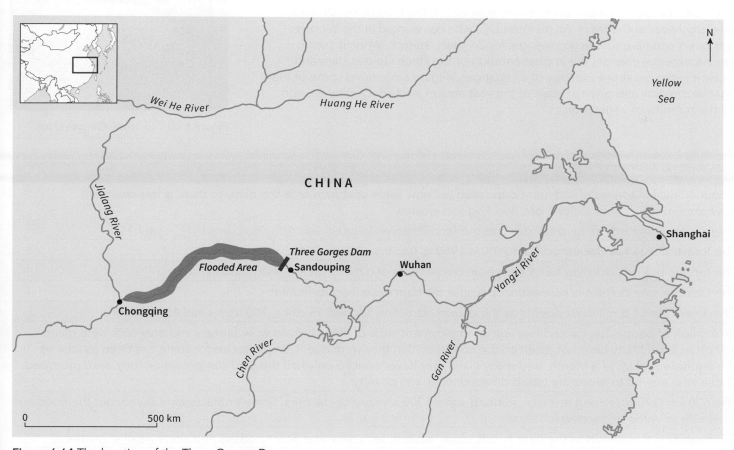

Figure 6.64 The location of the Three Gorges Dam.

Construction of the dam began in December 1994. It was opened in 2008 and completed in July 2012, having cost ¥180 billion (US$26 billion). The catchment area is 1 000 000 km^2 and the dam has a surface area of 1084 km^2). It is a development on a massive scale (Figure 6.65).

Positive and negative impacts

As well as producing electricity, the dam has other advantages. The river can now hold more flood water, which decreases flooding downstream of the dam and also allows larger ships to navigate the river. These larger barges also mean a reduction in carbon dioxide emissions by 630 000 tonnes. The Chinese government consider the project to be a huge success socially and economically as well as a major engineering feat. Considerable efforts have been made to restore tree cover upstream of the dam, especially after the 1998 Yangtze River floods. The dam has improved the control of flooding downstream, protecting large cities like Wuhan, Nanjing and Shanghai and the millions of people who live there, the farmland and China's most important industrial areas that are built beside the river. The dam also allows extra freshwater to be provided to the cities and farms in the dry season.

However, construction of the dam involved flooding historical sites and the relocation of 1.5 million people (Table 6.7). Biodiversity has also been affected due to the massive scale of the project and an increase in landslides. 57% of the plant species are endangered, some of which are very rare and important in traditional Chinese medicines.

The building of the dam has caused controversy both in China and around the world. George Davis, a tropical medicine specialist at the George Washington University Medical Centre in Washington DC, who has worked in the Yangtze River basin and neighbouring provinces for 24 years, stated: 'When it comes to environmental change, the implementation of the Three Gorges Dam and reservoir is the great granddaddy of all changes.' Figure 6.66 shows some of the negative impacts and gives an idea of the vast area of land affected by erosion and the removal of vegetation.

Figure 6.65 The Three Gorges Dam.

Negative impacts
About 40 million tonnes of sediment deposited will now settle upstream or in the dam, so there is less sediment downstream, which may cause more flooding and erosion.
There is an increased risk of landslides and tremors. Reservoir-induced seismicity is covered in Chapter 11.
The forested area has decreased from 20% in 1950 to less than 10% in 2012.
The turbine blades are killing fish. Changes in temperature and river flow are also harming fish.
The Chinese river dolphin is now extinct because the dam decreased its habitat.
China relocated 1.5 million residents as the dam construction flooded 13 cities, 140 towns and 1350 villages.
Relocation of people has caused massive unemployment; 40% of those moved were farmers and only 60% were given any other land. Many have not received the compensation they were due. Compensation for some has been as little as the equivalent of US$7 a month, and many claim they have received only half the land compensation they were promised. Those who moved to towns are being driven deeper into poverty.
The 600 km (370 mile) long reservoir flooded some 1300 archaeological sites. Some artefacts were saved, but the flooding inevitably covered undiscovered relics.
Biodiversity is threatened as the dam floods some habitats, reduces water flow to others and alters weather patterns.

Table 6.7 The negative impacts of the Three Gorges Dam.

Thinking like a geographer

Whose views should carry most weight: the farmer's, the government official's or the environmentalist's? Should the change in the lives of all those displaced be given importance while still going ahead with the project for the general good of the society? Contribute your findings to a class discussion.

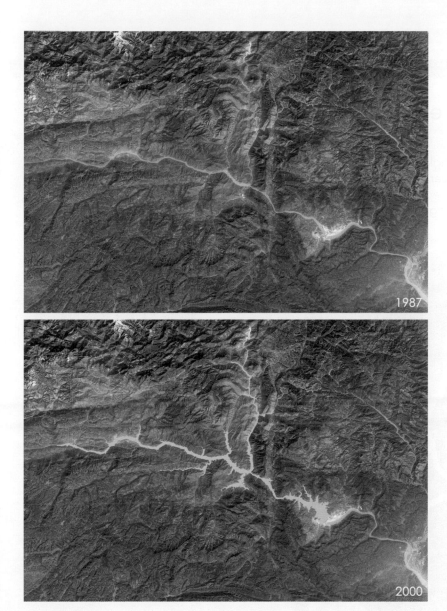

Figure 6.66 Before and after construction of the dam.

ACTIVITY 6.11

1   Explain why the Chinese government wished to proceed with the construction of the Three Gorges Dam.
2   Use a table like the one below to list the economic, social and political costs and benefits of the scheme and associated changes.

	Costs	Benefits
Economic		
Social		
Political		

3   How has the local community responded to the changes in the region? You may wish to investigate this further.

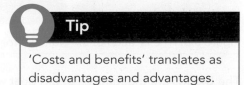

Tip

'Costs and benefits' translates as disadvantages and advantages.

6.8 The Norfolk Broads, an ecosystem at a local scale

The Norfolk Broads are located in the east of England (Figure 6.67), where rainfall totals around 650 mm per year and temperatures are mild. The Broads are a wetland environment, a local-scale ecosystem. This is a unique environment within Britain and one that is under great pressure.

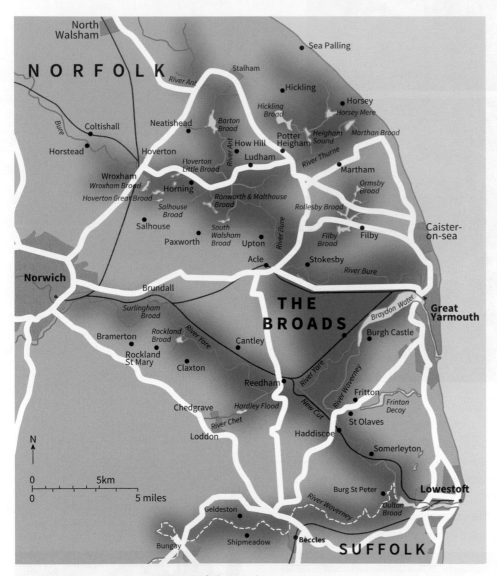

Figure 6.67 The location of the Norfolk Broads.

The Broads are the remains of old peat workings dating from Saxon and late Medieval times. They had to be abandoned when the sea level rose and flooded the hollows, creating the shallow lakes. Many of these lakes are connected by natural streams and rivers, whereas some have had artificial channels built. There are three main types of habitat: carr vegetation, fenland and open water (lakes and streams). Carr vegetation involves areas of woodland with species of alder and willow. In other areas, the Fens may give way to agricultural land.

The ecosystem contains a rich variety of plants such as reeds and water lilies, and animals such as geese, ducks and Chinese water deer. Some species, such as the fen orchid, are protected and unique to the environment. The reeds provide habitats for many birds, including the reclusive bittern. The open water is important for migratory wild fowl such as teal and tufted ducks.

For hundreds of years the wetland has been used by people for pastoral farming and fishing and for cutting reeds to thatch roofs (Figure 6.68).

Figure 6.68 Reed beds during cutting at Hickling, around 1886.

These activities were very much in harmony with the environment as they were sustainable. Today there is much less cattle grazing and reed cutting; these activities have been overtaken by tourism and agriculture, making management of the Norfolk Broads essential.

In the Norfolk Broads there are 3 national nature reserves and 36 Sites of Special Scientific Interest (SSSIs). Bure Marshes National Nature Reserve, for example, is recognised as a wetland of international importance.

Threats

Flooding from the sea and rivers are a threat to the Norfolk Broads. A modest rise in sea level could see the Broads disappear, with a total loss of the biodiversity. Already rising sea levels associated with climate change have seen a decline in species and habitats. Today there are demands for new housing and improved transport links. The main economic activities of agriculture and tourism also bring their problems and there is increasing pressure from a variety of sources including habitat loss, pollution of waterways and non-native species.

The marshland and fields close to the streams have been used for cattle grazing for centuries. However, the grazing has declined. Government incentives for land drainage, EU subsidies for arable crops and new technologies such as electric pumps have all encouraged farmers to switch to arable farming. Large areas of the marshes are now used for wheat growing, which reduces biodiversity and contributes to increasing eutrophication as fertilisers are washed into water courses. The increase in nitrogen and phosphorus encourages algal blooms that block out sunlight and prevent the oxygenation of the streams, causing aquatic life to die.

The waterways were once commercially important highways but today they are almost entirely used for a range of recreational activities mostly connected with boating and fishing (Figure 6.69). Tourism is economically valuable to the area and supports many local businesses such as boat hire companies, hotels and B&Bs, and boat builders. It is also a source of pressure on the fragile Broads.

Figure 6.69 Recreation on the Norfolk Broads.

Management

The Norfolk Broads missed out on designation as a National Park in 1948, but in 1989 the Broads Authority was given statutory status and management plans have been written, the most recent in 2011. The key principle for management of the Broads is sustainable development and the priorities for 2011–15 were:

- planning for the long-term future of the Broads in response to climate change and sea level rise
- working in partnership on the sustainable management of the Broads
- encouraging the sustainable use and enjoyment of the Broads.

A range of management strategies is shown in Table 6.8.

The management plans for the Norfolk Broads promote sustainable conservation. These go beyond protection of the area, but recognise the importance of tourism and agriculture to the local economy. The Broads are important sources of employment and tourism encourages local traditions and maintenance of the landscape. The challenge is to manage the pressures and land uses in the Norfolk Broads in a sustainable way that maintains the ecosystem and its biodiversity.

Problem	Development	Possible solution
Climate change	Possible increase in summer temperatures, drier summers and wetter winters.	A carbon reduction strategy for all developments in the Broads to reduce emissions of greenhouse gases; expand renewable energy production.
	Possible sea level rise, increasing flooding and polluting the freshwater ecosystems with salt water.	Coastal defences planned to 'hold the line', i.e. to maintain the current configuration of the coastline.
Reduced biodiversity	Changing distribution of habitats and species; net loss of biodiversity.	20-year Broadland Flood alleviation project includes plans to enhance biodiversity.
	Non-native species invade: the so-called 'killer shrimp', mink, signal crayfish and fast-growing non-native plants including floating pennywort, giant hogweed, Himalayan balsam, Japanese knotweed and parrot's feather.	A project ran from August 2012 to July 2013 in which leaflets were used together with signage throughout the Broads network to raise awareness of non-native species and showing people how to help stop the shrimp spreading.
		Implementation of the Broads Biodiversity Action Plan (BAP). Improving 800 ha of grazing marsh and creating 400 ha of biodiverse wetland habitat.
Water resources and quality	Increased demand for water for irrigation and the public water supply have resulted in lower water levels, with the threat of inundation by salt water which would threaten the freshwater ecosystem.	Possible access to alternative water supplies further away and water conservation measures, e.g. reduced use of irrigation and of water in homes and industry.
	The need to reduce nitrogen and phosphorus pollution mostly from chemical fertiliser use, which causes algal blooms and eutrophication.	Phosphorus stripping or removal by adding chemicals in sewage treatment works. Monitoring water quality by the National Rivers Authority. Farmers using fewer fertilisers.
	Removing algae to improve water quality.	The fish are removed and the water flea population allowed to increase to eat the algae. The fish are then replaced and eat the fleas. This is called biological manipulation.
Farming	Overuse of fertiliser to support the intensification of agriculture and the shift to arable farming. Eutrophication.	Reducing the use of fertiliser and maintaining traditional practices such as crop rotation and cattle grazing. Improved soil management to reduce erosion.
Reduction in reed and sedge cutting (Figure 6.70)	These activities help wetland diversity. They have declined in recent years, but demand is rising today.	Funding schemes and training initiatives to expand traditional sustainable industries.
Tourism and boating	Conflicts between water users such as water skiers, wind surfers, sailors, motorboats and fishing.	Zoning areas – some areas have restricted usage, e.g. water skiing is restricted to the River Yare and the River Waveney.
	Erosion of riverbanks and footpaths.	Coir rolls and textured mats stabilise riverbanks and encourage reeds to take root. Tree and scrub planting. Footpath repair.
	Silting of channel.	Dredging river channels, currently at a rate of 50 000 m^3 per annum.
	Lead pollution from fishing equipment.	Restricted use of lead weights.

Table 6.8 Management strategies for the Norfolk Broads.

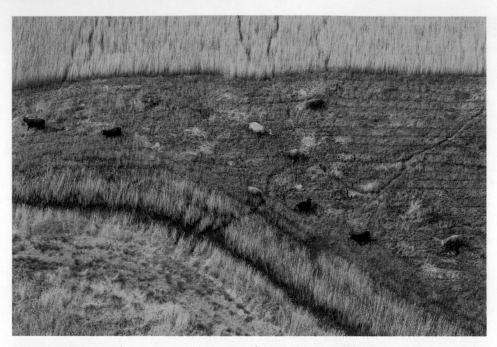

Figure 6.70 Livestock graze around an area of cut sedge at Hickling.

ACTIVITY 6.12

1 Summarise the nature and properties of the Norfolk Broads as an ecosystem.
2 How have human uses of the Norfolk Broads changed over time and become a threat to the ecosystem?
3 In what ways does the Broads Plan 2011 tackle the challenges faced by the Norfolk Broads and encourage sustainable development for the future?

 Look on **Cambridge Elevate** to investigate the Broads Plan 2011 and for more information on the Norfolk Broads, both on The Broads Authority website (www.cambridge.org/links/gase6057).

 For more activities on the Norfolk Broads, download Worksheet 6.7 from **Cambridge Elevate**.

Assess to progress

1   What is meant by the term 'trophic level'?   **1 MARK [A LEVEL]**
    A   The lowest level of a food chain, where energy is
        converted from the Sun.
    B   The amount of a chemical substance that has accumulated
        in an organism.
    C   The feeding level in a food chain.
    D   The amount of biomass at one level of a food chain.

2   Study Figure 6.71.
    a   Using Figure 6.71, give an example of a relationship with five
        trophic levels.
    b   Draw a pyramid of biomass to represent the five trophic levels.
    c   Explain why the pyramid is a better representation of the
        five trophic levels.   **6 MARKS [A LEVEL]**

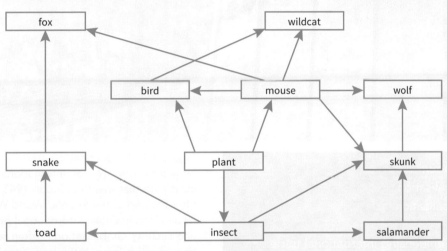

Figure 6.71 A model of a food web.

3   Discuss how human activities may impact on
    biodiversity and sustainability in natural
    ecosystems.   **20 MARKS [A LEVEL]**

To create a summary
table for your revision,
download Worksheet 6.8
from **Cambridge Elevate**.

Global systems and global governance

By the end of this chapter you should know:

- how to identify the dimensions of globalisation
- how to analyse factors influencing globalisation
- how global systems operate
- how to analyse patterns of and factors influencing international trade
- a case study of one transnational corporation
- how the global commons operate
- how Antarctica operates as a global commons
- how to make a critique of globalisation.

Figure 7.1 The UN headquarters in New York. The UN is an international institution that was founded in 1945, after the end of the Second World War. Its aim is to maintain international peace and security. Globalisation is often seen as a negative force, but international cooperation is a positive manifestation of globalisation.

Before you start…

You should know:

- globalisation is a powerful process that has economic, social, environmental and political impacts
- globalisation has aspects that need to be managed
- globalisation provokes different views on the need to manage its impacts.

7.1 Globalisation

Dimensions of globalisation

Globalisation is 'the growing interdependence of countries worldwide through the increasing volume and variety of cross-border transactions in goods and services and of international capital flows, and through the more rapid and widespread diffusion of technology' (International Monetary Fund).

Global systems refers to any organisation, groupings, or activities that link different parts of the world. TNC, for example, operate in two or more countries, linking their economies. Such relations or activities may provide opportunities, impact on inequalities and have an effect on people and the environment. Global governance refers to attempts to regulate global systems and activities, for example by the United Nations, International Monetary Fund and the World Bank. Their interventions may also have an impact on people and the environment.

The concept of globalisation developed in the 1960s after the Canadian academic Marshall McLuhan used the term **global village** to describe the breakdown of spatial barriers around the world. Globalisation refers to a range of processes and impacts that occur at a global scale, usually economic systems, but it can include physical systems (such as global warming) and socio-cultural systems (such as fashion, music and the film industry).

McLuhan argued that the similarities between places were greater than the differences between them, and that much of the world had been caught up in the same economic, social and cultural processes. He suggested that economic activities operated at a global scale and that other scales were becoming less important.

Globalisation is not new – many countries had empires from which they sourced raw materials and labour – but the current form of globalisation is more global, more integrated and has developed at a much faster rate than in the past.

There are three main forms of globalisation:

- economic: largely caused by the growth of transnational corporations (TNCs)
- social: the impact of western culture, art, media, sport and leisure pursuits on the world
- political: the growth of western democracies and their influence on poor countries, and the decline of centralised economies.

The KOF Index of Globalisation

The KOF Index of Globalisation was introduced in 2002 and covers the economic, social and political dimensions of globalisation. KOF defines globalisation as 'the process of creating networks of connections among actors at multi-continental distances, mediated through a variety of flows including people, information and ideas, capital and goods. Globalisation is conceptualized as a process that erodes national boundaries, integrates national economies, cultures, technologies and governance and produces complex relations of mutual interdependence.'

Figure 7.2 shows that the most globalised countries include many European countries, Canada, Australia and New Zealand. Larger economies such as the USA, China and Russia are not as globalised. The least globalised countries include many from sub-Saharan Africa, especially around the Horn of Africa, countries in conflict such as Afghanistan, and some low-income countries including Nepal and Myanmar.

More specifically, the three dimensions of the KOF Index are defined as:

- economic globalisation: characterised as long-distance flows of goods, capital and services, as well as information and perceptions that accompany market exchanges (36% of the globalisation index)
- social globalisation: expressed as the spread of ideas, information, images and people (38% of the globalisation index)
- political globalisation: characterised by a diffusion of government policies (26% of the globalisation index).

In addition to the indices measuring these dimensions, KOF calculates an overall index of globalisation and sub-indices referring to actual economic flows, economic restrictions, data on information flows, data on personal contact and data on cultural

Key term

global village: the world (globe) has been transformed into a 'village' by the almost instantaneous transmission of information, facilitated by improvements in ICT

Thinking like a geographer

Study Figure 7.2. How can the Index of Globalisation help us to understand development and underdevelopment?

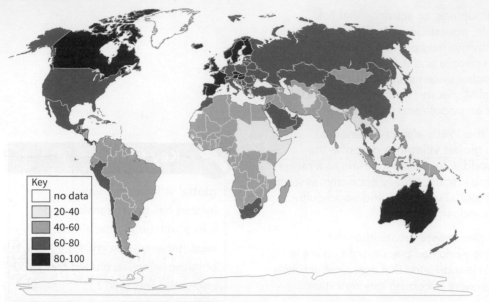

Figure 7.2 KOF Index of Globalisation, 2012.

proximity. In 2012 Ireland was identified as the most globalised country in the world, followed by the Netherlands and Belgium. The biggest jump in the KOF Index was made by the Czech Republic due to increased trade and foreign investment. Norway also improved its standing because of reduced trade barriers, whereas Cyprus fell three places on account of increased customs duties and capital transactions controls. The world's major economies (USA, China, Japan and Germany) tend to be more inward-looking and occur further down the globalisation index.

Economic globalisation

Broadly speaking, economic globalisation has two dimensions. First, actual economic flows, which are usually taken to be measures of globalisation; and, second, restrictions to trade and capital. Since the financial crisis of 2008, economic globalisation has made little progress.

Social globalisation

The KOF Index classifies social globalisation in three categories:

- Personal contacts: including international telecom traffic (outgoing traffic in minutes per subscriber) and the degree of tourism (incoming and outgoing) a country's population is exposed to. Government and workers' transfers (such as remittances and FDI) received and paid (as a percentage of GDP) measure whether and to what extent countries interact.
- Information flows: including the number of internet users, cable television subscribers, number of radios (all per 1000 people) and international newspapers traded (as a percentage of GDP).
- Cultural proximity: arguably the dimension of globalisation most difficult to grasp. According to one geographer (Tony Saich, 'Globalisation, Governance and the Authoritarian State') cultural globalisation refers mostly to the domination of US cultural products (Figure 7.3). However, there are many other companies and products that do not come from the USA: sushi, curry, Toyota and Sony spring to mind. KOF includes the number of McDonald's restaurants located in a country (Figure 7.4). In a similar vein, it also uses the number of IKEA stores per capita.

In 2012 Singapore had the highest social globalisation, followed by Ireland and Austria.

Figure 7.3 Disney merchandise in Brunei.

Figure 7.4 McDonald's sign in Tokyo.

Political globalisation

Political globalisation uses the number of embassies and high commissions in a country, the number of international organisations of which the country is a member and the number of UN peace missions in which a country has participated. In 2012 political globalisation was highest in Italy, followed by Austria and France.

Flows of capital

Figure 7.5 shows global flows of capital, 2002 and 2012.According to McKinsey & Company, one-third of financial investments are international transactions. In the next decade, global flows could triple, powered by rising prosperity and participation in the emerging world and by the spread of the internet and digital technologies. The flow of global finance increased from around \$2.5 trillion in 2002 to almost \$4 trillion in 2012, an increase of about 60%. The global pattern has also changed. In 2002 the dominant flow was between North America and western Europe, and there were important flows (but less in terms of % of global GDP) between Northeast Asia and both North America and western Europe. Most other flows were relatively small. By 2012, the dominance of North America/ western Europe had declined, and there was an increasingly important flow between western Europe and eastern Europe. The Chinese region had also increased in the size and number of flows that it was involved in. Overall, financial flows are becoming more connected regionally.

Flows of labour

Figure 7.6 shows the main migrant flows between 2005 and 2010. The countries are arranged by mean number of years of schooling. The pattern is quite clear: migrants are moving from countries with lower mean number of years of schooling to countries with higher mean number of years of schooling. In reality, migrants are moving from poorer countries to richer countries, where there are more job opportunities. The largest migrant flows are between Mexico and the USA (nearly 2 million migrants) and from India to the UAE (over 1 million migrants). Migrants' remittances are an important transfer between countries and are not always from high income countries (HICs) to low income countries (LICs) (Figure 7.7).

Physical and human

Suggest how physical and human geography may interact in the environment shown in Figure 7.3.

For more information and activities on the KOF Index of Globalisation, download Worksheet 7.1 from **Cambridge Elevate**.

Making connections

Migration can lead to a transfer of wealth from one country to another. How may host countries (destinations) try to limit the leakage of wealth to migrants' countries of origin? See section 10.5 Population change.

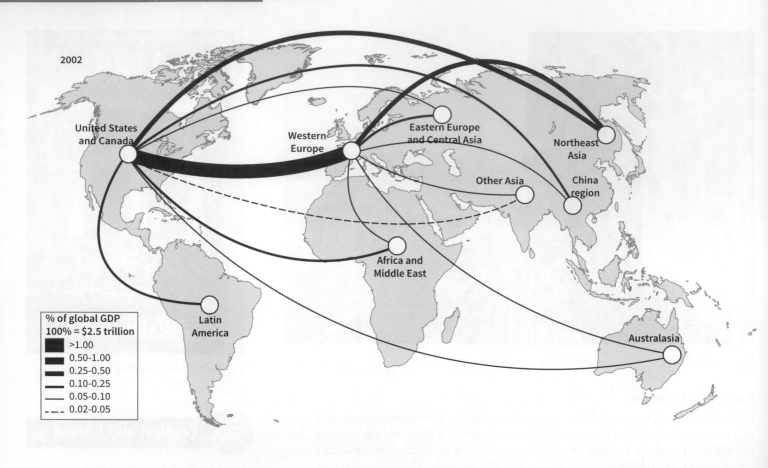

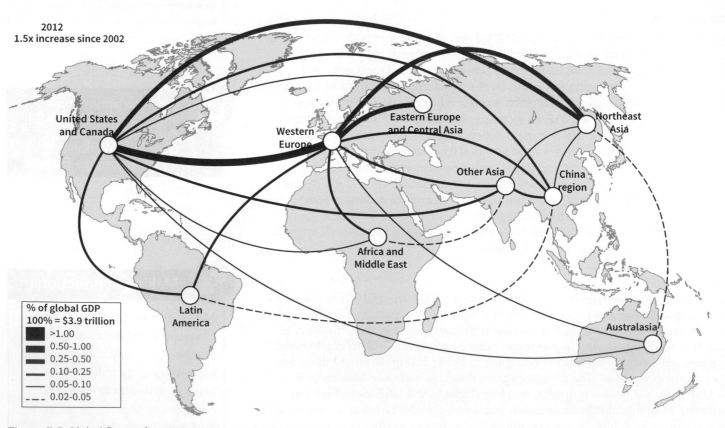

Figure 7.5 Global flows of capital, 2002 and 2012.

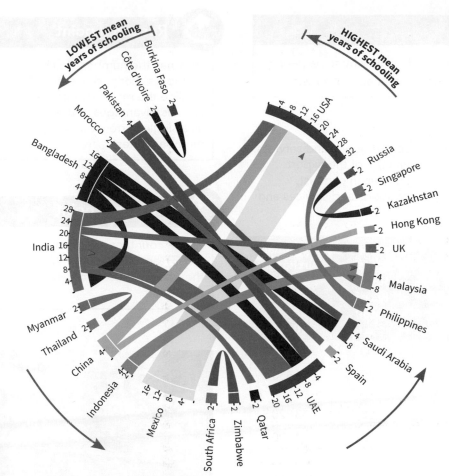

Figure 7.6 Main international flows of labour, 2005–10.

Research point

Imagine that you are an economic migrant working in a place near where you currently live. Find out how you could send money to your family, where you could do this from and what the cost is. Which method/company would you use? Justify your answer.

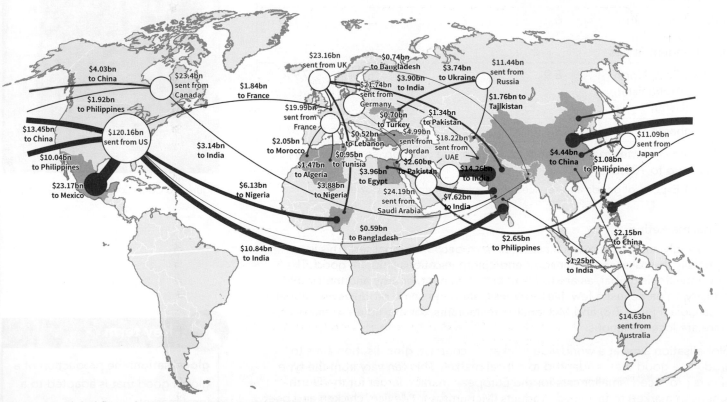

Figure 7.7 Global flow of remittances, 2011.

Thinking like a geographer

Figure 7.6 shows migration flows between countries. Explain why some people migrate from high income countries (HICs) to countries that are not HICs.

Flows of products, services and information

Table 7.1 illustrates many inequalities in the global export of goods and services, and in regional purchasing power. HICs account for over 60% of the export of goods and services and 50% of regional purchasing power. In contrast, sub-Saharan Africa accounts for just 2% of the export of goods and services and 3% of total purchasing power.

Region	Regional population (%)	Regional international trade (export of goods and services) (%)	Regional purchasing power (% of total)	Regional purchasing power ($/per head, 2013)
World	100.0	100	100	12350
High income countries	14.7	61	50	41650
G7	10.6	33	38	43820
Euro area	4.7	25	13	34020
Other Asia	49.0	17	26	6550
Latin America and the Caribbean	8.4	5	9	12670
Other Europe and Commonwealth Independent States	6.5	7	8	14170
Middle East, North Africa, Afghanistan and Pakistan	8.9	7	6	7990
Sub-Saharan Africa	12.5	2	3	2570

NB: Some countries may appear in more than one category so the numbers do not add up to 100%.

Table 7.1 Exports of goods and services and regional purchasing power.

Global marketing

Increasingly, many commercial activities have become globalised. This is especially the case where transport and communications links are good. The food industry is global, as are tourism, entertainment, energy and the clothing industry, to name just a few. Nevertheless, although some products are global – Coca-Cola (Figure 7.8) and McDonald's restaurants, for example – in many cases there are local variations.

Globalisation aims at a worldwide market. In contrast, **glocalisation** aims to produce a good that is adapted to a local market. This can vary from the type of cars produced (smaller cars for the European market, larger for the North American market) to fast food products (McBurritos in Mexico, chicken and beef rice wraps in China).

Research point

How has the number of EU members changed over time? Outline the main advantages and disadvantages of the euro as a single currency in many EU member states.

Research point

Which countries are members of the G7 and G8 groups? What are the roles of these groupings of countries?

Figure 7.8 Coca-Cola sign in Reykjavik, Iceland.

Key term

glocalisation: the production of a global good that is adapted to a local market

Case Study

7.2 Walmart and adaptation to globalisation

Walmart is the world's biggest retailer and the world's largest company by revenue. It was founded by Sam Walton, with the concept of 'low prices always' at the core of the business. The first discount store opened in 1962 in Rogers, Arkansas, USA. There are over 11 000 stores worldwide. Walmart has four main retail categories: Walmart Supercentres, Discount Stores, Neighborhood Markets and the huge Sam's Club members-only warehouses, which have a basic approach to retailing.

Walmart became an international company in 1991 and there are now over 6000 stores outside the USA in 26 countries (including China, Japan, Argentina and the UK). However, although Walmart is the model of a globalised company, offering global products to a global market, it has adapted, where necessary, to local conditions. This helps explain how it has been able to survive and thrive overseas. Walmart has made the necessary changes to adapt to local cultures and become involved in the local community. This is vital because social and cultural factors can represent large-scale barriers to success across borders.

Walmart in China

In 1996 Walmart decided to enter the Chinese market (Figure 7.9). As its development progressed, the company realised that Chinese tastes were different from those elsewhere. In particular, Chinese customers required leafy vegetables, which could only be purchased locally. This complicated Walmart's normal strategy of 'global centralised' purchasing. The vegetable section in Chinese Walmarts is double the size of that of American Walmarts and the products are different. In the Shenzhen Walmartin Guandong province, it is possible to purchase chicken feet, stewed pork ribs and pickled lettuce, products not normally found in American Walmarts.

Many products have to be sourced locally, partly because of the poor transport system in China and partly because of government regulations; Chinese rules state that products such as alcohol and tobacco have to be purchased from local suppliers. The result is that about 85% of products sold in Walmart China come from some 14 000 Chinese suppliers.

Walmart in Germany

Walmart entered the German market in 1988. At that time, Germany already had discount retailers such as Aldi and Lidl. Customer service was identified as one way that Walmart could differentiate itself from its competitors. Walmart took over approximately 100 hypermarkets in its first year.

In the USA, Walmart customers are met by friendly 'greeters', who smile and give them a shopping trolley in an attempt to personalise the shopping experience. This did not go down as well in Germany, where the greeters were regarded as superficial, and some stores removed them altogether.

One new development that took place in Germany was the introduction of 'singles' shopping nights' on Fridays in many German Walmart stores. This proved very successful: Friday night profits increased by 25% and at least 30 couples met during these events. The idea was transferred to a number of stores in Canada and South Korea. However, Walmart closed in Germany following disputes over labour costs.

ACTIVITY 7.1

1   Suggest the likely advantages for Walmart in operating in China.
2   Comment on the likely advantages for China in allowing Walmart to operate there.
3   Outline the potential conflicts that might arise from Walmart operating in China. Justify your answer.

 Look on **Cambridge Elevate** for more information on Walmart. Click on 'Our Story' to find out its history and click on 'Global Responsibility' for its latest *Global Responsibility Report* (www.cambridge.org/links/gase6058).

 For an activity on Walmart, download Worksheet 7.2 from **Cambridge Elevate**.

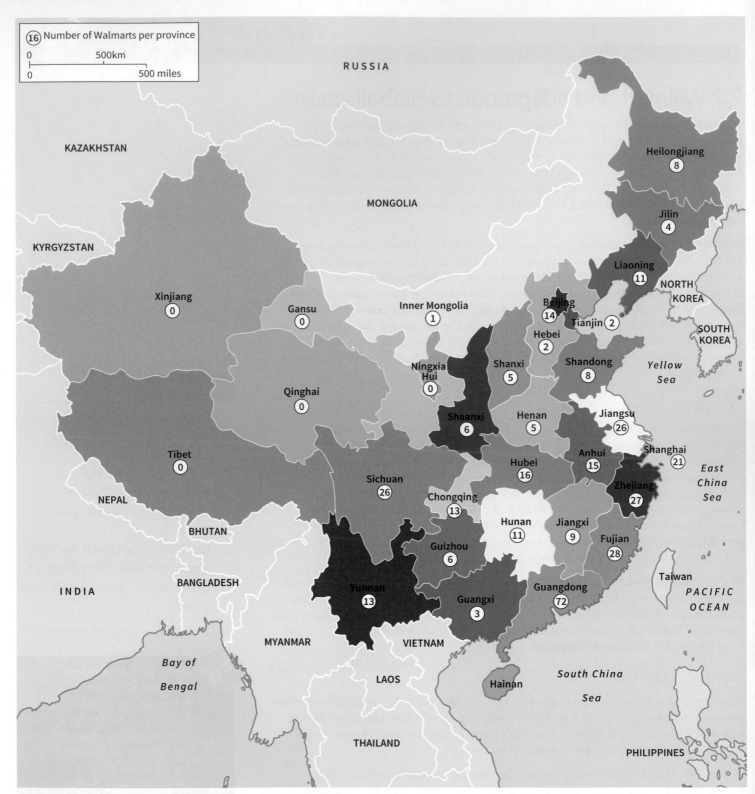

Figure 7.9 The distribution of Walmart in China.

Patterns of production, distribution and consumption

Before 1970 it may have been possible to generalise and state that much production, especially of primary products, occurred in low income countries which were transported to be consumed in high income countries. However, many previously 'poor' countries such as South Korea and Singapore have become 'rich' and many others such as Vietnam, Bangladesh and Pakistan are industrialising. As countries industrialise and become richer, patterns of consumption change, notably diet. Therefore, the global pattern of production, distribution and consumption are changing. Consider crude oil, for example. In the 1980s the main producers included the Middle East, the USA, Venezuela and the North Sea producers. The main consumers included North America, the EU and Japan. In the 2010s the main producers include the Middle East and North America, but Venezuela and the UK have declined. There are new producers such as Russia and China. The main consumers include the USA, China, Japan and India. As production and consumption change, the distribution has to adapt to changes in supply and demand.

On the other hand, analysis of the main producers and consumers of cocoa suggest that there is a low-income/high-income demand (Table 7.2). The same is true for coffee production and consumption, but not for tea production and consumption.

Producers	Tonnes (000s)	Consumers	Tonnes (000s)
Ivory Coast	1449	USA	770
Ghana	835	Germany	330
Indonesia	420	UK	223
Cameroon	225	France	218
Nigeria	225	Russia	205
Ecuador	192	Brazil	200
Brazil	185	Japan	160
Peru	69	Spain	107
Dominican Republic	68	Canada	89
Colombia	48	Italy	85

Table 7.2 The main cocoa producers and consumers, 2012–13.

Maths for geographers

Use Table 7.2 to calculate:

a the mean

b the range

c standard deviation

for cocoa producers and consumers. What do these results suggest about the producers and consumers of cocoa?

Factors in globalisation

There are many reasons why globalisation has occurred. These include improvements in transport and other forms of communications (such as the internet)leading to a 'shrinking world' (**time–space convergence**) (Figure 7.10), as well as the desire by transnational corporations (TNCs) to reach new markets, tap cheap sources of labour and use resources from a wide range of locations.

Investigate

Investigate a main street in your nearest town or city. How many of the shops or businesses belong to international companies? How many of the shops or businesses are local/independent companies? Comment on your findings.

Key term

time–space convergence: the time it takes to travel between places is getting shorter, so distant places are brought closer together in terms of the time taken to travel (and send messages) between them

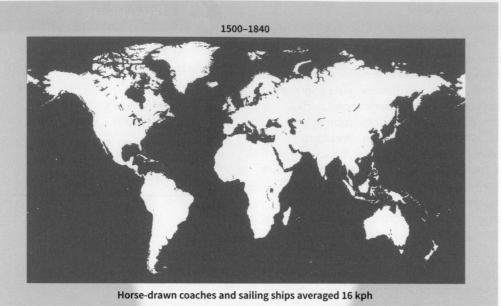

1500–1840

Horse-drawn coaches and sailing ships averaged 16 kph

1850–1930

Steam locomotives 105 kph; steam ships 57kph

1950's

Propeller aircraft 450–640 kph

1960's

Jet passenger aircraft 800–1120 kph

1970's

Supersonic aircraft 2300 kph

2010's

Sub-orbital aircraft 5600 kph

Figure 7.10 Time–space convergence.

Globalisation is associated with the rise of free market economies and the spread of democratic governments. In addition, the role of trading blocs, free trade and financial institutions such as the World Trade Organization (WTO), the International Monetary Fund (IMF) and the World Bank has helped the flow of capital, goods and labour around the world. At the same time, the increasing importance of TNCs has made some national boundaries seem less of a barrier. Nevertheless, there are others who believe that the power of globalisation is limited.

Financial systems

The global financial sector is often considered to be a model of globalisation. Since the 1970s, transnational flows of capital have increased dramatically. Activities such as banking, insurance, currency exchange and investment services have risen rapidly. The globalisation of finance has come about through deregulation, reform of services, development of communications technology and the evolution of tradable financial products. On the other hand, the world's financial system might not be as globalised as is widely believed. The global financial system is concentrated in a number of western economies and the bulk of the flows move between specialised districts in world cities, such as New York, London and Tokyo. Moreover, there are distinct circuits of money that are largely discrete and unintegrated. Nevertheless, there are important flows of money through remittances, foreign direct investment (FDI), loans, aid, repatriation of profit and trade.

 Look on **Cambridge Elevate** for a map of global remittances in 2010 on the Diverging Markets website (www.cambridge.org/links/gase6059).

Transport

The **frictional effect of distance** (or distance decay) suggests that areas that are closer together are more likely to interact with each other, whereas those that are further away are less likely to interact. However, there has been a reduction in the frictional effect of distance as improvements in transport have allowed greater distances to be covered in the same amount of time. In addition, improvements in ICT including Voice over Internet Protocol (VoIP) services such as Skype have brought places on different sides of the world together almost instantaneously.

A basic requirement for the evolution of international trade and the development of TNCs is the development of technologies that overcome the frictional effect of distance and time. The most important of these **enabling technologies** are transport and communications. Without them, today's complex global economic system would not exist.

Transport systems are the means by which materials, goods and people are moved between places. Communication systems are the means by which information is transmitted between places. Before the development of electricity in the 19th century, information could move only at the same speed and over the same distance as the prevailing transport system would allow. Electricity broke that link, making it increasingly necessary to treat transport and communication as separate, though closely related, technologies. Developments in both have transformed the world, allowing unprecedented mobility of materials and goods and a globalisation of markets.

Major developments in transport technology

The world has 'shrunk' in the time it takes to get from one part of the world to another. For most of human history, the speed and efficiency of transport were low and the costs of overcoming the frictional effect of distance were high. Movement over land was especially slow and difficult before the development of

 Key terms

frictional effect of distance: the theory that areas that are closer together are more likely to interact, whereas those that are further apart are less likely to do so

enabling technologies: inventions or innovations that allow a user or business to significantly impact the way they operate, such as the internet or barcode scanners

 Look on **Cambridge Elevate** for a map of cross-border investments on the Real Clear World website (www.cambridge.org/links/gase6060).

 Investigate

Investigate how long it would take and how much it would cost to send a book somewhere by courier (such as DHL), by plane, by boat or electronically. Comment on your findings.

the railways. The major breakthrough came with the invention and application of steam power and the use of iron and steel for trains, railway tracks and ocean-going vessels. The railway and the steamship enabled a new, much enlarged, scale of economic activity.

The mid to late 20th century saw an acceleration of this process of time–space convergence. The most important developments have been the introduction of commercial jet aircraft, the development of much larger ocean-going vessels (superfreighters) (Figure 7.11) and the introduction of containerisation, which greatly simplifies shipment from one mode of transport to another. Of these, the jet aircraft had the most influence, especially in the development of TNCs. It is hardly coincidental that the take-off of TNC growth and the take-off of commercial jets both occurred during the 1950s.

Security

Globalisation has had important impacts on aspects of human security – economic, military, environmental, cultural and psychological. In all of these aspects, globalisation can have both positive and negative impacts. However, it is not the only cause of human insecurity.

In relation to peace and security, increased global interdependence has promoted disincentives to war, especially among Organisation for Economic Co-operation and Development (OECD) countries. The growth of global governance has increased the possibility of arms control and conflict management. On the other hand, there has been continued intervention from high income countries (HICs) in conflicts in low income countries (LICs), especially when valuable resources are at stake. Globalisation (anti-westernisation) has also been blamed for the rise in nationalism and religious fundamentalism. Developments in technology have raised the destructive capacity of weapons and improvements in communications have raised the profile of some extremist groups (e.g. IS/Daesh).

In relation to the environment, globalisation has promoted ecological awareness and improved technology allows greater environmental monitoring. However, many global activities are polluting and lead to land use changes.

Communications

Both the time needed and the relative cost of transporting materials, goods and people have fallen dramatically as the result of changes in transport technology. However, these developments have depended, to a large extent, on parallel developments in communications technology. In the 19th century, rail and ocean transport needed electric telegraph and, later, the oceanic cable, for their development. Similarly, the far more complex global transport system of the present depends fundamentally on telecommunications technology.

Communications technologies are the key technology involved in transforming relationships on a global scale. Communications technologies are significant for all economic activities, but they are especially vital to those sectors and activities whose primary function is to collect, transform and transmit information. One of the most important catalysts to enhanced global communications has been the development of satellite technology. This has made possible remarkable levels of global communication of conventional messages, as well as the transmission of data. Its key element is the linking together of computer technologies with information-transmission technologies over vast distances. Not only are transmission costs by satellite insensitive to distance, but also user costs have fallen dramatically. Satellite communications are now being challenged by optical fibre cables. These systems have a large carrying capacity and transmit information at very high speed and with a high signal strength.

However, only very large organisations, whether business or government, have the resources to utilise fully the new communications technologies. For TNCs, they have

Figure 7.11 Superfreighters.

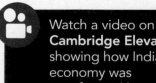

Watch a video on **Cambridge Elevate** showing how India's economy was transformed by advances in communications technology.

become essential to their operations. For example, Texas Instruments, the electronics TNC, has approximately 50 plants in some 19 countries. It operates a satellite-based communications system to coordinate, on a global scale, production planning, cost accounting, financial planning, marketing, customer services and personnel management. The system consists of almost 300 remote job-entry terminals, 8000 inquiry terminals and 140 distributed computers connected to the network.

According to Peter Dicken's *Global Shift*, technological developments in communications have transformed time–space relationships between all parts of the world. However, not all places are equally affected. In general, the places that benefit most from innovations in the communications media are the 'important' places, i.e. core areas. In contrast, the peripheral areas have benefited to a much lesser degree in terms of access to and use of new communications technologies. New investments in communications technology are market-related; they go to where the returns are likely to be high. The cumulative effect is to reinforce both certain communications routes at the global scale and to enhance the significance of the nodes (cities/countries) on those routes.

Figure 7.12 shows one year's worth of cross-border calls, as measured in minutes per person spent on international phone calls in 2012. There are a number of factors that help explain the pattern. One is the cost of an international phone call, which is relatively low in the USA, for example. A second is having the income to pay for the call. People in HICs are far more likely to call overseas than people in LICs. Of the total phone calls, 41% were from HICs to emerging economies; just 9% went in the opposite direction.

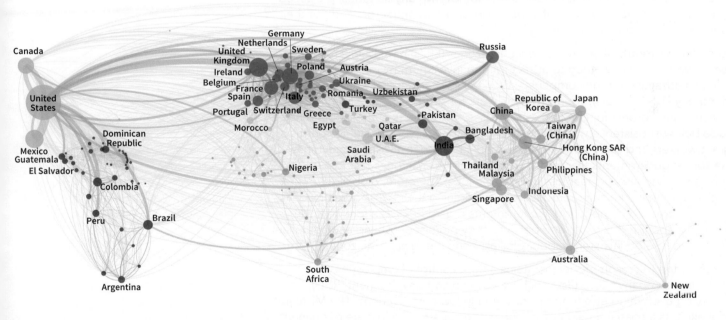

Figure 7.12 One year's worth of cross-border telephone calls.

Another factor relates to migration. The top two destinations of international calls placed from the USA were Mexico (the largest source of first-generation immigrants) and India (the third largest). The same kind of pattern appears elsewhere, between Hong Kong and China and between the UK and India. However, the map does not include computer-to-computer calls such as those via Skype, which accounted for about 34% of all international calling minutes in 2013.

The internet has become a powerful force for globalisation. Search engines allow users to access a vast amount of information from around the world. There are, nevertheless, barriers to access. Some lack access to computers or the internet, or do not have knowledge of the language used. Social media and internet search engines have led to a certain amount of cultural homogenisation. Equally, they can support bottom-up development and minority groups. For example, during the Arab Spring of 2010–11, people in the Middle East and North Africa were able to communicate instantly and without interference from the authorities. ICT enabled them to mobilise support and disseminate news to the outside world.

Management and information systems

Globalisation implies many changes to the nature of work and organisations. It has embraced 'flexibility', making it easier to replace career employees with (zero-benefit) temporary staff; it has 'outsourced' work to the lowest bidder; it has 're-engineered' its various processes in a less labour-intensive way; it uses new technology to cut out middlemen and move back-office jobs to wherever wages are lowest.

This contrasts with the earlier mode of production, the Fordist type with its mass production of uniform goods, assembly line and increasing productivity through economies of scale. Fordism began to decline in the 1970s.

The world has moved from an industrial to a post-industrial society and the focus has shifted from producing goods, such as steel and cars, to producing services, such as fast food and health. There has also been an increase in new technologies and in knowledge and information processing.

It was Nike that became associated with the no-limits spending on branding, together with complete disinvestment in its workers. Many major companies embraced the successful Nike model: they did not own any factories, produced their products through a variety of contractors and subcontractors and put their resources into design and marketing.

In some areas, freetrade or exportprocessing zones (EPZs) have been created. In these, governments have tried to attract foreign investment by making working conditions attractive for the companies. Workers in EPZs generally have a long working day (12–16 hours); young workers work for sub/contractors from HICs; contractors fulfil orders for companies in HICs. Other aspects of the labour market include below-subsistence wages, low-skill monotonous work, unstable contracts, migrant workers and short-term, unstable work.Fear and instability characterise these zones: governments fear loss of foreign factories, factories fear loss of superbrands, and workers fear loss of unstable jobs. Therefore, globalisation puts pressure on workers and producers by weakening their bargaining power as a result of increased competition. Governments regard EPZs as a foreign trade policynot a labour rights issue, and because they promised a cheap and compliant workforce to foreign investors, labour officials bend the rules in the zones.

In contrast, the Microsoft model maintains a tight control of employees who perform the company's core tasks such as research and development (R&D), outsourcing everything else to temporary staff in low-cost locations. The Microsoft model exhibits a spatial division of labour: in the country of origin are permanent, full-time workers with benefits and stock options, and in the periphery (mainly LICs) are temporary workers, many of whom are on relatively low wages. Some of the unhappiest workers are likely to be those working for the biggest brands, such as the 14 suicides at the Foxconn City Industrial Park in Shenzhen in 2010. Moreover, by hiring workers on temporary contracts, companies are bypassing the laws that provide benefits to workers and that prevent them from firing staff without cause. Moreover, there is a new breed of workers – 'temporary CEOs' – who move between multinational companies, earning multimillion dollar packages on the way in and out. For example, CEO George Fisher of Kodak cut 20 100 jobs and received a $60 million stock options grant.

The rise of the global economy has therefore meant a radical change in work and organisations. Although multinationals are creating economic growth, a healthy economy does not mean job stability or an increase in employment. Profits are put before people. Casual, part-time, temporary and low-wage work does not create commitment and loyalty.

Neoliberalism emphasises free markets, with prices set by markets, the liberalisation of trade, privatisation and consumer choice. The results are wide-ranging, including a huge increase in social and economic inequality, significant growth in extreme deprivation for LICs and an increase in the wealth of TNCs. On the other hand, there are many benefits to neoliberalism, including greater access to products, more competitive pricing and shareholder dividends.

Trade agreements

The WTO deals with the rules of trade between nations at a global or near-global level. Based in Geneva, Switzerland, the WTO has 153 members, representing more than 97% of total world trade. The WTO is:

- an organisation for liberalising trade
- a forum for governments to negotiate trade agreements
- a place for settling trade disputes
- a system of trade rules.

The WTO began was established on 1 January 1995, but its trading system is over 50 years older. Since 1948 the General Agreement on Tariffs and Trade (GATT) provided the rules for the system. The last and largest GATT round was the Uruguay Round (1986–94), which led to the WTO's creation. The GATT mainly dealt with trade in goods, whereas the WTO and its agreements cover trade in services and in traded inventions, creations and designs (intellectual property). The agreements provide the legal ground rules for international commerce, which aim to help trade flow as freely as possible. Nevertheless, trade relations often involve conflicting interests.

7.3 Global systems

World systems analysis is identified with Immanuel Wallerstein, author of *The Modern World-System*, and is a way of looking at economic, social and political development. It treats the whole world as a single unit, meaning that it examines the interrelationships between different sets of countries. Any analysis of development must be seen as part of the overall capitalist world economy, not adopting a country by country approach. Wallerstein argued that an approach that looked at individual countries in isolation was too simplistic and suffered from developmentalism. The developmentalism school assumed that:

- each country was economically and politically free (autonomous)
- all countries follow the same route to development.

As such, they were ethnocentric, believing that what happened in North America and Europe was best and would automatically happen elsewhere.

According to Wallerstein, the capitalist world system has three main characteristics:

- a global market
- many countries, which allow political and economic competition
- three tiers of countries (Figure 7.13).

Key term

Neoliberalism: an approach that favours privatisation, deregulation, free trade and a reduction in government spending

ACTIVITY 7.2

1 Define the term 'globalisation'.
2 Describe the variations in the KOF Index in Europe and Africa, as shown in Figure 7.2.
3 Distinguish between globalisation and glocalisation.
4 With the use of examples, explain the meaning of the term 'time–space convergence'.
5 Define the term 'frictional effect of distance'.

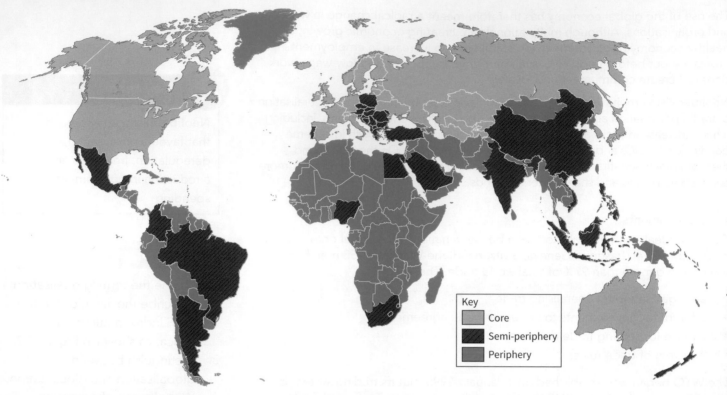

Figure 7.13 World systems theory.

The tiers are defined as:

- the core: largely higher income countries (HICs)
- the semi-periphery: a political label that refers to those countries where there are class struggles and social change, such as Latin America in the 1980s and eastern Europe in the late 1980s and early 1990s
- the periphery: identified with lower income countries (LICs).

Table 7.3 shows development data for six selected core, semi-periphery and periphery countries.

Development indicator	Core		Semi-periphery		Periphery	
	USA	UK	China	India	Afghanistan	DR Congo
GNP/capita ($)	54 600	39 500	12 900	5 900	1 900	700
Economic growth (%)	2.4	2.6	7.4	7.2	1.5	9.1
Population growth (%)	0.78	0.54	0.45	1.22	2.32	2.45
Infant mortality rate (‰)	5.87	4.38	12.44	41.81	115.08	71.47
Internet users/100 people	84.2	89.8	45.8	15.1	5.9	2.2
Doctors/1000 people	2.45	2.81	1.49	0.7	0.27	0.03
Population below poverty line (%)	15.1	15.0	6.1	29.8	36	63

Table 7.3 Development data for selected core, semi-periphery and periphery countries.

Thinking like a geographer

All statistics have their strengths and weaknesses. Outline the strengths and weaknesses of the statistics used in Table 7.3. Which one do you think is most valuable? Suggest reasons for your answer.

Wallerstein argued that capitalist development led to cycles of growth and stagnation. Stagnation is important for the restructuring of the world system and allows the semi-periphery to become involved in the development process.

According to the world systems approach, capitalism includes feudalism and socialism. They are extreme variations on the division of labour. As the world develops and changes, there will be either a swing towards a more socialist system or a transition towards a more unequal (feudal) system.

Unequal flows of people, money, ideas and technology within global systems

Flows of people, money, ideas and technology may bring benefits to the source as well as to the destination. For example, migrants may boost productivity in a country, as well as send remittances back to their families. As migrants tend to be young, educated and innovative, they bring skills and a hard work ethic to the destination. They also remove some of these qualities from the source region. The migration of highly trained IT workers or doctors to countries that offer higher wages is a net loss to the country of origin.

Although the single largest migration is from Mexico to the USA and the USA is the largest single destination, the largest regional migration is from south-east Asia to the Middle East. This is largely driven by the huge, oil-driven, construction boom occurring on the Arabian Peninsula.

The benefits of migration can be uneven, Qatar is an example of this. It has the highest proportion of migrant workers to domestic population in the world. Some 90% of the two million population are migrant workers, and Qatar is expected to recruit a further 1.5 million migrant workers to help build the infrastructure and stadia required for the 2022 Football World Cup. There are about 400 000 Nepalese workers in Qatar among the 1.4 million migrant workers working on a $137 billion building programme. As well as nine state of the art football stadia, Qatar is building $20 billion of new roads, a high speed rail network, and 55 000 hotel rooms to accommodate visiting fans. In addition, there is a new airport. This construction boom should be providing rich rewards for the workers. Many migrants who travel to Qatar have borrowed money to afford the transport, only to find themselves indebted to recruitment agencies and the conditions of their employment altered. Some are having to pay back their loans with an interest rate of over 35% – hence they end up being forced to work for very little pay. During 2012 and 2013, nearly 1000 workers from Nepal, India and Bangladesh died whilst working in Qatar, partly as a result of the working and living conditions.

An Amnesty International investigation revealed:

- evidence of forced labour on World Cup infrastructure projects
- salaries being withheld so that workers would not run away
- passports and ID confiscated
- overcrowded accommodation
- poor access to drinking water.

Thus, one of the world's richest countries is exploiting some of the world's poorest people in order to provide a global spectacle, the World Cup. The Nepalese ambassador to Qatar described the situation as an 'open jail'. Without official documentation, migrant workers are essentially illegal aliens, unable to leave their place of work for fear of arrest. They have few, if any rights. Under the Qartari *kafala* system, workers are unable to change jobs without their employer's permission. They are forbidden to form trade unions.

Nevertheless, there are many migrants that are working in construction, and women working in domestic service, that are treated well. Many of these do send remittances to their families.

In addition, according to defectors from North Korea, the North Korean government takes 70% or more of the earnings of migrants working on construction sites in Qatar. There are believed to be about 3000 North Koreans working in Qatar (and a further 65 000 working in Russia, China, Mongolia and the Middle East). The North Korean typically takes 70% of the earning, and once 'fees', food and accommodation are paid, the migrant labourers may receive 10% of their earnings. According to the Director of Anti-Slavery International, 'The conditions North Korean workers endure in Qatar – abuse of vulnerability, withholding of wages, excessive overtime – are highly indicative of state-sponsored trafficking for forced labour – a modern form of slavery'.

Unequal power relations

Unequal power relations enable some countries to drive global systems to their own advantage and to directly influence geopolitical events, while others are only able to respond or resist in a more constrained way. Examples of this are Chinese expansion in the South China Sea and the Yamal megaproject in Siberia.

Chinese expansion in the South China Sea

The South China Sea is a vital trade artery, accounting for about 30% of the world's trade passes, over £3 trillion in value. China's current behaviour there ignores international law, intimidates its neighbours and increases the potential for conflict with some of them and with the USA.

In 2015–16 China is alleged to have installed two launch batteries for surface-to-air missiles on Woody Island in the Paracel archipelago. China claimed its right to 'limited and necessary self-defence facilities'. The Paracels are also claimed by Vietnam and Taiwan. China insists that virtually all the sea belongs to it.

It also built over some coral reefs in the Spratly islands, creating artificial land on rocks and reefs also claimed by the Philippines, Taiwan and Vietnam. The construction, like the missiles, flouts the spirit of a declaration China signed in 2002 with the Association of South-East Asian Nations (ASEAN), in which the parties promised to 'exercise self-restraint' in the sea. China has built over 42 km of artificial land mass in the Spratly Islands to create land with facilities that could be used for military use, including an air strip with a 3000 m runway. The region is also rich in oil and gas.

In 2016 China delegates visited Itu Aba, the biggest natural island in the Spratly archipelago in the South China Sea, garrisoned by Taiwan but also claimed by China, the Philippines and Vietnam. Under the UN Convention on the Law of the Sea (UNCLOS), Itu Aba is a rock that cannot sustain human life, so it is entitled to 12 nautical miles of territorial waters, but not the 200-mile exclusive economic zone accorded to habitable islands.

Three approaches are being tried to moderate China's behaviour—legal, diplomatic and military. The legal case that the Philippines brought to the UNCLOS is to show that China's historic claim – a 'nine-dash line' on maps encompassing most of the sea (Figure 7.14) has no legal basis. Diplomatically,

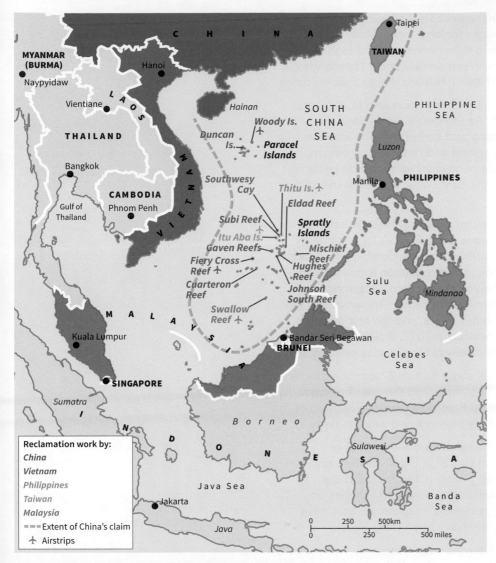

Figure 7.14 Geopolitical conflict in the South China Sea.

China prefers to negotiate with ASEAN members individually. As for military deterrence, a marked increase in defence spending across the region in recent years still leaves the USA as the only power capable of standing up to China.

The USA also wants to turn two Pacific Islands into a military training ground. Tinian and Pagan are two US territories that form part of the Commonwealth of Northern Mariana Islands. The US Navy has proposed using the two islands for live fire exercise for at least 16 weeks each year. Pagan has been largely uninhabited since a volcanic eruption in 1981, and would be used as a training ground for a potential conflict in the South and East China Seas.

The Yamal megaproject: an example of unequal power within a country

The Nenets are indigenous nomadic reindeer herders who have used the Yamal Peninsula for over 1000 years. The Yamal Peninsula extends from Northern Siberia to the Kara Sea. Yamal is a remote, wind-blasted region underlain by permafrost. The Nenets graze their reindeer in the Yamal during the summer, and move south during the winter. Some are semi-nomadic, residing in towns during the winter.

Some Nenets have abandoned their traditional way of life. Following the collapse of communism, many young adults left their villages for large cities. Many have failed to adapt to life away from nomadism, and there have been reports of high levels of unemployment, alcoholism and mental health problems. For the Nenets who retained their traditional ways, their lands and their herds are vital to their existence.

The Nenets are now facing threats from climate change and also from oil and gas exploration. The Arctic is changing fast. As temperatures rise and the tundra's permafrost thaws, it releases methane and carbon dioxide into the atmosphere. With ice melting earlier in the spring and not freezing until much later, the herders are being forced to change centuries old migration patterns. Melting permafrost is also causing some of the tundra's freshwater lakes to drain, which is leading to a decline in fish supplies.

Yamal holds Russia's (and the world's) largest natural gas reserves. An estimate of the gas reserves here is 55 trillion cubic metres (tcm). Russia's largest energy project in history puts the future of nomadic herding at considerable risk. Roads and pipelines are difficult for reindeer to cross, and oil pollution is threatening the quality of pasture and freshwater. The Russian corporation, Gazprom, is developing the region's huge oil and gas reserves, in a project known as the Yamal Megaproject. The project was first initiated in the 1990s, and the first of its gas supplies from the Bovanenkovo field was produced in 2012. A 570 km railway line from Obskaya-Bovanenk (the world's most northerly rail line) was opened in 2011.

Yamal has over 16 tcm of proven gas reserves and a further 22 tcm of expected ha reserves. Over 2500 pipelines will be built to transport the gas. Transport infrastructure is poorly developed in the Yamal Peninsula, so development of the region will require developments to the railway network and aviation network.

Oil and gas operations in the Yamal Peninsula destroyed over 64000 km^2 of tundra in just ten years of exploration. Fish yields on the River Ob have decreased, fish spawning grounds have been polluted; the River Ob used to provide 60% of the Former Soviet Union's fish catch; nearly 30 fisheries on tributaries of the Ob have been destroyed; reindeers' migratory routes have been bisected by railroads, and some reindeer have been shot.

According to a spokesperson from Survival International, 'Gazprom's website calls the Yamal Peninsula a strategic oil and gas bearing region of Russia. This sums up how they view the Nenets' ancestral homeland'. The statement concludes 'The Nenets people have lived on and stewarded the tundra's fragile ecology for hundreds of years. No developments should take place on their land without their consent, and they need to receive fair compensation for any damages caused'.

7.4 International trade and access to markets

Trends in the volume and pattern of international trade and investment

Globalisation is neither inevitable nor irreversible. Technology, especially transport and communications, has been the main driver of global economic integration over the past 200 years. Most of the 19th century and the early years of the 20th century produced the first great globalisation. Between 1914 and 1945, however, a period of dramatic 'deglobalisation' took place, during which the two world wars and the Great Depression resulted in many countries adopting more protectionist policies.

After the Second World War, globalisation resurfaced with the formation of the United Nations (Figure 7.15), the IMF, the World Bank and the GATT (later the WTO). These institutions were established to keep the peace and reduce economic nationalism.

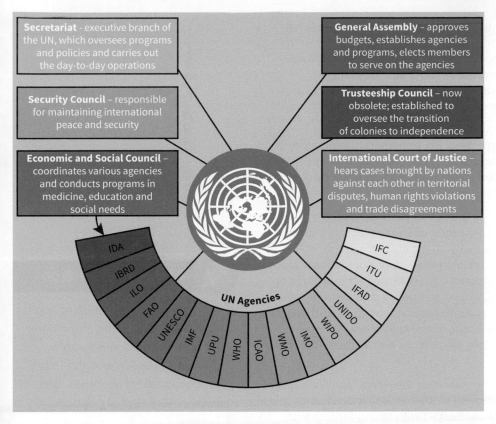

Figure 7.15 The structure of the United Nations.

International trade has grown tremendously over the last 30 years. The value of world merchandise trade increased by more than 7% per year on average between 1980 and 2011, reaching a peak of $18 trillion in 2013. Trade in commercial services grew at about 8% per year on average, accounting for $4 trillion in 2011. Since 1980, world trade has grown on average nearly twice as fast as world production.

Trading relationships

New players have risen to prominence in world trade, most notably large developing countries and rapidly industrialising Asian economies. Developing economies accounted for only 34% of world exports in 1980, but 47% in 2011. In contrast, the share of HICs dropped from 66% to 5%. China boosted its share in world exports from 1% in 1980 to 11% in 2011. In contrast, USA, Japan and the EU all recorded declining shares in world exports between 1980 and 2011. The share of South–South (emerging economies and newly industrialised countries, or NICs) trade in world trade rose from 8% in 1990 to 24% in 2011. The share of North–South trade also increased slightly, from 33% to 38% during this period, but trade among HICs (i.e. North–North trade) saw its share slide from 56% to just 3%.

Trade has tended to become more regionalised since 1990, particularly in Asia. The share of intra-regional trade in Asian exports rose from 42% in 1990 to 52% in 2011. The share of intra-regional trade in North America's exports increased from 41% to 56% between 1990 and 2000, before falling back to 48% in 2011.

The real nature of interdependence among economies can only be understood if trade is measured in terms of the value added by each location in the production process. International supply chains play a major role in today's world economy: traded goods and services contain inputs that may come from many different countries. Almost 30% of total trade consists of re-exports of intermediate inputs, indicating increased international interdependence through international production chains.

Look on **Cambridge Elevate** to read more from the UN website, about its values and its work (www.cambridge.org/links/gase6061).

If measured in value-added terms, the contribution of services to international trade is much higher. Services are key contributors to trade in goods, either in their role of facilitating international transactions or through their incorporation in the total production cost of goods. Economies import more and more intermediate goods and services to produce both for the domestic market and for exports. The more an economy integrates into international supply chains, the more its exports grow.

Several countries, mostly in the developing world, will experience favourable demographics but much depends on the education and integration of new entrants in the labour force. Others will need to cope with an ageing population and a shrinking working population.

Demography, investment, technology, energy and other natural resources, transportation costs and institutions are fundamental economic factors that all shape the overall nature of trade and explain why countries trade. The world is experiencing dramatic changes in the size and composition of populations. Many NEEs have experienced a demographic dividend – an increase in the proportion of young adult workers – whereas many HICs have an ageing population. Older groups in ageing countries spend more on communication, transport and health services. A younger population in countries accounts for goods and services such as recreation equipment, cars and mobile phones, as well as recreation and culture services.

Two other notable developments in the composition of the labour force are a rising share of educated workers and an increase in the female labour force. Female labour force participation is closely connected with falling fertility and rates vary widely (Figure 7.16).

Making connections

An increasing proportion of adults in relation to children and elderly is known as the 'demographic dividend'. Explain why this may be beneficial for countries. See section 10.8 Global population futures.

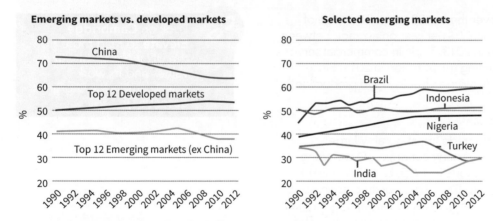

Figure 7.16 Female labour participation rates.

International migration is a component of demographic change. Migration can directly influence population growth by changing population levels in different countries. Emigration rates of highly educated individuals differ widely across sending countries, exceeding 40% in the Caribbean and in several sub-Saharan African countries. In general, emigrants from Africa and South and Central America tend to be relatively highly educated. Migrant networks promote trade between source and host countries in two ways:

• They reduce trade costs relating to informational, language and institutional barriers while facilitating the creation of business relationships.

• Migrants boost trade because they demand disproportionately more goods and services from their origin country.

Investment

Investment in physical infrastructure can lead to the emergence of new players in international trade. Public investment in infrastructure reduces trade costs and therefore could, for example, improve the situation of many sub-Saharan Africa countries in world trade. For instance, doubling the kilometres of surfaced roads or the number of the airports of a country's territory can boost trade by 13–14%. Domestic savings are also important for enhancing investment in physical capital. High savings rates should continue to provide funds for investment in infrastructure in middle-income countries. Foreign capital flows can complement domestic savings in promoting domestic investment. In addition, overseas development assistance and migrant remittances can help develop infrastructure in many LICs.

Technology

There have been significant changes in the geography of innovation. Although the technological gap between high and lowincome countries persists, R&D expenditure has become less concentrated. Although most innovation still occurs in manufacturing, R&D in services has increased faster since the early 1990s. R&D spending is highly concentrated. Nearly 90% of R&D investment takes place in the manufacturing sector. Nevertheless, R&D in services has grown in knowledge-intensive business services (KIBS).

Technological progress is a major factor in explaining trade. Technology affects trade by shaping comparative advantage and reducing trade costs. Countries tend to export products for which they have a home market advantage: that is, products with the greatest domestic demand.

Energy and other natural resources

Energy, land and water resources have a crucial bearing on the volume, pattern and growth of international trade, particularly as these resources are distributed unevenly. The link between national endowments of natural resources and exports is clearest in the case of energy and land resources. Typically, countries with energy reserves and land tend to export products that use these factors intensively. Countries with abundant supplies can also use control over their resources to support strategic and geopolitical objectives. This may lead to international tensions.

Increases in prices and the price volatility of natural resources can have negative effects on economic activity and international trade. For example, oil is a major factor of production, so an increase in the oil price reduces production and growth in energy-importing countries. Higher oil prices should expand output and growth in energy-exporting countries. In general, an increase in energy prices raises the prices of these energy-intensive products and reduces demand for them, thereby altering the commodity composition of trade for many countries. Volatility in oil prices tends to reduce trade flows because it increases the risks faced by importers.

The exhaustibility of some natural resources has frequently caused a degree of alarm that may not be entirely warranted. Over the last three decades, the stock of proven oil reserves rose by more than 140% and the ratio of reserves to global consumption increased from 11 to 19. Nevertheless, energy needs are projected to rise by nearly one-third by the year 2035, with most of the growth in demand coming from emerging economies. Higher energy prices are likely in the future.

Transport costs

Declining transportation costs can increase the range of goods available for international commerce. For example, estimates from Latin American countries

Making connections

Energy security refers to having a reliable supply of sufficient energy resources. How may energy security change over the next decade? See Chapter 11 Resource security.

suggest that a 10% decline in average transport costs would be associated with an expansion of more than 10% in the number of products exported and a 9% increase in the number of products imported. A delay of one week in shipments can reduce the volume of exports by as much as 7% or raise the delivered price of goods by 16%. Being landlocked and distant from markets adds significantly to transportation costs. Evidence suggests that, on average, being landlocked reduces trade volume by about 40%. The extent and quality of transportation infrastructure in source, destination and transit countries also have a major impact on transportation costs. The disadvantages of having poor transportation infrastructure are substantial.

The transportation sector is a service industry whose efficiency depends in part on how much competition is allowed in the sector. Lack of competition may arise from the existence of a natural monopoly but government policies are important too. Limited competition in maritime transport means LICs pay as much as 30% more in freight charges and consequently have some 15% less trade.

Innovation makes an important contribution to the reduction of transportation costs. The development of the jet engine reduced the cost of air transport more than tenfold, while containerisation accelerated delivery times (Figure 7.17).

Figure 7.17 Singapore's deep-water port opened the way for development in the country.

Customs and other border controls can create delays and increase trade costs. The potential reduction in costs through trade facilitation is significant and explains why this is a major part of the WTO's Doha Round negotiations. Many LICs suffer disproportionately from costly border procedures. The cost of importing into LICs has been estimated at some 20% higher than in HICs.

International trade is also linked to government systems. Most trade policies tend to be associated with more democratic countries. Political borders and political disputes reduce the volume of trade between countries. Trade – and globalisation more generally – facilitates the spread of ideas and innovation. This contributes to economic growth, but the spread of ideas and innovation also implies technological change. Successful integration in global markets therefore means the constant need for individuals and societies to adjust to changes in the competitive environment.

Differential access to markets

Differential access to markets varies with levels of economic development and trading agreement. Having access to a trading bloc, for example, increases the potential for trade, and so for economic and social well-being. Not having access to a trading bloc, or not being part of a trading agreement, limits the potential trade of a country, and that has implications for economic and social well-being.

Trading blocs

A trading bloc is an arrangement among a group of nations to allow free trade between member countries but to impose tariffs (charges) on other countries that may wish to trade with them. Examples of trading blocs include the European Union (EU), the Association of Southeast Asian Nations (ASEAN), the North American Free Trade Agreement (NAFTA) andthe Union of South American Nations (UNASUR) (Figure 7.18).

A trade bloc is a group of countries that share trading arrangements between themselves and are protected from external trade to some degree. Since the Second World War there has been an increase in the number of trading blocs. However, not all trading blocs have the same function and level of integration.

- Free trade areas: in these unions, members abolish tariffs and quotas on trade between themselves but have restrictions on imports from non-member countries. NAFTA is a good example of a free trade area.

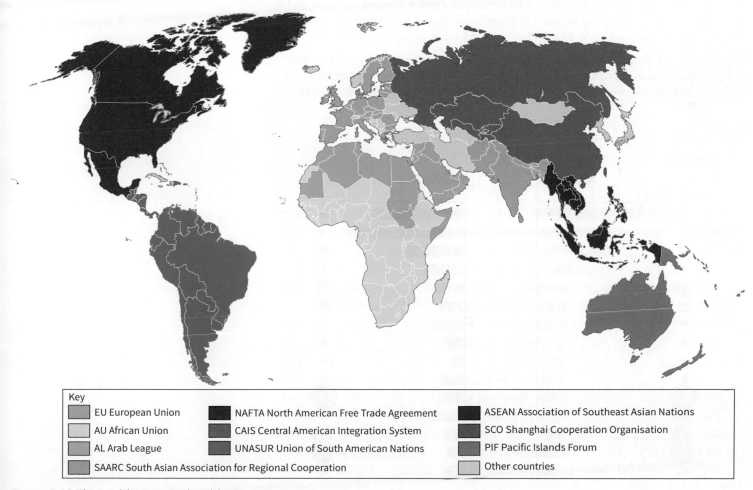

Key

EU European Union	NAFTA North American Free Trade Agreement	ASEAN Association of Southeast Asian Nations
AU African Union	CAIS Central American Integration System	SCO Shanghai Cooperation Organisation
AL Arab League	UNASUR Union of South American Nations	PIF Pacific Islands Forum
SAARC South Asian Association for Regional Cooperation		Other countries

Figure 7.18 The world's main trading blocs.

- A customs union: is a closer form of economic integration. As well as having free trade between members, all members operate a common external tariff on imports from abroad. Mercosur is a good example of a customs union.
- A common market: are customs markets which, as well as the free trade in goods and services, allow free movement of people and capital.
- An economic union: are groups of nations that not only allow the freedom of trade, and movement of people and capital, but also require members' common policies on such sectors as agriculture, industry and regional development. The European Union is an example of an economic union. When the UK joined in 1973, it joined a common market. With increasing integration, the common market became the European Economic Community (EEC), then the European Community, and finally, the European Union in 1993.

Look on **Cambridge Elevate** for more global trade graphics and an interactive graph from *The Economist* (www.cambridge.org/ links/gase6062).

Many trading blocs were established after the Second World War, as countries used political ties to further their economic development. Within a trading bloc, member countries have free access to each other's markets. Therefore, in the EU, the UK has access to Spanish markets, German markets, and so on. In return, Spain, Germany and other countries of the EU have access to the UK's market (Figure 7.19). Being a member of a trading bloc is beneficial as it allows greater market access – in the case of the EU, this amounts to over 500 million wealthy consumers.

Some critics believe that trading blocs are unfair as they deny non-members access to certain markets. For example, developing world countries have more limited access to the rich markets of Europe, which makes it harder for them to trade and develop. In order to limit the amount of protectionism, the WTO tries to promote free trade, which allows all producers in the world equal access to all markets.

The slowing of the Chinese economy and a sluggish recovery from the global financial crisis of 2007–08 have led to a long-term slowdown in world trade. The value of goods shipped around the globe has been shrinking on and off since early 2009.

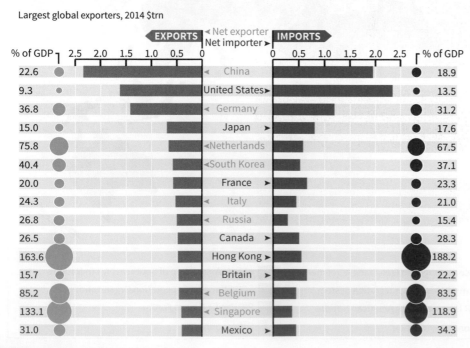

Figure 7.19 Trade flows, 2014.

Case Study

7.5 The Trans-Pacific Partnership

The Trans-Pacific Partnership (TPP) includes 12 countries in Asia and the Americas, including the USA and Japan but not yet China or South Korea. It is the biggest multilateral trade deal in 20 years.

What is the deal?

The TPP will apply to 40% of the world's economy. For exporters, 18000 individual tariffs will be reduced to zero. However, tariffs in the region were not that high to begin with. More important is the TPP's effort to free trade in services. The TPP promises greater access to markets for more service providers, which over time should provide a boost to productivity.

Several of the TPP's 30 chapters are devoted to protections for workers and environmental safeguards. There are clauses that attempt to slow deforestation and overfishing. All parties will also be compelled to follow the International Labour Organization's basic principles on workers' rights. They will be required to set a minimum wage and regulate working hours.

The TPP also attempts to limit the extent to which governments can favour state-owned enterprises. It could boost the world economy by $223 billion by 2025. The greatest impact will be felt not by the USA but by less developed members. The study estimates that Vietnamese GDP could rise by as much as an additional 10% over the same period.

In the long run, the partnership's impact will depend on whether or not its membership expands. Many commentators believe the USA pushed the TPP forward in order to increase its influence in Asia and reduce China's.

Look on **Cambridge Elevate** for more information on the TPP from the following websites:

- BBC (www.cambridge.org/links/gase6063)
- the *Guardian* (www.cambridge.org/links/gase6064).

Look on **Cambridge Elevate** for a map of member countries and a timeline of the TPP's development from the TPP website (www.cambridge.org/links/gase6065).

For more questions on the TPP, download Worksheet 7.3 from **Cambridge Elevate**.

ACTIVITY 7.3

1 Outline a case for China not to join the TPP.
2 Suggest reasons why the Republic of Korea (South Korea) is keen to join the TPP.

The nature and role of corporations (TNCs)

TNCs are organisations with operations in a large number of countries. Generally, headquarters are in HIC cities, R&D and decision-making are concentrated in growth areas of HICs, and assembly and production is located in LICs and NICs. TNCs provide a range of advantages and disadvantages for their host countries (Figure 7.20).

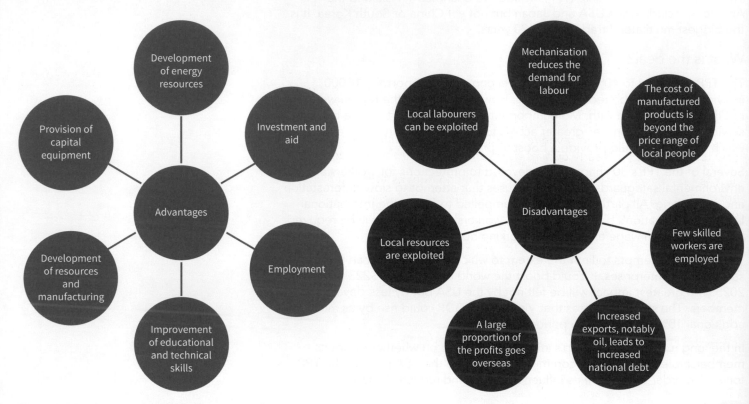

Figure 7.20 Advantages and disadvantages of TNCs.

TNC power

The sheer scale of the economic transactions that TNCs make around the world and the effect they have on urban, regional and national economies gives them tremendous power. Therefore, TNCs have become planned economies with vast internal markets:

- Up to one-third of all trade is made up of internal transfers of TNCs. These transfers produce money for governments via taxes and levies.
- Economic power comes from the ownership of assets.
- Over 70 million people are employed globally by TNCs.
- Although many governments in developing countries own their own resources, TNCs still control the marketing and transport of goods.

Reduced demand and increased competition create unfavourable economic conditions. In order to survive and prosper, TNCs use three main strategies:

- rationalisation: slimming down the workforce, which involves replacing people with machines
- reorganisation: improvements in production, administration and marketing, such as an increase in the subcontracting of production
- diversification: refers to firms that have developed new products.

The Tata group

The Tata group (Figure 7.21) is a family of companies encompassing cars and consulting, software and steel, tea and coffee, transport and power, chemicals and hotels. For example:

- Tata Steel is India's largest steelmaker and number ten in the world
- Tata Motors is among the top five commercial vehicle manufacturers in the world
- Tata Consultancy Services (TCS) is Asia's largest software company
- Taj Hotels Resorts and Palaces is India's biggest luxury hotel group by far
- Tata Power is the country's largest private electricity company
- Tata Global Beverages is the world's second-largest maker of branded tea.

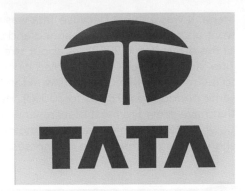

Figure 7.21 The logo of the Tata group.

The Tata group operates in over 80 countries and has a global workforce of about 395 000 people. There are over 100 operating companies, 28 of them listed on the Bombay Stock Exchange. Overall, the group earned 3.2 trillion rupees, or $67.4 billion, in revenues in 2009/10 and 82 billion rupees in profits (Figure 7.22). Nearly 60% of its revenue comes from outside India.

Just as Tata played a leading role in nation-building from its foundation in 1868 – creating India's first Indian-owned steel plant, power station, luxury hotel, domestic airline and sundry other firsts – it is now one of the stars of India's globalisation. Tata's state-of-the-art Ramanujan IT City is located in Chennai in southern India. This 10 ha site comprises an IT city that includes an IT Special Economic Zone (SEZ), luxury serviced apartments and an international convention centre.

Liberalisation

Liberalisation was both an opportunity and a threat for Tata. It was an opportunity because it enabled the group to compete in the international

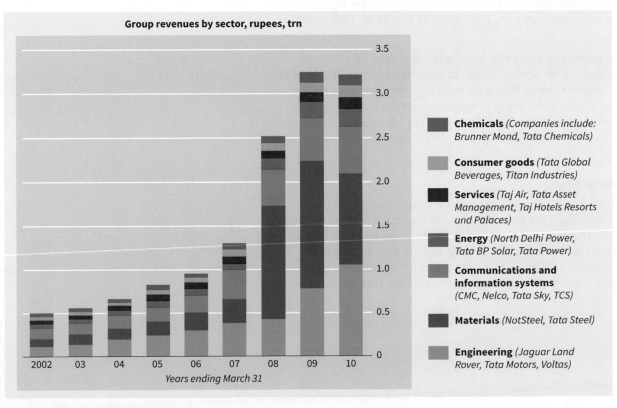

Group revenues by sector, rupees, trn

Years ending March 31

Chemicals (Companies include: Brunner Mond, Tata Chemicals)

Consumer goods (Tata Global Beverages, Titan Industries)

Services (Taj Air, Tata Asset Management, Taj Hotels Resorts und Palaces)

Energy (North Delhi Power, Tata BP Solar, Tata Power)

Communications and information systems (CMC, Nelco, Tata Sky, TCS)

Materials (NotSteel, Tata Steel)

Engineering (Jaguar Land Rover, Tata Motors, Voltas)

Figure 7.22 Tata's revenue by source and year.

arena. It was a threat because Tata was vulnerable to competition. Its companies were uncoordinated, overmanned and undermanaged. Ratan Tata (chairman of the group 1991–2012) set about streamlining the company. For example, Tata Steel has more than doubled its output since 1994 (from 3 million tonnes to 6.4 million) while cutting its workforce in India by more than half over the same period (from 78 000 to 30 000). He focused the group on six industries that have provided most of its revenues since 2000 – steel, motor vehicles, power, telecoms, information technology (IT) and hotels – and increased its shareholding in these core businesses.

 Look on **Cambridge Elevate** to read about Tata's Ramanujan IT City, from the Ramanujan IT City website (www.cambridge.org/links/gase6066).

Tata and globalisation

The group has embraced globalisation. The pace of foreign acquisitions has grown dramatically: in 1995–2003 Tata companies made, on average, one purchase a year; in 2004 they made six; and in 2005–06 they made more than 20. The scale of foreign acquisitions has also grown. Tata's takeover of Tetley Group, a British company, for $450 million in 2000 was the first of several acquisitions of well-known brands that announced the group's arrival in the global arena (Figure 7.23). In 2007 Tata Steel bought Corus, Europe's second-largest steelmaker, for $12.1 billion. A year later, Tata Motors paid $2.3 billion for Jaguar Land Rover (JLR).

In all, Tata has spent around $20 billion on foreign companies. Today it earns about three-fifths of its revenue abroad and employs more British workers than any other manufacturer. Two of its biggest companies, Tata Motors and Tata Communications, are listed on the New York Stock Exchange.

Tata has been busy in emerging markets, too. Tata Steel and Tata Motors have bought out or bought into several Asian companies such as Thailand's Millennium Steel and South Korea's Daewoo trucks. Diversified groups are the 'dominant' form of business in many emerging markets including Chile, Indonesia, Mexico, Pakistan and Thailand. In India Tata Motors has made the first Indian-designed car, the Indica, and the world's cheapest, the Nano (see below).

Corporate social responsibility

Tata has also established many of India's greatest institutions such as the Indian Institute of Science, the Tata Institute of Fundamental Research and the Tata Memorial Hospital. The organisation prides itself above all on its culture, which it argues is defined by three things: loyalty, dignity and what is now called corporate social responsibility (CSR). Tata trusts fundworthy causes, from cleanwater projects and literacy programmes to the various Tata institutions, all of which cost $97 million in 2010.

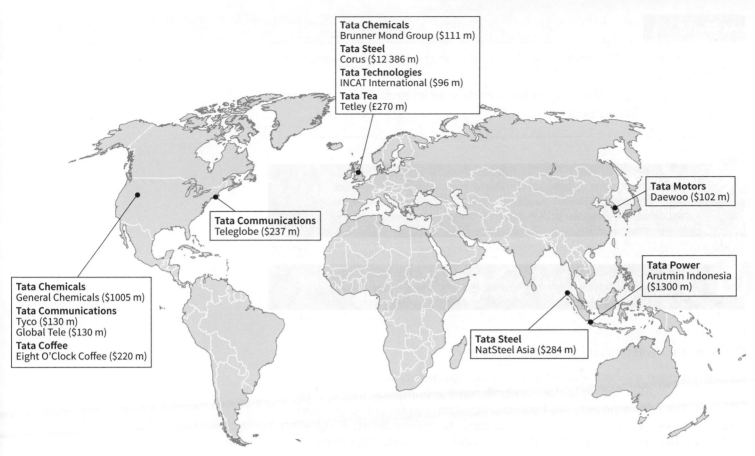

Tata Chemicals
Brunner Mond Group ($111 m)
Tata Steel
Corus ($12 386 m)
Tata Technologies
INCAT International ($96 m)
Tata Tea
Tetley (£270 m)

Tata Motors
Daewoo ($102 m)

Tata Communications
Teleglobe ($237 m)

Tata Power
Arutmin Indonesia
($1300 m)

Tata Chemicals
General Chemicals ($1005 m)
Tata Communications
Tyco ($130 m)
Global Tele ($130 m)
Tata Coffee
Eight O'Clock Coffee ($220 m)

Tata Steel
NatSteel Asia ($284 m)

Figure 7.23 Tata group – a selection of international acquisitions.

Jamshedpur, the home of Tata Steel, is, perhaps, the world's most successful company town. Tata Steel runs almost all the city's institutions, including a 980-bed hospital; a zoo, a giant sports stadium; academies for football, archery and athletics; golf courses; and the local utility company. Some critics claim that Tata is now placing profit at the expense of its once ahead-of-its-time philanthropy. For example, in 1912 the company introduced an eight-hour working day (the norm in the UK was then 12 hours). It introduced paid leave in 1920 (which became legally binding in India in 1945) and started a provident fund for its employees in 1920, which became law for all Indian employers in 1952.

The group is pursuing innovation on two levels. At the high end, Tata Chemicals is conducting research into nanotechnology and food science, but what has caught more attention is the group's commitment to 'frugal innovation': new products designed to appeal to poor people and the rising middle class. Tata's best-known frugal product, the Tata Nano, a 150 000 rupee car (about £1500), has run into problems: some cars have suffered from 'thermal incidents'. However, even if the Nano proves disappointing, frugal innovation looks promising overall. Tata Steel has made a prototype of a $500 house that can be bought in a shop and Tata's hotel company is building $20-a-night billets for India's army of commercial travellers. After theIndian Ocean tsunami in December 2004, TCS and Tata Teleservices joined forces to develop a weather-alert system for fishermen.

Look on **Cambridge Elevate** for more information on the Tata group, from the TATA group website (www.cambridge.org/links/gase6067).

ACTIVITY 7.4

1   Study Figure 7.22. Describe and comment on the revenue by sector for the Tata group.
2   Study Figure 7.23. Comment on the pattern of international acquisitions made by the Tata group.

Look on **Cambridge Elevate** to read about the Tata Trusts in its corporate brochure, *Leadership with Trust*. Consider how the group's current trusts compare with its earlier philanthropy (www.cambridge.org/links/gase6068).

For an activity about Tata's involvement in steel production in the UK, download Worksheet 7.4 from **Cambridge Elevate**.

Coffee: an international trade commodity

Coffee has been a valuable international trade commodity since the 1800s. The world coffee market has undergone a significant transformation over the last 50 years. The coffee industry has been characterised by new challenges such as climate change, risk management in response to price volatility, the growing cost of inputs, the sustainability of the sector and the development of world consumption.

Up until 1989 the coffee market was regulated by a series of International Coffee Agreements (ICAs) that were intended to manage supply and maintain price stability. This system subsequently collapsed and since 1990 the coffee market has been subject to the free market forces of supply and demand. Price levels during the regulated market period (1965–89) were relatively high. By contrast, the free market period beginning in 1990 had two sub-periods of markedly low price levels: 1989–93 and 1999–2004, although prices recovered strongly after 2004, reaching a 34-year high in mid-2011. In 2001 coffee prices were just one-third of their 1960 levels. This had a major impact on more than 25 million households in coffee-producing areas.

A number of factors help explain the fall in coffee prices such as the ending of the ICAs price regulation, fluctuating markets, growth in suppliers and increased market access of countries that re-export. Vietnam, for example, became a major coffee producer and exporter, increasing its production by 1400% and impacting a number of small producers. To overcome these weaknesses, price control, fair trade initiatives and economic diversification could all help. However, some countries including Burundi, Ethiopia and Uganda are relatively dependent on coffee, earning over 50% of their export earnings from this commodity.

The world's coffee market is dominated by four multinational corporations: Mondelēz International (formerly Kraft Foods who own Maxwell House), Nestlé, Procter & Gamble and the former Sara Lee Corporation (now split into Hillshire Brands and D.E Master Blenders 1753).

The WTO through its policies of free trade and liberalisation has a significant impact on coffee prices. Free trade is meant to benefit importers and exporters. However, large TNCs can force countries to compete against each other in a 'race to the bottom' by reducing the price at which they buy/sell. Small coffee producers are especially vulnerable.

The dynamics of world coffee production are generally characterised by considerable instability, with a large crop in one year frequently followed by a smaller crop the following year. Over the last 50 years, there has been steady growth in world production. South America remains the world's leading coffee producer, producing over 46% of the world total (Figure 7.24). Production follows a biennial cycle, with an alternating increase and decrease over successive years in Arabica production, whichaccounts for about 75% of Brazilian coffee production, as the trees require time to recover after a large crop. In 2012/13 coffee production in Central America was affected badly by coffee leaf rust. Over 2.7 million 60 kg bags of coffee were lost. Asia and Oceania have recorded the strongest production growth over the last 50 years, especially in the last 20 years. Vietnam has become an important coffee-producing nation, with production increasing dramatically since 1980. Between 1980 and 1989, it produced 451 000 60 kg bags of coffee and in 2012/13 the total amounted to 22 million bags.

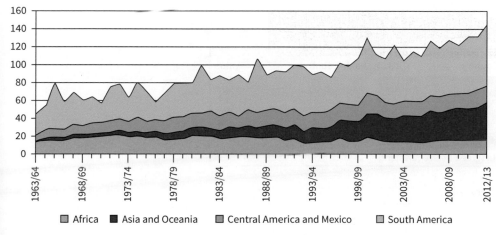

Figure 7.24 World coffee production by region, 1963–2013.

Production in Africa has exhibited negative growth over the last 50 years. During the regulated market period, many African countries benefited both from a guaranteed market in the European Union under the EU-ACP Agreements and from guaranteed prices for producers. The subsequent decline in production was initially attributable to structural factors given low yields and ageing coffee trees, as well as the economic liberalisation programmes implemented in the 1990s.

Exports

Total exports increased over the 50-year period between 1963 and 2013. Brazil exported 31.2 million bags in 2012/13 and Vietnam 20 million bags. There were also high growth rates in Peru, Nicaragua, Honduras, India and Ethiopia. Germany earned more than $1.4 billion in re-exports of 6.6 million bags. Re-exporting activities have continued to grow over the last 50 years and there is considerable value-added to the coffee imports. In exporting countries, most of the value is in the export of unrefined coffee.

World consumption (Figure 7.25) has increased on average by 1.9% per year over the last 50 years. The coffee industry was valued at around $170 billion in 2012. In exporting countries, most coffee is consumed at home, whereas in traditional importing countries out-of-home consumption accounts for the larger value produced. Domestic consumption in exporting countries has grown by about 3% per annum since the 1960s. Therefore, Brazil is not only the largest producer of coffee (Figure 7.26), it is also a relatively large consumer, globally. Total consumption in importing countries is slowing down. In contrast, consumption in emerging economies is growing considerably and shows potential for further expansion.

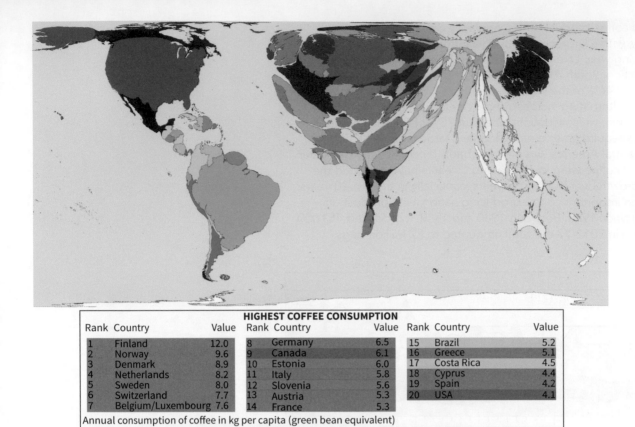

HIGHEST COFFEE CONSUMPTION

Rank	Country	Value	Rank	Country	Value	Rank	Country	Value
1	Finland	12.0	8	Germany	6.5	15	Brazil	5.2
2	Norway	9.6	9	Canada	6.1	16	Greece	5.1
3	Denmark	8.9	10	Estonia	6.0	17	Costa Rica	4.5
4	Netherlands	8.2	11	Italy	5.8	18	Cyprus	4.4
5	Sweden	8.0	12	Slovenia	5.6	19	Spain	4.2
6	Switzerland	7.7	13	Austria	5.3	20	USA	4.1
7	Belgium/Luxembourg	7.6	14	France	5.3			

Annual consumption of coffee in kg per capita (green bean equivalent)

Figure 7.25 World coffee consumption by country, 2007.

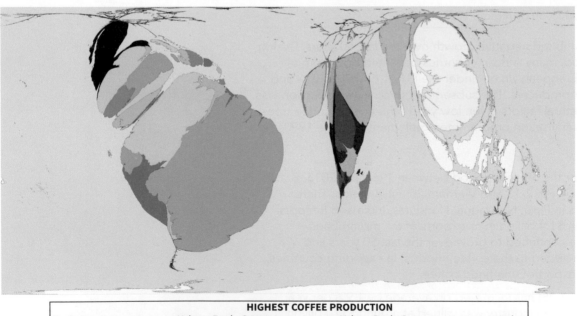

HIGHEST COFFEE PRODUCTION

Rank	Country	Value	Rank	Country	Value	Rank	Country	Value
1	Brazil	38.0	8	Guatemala	3.8	15	Nicaragua	1.3
2	Vietnam	14.5	9	Peru	3.4	16	Ecuador	1.1
3	Colombia	12.3	10	Honduras	2.9	17	Papua New Guinea	1.1
4	Indonesia	7.4	11	Ivory Coast	2.4	18	Venezuela	0.9
5	Ethiopia	4.9	12	Uganda	2.4	19	Kenya	0.8
6	India	4.7	13	Costa Rica	1.8	20	Cameroon	0.8
7	Mexico	4.2	14	El Salvador	1.4			

Annual production in millions of 60-kg bags of green coffee beans

Figure 7.26 World coffee production by country, 2007.

Maths for geographers

1 Use Table 7.4 to draw another scattergraphshowing the relationship between GNI and coffee consumption. Carry out a Spearman's rank correlation test to test for a statistical relationship between these two variables. For an explanation of these techniques, see Chapter 13, Geographical skills and techniques.

Country	GNI ($) (2015)	Annual coffee consumption (kg/capita)
Finland	40 700	12.0
Norway	67 200	9.6
Denmark	44 600	8.9
Netherlands	48 000	8.2
Sweden	46 200	8.0
Switzerland	58 100	7.7
Belgium	43 100	7.6
Germany	46 200	6.5
Canada	45 000	6.1
Estonia	27 900	6.0
Italy	35 100	5.8
Slovenia	29 900	5.6
Austria	46 600	5.3
France	40 500	5.3
Brazil	16 200	5.2
Greece	26 000	5.1
Costa Rica	14 900	4.5
Cyprus	30 900	4.4
Spain	33 800	4.2
USA	54 400	4.1

Table 7.4 Data on GNI and coffee consumption.

2   Use Table 7.5 to draw a scattergraphshowing the relationship between GNI and coffee production. Carry out a Spearman's rank correlation test to test for a statistical relationship between these two variables.

Country	GNI ($) (2015)	Annual coffee production (millions of 60 kg bags)
Brazil	16 200	38.0
Vietnam	5 700	14.5
Colombia	13 500	12.3
Indonesia	10 700	7.4
Ethiopia	1 600	4.9
India	5 800	4.7
Mexico	18 000	4.2
Guatemala	7 500	3.8
Peru	11 900	3.4
Honduras	4 700	2.9
Ivory Coast	3 100	2.4
Uganda	1 900	2.4
Costa Rica	14 900	1.8
El Salvador	8 100	1.4
Nicaragua	4 800	1.3
Ecuador	11 300	1.1
Papua New Guinea	2 500	1.1
Venezuela	17 800	0.9
Kenya	3 100	0.8
Cameroon	3 000	0.8

Table 7.5 Data on GNI and coffee production.

3   Compare the results for the two graphs and the correlations you have produced. Comment on your findings.

Challenges

Price fluctuations are a major source of uncertainty and vulnerability for coffee producers. Production costs – such as labour, fertilisers, pesticides – can be variable. Coffee is a labour-intensive industry: as the agricultural workforce ages, the cost of labour is therefore rising. Coffee trees are also vulnerable to pests such as coffee leaf rust and coffee berry borer.

Investigate

Investigate the ways in which Fairtrade farmers have better working conditions than those who are not involved in the Fairtrade Foundation.

For questions about the Fairtrade Foundation, download Worksheet 7.5 from **Cambridge Elevate**.

ACTIVITY 7.5

1 Describe the main features of global trade. Identify the main ways in which it is changing.
2 Using examples, briefly explain *three* factors that influence global trade.
3 Outline the advantages and disadvantages of TNCs.
4 Study Figure 7.24. Describe and comment on the growth in world coffee production by region.
5 Study Figure 7.25. Describe and suggest reasons for variations in coffee consumption by country.
6 Study Figure 7.26. Describe and suggest reasons for variations in coffee production by country.

 Look on **Cambridge Elevate** to find out about the aims and success of Fairtrade coffee, from the Fairtrade website (www.cambridge.org/links/gase6069).

How international trade and variable access to markets impacts people's lives

There are winners and losers as a result of international trade and access to markets. Rich countries generally have greater market access and high value exports compared with poorer countries. Many low income countries export low value products (such as agricultural products, e.g. unprocessed coffee beans) and workers in low income countries generally receive low wages. In contrast, the same product may be processed or refined in a high income country, adding value to the good. Many workers in high income countries receive competitive incomes, and so levels of wealth in high income countries are much greater than in low income countries. Consequently, the goods that a person from a low income country can afford to buy are much less varied, and a higher proportion of their expenditure is on essential goods (food, clothing and energy, for example). In contrast, for those in high income countries, a lower proportion of their earnings is spent on essential goods, and more on 'luxury' goods or inessentials.

 For an activity on trading patterns, download Worksheet 7.6 from **Cambridge Elevate**.

7.6 Global governance

Some analysts believe that nations are far less important than they once were. They argue that the increasing flow of people, capital, goods and ideas across international boundaries illustrates the demise of the nation state. At the same time, the growth of trading blocs and TNCs heralds a new world order in which individual countries are less important than before.

 Making connections

Globalisation is one of the key developments in geography over the last 50 years. However, some commentators disagree that this is the case. How do globalisation sceptics, transformationalists and hyperglobalists differ in their views about globalisation? See section 7.8 Globalisation critique.

Regulating global systems

Attempts are made to govern and regulate global systems. Figure 7.27 shows the agencies that attempt to regulate these systems.

\Much of the trade and money exchange that takes place is run by stock exchanges and the world's main banks. For example, Barclays Capital is the investment-banking sector of Barclays Bank. It deals with over £360 billion of investment through its 33 offices located worldwide. Its regional headquarters are located mostly in HICs such as London, Paris, Frankfurt, New York and Tokyo. Hong Kong is the exception, although it is also an important financial centre like most of the other cities on the list. There is widespread criticism that many of the regulatory bodies (Figure 7.27) have limited power and that when faced with a powerful HIC or TNC they capitulate.

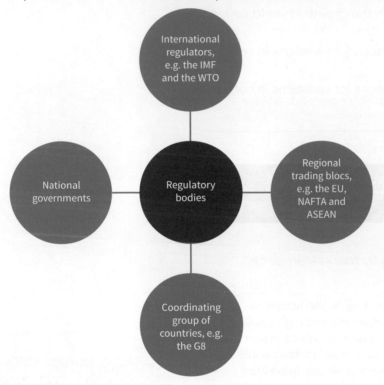

Figure 7.27 Regulatory bodies.

The World Bank

The World Bank is a source of financial and technical assistance to developing countries around the world. Its mission is to fight poverty by providing resources, sharing knowledge and building capacity. It comprises two unique development institutions owned by 186 member countries, the International Bank for Reconstruction and Development (IBRD) and the International Development Association (IDA).

The World Bank was established in 1944, and has its headquarters in Washington DC. It has more than 10 000 employees and more than 100 offices worldwide. Until 1967 the bank undertook a relatively low level of lending. From 1968 to 1980 the bank focused on the needs of people in the developing world, and greatly increased the size and number of its loans to borrowers. Bank policy shifted toward measures such as building schools and hospitals, improving literacy and agricultural reform.

The period 1980–89 was dominated by lending to service third-world debt. Structural adjustment policies (SAPs) aimed at streamlining the economies of developing nations were a large part of World Bank policy during this period.

Since 1989 its policy has changed, and its current focus is on the achievement of the Millennium Development Goals (MDGs), lending primarily to middle-income countries. The Bank's mission is to aid developing countries and their inhabitants to achieve development and the reduction of poverty, including achievement of the MDGs, by helping countries develop an environment for investment, jobs and sustainable growth, thus promoting economic growth through investment and enabling the poor to share the fruits of economic growth.

Criticisms of the World Bank

The World Bank has long been criticised by non-governmental organisations and academics, who argue that its free-market reform policies are harmful to economic development. In *Masters of Illusion: The World Bank and the Poverty of Nations* (1996), Catherine Caufield argued that western practices are adopted and traditional economic structures and values abandoned. A second assumption is that poor countries cannot modernize without money and advice from abroad.

Another criticism of the World Bank is the way in which it is governed. While the World Bank represents 186 countries, it is run by a small number of rich countries. In addition, the World Bank has dual roles that are contradictory; that of a political organisation and that of a practical organisation. As a political organisation the bank must meet the demands of donor and borrowing governments. As a practical organisation, it must be neutral, specialising in development aid, technical assistance and loans. Moreover, critics say that it focuses too much on the growth of GDP and not enough on living standards.

Some analysis shows that the World Bank has increased poverty and has been detrimental to the environment, public health and cultural diversity. It has also been suggested that the World Bank is an instrument for the promotion of US or western interests in certain regions of the world. One of the most significant criticisms of the World Bank has been to do with the effect of its structural adjustment programmes (SAPs).

The International Monetary Fund

The International Monetary Fund (IMF) is the international organisation that oversees the global financial system by following the economic policies of its member countries, in particular those with an impact on the exchange rate and the balance of payments. Its stated objectives are to stabilise international exchange rates and facilitate development.

Created in July 1944, the International Monetary Fund started with 45 members but it now has 186. Member countries contribute to a pool, from which other member countries with a payment imbalance may borrow on a temporary basis. The IMF was important when it was first created because it helped the world stabilise the economic system. The IMF's influence in the global economy steadily increased as it accumulated more members.

To deal with the 2008 global financial crisis, the IMF agreed to sell some of its gold reserves. In addition, in 2009 at the G20 Summit in London, it was decided that the IMF would require additional financial resources to meet the prospective needs of its member countries during the ongoing global financial crisis. The G20 leaders pledged to increase the IMF's supplemental cash tenfold to $500 billion, and to allocate to member countries another $250 billion via special drawing rights.

Member states with balance of payment problems may request loans to help fill gaps between what they earn and/or are able to borrow from other lenders and

Look on **Cambridge Elevate** to learn more about the World Bank. Click on the Financial crisis button to find out more about the debt crisis and the bank's response (www.cambridge.org/links/gase6070).

Look on **Cambridge Elevate** for more information about the IMF, from the IMF website (www.cambridge.org/links/gase6071).

what they need to spend in order to operate. In return, these countries usually launch reforms such as structural adjustment programmes.

Criticisms of the IMF

Criticisms of the IMF include the following:

- IMF policymakers have supported military dictators friendly to American and European corporations, and appear unconcerned about democracy, human rights and labour rights.
- One of the main SAP conditions placed on troubled countries is that the governments sell up as much of their national assets as they can, normally to western corporations at a big discount.
- The IMF sometimes advocates austerity programmes, increasing taxes even when an economy is weak, in order to generate government revenue.
- The IMF's response to a crisis is often delayed, and it tends only to react to them (or even create them) rather than prevent them.
- Historically the IMF's managing director has been European (and the president of the World Bank has been from the USA). The IMF is for the most part controlled by the major western nations.

Structural adjustment programmes

Structural adjustment programmes (SAPs) were designed to cut government expenditure, reduce the amount of state intervention in the economy, and promote liberalisation and international trade. SAPs were explicit about the need for international trade. They consist of four main elements:

1 Greater use of a country's resource base.
2 Policy reforms to increase economic efficiency.
3 Generation of foreign income through diversification of the economy and increased trade.
4 Reducing the active role of the state.

However, some people argue that these measures have made the situation worse.

The measures were sometimes divided into two main groups: the stabilisation measures, short-term steps to limit any further deterioration of the economy (e.g. wage freeze, reduced subsidies on food, health and education); and adjustment measures, longer-term policies to boost economic competitiveness (tax reductions, export promotion, downsizing of the civil service, privatisation and economic liberalisation).

There have been a number of Caribbean countries, for example, that have experienced SAPs. The government of Barbados had to cut wages in the public sector by 8%, and increase taxes, as well as increase bus fares by 50% as conditions for securing a loan from the IMF and World Bank. Spending on social welfare is often reduced in return for IMF/World Bank loans, and this may have a negative effect on health care for women and children, in particular.

The United Nations

The United Nations is an intergovernmental organisation to promote international co-operation. It was established in 1945 after the Second World War, in order to prevent another such conflict. It began with 53 member states and now has 193. Its objectives include maintaining international peace and security, promoting human rights, fostering social and economic development, protecting the environment, and providing humanitarian aid in cases of famine, natural disaster, and armed conflict. By the 1970s its budget for economic and social development outstripped its budget for peacekeeping.

The UN has five principal organs: the General Assembly (the main deliberative assembly); the Security Council (for maintaining peace and security); the Economic and Social Council (ECOSOC) (for promoting international economic and social co-operation and development); the Secretariat (for providing studies, information, and facilities needed by the UN) and the International Court of Justice (the primary judicial organ, located in the Hague). Its subsidiary organs include the Food and Agriculture Organisation, the International Labour Organisation, the World health Organisation, the World food Programme, UNESCO and UNICEF.

The UN sends peacekeepers to regions where armed conflict has recently paused or ceased. The UN also promotes and encourages respect for human rights and for fundamental freedoms for all without distinction as to race, sex, language, or religion. Another primary aim of the UN is 'to achieve international co-operation in solving international problems of an economic, social, cultural, or humanitarian character'. In 2000, the 192 United Nations member states agreed to achieve eight Millennium Development Goals by 2015.

Millennium Development Goals

1   Eradicate extreme poverty and hunger.
2   Achieve universal primary education.
3   Promote gender equality and empower women.
4   Reduce child mortality.
5   Improve maternal health.
6   Combat HIV/AIDS, malaria, and other diseases.
7   Ensure environmental sustainability.
8   Develop a global partnership for development.

Some commentators believe the organisation to be an important force for peace and human development, while others have called the organisation ineffective, corrupt, or biased.

Interactions between different scales of governance

Although there is no global government, there are global institutions such as the IMFD, United Nations and the World Bank, as well as international institutions such as the New Development Bank (formerly the BRICS Development Bank). In addition, there are multi-government organisations, such as the EU, that are political unions as well as economic unions. These organisations may make decisions which alienate governments at other scales; for example, the IMF and Greece, or the EU and the UK over migration.

Within nations, there may be conflict between regions or calls for independence, for example the Scottish referendum for independence from the UK. There are also local conflicts between local stakeholders, national governments and TNCs – the Canadian First Nation Peoples in relation to their traditional lands and energy developments or the Australian indigenous people moved from their lands in the Galilee Basin in order to make way for the Indian company Adani to develop Australia's largest coal mine. Some local communities, or even nations, may appeal to a higher level of governance for aid or arbitration – although it is argued that some international groupings (e.g. the EU) and global groupings, such as the World Bank and the IMF, have their own interests and agendas.

7.7 The global commons

The **global commons** refers areas that lie outside the political reach of any nation state. According to the United Nations Environment Programme (UNEP), there are four global commons: the high seas, Antarctica (Figure 7.28), the atmosphere and outer space. The global commons require management and protection.

Key terms

global commons: the Earth's shared and unowned natural resources, such as the oceans, the atmosphere and outer space

the tragedy of the commons: the decline of common resources, such as ocean fish stocks, when the rate of use exceeds the rate of natural replacement and regeneration

Figure 7.28 Antarctica is a global common.

Renewable resources such as fish need not be depleted provided that the rate of use does not exceed maximum sustainable yield; in other words, if the rate of use is within the limit of natural replacement and regeneration. If resources become over-exploited, depletion and degradation will lead to scarcity. If more than one nation is exploiting a resource, which is clearly the case in the fishing industry, resource degradation is often the result.

Making connections

Antarctica has many resources that may be useful for modern societies. Why are its resources likely to be under severe development pressure in the future? See section 11.5 Energy security.

Garrett Hardin, the American ecologist, suggested a metaphor, **the tragedy of the commons**, in 1968, to explain the tendency. This refers to the way that there may be little control over the way common resources are used and how the selfish acts of a few individuals can destroy the resource for others. In any given ocean, a number of nations may be fishing. Apart from the seas close to land, where there is an exclusive economic zone (EEZ), no country owns the oceans or the resources that they contain. However, countries may use their resources and, if one country takes more fish from the oceans, their profits increase. Other countries do not benefit from this action. To maintain the same relative profitability, other countries may in turn increase their catch, so that they are not losing out relative to their competitors. The 'tragedy' is that other countries feel compelled to increase their catch in order to match the scale of the country that initiated the increase. Therefore, the rate of use may exceed maximum sustainable yield and the resources may become depleted. Although simplistic, the tragedy of the commons explains the tendency to over-exploit shared resources and the need for agreements over common management.

Antarctica as a global common

Antarctica is one of the world's last great wilderness. It has an important influence on global climate and on food resources (especially fish), it is a growing tourist destination and it may contain valuable minerals. However, Antarctica is unique in the way that it is managed and conserved. It is experiencing environmental degradation on account of pollution and global warming. There are also pressures on its resources, from fishing to mineral resources.

Climate and climate change

Antarctica is the coldest, driest, windiest and highest continent. Temperatures vary with altitude, latitude and proximity to the sea (Figure 7.29). Mean annual temperatures range from below −40°C in the interior to around 0°C in summer and from −10°C to −20°C in winter around the coast. The interior receives less than 50mm of snow per annum.

Look on **Cambridge Elevate** for more information on Antarctica, from the Last Ocean website (www.cambridge.org/links/gase6072).

Making connections

There are many types of ice mass, ranging from ice sheets and ice caps to mountain and valley glaciers. Why are some types of ice mass more vulnerable to climate change? See section 4.3 Systems, processes and landscapes.

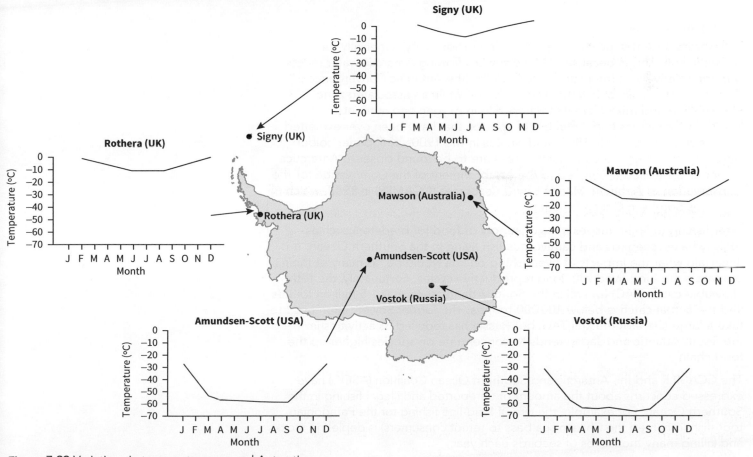

Figure 7.29 Variations in temperatures around Antarctica.

Antarctica is experiencing climate change. For example, since the 1960s rainfall and snowmelt have increased in the Marguerite Bay Area of the Antarctic Peninsula. There has also been a decline in snow cover in the area. These characteristics (more rainfall, more snowmelt and reduced snow cover) are characteristic of the Antarctic Peninsula as a whole. Temperatures have risen by about 2.5 °C and the period of snowmelt has extended by up to three weeks. The warming found in the Antarctic Peninsula does not extend to the upland interior.

The Intergovernmental Panel on Climate Change (IPCC) has predicted that global mean air temperatures will rise by 2 °C by 2100. The range of predicted rise is between 1.5 °C and 3.5 °C, depending on computer model. Sea levels are predicted to rise by about 50 cm (estimates range from 15 cm to 90 cm). Other changes could include increased variability in weather events, with more extreme events. As the climate warms, there is likely to be:

- increased snowfall in central Antarctica
- increased rainfall in coastal margins
- increased melting of low-lying snow and of snow in the Antarctic Peninsula
- a reduction in sea ice around Antarctica
- the collapse of ice shelves around the Antarctic Peninsula.

In 2015 NASA reported that Antarctica was gaining more ice than it had lost. However, some places such as the Antarctic Peninsula and West Antarctica were losing ice while other areas were gaining, such as the eastern part and the interior. Researchers from Germany suggested that ice in West Antarctica could be unstable enough to cause sea level rise of between 1 and 3 m.

Fishing and whaling

The waters off Antarctica are high in marine productivity, especially for Antarctic krill. This is because cold, northward flowing Antarctic water meets with the relatively warmer subantarctic water (the Antarctic Convergence). The cold water sinks below the warmer water, while an associated zone of upwelling and mixing creates waters rich in oxygen and nutrients. The Southern Ocean has had a number of species that have been over-exploited such as seals in the early 1800s and whales in the 1900s. Krill prefer colder water so the richer, more productive seas are to be found closer to Antarctica. Earlier uncontrolled fishing led to the establishment of the Commission for the Conservation of Antarctic Marine Living Resources (CCAMLR) in 1982, which regulates Southern Ocean fisheries.

Over-fishing of krill removes a major supply of food for predators such as seals, whales, seabirds and carnivorous fish living in the Southern Ocean. It is uncertain what the impacts of over-fishing on krill would be, as many of their predators are long-lived with long reproductive cycles. Fortunately, the total allowable catch (TAC) for krill in the South Atlantic section is 1.5 million tonnes and the actual catch is below 100 000 tonnes. The former Soviet Union used to take a large share of the krill TAC, but Russia has reduced its activities in the South Atlantic and Japan tends to concentrate on species higher up the food chain.

The CCAMLR and the Antarctic and Southern Ocean Coalition (ASOC) have expressed concerns about the amount of unreported and illegal fishing in the Southern Ocean. For example, the use of long-line fishing for the Patagonian toothfish (renamed the Chilean sea bass to tempt consumers) is depleting stocks and killing many thousands of seabirds each year.

Whaling in Antarctic waters has a long history. Humpback whales were caught first due to their large numbers. As technology improved, whalers went further out to sea and blue whales became the main target species. Whaling stopped during the Second World War but resumed afterwards and, by the early 1950s, the blue whale population had been decimated. Whalers then turned to fin whales, whose numbers collapsed within a decade. In 1982 the International Whaling Commission (IWC) banned commercial whaling globally. The former Soviet Union and Japan continued commercial whaling until 1986/7, and Japan continues to kill around 300 minke whales a year for what they claim are scientific purposes. Overall, it is believed that some 1.3 million whales have been killed in the Southern Ocean.

Tourism

Tourists first visited Antarctica in 1958 and numbers have grown dramatically since. Antarctic tourism raises many issues. Of particular concern is how to protect the Antarctic wilderness while giving people the opportunity to experience its beauty for themselves (Figure 7.30). It has been suggested that tourism will inevitably lead to the degradation of the Antarctic environment and should be stopped. An alternative argument is that everyone has the legal right to visit the continent and that visitors will become advocates for protecting the continent.

In 1991 the International Association of Antarctica Tour Operators (IAATO) was set up. This organisation draws up guidelines on the numbers of people allowed to visit the continent at one time. Since 2011 ships cannot use heavy fuels to visit Antarctica and since 2013 a new Polar Code limits the number and size of ships visiting. Ships with more than 500 tourists cannot berth on Antarctica and no more than 100 tourists are allowed there at any one time (Figure 7.31). However, there have been some incidents involving cruise ships in the sea ice off the coast.

Look on **Cambridge Elevate** for more information fishing in the Ross Sea, from the Last Ocean website (www.cambridge.org/links/gase6073).

Figure 7.30 Antarctica's dramatic scenery.

 Physical and human

Outline ways in which human activities may be affecting the physical environment shown in Figure 7.30.

Figure 7.31 The Polar Code limits the number and size of ships visiting Antarctica.

Mineral resources

Some scientists believe that Antarctica may contain a similar quantity of rich mineral deposits to South America or southern Africa. However, no large area of mineral resources has, as yet, been identified. Nevertheless, some gold, silver, iron and coal has been discovered there. The Environmental Protocol to the Antarctic Treaty came into force in 1998 and bans commercial mining activity in Antarctica. Indeed, there would be many problems in trying to develop Antarctica's resources, including:

- very low temperatures, making the functioning of machines difficult
- remoteness and large distances involved
- lack of daylight hours
- lack of water
- high wind speeds
- high set-up costs.

Nevertheless, these are not impossible conditions.

Trying to exploit offshore oil and gas deposits would be difficult on account of the depth of the continental shelf (500–1000 m), stray icebergs and seasonal growth of sea ice. Since oil was discovered on the Falklands Plateau, there may be a greater chance of oil being found under the continental shelf of Antarctica.

Mineral exploitation in Antarctica is controversial. Although there are mineral occurrences in Antarctica, none are known in commercially viable quantities. The technical, economic and environmental difficulties of extracting minerals are immense.

The developing governance of Antarctica

Global commons require management by international organisations. As we have seen, there are a number of international government organisations involved in the governance of Antarctica, including the United National Environment Programme (UNEP) and the the International Whaling Commission. However, international management may be seen to be slow in response to potential conflicts over common resources. Some individuals may also feel that International Government Organisations do not represent their own demands. Consequently, some NGOs have an important role in monitoring threats to Global Commons. They also represent many individuals, who may support or subscribe to particular NGOs, and help their operations.

The role of NGOs in monitoring threats and enhancing protection of Antarctica

The Antarctic Treaty was signed in 1959 and came into force in 1961. Under the Treaty, Antarctica is used for peaceful purposes only and the environment is protected (Table 7.6). Research is the major activity undertaken although, in summer, fishing and tourism also take place. Forty-six countries have now signed the Treaty, representing over 80% of the world's population. Of the many countries that have taken part in the exploration of Antarctica, only seven have staked territorial claims in the region.

The Antarctic Treaty has been in operation for nearly 50 years and is regarded by many people as an outstanding example of international cooperation. Some nations that have not signed up to the Antarctic Treaty believe it is a 'rich man's club' and in the past have proposed that the continent should be managed by the United Nations as a global heritage for mankind.

The Antarctic Treaty governs the continent and its surrounding ocean, but it can be slow to achieve results because consensus-based decision-making is required. The decision by the CCAMLR to endorse the creation of a network of MPAs in the Southern Ocean by 2012 represents a major step forward for marine conservation. Any MPA network in the Southern Ocean must include a

The Antarctic Treaty
Military activities (e.g. military manoeuvres) in Antarctica are prohibited, although military personnel and equipment may be used for scientific research or other peaceful purposes.
Freedom of scientific investigation and cooperation in Antarctica shall continue.
Free exchange of information on scientific programmes and scientific data.
Existing territorial sovereignty claims are set aside. No new territorial claims can be made while the Treaty is in force.
Nuclear explosions and radioactive waste disposal are prohibited in Antarctica.
The Treaty applies to all land and ice shelves south of latitude 60 °S, but not to the high seas within the area.
All Antarctica stations and all ships and aircraft operating in Antarctica have to be open to inspection by designated observers from any Treaty nation.
Personnel working in Antarctica shall be under the jurisdiction only of their own country.
Treaty nations will meet regularly to consider ways of furthering the principles and objectives of the Treaty.
The Treaty may be modified at any time by unanimous agreement.
The Treaty must be ratified by any nation wishing to join.

Table 7.6 A summary of the Antarctic Treaty.

large protected area in the Ross Sea. The Ross Sea represents humanity's best remaining chance to preserve a mostly intact open-ocean ecosystem.

Within the CCAMLR, ASOC is the only accredited environmental NGO. It is composed of diverse organisations interested in the Antarctic environment. Since 2000, it has been urging the CCAMLR to develop criteria for a network of MPAs in the Southern Ocean, notably the inclusion of the Ross Sea. ASOC also played a critical role in raising public awareness and driving public opinion about the mining discussions, promoting the idea of Antarctica as a World Park. The CCAMLR was the first organisation involved in the regulation of fisheries to conceive of itself as protecting an ecosystem rather than simply managing individual stocks to maximise yield.

The Protocol on Environmental Protection to the Antarctic Treaty (also known as the Antarctic Environmental Protocol or the Madrid Protocol) provides for comprehensive protection of the Antarctic environment and dependent and associated ecosystems. The Treaty was signed in 1991 and came into force in 1998. It will be open for review in 2048. Key aspects of the Treaty include:

- the protection of the Antarctic environment as a wilderness with scientific and aesthetic value is a fundamental consideration of all activities that occur in the area
- any activity relating to mineral resources, other than scientific research, shall be prohibited
- environmental assessment is required for all activities, including tourism.

Thirty-three countries have signed and ratified the Protocol and a further eleven have signed, but not ratified the Protocol.

In order to promote the protection of the Antarctic environment and dependent and associated ecosystems, and to ensure compliance with this protocol, the Antarctic Treaty Consultative Parties shall arrange, individually or collectively, for inspections by observers. Observers are: (a) observers designated by any

Antarctic Treaty Consultative Party; and (b) any observers designated at Antarctic Treaty Consultative Meetings to carry out inspections.

Parties shall co-operate fully with observers undertaking inspections, and shall ensure that during inspections, observers are given access to all parts of stations, installations, equipment, ships and aircraft open to inspection under Article VII (3) of the Antarctic Treaty, as well as to all records maintained there.

International Whaling Commission

The International Whaling Commission (IWC) is the global body charged with the conservation of whales and the management of whaling. The IWC currently has 88 member governments from countries all over the world. Uncertainty over whale numbers led to the introduction of a 'moratorium' on commercial whaling in 1986. The IWC established the Southern Ocean Whale Sanctuary in 1994. The sanctuary surrounds Antarctica and bans all types of whaling there. However, there has been dispute over the legality of the sanctuary, with Japan disregarding the sanctuary and hunting whales under the guise of 'scientific research'.

Although the IWC does not regulate a special permit for whaling, Article VIII does stipulate that any country undertaking special permit whaling should report to the IWC each time a permit is issued. It also states that the scientific information produced by the special permit whaling should be presented, at least annually, to the commission. Japan has announced it will resume whaling in the Antarctic in 2016 after a break of more than a year. Despite an International Court of Justice (ICJ) ruling that Japan cease all whaling, Japan plans on catching 333 annually in the Antarctic Ocean. Since 2005, it has killed over 3600 whales. Thus Japan is either 'bending the rules' or is exploiting a 'loophole' in the legislation.

Marine parks

In 2015 plans to create two huge marine sanctuaries in Antarctica failed for a third time after Russia and Ukraine blocked the bids. The meeting of the CCAMLR had sought to protect the Ross Sea and an area off east Antarctica from exploitation. Plans for a marine reserve in the Ross Sea have been under discussion for a decade and have been blocked on several previous occasions, with the main sticking point being restrictions on fishing. The Ross Sea shelf and slope is an area of stunning natural beauty and a haven for wildlife, with more than 40 endemic species and one group of fish that appears to have evolved there. According to ASOC, it comprises 3.3% of the area of the Southern Ocean, but it provides habitat for significant populations of many animals including 38% of the world's Adelie penguins, 26% of Emperor penguins, more than 30% of Antarctic petrels, 6% of Antarctic minke whales and perhaps more than 30% of Ross Sea killer whales. Although governments have set a goal of extending protected areas to 10% of the world's oceans, the CCAMLR has established just one MPA in the Antarctic so far.

Look on **Cambridge Elevate** for a short video from Vimeo on Antarctica (www.cambridge.org/links/gase6074).

A revised proposal by the USA and New Zealand – reducing the scale of the Ross Sea reserve by 40% to about 1.25 million km² – had been thought more likely to succeed at the CCAMLR's meeting in Hobart in October 2014. There was also a proposal to create a protected zone of 1.6 million km² off east Antarctica. The two zones were intended to conserve parts of the Southern Ocean from fishing, oil exploration and other commercial exploitation, but they were both blocked by Russia and Ukraine, while China withdrew support for the proposal.

The Greenpeace vision of Antarctica as a World Park

The environmental group Greenpeace campaigned for the creation of Antarctica as a World Park. It is guided by four principles:

- the recognition of the intrinsic value of the continent as the world's last great and near-pristine wilderness
- the protection of all wildlife and ecological communities within the area below the Antarctic Convergence
- the use of the continent only for high quality scientific activity, emphasising cooperation among scientists from all nations
- maintaining the continent as a zone of peace, free of nuclear and other weapons, and of all military activity.

The following activities, deemed detrimental to the environment, would be prohibited:

- mineral and oil exploitation
- military and nuclear activities
- disposal of radioactive and toxic waste
- killing and interfering with marine mammals, birds and plant life.

A range of activities were to be carefully monitored:

- scientific research
- tourism and non-governmental activities
- the commercial exploitation of marine resources (except mammals and birds, which should be completely protected)
- the construction and decommissioning of stations and logistical support facilities
- the operation of all scientific bases, including fuel use, waste disposal and other logistics.

For an activity on Antarctica as a global common, download Worksheet 7.7 from **Cambridge Elevate**.

Look on **Cambridge Elevate** for more information on Greenpeace's World Park from the Greenpeace website (www.cambridge.org/links/gase6075).

Look on **Cambridge Elevate** for more details about MPAs from the Antarctic and Southern Ocean Coalition (www.cambridge.org/links/gase6076).

ACTIVITY 7.6

1 Explain the meaning of the term 'global commons'.
2 Study Figure 7.28. Describe the variations in temperature in Antarctica and suggest reasons for these variations.
3 Briefly explain the impacts of the following on Antarctica:
   a fishing and whaling
   b climate change.
4 Outline the ways in which Antarctica has been managed. How successful have these been?

For questions on the threats to Antarctica, download Worksheet 7.8 from **Cambridge Elevate**.

For an activity on MPAs, download Worksheet 7.9 from **Cambridge Elevate**.

How global governance affects people's lives

Global governance has many impacts on people's lives. While it might seem at first that global governance is directed at nations (for example, structural adjustment plans) or economic sectors (for example, the whaling and fishing industries), ultimately the decisions taken at a global or international level have an impact on individual's lifestyles and quality of life – for example, how much fish can be caught, the age at which people are able to retire, and so on. Some individuals and organisations will benefit from global governance decisions whereas others are disadvantaged by them. Some may argue that the protection of Antarctica and its resources prevent some countries or TNCs from using the resources it contains, thereby impacting on the quality of life of some people. On the other hand, it can be argued that the preservation of Antarctica benefits all human-kind. It depends on which resources are protected, who the potential beneficiaries are, and the environmental philosophy of the decision-makers.

7.8 Globalisation critique

Globalisation brings many benefits such as economic growth, development, integration and stability. Nevertheless, there are many disadvantages including increased inequalities, injustices, conflict and environmental impacts. Thus, there are a number of different views of globalisation, the most common of which are those of the hyperglobalists, the sceptics and the transformationalists. Each group has a different view of the significance of globalisation and its impact on cultural diversity.

Hyperglobalists

Hyperglobalists believe that this is a new geographical era. They argue that the nation state is no longer important; instead, there is a single global market supported by transnational networks of production, trade and finance. They believe that forms of government above the level of the state – for example, trading blocs such as the EU – are increasingly important.

Hyperglobalists see in this the erosion of the power of the state and therefore the victory of capitalism over socialism. This view was widely supported following the collapse of the former Soviet Union, when socialist hyperglobalists saw globalisation as aggressive and regressive.

Hyperglobalists believe that economic forces are dominant in an integrated global economy and suggest that there is a new world order based on consumerism. They believe that this is leading to a spread of liberal democracy. They also take the line that globalisation leads to homogeneity of culture – the Americanisation of the world economy and culture.

However, the global financial crisis of 2007–08 and the involvement of national governments in an attempt to support their economies suggest that the nation state is not yet dead and that hyperglobalists may have to modify their view.

Sceptics

Sceptics question whether globalisation is anything new. They believe that the world was just as integrated in the 19th century. They also claim that if the hyperglobalists are correct, there would be uninterrupted flows of labour, trade and capital. However, labour is relatively immobile and protectionist policies limit the amount of free trade. Sceptics believe that national governments are still the most important players. The rise of China, India and Iran as emerging powers is due, in large part, to government policies. In addition, trading blocs promote regionalism rather than globalisation.

Sceptics take the stance that the neoliberal hyperglobalists are only interested in increasing their market share in the new global economy. This leads to the marginalisation of the poor. The sceptics' view is that cultural heterogeneity will continue, although homogeneity of culture may occur within a single nation, such as China or Iran.

Transformationalists

The hyperglobalists and the sceptics represent two extremes of the globalisation continuum. The transformationalists lie somewhere in between. These academics believe that globalisation is real and it is changing society. They consider that such change is an extension of colonial relations. They also believe that the role of national governments is changing rather than being made redundant.

Cultural exchanges lead to hybrids. Politically, nation states have to take into account international and supranational bodies, such as the European Parliament. Economically, production, trade and finance are interlinked in global networks. According to transformationalists, the state is also actively engaged in its own economic and cultural issues, which produces diversity and increased unevenness. There is therefore more differentiation in global society, politics and economies.

	Hyperglobalist	**Sceptic**	**Transformationalist**
What is happening?	The global era	Increased regionalism	Unprecedented interconnectedness
Central features	Global civilisation based on global capitalism and governance	Core-led regionalism makes globe less interconnected than in late 19th century	'Thick globalisation': high intensity, extensity and velocity of globalisation
Driving processes	Technology, capitalism and human ingenuity	Nation states and the market	'Modern' forces in unison
Patterns of differentiation	Collapsing of welfare differentials over time as market equalises	Core-periphery structure reinforced, leading to greater global inequality	New networks of inclusion/exclusion that are more complex than old patterns
Conceptualization of globalisation	Borderless world and perfect markets	Regionalization, internationalisation and imperfect markets	Time–space compression and distancing that rescale interaction
Implications for the nation state	Eroded or made irrelevant	Strengthened and made more relevant	Transformed governance patterns and new state imperatives
Historical path	Global civilisation based on new transnational elite and cross-class groups	Neo-imperialism and civilisational clashes through actions of regional blocs and neoliberal agenda	Indeterminate: depends on construction and action of nation states and civil society
Core position	Triumph of capitalism and the market over nation states	Powerful states create globalisation agenda to perpetuate their dominant position	Transformation of governance at all scales and new networks of power

Table 7.7 Three theses of globalisation – a schema.

ACTIVITY 7.7

1   Briefly describe the three viewpoints of globalisation. Giving reasons, justify the one that you believe to be correct.

Assess to progress

1   Describe one index of globalisation.   `4 MARKS [A LEVEL]`

2   Using examples, explain how it is possible to manage common resources.   `6 MARKS [A LEVEL]`

3   Study Figure 7.6. Examine the relationship between mean years of schooling and migration.   `6 MARKS [A LEVEL]`

4   Explain why remittances may be more effective at reducing inequalities than trade.   `6 MARKS [A LEVEL]`

5   'Globalisation creates opportunities for everyone.' Discuss this statement.   `20 MARKS [A LEVEL]`

Tip

There are two distinct parts in question 4 that you must cover: why remittances are useful to people or households and why some people do not benefit from trade. Use examples to support the points you make.

Tip

Question 5 asks for a discussion, so you should cover both sides of the argument, i.e. that globalisation creates opportunities for everyone, as well as the view that some groups of people are disadvantaged by globalisation. You should use examples to back up your points, even though the question does not directly ask for them.

8

Changing places

By the end of this chapter you should know:
- some of the ways in which geographers have defined place
- how places are represented in a range of different ways
- how these representations are constructed and shaped by internal and external forces over time
- quantitative and qualitative techniques to investigate the character of your local place in comparison to one further away.

Figure 8.1 Regeneration in Stratford, London. Who do you think benefits from this redevelopment and who loses out?

Before you start…

You should know:

- that place has always been important to people
- how different places are **perceived** affects how people interact and behave in them
- how our **perceptions** of place can be changed and manipulated, which can result in both positive and negative consequences.

 Key terms

perceive: to consider/view/regard

perception: how something is viewed, regarded or considered

8.1 The nature and importance of places

The term 'place' is used in many ways in geography. Geographers have always been interested in studying places, and the word 'place' has a number of specific meanings that are complex. Economic geographers are interested in how and why places become sites of economic activity, while political geographers consider why certain places become sites of unrest or legislative power. Considering place more widely, we might ask why people choose to live in one place over another, why they might avoid certain places or why some places hold special meaning for them. This section introduces the concept of place and considers a range of factors that inform how we think about different places.

Geographers have defined place in different ways

The geographer Yi Fu Tuan (1977) contrasts place with the allied concept of space, stating that 'Place is security' while 'Space is freedom', suggesting that while space is infinite, place is bounded, identifiable and something to which humans can become emotionally attached. Similarly, John Agnew (1989) defines place as a 'meaningful location'.

Defining place

Place can be understood in several ways:

- A point in space, such as a location on the Earth's surface.
- Somewhere that can be mapped, represented or measured.
- Something concrete, with elements that make it identifiable, such as a name. For example, there are thousands of rivers in the world but only one 'Amazon' or 'Ganges'.
- Somewhere local because it can be identified as being 'here' and not somewhere else, and therefore differentiated from other places.
- Somewhere meaningful; a space that has no meaning cannot be a specific place.
- Associated with human behaviour, history and culture, whether personal/ individual or collective. This means that they often evoke emotional responses as sites of symbolism, memory or nostalgia.

Places may be spatially constructed to create an emotional response, for example, the arrangement of rooms, corridors, windows and décor of a building may combine to create a welcoming place, or one that is intimidating.

Places are represented in a range of different media such as text, images or performance. These representations can express and shape how we understand a place and give it meaning.

Tip

It would be useful at the start of this chapter, to start thinking of the places that are important to you personally. Why do they matter so much to you, and how does the fact they have (or haven't) changed in your lifetime change the way you feel about them?

ACTIVITY 8.1

1 a Outline the main characteristics of the place shown in Figure 8.1.
   b In what ways does it suggest that this place is changing?
   c Suggest why people might be attracted to live in this place or to leave it.
2 a Briefly outline the concept of place.
   b Suggest why place is important in human life and experiences.

Divisions of place

The perceptions of place vary with individuals. We bring our unique personal histories, thoughts and feelings to bear on our perception of places and their meanings. The following terms offer some ways to begin to think about different types of place.

Insider and outsider

The way we understand different places depends on the level to which we are attached to them. A tourist visiting London may have a very different perception of it than someone who commutes there every day. They in turn are likely to see it differently to someone who has lived there for many years. Geographer Edward Relph described these different responses to place in terms of **insider** and **outsider** perspectives. When we live in a place, we become familiar with the streets and buildings, and also its rhythm: the opening times of shops, the habits of our neighbours, bus timetables, refuse collections and so on. This familiarity makes us feel 'at home' because we are able to negotiate the place easily, and may make us 'insiders'. Those who are new to a place, such as tourists or refugees, are often considered 'outsiders'. It is still possible to become an outsider even in a place one knows well. Becoming homeless, for example, changes a person's experience and understanding of a place and the treatment they receive from the rest of the community. Even those who live and work in a place may not feel 'at home' there. Any section of the community that is marginalised or experiences prejudice or discrimination may feel themselves to be outsiders. For example, ethnic minorities or lesbian, gay, bisexual and transgender (LGBT) people in small rural communities.

Public and private

Another way in which geographers think about place is in terms of those that are privately owned and those that are open and accessible to the public. For example, a **freehold** house would be an example of a **private** place, whereas a street or civic square would be a **public** one. Not all space is easily divided into distinct categories (Figure 8.2). Many privately owned places allow the public to have some access. Shopping centres may seem open to the public but the presence of security guards and CCTV make it very clear that consumers must obey certain behavioural rules in order to be admitted. Public places often have powerful symbolic meanings; we may think of those places where people gather to celebrate national events or hold demonstrations. The Occupy Movement is a group that has protested against social and economic inequality. One of its most effective methods of protest is through the occupation of significant public places.

Key terms

insider: the perspective of someone who knows a place well and is familiar with not only its topography but also its daily rhythms and events

outsider: the perspective of someone who does not know a place well (e.g. a visitor) or someone who is marginalised in a community, such as the homeless or people from minority groups

freehold: a type of tenure (ownership) in which the owner has outright ownership of the property and the land on which it stands

private space: a space that is privately owned and public access may be prevented or limited

public space: space that is open and accessible to the public

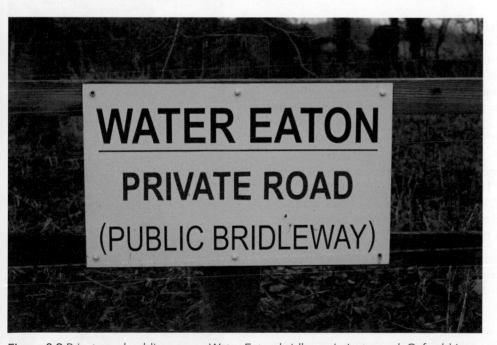

Figure 8.2 Private and public space – Water Eaton bridleway/private road, Oxfordshire.

Far and near places

The frictional effect of distance is a concept that states that places near to each other have greater interaction, whereas those that are further apart have less interaction. This is true up to a point. It also means that we generally know more about places that are close by, and less about places further away. However, developments in ICT are changing this, as are improvements in transport. Increasingly, time–space convergence (compression) is occurring, whereby places that are far apart in distance may be getting closer in terms of travel time between them. There are two case studies at the end of this chapter – one is on an urban area and the other is on a remote rural area.

Experienced places

When we have actually visited and 'experienced' a place, we see them differently. If a British family from Leicester travels to Delhi to visit relatives every year, it may be that they know the Indian capital better than London, which they rarely visit despite its relative proximity. In this case, although Delhi is geographically 'far', having experienced it many times makes it seem 'nearer'. It is experience that turns undifferentiated space into 'place'; from somewhere that we have a vague idea about based on representations, to one that we know at first hand and to which we attach meaning. While we often choose to revisit places that we like and feel comfortable in, this does not necessarily mean that the places that have meaning for us are always associated with positive feelings. Tuan introduced the concept of **topophilia** (love of place) and **topophobia** (fear of place). Certain places can evoke very mixed feelings. For example, Auschwitz would provoke topophobia in many people. On the other hand, it exerts a strong fascination for the thousands of people that visit every year.

 Making connections

In what ways has time–space convergence made the world a smaller place? See section 7.2 Case Study: Walmart and adaptation to globalisation; in particular Figure 7.10.

Media places

The places that we have experienced differ from those places that we know only through media such as literature, film or art. We may be particularly attached to fictional places such as Hogwarts or Narnia, precisely because we have a strong sense of 'what these places are like' that cannot be ruined by the actual reality falling short of our expectations. The attraction of such places is strong. Tourists visit places used as film or television locations, seeking to connect with the fictional places (Figure 8.3). Tourists to New Zealand can visit the locations used to create J.R.R. Tolkien's Middle Earth in *The Lord of the Rings*, with some using these areas to relive the events of the films through live action role play. Many of these fictional associations are enduring. *The Prisoner*, a popular British spy show which aired on television in the 1960s, still brings visitors to the village of Portmeirion in north Wales (Figure 8.4), where they can stay in hotel rooms used in the programmes and even attend an annual music festival based in part around characters and catchphrases from the series.

Although some of these places are fictitious, the development of theme parks around them is very real for the people who live and work there. For example, Disney films are fantasy but Disney has had a major impact on places and economies in the USA, France and Japan.

Whether or not the 'real' place matches up to their preconceived expectations, we can see how places come to be imbued with different meanings depending on how they are represented.

Occupy St Paul's, 2012

Occupy London was an anti-capitalist protest in London. The protesters had originally intended to camp outside the London Stock Exchange. Instead, they formed a camp outside St Paul's Cathedral in October 2012 (Figure 8.5). The protest was in solidarity with Occupy Wall Street, in New York. Protesters were

 Key terms

topophilia: a strong sense of place or love of particular places

topophobia: a fear or dread of certain places

Figure 8.3 Platform 9 ¾ at King's Cross Station, London.

Figure 8.4 Portmeirion in north Wales; the whole place represents the vision of architect Clough Williams-Ellis who planned, designed and built the village between 1925 and 1975.

evicted in February 2013, with 20 arrests being made. Following eviction, the protesters moved to Salvation Army offices near the Millennium Bridge, but the police moved them on.

Occupy Wall Street (OWS), New York, was an anti-capitalist protest which focused on inequality. Protesters used the slogan 'we are the 99%', bringing attention to the huge profits and inequalities generated by the financial services.

ACTIVITY 8.2

1 a Define the terms 'insider' and 'outsider'.
  b Research your local press to find examples of who is considered to be an 'insider' and who is considered to be an 'outsider' in your home area. Explain why the 'outsiders' are considered to be 'outsiders'.
2 a Evaluate the definitions of 'place' provided in this chapter.
  b Which definition do you consider to be (i) most satisfactory and (ii) least satisfactory. Justify your choices.
3 Comment on the contrasts in private and public space as shown in Figure 8.2.
4 Outline the likely living conditions that protesters experienced between October 2012 and February 2013.
5 Suggest why a protest in an urban place may be easier to attend, compared with a protest in a rural place.

Figure 8.5 Occupy St. Paul's Cathedral, London.

Places change as a result of factors from both within and beyond them. **Endogenous** factors are found *within* places. They are related to the location of the settlement, the topography of its setting and the physical geography of its surroundings. A small rural village such as Malham in the Yorkshire Dales will have particular land-use, local stone used in constructing its houses and limited infrastructure. Its demographics and the economic activity of its residents will be very different to larger urban places such as Leeds. All places, however, evolve over time, as buildings change, vegetation grows to change a view, and properties change hands.

Exogenous forces come from outside. These include the changing nature of farming as a result of outside pressures, migration of people into the village, and young people leaving to study or work. Tourism brings temporary visitors, who then drive change in the use of buildings to accommodation, or providing visitor services. Over time, the village becomes a very different 'place' while remaining in the same geographical location.

Rural and urban places

Rural places are often associated with wholesome living and simplicity, and 'getting back to nature'. In contrast, urban living is typified as hectic and stressful but more culturally sophisticated. Although the image of an idyllic country life is often sold as an antidote to the city, the reality seen by those who live and work in rural areas can be quite different. For the farm worker facing a range of social and economic hardships, from poor harvests and low profits from supermarket price-fixing to a lack of amenities such as broadband connection and a sense of isolation, the reality can be quite different. A lack of access to gas mains may result in a reliance on more expensive bottled gas or oil for heating, and having to use septic tanks when access to drainage systems is unavailable. Moreover, expensive and limited public transport, closure of rural Post Office branches, shops, pubs and schools makes access to amenities and services problematic, especially for those without access to a car.

Many geographers and sociologists have written about the differences in rural and urban areas. However, so rapid is the change affecting rural communities that some

Research point

Use the internet to find out more details about Occupy Wall Street and other Occupy movements:

1 When was Occupy Wall Street?

2 What were the protesters protesting about?

3 What is meant by the phrase 'we are the 99%'?

4 What impact did the Occupy Movement have?

Key terms

endogenous: factors within a place that help shape its character (e.g. location and topography)

exogenous: factors from outside a place that force a change in a place's character (e.g. its relationships with other places)

geographers have claimed that there are no significant differences between rural and urban populations in the life they lead, in their hopes and aspirations, and in their attitudes. The cause of this change has been the decline of traditional rural economic activities combined with the growth of material and personal mobility.

One of the earliest and best-known classifications of urban and rural is that of the German geographer, Ferdinand Tonnies. The urban extreme was called the **gesellschaft** and the rural extreme **gemeinschaft**. He described the rural ideal as an unchanging, peasant society, organised in small inward-looking, idyllic communities, based on kinship and supported by subsistence agriculture. By contrast, the urban gesellschaft is the ever-changing life of the large cosmopolitan, commercial city (Table 8.1). It is clear that Tonnies's classification is over-simplified, and it is arguable whether any settlements could ever match the strict criteria for the rural gemeinschaft. His model is, however, a useful starting point for comparative studies. According to sociologist Louis Wirth (1938), urban lifestyles were 'impersonal, superficial, transitory and segmented'.

Tonnies's model has been adapted to show the main characteristics of rural communities. Unlike urban settlements, in traditional rural communities there is:

- much interaction between individuals
- a distinct nucleus centred on the village
- involvement in village-based activities
- a heightened local awareness and a sense of belonging
- shared attitudes.

Social characteristics	Rural – gemeinschaft	Urban – gesellschaft
1 Dominant social relationships based on kinship, locality and neighbourliness	Fellowship – a sharing of responsibilities and fates, a common purpose	Commerce, specified functions, formal and limited responsibilities
2 Ordering of social institutions	Family life, rural village life	City life, national life, cosmopolitan life
3 Characteristic forms of wealth	Land	Money
4 Central institutions and forms of social control	Family law, extended family groups, customs, religion	The state, convention, political legislation, public opinion
5 Status role	Everyone's role is fully integrated in the system	Roles based on specific relationships, status based on personal achievement

Table 8.1 Major characteristics of gemeinschaft and gesellschaft.

According to the geographer Ray Pahl (1966), 'the terms rural and urban are more remarkable for their ability to confuse than their power to illuminate'. He used the term 'metropolitan village' to describe villages that had become suburbanised. An increasing number of middle-class commuters moved into rural settlements, causing their characteristics to change. Urban and rural are no longer defined by place or location, but by way of lifestyle and behaviour. Hence, it is increasingly difficult to distinguish between urban and rural. Although two extreme forms can be identified, it is better to think of an **urban–rural continuum**.

Key terms

gesellschaft: the urban extreme – the ever-changing nature of large, cosmopolitan commercial cities

gemeinschaft: the rural extreme – a peasant society which is inward looking, an idyllic community, based on kinship and supported by subsistence agriculture

For an activity on rurality download Worksheet 8.1 from **Cambridge Elevate**.

Key term

urban–rural continuum: the range of settlement types from extremely urban to extremely rural

Despite the existence of the Rural–Urban Classification, it is not always easy to determine where the urban ends and the rural begins. Some geographers have explored the constantly shifting borders between such places. These **edgelands** include wasteland and industrial estates that exist in the borders between the urban and rural but cannot be easily defined as belonging to one or the other. These places are described as **liminal**, meaning in between.

Place as home

'Home is where you can be yourself.' (Tim Cresswell)

One of the most familiar examples of place is at a very small scale – the idea of home, a place to which people typically feel a strong sense of attachment. This can be the building that they call home – or it could be the local settlement in which they live. For others, they may feel 'at home' or safe within their home, but unsafe within the locality. It is a place where a person can withdraw from the pace of the world around them and have some control over their immediate environment, choosing how to decorate and run their home.

An attachment to one's home can be particularly important for those groups that may feel 'less at home' in their local area. Older people, for example, may feel secure and comfortable in their home where they may be less troubled by a lack of mobility or the rapid pace of change. Similarly, for groups such as traveller communities, home is likely to be more closely associated with their caravans and vehicles than with any particular town or village. Again, it is important to avoid sweeping generalisations; while home can connote security and comfort for some, for others it may be a place of drudgery, abuse or neglect.

Placelessness

We can identify the things that make a place unique or different to those around it, but some geographers have identified ways in which this uniqueness is increasingly under threat. The increase in transport and communications technology has meant that even places that are far away are brought closer, and the spread of multinational business means that everything from the clothes we buy to the ingredients of our dinner are made, farmed or processed all over the world. The geographer Doreen Massey called this global interconnectedness 'time–space compression' and identifies that it has complicated our understanding of the unique characteristics of place and how we relate to them. There are many examples of places that look, feel, sound and even smell the same wherever we are in the world. Shopping centres, fast-food chains, service stations, airports and chain hotels are often cited as examples of places that are somehow '**placeless**'. These are places that can feel detached from the local environment, and tell us very little about where we are located. For example, airport departure lounges look similar around the world, with their crowds of travellers of every nationality and luxury brand boutiques. On a connecting flight where we do not have the opportunity to exit the airport building or see the landscape, the only indication as to the identity of the country we are in may come from the language used in signage.

Thinking like a geographer

Geographers consider different perspectives. For example, in any place, there are some people who feel a strong sense of belonging and others who do not. For your home city or county, identify some groups of people or individuals who may not feel a strong sense of belonging, and suggest reasons why that may be the case.

Key terms

edgelands: places where the borders between urban and rural are difficult to define/classify

liminal: in between

Tip

How can artists, authors, poets and musicians contribute to creating a sense of place? In what ways do they achieve this? Try to use examples that are local to your home region. Find out about local artists, authors, poets, musicians and so on. Your local newspaper is likely to carry information about events featuring local artists.

Key term

placeless: a place that is indistinguishable from other such places in appearance or character

To read about and complete an activity on stateless people, download Worksheet 8.2 from **Cambridge Elevate**.

Making connections

How has time–space convergence (compression) affected globalisation? See Chapter 7 Global systems and global governance.

ACTIVITY 8.3

1   Distinguish between topophilia and topophobia.
2   a   Describe the main characteristics of three examples of places or located places where you would experience topophilia, and three places where you are likely to feel topophobic.
    b   Briefly explain why the places you described create a strong sense of emotion.
3   a   Briefly describe the main characteristics of a media place that you are familiar with.
    b   Outline the ways in which a sense of place has been created.

> **Tip**
>
> Relate the information in this section to your local place study and your contrasting one. For each place study, consider:
>
> • What type of place is it?
> • What factors contribute to its character?

8.2 Changing places – relationships and connections

Recent changes in rural settlements in the UK

Most rural settlements in the UK have changed in recent decades. Many have grown in size whereas others have declined in size. Many have changed function, moving away from agriculture and towards commuting. However, others have retained a recreational-tourist function. There is, thus, great diversity, in the UK's rural settlements.

Making connections

Factors contributing to the character of places include endogenous (local) factors such as physical geography, history, land-use, built environment, infrastructure and population. External (exogenous) factors include relationships with other places (e.g. out-migration and in-migration). Change may be brought about by individuals, local governments, national governments, TNCs and MGOs and NGOs. Detailed examples of the dynamics of changing places are provided by the case studies of urban change in Stratford, London, and rural change in the Blasket Islands, Kerry, Ireland.

The key factors explaining rural change are:

• changes in improvements in transport
• changes in increased standards of living
• changes in decreased size of households.

Counter-urbanisation is an extension of suburbanisation. Although they may live in rural areas, the newcomers bring with them urban attitudes and lifestyles. In addition, house prices increase. Industry and retailing are also moving to the rural areas. It is possible that counter-urbanisation will lead to a more even distribution of population in the industrialised nations in the next 50 years. Indeed, it is difficult to see how inner cities can become as attractive to people as the smaller towns and rural areas.

Key term

counter-urbanisation: the movement away from large urban settlements to smaller urban settlements and rural settlements

Those who have moved into rural settlements include:

- families who prefer a safer, more pleasant environment
- commuters who prefer living in smaller settlements but whose jobs are elsewhere
- retired people
- careerists moving to the region as part of their career but whose residence is only temporary
- small-scale entrepreneurs and self-employed people who live in an area they consider offers a good quality of life.

There are a number of reasons to explain the movement to small towns and rural areas, including a growing dissatisfaction with urban lifestyles, an increase in car ownership and improving technology, which has allowed industries to become 'footloose'. One of the greatest changes has been the improvement in transport, both public and private. There is a clear relationship between the type and rate of change in rural settlements and the distance from large urban areas (Figure 8.6). The most accessible villages have grown the most.

Many villages in the UK have grown considerably and have lost their original character, form and function. These are often described as dormitory, commuter or **suburbanised villages** (Table 8.2). The Gower and Purbeck villages are good examples. Villages without good transport links or beyond the distance of commuting have tended to retain more of their original character. However, although the size of the population may not change much, the composition does. The younger generation move out to be replaced by retired people, even though the villages may lack some necessary facilities.

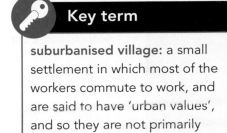

Key term

suburbanised village: a small settlement in which most of the workers commute to work, and are said to have 'urban values', and so they are not primarily interested in the rural economy

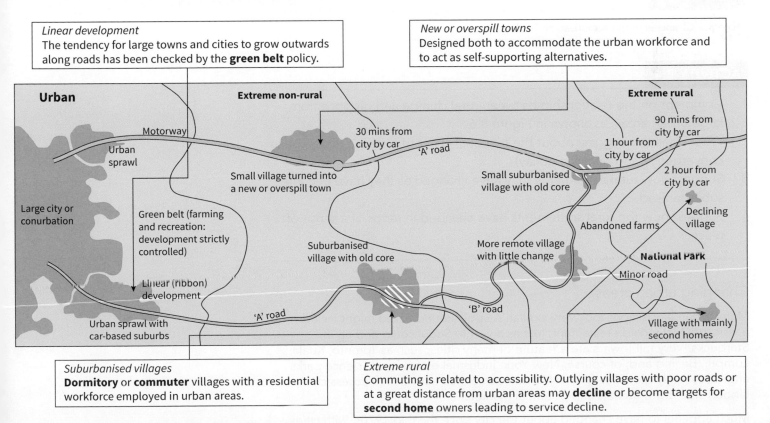

Linear development
The tendency for large towns and cities to grow outwards along roads has been checked by the **green belt** policy.

New or overspill towns
Designed both to accommodate the urban workforce and to act as self-supporting alternatives.

Suburbanised villages
Dormitory or **commuter** villages with a residential workforce employed in urban areas.

Extreme rural
Commuting is related to accessibility. Outlying villages with poor roads or at a great distance from urban areas may **decline** or become targets for **second home** owners leading to service decline.

Figure 8.6 Rural change and distance from large urban areas.

Villages in national parks or areas of attractive scenery, such as Snowdonia and the Gower Peninsula, are being affected by the increased incidence of second homes. This situation has led to conflict between visitors and locals. Locals are priced out of the housing market, and holidaymakers or weekenders are made to feel unwelcome as a result.

In the most remote areas of the UK, there are few opportunities. As a result, out-migration is prevalent and service provision, such as schools, is declining. Villages may go into decline and eventually the whole settlement may be abandoned.

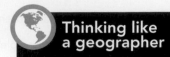

Thinking like a geographer

How might the model in Figure 8.6 change in each of the following situations?

a   In a low-income country.

b   In a country in conflict.

	Original village	Suburbanised village
Housing	Detached, stone-built houses with slate/thatch roofs. Some farms. Most over 100 years old. Barns.	New, mainly detached or semis. Renovated barns or cottages. Expensive planned estates, garages.
Inhabitants	Farmers and labourers employed in primary or manual jobs.	Professionals/executives, commuters. Wealthy with young families, or retired.
Transport	Bus service, some cars. Narrow, winding roads.	Decline in bus services as most families have one or two cars. Better roads.
Services	Village shop, small junior school, public house, village hall.	More shops, larger school, modern public houses and/or restaurant.
Social	Small, close-knit community.	Local community swamped. Village may be deserted during the day.
Environment	Quiet, relatively pollution-free.	More noise and risk of more pollution. Loss of farmland and open space.

Table 8.2 Changes in the suburbanised village.

ACTIVITY 8.4

1   Comment on the relationship between rural change and distance from large urban areas, as shown in Figure 8.6.

2   What does this suggest about the frictional effect of distance (time–space convergence and distance decay)?

3   Suggest how rural settlements may have changed as they have become suburbanised.

4   Suggest how the rural settlements have changed in terms of a sense of place.

Changing urban areas

Many urban landscapes look very similar. A stroll around Tokyo might include a visit to a McDonald's restaurant, just as a visit to Seoul could end up in Starbucks. Very tall towers are a feature of many cities, such as Toronto, Kuala Lumpur, Beijing and, of course, New York. Industrial estates and science parks are increasingly globalised, as TNCs outsource their activities to access cheap labour, vital raw materials and potential markets.

Much appears to have changed about the city since the mid 1970s, with cities having undergone dramatic transformations in their physical appearance, economy, social composition, governance, shape and size. So are urban areas around the world converging in form? Are we seeing a globalised urban pattern or do local and national characteristics still prevail?

Take Los Angeles, for example. In this city, there is a dazzling array of sites in compartmentalised parts of the inner city. For example, the Vietnamese shops and traditional Chinese-style housing of Chinatown, the pseudo-Bohemian of artists' lofts and galleries, the wholesale markets, the urban homelessness in the Skid Row district, the enormous murralled barrio (shanty town) stretching eastwards towards east Los Angeles and the intentionally gentrifying South Park redevelopment zone. Many large cities have their Chinatowns and other ethnic/racial areas. Individual cities are anything but homogeneous. As cities become globalised, they are more heterogenous (diverse). Ironically, this diversity is making cities around the world more similar in certain ways, e.g skyscrapers, metro systems, TNCs present, retailers present etc.

The post-industrial city is regarded as a more flexible, complex and divided city than its predecessor. The result is a patchwork city of different ethnic enclaves, economic areas and residential areas, where the boundaries between city and country (both physical and social) are difficult to define. Consequently, an array of new terms has emerged to describe the post-industrial city and its attendant spatial forms: the splintered city, the edgeless city, the urban galaxy, the spread city.

The Los Angeles school of geographers are very pessimistic about the development of their city, and see it as teetering on the verge of meltdown. They talk about the death of cities, ecological disaster, terrorism, inequality and dysfunction.

The evolution of uniform urban landscapes (the **homogenisation** of landscapes) is due to a number of interacting factors:

- improvements in ICT so that people in cities around the world are aware of opportunities
- the increase in international migration and the spread of ideas and culture
- time–space convergence, which allows improved interactions between places in a decreasing amount of time
- the desire of global brands (TNCs) such as Coca-Cola, McDonald's and Starbucks to reach new markets
- improvements in standards of living and aspirations to be part of a global network of urban centres
- globalisation of economic activity, culture (art, media, sport and leisure activities) and political activity.

Seoul – homogenised or independent?

Seoul is a good example of the debate on the homogenisation of urban landscapes. On the one hand, it fits the theory of a homogenised landscape – there are global firms (such as McDonald's) in Seoul, just as there are Korean firms such as Hyundai and Samsung located in other countries. The Central Business District (CBD) is characterised by skyscrapers and international firms such as Barclays and 7-Eleven (Figure 8.7). There are high-rise apartments and edge-of-town developments, and decentralisation, such as at Gyeonggi-do and Pangyo on the south side of Seoul.

On the other hand, there has been a massive urban redevelopment centred on the restoration of the Cheong Gye Cheon River in downtown Seoul. This project has been more than just the restoration of a river; it has a historic, cultural and touristic–economic value. Murals along the side of the river recount some of the

Key term

homogenisation: the process whereby places and social characteristics become more similar to each other so that they eventually become indistinguishable

ACTIVITY 8.5

1 Suggest ways in which central Seoul has become similar to many other central areas in large cities around the world.

2 a Study Table 8.2. Suggest why the characteristics of the suburbanised village have changed from the original village.

   b Suggest how Soja's perspectives of place may add to an understanding of the sense of place experienced by original residents and newer residents.

most important events to occur in Seoul over the last 600 years, and the river has become an important focus for Seoul residents and visitors – rather like Trafalgar Square in London – partly because it is stressing the individuality and uniqueness of Seoul, and of Korea.

Making connections

To what extent are urban areas becoming more similar? See Chapter 9 Contemporary urban environments.

Figure 8.7 Downtown Seoul – much like most large cities.

Economic change and social inequalities in Detroit

Detroit is the largest city in Michigan, a Midwestern US state. During the 20th century, the city underwent considerable economic and social change (Figure 8.8). In 1960, Detroit had the highest per-capita income in the US. In 2013, 36% of the population was categorised as living below the poverty level.

In 1960, the annual homicide rate was 10.3 per 100 000 residents. In 2000 it was 41.6 per 100 000 residents. From 2012 to 2014, Detroit was the most dangerous city with a population over 200 000 in the US.

Tip

Relate the information in this section to your local place study and your contrasting one. For each place study, consider:

- the ways in which the place has changed or stayed the same
- how relationships and connections have contributed to these changes
- the ways in which the changes have affected people's lives.

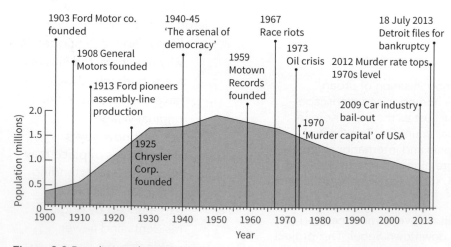

Figure 8.8 Population change in Detroit, USA, and a number of key changes in the city and its economy.

ACTIVITY 8.6

1 Suggest reasons for the growth of Detroit between 1900 and 1930.
2 In what ways may the growth of Detroit's economy have influenced its 'sense of place'?
3 Suggest reasons for the decline in Detroit's population from about 1950.
4 In what ways might the 1973 oil crisis have contributed to Detroit's decline?
5 Suggest how Detroit's 'sense of place' changed between 1950 and 2012/13.
6 How might the 'sense of place' change in future years? Suggest ways in which Detroit could rebrand itself as a 'city of opportunities'.

8.3 Changing places – meaning and representations

A sense of place

One of the most important concepts to grasp when studying place is the idea of a 'sense of place'. This is not a new idea; many cultures throughout history have recognised that certain locations can have a distinctive character or atmosphere that makes them important. Think, for example, of the prehistoric builders of Stonehenge, the huge **geoglyphs** drawn by the ancient Nazca people of Peru or the sacred landscapes of the Aborigines (Figure 8.9).

A sense of place can be defined as the feelings of attachment we have to certain places. Many factors may shape our sense of place. Our reactions may be influenced by what we see in the built environment; we may find a place, its architecture, streets or landscaping beautiful. We might become fond of a place where we work or enjoy leisure activities. We may associate a place with pleasant memories, a beach with childhood memories or the house of a friend with memorable celebrations.

Tuan notes that sense of place can be positive or negative; we may deliberately avoid walking down dark alleyways or travel out of our way to circumvent places we associate with negative experiences. A sense of place can also apply to places at varying scales. Small, personal spaces such as our bedroom, desk or locker might be imbued with a sense of place just as we might associate a sense of place with whole regions or countries. In some extreme cases, people are willing to use violence to uphold their perception of what makes a place special. In Afghanistan, for example, the Taliban seek to expel all Western influence to create a place in which only Islamic culture exists.

Gaining a sense of place: What gives a place its identity?

Sense of place can be very powerful in determining how people perceive and interact with different environments. How do we go about understanding our own sense of place and that of others? Formal techniques for gathering data such as census statistics and cartography can only get us so far. We may be able to collect information on the size, topography or demographic make-up of a place, but such statistics cannot tell us how people *feel* about them. Geographer Edward W. Soja describes the quantitative approach as a **firstspace** perspective. This means an attempt to understand a place in terms of *quantitative* analysis, looking at what is physically present in a place and is empirically measurable. A sense of place can also be expressed through other means, such as in art, photography, travel writing, blogs and interviews using any type of media that expresses how individuals feel about a place. Soja terms these expressions as **secondspace** representations. These are *subjective* accounts of personal experience and capture a sense of place in a way that firstspace accounts cannot. Finally, one of the most useful ways to understand a place is to consider both quantitative and qualitative data or, as Soja

Figure 8.9 Uluru – spiritual home of Australia's indigenous population.

Key terms

geoglyph: large motifs or designs carved into rocks or drawn on the ground such as the White Horses of southern England or the Nazca art in Peru

firstspace: the quantitative analysis of a place (e.g. demographic data and socio-economic data)

secondspace: qualitative data for how people feel about a place

calls it, a **thirdspace** reading. In this way we build a richer image of what a place is like and how it is experienced and perceived. For an explanation of quantitative and qualitative data, see Chapter 12 Fieldwork.

Throughout our lives, we encounter places which become important to us. Some reveal themselves through repeated visits, or by living in them for prolonged periods of time. The continuity of experience can also lead to us losing sight of some of their special character. Memories of seaside holidays can give us a 'rose-tinted' view of places, which may have changed beyond recognition. Flowers taped to a lamp post may also be a visual symbol of a location which for one family means grief and loss, which others would walk past without understanding the added significance.

Relationships and connections: perspectives on Ellis Island and London

Ellis Island is an island situated in Upper New York Bay in the Port of New York and New Jersey, USA. It was the gateway for millions of immigrants to the USA as the nation's busiest immigrant inspection station from 1892 until 1954 (Figure 8.10).

Katie Bourke who arrived in 1921:

> We were herded on board the boat, Cedric. It was a terrible crossing, lots of people fell ill. When we got to America we passed through a vast centre (Ellis Island) where there were people from all over the world, speaking every language. Some were refused entry. I admit I was so pleased to go to Aunty Josie's (a resident of New York). Still, it felt like a temporary prison – luckily I was released!

Mary Bourke (granddaughter of Katie):

> Ellis Island is amazing. It is so atmospheric. I find it hard to believe that Granny passed through here … it must have been tough leaving home forever, but at least she had family here. Others were not so fortunate. It does make me think about current migrants and refugees. This is more than just a tourist attraction.

Key term

thirdspace: a combination of both quantitative and qualitative data for a place

Thinking like a geographer

In what ways do you think each of the following influences people's perception of place?

- Level of wealth
- Level of education
- Age
- Access to media

Research point

Find out why Uluru is important to Australia's indigenous population. Find out about 'dreamtime'. Comment on the implication of this for tourism at Uluru. Give at least two different perspectives and justify your answer.

Figure 8.10 Ellis Island immigration hall, New York, USA, now a tourist destination.

Dickens's London

Little Dorrit

> It was a Sunday, gloomy close and stale … Melancholy streets in a penitential garb of soot, steeped the souls of people who were condemned to look at them out of windows in a dire despondency. Nothing to see but streets, streets, streets. Nothing to breathe but streets, streets, streets. Nothing to change the brooding mind or raise it up.

Bleak House

> Fog everywhere. Fog up the river, where it flows among the green aits* and meadows; fog down the river, where it rolls defiled among the tiers of shipping, and the waterside pollution of a great (and dirty) city. Fog on the Essex marshes, fog on the Kentish heights.

> (*ait is a small island)

Great Expectations

> … those long reaches below Gravesend, between Kent and Essex, where the river is broad and solitary, where the waterside inhabitants are very few, and where lone public houses are scattered here and there …

ACTIVITY 8.7

1   Using the quotes from Dickens, describe how he portrays the physical and human geography of London and the Lower Thames Valley.
2   For a place that you have experienced, compare the sense of place conveyed by direct experience with that conveyed by one other medium (e.g. travel brochure, novel, film).
3   Using one piece of media, such as a film, photography, art, novel or song, outline how it conveys a sense of place.

 For an activity on creating a sense of place using *The final problem*, download Worksheet 8.3 from **Cambridge Elevate**.

Meaning and representation

Our reaction to and perception of place is always changing, as both places and ourselves change over time. However, there are a number of ways in which our perception of place can be deliberately managed and manipulated. External agencies such as governments, corporate bodies or local groups may all have a vested interest in trying to change the way we feel about certain places, what they mean to us and therefore how we as individuals, groups, businesses or institutions behave in them.

Shopping centres and management of place

Shopping centres are designed using well-known tricks to manage our behaviour. Designers arrange escalators so we have to walk past certain shop fronts; they install hard seats so that we do not linger too long in any one area; there are no drinking water fountains, so we buy expensive drinks; bright lighting and no clocks means we forget the amount of time we are spending inside. Sometime this manipulation may be more subtle – retail planners and developers create spectacular places deliberately to make people want to spend longer amounts of time there, to have 'a day out'. Rather than simply carry out their shopping, the shopping centre becomes a leisure destination where one can shop, eat and go to

Research point

Visit the Statue of Liberty and Ellis website and find out whether you have any relatives who passed through Ellis Island, or whether people from your area passed through. How would the discovery that your relatives were connected with this place change your own thoughts on it?

Look on **Cambridge Elevate** for a link to the Statue of Liberty and Ellis website (www.cambridge.org/links/gase6077).

Tip

If you have a favourite author or artist, use some of their work to help support your study of changing places.

Research point

Using your favourite author/artist/musician, or a local one, describe and explain how they manage to create an image of a located place.

Making connections

To what extent has globalisation eroded our sense of place? See Chapter 7 Global systems and global governance.

the cinema all in one place and in so doing, spend more money (Figure 8.11). This type of development has been termed **hyper-reality** and the **'ecology of fantasy'**.

Figure 8.11 The Trafford Centre, Manchester.

There is a huge industry that sets out to reimagine places, to create 'uniqueness' in order to attract attention, visitors and money. Landscapes can be engineered, their culture commodified, often for financial gain. There are numerous ways in which a place can be shaped or **rebranded** to alter our perceptions of it. One way of rebranding a place, particularly if it has been associated with some sort of stigma or uncomfortable historical memory, is to rename it. An example is the renaming of Windscale Nuclear power station to Sellafield after the terrible leak and contamination of the area, caused by a fire in 1957. Urban areas in decline are often **regenerated** in order to improve their image, attract economic investment and improve the quality of life experienced by those who live there.

Heritage organisations may protect certain buildings and landscapes through regular maintenance and upkeep, but they can sanitise and regulate places in ways that irretrievably change their meaning. Country houses, for example, which were once busy working estates and family homes become museums, places in which people no longer live and a certain version of the past is preserved from change. Even natural landscapes can be turned into neat, highly managed visitor attractions where people must not veer from the gravel path or away from the marked route.

Places are also represented in different ways by a range of media. Advertising agencies represent appropriate places, for example car adverts always feature open roads free of cars, often in dramatic upland scenery. If the car is a 4x4, this may then transform into an urban jungle to show the versatility of the vehicle. Our memories of places can be triggered by music or songs, particularly classical symphonies which are sometimes named after places. The landscape photography of Ansel Adams captured US National Parks at a particular moment in time, but his images of Yosemite could mostly still be taken today from the same locations.

Tourist agencies use particular wording to describe places in a way which connects with our emotions, or our perceptions of a place we may never have visited. The sea is usually 'crystal clear', for example. The reality of some seaside resorts as shown by statistics on social inequality in the census, may be at odds with our memories of these places from visits made when we were small children. They are perhaps 'edgier' than we remember them.

Key terms

hyper-reality: a condition where what is real and what is fiction is blurred so that no clear distinction between the two can be made

ecology of fantasy: a term associated with Margaret Crawford (1988), in which she described theme parks as public spaces that have become a commodity – the underlying theme is consumption – a kind of disguised shopping centre

rebranding: a form of marketing in which a new development or redevelopment uses a new name, image, symbol, design or combination thereof for an established feature with the intention of developing a new, differentiated identity in the minds of consumers, the public, investors, competitors and other stakeholders

regeneration: a form of renewal and redevelopment of a run-down area; regeneration aims to improve the conditions of an area and the quality of life experienced by those who live there

ACTIVITY 8.8

1. a Describe the main characteristics of a large/regional shopping centre in your home location.
   b How would you describe the shopping centre in terms of
      i   private and/or public place
      ii an example of hyper-reality/ecology of fantasy?
   c Identify ways in which retail centres may try to create a 'sense of place'.
2. Consider a place of tourist interest close to your home location.
   a If you were to visit the place, would you still fee like a tourist?
   b What demographic or socio-economic group is the attraction targeted to?
   c How would you adapt the attraction so that it was of interest to a wider range of people and how would that change the character of the place?

Why are places manipulated, and by whom?

Decisions to manipulate or change the perception of a place may be motivated by a number of different factors including:

Social
- To change negative stereotypes.
- To encourage people to move, live and work in an area.

Economic
- To attract inward investment.
- To improve job opportunities.

Environmental
- To improve the quality of the built environment by removing derelict buildings, wasteland and so on.

Political
- To raise the status of a place, which can in turn give political gain.
- To rebrand, make more attractive, possibly attract inward investment, and to improve the environment for those living in the area.

Government – Lea Valley, Olympic Park

The Lea Valley is an area with a thriving industrial heritage. Running through Hertfordshire, Essex and Greater London, the River Lea and its marshland form a natural area some 2 km wide and 20 km long.

Much of the Lea Valley's industrial past was linked to the availability of water and the production of gunpowder, ceramics and more recently electronic goods. However, much of this industry has now gone and a brownfield site left in its place, which has been redeveloped into a site of leisure, retail and housing. Ian Sinclair discusses the controversy surrounding the redevelopment of the empty Royal Small Arms Factory on ex-Ministry of Defence land at Enfield Lock. Despite the ground being contaminated with high levels of chemicals from previous industrial use and a range of health complaints among local residents, the development went ahead with the factory being rebranded as 'Enfield Island Village, an exciting new village community'. Little reference is made to the problematic past on the Lea Valley website, which promotes a wholesome image of the park as a place for health with the slogan 'For nature, sport and discovery'.

The development of adventure tourism in New Zealand

Figure 8.12 Adventure tourism in New Zealand.

This example illustrates some of the key actors involved in the production of a tourism place. The New Zealand tourism board has invested heavily in a new countrywide marketing strategy known as 'Brand New Zealand' (Figure 8.12). Private companies in Queenstown, known as the 'adventure capital of the world', have played a part in it. The town contains everything that the adventure seeker could want, including the popular Awesome Four adventure combination of helicopter flight, whitewater rafting, high-speed jet boating and bungee jumping. Thus, Queenstown is branded as an appropriate place for exhilarating, fresh and unsullied experiences. New Zealand's tourist board has also taken advantage of its connection with the filming of *The Lord of the Rings* and *The Hobbit* trilogies, by re-branding itself as 'Middle Earth', aligning itself with a fictional place which for many fans of the books and films feels real.

The US National Park Foundation

There is a growing trend for big businesses to 'sponsor' certain types of environment in order to enhance their brand image. The US National Park Foundation has a number of corporate sponsors, including American Express, Budweiser, Disney and Coca-Cola. Such relationships may have a number of positive benefits. For example, Disney pays for half a million children to visit the national parks each year. However, consider the ethical implications of a company like Coca-Cola sponsoring spaces for health and exercises.

City branding – Las Vegas as Sin City

City branding creates a single brand for the city and extends it to all its offerings and interactions. From a customer point of view, this creates a unique picture of the city at every level of interactions. City branding has the power to turn a city into a place where people want to live, work and visit.

In the 1950s, Las Vegas even made a virtue of its location close to nuclear testing sites, and people came for parties to coincide with the detonation of bombs, with bars offering special 'atomic cocktails'. Las Vegas is branded as 'Sin City' because of its association with gambling, bookmaking, easy marriage, easy divorce, sex shows, strip clubs, cabarets, clubbing and 24-hour liquor sales ('What happens in Vegas, stays in Vegas.'). In former days, it was known also for organised crime and police and political corruption.

 Making connections

To what extent should transnational corporations (TNCs) and multi-government organisations (MGOs) sponsor aspects of a nation's heritage? See section 7.4 International trade and access to markets to see how some TNCs adapt their services in different countries. There has also been some criticism of the cultural appropriation of local symbols and artifacts by companies to help promote their products. Can you identify some examples of this?

 Tip

Relate the information in this section to your local place study and your contrasting one. For each place study, consider:

- the meanings that the place has for different people
- how the place is represented.

8.4 The Carpenters Estate, Stratford, UK

Figure 8.13 Carpenters Road, Stratford, UK *c.*1930s.

> **Tip**
>
> This place study explores the developing character of the Carpenters Estate in Stratford. While reading this place study, you might want to think how it relates to a place local to you. How is it similar and how is it different?

> **Physical and human**
>
> Suggest ways in which physical geography of the area (landforms, features) has influenced the human geography (e.g. settlement and industry). To what extent has human geography influenced the physical geography of the Stratford area?

Stratford is a town in the London Borough of Newham. It is approximately 10 km east of the centre of London (Charing Cross). During the 19th century, it was an industrial suburb famous for its rail works and heavy industries (Figures 8.13 and 8.14a). However, partly as a result of overseas competition and changes in transport and technology, Stratford began to decline in the 20th century. It was heavily bombed during the Second World War, so that by the mid- to late-20th century it was in need of regeneration. London won the bid for the 2012 Olympic and Paralympic Games, partly on the back of its regeneration plans for Stratford and the East End (Figure 8.14b). Stratford is now a major commercial and retail centre, with a population of around 100 000. However, not all of Stratford has been regenerated to date.

Stratford has good transport links (Figure 8.15). Stratford City is London's best connected transport hub outside Zone 1 served by HS1, Jubilee and Central Lines, and DLR commuters can be in Canary Wharf in 15 minutes. In 2018, the area will be given a direct link to Heathrow via Crossrail.

> Watch the video on **Cambridge Elevate** about the history of East London.

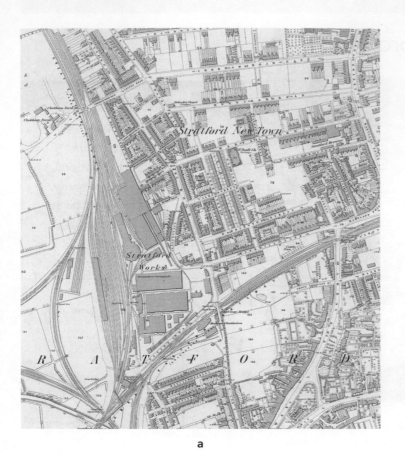

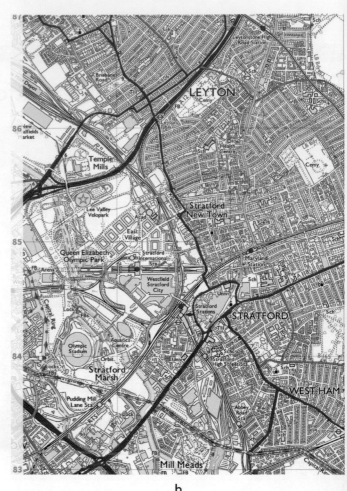

a

b

Figure 8.14 Ordnance Survey map extracts of Stratford, London: a 1867 and b 2016 at 1:25 000.

ACTIVITY 8.9

1   Describe the main characteristics of the Stratford area in the 1930s, as shown in Figure 8.13.
2   How did Stratford change between 1867 and 1930, as shown in Figures 8.14a and 8.13 respectively.
3   Describe and comment on the urban regeneration that is shown in Figure 8.14b.

Figure 8.15 The tube station at Stratford, London.

As Figures 8.13 and 8.14 illustrate, there has been considerable change in Stratford, from an industrial- to a post-industrial economy. This is due to a combination of deindustrialisation, globalisation, the development of a finance-orientated service sector, good transport communications, as well as large-scale urban regeneration. Nevertheless, there is much inequality in the area. Expensive developments such as Stratford Plaza and Stratford Halo contrast with areas that have had little recent regeneration, such as the Carpenters Estate.

The Carpenters Estate

The Carpenters Estate was first established in the late 19th century. The close proximity of jobs and housing, and the tendency of families to remain in the area, created the sense of a self-contained community, with a strong neighbourhood identity. The Carpenters Company strengthened this sense by investing in the local school, public house and community centre.

Like much of Stratford, the Second World War had a major impact on the Carpenters Estate. The area's close proximity to the railroads and its many factories made the area a key target during air raids, and much of the Carpenters Estate was destroyed or damaged. The lack of funding through to the 1960s resulted in the estate becoming increasingly rundown. In the late 1960s, the borough constructed a number of terraced houses and three 22-storey tower blocks, providing over 700 housing units between them (Figures 8.16–8.18).

> ### Tip
>
> Thinking about the subject of your own place study, what do you know about its:
>
> - transport facilities
> - infrastructure
> - economy
> - history?
>
> What data could you use to find out?

ACTIVITY 8.10

1   Study Figures 8.16–8.18. Suggest different reasons why developers may wish to regenerate the Carpenters Estate.

Figure 8.16 Old and new – the Carpenters Estate, Stratford: Doran Walk and the new Stratford Plaza (on extreme right).

Figure 8.17 Lund Point, Stratford, with the Athlete's Village in the background.

Figure 8.18 Carpenters Arms, Stratford, symbol of a decaying neighbourhood.

The population of the Carpenters Estate is among the most deprived in all of England. Newham is one of the most deprived boroughs in London. Unemployment is higher than the London average, over one-third of the residents are paid below the London living wage and some 29% of jobs within the borough are low paid. Newham Council has concluded that residents in the borough live in overcrowded and poor housing conditions, and it is therefore necessary to initiate the process of regeneration that looks to improve, transform and revitalise the area.

 Download Worksheet 8.4 from **Cambridge Elevate**, and compare the census data for Stratford, Newham and London (2011) to the census for your home area.

Maths for geographers

Overview of Boroughs

		Inequality		Homeless		Housing		Workless		Low pay		Benefits		Education		Average
		1	2	3	4	5	6	7	8	9	10	11	12	13	14	15
Outer East & Northeast	Barking & Dagenham															
	Bexley															
	Enfield															
	Greenwich															
	Havering															
	Redbridge															
	Waltham Forest															
Inner East & South	Hackney															
	Haringey															
	Islington															
	Lambeth															
	Lewisham															
	Newham															
	Southwark															
	Tower Hamlets															
Inner West	Camden															
	Hammersmith & Fulham															
	Kensington & Chelsea															
	Wandsworth															
	Westminster															
Outer West & Northwest	Barnet															
	Brent															
	Ealing															
	Harrow															
	Hillingdon															
	Hounslow															
	Richmond															
Outer South	Bromley															
	Croydon															
	Kingston															
	Merton															
	Sutton															

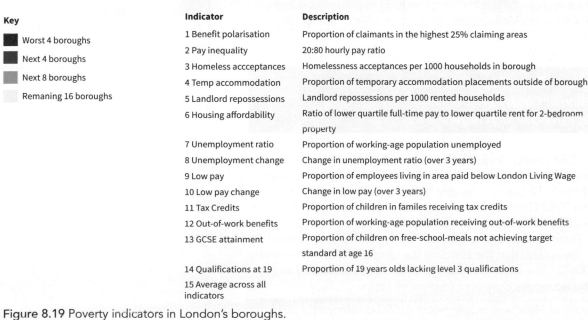

Key

- Worst 4 boroughs
- Next 4 boroughs
- Next 8 boroughs
- Remaning 16 boroughs

Indicator	Description
1 Benefit polarisation	Proportion of claimants in the highest 25% claiming areas
2 Pay inequality	20:80 hourly pay ratio
3 Homeless accceptances	Homelessness acceptances per 1000 households in borough
4 Temp accommodation	Proportion of temporary accommodation placements outside of borough
5 Landlord repossessions	Landlord repossessions per 1000 rented households
6 Housing affordability	Ratio of lower quartile full-time pay to lower quartile rent for 2-bedroom property
7 Unemployment ratio	Proportion of working-age population unemployed
8 Unemployment change	Change in unemployment ratio (over 3 years)
9 Low pay	Proportion of employees living in area paid below London Living Wage
10 Low pay change	Change in low pay (over 3 years)
11 Tax Credits	Proportion of children in familes receiving tax credits
12 Out-of-work benefits	Proportion of working-age population receiving out-of-work benefits
13 GCSE attainment	Proportion of children on free-school-meals not achieving target standard at age 16
14 Qualifications at 19	Proportion of 19 years olds lacking level 3 qualifications
15 Average across all indicators	

Figure 8.19 Poverty indicators in London's boroughs.

Figure 8.19 shows 14 indicators of poverty for London's 32 boroughs.

1 Create a table/spreadsheet showing the 14 indicators and the 32 boroughs. Add a final column for the total score.
   • Award one point if a borough is among the worst four boroughs.
   • Award two points if a borough is in the next four worst boroughs.
   • Award three points if a borough is in the next eight boroughs.
   • Award four points for the top 16 boroughs.
   • Add up the scores for each borough.
2 Which are the most deprived and the least deprived boroughs? How does Newham compare with the other boroughs?
3 Work out the mean, mode, median and range for deprivation in London boroughs.
4 How accurate is the method that you have used?
5 How could you improve your analysis?
6 What conclusions can you draw about inequalities in London?
7 Using your results, conduct a Chi-square test to see whether there is a significant difference in the level of inequality in London boroughs. The expected value should be the mean value for all boroughs; the observed value is the total value for each borough. For an explanation of how to conduct a Chi-square test, see Chapter 13 Geographical skills and techniques.

Look on **Cambridge Elevate** for more details on the Carpenters Estate from the following websites:
• The Carpenters Estate, Common Ground (www.cambridge.org/links/gase6078)
• Home2Home: Down Carpenters' Way, Part 1 (www.cambridge.org/links/gase6079).

Regeneration prospects

The Carpenters Estate is potentially undergoing a substantial social and spatial transformation. Its location adjacent to the Olympic Park and Stratford City (Figure 8.20) have created immense development pressures. A large number of luxury developments has introduced a new, richer population to the area. Local authorities are passing their responsibilities for social housing to private housing associations, and property development interests place pressures on vulnerable communities.

Tip

Thinking about the subject of your own place study, what are its prospects for the future? Are there any plans for redevelopment?

Watch the videos on **Cambridge Elevate** about:
• the regeneration of Canary Wharf
• problems that can occur with regeneration.

Regeneration schemes in East London include the London Docklands Development Corporation, and more recently the London 2012 Olympic and Paralympic Games. The promised 'legacy' of the 2012 Games was that 'within twenty years the communities who host the 2012 Games will have the same socio-economic chances as their neighbours across London' (London Organising Committee of the Olympic and Paralympic Games). Plans for the regeneration in Stratford have been around since 2000/01. By 2004, it was clear that the building standard of much of the estate was in poor repair. By 2006/07, the work to repair the estate was considered too expensive. After 2008, the economic downturn (recession) set in.

In 2011, it was estimated that Newham would need 20 000 dwellings by 2016 to meet the existing housing needs. Newham's housing policy places strong

Figure 8.20 Carpenters Estate, Stratford, with part of the Olympic Park in the background.

Figure 8.21 Stratford Plaza, London.

emphasis on high quality and affordability. However, regeneration in Newham aims to transform a number of areas into what has been named an 'Arc of Opportunity', London's Manhattan. A part of Stratford has been revamped, known as 'New Stratford' – a place that offers a 'golden opportunity' for property investors. The Stratford City development will feature a large shopping mall, hotels, offices and housing (Figure 8.21).

Regeneration of Stratford – some benefits

Planners are building a city within a capital city. Over £9 billion has been invested in Stratford, making it London's largest single regeneration project. There are many developers pouring cash into Stratford.

An accelerated process of urban regeneration has taken place in East London during the past decade. The Queen Elizabeth Olympic Park (the former Olympic Park) has brought more open space and wildlife habitats to Newham. iCity has been confirmed as the occupier of the Press and Broadcast Centre with tenants including BT Sport, Loughborough University London and Infinity.

By 2020, the economic impact of the London 2012 Olympic and Paralympic Games is estimated to be £28 billion to £41 billion in Gross Value Added (GVA). Oxford Economics has predicted that by 2030 the area will be one of the UK's most important growth drivers, and a net contributor to public finances worth £5.4 billion a year. East London is also expected to accommodate half of London's population growth and nearly a quarter of its growth in jobs to 2031.

Westfield is the largest urban shopping mall in Europe. It attracted nearly 50 million visitors in its first year of opening, providing more than 10 000 permanent jobs. There are over 250 top high street and designer brands, as well as eateries, a cinema, casino and bowling alley.

According to Newham Council, there are some 20 000 new homes being built. Manhattan Loft Gardens, which overlooks the Olympic Stadium, is a £200 million, 42-storey statement in glass and terracotta, incorporating 248 apartments. When it completes in 2016, it will be the tallest and most

Tip

Thinking about your own place study, try to explore advantages and disadvantages of recent changes in the area.

expensive building in Stratford, with prices double the local going rate. A one-bedroom flat will cost from £565 000 for 618 sq ft, and a two-bedroom unit will cost from £695 000 for 810 sq ft. LandProp, IKEA's property arm, has developed 1200 new homes. The former Athletes' Village, rechristened East Village, is being converted into some 2800 apartments by QDD, a joint venture between Qatari Diar and Delancey. The 25-storey Stratford Plaza by Telford Homes contains 198 units. These have all been sold, around three-quarters to overseas buyers, and the total revenue for the development topped £60 million. The Stratford Halo is a complex of six new buildings with a central tower of 43 storeys. Around 294 of its 706 apartments are earmarked as affordable for low-income Londoners.

Research point

There is a wealth of geospatial data available for many local places. You should be able to contrast this place study with your own home area. Use websites such as DataShine, or CDRC Maps to explore the nature of your home area in great detail using up to date statistics.

The Stratford area of London has undergone great change in recent years, and will continue to change for some time to come.

There are also plans for the University of East London and Birkbeck College to open a new campus. The Victoria and Albert Museum, Sadlers Wells and the University of Arts London are each building world-class institutions on the Olympic Park. From August 2016, West Ham United Football Club will be the anchor tenants for the Olympic Stadium.

All of these developments create jobs in construction (builders, carpenters, electricians, plumbers, drivers) and there are many multiplier effects, such as increased spending in local premises and increased demand for housing. Some of these may be short term, but many are long term.

Other impacts of regeneration

There have been a number of impacts of regeneration, such as increased investment, new housing, improved infrastructure and new business opportunities. However, there has also been relocation, polarisation, privatisation and fragmentation.

Newham Borough Council has relocated many local residents. It claims that 70% of residents from the tower blocks have been rehoused within E15. This has left the tower blocks and Carpenters Estate mainly empty. At the start of 2016, around 200 residents still occupied the estate. The Council relocated residents because of health risks from asbestos used in the tower blocks. However, some residents believed that the relocation was actually a form of 'social cleansing'. They argued that the tower blocks cannot have been considered unsafe because the BBC and Al Jazeera used a number of floors during the 2012 Olympic and Paralympic Games to film TV footage.

Polarisation may develop as new developments may create two separate worlds within the neighbourhood. The interior of the site will still be home to the existing population, with both private owners and council tenants in the

Key term

social cleansing: the removal from the area of members of a social class considered 'undesirable'

remaining low rises. Surrounding them will be a curtain of new developments with new, mostly wealthier residents.

The new developments have focused almost entirely on providing private spaces, omitting an essential component of a neighbourhood. Ironically, many of the residents of Lund Point and Dennison Point were leaseholders – having bought their properties during the 'right to buy' scheme of the Thatcher Government (1980s). However, during the early talks about regeneration, it was suggested that leaseholders would have to pay for the cost of refurbishment. At a cost of £120 000 to upgrade each property, this was more than their average value. Consequently, many leaseholders sold their properties and moved out of Stratford.

The exodus of most of the Carpenters Estate tenants threatens to be yet another fragmentation of the community. The current residents of the estate will most likely live in many separate places.

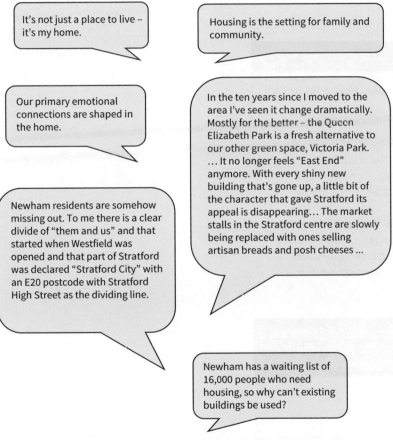

Figure 8.22 Comments made by Newham residents about housing in Newham, and the changes taking place there.

Some residents claim that perfectly adequate housing is going to waste. The Focus E15 Mothers are a group of young women originally housed in the mother and baby unit at the Focus E15 Hostel. They opened up a group of homes scheduled for demolition to highlight the lack of low-cost housing for people in Newham in particular, and across London in general. Some of the flats were in Doran Walk (Figure 8.16). One greater London Assembly Member stated:

We are seeing all too many perfectly serviceable social housing estates face demolition when refurbishment would be the obvious solution. I've worked with local residents to stave off demolition at Carpenters for several years now, going back to the time of the Olympics bid, and applaud the current protest. These homes should be lived in.

Some people have claimed that the rights of the remaining Carpenters Estate residents contrast with the regeneration plans pursued by Newham Council and private developers. The affordability of housing in Newham has become an issue of concern at the estate. Many residents who were interviewed by members of University College London (UCL) expressed fears that Stratford will become unaffordable after regeneration (Figure 8.22). Property and land values have presented an upward trend ever since London was awarded the Olympic Games and the redevelopment of Stratford began. The proposed regeneration plan has threatened job security, raised the cost of living and damaged community networks, placing obstacles in residents' paths to achieving greater levels of well-being.

Tip

Thinking about your own place study, can you interview local residents to find out their experiences of living in the area?

The Newham Masterplan's motto is 'Making Newham a place where people live, work and stay'. Newham's 20-year Sustainable Community Strategy sets out a clear vision of an active civil society, characterised by residents who participate in local decision-making. Carpenters Estate has epitomised this kind of active and connected community. Residents are active in volunteering, take pride in their neighbourhood and organise community social events. However, the way in which regeneration has been pursued has undermined both active citizenship and community cohesion on the Carpenters Estate.

Look on **Cambridge Elevate** for a link to Neighbourhood Statistics and investigate types of deprivation in Newham. The postcode for Carpenters Estate is E15 2JL (www.cambridge.org/links/gase6080).

ACTIVITY 8.11

1   Using the resources in this section, explain why the Stratford area of London declined as an industrial hub.
2   Explain why it became the focus of a regeneration project.
3   Comment on the winners and losers of the regeneration project.
4   Suggest how the 'sense of place' has changed in Stratford in recent years.
5   Evaluate the advantages and disadvantages of regeneration in Stratford.
6   How might developers and members of local government respond to the viewpoints in Figure 8.22?

8.5 The Blasket Islands

The Blasket Islands are a group of islands found off the south-west coast of Ireland. They are part of an Irish-speaking region, known as a Gaeltacht (Figure 8.23). Table 8.3 shows the mean temperatures and rainfall for the region.

Tip

This place study examines a place that is very different to the Carpenters Estate in Stratford. As you read through it, consider the similarities and differences with either the Carpenters Estate or your own local place study.

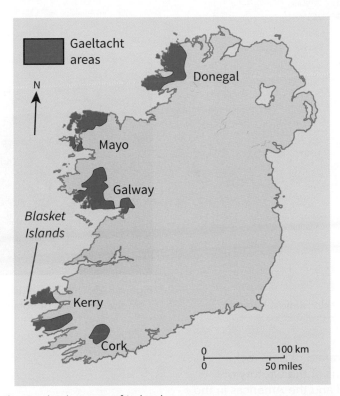

Figure 8.23 The Gaeltacht areas of Ireland.

	Jan	Feb	Mar	Apr	May	Jun	Jul	Aug	Sep	Oct	Nov	Dec	Year
Mean temp. (°C)	7.3	7.2	8.2	9.4	.11.6	13.8.	15.4	15.4	14.1	11.7	9.3	7.8	10.9
Rainfall mm	173.8	123.7	123.8	96.7	93.5	95.3	99.0	114.9	125.4	177.1	169.3	164.9	1557.4

Table 8.3 Climate data for Valentia Observatory, Ireland.

There are six main islands (Figures 8.24 and 8.25). Beginish is closest to the mainland. This is a small flat island with relatively good grazing potential. One mile further out to sea is Great Blasket Island, a high, narrow island, approximately 5 km by 1 km. Most of the houses here were located above the tiny harbour and the long White Strand (An Traigh Mhor, grid square 2798). Another beach, Gravel Strand, was used as an area to pull up boats, for shearing sheep and for the collection of seaweed from the rocks.

Inishvickillane (Inis Mhic Aoibhleáin) is the most fertile island and was used for lobster fishing in the summer and mackerel fishing in winter. Island of the Quern (Inish na Bro) is a rugged hogs-back with a headland perforated by the

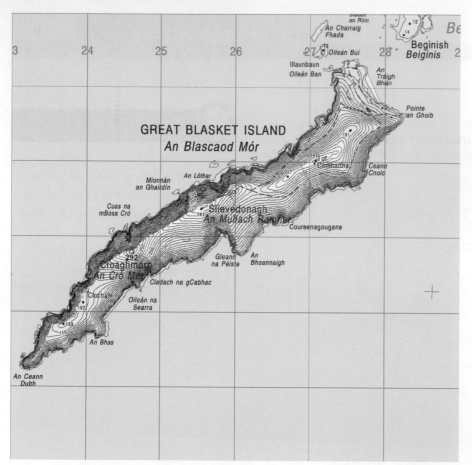

Figure 8.24 1:50,000 OS Ireland map extract of the Great Blasket Islands, Ireland.

Figure 8.25 The Blasket Islands looking from the mainland of Ireland.

Tearaght, the most westerly of the islands, which is a pyramid of bare rock. Inishtooskert (Inis Tuaisceart) to the north, has the remains of the Oratory of St. Brendan, who is reputed to have sailed to Greenland and the Americas in the 6th century (*The Brendan Voyage*, Tim Severin).

Great Blasket Island has a vegetation cover of furze (gorse), heather and peat bog. Sheep, cattle and rabbits grazed on the scarce pasture, and turf (a form of fuel) was cut from the peat bog of Mountain of the Fort (Sliabh an Duna). A small valley passes through the old village and there are species present such as holly, ivy and goat willow. The Blaskets have a large population of rabbits. There is a rich seabird population including puffins, shearwater, guillemots, storm petrels and razorbills.

ACTIVITY 8.12

1   Outline the opportunities and constraints offered by the Blasket Islands for people.

According to the historian Charles Smith (1756), Great Blasket was uninhabited until about 1710. The number of people living year-round on the islands has fluctuated over time. There were about 140 people living there before the Great Famine in 1845–49 (Figure 8.26a), but after the famine numbers fell to about 100. Island life was considered to be a constant struggle – the 3-mile crossing from the mainland was followed by a 5-mile walk to reach a priest or 12 miles to find a doctor.

The population peaked in 1916 at 176, and then declined until 1953 when the island was abandoned (Figure 8.26b). There has been a recent (post-2000) growth in population, especially in the summer, linked with tourism, cultural tours and educational visits.

For information on the demographic history and characteristics of Great Blasket Island, and activities related to these datasets, download Worksheet 8.5 from **Cambridge Elevate**.

ACTIVITY 8.13

1 Describe the location of the residences, shown in Figure 8.26a, and the changes in the distribution of housing in Figure 8.26b.

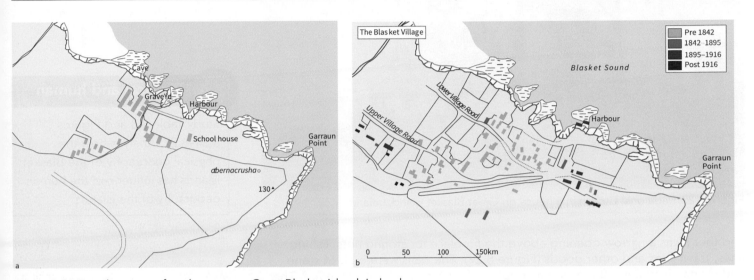

Figure 8.26 Development of settlements on Great Blasket Island, Ireland.
a 1842 – the settlement on Great Blasket Island, Ireland.
b Changes in the settlement on Great Blasket Island, Ireland, pre 1842–post 1916.

The islanders survived mainly on fish, some potatoes and a patch of oats or rye. Some islanders had a cow or two. Barter for products was common. Islanders used seaweed and mussel shells as fertiliser, and a limited amount of dung. The island was held in common by all the islanders with turbary rights (the ancient right to cut turf or peat) and a right to hunt rabbits. There were no horses on the island, only donkeys. These were used to carry turf from the mountain, and sand and seaweed from beach. From 1905, when visitors began to stay on the island, some extra vegetables, such as carrots, onions and turnips, were grown.

The lives of the islanders were transformed by curraghs (canoes) – they allowed them to become fisher folk. Mackerel was the main catch until the 1870s, when pilchards replaced them. In the 1920s, the islanders began to fish for lobsters and crayfish. Dingle on the mainland was the main market until a French sea merchant, Pierre Trehiou, came to the islands and began to buy lobsters direct from the islanders. Occasionally, there was exchange of goods such as nets, tobacco and rum. Some of the islanders learnt a few French phrases and to count in French.

In the 1930s, the islands began to decline in population as many of the young were loath to marry and stay. Many emigrated to the USA, settling in Massachusetts, and elsewhere. In some cases, entire households emigrated.

At its peak, Great Blasket Island contained 30 houses. In 1909, the Congested Districts Board built five two-storey houses at the top of the village (Figure 8.26b). These looked down on the rest of the village. Most of the traditional houses had a similar layout – there was a room behind the fireplace. The kitchen had to be big enough to accommodate animals in bad weather,

Making connections

In what ways did the Blasket Islanders mirror the global governance of resources? See section 7.6 Global governance.

Figure 8.27 Traditional kitchen in a house on Great Blasket Island, Ireland.

Physical and human

Study Table 8.3 and Figures
8.24–8.27. Analyse how the
physical geography of the Blasket
Islands has influenced the human
geography of the islands.

and there was a narrow opening above the fireplace for storing nets, fishing
lines, trawl lines and other goods (Figure 8.27). The walls were built of stone
and mortar, with earth floors and a couple of flagstones in front of the fire. The
earth floors were constantly damp. To keep them dry, they spread sand from
the beach on them a couple of times each day. The roofs were mainly built
from rushes.

Food

When the potato crop failed during the famine, the islanders suffered like
most communities on the mainland. However, they also had fish to rely on.
Consequently, some mainland farmers migrated to the Blasket Islands during
and after the famine. The island had no shop – the islanders had to travel by
boat to the mainland for any flour and household goods that they may have
needed.

Sheep were an important indicator of a household's wealth. There was a saying
on the island: 'a sheep to sell, a sheep to shear, and a sheep to eat'. Sheep
were therefore useful as a source of money, barter, wool and food. Twice yearly
households killed a sheep and cured a portion of it. Fish were boiled. Sealskins
were used as floor mats. Oil extracted from seals' livers was used for healing
wounds and other injuries. Shellfish, such as limpets and periwinkles, and sea
lettuce and seaweed (carrageen) were favoured delicacies. Rabbits were caught
and seabirds' eggs were collected as a food source.

In the 19th century, most islanders would have had two meals a day, both
consisting of potatoes and fish, and some milk if they were fortunate to own a
cow. In the 20th century, and the advent of tea to the island, islanders began to
have four meals a day.

Recreation and social activities

The village on Great Blasket was divided into two sections – the upper village
and the lower village, where life was considered to be better. Some of the

island's famous authors, such as Peig Sayers, Maurice O'Sullivan and Tomas O'Crohan, poets, musicians and singers resided there. Nevertheless, the upper village had its own important residents, such as the King of the Blaskets (the village elder), and famous visitors, such as J.M. Synge and Robin Flower. The nightly gathering to discuss events took place in the Dail (parliament) which was based in the upper village. Most importantly, the village well was located in the upper village – hence women congregated there by day, fetching water, washing clothes and just talking.

In winter, the island was wet and dreary (Table 8.3), but it was the time for fiddle (violin) music, dancing and for the storytellers to tell their tales. The storytellers were the caretakers of an oral tradition. However, they lost their audience. The radio took away their voices, the printed page took away their memories and the TV, and later the internet, took away their images. The tradition of storytelling was very important on the Blasket Islands, Tomas O'Crohan published in Irish his autobiography of a Great Blasket islander, one of the most notable books written in Irish. It was translated as *The Islandman* by Robin Flower.

Visitors and their influence

There were few visitors to Great Blasket Island until the 20th century. The Norwegian Carl Marstrander visited in 1907, stayed on the island, worked and laboured with the islanders. He gave the islanders a new perspective of life and helped them appreciate their own culture. Robin Flower, a scholar from the British Museum, came to the island to learn Irish.

Writing in 1951, George Thompson stated 'as for the Blasket Islands, all the old people … are gone; the school was closed many years ago and the village in ruins. The population has been reduced to five households, comprising 21 persons, with only one child. The mainland is being devastated in the same way. Nearly all the young people have emigrated.'

Two years later the island was deserted – the remaining people having been evacuated by the Land Commission to less productive holdings on the mainland. In 2015, the last Blasket Islander, Dr Mike Carney, died. He was one of the strongest campaigners for conservation of the unique heritage of the Blasket Islands, yet he also wrote a letter to the Irish president requesting evacuation from the island. This followed the death of his bother Sean from meningitis in 1947, when it proved impossible to get a doctor or a priest from the mainland due to bad weather. By then, government inertia, the decline of the fishing industry and continuing depopulation led Carney to believe that evacuation was the best option for the islanders.

Ironically, in 1974 the Irish TD (Member of Parliament) Charles Haughey bought one of the Blasket Islands, Inishvickillane, and built a mansion on it. So, the investment that the government had failed to provide was now provided by a politician for his own family.

Rebirth and the revival of the traditional culture

In 1989, Great Blasket Island was declared a National Historic Park by the Irish government and has since been managed by the Ireland's Office of Public Works. Kerry County Council adopted a conservation plan for the islands in 2012. The Local Area Plan calls for strict preservation of the cultural and natural landscape of the islands.

Since 1953, only local fishermen and those engaged in providing tourist facilities as well as a limited number of holidaymakers have occupied the island in the summer months. The island has made a significant impact on Ireland's cultural heritage. In particular, the contribution of islanders to Irish literature, who wrote about life on the island. The island has long been associated

To learn about gaining a sense of place from a song, download Worksheet 8.6 from **Cambridge Elevate**.

with the essence of Irish language and culture, and has traditionally been a destination for those interested in studying the Irish language, culture and folklore of the area.

Growth and future development

Permission has been granted for the upgrading and construction of new piers at both Dunquin and on Great Blasket. The construction of these piers is subject to the availability of government funding.

Increased access may generate demand from landowners for residential and holiday home developments, which would be damaging to the landscape. With the exception of a limited number of habitable houses and a small hostel, residential uses are not currently available on the island. This has allowed the island's natural and cultural heritage to remain intact.

Tourism

The island is a popular tourist destination, appealing to visitors interested in island literature and history, and those who visit to enjoy the unspoiled beauty of the island. In order to protect the islands' environment, the number of visitors in any one day is capped at 400 people. Currently, tourist facilities comprise a hostel, a café, a craft shop (Figure 8.28) and a weaver's shop. Passenger ferries to Dunquin (Dún Chaoin) operate from a small pier from April to October (Figure 8.29). Museum of the Blasket Islands (Ionad an Bhlascaoid Mhóir) is located in Dunquin (Dún Chaoin) and the Blasket Centre provides exhibitions and presentations on life.

The diverse range of attractions on the island has resulted in the development of cultural, recreational and ecological tourism as the primary land use. The island's overriding value, however, is as a heritage asset of national and international importance. The development of tourism, though important, is a secondary objective. The Local Area Plan supports ecotourism, which underpins conservation and sustainability and avoids exploitation but, at the same time, recognises the need for socio-economic benefit for the local community granted in 2008 for a new café and service building. There is, however, no public sewage infrastructure on the island. Any development needs to be serviced by a private water supply.

ACTIVITY 8.14

Answer the following questions using the resources provided in this place study.

1   Explain why the Blasket Islands were abandoned.
2   Why has there been a resurgence in activity on the islands?
3   In what ways has a 'sense of place' helped in the rebranding and redevelopment of the Blasket Islands?

Look on **Cambridge Elevate** for more information about the Blasket Islands from the following websites:

- Ecotourism on the Blasket Islands (www.cambridge.org/links/gase6081)
- Visiting the Blasket Islands (www.cambridge.org/links/gase6082)
- Accommodation on the Blasket Islands (www.cambridge.org/links/gase6083)
- Café menu (www.cambridge.org/links/gase6084)

Figure 8.28 Restored house now used as Great Blasket Island's craft shop, Ireland.

Figure 8.29 Restored housing and one of Great Blasket Island's ferries, Ireland.

8.6 Undertaking place studies

In the AS and A Level courses, you are required to undertake two place studies: a local place study to explore the developing character of a place local to you, and a contrasting place study to explore the developing character of a contrasting and distant place. This section suggests some methods that you could use.

Methods of data collection

- Aerial photographs and satellite imagery: Aerial photographs such as that of Stratford (Figure 8.13) can provide a very useful snapshot of a place. In Figure 8.13 there is a clear depiction of industry, housing, transport infrastructure and the location of a canal/waterway. It is possible to make links between the physical environment and the human environment. Aerial photographs from different year groups can show changes over time – Figure 8.1 shows change to part of the area in Figure 8.13. Satellite images and aerial photographs can provide valuable sources of information in field studies because they can show elements of the landscape which are not found on OS maps, such as water quality, and landscape changes by comparing images taken at different times of the year or over longer time periods.

  Sources of aerial photos include Google Earth, NASA, USGS, Flash Earth, Universe Today. and Apollo Mapping. The University of Dundee has a major collection of satellite images, as does NASA.

- Census data: this has been collected in Great Britain every ten years since 1801, with the exception of 1941 due to the Second World War. It provides a wide range of data on features such as household size, occupation, housing tenure and so on. When using census data, it is best to use them over a long period of time as these show patterns of greater contrast. Similarly, the use of ten-year gaps, such as 1891, 1901, 1911 and so on, shows trends in the development in village growth.

- Ordnance Survey (OS) maps: these can show how a settlement has grown over time. Most county libraries contain maps that go back to the 18th and 19th centuries – useful for finding out what the settlement looked like at a very early stage. It is best to show the pattern of growth in the settlement over as long a period as possible.

- Kelly's Directories: these provide data on the number and services and industries in settlements (Figure 8.30). You can use these with surveys based on observations to show the changes in services and rural-based industries.

- County Planning Reports: these show how county plans change over time or village developments and transport developments. For example, the BABTIE Reports are reports of the Berkshire highways and planning consultants, showing how transport in the county has changed over a long period of time. You can then relate to changes in the settlement pattern.

- Old photographs, postcards and other memorabilia: you can use these to show how settlements have adapted to change.

Tip

It might seem more difficult to obtain data about your distant and contrasting place study, but you can obtain data from Google Earth (maps and aerial photographs), internet searches, online local newspapers, Ordnance Survey maps, census data, published books and articles.

Alexander Frederick John, surgeon, Grove Terrace
Alexander Horace, architect and surv. Rokeby House, Broadway
Astley Peter Hyde, tailor, Broadway
Atkin Charles, beer retailer, Forest Gate
Ault Henry, boarding school for gentlemen, Grove House, Forest Lane
Austin Thomas, upholsterer, High Street
Avery Thomas, straw hat maker, Broadway

Figure 8.30 Extract from Kelly's Directory.

- Oral sources such as interviews, reminiscences and songs: these could be done face-to-face with people who are known to you, or in the street with strangers. Consider local poets and songwriters, who may have written songs about local places. It is not just the Blasket Islands which have a strong oral tradition.

Tip

Smartphones can be used to record interviews, and there are also free apps and software which can be used to edit these and make them available for others to hear.

Primary data collection includes surveying the area. This covers land use, the age of the buildings, the type of buildings, their function, the amount of land they cover and any geographic patterns that exist. It is important to record the number and type of services.

Questionnaires and surveys are also important. You can use simple questionnaires to determine the proportion of people who work in the village or work in a nearby town, who use local services such as shops, who use local schools, who use local general practitioners (GPs) and so on. It is possible to determine the sphere of influence of a particular service by the use of questionnaires and delivery rounds. For more information on primary data and questionnaires, see Chapter 12 Fieldwork.

Quantitative and qualitative data

Quantitative data refers to numerical data that can be quantified and is measurable (objective), such as population numbers. Qualitative data refers to data in nominal form (named), which illustrates a view and is open to interpretation (subjective), such as interviews.

Settlement growth

Settlements change over time. One way we can observe this is through the type of housing (Figures 8.31, 8.32 and 8.33). A building survey will show the approximate age of houses. Alternatively, you can use OS maps.

Both types of data will be useful in your place studies.

Figure 8.31 Georgian town house. Houses built in the 18th and 19th centuries are very grand. These houses are usually large and centrally located; they often have three or more floors and a cellar.

Figure 8.32 Victorian terrace. Houses built in the Victorian era were built using slate, iron and bricks. On a map, the road network is very geometric or uniform and housing is tightly packed.

Figure 8.33 Interwar housing, largely built in the 1930s, is characterised by semi-detached and detached housing with bay windows and enclosed front and back gardens. Many houses also have their own garages.

Fieldwork investigation

Investigate the growth of a small town in your home region. You could use OS maps from different years to show the expansion of the settlement. You could also study the age and type of housing by visiting the area or using Google Street View. You could use census data to investigate socio-economic changes over time.

ACTIVITY 8.15

1   To what extent do the changes that you identify conform to the changes shown in Figure 8.6?

Comparing residential areas

Residential areas vary greatly. Some areas are pleasant places to live whereas others are less so. Housing quality and desirability are affected by positive and negative **externalities**. Positive externalities include green areas, good accessibility, recreational areas, amenities and quality of housing. Negative externalities include high crime rates, heavy traffic, low flying aircraft, and pollution.

There are several ways to compare residential areas. Primary data methods include:

*   Questionnaires: you can give residents a questionnaire to assess their attitudes to their housing, and their perceptions about other areas.
*   Environmental surveys: you can use these to examine intangible factors (their views on the attractiveness, sense of community, maintenance, cultural/historic value), externalities (landscape quality, derelict land, litter, presence of amenities, industrial premises, noise, schools) and index of decay (deterioration of buildings, peeling paint, broken glass, broken gutters, structural damage, vandalised buildings).
*   Land use survey: you can conduct a survey to estimate the percentage of land that is residential, industrial, retail, commercial and other. Record the age and type of housing. Take photographs and then annotate them.

Secondary data collection methods include census data, at ward and enumeration district levels. Local newspapers and national newspapers have articles and property sections that are useful for comparing house prices. Ask estate agents about the status of the area and house prices. For a more detailed explanation of primary and secondary data, see Chapter 12 Fieldwork.

Fieldwork investigation

Make a comparison of the externalities of two or more different areas near to where you live, or where you go to school/college. On a map, plot positive and negative externalities. You may decide to give different factors a weighting. For example, access to open space may be considered by some to be more important than access to a public library.

Key term

externality: a factor that cannot be changed by an individual but has a bearing on their quality of life (e.g. access to open space, presence of good schools)

ACTIVITY 8.16

1   Is there any significant correlation between house prices and externalities?

Assess to progress

1   Table 8.4 provides details on Council Tax for different areas of London,
    London as a whole and England.
    (The Council Tax is a tax on domestic properties collected by the local
    authorities.)

Council Tax Band (Value of property)	Newham	Merton	Harrow	London	England
A (up to £40 000)	4.80	1.30	0.56	3.48	24.89
B (up to £52 000)	30.44	9.94	3.91	13.57	19.58
C (up to £68 000)	45.35	26.19	21.44	27.60	21.76
D (up to £88 000)	15.71	33.69	31.78	25.49	15.31
E (up to £120 000)	28.90	15.99	25.09	15.11	9.44
F (up to £160 000)	0.69	6.15	8.90	7.56	4.99
G (up to £320 000)	0.11	4.82	6.98	6.02	3.51
H (over £320 000)	0.03	1.91	1.33	1.72	0.57
Vacant/second home	–	–	1.90	4.60	4.70

Table 8.4 Council Tax for selected areas.

Choose the correct statement from options **A** to **D**.   1 MARK [AS LEVEL]
Table 8.4 shows that:
A   Newham is a suburban area.
B   Newham has proportionally more Band A properties
    than London as a whole.
C   There are no properties values over £320 000 in Newham.
D   Newham has fewer average priced properties (B and D) compared
    with the national average.

2   Study Figure 8.34 (The Old School). Describe how the land use
    has changed over time, and suggest reasons why
    this has occurred.   6 MARKS [A LEVEL]

Figure 8.34 The Old School, Woodstock, Oxfordshire.

3   For your local area, identify a qualitative source that you have used in your study of place. This could include photographs, maps, a painting, song, poem, text source or a newspaper article.
    Describe the nature of the information provided about your chosen place, and explain how it helped you to understand the character of that place.   6 MARKS [AS/A LEVEL]

4   Describe how different people may have different views about the same place, and discuss how those views may be supported with the use of qualitative and quantitative data.   20 MARKS [A LEVEL]

Contemporary urban environments

Figure 9.1 Tokyo in Japan has the largest urban population in the world at over 37 million residents.

By the end of this chapter you should know:

- the features of urbanisation in contrasting areas of economic development
- the emergence and characteristics of megacities and world cities and their regional and global roles
- what social and economic issues are associated with urbanisation
- what effect urban environments have on local weather, climate and drainage
- what environmental problems are associated with urban areas, such as atmospheric pollution and waste disposal, and strategies to manage these problems
- the features of and strategies for developing sustainable urban growth and living.

Before you start...

You should know:

- urbanisation is a global phenomenon
- the cause and pace of urban change are different for more and less developed economies
- there are different functions within a settlement, each having their own characteristics, which can change over time as an area develops.

9.1 Urbanisation

Urbanisation will be a familiar geographical term for many. It is often used in news reports and on the internet, but it can be a confusing process.

Urbanisation is the growth in the proportion of a country's population that live in an urban environment compared to a rural environment. It plays an important role in a country's industrialisation.

The United Nations (UN) estimated that in 2008 the world reached a tipping point, as for the first time in human history, more than half the population (3.3 billion people) lived in urban areas. Planet Earth had become an urbanised planet.

Urbanisation is a dynamic geographical process, influenced by many different factors and operating at a global as well as regional scale.

Key term

urbanisation: the growth in the proportion of a country's population that live in an urban environment compared to a rural environment

Urbanisation and its importance in human affairs

Urbanisation should not be seen as just a modern phenomenon, where people are moving from the rural countryside to urban areas. The process is having a profound effect on human affairs and is rapidly changing the social structure of human society, on a scale not witnessed before. In the last century alone, when looking at the world trend, the dominant rural culture has been replaced by a predominantly urban culture and this is predicted to continue, as illustrated in Figure 9.2. Rates of urbanisation have been most rapid in the poorest regions of the world.

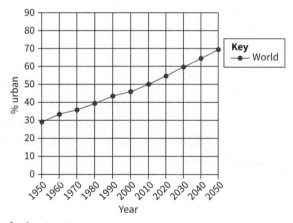

Figure 9.2 Rates of urbanisation.

While the process of urbanisation currently experienced is unprecedented, there have been similar changes in the past that have had profound effects on human affairs. For example, the change from a predominantly hunter-gatherer lifestyle to one of farming promoted the development of the first village settlements. These village settlements had distinct characteristics such as close family ties and a communal bond. The move away from these village or rural settlements has changed the way in which the human population lives in cities, which could be characterised as developing a competitive behaviour and distant family ties.

The impact of urbanisation

In the UK, the agricultural and industrial revolution in the late 18th century saw the beginning of urban population growth. In England, the proportion of the population that lived in cities grew from 17% in 1801 to 72% in 1891. This dramatic change led to changes in lifestyle as well. Workers were no longer tied to the land and could seek employment in the developing cities of London, Manchester and Birmingham. As urbanisation continued, improved public transport links followed and cities expanded. Cities became trading hubs, able to trade across continents, opening up further new opportunities.

Improved status for women

The process of urbanisation has also created opportunities for women that are often not available in the rural areas, particularly in the lower-income countries. In urban areas women are engaged in greater numbers in paid employment or education. While greater opportunities do exist, in places there is still unequal pay or status for women.

Global patterns of urbanisation since 1945

Between 1945 and 2014, the urban population of the world grew from an estimated 0.75 billion to an estimated 3.9 billion (Figure 9.3). At the end of 2014, there were five times more people living in urban areas than there were in 1950. In 1950, it was estimated that 29% of people lived in urban areas, rising to 49% in 2005, while in 2030 the figure could rise to 60%.

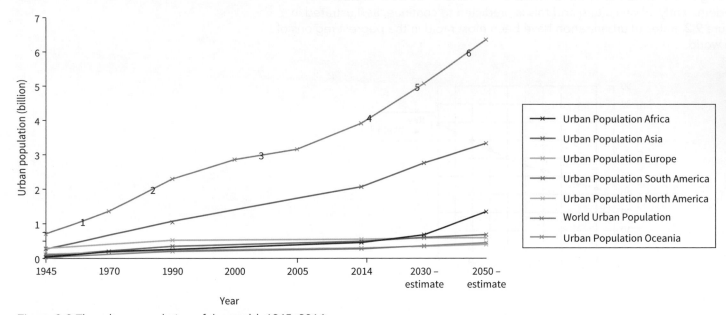

Figure 9.3 The urban population of the world, 1945–2014.

The average annual rate at which worldwide urbanisation occurred from 1945 to 2014 was 2.58%. When compared to the annual rate of population growth over the same period of 1.65%, we can see that the world population was urbanising rapidly in comparison to population growth.

The number of years for each successive billion to be added to urban population is slowly reducing, but is still quicker than the time taken to reach the first billion (Table 9.1).

The most urbanised regions of the world include North America (82% living in urban areas), Latin America and the Caribbean (80%) and Europe (73%). By contrast, Africa and Asia remain predominantly rural, with 40% and 48% of their respective populations living in urban areas. Although Asia has a

Population (billion)	Year when reached	Number of years it took to increase by 1 billion
1	1959	
2	1985	26
3	2002	17
4	2016 (est.)	14
5	2029 (est.)	13
6	2045 (est.)	16

Table 9.1 Urban population milestones.

Maths for geographers

Refer to Table 9.1.

1 Plot a graph of the data shown in Table 9.1.
2 How does using log paper change the shape of the graph? Is this important?
3 Under which circumstances would log paper be used by geographers?

lower percentage of people living in urban areas, it is home to 53% of the world's urban population.

While all regions of the world are expected to become further urbanised in the future, the continents of Africa and Asia are urbanising faster than the other regions and are projected to become 56% and 64% urban, respectively, by 2050.

During the same period of time, 2014–50, three countries are expected to account for 37% of the world's urban population growth: India, China and Nigeria.

The growth of urban dwellers in these three countries is predicted to be:

- India 404 million
- China 292 million
- Nigeria 212 million.

To put this into context, a further seven countries are each expected to add 50 million urban dwellers during the same time: the Democratic Republic of Congo, Ethiopia, Tanzania, Bangladesh, Indonesia, Pakistan and the United States of America. This highlights the concentration of urban dwellers in India, China and Nigeria (Figure 9.4).

Making connections

How will the growth of urban populations in the future affect the environment? See section 8.3 Changing places – meaning and representations.

357

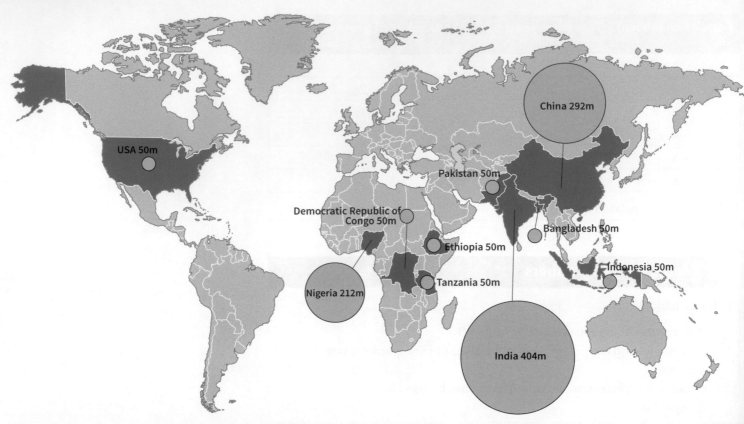

Figure 9.4 World map showing predicted growth of urban dwellers in ten countries, 2014–50.

ACTIVITY 9.1

Years	Average annual rate of change (%)
1950–70	2.96
1970–90	2.63
1990–2014	2.21
2014–30 (est.)	1.66
2030–50 (est.)	1.13

Table 9.2 Average annual rate of world urbanisation.

1   Look at Table 9.2. Describe how world urbanisation has changed between 1950 and the present day.
2   Explain why this change might be occurring.
3   The Unicef website has a section called 'An Urban World', showing population growth in the past and projected population growth up until the year 2050. Visit this section and run the simulation. What areas of the world will experience continued growth? Remember to identify countries and regions.
4   What issues might this uneven urbanisation create in different areas of the world?

 Look on **Cambridge Elevate** for 'An Urban World' from Unicef and run the simulation (www.cambridge.org/links/gase6085).

 You can represent data using proportional circles. For an activity on proportional circles, download Worksheet 9.1 from **Cambridge Elevate**.

Suburbanisation

When villages and towns are engulfed into larger urban areas, or agglomerations, geographers call this process **suburbanisation**. This process occurs as urban residents choose to move away from the urban centre where they work. There are several push and pull factors that can be associated with suburbanisation.

The pull factors include:

- greater open spaces and a desire to live in a cleaner environment
- a wider range of employment opportunities in the suburban areas
- lower house prices compared to the urban centre.

Push factors include:

- increasing traffic and pollution in the urban centre
- a perception that the urban centre offers a lower quality of life than the suburbs
- a desire to move away from industry.

Suburbanisation changes the character of the area, and puts pressure on **greenfield sites** and the surrounding wildlife. While the areas are predominantly residential, characterised by larger gardens and greater open spaces than found closer to the urban centre, small-scale industries can also be found here providing employment opportunities.

Suburbanisation could not have happened were it not for developments in local transport infrastructure. People will not move to an area if commuting to the nearby urban centre is difficult. The development of the railways in the 1850s in the UK encouraged suburbanisation, as did the expansion of the London Underground, leading to the growth of 'Metro-Land'.

'Metro-Land' was the term used by the marketing department of the Metropolitan Railway housing department from 1919. Unlike the other railway companies at the time, the Metropolitan Railway did not need to relinquish land it had acquired to build the railway. The counties of Buckinghamshire, Hertfordshire and Middlesex developed into London suburbs as the Metropolitan Railway developed surplus land into housing estates. The more notable estates developed were:

- Kingsbury Garden Village, near Neasden
- Wembley Park
- Cecil Park
- Harrow Garden Village.

The extension of the Piccadilly Line led to the development of Bedford Park, described as London's first garden suburb. The estate was built by Jonathan Carr, a cloth merchant, who chose Bedford Park as a site to develop 400 houses because of the close proximity of the newly opened Turnham Green station in 1875 (Figure 9.5). The suburb is now situated in Zone 3 of the London Underground network.

Suburbanisation leads to the growth of suburbs like Bedford Park. **Suburbs** are areas on the edge of cities, close enough for commuters to reach the city centre. This outwards development shows urbanisation is happening, as the city expands and encroaches on the countryside. As suburbs grow, they attract people from the nearby rural areas, as well as those from the inner city and **CBD** areas.

Counter-urbanisation

Cities are dynamic places in which to live. There is a flow of people moving into as well as out of the city. In recent times there has been an increasing movement

Key terms

suburbanisation: the growth of areas on the fringes of cities

greenfield sites: undeveloped countryside areas

suburb: an outlying district of a city

CBD: central business district

Figure 9.5 Turnham Green Station was opened to serve one of London's first suburbs, Bedford Park.

Investigate

Investigate how your local area will be developing in the future. Which areas are earmarked for development? Assess the strengths and weaknesses of the plans.

of people away from the city, called counter-urbanisation, which has three main driving forces:

- demographic
- social
- economic.

The demographic driving force in the UK has been the migration of people living in the cities to smaller urban towns beyond the green belt. Higher-income groups of retirement age have increased counter-urbanisation in coastal towns and in towns within National Parks, such as the Lake District.

People moving away from the city are driven by a desire to have a better quality of life, typified by perceptions of a cleaner and quieter area, without the issues of crime and lack of opportunities associated with urban areas.

Motorways and connected rail services, as already discussed, make commuting to cities easier so people can afford to live further afield. The growth of reliable and quick internet services has led to an increase in people working from home. This has benefits for both the employee and the employer. For the employee, commuting costs are lower, and some flexibility in working hours could exist. For the employer, greater numbers of staff working from home can result in the need for smaller office space and equipment, therefore lowering overheads, particularly in the cities where office space is sold at a premium.

The New Towns Act of 1946 encouraged counter-urbanisation from major conurbations with the building of New Towns such as Milton Keynes and Basildon.

Figure 9.6 shows that in the 1950s, Basildon was a small hamlet with land nearby where Londoners would buy and develop a small plot to use as a weekend retreat to the countryside.

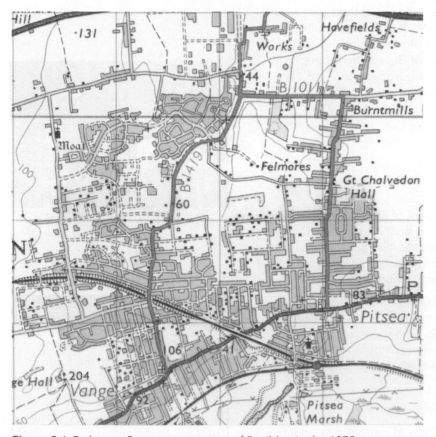

Figure 9.6 Ordnance Survey map extract of Basildon in the 1950s.

For a GIS mapping activity, download Worksheet 9.2 from **Cambridge Elevate**.

Research point

Research in detail the New Towns Act of 1946. Which sites were developed as New Towns? Consider how you would measure the success of the New Towns.

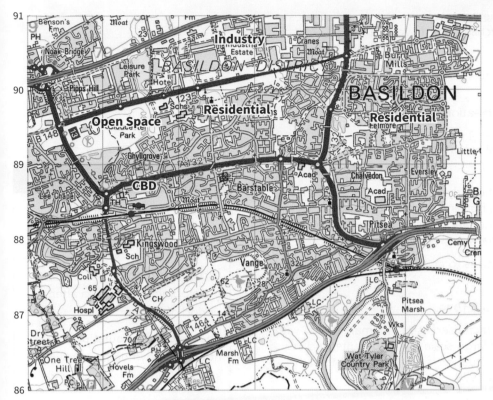

Figure 9.7 OS 1:50000 map of Basildon in 2016.

The New Towns Act of 1946 saw Basildon transformed into a new town, with residential areas around a CBD and industry on the outskirts (see Figure 9.7). New Towns such as these are often called commuter towns or dormitory towns as people sleep and live in these towns but work elsewhere, although the original intention was for the New Town to provide all the local employment.

Urban resurgence

From the 1950s to the 1970s the UK's cities were in decline, both demographically and economically. The decline was linked to outdated infrastructure: housing was seen as inadequate compared to the conditions in the suburbs and New Towns, and industrial areas were no longer fit for purpose. This began a cycle of dereliction. Large inner city areas, such as the Docklands in London, became abandoned as industries and businesses left and the area was left to slowly decay. This in turn led to a number of social, economic and environmental problems which reached a crisis point in the 1980s with an increase in riots, increased crime and racist attacks.

Key problems in the inner cities at this time included:

*   environmental problems – pollution, vandalism, poorly built tower blocks, overcrowding and a lack of open spaces
*   economic problems – unemployment, poverty, low incomes, lack of space for new industries and poor access
*   social problems – increased crime rates, falling birth rates, high concentration of ethnic groups and concentrations of the very young and very old.

To counter these problems, successive governments have introduced policies targeting these inner city areas. The overarching aims have been to:

- improve housing conditions
- create new jobs and training opportunities for local people
- encourage private sector investment
- enhance the environment through the creation of open green spaces
- convert derelict buildings and industrial areas into new usable areas through the process of **gentrification**.

After decades of decline, in the 1990s, particularly in the inner city, some cities witnessed a slow resurgence in population, housing prices and employment, particularly cities such as London, Manchester and Paris. This slow resurgence has been as a result of several different initiatives.

There have been several government initiatives to encourage **urban resurgence** in the UK.

Urban policy and regeneration in Britain since 1979

Urban regeneration in Britain has been characterised as being 'market-led', with the private sector being heavily involved in large-scale developments, and in the development of policies. However, the situation is more complex than this suggests and changes can be tracked since 1979.

Urban Development Corporations (UDCs) – 1980s

The Conservative victory in 1979 led to a major change in how regeneration was organised in the UK. Before 1979, regeneration was led by the public sector. The government of the time recognised that regeneration in the UK required drastic action, not capable of being solved by the local authorities on their own. The solution was to create agencies that would regenerate specific areas, the Urban Development Corporations (UDCs), focusing on:

- the physical redevelopment of derelict land
- securing private capital and private sector expertise in redeveloping the area.

The first UDCs to be created, in 1981, were in London Docklands and Merseyside. Twelve UDCs were created in the 1980s and 1990s and locations also included Don Valley in Sheffield and Cardiff Bay. UDCs were a property-led regeneration, as derelict land was acquired, restored and then sold to private businesses. Public money was used to pump-prime private investment in the areas. In the London Docklands for example, the government spent £1.86 billion through the UDC, but by 2000 private investment was estimated to be worth £6.67 billion.

The 12 UDCs delivered 27 000 new homes and office space covering 5.4 million m². In addition, 150 000 jobs were created. It is generally agreed that while the UDCs were a success, bringing economic development to an area, local people and their needs were often ignored.

Enterprise zones (EZs)

These areas were set up in 1981 to try to create development in areas of high **unemployment**. Taxes were reduced for businesses moving into the EZs, to encourage start-ups. However, while EZs were successful in part, they tended to result in businesses relocating to the EZs rather than new start-ups entering the area, so new job opportunities were limited.

Key terms

gentrification: the renewal of an area leading to an influx of affluent people

urban resurgence: the development of an area after a period of decline

unemployed population: those not in employment but actively seeking and available for work

City Challenge – 1991

A change of focus occurred in 1991, when local authorities were given more control by the Conservative government to regenerate local areas. City Challenge was a partnership between local authorities and the private sector. The main difference between the UDC policy was that local communities were more involved. For funding to be awarded, companies had to demonstrate how the redevelopment would affect the area and the local authority as a whole. Funding was also allocated based on the quality of the partnership between the local authority and the private sector company; not necessarily on the need for regeneration. City Challenge could be seen as a coordination through the physical regeneration of an area to:

- physical infrastructure
- job creation
- social regeneration.

The Labour policy – 1990s

When the Labour Party came to power, the regeneration of areas was addressed by focusing on:

- community
- neighbourhood
- urban design.

To involve the community, Local Strategic Partnerships were set up. Their purpose was to involve a broader range of the local population when forming the local policy for regeneration and development.

In order to be more specific in targeting areas that needed regeneration, particularly the most deprived areas, Neighbourhood Renewal and Community Development programmes were set up. These would be managed by the Local Strategic Partnership.

Urban design was the third area to be addressed by the Labour government. A greater focus on environmental quality of urban areas was taken, which led to the architect Richard Rogers being commissioned to lead the Urban Task Force. The task force was asked to report on how regeneration should be tackled, and its report outlined the importance of the physical and visual aspects of urban regeneration. Urban Regeneration Companies (URCs) were intended to deliver the regeneration.

Current urban resurgence initiatives

Partnership schemes

More recent regeneration schemes have been achieved through partnerships between the private and public sectors. These schemes aim to achieve social and economic development as well as physical development. The *New East Manchester (NEM)* is one such partnership between Manchester City Council, the North West Development Agency and the Homes and Communities Agency. The aim of the partnership is to redevelop 20 km² of inner Manchester (Figure 9.8).

The East Manchester area contains the neighbourhoods of Ancoats, Miles Platting, Beswick, Openshaw, Clayton, Newton Heath and Gorton. In the 19th century the area was home to manufacturing industries, such as textiles, steel and engineering, along with residential areas to accommodate the large workforce. During the 1970s and 1980s, the area witnessed a wide-scale economic decline, losing 60% of its economic output. There was a loss of 33 000 jobs during that period and the population declined sharply. As a result, East Manchester entered the 21st century with large vacant plots of land and

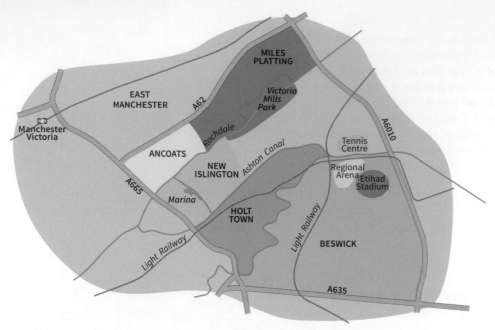

Figure 9.8 A map of the New East Manchester Development Area.

low-value housing, leading to a low housing demand. A **negative multiplier effect** developed where lower wages and higher unemployment led to a reduction of local services, such as retail shops, banking and schools. The neighbourhoods became dilapidated. The area, focusing around the Etihad Football Stadium (built for the 2002 Commonwealth Games and now home to Manchester City Football Club), has been widely developed. Between 2002 and 2010:

- 5000 new were homes built
- 6500 homes were renovated
- three new shopping areas were created, incorporating health centres and open spaces
- three new secondary schools were built
- 200 000 m² of commercial floor space was created
- community gardens were established
- 6200 local jobs were created and a further 600 people retrained.

The improving social conditions for the local population can be seen by the reduction in the percentage of working residents that claim benefits, which has fallen from 40% to 33%, and the increasing educational standards of school leavers in the area.

The development of the London Docklands in the 1990s, the redevelopment of Stratford as part of the 2012 Olympic Games and its continued redevelopment, are evidence of the resurgence in London, along with the Shard, which in 2015 was the tallest inhabited building in western Europe (Figure 9.9).

The Shard and the Westfield Centre in Stratford are examples of buildings that have a diversity of uses. The Shard offers opportunities for exclusive penthouse apartments, offices, a 200-bedroom hotel and six bars and restaurants, whereas the Westfield Centre in Stratford offers retail spaces, as well as leisure in the form of a casino.

One of the newest development projects to be undertaken in London is Battersea Power Station, in south-west London.

Investigate the geography of New East Manchester further using GIS by downloading Worksheet 9.3 from **Cambridge Elevate**.

Key term

negative multiplier effect: a downward spiral of events that follow the decline of investment in a region such as decreased spending, the loss of other jobs and out-migration

Figure 9.9 The Shard, London: a vision of a vertical city.

Battersea Power Station and resurgence in south-west London

Battersea Power Station is another example of how urban spaces are being developed, but also of how such developments are key to the wider resurgence of the area. The power station, on the south bank of the River Thames, was a coal-powered power station built between 1930 and 1950 (Figure 9.10). Built with four distinctive chimneys and art deco interior, it is a Grade II listed building. It ceased generating power in 1983, but has become a well-known London landmark. The project is being financed from Malaysia's property development and investment businesses, S P Setia Berhad, Sime Darby and Employees Provident Fund.

The development of the 40-acre site is a blend of shops, cafes, art and leisure facilities, as well as residential accommodation and office space (Figure 9.11). The development will not only save the Grade II listed building, including the replacement of the iconic chimneys, but also connect this part of London, which has been derelict for decades, to the city with the building of an extension to the London Underground.

The development of Battersea Power Station should be seen as part of the larger redevelopment of Clapham, Battersea and Wandsworth, making this area of London increasingly desirable.

The area stretches from Vauxhall in the north-east to Putney in the south-west. Housing in the area includes large riverside developments, Victorian spacious mansion flats and tiny terraced cottages, and grand villas overlooking Clapham and Wandsworth Commons. This range has helped to attract young professionals with expanding families. The excellent railway and Underground links make commuting to the City or the West End very easy, with the nearby Clapham Junction being one of Europe's busiest railway stations.

The area has a rich history and this is reflected in the diverse population that now settles there. Young professionals, students and recent immigrants mix with Londoners who have called the area their home for the last 60 years.

 Look on **Cambridge Elevate** to find out about the development of Battersea Power Station (www.cambridge.org/links/gase6086).

ACTIVITY 9.3

1 Visit the Battersea Power Station development website and answer the following questions.
   a What is planned for the 40-acre site?
   b Evaluate how the redevelopment meets the needs of the local community.
   c To what extent does the redevelopment link to the wider development of this part of London?
   d How is this approach to developing an area different to the UDC approach?

 For more questions, download Worksheet 9.4 from **Cambridge Elevate**.

Figure 9.10 The Battersea Power Station before its closure in 1983.

Figure 9.11 An artist's impression of the finished project.

Megacities

At the start of the 20th century, geographers classified cities by their population. For example, the term **millionaire city** was used to describe a city with a population greater than one million. In 1900, the world's biggest cities were predominately in Europe and North America, with 12 cities classed as millionaire cities. By 2015, the number of millionaire cities had reached over 500!

Some of the world's largest cities have merged with other nearby cities to form city regions, or urban agglomerations. Tokyo grew and merged with the city of Yokohama. A city with a population of over 10 million people is known as a **megacity**. In 1950, there were only two megacities in the world: New York and Tokyo. The growth of megacities was centred in the developed world. By 1990, there were ten megacities in the world, home to some 153 million people.

Since the 1990s, the world's megacities have increasingly been located in less developed regions, for example São Paulo, Mexico City and Mumbai. By 2000, 75% of megacities were found in the developing world. By 2015, there were over 30 megacities, home to over 450 million people:

- 18 in Asia
- four in South America
- four in Africa
- three in Europe
- two in North America.

Although megacities contain over 10 million people, when we look at the population of the world as a whole, the percentage of people that live in megacities is still small, with only 12% of the world's urban population. The UN predicts that by 2030 there will be 41 megacities.

Key terms

millionaire city: a city with over one million inhabitants

megacity: metropolitan area with a total population in excess of 10 million people

Tip

Ensure that you are familiar with different data presentation techniques, such as choropleth, isopleth and proportional symbol maps and pie charts, as you will be expected to interpret data from a range of sources.

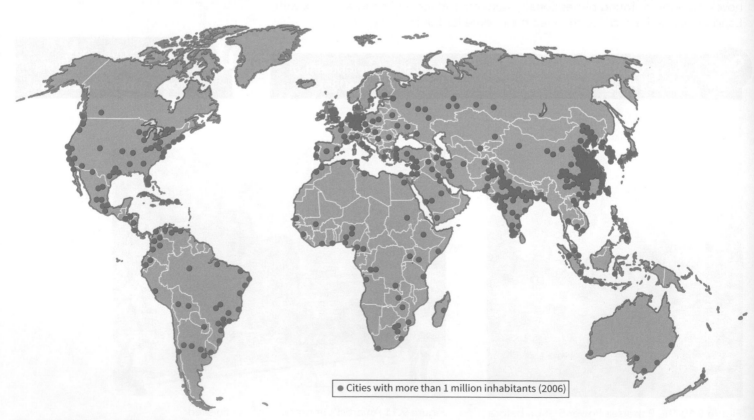

● Cities with more than 1 million inhabitants (2006)

Figure 9.12 The world's millionaire cities in 2006.

Tokyo was the world's largest megacity in 2015 with 38 million people, but its population is predicted to decline slowly to 37 million by 2030. Overall, megacities are growing slowly (Table 9.3). Of the 28 megacities identified by the UN in 2014, between 2010 and 2015:

- eight experienced a growth rate of below 1%
- ten grew by over 3%.

Research point

Research the growth of megacities in Africa. What opportunities and challenges do these megacities bring the region?

For questions on megacities, download Worksheet 9.5 from **Cambridge Elevate**.

Megacity	Population in 2014 (thousands)	Growth rate (%) (2010–15)
Tokyo, Japan	37 833	0.6
Delhi, India	24 953	3.2
Shanghai, China	22 991	3.4
Mexico City, Mexico	20 843	0.8
São Paulo, Brazil	20 831	1.4
Mumbai, India	20 741	1.6
Osaka, Japan	20 123	0.8
Beijing, China	19 520	4.6
New York, USA	18 591	0.2
Cairo, Egypt	18 419	2.1
Dhaka, Bangladesh	16 982	3.6
Karachi, Pakistan	16 126	3.3
Buenos Aires, Argentina	15 024	1.3
Calcutta, India	14 766	0.8
Istanbul, Turkey	13 954	2.2
Chongqing, China	12 916	3.4
Rio de Janeiro, Brazil	12 825	0.8
Manila, Philippines	12 764	1.7
Lagos, Nigeria	12 614	3.9
Los Angeles, USA	12 308	0.2
Moscow, Russian Federation	12 063	1.2
Guangzhou, Guangdong China	11 843	5.2
Kinshasa, Democratic Republic of the Congo	11 116	4.2
Tianjin, China	10 860	3.4
Paris, France	10 764	0.7
Shenzhen, China	10 680	1.0
London, United Kingdom	10 189	1.2
Jakarta, Indonesia	10 176	1.4

Table 9.3 Megacities and their population growth.

World cities

Some cities have developed to play a critical role in the economic well-being of the global economy, with only 100 cities accounting for 30% of the world's economy!

These cities are seen as hubs through which trade, wealth, culture and scientific innovation flow, and are classed as **world cities**. These world cities allow global markets to operate at key locations, and play a disproportionately important role globally.

World cities have an important role to play in regional economies (see Figure 9.13) as well as in the global economy. World cities can be seen as resource centres and learning centres. Cities will often grow as companies access the skills and knowledge of the population, and use this to develop new concepts and products. By using the population as a resource, enterprises will start to flourish and other companies will be attracted to the city as a result. This promotes the city as a learning centre, an area where new ideas are developed within universities and science parks. In a world city, science parks and universities will encourage people to communicate and share ideas, sparking innovation. This is the process of **spatial proximity**.

World cities also play an important role in:

- politics
- migration
- business and trade
- transport.

World cities play an important role in world politics. They participate in and influence international events such as G8 summits (annual meetings between the leaders of Canada, France, Germany, Italy, Japan, Russia, the UK and USA). Politicians from world cities use their influence to drive trading negotiations and develop economic links with other countries. The former London mayor, Boris Johnson, for example, used his role to promote businesses and trade in China during the Beijing Olympics of 2008.

World cities attract a well-qualified and skilled workforce from around the globe. This results in a diverse population which adds to the spatial proximity that already exists in the city.

Key terms

world city: a city that acts as a major hub or centre for finance, trade, business, politics, culture, serving not just the country or region but the world

spatial proximity: the development of innovation due to the close geographical locations of universities and industry

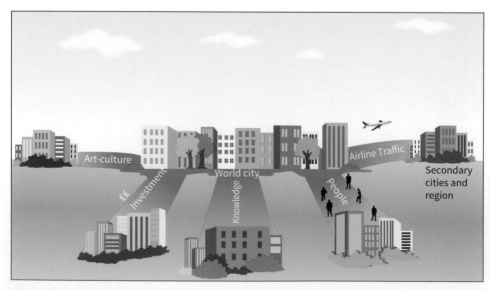

Figure 9.13 The role of a world city.

The movement of people is supported by the flow of business and trade through the world cities. While few world cities produce their own manufactured goods, the headquarters of international companies are often located in the world cities and their decisions will affect large parts of the world. World cities will often have different specialist roles within the business and trade sector. London and New York, for example, specialise in the financial markets, while Tokyo dominates the trade sector and Singapore the container and shipping trade.

World cities can be seen to share common characteristics:

- The manufacturing and distribution of goods have been **outsourced** to other cities or countries.
- The labour force, although varied, is primarily polarised. Jobs are available that require high levels of skill, education and training, but in return offer the employee high rewards. At the other end of the spectrum there are the support jobs, which are semi-casual, often low paid and offer limited career development. This polarisation will be reflected in the characteristics of the residential areas within the city.

Key term

outsource: the employment of other people, for example from overseas to do jobs previously done by people in the home country

Economic, social, technological, political and demographic processes associated with urbanisation and urban growth

Urbanisation was seen in the past as the result of industrial development. Investment in the industrial sector led to employment opportunities in urban areas. These opportunities produced a steady flow of migrant workers, which in turn kept wages low, maximising profits and leading in turn to further economic growth. As people moved from agricultural labour to more specialised and skilled labour, urbanisation was seen as driving economic conditions.

As cities are the focus of economic growth for a country, urban residents often have better access to education, healthcare and transportation, as well as clean water and other basic services compared to rural residents.

As the examples of megacities and world cities illustrate, urbanisation and urban growth develop areas economically. In the UK, cities have traditionally developed economic growth points ranging from the CBD, to the high street, to smaller local parades of shops through to the local corner shop. Town centres undergo constant change as they try to attract new customers and combat the loss of customers to regional shopping centres (e.g. Bluewater or the MetroCentre) or to the internet. To encourage more people into the town centre, pedestrianisation and improvements in public transport have occurred. These developments, coupled with an increase in bars and restaurants, have sought to improve the town centre environment and increase the economic prosperity of the area.

Tip

Keep up to date with urbanisation issues by reading both print- and web-based media. Use the favourite feature on Twitter to develop a personal summary of news features.

Technological advances have led to buildings being built in excess of 500 metres high. The Burj Khalifa in Dubai stands at 828 m while the Shanghai Tower in China stands at 632 m tall. Major cities are now developing upwards, as new advances in technology allow for ever-taller buildings. These buildings are not just for office space, but are designed with a mixture of office, residential and commercial space.

Natural increase can have a significant impact on urban growth, particularly in countries where the fertility rates are high. The United Nations highlights that for developing countries, natural increases make a larger contribution to urban population growth than internal migration. Migration continues to be an important component of urbanisation. In developing countries, the transition from a rural to an urban population is being achieved at a much faster rate than the UK and other early industrialised countries experienced, accomplishing the change within decades, as is the case with Latin American countries.

The two demographic processes associated with urbanisation are **rural-to-urban migration**, and changes to **natural population change**. With people moving to the cities from the countryside, a net migration gain occurs in the urban areas, and a net migration loss occurs in rural areas. This change is more pronounced in areas of lower economic development. Although, as discussed earlier, in the more developed economies of the world, demographically, people are slowly moving away from the city and returning to the countryside.

An urban culture develops within the city environment, with inhabitants sharing common social and behavioural characteristics connected to the city in question. The social factors caused by urbanisation are discussed at greater length later in the chapter.

Politically, urban areas are becoming more influential in national and, if a world city, international affairs. In 2014, regional councils in the UK agreed to allow Greater Manchester the power to elect its first mayor, who will oversee transportation, social welfare, housing and police budgets.

Urban change: deindustrialisation, decentralisation and the rise of the service economy

Deindustrialisation is a process that brings about social and economic change, due to the removal of industrial activity in a country, region or area. Typically, heavy industries such as the coal industry or the manufacturing sector are affected the most. The process of deindustrialisation is a debated one, and there are currently four possible definitions:

1   A decline in the output of goods or employment in the manufacturing sector. This definition has its drawbacks as it does not take into account seasonal declines of employment or short-term declines.
2   A shift from a manufacturing base in an area to a service sector employment base. This can also be misleading as employment or output in manufacturing could still be increasing in such an area, even if the percentage of people working in the manufacturing sector has reduced.
3   There is a decline in export trade, so that imported goods become the dominate feature of an area.
4   Developing from the greater importance of imported goods, a trade deficit occurs, resulting in the inability to pay for imports to produce manufactured goods in the country in question.

Figure 9.14 Manufacturing becomes less important as deindustrialisation occurs.

Research point

What links between urban characteristics, community and historical event exist in your local area? Define and justify the characteristics of your nearest urban area. Use a GIS package to present your findings.

Key terms

rural-to-urban migration: the movement of people from the countryside to the city

natural population change: the difference between birth rate and death rate; it illustrates how much the population will increase or decrease per thousand per years of the population

deindustrialisation: fall in the percentage contribution of secondary industry to an economy in terms of value of input to GDP and importance as an employment sector

Deindustrialisation in the UK has seen an increase in business services, retail and finance, as employees move out of factories and into offices or stores. Countries like China are now the industrial heartland of the global economy, as they can produce manufactured goods cheaply. The rise of ICT has also seen the cost of logistics reduce, making the shipping of goods from countries like China even cheaper.

Deindustrialisation in the UK

In 2015 there were around 2.6 million people working in the UK's manufacturing sector. In the late 1970s this figure was 5.2 million and accounted for 25% of all jobs in the UK, while today manufacturing accounts for only 8% of all jobs.

While the proportion of manufacturing output in the UK has dropped since the 1970s, by about a third to now stand at 10% of the natural output, in fact the total manufacturing output in the UK has increased in size since the 1970s. The UK is currently the seventh largest manufacturer in the world, further highlighting the difficultly in defining deindustrialisation (Table 9.4).

Decentralisation

Decentralisation is a process currently taking place in urban areas, where functions once centred within the central location or authority are dispersed.

In the UK, the Conservative government is pursuing a policy of decentralisation. The Rt Hon Greg Clark MP, speaking at a Local Government Association conference, outlined the reasons for the government's plan to decentralise:

As we recover from the recession and look to the future, it's clear that for our country to succeed to the maximum extent possible, for us to fulfil our potential, every part of the country needs to be successful – not London alone.

Since no two places are the same – South Holland cannot be confused with Dudley, nor Cornwall with Middlesbrough – it should be obvious that a central plan for everywhere won't work anywhere.

To have ministers and officials calling the shots from the centre is to miss out on the knowledge, the drive, the connections, the leadership that local government can give.

Rank	Country	GDP
1	China	4422042
2	United States	3327015
3	Japan	1269492
4	Germany	1084533
5	Russia	668686
6	Brazil	644729
7	United Kingdom	618481
8	South Korea	563946
9	India	528335
10	France	520981

Table 9.4 Manufacturing countries by GDP $ millions.

To achieve decentralisation, the Cities and Local Government Devolution Bill came into effect on 29 May 2015. This bill devolved new powers to local authorities, with the aim of stimulating growth in towns and cities by allowing those areas to identify the needs instead of Whitehall.

One of the first areas to take advantage of such decentralisation was Greater Manchester. Decentralisation will allow Greater Manchester decision-making powers on local issues such as economic development, transport, housing and public services. A locally elected mayor of Greater Manchester will take office in May 2017. The first interim mayor for Greater Manchester is Tony Lloyd.

The rise of the service economy

The service sector dominates the UK economy and accounted for 77% of the economy in April 2015. This rise in the service sector has been influenced by increased foreign investment and increasing demand at home. The rise of the service sector has also been helped by the slow growth in recent years of the manufacturing and construction industries.

The service sector is often referred to as providing 'soft' parts of the economy, as the production is often not end-products but, rather, intangible goods such as:

- advice
- experience
- access to information
- entertainment.

With such a broad range of intangible goods within the service sector, defining which industries are within the sector can at times prove difficult. However, the following industries are generally regarded as being situated within the service industry.

Examples of tertiary industries may include the following:

- entertainment
- government
- telecommunications
- hospitality industry/tourism
- mass media
- healthcare/hospitals
- public health
- information technology
- waste disposal
- financial services/banking
- insurance
- investment management
- accounting
- legal services
- gambling
- retail sales
- real estate
- education.

In the UK, over the last 100 years, there has been a shift from the primary and secondary sectors to the service or tertiary sector.

Table 9.5 illustrates the importance that the service sector has on the UK economy, by highlighting how much each industry contributed to the UK economy in 2011.

Sector	Contribution in 2011
Education	£84 556 million
Health	£104 026 million
Finance	£116 363 million
Hotels and restaurants	£36 554 million
Real estate	£143 641 million
Transport	£59 179 million
Retail	£151 785 million

Table 9.5 Contribution to UK economy per service sector industry.

9.2 Urban forms

The growth and development of London has highlighted the many factors that have shaped the urban characteristics of London. As a result of these complex factors, there is not one particular urban form that fits all urban environments across the world.

Even in a city like London, the urban characteristics are not uniform across the city. Areas will have characteristics that are often unique to that area. Little Venice is located north of Paddington. This part of London takes the form of canals (the Grand Union Canal and Regent's Canal) along with waterside cafes and restaurants. The area has a tranquil atmosphere, with narrowboats the dominate feature.

Contrast this with Mile End, a district within east London and part of Tower Hamlets. This part of London is characterised by a wide variety of architecture, influenced by a long history of migration into the area. The Jewish community which arrived in the 19th century directly influenced the now characteristic Sunday markets in the area, such as Petticoat Lane. The Jewish community at the time was able to obtain a dispensation given by the government to trade on Sundays. Later the area became well known for curry houses in Brick Lane, as Bangladeshi communities settled in the area.

Physical and human factors in urban forms

The term 'urban form' relates to the physical characteristics that go towards making up an urban area. This will include the:

- shape
- size
- density of population
- configuration of the settlement.

The urban form has been shaped since settlements were first made, and is an evolving process in response to social, environmental, economic and technological developments.

This can be viewed and studied at different scales, ranging from the regional scale to the smallest street scale.

The UK's urban form at present is characterised by:

- dispersed, very small settlements comprising a few dwellings
- small towns and villages
- 56 towns and cities with more than 125 000 people in a continuous built-up landscape
- 64 'primary urban areas' – areas that have populations over 125 000
- six large metropolitan areas (Birmingham, Leeds, Liverpool, Manchester, Newcastle-Upon-Tyne and Sheffield)
- one built-up megacity region (London and the Greater South East).

Urban environments are affected by both physical and human factors (Table 9.6). Some of these factors will have been very important historically, when settlements were first established, while others become more important in the modern urban environment.

Physical factors	Human factors
Wet points: areas that have a good water supply.	Trading centres: areas grow as a result of trade, increasingly on a global scale.
Dry points: areas that are away from the risk of flooding – this may change in the future due to rising sea levels.	Government policy: the focus of regeneration will often result from government ideologies of the time.
Gap towns: towns located in between two areas of high land.	
Resources: were often important for industry, e.g. villages such as Aberfan in the Welsh Valleys being close to accessible coal reserves. This is becoming less important as the service sector in the UK dominates.	

Table 9.6 Factors affecting settlement location.

Urban characteristics in contrasting settings

Urban characteristics are not uniform across the globe. In highly developed economies, the current trend in urban planning and design is to create **sustainable** environments that are built with the needs of the inhabitants in mind. The term **walkable urbanism** is becoming popular with urban planners, as they seek to reduce the environmental impact by designing cities that are smarter. Sustainable transport is a key design element, allowing residents to drive less and walk more. These newer city areas are compact, designed around the concept of circular flow land use management – the development of **brownfield sites** and infilling derelict land to reduce the development of greenfield sites. New housing is a blend of the surrounding traditional architecture and more classical designs.

In sustainable construction, the recent movement of New Classical Architecture promotes a sustainable approach towards urban construction that appreciates and develops smart growth, walkability, architectural tradition and classical design.

Jakriborb is a housing estate in Hjarup, southern Sweden, which utilises the New Classical Architecture approach. Building started in the late 1990s and has continued ever since. The town is a mixture of traditional and New Classical

Key terms

sustainable: that which is capable of being maintained into the foreseeable future without prejudice to its own continuation or damage to the environment

walkable urbanism: an urban design movement which encourages planners to design urban spaces that encourage walking and exploring

brownfield site: land that has previously been used, suffered decline and is now available for redevelopment

Figure 9.15 Narrow winding streets in Jakriborb, Sweden, promote walkability.

Figure 9.16 An aerial photograph of the Kenyan capital, Nairobi, showing Kibera, a huge informal settlement that is thought to be home to up to one million people.

Architecture. To increase walkability, the roads in Jakriborb are deliberately narrow (Figure 9.15). In 2003, the population of the town was 500 families, with plans to expand the site by ten times the current size. However, the developers limit the number of new apartments built each year, in order for the town to grow organically into a city.

The urban characteristics in less economically developed areas of the world differ to those in economically developed areas, such as Jakriborb. The speed and scale of urbanisation creates issues of poor-quality housing and housing demand outstrips supply. This leads to the growth of **informal settlements**, creating further environmental and social issues as there is a lack of services and employment.

In Nairobi, Kenya, for example, the continued pace of urbanisation has led to over half of the inhabitants living in informal slums (Figure 9.16). A typical slum-dwelling of only 3–6 m² may be occupied by five or six people. As a result of this overcrowding and the lack of basic sanitation in the slums, waterborne diseases, diarrhoea and tuberculosis (TB) are common.

New urban landscapes

A recent report for the Government Office for Science entitled 'What are future cities?' identified a range of different names used when describing cities that have an environmental, social or economic focus. Cities that focus on being environmentally sustainable for example, might be termed garden cities, sustainable cities or even smart cities. It is therefore important to have an awareness of these different terms when researching the urban landscape topic (Table 9.7).

Town centre mixed developments

When redeveloping town centres, the current trend is to develop the town centre so there is a combination of residential, commercial, cultural, institutional, or industrial uses. These functions are designed to be physically and functionally integrated, with free-flowing pedestrian access. The Shard is an example of mixed-use development in central London.

Key term

informal settlement: a settlement where housing has been built on land to which the occupants have no legal right

Look on **Cambridge Elevate** to maintain an up-to-date perspective on urban landscapes, from the Government Office for Science (www.cambridge.org/links/gase6087).

Environmental	Social	Economic
garden cities	participative cities	entrepreneurial cities
sustainable cities	walkable cities	competitive cities
eco cities	integrated cities	productive cities
green cities	inclusive cities	innovative cities
compact cities	just cities	business-friendly cities
smart cities	open cities	global cities
resilient cities	liveable cities	resilient cities

Table 9.7 Different terminology used to describe UK cities.

Cultural and heritage quarters

In an attempt to promote growth in cities, many UK cities have developed cultural and heritage areas or quarters. These areas focus on cultural or heritage themes, such as the arts and the creative industries, in order to revitalise the area.

Fortress developments

Fortress developments can be defined as urban developments that have a high focus on security measures. This focus has been driven in part by a 2009 Home Office review, where soft targets such as schools, major events and shopping centres were seen as vulnerable to attack. The concept can be traced back to the work of Oscar Newman and his idea of defensible spaces.

Recent government policy in 2012 required new developments to focus on high security as part of the design brief. This prerequisite covers a range of urban settings from town centres, schools and hospitals to housing. The policy has resulted in a growth of fortress developments that are often characterised by:

- high fences or walls
- CCTV
- security bollards, roller shutters and grilles
- electronic locking systems
- clear boundary lines between different territories.

The current trend is also linked to crime rates, meaning that schools, in particular, will have a militarised feel to their design in areas of high crime.

The wider development of the Battersea and Wandsworth area includes the location of the new American Embassy in 2017, which incorporates elements of fortress design. The new building will be surrounded by a landscaped moat, creating a defensible space without the need for high fences.

Gentrified areas

Gentrified areas are the result of gentrification, a process that can be seen as controversial. It is characterised by the shift of an urban community in an area, to be displaced by higher-income residents or businesses. While some see the displacement of poorer communities as a negative impact of gentrification, others see the process as simply rejuvenating a once wealthy area that has undergone decline to prosperity again. In an area undergoing gentrification, average incomes rise, as wealthy residents are attracted to the area. Poorer residents are often unable to pay increased rents and have to relocate to cheaper and more-affordable areas.

Visit **Cambridge Elevate** to view a Google map which has been created to show the different cultural quarters. Could you design your own map for a local cultural or heritage quarter, adding photos and descriptions (www.cambridge.org/links/gase6088)?

Key term

fortress developments: city developments that integrate greater security into the design of the building or landscaping

Edge cities

Since the Second World War, there has been an increase in **edge cities** in the UK. Major cities and towns are now surrounded by retail, leisure, industrial and business parks, warehousing, ring roads and large employment buildings. Motorway interchanges often provide excellent transport links.

The concept of the post-modern western city

The post-modern western city is characterised by a return to flowing lines in the cityscape with peaked, triangular and multi-levelled roofs. More emphasis is on ornamentation, rather than the modernist architecture of the 1970s which was characterised by shaped edges and geometry.

The features associated with modern and post-modern cities are summarised in Table 9.8.

	Modern city	Post-modern city
Urban structure	Dominant commercial centre and a steady decline in land values away from centre.	A multi-nodal structure, containing hi-tech corridors and post-suburban developments.
Landscape	A landscape dominated by very functional architecture.	A landscape where the architecture is more of an expression of art than function (Figure 9.17). There is also a greater use of heritage.
Economy	Industrial economy focusing on mass production and economies of scale.	A service-sector based economy that focuses on niche markets. A globalised economy. Telecommunications dominate.
Planning	Cities planned in totality rather than in smaller sections. Urban open spaces planned and shaped for social needs.	Cities planned in fragments, and focusing on the aesthetic needs rather than social needs (Figure 9.18).
Culture and society	Divisions of class found within the city. A large homogeneity across the city ethnically.	Ethnic diversity, resulting in a city that is highly fragmented culturally, with a high degree of social polarisation in some areas. Groups distinguished by their consumption patterns.

Table 9.8 The characteristics of modern and post-modern cities.

Figure 9.17 An example of post-modern architecture: City of Arts and Sciences in Valencia in Spain.

Figure 9.18 London is an increasingly post-modern city characterised by the new dynamic flowing skyline.

🔑 **Key term**

edge cities: a concentration of business, shopping, and entertainment outside the traditional central business district

9.3 Social and economic issues associated with urbanisation

In the UK, the process of urbanisation has led to unexpected social and economic issues, largely focusing on poverty, unemployment, social unrest and crime. Danny Dorling highlighted the scale of inequality within the UK by suggesting that people could be living in different parts of Britain, or in different parts of the same city, but in reality are living in completely different worlds, with different expectations and accepted norms. The decline of the inner-city areas has attracted government and private investment to combat these issues, with differing levels of success. However, it is not just the inner-city areas that suffer.

Inner-city estates are often acutely affected by social and economic issues. There are often deprived areas, where low educational attainment and high unemployment is the norm. These areas also see a concentration of crime, poor health and diet, as well as social issues such as family breakdowns or race-related crime.

Crime is seen by residents as a constant threat, while obtaining full-time employment is difficult. The fabric of the area is typically characterised by cheap housing stock, constructed from poor-quality materials available in the 1950s and 1960s. These materials have not lasted the test of time, and are now deteriorating badly. Where high-rise flats were built, residents have a sense of isolation and a lack of community. Poor access and maintenance encourage crime.

Car ownership, and the lack of it, also highlights the sense of isolation. Low employment and low wages mean that people feel that they are not able to make use of public transport, reinforcing the sense of isolation.

As the difference between the high and low earners increases, the pattern of wealth in a city changes. The wealthy start to move to the more exclusive areas of the city. These areas will have larger housing, better access to green open spaces and a cleaner environment. The best schools will also be in these wealthier areas. For the lower-income families, the opportunity to move to the wealthier areas becomes increasingly more difficult as the gap between rich and poor widens.

In the UK, one in five people live in poverty according to a recent Oxfam report. Peter Townsend defined poverty in relation to the accepted standards present in the location within which someone lives. Individuals, families and groups in the population can therefore be in poverty when their diet, living conditions, amenities and social activities are below those that are customary in the area or country in which they live.

Poverty can result in:

* reduced access to education
* reduced access to housing
* poor nutrition
* higher incidences of crime
* less access to green areas.

Issues associated with economic inequality can be illustrated using two contrasting urban areas: London in the UK and Bangalore in India. Within both cities there are considerable differences in typical incomes.

London inequalities

London is the most unequal region in the UK: 16% of the population of London are in the poorest tenth of the population nationally, and 17% are in the richest tenth. Across London, Kensington and Chelsea has the greatest difference between top and low earners of any borough. The top earners can command at least £41 per hour on average, while the lowest earners can expect to receive only £12 per hour.

The *London Poverty Profile 2015* provides statistics on poverty and inequality indicators. In 2015:

* 27% of Londoners were living in poverty (after housing costs are taken into account).

- 27 000 landlord possession orders allowing landlords to immediately evict tenants took place. This rate was more than double the rest of England.
- 48 000 households were living in temporary accommodation.

Lack of security in housing has a considerable impact of the quality of life for those affected. Homelessness is the most obvious issue, but lack of housing security can also affect school attendance and the ability to gain employment.

The 2011 census reveals that there are several issues of inequality that can be seen within London.

Figures 9.19 and 9.20 illustrate that within London there are clear patterns of economic activity that can be linked to a Londoner's country of birth. Figure 9.19 shows that foreign-born Londoners with the highest economic-activity rates are from New Zealand, Australia and Lithuania. The figure also highlights that Australian-, New Zealand-, South African- and Canadian-born Londoners work principally as full-time employees.

Londoners from EU accession countries are more likely to be self-employed than those from other parts of the world. For example, Romanians have the highest self-employment rate at 44%.

Figure 9.20 shows the countries of birth of Londoners with the lowest economic-activity rates. Turkish-born Londoners form the largest group of part-time workers at 17%. Unemployment rates for the groups with the lowest economic-activity rates are high, as you would expect, with Somali-born Londoners the highest at 17%.

When looking at the employment, unemployment and **economically inactive** figures for each London borough, the data again highlight a number of inequalities. In Newham, 57% of the population aged 16–74 were in

Key term

economically inactive population: those not in work and not seeking work nor available for work

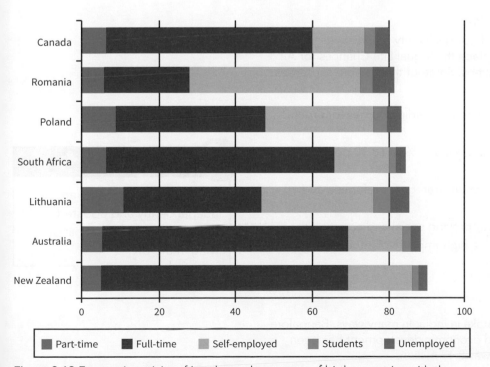

Figure 9.19 Economic activity of Londoners by country of birth: countries with the highest economic-activity rates.

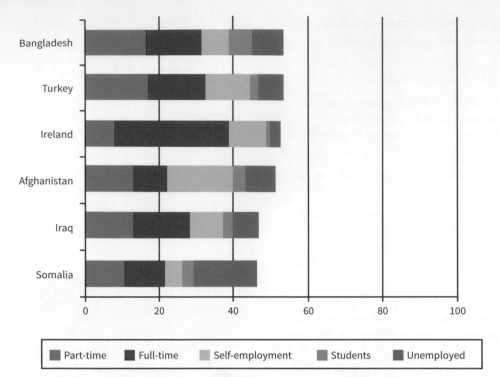

Part-time ■ Full-time ■ Self-employment ■ Students ■ Unemployed

Figure 9.20 Economic activity of Londoners by country of birth: countries with the lowest economic-activity rates.

ACTIVITY 9.4

Visit the Londonmapper website to explore wealth and poverty in London using GIS mapping.

1   Visit Londonmapper.
2   Load the Wealth and Poverty interactive map.
3   Explore the data presented on the map. Is poverty in London evenly distributed? What factors might be driving the pattern you have identified?

Use the GIS website. Chose various different data variables to investigate the inequities that exist in London. Prepare a number of PDF maps to help you critically assess the extent of inequality within London.

employment, compared to 73.2% in Wandsworth. Unemployment rates also vary across the city from 3.1% in Richmond upon Thames to 7.7% in Barking and Dagenham, and the share of those who are economically inactive spans a low of 22.8% in Wandsworth to a high of 35.8% in Newham.

Strategies to manage inequalities in London

The inequalities in London are being tackled using a variety of initiatives. In 2012, the Greater London Authority put in place the 'Equal Life Chances for All' initiative aimed at tackling London's inequalities. Some of the notable successes that this initiative has achieved include:

- a four-year affordable homes building scheme providing homes for around 250 000 Londoners
- increasing the London **Living Wage** by more than 5% to £8.30 per hour to tackle poverty in London
- developing 'London Enriched', an integration strategy for refugees and vulnerable migrants
- building stronger neighbourhoods and improving social and community cohesion by introducing 'Team London', a high-impact volunteering scheme.

Bangalore, India

Bangalore is the capital of the state of Karnataka in India. In many ways, Bangalore is of India as a whole. Population growth and economic development has been rapid. The population of Bangalore in 2011 was 8.43 million.

The growth of Bangalore has in part been due to the growth of the technology industry. The city is known as the 'Silicon Valley of India', bringing a significant urban-to-urban migration of technology professions to Bangalore, as well as a

Key term

Living Wage: an hourly rate set independently and updated annually based on the cost of living in the UK

rural-to-urban migration of the rural poor as they seek a better life in the city, as well as employment.

As with other cities, different factors have been critical in the growth of the technology industry in Bangalore:

- Bangalore University's ability to provide well-qualified science graduates
- the growth of outsourcing from the West to India, in particular the growth of call centres for banks and major retail companies
- India establishing Bangalore as a **Special Economic Zone (SEZ)** where export tariffs were removed and taxes for businesses reduced.

Bangalore is also a city of inequality (Figure 9.21). For the wealthy population who make their wealth from technology, housing and living conditions are good. The richest 2% of the population have a monthly income that is 37 times more than the bottom 30% poorest people.

For the poorer workers such as construction workers, housing conditions are poor, with the increase in slums a real issue. Official statistics suggest that 16% of Bangalore's population live in the slums, but some experts place this figure even higher at 25%. There are at least 600 slum areas, fuelled by increasing rural-to-urban migration. While the wealthy have comfortable lifestyles, the poorest in Bangalore often have to involve all the family in work, including children, to make ends meet. Even this is often not enough, and families resort to informal sectors for finance.

One of the major inequalities in Bangalore is the **caste system**. This is a class system in India, found mostly among Hindus, whereby social class is defined by birth. Dalits have the lowest status and often work in unpleasant jobs for low pay. The name Dalit means 'oppressed'. Those of a Dalit caste often suffer discrimination, poverty and segregation. Such discrimination is in decline but is still deeply rooted in India.

Strategies to manage inequalities in Bangalore

While both London and Bangalore have inequality issues, in absolute terms, the inequalities faced in Bangalore are worse than those in London.

Bangalore is planning for the future. The city's government plans to decentralise by building new towns on the edge of the city and to reduce the slum areas by

Key terms

Special Economic Zone (SEZ): a designated area within a country that has favourable economic regulations to encourage investment

caste system: traditionally a Hindu social division system; each caste is afforded different privileges and limitations

Watch the video on **Cambridge Elevate** about housing and conditions for the poor in Bangladesh.

Look on **Cambridge Elevate** to read more about Bangalore in 'City of the future' from Citizen Matters (www. cambridge.org/links/ gase6089)

Figure 9.21 Bangalore: a city of inequalities – wealth and slums.

providing new areas for workers to live. It is keen to make Bangalore less reliant on the technology sector and to diversify into manufacturing. Several challenges still need to be tackled:

- building sufficient housing to match migration rates that is affordable for local people, particularly construction workers
- providing sustainable energy: many IT companies have their own generators as the city's energy supply is so unreliable
- improvements to the transport system – new highways and flyovers have been planned, but can modern mass transit systems be integrated into the present road system?

ACTIVITY 9.5

1 Produce a presentation comparing the issues facing London and Bangalore. Can both cities learn from each other?

For an activity about Bangalore, download Worksheet 9.6 from **Cambridge Elevate**.

Making connections

Does population growth affect the social/economic characteristics of a city? See section 8.2 Changing places – meanings and representations.

9.4 Urban climate

The impact of urban forms and processes on local climate and weather

The urban environment influences and affects the weather and climate conditions experienced by urban dwellers, including:

- temperatures
- precipitation
- wind
- air quality.

Urban temperatures

Take a close look at a weather forecast map of the UK and you will see that large cities are often warmer than the surrounding countryside. This is known as the **urban heat island (UHI) effect**. The temperature difference is most noticeable at night, when winds are weak, and during the summer and winter months.

Higher temperatures in cities are due to the way humans have modified the urban landscape. In the cityscape, materials such as concrete and asphalt are used that effectively store shortwave radiation. During the day, these urban surfaces absorb solar radiation. Concrete can store 2000 times more heat than an equivalent volume of air. The energy is then slowly released as longwave radiation during the night.

The city landscape also contributes to the UHI effect (Figure 9.22). Cities have less natural vegetation to offer shade and evapotranspiration. The lower albedo of pavements and roofs compared to the countryside also means greater absorption of heat. Cities also produce waste heat, from lighting, air

Key term

urban heat island (UHI) effect: the increased temperature in urban areas compared to surrounding rural areas

Physical and human

Consider how the growth of a city might affect the severity of the UHI effect. How could developers plan to reduce the UHI effect?

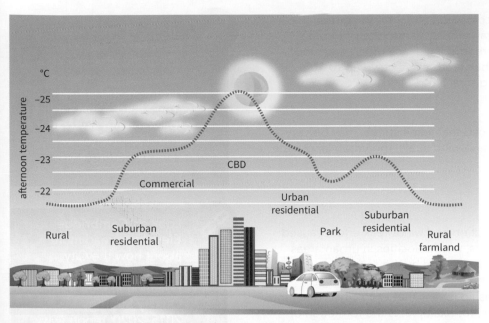

Figure 9.22 Afternoon temperatures in urban, suburban and rural areas. The temperature peaks in the CBD, illustrating the urban heat island effect.

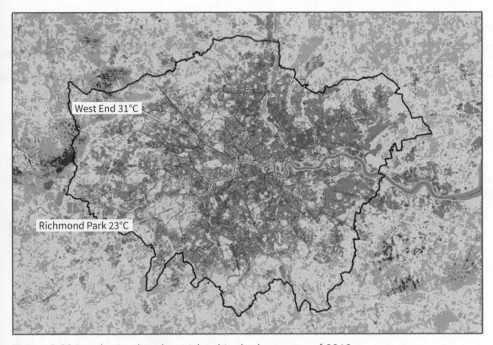

Figure 9.23 London's urban heat island in the heatwave of 2013.

conditioning units and electrical devices, which all further contribute to the UHI effect (Figure 9.23).

The UHI effect can be reduced by the use of **green roofs** and lighter coloured surfaces. These lighter surfaces reflect more sunlight and absorb less heat, thus reducing the UHI effect.

Precipitation

Urban environments also influence local meteorology. The UHI effect increases convection, leading to showers and increasing the chance of possible

 Key term

green roof: a roof of a building that is partially or completely covered with vegetation such as grass to promote wildlife and reduce insulation costs

thunderstorm development by up to 25% compared to surrounding rural areas. Low pressure caused by this uplift draws moist air into the city from the surrounding countryside, leading to increased incidence of fog and cloud formation and the increased risk of rain. Urban areas can receive up to 10% more frequent cloud cover than surrounding rural areas.

Wind

If you have visited a city, you may have noticed that some streets may be very windy, but once you turn the corner there is no wind at all! The urban landscape can influence the wind by:

- increasing or decreasing wind speed
- altering wind direction.

Wind velocity is generally reduced by the friction and windbreak effect caused by buildings in cities. Compared to rural areas, wind velocities in urban areas can be 30% lower. However, as wind speed is affected by the roughness of the buildings, and wind direction by the position and height of the buildings in relation to each other, this complex relationship means that each city is different. The overall pattern in a city with skyscrapers, for example, is the formation of **urban canyon winds**, as buildings increase the street-level winds which then separate and travel down various streets. The buildings here are acting like canyon walls.

Air quality

In cities, large quantities of solid impurities and gasses are emitted by the burning of fossil fuels from car exhausts and industry. Compared to rural areas, cities can have a number of air quality issues, including:

- ten times more nitrogen oxide
- 200 times more sulphur dioxide
- ten times more hydrocarbons
- twice as much carbon dioxide.

These pollutants can increase cloud cover and precipitation, and lead to an increase in smog. Such issues cause real problems for residents of Beijing, for example.

Pollution reduction policies

Many cities are now taking greater steps to combat and reduce pollution levels, partly as a result of increased public awareness of the issue. London, for example, has some of the highest levels of pollution in the UK. With national health objectives not being met, the whole of the city has been declared an Air Quality Management Area.

To manage the level of pollutants, a number of strategies have been put in place, including:

- the adoption of zero emission capable buses and taxis across London
- the introduction of an Ultra Low Emission Zone (ULEZ) in central London
- working with major city businesses to phase out standby generators that run solely on diesel
- issuing fixed fines for unnecessary vehicle engine idling in the Square Mile and erecting street signs in areas of concern (Figure 9.24)
- recognising and rewarding good practice by businesses
- increasing public awareness of air quality
- monitoring the impact of measures to reduce pollution.

 Look on **Cambridge Elevate** to read more about the effect of tall buildings on wind direction and speed in 'The Shard: What's it like to live near a skyscraper?' from the BBC (www.cambridge.org/links/gase6090).

 Look on **Cambridge Elevate** to read more about how the City of London is tackling pollution in their 'Air Quality Strategy 2015–2020' report (www.cambridge.org/links/gase6091).

 Key term

urban canyon winds: wind created by narrow urban streets and high office blocks funneling the wind between them

YOU are the key to cleaner air

Please switch off your engine while waiting and breathe a little easier

Idling engines waste fuel and money as well as creating pollution. Help us to improve air quality by switching your engine off when parked.

www.cityoflondon.gov.uk/air

Figure 9.24 Posters can encourage the public to do what they can to reduce air pollution.

Tackling air pollution in Beijing, China

Beijing issues first pollution red alert

A red alert – the first in Beijing, was issued as smog engulfed the capital city in December 2015. The alert began on Tuesday at 7am, and as a result millions of factories and construction sites were shut down.

The Chinese capital, Beijing, has been one of the most polluted cities in the world for many years. There are many different sources of pollutants that are affecting Beijing. Foe example, Beijing is home to over 5 million motor vehicles. In 2013, it was estimated that motor vehicles in Beijing consumed over 7 million tons of fuel, producing 900 000 tons of emissions, including 77 000 tons of hydrocarbons and over 80 000 tons of nitrogen oxides. Since 2013, this figure has continued to rise. In October of 2015 a white paper outlined the extent of pollution in Beijing caused by its transportation network, shown in Figure 9.25.

Figure 9.25 illustrates that transportation accounts for 86 percent of carbon monoxide in Beijing, and therefore if air pollution is to be addressed, then changes to the emissions from transportation is key to a successful outcome. These pollutants not only threaten public health and reduce air quality, but also contribute significantly to climate change.

A key issue that Beijing has had to face since 2000 is the growth in the number of vehicles within the city. In 2004 the city had two million vehicles, but by 2010 this figure had reached five million. Early attempts to reduce the number of vehicles on the roads of Beijing occurred in 2008 when vehicle use was restricted between the hours of 8.00 p.m. and 7:00 a.m. on a week day. This had little effect on pollution levels however as vehicle numbers still rose.

To tackle the air pollution issues in Beijing for the 2008 Olympics, a temporary road space rationing policy was introduced. Cars with an even number on their licence plate were able to drive on roads on one day (Figure 9.26), while cars with an odd last number on their licence plate were able to travel on roads the next day.

In 2011, a new vehicle quota was introduced in Beijing in a further attempt to reduce the impact on air pollution. A total of 240 000 new vehicle registrations was permitted in 2011 to 2013, through a vehicle lottery. This number was reduced to 150 000 in 2014, with the aim of capping the total number of

Look on **Cambridge Elevate** at the article 'Beijing issues first pollution red alert as smog engulfs capital' from the *Guardian* (www.cambridge.org/links/gase6092).

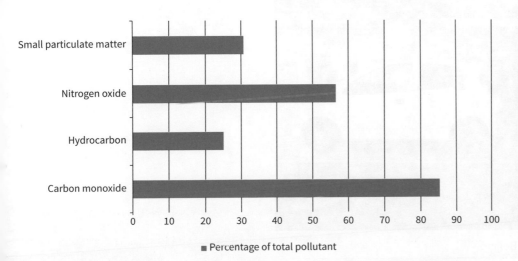

Figure 9.25 The percentage of total pollutants caused by transportation in Beijing.

Figure 9.26 This car in Beijing has an even ending licence number, restricting its use on public roads to every other day.

vehicles in Beijing to 6 million by 2017. The lottery system occurs on the 26th of every month. The Traffic Management Bureau enters all eligible vehicle registrations into the lottery and then selects a certain amount of them randomly.

The Chinese government has recently taken further steps to reduce the pollution, with a series of measures and long-term goals aimed at reducing pollution emissions.

Remote sensing

To ensure that vehicles are meeting the required emissions levels, remote sensing has been adopted on the streets of Beijing, particularly at night. Traffic is scanned at night, with the licence plate number and emissions recorded. This data is then compared to the required level of emissions allowed for the vehicle. While the accuracy of this system is still to be improved, it is hoped that in the future it will provide a useful system to further combat vehicle emissions.

Traffic restrictions

The success of the 2008 number plate restrictions has led to the continuation of the restrictions, but only when the local weather forecast in Beijing predicts at least three days of consecutive severe air pollution.

Green energy

Beijing is also tackling car emissions, by promoting electric vehicles (Figure 9.27), and producing cleaner fuel. These new energy vehicles also have large tax breaks, equivalent to 10% of the total cost of the vehicle, making them much more affordable to the general public. To further encourage the use of electric cars, 18% of any new car parking areas must be for electric cars, with public charging posts. In 2014, 1000 public charging points were built, while 8500 electric vehicles were introduced to the the public transport system between 2014 and 2015.

Figure 9.27 Electric car charging station in Beijing.

New environmental laws

In January 2015, a new environmental protection law took effect. The law fines polluters, and in the first six months, fines worth US$18.3 million were issued. The last coal-fired power station in the city is set to close by 2017 to be replaced by four gas-fired plants by 2016. Solar power plants have also been heavily invested in recent years, with 14 gigawatts of solar power being installed, increasing to almost 18 gigawatts by the end of 2015. In the same period, the USA installed just 7.3 gigawatts of solar power, illustrating China's commitment to renewable energy

Efforts in Beijing and in China in general appear to be working. Carbon dioxide emissions for China declined in 2014 for the first time in ten years, while total emissions are predicted to fall from 2025, although as Figure 9.28 indicates, it maybe some time yet before the population of Beijing sees an improvement in air quality.

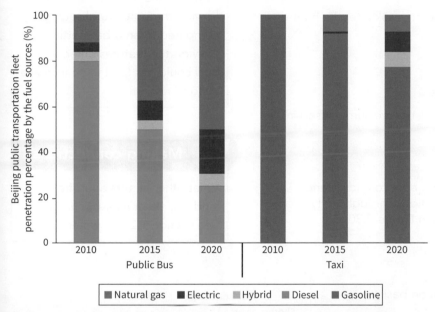

Figure 9.28 The proportion of power sources used across Beijing's public transport network.

9.5 Urban drainage

Rivers play an important role in our cities. In doing so, however, rivers within urban areas have been altered from their natural state. In Germany, only 21% of rivers are still in their natural state or are only slightly or moderately altered. Changes can of course provide benefits, but also lead to rivers losing their economic value and create issues of flood management, drainage and waste management.

Urban precipitation and water movement through urban catchments

At the catchment level, urban environments transform the natural hydrological system (see Chapter 1 Water and carbon cycles) through the building of impervious surfaces such as roads and pavements and storm water drains. At a local river scale, river water and sediment quality are affected by a higher concentration of storm water, brought by drains and gutters, wastewater and pollutants.

Urbanisation has increased the risk of flooding. With the increasing use of concrete and tarmac, water cannot infiltrate and surface runoff is increased. In urban areas, rivers are often **canalised** or run through **culverts**. This reduces friction and water is carried away more quickly. Gutters and drains have a similar effect. All can lead to problems further downstream as water arrives much quicker than from a more natural river environment, leading to increased flood risks.

Urban rivers suffer from lower water quality than rivers flowing in a rural setting. The main cause of this is discharge from sewage overflows and storm water.

River flow regimes within urban areas point to the development of an urban hydrology, which is characterised by:

- an increase in total runoff
- an increase in the frequency of flooding
- a decrease in the lag time (time taken for the river to peak after the highest rainfall)
- an increase in peak discharge
- a lack of seasonal variations
- a decrease in the base, or normal flow of the river.

The differences in urban and rural discharge characteristics are summarised in Figure 9.29.

The urban water cycle

When studying rivers within an urban setting, it is important to understand the differences in the water cycle that occur as a river flows through a city. The components of the urban water cycle are shown in Figure 9.30.

Issues associated with catchment management in urban areas

To manage the issues created within the urban drainage basin, several approaches can be taken, including:

- sustainable urban drainage systems (SuDS)
- river restoration and conservation.

While these approaches can benefit the river and the drainage basin as a whole, it is important to remember that they too will have an impact on the surrounding area, and this needs to be considered.

Sustainable urban drainage systems (SuDS)

Urban rivers can be prone to increased flooding, as vegetation is replaced by impermeable surfaces, leading to water being directed quickly to rivers instead of infiltrating into the surface.

Sustainable urban drainage systems (SuDs) are designed to replicate the natural environment to drain water slowly back into rivers, therefore reducing the likelihood of flash flooding.

SuDs have the following characteristics:

- easy to manage
- resilient to use
- environmentally attractive
- require little or no energy.

Key terms

canalise: straighten a section of a river

culvert: a tunnel carrying a river underground; the River Fleet in London is largely found underground in culverts

Physical and human

Consider the features of a river flowing through a rural setting compared to an urban setting. How do the features differ, and how could this lead to an increase in flood risk?

Making connections

What other factors apart from land use affect river discharge? See section 1.2 The water cycle.

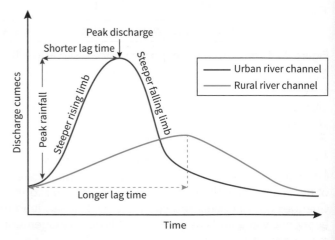

Figure 9.29 The effect of the urban environment on river discharge.

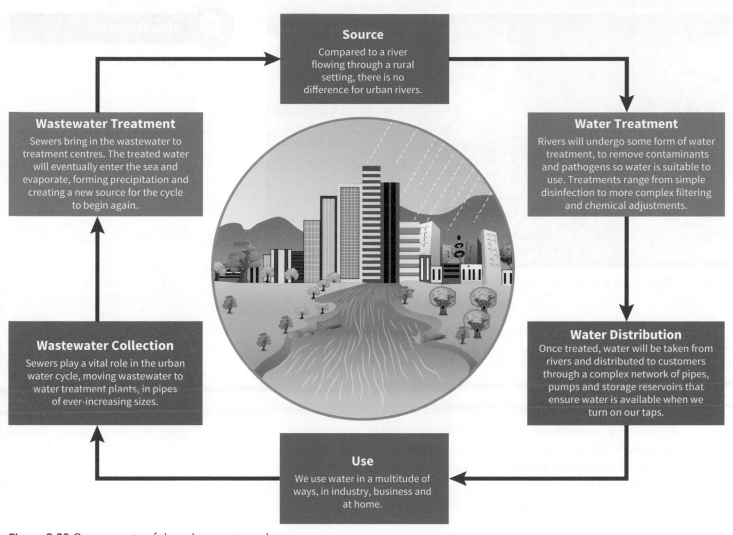

Source
Compared to a river flowing through a rural setting, there is no difference for urban rivers.

Water Treatment
Rivers will undergo some form of water treatment, to remove contaminants and pathogens so water is suitable to use. Treatments range from simple disinfection to more complex filtering and chemical adjustments.

Wastewater Treatment
Sewers bring in the wastewater to treatment centres. The treated water will eventually enter the sea and evaporate, forming precipitation and creating a new source for the cycle to begin again.

Water Distribution
Once treated, water will be taken from rivers and distributed to customers through a complex network of pipes, pumps and storage reservoirs that ensure water is available when we turn on our taps.

Wastewater Collection
Sewers play a vital role in the urban water cycle, moving wastewater to water treatment plants, in pipes of ever-increasing sizes.

Use
We use water in a multitude of ways, in industry, business and at home.

Figure 9.30 Components of the urban water cycle.

SuDs can take on many different forms, including dry basins (only to be filled when it is raining), rain gardens which are similar to dry basins but with shrubs planted in them, filter drains and bioretention basins. These are shallow depressions filled with gravel or sand, often with grass placed over the top. Green roofs are also SuDs, as is permeable paving as shown in Figure 9.31. Permeable paving has the advantage of allowing water to pass through the paving, reducing surface runoff while at the same time trapping suspended solids and filtering pollutants from the water.

It is important to remember that SuDs are not designed to reduce flooding in areas where they are deployed. SuDs are designed to reduce the impact of flash floods, which may occur in another area.

River restoration and conservation in damaged urban catchments

River restoration has two main aims:

• to improve the quality and function of rivers
• to restore the river so it can support healthy and thriving ecosystems.

Restoration can occur at different scales. At the larger scale, a restoration project could include an entire flood plain. Buildings might be removed and water channels brought back to more natural courses.

Investigate

Which areas close to you have SuDs? Why are they placed there? Will this reduce flooding in the future?

Figure 9.31 This paving is permeable, allowing water to pass through and reducing runoff.

On a smaller scale, a section of river might be restored by removing hard engineering and replacing it with more natural features. Restoration can be seen to work in conjunction with SuDs and other development projects within the urban environment.

The typical benefits that river restoration can bring to an area include:

- improvements in the quality of housing and the surrounding landscape
- more sustainable transport options, including footpaths and cycle ways
- opportunities for education and informal learning about the environment through visitor centres
- improvements in local people's health and well-being
- reduction in flood risk
- creation of green space corridors
- increasing access to nature and recreation
- improvements in river and riverbank biodiversity
- improvements to water quality and land drainage.

River restoration – the River Marden, Calne project

The River Marden flows through the town centre of Calne, in Wiltshire (Figure 9.32). In the past the river had been straightened and culverted. This led to a series of issues:

- no public access to the river bank
- concrete channels were deemed unattractive
- the local community had lost its connection with the river
- a risk of flooding to the town centre.

The restoration work centred on creating a double meander along a 100m length of the river, with the inner bend of the meander created using gravel shoal. This involved removing the old artificial channel and weirs, and re-meandering the channel. Natural stone was used to stabilise the river and to also create harmony with the local environment.

The project was a joint venture led by the district council, Calne Town Council, the River Restoration Centre and Nicholas Pearson Associates, as part of a wider rejuvenation of the town centre at a cost of £5.1 million.

Figure 9.32 The town of Calne, showing the course of the River Marden.

To encourage public access to the river, seating and planting was placed on the riverbanks. A local action group, Castlefields Canal and River Park Association (CARP), was set up to develop and improve the environment, and to provide public amenities for recreation and leisure.

To improve flood protection, the restored river now has a wider channel which can accommodate higher flows. The seating and planting areas are designed to be submerged (Figure 9.33). Since completion, the river restoration project has been a success with the local population. The 100 m stretch of river is now used for an annual charity duck race.

ACTIVITY 9.6

1 Visit the European Centre for River Restoration (ECRR) website and go to the 'Riverwiki' page. Use the map to locate the river restoration case studies that have occurred within Europe.
    Choose a river restoration project near where you live and produce your own case study. Use the following headings as a starting point:

    a   The need for restoration
    b   What was done to the area/river
    c   What have been the benefits?

    Try to use a variety of maps and images to support your work. Annotating photographs is an excellent way of developing a geographical argument and showing that you have understood the issues.

Figure 9.33 The River Marden at Calne, after restoration.

 Look on **Cambridge Elevate** to find out about different river restoration case studies in 'Riverwiki' on the ECRR website (www.cambridge.org/links/gase6093).

9.6 Other contemporary urban environmental issues

There are many environmental problems that occur in urban areas. These problems will differ depending on the size and scale of the urban area, as well as the level of development of the city in question. We have already discussed the issue of atmospheric pollution in Beijing and the dereliction of the London Docklands and subsequent resurgence. This section will focus on waste disposal.

Waste is an issue that faces every city in the world. In this section, using the examples of London and Bangalore, the environmental problems associated with waste will be explored.

Urban waste and its disposal

In England, 177 million tonnes of waste is produced each year. Not only is the issue an environmental one, but it is also a political one. The UK government has issued all local authorities with targets to reduce the amount of waste entering landfill. If these targets are not met, local authorities are fined. The UK government is also influenced by EU policy. The EU has set a limit on the amount of biodegradable waste that can enter landfill sites. To reach this target, the UK government imposes a £32 per tonne tax to reduce the amount of biodegradable material entering landfill sites.

As cities become more prosperous, the amount of waste generated also increases. For example, 90% of all products brought and used in London become waste within six months!

In London, every household produces over a tonne of waste each year. Traditionally, waste in London was buried in landfill sites. This was a cheap option, but finding sites to bury the waste became increasing difficult. As a result, waste started to travel outside the city for disposal, particularly in the Home Counties (e.g. Essex) in disused quarries.

Bangalore produces 20 000 tonnes of e-waste a year from the dominant IT sector in the city, and it is increasing by 20% year on year. Up to 90% of this waste is removed using the informal sector. Local businesses employ low-paid workers to sort and incinerate the e-waste. Due to a lack of regulations, workers are often unaware of the safety measures needed to work with e-waste. As a result, lead, mercury and other toxins are released into the environment. Workers use acid to extract precious metals from hardware, with no or very limited specialist clothing. Any remaining waste is then dumped, allowing the remaining pollutants to seep into the groundwater.

Strategies to manage these environmental problems

In London, the strategies to manage these environmental issues focuses on the use of landfill sites, incineration and recycling, while in Bangalore greater measures are needed to police dumping of e-waste by the informal sector, and increase the levels of recycling.

Landfill sites

Landfill sites, if well managed, are an inexpensive way of getting rid of waste. Modern landfill sites are built with clay or plastic linings to reduce the leaching of toxic liquids into the environment. Waste is compacted and covered to reduce the attraction to vermin. Gases, such as methane and carbon dioxide, are sometimes collected and burnt to generate electricity (Figure 9.34).

Thinking like a geographer

Being able to evaluate a topic from different points of view is a key *Thinking like a geographer* trait. India is a major destination of waste imports, from areas such as the USA, Japan and the EU. Should these countries stop exporting their waste to India and process it themselves?

Figure 9.34 The covered landfill site in Aveley, Essex, produces methane which is collected at this plant; the plant has the advantage of preventing gas from leaking into nearby homes.

Incineration

Some waste does not end up in landfill sites, but instead is incinerated, turning the waste into gas, heat, steam and ash. Incineration of hazardous material such as medical waste is a practical solution, but is not without controversy. Burning of waste causes the release of gaseous pollutants into the atmosphere.

Waste reduction

A key method of reducing waste is to prevent materials becoming waste in the first place. This is known as waste reduction. Several different methods of waste reduction exist, including:

- reusing second-hand products
- repairing broken products such as televisions
- using bags for life instead of single-use carrier bags
- designing products that involve less packaging, for example eco-coffee refills.

The issue with single-use carrier bags

From October 2015, a 5p charge was levied on single-use plastic bags in large shops in England (a 5p charge for carrier bags had already been in place in Scotland, Wales and Northern Ireland). In 2013, supermarkets alone had given out 8 billion single-use carrier bags across the UK. This is approximately 57 000 tonnes in single-use carrier bags each year. The effect of the charge in Wales between 2010 and 2013 resulted in a fall in carrier-bag usage of 79%.

Recycling methods

It is now a common sight in many towns and cities to see waste recycled at the kerbside, with householders using different coloured bins to dispose of different types of refuse. There is an ever-increasing pressure on households to recycle more, in order for the local authorities to meet UK and EU recycling targets. There are three different methods of recycling.

Physical reprocessing

This is the sorting of recycled materials so that the raw materials can be reprocessed to make new products. Different local authorities will have different methods of physical reprocessing. Some local authorities ask for all recyclable material to be placed in pink sacks, including paper, cardboard and plastics. These sacks are then sent to a reprocessing plant where it is sorted into the different materials. Some local authorities ask for separate collections of paper and glass, placing more responsibility on households.

Biological reprocessing

Biological waste such as garden waste, plant material and food scraps can be recycled by composting. After composting, the resulting organic material can be sold as soil improver or compost to local households or used in local parks or agricultural projects.

The recycling of e-waste in Bangalore

One of the problems limiting further recycling of e-waste in Bangalore is that most recycling technologies have been designed for large, economically developed companies, not the informal sector. Greater efforts are now being made to produce systems that require low maintenance and low technology, such as a system that uses bicycle power to sort copper from circuit boards.

Water pollution and strategies to manage it

Water pollution can be defined as the contamination of water bodies. This will occur when there is inadequate treatment of pollutants before they directly or indirectly enter the water bodies. It is not just the water that is affected. Plants and organisms are also affected. It is rare that water pollution will only affect one or two species; normally the whole biological community is affected.

Water is seen as polluted when it can no longer support human use, such as for drinking, or there is a shift in the ability to sustain aquatic life.

Water pollution is a major global concern and is one of the leading causes of death or disease across the globe. Around 14 000 people are killed daily due to a water pollution related illness, while in India alone it has been estimated that nearly 600 people die every day due to illnesses connected with water pollution.

The rivers within the cities of China are heavily polluted, with recent reports suggesting that around 90% of the water in Chinese cities is polluted to a degree, while half a billion people in China still do not have access to safe drinking water. Some rivers were so polluted in 2007, that the head of China's national development agency commented that for seven of the largest rivers in China, about a quarter of those rivers were polluted enough to harm the skin. This issue is linked to the rapid urbanisation of China. It was not until the early 1980s that China built its first municipal wastewater treatment plant in the city of Nanjing. By 2015 waste treatment rates had reached:

* 100% for municipalities, provincial capital cities and specifically designated cities
* 85% for other cities
* 70% for counties
* 30% for towns.

It is not just the recently industrialised nations that face water pollution issues. In the USA a recent report outlined that around 50% of streams and lakes were polluted, while 30% of estuaries and bays could also be classified as polluted.

ACTIVITY 9.7

1 Summarise what the governments of the UK and India are doing to reduce the dumping of e-waste. Critically assess the level of success of the polices introduced.

Water pollution can be caused by three main sources:

- chemicals
- pathogens
- physical changes – temperature.

Chemical pollution

Chemicals, such as calcium and sodium, occur naturally in water bodies. The concentration of the chemicals is the key factor in determining the level of pollution. Even naturally occurring chemicals, in a high concentration, will cause pollution.

The main issue regarding chemical pollution is the depletion of oxygen and increase in **turbidity**. The turbidity of the water, the amount of suspended load in the water body, will block sunlight, affecting plant growth and can clog the gills of fish.

When chemical pollution in a water body occurs, eutrophication can develop. This is an increase in the concentration of chemical nutrients in the ecosystem of the water body, to such a degree that it results in an increase in the growth of algae. This can develop into algal blooms, which reduce the level of oxygen in the ecosystem.

Thermal pollution

This is the rise or fall in a natural body of water caused by human influence. Increased temperature in water decreases oxygen levels, and in turn can kill fish and affect the ecosystem. Urban runoff can increase thermal pollution, as can the release of very cold water from the base of reservoirs into rivers. Power stations and industrial plants often use water as a coolant, and the release of this water back into the rivers can also led to thermal pollution.

Thermal pollution from urban runoff can be controlled by diverting the runoff into storm water drains, which direct the water into the groundwater to be absorbed.

Pathogen pollution

This is the pollution of water bodies by inadequately treated sewage entering the water. In low-income countries and in older cities, poorly designed or maintained sewage treatment works can lead to pathogens entering the water supply. Some cities have a combined sewage system, whereby in times of intense storms, storm water flows into sewers, which then take both the sewage and the storm water into local river courses.

In high-income countries, city sewage systems are often treated using centralised sewage treatment plants. If well designed, these plants can remove 90% of the pollutants within the sewage. Treatment plants with secondary systems, as shown in Figure 9.35, are even more effective at removing pollutants.

In cities with combined sewer overflow systems, several approaches can be used to reduce pollution:

- Developing greater groundwater storage of storm water.
- Repairing and replacing leaking pipes and equipment.
- Increasing the capacity of the sewage system.

Education can play an important role in reducing pollution. The UK Environment Agency aims to raise a greater awareness of the ecological impact of contaminating surface drains with pollutants such as oil. In efforts to reduce the number of people who use surface drains to dispose of pollutants the campaign 'Only rain down the drain' is used in conjunction with the yellow fish symbol. It is hoped that this symbol will remind people that any waste poured into the drain will go directly to the nearest water course, causing pollution and affecting wildlife.

Key term

turbidity: the cloudiness of a fluid caused by large numbers of suspended particles

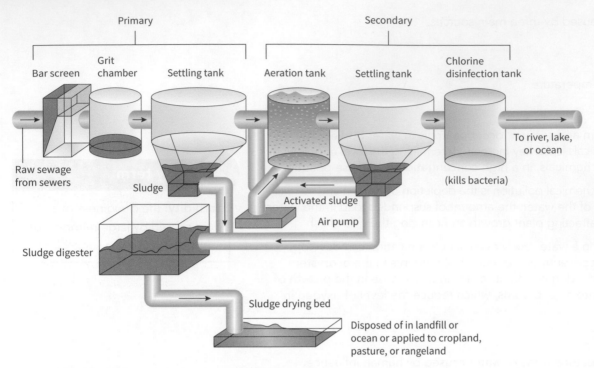

Figure 9.35 A typical sewage treatment plant with primary and secondary systems.

Dereliction

Dereliction is the act of abandonment. In the urban environment, dereliction can occur for a number of reasons:

- out-migration
- decline in housing quality
- the impact from past urban planning decisions
- a loss of industry.

The out-migration of skilled people from an urban area will leave behind a lower-skilled and less-qualified population. This is often linked to the process of suburbanisation, which has been discussed earlier in this chapter. With a greater percentage of lower-skilled people, the area will become economically less active and unemployment rates will increase.

Pre-war buildings are often expensive to maintain. Eventually owners are unwilling to pay for the maintenance, tenants move out and the area becomes abandoned. An increase in population density can also lead to a lowering of the housing quality, leading to a lower quality of living.

The impact of past urban planning decisions can lead to a decline in an area, and ultimately dereliction. Narrow streets, and a lack of infrastructure were among the issues that led to a lack of investment in the London Docklands until the LDDC developed the area.

The decline in manufacturing, or the loss of an industry completely, can also lead to dereliction. This can result from a change in government policy or support or a change in the availability of raw materials or profitability of the industry, as was the case in the coal industry in south Wales. In the USA, Detroit was regarded as a manufacturing city, but as globalisation increased and work was relocated to Asia, large areas of Detroit became derelict (Figure 9.36), becoming known as the Rust Belt.

Key term

dereliction: an area that has become abandoned or dilapidated

Figure 9.36 The Michigan Central train depot, closed in 1988 and remains vacant, although an $80 million renovation project is currently underway.

9.7 Sustainable urban development

Urban ecological footprints

For over 40 years, humanity has demanded more from nature than it can replenish. Current statistics suggest that we would require 1.5 Earths to produce the ecological services we currently use.

The **ecological footprint** totals all of the ecological services that people demand. These include:

- biologically active land and ocean:
  - crops
  - grazing land
  - built-up areas
  - fishing grounds
  - forestry products
- areas of forest needed to absorb additional carbon dioxide.

This is expressed in a common unit called a global hectare (gha). As Figure 9.37 illustrates, carbon has dominated the ecological footprint since the 1960s and this trend is set to continue well into the 21st century.

While technological advances have helped to increase the average yields per hectare from 9.9 billion global hectares to 12 billion global hectares between 1961 and 2010, the world's human population during that time also increased from 3.1 billion to 7 billion (Figure 9.38). This resulted in a reduction in the global

> **Key term**
>
> **ecological footprint:** measures the area required to supply the ecological services used by the population, measured in global hectares (gha)

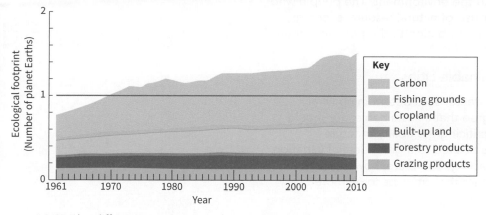

Figure 9.37 The different components of the ecological footprint.

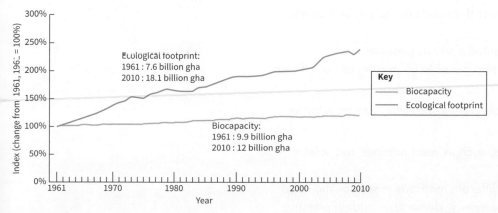

Figure 9.38 The fragile relationship between population, ecological footprint and biocapacity.

ecological capacity to just 1.7 gha. The issue here is with an ever-decreasing ecological capacity, and an increasing ecological footprint. How will the gap be bridged?

The driving force behind the increase in the global ecological footprint is cities. This is fuelled by the ever-increasing consumption of resources and the production of waste, along with the increase in population. In fact cities account for over 70% of global carbon emissions (UN HABITAT, 2011). However, cities can also help to lead the way in reducing the ecological footprint through better resource management. In Stockholm, for example, 75% of residents now use public transport. This has been achieved through the implementation of a congestion tax and better urban planning including a focus on 'walkability'and cycle lanes. Mexico City has invested heavily in a reforestation programme, with 2 million trees planted each year in the hope of improving the forest and wetland areas. Meanwhile in Singapore, rainwater collection and recycling now accounts for 50% of the city water supply. Urbanisation should not necessary mean the increase in the global ecological footprint. With wise planning and a greater emphasis on sustainable lifestyles, urbanisation can help to reduce the ecological footprint.

This chapter began by saying that for the first time in human history, the world had become an urban one, with over 50% of people living in urban areas. What does this mean for our futures, and how can the pressures of living in urban areas be balanced by a desire to live in a more sustainable fashion?

A sustainable city, sometimes referred to as an **eco-city**, is a city that has been designed to limit the impact it has on the environment. The people who live in a sustainable city will minimise their use of natural resources, energy, water and food and, as a result, limit their contribution to the pollution created by the city.

Strategies for developing more sustainable cities

While there is, as yet, no agreed set of characteristics determining what makes a city a sustainable one, experts agree that a sustainable city should meet the needs of the present without sacrificing the ability of future generations to meet their own needs. This has led to a great deal of variation between cities in working towards sustainability. There are, however, some guiding principles that can be used to ensure that cities become more sustainable. A city must:

- have the ability to use the surrounding countryside to feed the urban population, to reduce the distance from field to fork
- use renewable sources of power to meet the needs of the population and industries within the city
- reduce the ecological footprint to as small a size as possible
- produce the smallest amount of pollution possible by making use of efficient recycling methods.

To achieve these principles, a number of different approaches can be adopted, including:

- developing renewable energy sources, such as wind turbines and solar panels
- building into the urban environment different methods to reduce the need for air conditioning, which is a massive energy demand, including planting trees, water features and increasing green open spaces to counter the UHI effect (see the earlier section on Urban climate)

Key term

eco-city: a city that aims to provide a healthy environment for its inhabitants without using more resources than it replaces

Making connections

What links can be made between sustainable cities and natural resource availability? See section 11.2 Natural resource issues.

- improving public transport, creating more mass transit systems (e.g. bus lanes) and cycle lanes, as well as increasing pedestrianisation to reduce car emissions
- using green roofs on new builds and zero-energy buildings (see the London BedZED case study later in this section)
- greater use of sustainable urban drainage systems (see the earlier section on Urban drainage).

Creating sustainable cities is a long process. As cities expand and redevelop, it is in these areas that sustainability becomes the focus, until gradually the city as a whole will become more sustainable. There are, however, challenges. Sustainability is not a cheap option. It requires careful planning and, to some extent, compromise to balance the needs of people now and the needs of future generations, without damaging the environment.

Sustainable urban living has been created in both London and Bangalore. Each city has taken a different approach.

Concept of liveability

The concept of liveability is a simple one, and can be defined as which locations around the world provide the best and the worst living conditions. The Economist Intelligence Unit produces a report each year summarising the liveability of cities across the world. Investigating the liveability of cities raises important geographical questions about access to water, energy and education, for example, and also illustrates the importance of making links and seeking connections between social, economic and political factors. The unit uses key characteristics to assess the level of liveability within cities:

- stability
- healthcare
- culture and environment
- education
- infrastructure.

The five characteristics are scored as either: acceptable, tolerable, uncomfortable, undesirable or intolerable. A weighting system is then applied, which sees, for example the education score accounting for 10% of the liveability score while culture and the environment accounts for 25%. This allows an overall score out of 100 to be produced. The Economist Intelligence Unit has devised a rating scale for each characteristic as shown in Table 9.9.

Table 9.10 highlights the top and bottom 10 cities in the world in terms of liveability according to a recent report by the Economist Intelligence Unit.

Research point

To what extent do you agree with the characteristics chosen to investigate liveability and the rating given? How would you measure these characteristics so the data is comparable?

Rating	Description
80–100	There are few, if any, challenges to living standards
70–80	Day-to-day living is fine, in general, but some aspects of life may entail problems
60–70	Negative factors have an impact on day-to-day living
50–60	Liveability is substantially constrained
50 or less	Most aspects of living are severely restricted

Table 9.9 Rating scale from the Economist Intelligence Unit.

The top ten cities

(100=ideal; 0=intolerable)

Country	City	Rank	Overall Rating (100 = ideal)	Stability	Healthcare	Culture & Environment	Education	Infrastructure
Australia	Melbourne	1	97.5	95	100	95.1	100	100
Austria	Vienna	2	97.4	95	100	94.4	100	100
Canada	Vancouver	3	97.3	95	100	100	100	92.9
Canada	Toronto	4	97.2	100	100	97.2	100	89.3
Australia	Adelaide	5	96.6	95	100	94.2	100	96.4
Canada	Calgary	5	96.6	100	100	89.1	100	96.4
Australia	Sydney	7	96.1	90	100	94.4	100	100
Finland	Helsinki	8	96.0	100	100	90	91.7	96.4
Australia	Perth	9	95.9	95	100	88.7	100	100
New Zealand	Auckland	10	95.7	95	95.8	97	100	92.9

The bottom ten cities

(100 = ideal; 0 = intolerable)

Country	City	Rank	Overall Rating (100 = ideal)	Stability	Healthcare	Culture & Environment	Education	Infrastructure
Cote d'Ivoire	Abidjan	131	45.9	30	45.8	54.2	50.0	53.6
Libya	Tripoli	132	44.2	45	41.7	37.0	50.0	51.8
Cameroon	Douala	133	44.0	60	25.0	48.4	33.3	42.9
Zimbabwe	Harare	134	42.6	40	20.8	58.6	66.7	35.7
Algeria	Algiers	135	40.9	40	45.8	42.6	50.0	30.4
Pakistan	Karachi	136	40.9	20	45.8	38.7	66.7	51.8
Nigeria	Lagos	137	38.9	25	33.3	53.5	33.3	46.4
PNG	Port Moresby	138	38.9	30	37.5	44.2	50.0	39.3
Bangladesh	Dhaka	139	38.7	50	29.2	43.3	41.7	26.8
Syria	Damascus	140	30.5	15	29.2	44.7	33.3	32.1

Table 9.10 The ten top and bottom cities in terms of liveability, as ranked by the Economist Intelligence Unit.

ACTIVITY 9.8

Using the information from Table 9.10, use a GIS package to produce a world map to show the data. Then consider these questions:

1   What trends can be seen?
2   Do certain regions dominate the bottom liveability cities?
3   Add another layer of data to your map, such as education or healthcare. Does a pattern develop as a result?

9.8 London – Beddington Zero Energy Development (BedZED)

Beddington Zero Energy Development (BedZED) is a sustainable housing development in Hackbridge, London (Figure 9.39). It is in the borough of Sutton, 3 km north-east of the town of Sutton. Built between 2000 and 2002, BedZED consists of 82 houses, 17 apartments and 1405 m² of workspace.

The housing development has taken on many of the characteristics of a sustainable city, and was primarily designed to create zero carbon emissions. The development was designed by Bill Dunster and led by The Peabody Trust. The local authority sold them the land below the market value to make the development economically viable as well as sustainable.

To minimise the impact of the build on the physical environmental conditions, construction materials were sourced locally where possible. Local was defined as within a 50-mile radius of the BedZED development, and materials were either recycled or made from renewable materials. This led to a decrease in the energy required for transportation. One of the few materials that were sourced outside the 50-mile radius was the triple-glazed window units, which were constructed in Norway. All of the wood that was used for the project was approved by the Forest Stewardship Council or comparable internationally recognised environmental organisations.

In order to increase the sustainability of the project further, the houses were arranged to be south facing, in order to maximise the heat from the sun. Sunspaces were created on these south-facing sides to provide an added layer of natural insulation and heating source, although in practice these have not been as successful as planned.

Figure 9.39 Housing and industrial units in BedZED.

Workspaces are north facing, creating a cooler location reducing the need for energy sapping air conditioning units. Extra heating is provided by a centralised heating plant, which uses off-cuts from tree surgery waste that would have otherwise been destined for landfill sites in the area. While issues have occurred with the reliability of the system, it has still helped to reduce overall energy consumption. The development produces an estimated 37% less carbon dioxide from gas and electricity than the average development of an equivalent size.

Economic well-being has been a key feature of the development. As a result of the 30 cm-thick wall insulation and the south-facing properties, heating costs are 88% less than a comparable sized house. By recycling and using water harvested from the BedZED site, mains water consumption has been reduced by 50%, or 67% in homes with power showers. Savings are not limited to just heating and water. Electricity use was 25% less than the UK average, and 11% of this was produced by the BedZED solar panels, further increasing the savings to residents.

There have also been a number of social benefits as well. Due to the Green Transport Policy that was planned at the beginning of the project, with an electric car charging point, cycle storage built into the complex and local and affordable public transport nearby, residents' car journeys are 65% less than the local average. There is also greater social connection between residents. The BedZED residents claim to know on average 20 of their neighbours by name; the local average is eight.

Affordable housing was another key social aim of the project, particularly for people on lower incomes. Half of the homes in the development are for shared home ownership or low cost rent.

Key features of the development include:

- 82 homes
- 1405 m² of work space
- 777 m² of solar panels
- apartments are south facing and triple glazed
- rainwater is collected and reused
- building materials for the development were recycled or renewably sourced within 56 km of the site – with the exception of the triple-glazed windows, which came from Norway
- waste recycling is an integral part of the kitchen design to encourage the residents to recycle
- electric cars use is encouraged by the availability of charging points in the car park; residents are also encouraged to car share
- green roofs are used to further insulate the housing, and to provide spaces for residents to grow their own produce

ACTIVITY 9.9

1 Explain how the UK government is encouraging eco-living through the use of grants and initiatives.

 For an activity on the BedZED development, download Worksheet 9.7 from **Cambridge Elevate**.

9.9 Bangalore – Samskruti Hoysala development

Bangalore is the capital of the state of Karnataka in India. In 2016, Bangalore had a population of over 11.5 million and was the third-most populous city in India.

Economic and social well-being

Most of the economic activity in Bangalore is based around the booming technology industry, which attracts highly educated workers. In 2016, the literacy rate in Bangalore was 89%, compared to India's overall literacy rate of 75%. Workers in the technology industry are well paid and have comfortable lifestyles. However, workers in other industries such as construction receive much lower wages and are often forced to live in unsafe conditions. In Bangalore, 16–25% of the population live in slums. There is considerable economic inequality in the population (see 9.3 Social and economic issues associated with urbanisation), which has contributed to inequality in social well-being.

Nature and impact of physical environmental conditions

Vegetation in Bangalore, particularly trees, is vitally important to the well-being of the city inhabitants and for those living in the slums. However, rapid urbanisation is threatening the vegetation that is still present. Vegetation plays an important role in supporting nutrition and healthcare, particularly when species are planted that have medicinal use. The drumstick tree, for example, is locally known as the 'miracle tree'. The fruits and leaves provide rich sources of proteins, vitamins and minerals. As a result, the trees help to meet the nutritional deficiencies found within the slum areas. With the growth of the city ever increasing, the pressure to retain vegetation is increasing. As well as the health benefits, trees in the slum areas are of particular importance as they provide spaces for social activities; for example, children playing games and adults socialising, as well as domestic activities such as washing and drying of clothes. The reduction of green spaces in Bangalore has led to a number of innovative types of gardening across the city, using plastic bags, buckets and old kitchen utensils to grow kitchen gardens.

Environmental sustainability

In a city where providing safe housing for all of the population is a challenge, environmental sustainability has not traditionally been a priority. However, as the population of Bangalore has become wealthier and concerns over climate change have increased, sustainability has become more important.

In 2010, the government of Karnataka launched the Bangalore Climate Change Initiative – Karnataka (BCCI-K). The initiative aims to encourage the development of low-carbon sustainable development in the state. As well as top-level policies, environmental sustainability is influencing decisions at lower levels too. Sustainable housing developments such as the Samskruti Hoysala development are becoming more common.

The Samskruti Hoysala development consists of 38 apartments located near the IT hub in the Doddakannelli district of Bangalore (Figure 9.40). The development aims to be sustainable in five key areas:

- water
- space
- energy
- community
- health.

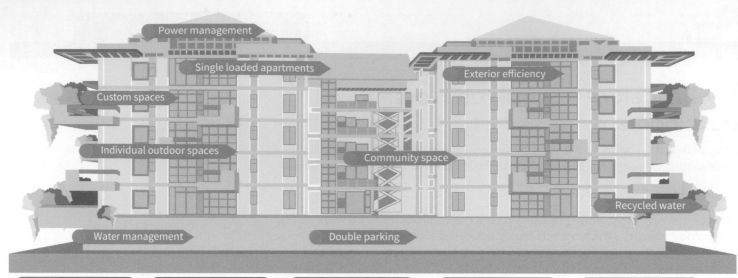

| **Rainwater harvesting**
Providing the majority of the water needs for each apartment. | **Double parking**
Allowing two cars to occupy one space. | **Community space**
A central space for people to relax and interact, to include a swimming pool, barbeque area and living walls of vegetation. | **Energy**
Solar panels to provide much of the energy requirements. | **External walls**
Layering of the external walls and the different colour shades help to minimise heat loss. |

Figure 9.40 Sustainable living in Bangalore: Samskruti Hoysala.

In order to conserve water, a **rainwater harvesting** system is in place to collect 350 000 litres of rainwater. This reduces the demands for water from the city-wide resources. **Grey water** is used for irrigation and flushing. Rainwater harvesting, combined with solar heating, provides hot water for each apartment.

Energy is provided by solar panels on the roof of the apartments, as well as being supplemented by the use of **hybrid green energy** from the National Grid. The external walls of the apartment block are designed to further reduce the use of energy.

The health of the inhabitants has also been considered when designing the apartments. Each apartment has a green terrace area, where fruits and vegetables can be grown, which use the rainwater harvesting system as a water source.

To encourage community interaction, a central space has been created, which includes a swimming pool, walking parks and landscaped walls. To save space, a system of double parking will be used so two cars can be allocated per apartment (Figure 9.41).

Key terms

rainwater harvesting: a system to collect the rainfall and use it in buildings and gardens

grey water: used water from bathroom sinks, showers and washing machines

hybrid green energy: producing energy using two renewable energy sources

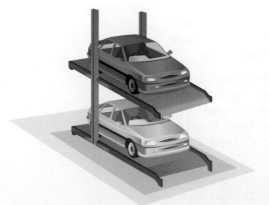

Figure 9.41 Double car-parking system in Samskruti Hoysala.

Assess to progress

For a revision activity, download Worksheet 9.8 from **Cambridge Elevate**.

1 What are the likely pull factors that lead to suburbanisation?
  A A greener, cleaner environment with a wider range of employment opportunities.
  B Rising house prices in the urban centre.
  C A desire to move away from industry.
  D Increasing traffic and pollution in the urban centre. **1 MARK [AS/A LEVEL]**

2 Which is not a driving force of counter-urbanisation?
  A An increasing ageing population of a country, leading to higher income retirement age groups moving to coastal towns.
  B A reliable commuter service providing the freedom to live further from the place of employment.
  C The decline of industry and services in the CBD leading to greater levels of unemployment.
  D House prices in rural areas increasing as a result of second homes being bought. **1 MARK [AS/A LEVEL]**

3 Outline potential impacts of suburbanisation on rural villages. **3 MARKS [AS LEVEL]**

4 Explain the advantages of using sustainable urban drainage systems (SuDS) in an urban area. **9 MARKS [AS/A LEVEL]**

5 Using Figure 9.42 and your own knowledge, assess the threat to health presented by air pollution in cities, and the degree to which air pollution can be reduced in an area that you have studied. **9 MARKS [A LEVEL]**

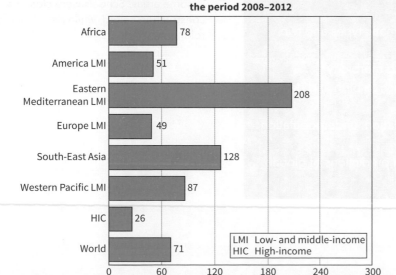

Figure 9.42 Air pollution levels in cities by region. The WHO recommended safe level of PM10 = $20\,\mu g/m^3$ annual mean.

6 Assess the opportunities and challenges associated with sustainable development in urban areas. **20 MARKS [AS/A LEVEL]**

Population and the environment

By the end of this chapter you should know:

- global populations are influenced by climate, soils, topography and resource availability
- global patterns of food production and consumption and the concerns over global food security
- the characteristics and distribution of two major climatic types and two zonal soils
- global and regional patterns of health, mortality and morbidity
- population change as a result of natural change, such as birth and death rates, and migration change
- population ecology and the concepts of overpopulation, underpopulation and optimum population
- contrasting perspectives on population growth and predictions of global population change under different scenarios.

Figure 10.1 Air pollution is a growing global problem. In December 2015, Beijing in China issued its first ever red alert over hazardous pollution levels, which were up to 40 times the safe level in some areas. Schools were closed and construction halted, while people were told to stay indoors.

Before you start...

You should know:

- population measures include birth rates, death rates, infant mortality and life expectancy
- the world's population is expanding, with the greatest increases seen in low income countries (LICs)
- different food is produced in different places, depending on factors such as climate; food is then transported between countries through trade

- population numbers and movements have implications for the provision of food, water and energy supplies
- levels of health and disease vary between places.

10.1 Introduction

Human populations can be described using **population distribution** and **population density**. Population distribution is the spread of people over an area. People are rarely evenly spread, but are more likely to be found in clusters around towns and cities. Distribution is therefore a description of the spread of people. Population density measures the number of people within an area. High population densities are found where there are many people clustered together and low population densities are found where fewer people live in close proximity to one another.

Birth rates, **fertility rates**, death rates, infant mortality and life expectancy all measure human populations. Each of these measures changes over time and each is influenced by development processes operating within a country. For example, India has seen steady economic growth since the turn of the century. Between 2000 and 2013, the following changes have taken place within India's population:

- birth rates fell from 21 to 20 births per thousand
- the fertility rate decreased from 3 to 2 births per woman
- the infant mortality rate decreased from 43 to 38 deaths per 1000 live births
- life expectancy increased from 62 to 66 years (Figure 10.2); by 2014, 5.8% of India's population were 65 years of age or older
- the death rate remained low, at 8 deaths per 1000 people.

People can survive only if environmental conditions are suitable for their existence. Key elements within the physical environment that determine the characteristics and rates of change within a population include:

- Climate: extremes of temperature limit population growth. Too much or too little rainfall also presents challenges. Desert and polar environments often have low population densities. Mauritania in western Africa has a population density of just 3.36 people per km². Around 90% of the country consists of desert, so one-third of the population lives along the south-western coast.
- Soils: the presences of fertile soils is necessary to grow food. Permafrost (see Chapter 6, Glacial systems and landscapes) can also prevent access to the soil. Food can be imported, so this factor is less critical for wealthier nations. Greenland has a population density of just 0.03 people per km². Most of the country is covered in ice or permafrost, so people live mainly along the south and west coast where the soils are suitable for farming.
- Topography: the shape of the land determines people's ability to create lasting settlements and access other places and resources. Mountainous areas often have sparse populations. Bhutan is a country that sits within the eastern Himalayan mountains. It is also landlocked, with India to the south and China to the north. It has a low population density of around 16.52 people per km².
- Resource distributions: access to food, water and energy resources are needed to sustain human communities. Namibia in southern Africa has a population

Key terms

population distribution: the pattern of where people live

population density: the number of people living in an area, usually given as the number of people per km²

fertility rate: sometimes called total fertility rate (TFR), this is the average number of children that are born to a woman during her lifetime

Figure 10.2 Economic development in India has meant that life expectancy has increased from 62 to 66 years between 2000 and 2013.

density of just 2.56 people per km². The Namib Desert spreads across a large part of the country, so water shortages are commonplace. Lack of suitable grazing has forced many farmers to sell cattle, meaning food is becoming scarce. Competition for good pasture land is creating tribal conflicts.

Global patterns of population

World population reached 7.3 billion people in 2015, with estimates suggesting there are an additional 80000 people on the planet every day. This takes into account the number of people being born and the number of people dying. The most populous countries in 2015 were China (1.3 billion), India (1.2 billion) and the USA (0.3 billion). The global population has seen **exponential growth** over time (Table 10.1), although the increase in numbers has not taken place evenly.

Global population densities for 2014 are shown in Figure 10.3. Of the most populous countries (China, India and the USA), both China and India have high population densities. The USA has large numbers of people but, at 9.63 million km², it also has a greater land area than both China and India. Several smaller countries, such as the UK, Germany and Italy, also have high population densities.

Some parts of the world have seen population growth while others have seen population decline. Table 10.2 shows the annual percentage population growth rate for nine countries. High income countries (HICs) have the lowest annual growth rate, whereas low income countries (LICs) have the highest annual growth rates. The growth rates for middle income countries (MICs) fall between these two.

The depletion of energy resources leads to the exploration, exploitation and development of new resources. This creates flows of people between places. The availability of water resources also determines the population within an area. The availability of resources is explored in Chapter 11 Resource security.

Key term

exponential growth: when the rate of increase becomes ever more rapid in proportion to the size of the population

Year	Population (billions)
1800	1.1
1850	1.4
1900	1.8
1950	2.6
2000	6.1
2050 (UN estimate)	9.6

Table 10.1 World population growth, 1800–2050.

Making connections

Population change is affected by both human and physical processes.

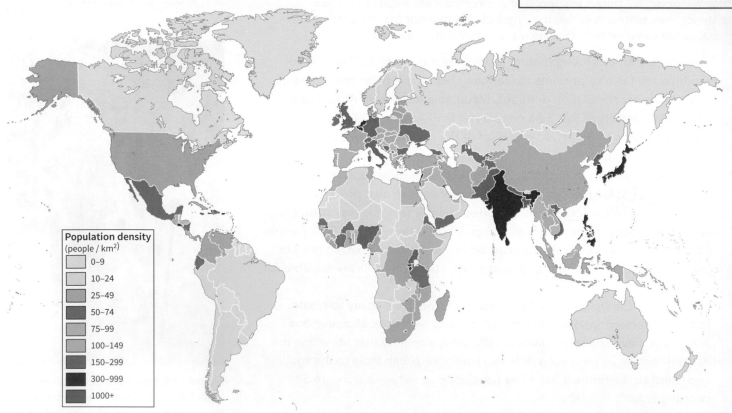

Population density
(people / km²)

- 0–9
- 10–24
- 25–49
- 50–74
- 75–99
- 100–149
- 150–299
- 300–999
- 1000+

Figure 10.3 Global population densities, 2014.

Country grouping	Country	Population growth rate, 2011–15 (annual %)
HIC	Germany	0.3
	Japan	−0.2
	UK	0.6
MIC	Brazil	0.9
	Morocco	1.4
	Turkey	1.2
LIC	Afghanistan	3.0
	Niger	4.0
	Tanzania	3.2

Table 10.2 Annual population growth rates for selected countries.

Global and national organisations, such as the UN and national governments, may attempt to manage flows of people through development projects, birth control programmes or migration policies. Chapter 7 Global systems and global governance looks at these organisations in more detail.

10.2 Environment and population

Food security is an increasingly important issue. Both global food production and calorie intake per capita have increased over the last decade. Within this, regional patterns have emerged. The UN estimates that there will be 9.6 billion people on the planet by 2050. This increase in numbers will see an increase in the demand for food.

Global and regional patterns of food production and consumption

Around half of the exploitable land surface in the world is now used to produce food (Figure 10.4). Usable land surface is limited in supply, so we have diminishing capacity to create more farmland.

Look on **Cambridge Elevate** for more information on population change from the following websites:
- Worldometers (www.cambridge.org/links/gase6094)
- The World Bank (www.cambridge.org/links/gase6095)
- World Population Review websites (www.cambridge.org/links/gase6096)
- Population Matters (www.cambridge.org/links/gase6097)
- UN data (www.cambridge.org/links/gase6098)
- Population Reference Bureau (www.cambridge.org/links/gase6099)
- Index Mundi (www.cambridge.org/links/gase6100).

Key term

food security: when people have enough affordable and nutritious food to eat

Figure 10.4 Around half of the usable land on the planet is used to grow food.

Different parts of the world specialise in producing different foods and some general trends are as follows:

- Much of our global food supply originates in Asia. Asian countries produce the most cereal crops (e.g. oats and corn), wheat, rice, sugar, meat, milk and fish. Within Asia, China and India are the largest producers of meat, fish and milk.
- South America grows the most oil crops.
- North American grows the most coarse grain (used for animal feed and brewing).
- Europeans grow the most barley and are the second biggest producers of pork, milk and fish.

The countries that produce the most food are not always the countries that consume the most food. Trade between different nations enables the food produced in one country to be transported elsewhere.

Food consumption is measured through calorie intake; an average person needs to consume between 2000 and 2500 calories a day in order to maintain their weight and remain healthy. Average calorie intake for every part of the world has increased since the 1990s and is expected to continue to rise by 2030 (Table 10.3).

Region	1997–1999	2015	2030 (est.)	% increase over time
World	2803	2940	3050	8.1
Developing countries	2681	2850	2980	10.0
Near East and North Africa	3006	3090	3170	5.2
Sub-Saharan Africa (excluding South Africa)	2195	2360	2540	13.6
Latin America and the Caribbean	2824	2980	3140	10.1
East Asia	2921	3060	3190	8.4
South Asia	2403	2700	2900	17.1
Industrialised countries	3380	3440	3500	3.4
Transition countries	2906	3060	3180	8.6

Table 10.3 Per capita food consumption (kcal per person per day).

- People in industrialised countries consume more calories than they need. The World Health Organization (WHO) has identified a 'double burden of malnutrition' whereby HICs and LICs are both facing malnutrition. People in HICs are eating food that is high in calories but low in nutrients.
- South Asia has seen the biggest increase in calorie intake, which mainly originates from an increase in wealth and improved food security in China.
- Sub-Saharan Africa has seen the second biggest increase, although average food consumption here remains much lower than the world average and under-nutrition is commonplace. Some countries such as Chad and Tanzania have calorie intakes that are much lower than this average. The World Bank produces a measure called the depth of the food deficit that indicates the difference in calories between average food consumption and average food requirements. In 2014 the depth of food deficit for Chad was 264 calories and for Tanzania 258 calories.

 Key terms

malnutrition: consuming an unsuitable amount of energy, protein and nutrients

under-nutrition: consuming too little food, leading to loss of body weight

depth of the food deficit: a measure of the difference between average food consumption and average food requirements (in kilocalories per person per day)

ACTIVITY 10.1

1 Explain the causes and effects of the 'double burden of malnutrition'.
2 How is level of wealth related to food security?
3 To what extent is 'average calorie intake' useful when studying food security?

Agricultural systems and agricultural productivity

Agricultural production is a system with inputs, processes and outputs (Figure 10.5).

Inputs to the farming system can be physical, such as climate, relief and soils. Physical inputs are outside of the farmer's control, but with some expense they can be adapted to suit the farmer's needs, such as the use of irrigation systems to increase water supplies. Inputs can also be human, such as machinery, labour and animal feed. These inputs require **capital investment**, but the farmer can sometimes ease these costs, for example by sharing machinery with other farmers through a **cooperative**.

Processes are the activities that take place on the farm. Farms can be arable, pastoral or mixed. Arable farms grow crops such as wheat, rice and cotton. Ploughing, seeding (drilling) and harvesting are processes that take place on arable farms. Pastoral farms involve rearing animals such as cows, pigs or chickens. Shearing, milking and moving cattle to new grazing are all processes that take place on pastoral farms. Mixed farms involve growing crops and rearing animals. Mixed farms carry out both arable and pastoral processes. Arable, pastoral and mixed farming systems can be further subdivided into other categories:

- Intensive farms have large inputs of labour, machinery, technology or capital. Smaller areas of land are often used. Productivity is high, with large outputs per area of land. Negative outputs can be high on account of the intensive use of **agrochemicals**.

Key terms

capital investment: funds invested in a firm or enterprise for the purposes of furthering its business objectives

cooperative: a group that works together to share costs and maximise profits

agrochemicals: artificial pesticides and fertilisers that are used in farming

Farming is a system, with inputs, processes and outputs

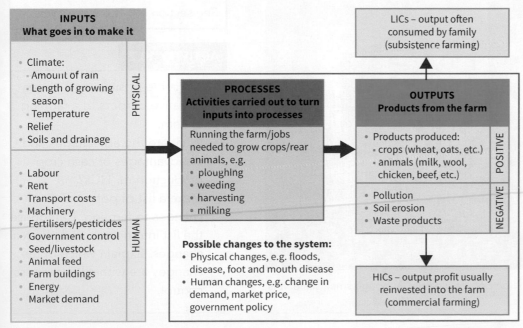

Figure 10.5 Farming as a system.

- Extensive farms have lower inputs of labour, capital and machinery per area of land. Large areas of land are used, often to monoculture. Yields are lower per area than intensive farming.

- Commercial farms are run to make a profit. Commercial farms can range in size from family-run operations to enterprises backed by **transnational corporations (TNCs)**. Produce is sold for as much profit as possible. **Cash crops** are a form of commercial farming as crops are grown purely to make a profit.

- Subsistence farms are run for personal consumption. They have small inputs of capital and large inputs of labour. They are often associated with LICs, but the growth of **urban and peri-urban horticulture (UPH)** (Figure 10.6) is leading to an increase in subsistence farming in some HICs. There are few negative outputs, but little or no surplus produce to sell.

- GM and organic farms are newer models of farming. The crop varieties used on GM farms have had been genetically modified to improve their characteristics. For example, Golden Rice contains two genes from daffodil flowers that give the food more A vitamins than other rice varieties. Inputs to a GM farm therefore include **biotechnology** and the food produced can have higher yields, better disease resistance or be more nutritious than food grown on traditional farms. Organic farms are run with environmental sustainability in mind. Inputs include natural fertilisers and pest control. Although outputs decline initially, research has shown that yields eventually improve. Outputs include foods that contain fewer artificial chemicals.

Changes to farming systems can create difficulties for farmers as they are often outside their control. Physical changes include floods and animal diseases, and human changes involve government policies or changes in demand.

Figure 10.6 UPH is carried out by 800 million people globally. Although small scale, it is 15 times more productive than rural farms.

Key terms

transnational corporations (TNCs): large companies that operate across national boundaries

cash crops: a crop produced to sell rather than for the farmer to consume

urban and peri-urban horticulture (UPH): subsistence farming that takes place on small plots of land within and around the edge of cities

biotechnology: the science behind genetic modification

Making connections

Agricultural systems operate through inputs, processes and outputs. The same can be said of most physical geography systems. For example, drainage basins have inputs in the form of precipitation, processes in the form of water flows and outputs in the form of evapotranspiration. See section 1.2 The water cycle.

ACTIVITY 10.2

1   List some positive and some negative outputs of a farming system.

2   What are the advantages and disadvantages of cash crop production for LICs?

3   Make a list of potential changes to farming. Categorise the list into human and physical changes. Explain which of the changes are within the farmer's control.

Key physical environmental variables – climate and soils

In reality, combinations of agricultural systems occur, such as intensive commercial farming. Different types of farming take place in different parts of the world (Figure 10.7). To some extent, these patterns are determined by human factors such as level of wealth and access to resources. However, food production also has a direct relationship with environmental factors. The key environmental variables determining agricultural systems are climate and soils.

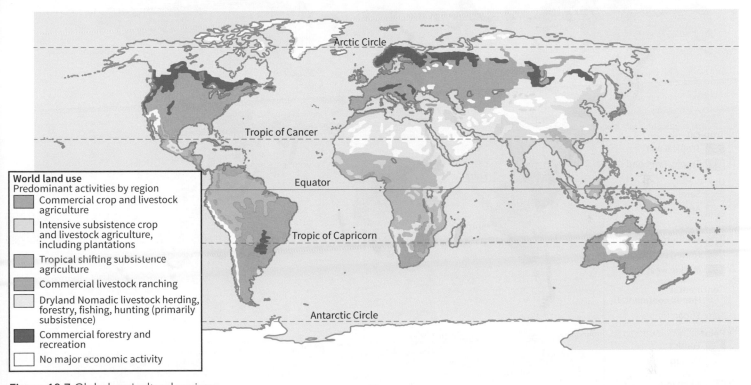

Figure 10.7 Global agricultural regions.

Most crops require certain climatic and soil conditions in order to grow well. Rice and potatoes are both commercially grown crops. Rice grows where rainfall is high as it needs a period of time standing in water. Temperatures between around 16 and 27 °C are ideal. Rice grows best in fertile **alluvial soils** found within the flood-prone regions of river basins. Clay soils are ideal as they have better water retention. Potatoes require much less water than rice. Too much rainfall can cause potato blight, a disease that destroys potato crops. They also grow best when temperatures are cooler, at around 18 to 20 °C. Potatoes prefer loose, sandy soils that drain freely. They also need soils that are rich in nutrients.

Figure 10.7 shows that commercial crop and animal production is more difficult around polar regions, as much of the agriculture to the northern extent of Russia, Canada and Alaska is **nomadic cultivation**. It also suggests that very dry regions, such as the Sahara Desert and the Namib Desert, are difficult to farm commercially. In terms of soils, the polar regions are also prone to permafrost, which prevents **sedentary cultivation**. Arid soils are too dry and mountainous soils, such as those found in the Rocky Mountains, the Andes and the Himalayas, are often too thin and therefore unsuitable for agriculture.

 Key terms

alluvial soils: fertile soils deposited when a river floods

nomadic cultivation: when a farmer moves from one place to another to find water supplies and better pasture land

sedentary cultivation: farming that occurs in one place

Climatic types

Global climatic types (Figure 10.8) result from the variety of climatic conditions found across the world. This section focuses on two major climatic types: semi-arid and Mediterranean.

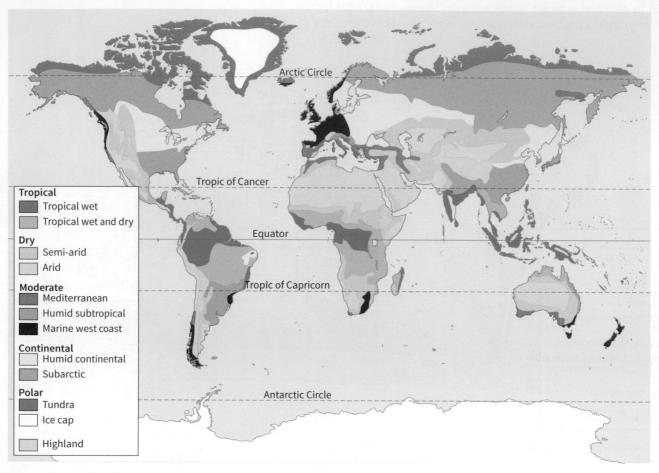

Figure 10.8 Global climate types.

Semi-arid climates

Semi-arid climates are found near the equator, between the Tropics of Cancer and Capricorn. They lie beside the arid hot desert regions of North and South America, Africa, Southern Asia and Australia.

Semi-arid regions are characterised by savanna vegetation, which consists of tall grasses and occasional woody trees (Figure 10.9). They are an area of transition between wet, tropical rainforests and dry, hot deserts. In some years they receive enough rain to support some agriculture, but they can also experience long periods of drought. Rainfall is seasonal and averages 25 to 50 cm per year, depending on the location. Vegetation growth does take place within the wet season, but water levels are insufficient to sustain many plants other than grass. Fires commonly destroy this grass during the dry season, so almost all species have adapted to survive these fires. Temperatures in semi-arid regions are determined by latitude; the semi-arid regions of North America are much cooler than those found in Africa.

The Sahel is a long strip of land that lies beneath the Sahara Desert in Africa. It has a semi-arid climate and savanna vegetation. The countries of Burkina Faso, Chad, Mali, Mauritania, Niger and Senegal lie within this region. Agriculture is the most important form of economic activity for these countries and

Figure 10.9 Savanna grassland in Kenya. Semi-arid regions have little rainfall, so can only support grasses and the occasional woody tree.

consists of three systems of farming: pastoral (including sedentary, nomadic and seasonally nomadic), **rainfed** mixed and irrigated mixed. Crops include millet, cowpea, sorghum, cotton and groundnut; livestock involves rearing cattle, sheep, goats and camels. Farming is unreliable in this region because of the climate. As a result, **food insecurity** is widespread and many suffer malnutrition.

Like many other areas with a semi-arid climate, the Sahel faces increasing challenges over time. Population growth is outstripping food supply. Niger and Mali have the highest birth rates globally and population across the Sahel as a whole is expected to triple in the space of just 40 years. In 2013 the population of the region was around 100 million and it is estimated to rise to 340 million by 2050. In addition to this, climate change is making rainfall levels less reliable and therefore agriculture is becoming more difficult. Since 1950 the Sahel has seen a marked decrease in rainfall levels and between 1970 and 1993 there were 20 years of widespread and severe drought. A study in 2015 reported that global warming had actually caused rainfall levels in the Sahel to begin to increase again (Figure 10.10). It suggested that the droughts of the 1970s and 1980s were being replaced by increased precipitation due to the northerly migration of tropical rainfall belts.

Mediterranean climates

Mediterranean climates are warm coastal regions found between 30 and 45° in latitude. The name comes from the Mediterranean Sea, although this climate type can also be found along sections of coastline in North and South America, Africa and Australia.

The vegetation of Mediterranean regions is characterised by shrubs, thorny bushes and small trees (Figure 10.11). Mediterranean climates have summer and winter seasons. Summers are warm to hot and very dry, and winters are mild to cool and wet with occasional snow falling in higher altitudes. Mediterranean climates receive around 50 cm of rainfall a year. Vegetation found in this climate type tends to be small and drought resistant. Fruit trees, grapevines, figs, olives and citrus fruits grow well.

Key terms

rainfed: using water that originates from rainfall

food insecurity: when people do not have reliable access to a sufficient quantity of affordable, nutritious food

415

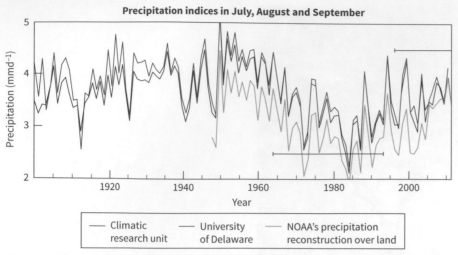

Data was collected between June to September, which is when seasonal rains fall. The three different lines show three different datasets.

Figure 10.10 Annual rainfall averages in the Sahel, 1900–2012.

Figure 10.11 Mediterranean regions have seasonal rainfall, so plants are low growing and drought resistant. In California, this type of vegetation is given the name 'Chaparral'.

The Mediterranean Basin is an area that surrounds the Mediterranean Sea, in between Europe and Africa. It has a Mediterranean climate and low-growing vegetation. The countries of Portugal, Spain, France, Italy, Greece, Turkey, Algeria and Tunisia lie within this area. Tourism brings in a lot of money for these countries, but agriculture is still important. Intensive **viticulture**, or grape cultivation, takes place and this supports the wine, sherry and port industries. Citrus fruits, olives and figs are also cultivated here; their long roots, sparse foliage and waxy-skinned fruits grow well in this type of climate. Pastoral farming is not as common because grass has shallow roots and does not grow well here, so grazing land is scarce. Farming is reliable in this region and food security is high, so large numbers of people can be supported.

Places with Mediterranean climates are facing increasing challenges over time. The biggest threats come from development, as these areas are in warm, coastal locations that are desirable for accommodation and tourism. In addition, climate change is shifting climate belts; a warming of just 2 °C could lead to arid and semi-arid climate belts encroaching on the Mediterranean Basin, resulting in an increasingly dry climate. The Mediterranean Sea is warming at a faster rate than other bodies of water, which is affecting marine life such as sea grass and dolphins. Rainfall levels have been decreasing during the winter months (Figure 10.12), which means that **groundwater aquifers** are not being recharged and therefore less water is available for the growth of crops during the summer months. These trends mean that greater levels of irrigation are required for agriculture to continue at current levels in the Mediterranean Basin.

 Key terms

viticulture: the cultivation of grapevines for wine-making

groundwater aquifers: rocks beneath the ground that store water

parent material: the rock underlying a soil

topography: the shape of the land

profile: a cross-section of soil

 To recap on semi-arid and Mediterranean climatic types, download Worksheet 10.1 from **Cambridge Elevate**.

Zonal soils

Soil takes hundreds of years to form. It consist of weathered rock, organic material, water and air. The type of soil found in an area is dependent on climate, **parent material**, **topography**, living organisms and time. Zonal soils are those that have been forming for long periods of time under the influence of climate and vegetation. They have developed a **profile** with well-defined features. The UN's

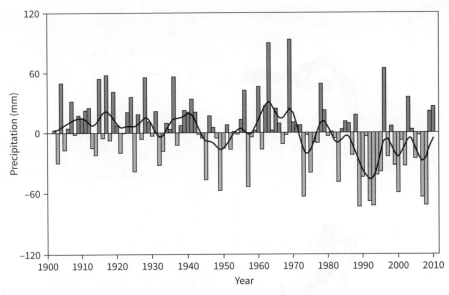

The average rainfall is shown by 0. The bars above show years with higher than average rainfall and the bars below show years with lower than average rainfall.

Figure 10.12 Winter rainfall averages in the Mediterranean Basin, 1902–2010.

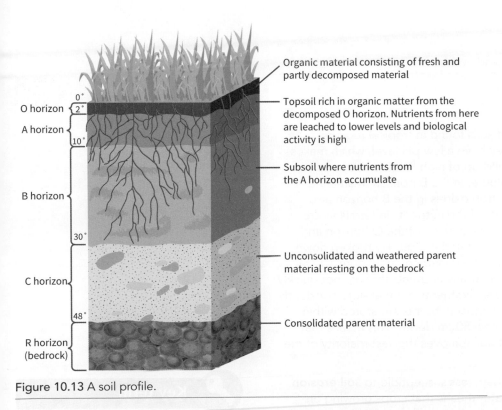

Organic material consisting of fresh and partly decomposed material

Topsoil rich in organic matter from the decomposed O horizon. Nutrients from here are leached to lower levels and biological activity is high

Subsoil where nutrients from the A horizon accumulate

Unconsolidated and weathered parent material resting on the bedrock

Consolidated parent material

O horizon
A horizon
B horizon
C horizon
R horizon (bedrock)

Figure 10.13 A soil profile.

Food and Agricultural Organization (FAO) has a global classification system for zonal soils, based on their characteristics. It identifies soil horizons, or horizontal bands, within soils using the symbols O, A, B, C and R (Figure 10.13).

Ferralsols and podsols

Figure 10.14 shows the distribution of two of the FAO's key zonal soils: ferralsols and podsols. The geographical location of these soils indicates that their formation has primarily been as a result of climate.

Figure 10.14 The global location of ferralsols and podsols.

Ferralsols are deep, intensively weathered soils found in tropical regions. They are often red or yellow in colour. They have a low pH level, which makes them acidic. Low soil pH promotes the build-up of high levels of iron and aluminium compounds (which become soluble) in the B horizon, restricting access to nutrients in the lower soil levels. Iron oxides in the B horizon also contribute to the accumulation of clay. Most of the nutrients in ferralsols are found in the organic material deposited on the surface of the O horizon and within the upper levels of the A horizon. This material is quickly broken down in high temperatures, which gives these layers a darker colour (Figure 10.15). Rainfall in this region is high, which means that any nutrients that are not quickly absorbed by roots are leached out of the soil. Nutrients are therefore constantly cycled between vegetation and the topsoil; most nutrients are stored within the biomass and very few can be found below 50 cm depth. This means that vegetation clearance on the surface of the soil removes the vast majority of the nutrients.

Ferralsols are well-drained, which makes them less susceptible to **soil erosion**. However, their limited capacity to store water means that crops growing on this type of soil are more prone to drought conditions. Shifting cultivation and grazing are common forms of agriculture practised on ferralsols. Permanent cultivation requires high fertiliser use and liming to raise the pH level of the soil. Complete removal of vegetation would interrupt the nutrient cycle, cause a rapid decline in soil fertility and make the soil prone to erosion. Successful use of ferralsols includes the use of permanent vegetation cover, such as black pepper and rubber plantations in Brazil, or mixed cropping to eliminate the potential for bare soil during harvests, such as the use of both tree (coconut and oil palm) and cereal crops in Indonesia.

 Key term

soil erosion: the loss of soil through natural forces such as wind or rain

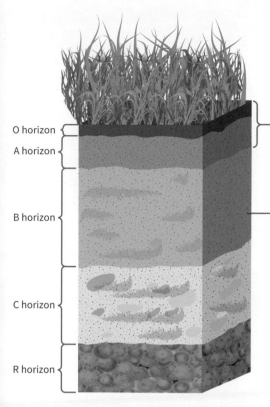

O horizon

A horizon

B horizon

C horizon

R horizon

Most of the nutrients are found in the organic material deposited on the surface of the O horizon and within the upper levels of the A horizon

Low soil pH promotes the build-up of iron and aluminium. Iron oxides contribute to the accumulation of clay. Red or yellow in colour

Figure 10.15 Ferralsols are deep. They are often red and yellow in colour, with dark O and A horizons.

Podsols are mature soils, taking between 3000 and 5000 years to develop. They have clearly defined horizons (Figure 10.16) and are found mainly where precipitation levels are high and temperatures are cool (e.g. the **boreal zone** and **temperate zone**). They are a mix of dark and ash-grey horizons and they sometimes have red iron compounds. They have a low pH level, which makes them acidic. Podsols have dark O and A horizons; evergreen trees grow well in this climate and soil pH and they deposit leaf litter throughout the year. Lower temperatures mean that both the decomposition of litter and the growth of vegetation is slow. Nutrients are therefore stored for long periods of time in the O and A horizons. Beneath the A horizon is an E horizon, or a zone of **eluviation**, where severe leaching has taken place. High acidity makes iron and aluminium compounds soluble. In Podsol soils these accumulate in the B horizon to form a thin hardpan layer, which can be orange in colour. This hardpan hinders drainage and creates waterlogging. The C horizon consists of weathered bedrock with very little organic material.

Podsols are low in nutrients and very acidic, which makes them unsuitable for arable farming. They occur in regions that are cool and wet, so their location is also incompatible with growing crops. Deep ploughing to remove the iron hardpan, along with the continuous use of fertilisers and lime, are measures that can be taken to enable crop cultivation. Many areas with podsolic soils are used for forestry, recreation or extensive grazing.

Key terms

boreal zone: a cold region to the south of the Arctic

temperate zone: a region with mild climate found at mid-latitudes

eluviation: the movement of soil material from upper to lower horizons by the downward movement of water

ACTIVITY 10.3

1 Create annotated diagrams of ferralsols and podsols. Outline the similarities and differences in their characteristics and use.

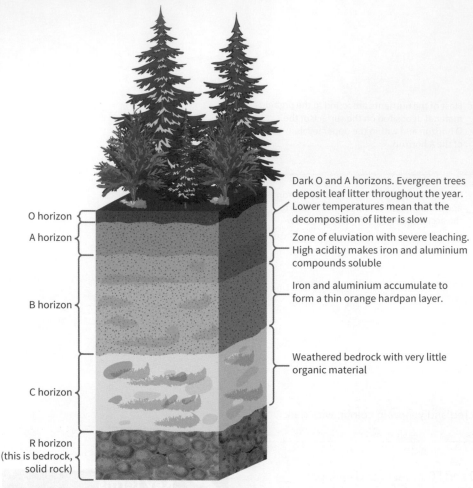

O horizon

A horizon

B horizon

C horizon

R horizon
(this is bedrock,
solid rock)

Dark O and A horizons. Evergreen trees deposit leaf litter throughout the year. Lower temperatures mean that the decomposition of litter is slow

Zone of eluviation with severe leaching. High acidity makes iron and aluminium compounds soluble

Iron and aluminium accumulate to form a thin orange hardpan layer.

Weathered bedrock with very little organic material

Figure 10.16 Podsols have well developed horizons. They often have a bleached E horizon and an orange hardpan within the B horizon.

 Look on **Cambridge Elevate** to find out about the soil in your locality. Go to the UK Soil Observatory website and use the Map Viewer and use the Map Layers function at the top right to find out about the soil type, acidity, moisture and biodiversity for your postcode. Zoom out to get an overview after you have selected each layer (www.cambridge.org/links/gase6101).

 Making connections

Through the study of hot deserts and cold environments, we learn more about climate and soils. The water balance within hot deserts affects soil moisture levels and therefore the capacity to grow food. Desertification further hinders food production and may lead to out-migration. In cold environments, permafrost hinders food security. See Chapter 2 Hot desert systems and landscapes and Chapter 4 Glacial systems and landscapes.

 Physical and human

List the ways that soil type affects human activities.

Soil problems

Soil degradation can occur as a result of erosion, waterlogging, salinisation and structural deterioration. Soil is a finite resource as it takes a long time to form. Agricultural productivity has a direct relationship to soil quality. Any loss or degradation of soil is therefore a key issue for human survival.

Figure 10.17 Gullies formed as a result of soil erosion in Ukraine. Poor land management has led to the erosion of over 500 million tonnes of soil, resulting in a loss of agricultural productivity.

Soil erosion

Soil erosion is the relocation or loss of topsoil through natural forces such as wind and rain, and human activities such as deforestation and **tillage**. Wind erosion is most common in arid and semi-arid regions or places that experience seasonal rainfall. Water erosion is found in areas of high rainfall. Its effects can be spread evenly across the land or concentrated through the formation of **rills** and **gullies** (Figure 10.17). Tillage includes poor land management techniques such as the complete removal of vegetation or excessive cultivation.

Soil erosion is usually a slow process when it occurs naturally, but is more rapid when it is brought about by humans. Accelerated erosion is the most serious form of soil degradation affecting the planet. Western European countries, China and the USA have particularly high levels of soil erosion on account of human activity. Soil erosion is a global problem that affects both agriculture and the natural environment. It reduces crop yields and increases the cost of growing food. This is because it reduces the water retaining capacities of the soil, washes away plant nutrients and creates a lack of uniformity across fields, making it difficult for farmers to rectify any problems.

The most effective way to manage soil erosion is through the provision of surface cover. When vegetation covers the soil, it protects it from the impact of the wind and rain and it absorbs water that would otherwise run off the land. Farmers can help to prevent soil erosion by **conservation cropping**, which avoids disturbing the soil and leaving the land fallow. They can also create structures like contour banks, which restrict the downhill flow of water.

Waterlogging

Waterlogging occurs where there is an excess of water in the soil. It is a natural problem that can be caused by heavy rainfall, high runoff, underlying impermeable subsoil or bedrock, and irrigation. Waterlogged soils are a problem for many countries, even those without an excess of rainfall. Areas that have a high water table (within 2 m depth) are more prone to waterlogging. For example, 90% of Egypt is desert, yet the water table lies only 80 cm below the surface for much of the country, creating waterlogging problems.

Key terms

tillage: land used for cultivation

rills: shallow channels cut into the soil by running water

gullies: deep channels cut into the soil by running water

conservation cropping: the practice of minimising soil disturbance, planting crops early and retaining stubble (stems left over after harvesting)

Waterlogging inhibits agricultural productivity. Air spaces become filled with water, which prevents the plants roots from respiring and causes them to rot. Soil temperatures decrease as wet soil is slow to warm up. Waterlogging therefore causes low yields, crop diseases and total crop failure. The problem is often not apparent on the surface of the soil until crops begin to die. By this point it can be too late for the farmer to remedy the situation.

The use of drainage channels is a good way to reduce waterlogging as they allow the water flow away. Other methods include growing crops that are tolerant to waterlogged soil and planting crops earlier so that they are mature enough to withstand wet conditions.

Salinisation

Salinisation is the accumulation of salt within soil and it has both natural and human causes. Natural causes include low precipitation or high temperatures, leading to high levels of evaporation. When water is drawn up through the soil and evaporated from the surface, it leaves behind any salts that were dissolved within it. Sea level change can also draw saltwater into the soil. Human causes include the **over-abstraction** of groundwater, which can lead to saltwater **saltwater intrusion**. In addition, the use of irrigation in warmer climates can lead to high salinity. Irrigation takes place today on an estimated 200 million hectares of the world's agricultural land. The UN suggests that, as a result of this, around 40 million hectares of land globally are either waterlogged, excessively saline or a combination of both.

Salinity is reducing agricultural productivity in many places. Under normal conditions, osmosis enables water to move from the soil to the plant. Salinisation inhibits osmosis and makes it difficult for plants to absorb soil water. Some plants, such as cotton and sugarbeet, are more tolerant of high salt levels, whereas others, such as peas and beans, are not. In extreme cases, a crust of salt forms on the surface of the soil (Figure 10.18). In less extreme cases, the problem of salinisation is not simple to diagnose as symptoms are not obvious, so the true cost in terms of productivity is unknown. In the San Joaquin Valley of California, irrigation has created problems with soil salinity. This is affecting crop yields, the quality of drinking

Key terms

over-abstraction: taking too much of something, such as too much water from groundwater supplies

saltwater intrusion: the movement of saline water (e.g. seawater) into freshwater supplies

Figure 10.18 Salinisation can lead to the formation of a salt crust. This has happened on the border of Kazakhstan and Uzbekistan, where diverted river water has led to a reduction in size of the Aral Sea.

water and therefore public health. Direct costs are estimated to reach $1 billion to $1.5 billion by 2030, with indirect costs and job losses adding to that figure.

Managing salinisation involves adjusting the amount of water entering and leaving the soil to ensure that any flow of water is in a downwards direction. Lowering the water table can reduce evaporation from the soil and lower soil salinity levels. This can be achieved by increasing the amount of vegetation so that more moisture is absorbed, extracting groundwater supplies and installing drainage systems below the surface of the soil.

Structural deterioration

Soil structure refers to the manner in which soil **aggregates** are arranged. The spaces in between soil particles are called pore spaces and these allow air, water and nutrients to move through the soil. A good soil structure is aggregated, which means the soil is resistant to erosion, and contains lots of pore spaces, which give good aeration and drainage. A poor soil structure has no noticeable aggregation and contains fewer pore spaces.

Soil structure changes over time, depending on weather conditions and land management. A deterioration of soil structure can occur as a result of many factors. Soil compaction, from the use of heavy farm machinery or overgrazing, damages soil structure as it removes pore spaces. Pore spaces can also be removed through prolonged wet conditions, which cause clay particles within the soil to expand, or the use of agrochemicals, which destroy soil biota that would otherwise naturally aerate the soil. In addition, the loss of organic matter, through the annual harvesting of crops, can reduce aggregation and leave soil exposed to the forces of the wind and rain.

The deterioration of soil structure is managed by increasing vegetation cover so that more organic matter is produced. Organic matter causes soil particles to aggregate or combine together, which increases the number of pore spaces. The use of heavy machinery should also be avoided to reduce further compaction.

Strategies to ensure food security

Food security gives access to affordable and nutritious supplies of food. Steps can be taken to ensure food security, focusing on improved food production or the reduction of food waste:

- Irrigation increases crop yields between 100 and 400%. Introducing irrigation into all countries could significantly increase global crop yields and bring food security to many countries.
- The Green Revolution is the transfer of farming methods, such as agrochemicals, mechanisation and high-yield crop varieties, from developed to developing countries. More recently, the 'New' Green Revolution has led to the development of seeds that can tolerate specific conditions such as drought and salinity ingress. This is biotechnology – the genetic modification of plants and selective breeding of animals to produce beneficial characteristics such as higher yields.
- **Aquaculture** is the farming of aquatic plants and animals. Through fish farms (Figure 10.19), species numbers can be controlled and boosted, which is better than traditional fishing techniques where species can be overfished. Sustainable fishing is the use of traditional fishing techniques, but catching fewer fish and avoiding bycatches. This allows marine species to repopulate.
- **Aeroponics** and **hydroponics** are techniques for growing plants without the need for soil. Aeroponics involves plants suspended with their roots hanging

Thinking like a geographer

How might soils be improved or destroyed through hazards such as volcanoes or flooding?

Look on **Cambridge Elevate** for more information on soils and agriculture from the following websites:.

- UK Soil Observatory (www.cambridge.org/links/gase6102)
- Food and Agriculture Organization of the United Nations (www.cambridge.org/links/gase6103).

Key terms

aggregates: particles that bind together

aquaculture: farming the seas

aeroponics: growing plants in air that contains a mist of water and nutrients

hydroponics: growing plants in material other than soil, such as pebbles and sand

Figure 10.19 A fish farm in a fjord (a type of deep-water estuary) in Montenegro. This area is particularly good for the production of mussels, oysters, sea bass and sea bream.

in air saturated with water and nutrients. Hydroponics entails plants grown in materials other than soil (e.g. sand or pebbles), with water and nutrients flowing through them. This could bring food security to areas that have poor soil or high levels of soil erosion.

- Urban farming refers to food grown in cities. Productivity from gardens and allotments can be up to 15 times greater than traditional farms. UPH is improving food security in HICs, MICs and LICs.

- Reducing food waste. This is higher in developed nations, where farms, supermarkets and individual households throw away both edible food and food that has been allowed to go out of date, or food that doesn't conform to the shapes or sizes that customers prefer. Reducing food waste means that more food would be available for consumption.

One country that has begun to tackle the issue of food security is Niger, which is a low income country with an agriculture-based economy. In 2012 a government initiative called 3N (Nigeriens Nourish Nigeriens) led to the use of improved seed varieties, better irrigation and the transfer of surplus milk from the north to the south of the country. Food insecurity has decreased and Niger's GDP growth, which is driven by agriculture, increased from 4.1% in 2013 to 7.1% in 2014.

10.3 Environment, health and well-being

Studies show that a healthy environment improves well-being and quality of life. The characteristics of a healthy environment differ between developed and developing nations.

Global patterns of health, mortality and morbidity

WHO measures global levels of **health** through two measures: healthy life expectancy (HALE) and disability-adjusted life years (DALYs). HALE is a version of life expectancy that measures *healthy* life expectancy. This is the average number of years that the average individual lives in full health. Figure 10.20 shows global HALE data for 2012. The pattern shows how the USA, Europe and Australia have healthy life expectancies of over 70 years. On average,

Key term

health: mentally or physically free from illness or injury

Figure 10.20 Global HALE data, 2012.

Key
HALE at birth
< 50
50–59
60–64
65–69
70–76
Not applicable
Data not available

populations in these countries enjoy long and healthy lives. On the other hand, in sub-Saharan Africa the healthy life expectancy is less than 50 years. Here, people can expect to live only until they are 50 before they suffer health issues.

In 2015, scientists at King's College London developed a test to show how well someone is ageing. The information was intended to match organs to donors and avoid transplanting older organs. The 'healthy ageing' formula showed an extensive range in **biological age** scores of people born during the same year, suggesting that a person's biological age is very different to his or her chronological age. This concept is similar to the theory of DALYs. These measure the gap between current levels of health and ideal health. One DALY is the equivalent to one fewer year of 'healthy' life. DALYs are calculated using the years of life lost (YLL) due to early death and the years lost due to disability (YLD). The formula is:

$$DALY = YLL + YLD$$

Figure 10.21 shows global DALY data for 2012. The pattern is similar to the HALE data, in that more developed countries have lower DALY scores. This means that current levels of health in these countries are closer to 'ideal'.

HALE and DALY measures are determined by **morbidity**, or the prevalence of illness. There are two main types of illness or disease:

- **Non-communicable illnesses** are medical conditions or diseases that are non-infectious or non-transmissible.
- **Communicable (infectious) diseases** are conditions that are passed on from person to person.

Figure 10.22 shows the global pattern of non-communicable illnesses. This data includes diseases such as cancer, diabetes, chronic respiratory and cardiovascular

Key terms

biological age: the age of someone's body, regardless of their chronological age

morbidity: how often a disease and poor health occurs in a specific area; co-morbidity is when people have two or more medical conditions

non-communicable illnesses: medical conditions or diseases that are not infectious or transmissible from person to person

communicable (infectious) diseases: illnesses that can be passed on to others

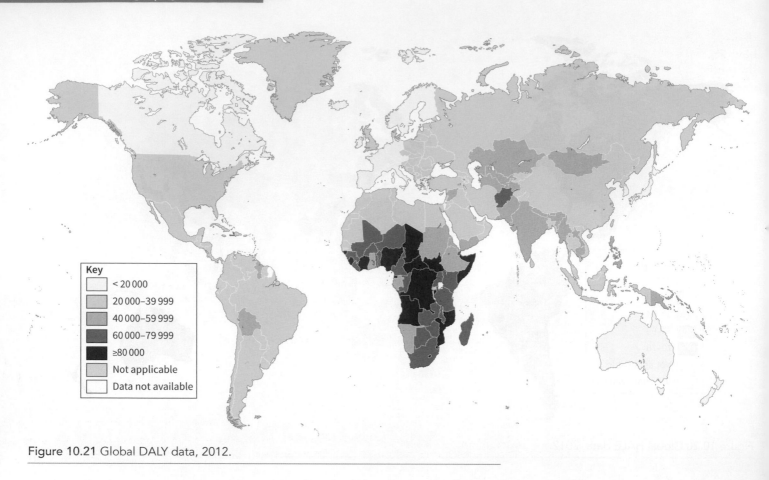

Figure 10.21 Global DALY data, 2012.

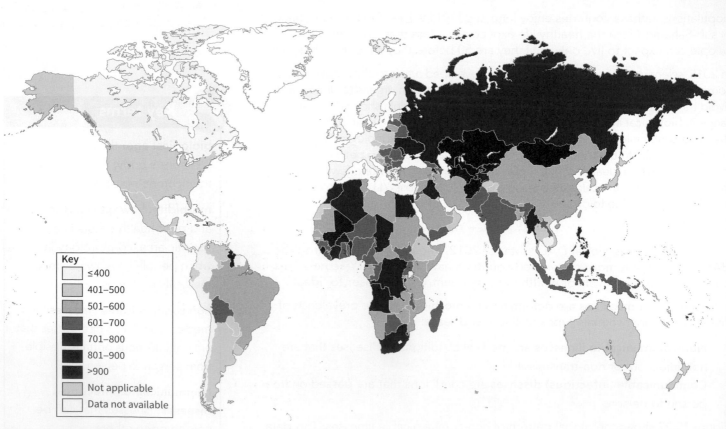

Figure 10.22 Global patterns of non-communicable illness, 2012.

diseases. The global patterns show more economically developed countries have fewer deaths from non-communicable illnesses. This suggests either that those particular diseases are a result of a certain environment or that they are better prevented in certain parts of the world.

Within the non-communicable statistics, several patterns exist:

- Cancers are found throughout the developed and developing world. The highest prevalence of cancer is found in developed countries such as the USA, France and Australia, but the most deaths from cancer are found in countries such as Kazakhstan, Mongolia and Uruguay. Breast, prostate and lung cancers are more common in developed countries, whereas liver, stomach and cervical cancers are more common in developing countries.
- Diabetes is found throughout the world. The highest prevalence is in Middle Eastern countries such as Saudi Arabia and Oman; changing diets throughout the Arab world are leading to an overall increase in diabetes. The most diabetes-related deaths are found in Africa and South America.
- Chronic respiratory diseases are found throughout the world, but are most likely to lead to death in African and south-east Asian countries. Asthma is most prevalent in the USA, Canada, the UK, Australia and Brazil. Other conditions such as chronic obstructive pulmonary disease (COPD) are seeing the biggest increase in emerging economies such as China and India.
- Cardiovascular or heart disease is the number one cause of death globally. Over three-quarters of deaths from heart disease now occur in low and middle-income countries. The highest number of cardiovascular-related deaths take place in north Asian countries.

Figure 10.23 shows the global pattern of infectious illnesses. These statistics include diseases such as HIV/AIDS, tuberculosis (TB) and malaria. The global patterns show a greater probability of infection in tropical regions. This suggests that infectious diseases are more prevalent in warmer environments.

Within the infectious disease statistics, several patterns exist:

- HIV/AIDS has spread throughout the world. The disease is often sexually transmitted and does not correlate with environmental conditions; indeed many studies have mapped the spread of HIV/AIDS via the movement of humans such as African trucking routes. Countries with the greatest numbers of people living with HIV/AIDS are India, Kenya and the USA.
- TB is a serious bacterial infection spread via coughs and sneezes. Prevalence of TB is low in many countries, particularly those who vaccinate children against the infection. However, the risk of developing TB is thought to be between 26 and 31 times greater in those infected with HIV. TB incidence rates are highest across Africa and Southeast Asian countries.
- Malaria is a tropical disease spread by mosquitos infected with the plasmodium parasite. Malaria infections are found at lower latitudes, but the disease is preventable through medication and physical barriers such as mosquito nets. The highest rates of malaria are found in sub-Saharan Africa.

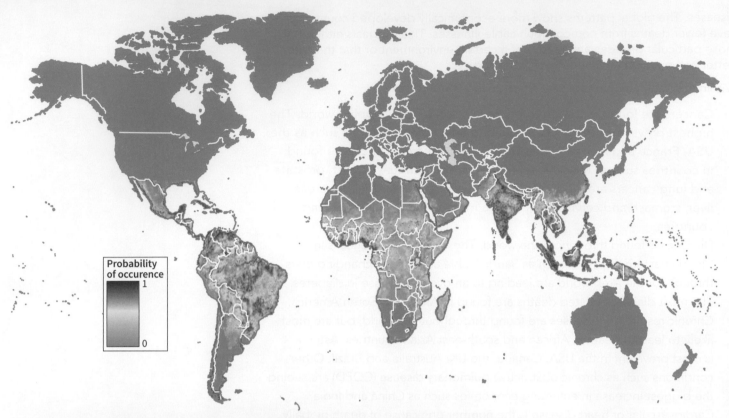

Figure 10.23 Global patterns of infectious disease, 2013.

Look on **Cambridge Elevate** for more details on the communicable and non-communicable patterns of disease from the following websites:

- Global Cancer Incidence (www.cambridge.org/links/gase6104)
- Centers for Disease and Control Prevention (www.cambridge.org/links/gase6105)
- UN AIDS (www.cambridge.org/links/gase6106)
- Health Policy Project (www.cambridge.org/links/gase6107).

Mortality is a measure of death rates. High levels of morbidity do not necessarily lead to high levels of mortality; the relationship between the two is determined by standards of healthcare. Countries providing the best standard of living and healthcare have higher life expectancies. However, people cannot live indefinitely and ageing populations increase death rates. Figures 10.24 and 10.25 illustrate this. Figure 10.24 shows how global life expectancy values are highest in Canada, the USA, western Europe and Australia. Figure 10.25 shows how these countries have higher death rates than parts of Africa and South America.

Mortality is not exclusive to elderly people. In some countries, younger and middle-aged people are just as likely to die. Both infant and maternal mortality rates are much higher in less developed countries, particularly across African nations.

Average annual of years
to be lived by a group of
people born in the same year

- 46–53
- 53–60
- 60–66
- 66–73
- 73–79
- 79–84
- 84–90
- 90–95
- no data

Figure 10.24 Global life expectancy levels, 2014.

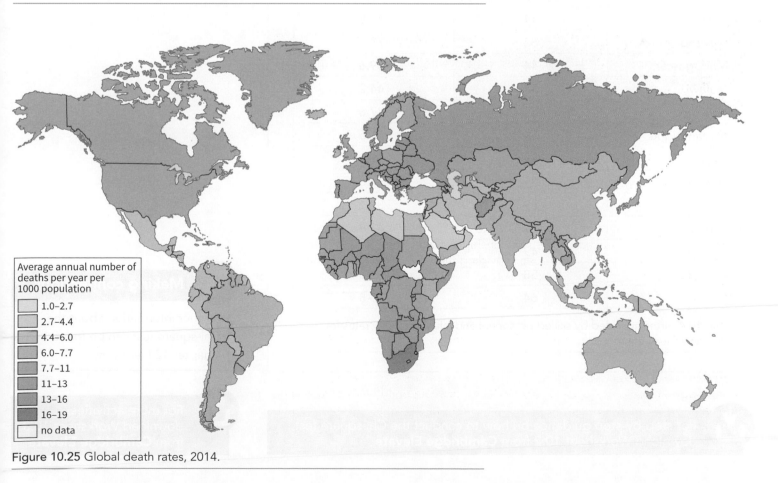

Average annual number of
deaths per year per
1000 population

- 1.0–2.7
- 2.7–4.4
- 4.4–6.0
- 6.0–7.7
- 7.7–11
- 11–13
- 13–16
- 16–19
- no data

Figure 10.25 Global death rates, 2014.

Maths for geographers

We can investigate the relationship between infant mortality and maternity care using the Chi-square test. Use Table 10.4 to work out whether or not there is a statistical relationship between the two variables in selected African countries.

Country	Births attended by skilled personnel (%)	Infant mortality rate (per 1000 births)
Algeria	97	21.6
Angola	49	101.6
Benin	81	56.2
Botswana	99	36.3
Burkina Faso	66	64.1
Burundi	60	54.8
Cameroon	64	60.8
Chad	14	88.5
Eritrea	32	36.1
Ethiopia	10	44.4
Gabon	89	39.1
Gambia	57	49.4
Kenya	44	47.5
Lesotho	62	73.0
Madagascar	44	39.6
Malawi	87	44.2
Mali	57	77.6
Mozambique	54	61.5
Niger	29	59.9
Nigeria	35	74.3
Rwanda	69	37.1
Senegal	51	43.9
Tanzania	49	36.4
Uganda	58	43.8
Zambia	64	55.8

Table 10.4 Births attended by skilled personnel and infant mortality rates for selected African countries.

Making connections

Further information about the Chi-square test can be found in Chapter 12 Fieldwork.

For step-by-step guidance on how to conduct the Chi-square test, download Worksheet 10.2 from **Cambridge Elevate**.

For more activities, download Worksheet 10.3 from **Cambridge Elevate**.

Epidemiological transition

Epidemiological transition refers to changes in the pattern of mortality and morbidity as a country experiences social and economic development. Low income countries have high infant and child mortality rates, caused by infectious diseases, poor living conditions and food insecurity. High income countries have largely eradicated the conditions that lead to high rates of infant and child mortality through social and economic progress, such as education and increased affluence. These countries are more likely to experience degenerative diseases, which are those associated with the process of ageing, or human-induced conditions, e.g. those attributed to smoking or stressful lifestyles.

Environmental variables and diseases

Most diseases occur as a result of either genetic or environmental factors. An estimated 70 to 90% of risk from disease is due to environmental factors. There are a wide range of environmental triggers, including:

- Latitude and climatic conditions. A place's position on the planet determines its climate. Warmer climates closer to the equator encourage diseases such as malaria and dengue fever (a debilitating viral disease transmitted by mosquitoes). Cooler climates closer to the poles may increase the chances of contracting illnesses such as hypothermia and influenza.
- Air pollution. Outdoor pollution comes from industry and transport and indoor pollution can originate from tobacco smoke and the burning of solid fuels. Exposure to air pollution is difficult to avoid and often higher in urban areas. Air pollution caused an estimated 3.7 million premature deaths globally in 2012. Around 88% of these deaths occurred in low and middle income countries. Improving the quality of air can reduce rates of strokes, heart disease, lower respiratory infections, lung cancer and asthma.
- Topography. This refers to the shape of the land, which can determine drainage conditions and levels of oxygen in the air. Poor drainage and unsafe water supplies can cause diseases such as diarrhoea and schistosomiasis (a type of infection caused by parasites that live in freshwater) and cholera. An estimated 2 million people die annually from diarrhoea and around 260 million people globally are thought to be infected with schistosomiasis. The WHO suggest that 4% of the global disease burden could be avoided by improving water quality and hygiene. At higher altitudes, the air contains less oxygen. Mountain sickness and High-altitude pulmonary edema (HAPE) can affect those not acclimatised to such conditions. These illnesses affect the brain and lungs and can be fatal.
- Overcrowding. This is where too many people live in too small a space. Overcrowding can lead to unsanitary living conditions and can enable diseases to spread quickly. This can increase the spread of diseases such as acute respiratory infections and meningitis.

WHO has identified diseases that have the largest health burden (measured in DALYs) as a result of environmental factors. These are shown in Table 10.5.

Disease	Environmental incidence and impact	DALYs per year
Diarrhoea	Unsafe water and poor sanitation and hygiene.	58 million
Lower respiratory infections	Indoor and outdoor air pollution.	37 million
Unintentional injuries other than road traffic injuries	Industrial and workplace conditions.	21 million
Malaria	High temperatures. Poor drainage and land use management. Poor housing conditions and lack of protection from mosquitos.	19 million
Road traffic accidents (RTAs)	High car use. Poor design of transport systems and urban areas.	15 million
Chronic obstructive pulmonary disease (COPD)	Exposure to workplace fumes and dust. Indoor and outdoor air pollution.	12 million
Perinatal conditions	Unsafe water and poor sanitation and hygiene.	11 million

Table 10.5 Diseases with the largest health burden that are caused by environmental factors.

In terms of mortality, many of the same environmentally triggered diseases also cause the highest number of deaths. However, the rank order changes; although environmental factors cause these diseases, the number of fatalities is affected by factors other than the environment. For example, the steroids used to treat COPD can lead to other illnesses, such as osteoporosis and a thinning of the skin. Cardiovascular diseases and diarrhoeal diseases rank the highest in terms of mortality. Lower respiratory infections and cancers also cause high rates of mortality. Although unintentional injuries and RTAs result in high DALYs, they actually have lower mortality rates as sufferers do not always die as a result of their injuries.

For more questions on the health burden, download Worksheet 10.4 from **Cambridge Elevate**.

The global distribution of a biologically transmitted disease: malaria

Malaria infects around 500 million people yearly and causes over 1 million deaths. Globally, around 3.2 billion people are at risk of contracting the disease (Figure 10.26). Tracking cases of malaria can be difficult; estimates suggest that as few as 14% of global malaria cases are detected in some years. Around 90% of deaths occur in Africa, where an estimated one child death per minute occurs through malaria, although Asia, Latin America and the Middle East also experience the disease.

Malaria is an infectious disease that is both preventable and curable. It is biologically transmitted by *Plasmodium* parasites carried by mosquitos, or 'malaria vectors'. Humans contract malaria through the bite of infected mosquitos (Figure 10.27), which often happens at night. The spread of the disease depends on environmental and human factors.

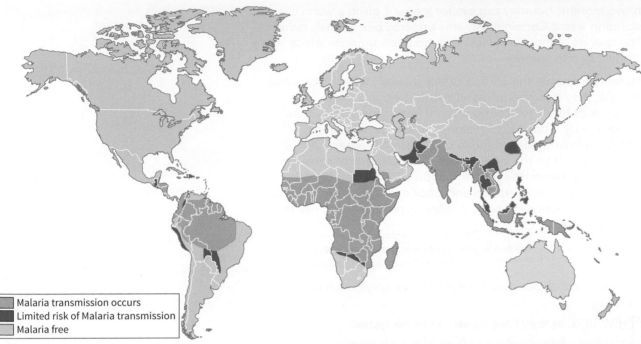

Malaria transmission occurs
Limited risk of Malaria transmission
Malaria free

Figure 10.26 Areas most at risk from malaria.

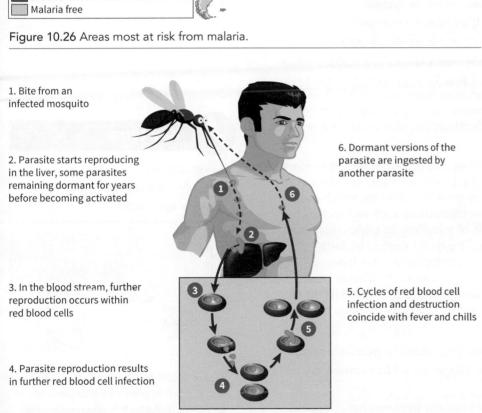

1. Bite from an infected mosquito

2. Parasite starts reproducing in the liver, some parasites remaining dormant for years before becoming activated

3. In the blood stream, further reproduction occurs within red blood cells

4. Parasite reproduction results in further red blood cell infection

5. Cycles of red blood cell infection and destruction coincide with fever and chills

6. Dormant versions of the parasite are ingested by another parasite

Figure 10.27 The spread of malaria from mosquitos to humans.

Malaria is primarily an environmentally triggered infection. The local natural environment is responsible for the existence of the mosquito and the *Plasmodium* parasite. Mosquitos breed in warm, shallow water such as puddles, rice fields and even animal footprints. This means that malaria is widespread in tropical and subtropical regions, where the sun is strong enough to heat surface water. Transmission can be seasonal, occurring during or after rainy seasons. The spread of malaria is greatest where mosquitos are able to live longer. Mosquitos often die within two months, but they can live for longer if given a warm climate with plenty of standing water. Certain mosquitos prefer to bite animals rather than humans. The species of mosquito most commonly occurring in Africa lives a long time and prefers to bite humans.

Socio-economic factors enable the spread of the disease. When mosquitos bite infected people, they become infected themselves and spread the disease on to other people. A greater number of infections occur where people have low immunity. This makes malaria more prevalent within endemic areas that are holiday destinations or places where people migrate to. People exposed to the disease over long periods of time often develop partial immunity, hence the high infection rates among children. Overcrowding, high rates of urbanisation and poor quality housing all enable the rapid spread of the infection. Specific groups of people are at risk from malaria infection, including:

- young children living in affected areas who have not yet developed immunity
- pregnant women; malaria causes high rates of miscarriage, maternal death and low birth weight
- people with HIV/AIDS, as they have weaker immune systems
- travellers from malaria-free countries as they have no immunity
- returning immigrants who have been living in non-endemic areas.

Malaria is an acute febrile illness, which means that it results in a sudden onset of fever. Symptoms usually appear between 7 and 15 days after the mosquito bite. Symptoms can initially be mild and difficult to diagnose, such as headache and vomiting. However, the disease can become very severe within just 24 hours and often leads to death. **Asymptomatic infections** can also occur as a result of people developing partial immunity.

Malaria has implications for individuals, families and governments. It hinders economic development and has a direct impact on health and well-being. People buy mosquito nets and medication to treat the disease, which means that they have less money to spend on other necessities such as food and education. Additional costs occur as a result of travelling to clinics, lost work and school days and the expense of burials. The direct cost of malaria – through prevention, cure and loss of national productivity – has been estimated at $12 billion per year. The indirect costs in terms of economic development, health and well-being are much greater and more difficult to calculate. For this reason, health bodies, charities and governments have taken steps to reduce infections:

- Prevention: anti-malarial medicines can be prescribed to people visiting affected areas temporarily (Figure 10.28). Diagnosis and treatment prevents deaths and helps reduce transmission.
- Management: controlling vectors reduces malaria transmission. Sleeping beneath insecticide-treated mosquito nets (ITNs) or indoor residual insecticide (IRS) spraying can both be effective.
- Eradication: malaria elimination is achieved when cases of malaria have been reduced to zero. Eradication occurs when the reduction of cases to zero becomes permanent. Although malaria cases are decreasing among 55 countries, only 4 countries have eliminated the disease (the UAE, Morocco, Turkmenistan and Armenia).

Key term

asymptomatic infections: when an infection is present but there are no symptoms

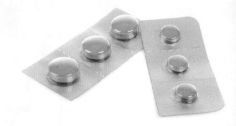

Figure 10.28 Malarone is one form of medication prescribed to prevent and treat malaria. It is taken over three consecutive days to kill parasites in the body.

ACTIVITY 10.4

1   For an infectious disease that you have studied, outline the environmental triggers and the impacts on health and well-being.

The global distribution of a non-communicable disease: lung cancer

There are over 200 recognised types of cancer, which is also known as malignant tumours and neoplasms. The disease is caused by the presence of abnormal cells within any part of the body. These cells divide and grow in an uncontrolled manner and some are able to spread to other parts of the body. Cancer can be fatal, but research has led to new medication that can treat the disease. Different types of cancer have different prevalence and survival rates.

Lung cancer is amongst the five most common cancers in men and women, making up 13% of all cancers diagnosed. The diseases causes an estimated 1.59–1.82 million deaths globally. Lung cancer largely affects wealthier and industrialising nations (Figure 10.29). Mortality rates vary between countries, but are higher than for other types of cancer.

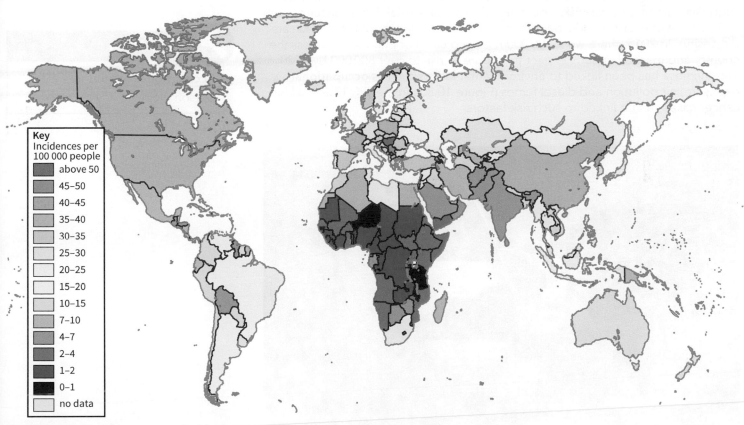

Key
Incidences per 100 000 people
- above 50
- 45–50
- 40–45
- 35–40
- 30–35
- 25–30
- 20–25
- 15–20
- 10–15
- 7–10
- 4–7
- 2–4
- 1–2
- 0–1
- no data

Figure 10.29 Global lung cancer incidence.

The most important risk factor for lung cancer is tobacco, which causes an estimated 70% of deaths from all cancers. This is a lifestyle-related factor as tobacco is inhaled through smoking, either directly or through being in the company of smokers. However, the percentage of adults smoking is higher for many LICs than

HICs. In Sierra Leone, 55% of adults smoke, yet lung cancer incidences are low at 1.52 cases per 100 000 people. In the USA, 21% of adults smoke, yet lung cancer incidences are high at 38.35 cases per 100 000 people. This is because ageing is a key factor for the development of cancer. The ability of the body to repair cells becomes less effective as a person ages. In the UK, six out of every ten cases of lung cancer occur in people aged 70 or above. The life expectancy in Sierra Leone is only around 45 years, meaning that people do not live long enough to develop the disease. This means that lung cancer also has economic causes as lower life expectancies in LICs prevent higher rates of prevalence.

Funding for cancer research has also impacted upon the morbidity and mortality rates for lung cancer. In the UK funding for breast cancer research is far higher than for lung cancer and yet survival rates for breast cancer are much better than for lung cancer. This is due in part to the nature of the illness; lung cancer sufferers are often too ill to participate in medical trials. However, it is also about how well different cancer charities raise funds and are perceived by the public. An example of this is the Pink Ribbon Foundation, which creates successful high profile campaigns that raise public awareness and therefore money.

Lung cancer has also been linked to the physical environment. Some studies have shown how migrants moving from countries with low prevalence rates to countries with high prevalence rates soon develop the same risk level. This suggests that lung cancer risks could also be environmental. Lung cancer occurs in 36.07 out of every 100 000 people in China and incidences of the disease are increasing. In 2015, there were 700 000 reported cases of the disease across the country and medical experts expect this figure to rise to over 800 000 by 2020. This increase has been linked to environmental factors such as **occupational** exposure, air pollution and diesel fumes (Figure 10.30). In the UK, 13% of all lung cancer cases can be linked to such risk factors.

Key term

occupational: related to a person's job

Figure 10.30 Diesel fumes and exposure to air pollution has been linked to increased lung cancer prevalence in China.

Lung cancer has low survival rates, with older people having the lowest chances of survival. In the UK fewer than 10% of sufferers live for more than five years. Many of these will have significantly reduced lung capacity, meaning that they require extra oxygen from portable tanks. Such measures are restrictive to a person's **mobility**. Those who survive for longer are also ten-times more likely to develop another form of cancer. Only 1% of sufferers go on to survive long-term and in good health. Experts think that this is due to late diagnosis; over 67% of cases in the UK are diagnosed at a late stage.

Lung cancer is treated through **radiotherapy, chemotherapy** or surgery to remove parts of the lung. In some cases, an entire lung may be removed. Advances in **keyhole surgery** have now made this process less intrusive. As survival rates are so low, prevention of the disease is better than cure. Governments have used mitigation strategies to reduce rates of lung cancer. The reduction of tobacco inhalation can be achieved through prohibiting smoking in public areas, banning tobacco advertising and funding education projects and 'stop smoking' clinics. Cleaner air can be achieved through tighter legislation governing industry and incentives, such as lower taxation on cleaner road vehicles.

Combating disease

International agencies and non-governmental organisations (NGOs) play a key role in promoting health and combating disease at a global scale. Many international agencies and NGOs work to improve standards of living, health and well-being.

- The Department for International Development (DFID) is a UK government agency that works to end extreme poverty. It operates in 28 countries across Africa, Asia and the Middle East and carries out ongoing projects and responds to humanitarian emergencies. One example of the DFID's work can be seen in Nepal, where in March 2016 £4.5 million was used to fund water and sanitation projects in earthquake-affected parts of the country.

- The World Health Organisation (WHO) is an agency of the United Nations that works to improve public health levels globally. The WHO was established in 1948 and is funded by its member states. The WHO gather and publish health statistics and work in individual countries to improve conditions. One example of the WHO's work is in March 2016, where a vaccination project was funded to reduce a yellow fever outbreak in Angola.

- The Bill & Melinda Gates Foundation is an NGO set up in 2000. Bill Gates was the co-founder of Microsoft. The couple use money that they earned from the Microsoft venture to fund projects that enhance global levels of health care and reduce global poverty. The foundation has provided additional funding for many projects. One example is the Alliance for a Green Revolution in Africa (AGRA), where in 2015 $264.5 million was given towards improving seeds and soil for African farmers, so that rural families can remain healthy and prosperous.

Key terms

mobility: the ability to move freely

radiotherapy: a treatment for cancer that uses X-rays or similar forms of radiation

chemotherapy: a treatment for cancer that uses chemicals or drugs that destroy malignant cells

keyhole surgery: operations carried out through small incisions, using special fibre optic instruments

10.4 The relationship between place and health

Those living in regions affected by extreme poverty, conflict or natural disasters understand the relationship between place and health. Deprivation, war, flooding, tsunamis and earthquakes have obvious detrimental effects on individuals and newspapers often report such impacts. The relationship between place and well-being is perhaps less obvious in wealthier, more stable parts of the world. Here, we look at the value of place in terms of sustainability, environmental quality, access to green spaces and architecture.

Green spaces

Research suggests that the value of green spaces is greater than that of pay rises or promotions. Access to permanent areas of green space has long-term benefits to public health, it increases standards in education and it reduces the burden on national health services. The sustainable nature of these benefits was even found to last longer than large wins on the lottery.

Green spaces improve schoolchildren's mental development, study finds

Research on primary school children in Barcelona suggests a boost in short-term memory from nearby vegetation, due in part to reduction in traffic pollution.

The researchers found that each degree of increase in surrounding greenness led to a 5% improvement in the development of short-term, or working,

memory over one year. It also improved the progress of 'superior working memory' – the ability to update memories with changing information – by 6%, and reduced inattentiveness. Analysis suggested that carbon from traffic fumes might account for up to 65% of the trend.

Look on **Cambridge Elevate** to read the article in full from the *Guardian* (www.cambridge.org/links/gase6108).

The UK National Ecosystem Assessment values the health benefits of living close to green spaces to be up to £300 per person per year. The UK aims to achieve the new UN **sustainable development goals (SDGs)**. As such, the country should value human and environmental well-being. An improved environment leads to a healthier population that is more able to work and less likely to need expensive healthcare. A UK government white paper published in 2011 was the first of its kind to give communities the power to designate protected green spaces. Following on from this, the government carried out research into the benefits of green spaces to the city of London. They found that people with access to **green infrastructure** had better mental and physical health and also felt part of a stronger society (Figure 10.31).

Key terms

sustainable development goals (SDGs): UN goals that came into force at the end of 2015; they are international development targets to be achieved by 2030

green infrastructure: a network of green spaces, both rural and urban, that are essential to the well-being and quality of life of communities

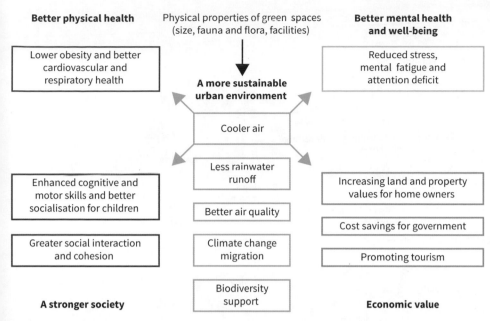

Figure 10.31 The benefits provided by access to green spaces.

Table 10.6 shows the percentage of green spaces for selected world cities. Singapore is the greenest world city and London ranks third place. Almost 4450 ha of public green spaces are found in and around London, containing an estimated 2800 trees (Figure 10.32). Around 200 of the green spaces are classed as 'small' spaces within the city. A further 14 are classed as 'large' spaces around the edge of the city.

Some green spaces within London were planned and others happened as a result of events such as the Great Fire of London (1666) and the Blitz (1940s). Table 10.7 shows the benefits of these green spaces to Londoners. In summary:

- The air is cooler as a result of shade.
- Runoff is lower, reducing flood risk.
- The air quality is better through the absorption of pollutants.
- Obesity, heart and lung health issues are reduced.
- The aesthetic impact of green spaces has a positive psychosomatic effect and reduces stress, lowers blood pressure, and alleviates cognitive disorders.
- Spaces allow children to play and social interaction among adults to take place. This also reduces obesity and stress levels.
- The government saves money through reduced need for healthcare facilities.

City	%
Singapore	47.0
Sydney	46.0
London	38.4
Johannesburg-Gauteng	24.0
Berlin	14.4
New York	14.0
Paris	9.4
Tokyo	3.44
Shanghai	2.6
Mumbai	2.5
Istanbul	1.5

Table 10.6 The percentage of green space found in selected world cities, 2012.

The Bankside Open Spaces Trust

Southwark is a borough located in central London. It is the 41st most deprived local authority in England and the 12th most deprived borough in London. Almost one-third of children live in poverty. These statistics suggest that a high percentage of residents in Southwark are likely to experience mental health issues, type 2 diabetes and heart failure. The area is densely populated and ethnically diverse; over 30% of residents were born outside the EU and over 300 languages are spoken. An inability to communicate in English is a recognised barrier to accessing health care in the UK. There is a high turnover of residents in Southwark, many of whom are young. Most residents are economically active, although women and black and minority ethnic groups have the highest rates

Figure 10.32 London's green open spaces house around 2800 trees.

	Evidence		Impact			
	Large spaces	Small spaces	City of London residents and workers	City of London businesses	London residents and workers	London businesses
Air cooling	✓✓✓				✓✓✓	
Reducing rainwater runoff	✓✓	✓✓	✓✓	✓✓	✓✓	✓✓
Pollutant absorption	✓✓	✓✓	✓✓		✓✓	
Space for exercise	✓✓		✓		✓✓	
Better air quality	✓✓		✓		✓✓	
Aesthetic experience/'restorative' power	✓✓	✓✓	✓✓		✓✓	
Space for play and challenge (children)	✓✓				✓✓	
Space for social interaction and meeting	✓	✓			✓	
Cost saving for government (capture of environment and health benefits)	✓	✓				

Table 10.7 The benefits of access to green spaces in London.

of unemployment. Poor quality housing and homelessness create many health issues and Southwark Council aims to build more affordable housing to alleviate this situation.

Research carried out by Guy's and St Thomas' Charity found that many residents in Southwark do not prioritise their health. The survey highlighted an unmet need in relation to mental health, which was leading to further health issues. Southwark has a 're-ablement service', which offers free council services to help people to regain skills and confidence, particularly following a period of illness or admission to hospital. Services can be put in place for a period of around 6 weeks and studies have found that this form of intervention can help to reverse negative attitudes towards health and prevent further illness.

The Bankside Open Spaces Trust (BOST) is a charity run with the help of local people in the north of Southwark. BOST is improving access to open spaces through a network of public parks and community gardens. Some of BOST's key achievements are as follows:

- It holds sports days, open days, fundraising activities, planting events, music and festive entertainment and flower and vegetable shows. These help to maintain the quality of the environment and bring the community together.
- BOST works with local primary and secondary schools and has set up family food-growing clubs. These improve access to healthy food and encourage healthy eating.
- It carries out training and offers work experience placements. Many have been given to homeless people or those who have suffered severe mental health issues. This helps vulnerable people to get back into work.
- BOST has created 'Edible Bankside', a food-growing project that aims to improve aspects of diet, health, motivation, employability and social inclusion for at least 350 residents.

'I've met so many people here today, it's been amazing! I'm so happy that I came. My son really loved planting the vegetables, I'm really up for gardening.'

ACTIVITY 10.5

1 Explain three ways that green spaces improve public health.

Look on **Cambridge Elevate** to find more about the Bankside Open Spaces Trust. Outline how and why the charity is helping to improve levels of health in Southwark (www.cambridge.org/links/gase6109).

10.5 Population change

On a national, regional or local scale, population change happens through a combination of natural processes and the effects of migration.

Natural change

Several factors interrelate to bring about natural changes in population levels. Differences in birth and death rates lead to a **natural increase** or **natural decrease**. Natural increase is calculated by subtracting the death rate from the birth rate. It is shown as an increase or decrease in the number of people per thousand. Many different factors lead to changes in birth and death rates, including:

- Health: access to safe, clean water and sanitation results in lower death rates. The spread of infectious diseases and poor living conditions lead to higher death rates.
- Education: health education reduces death rates, whereas sex education and family planning can reduce birth rates. Higher levels of education among women leads to more women in the workplace, which can result in fewer births.

Key terms

natural increase: when births are higher than deaths and the population grows

natural decrease: when deaths are higher than births and the population gets smaller

- Social provision: public sewerage systems, piped water and care for the elderly are examples of social provision that decrease death rates. The availability of maternity services and childcare has implications for birth and infant mortality rates.
- Cultural preferences: in some cultures, having many children is encouraged. Certain cultures and religions forbid contraception and abortion. In both instances, fertility rates increase, but death rates may also increase through the incidental spread of sexually transmitted infections (STIs).
- Political factors: some governments recognise the need to manage population levels and either incentivise or discourage pregnancy. The Japanese government has introduced 'family care leave' laws for couples with children and have funded match-making events in an attempt to improve fertility rates. During times of conflict, birth rates often fall and death rates often increase.
- Environmental factors: natural disasters, climate, the availability of resources and levels of pollution lead to changes in birth and death rates. Age UK estimates that 28000 elderly people in the UK die yearly as a result of cold weather.

The demographic transition model

The demographic transition model (DTM) shows natural changes to populations (Figure 10.33). It provides an insight into how birth rates, death rates and total population change over time. There are five stages to the model and it is assumed that all countries will move through the model as they become more developed.

The stages of the DTM

The five stages of the DTM are as follows.

Stage 1: High stationary

This stage has high birth and death rates and a stable but low population.

- High birth rates are due to a lack of contraception and family planning. High infant mortality also encourages the birth of more children.
- High death rates are due to poor levels of hygiene or a lack of health facilities. Disease and famine may be commonplace.

Investigate

The UK birth rate grew from 10.88 per thousand in 2004 to 12.22 per thousand in 2014. Investigate the causes of this increase. Which localities, regions or social groupings saw the largest increases in births? What will be the implications of these changes? Visit the UK Data Explorer website to find out more.

Look on **Cambridge Elevate** for more information on the UK Data Explorer website (www.cambridge.org/ links/gase6110).

Making connections

An increase in population leads to an increase in the demand for water. Which strategies can be put in place to manage water consumption and improve water security? See section 11.3, Water security.

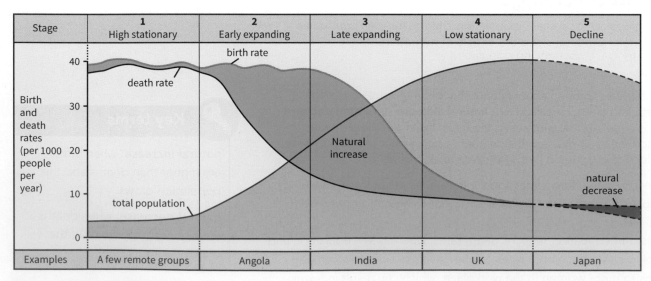

Figure 10.33 The demographic transition model.

Stage 2: Early expanding

This stage has a high birth rate and a declining death rate. The population expands rapidly.

- Birth rates remain high.
- Death rates begin to fall. This is due to a combination of factors such as improved healthcare, better hygiene and better nutrition.

Stage 3: Late expanding

This stage has a falling birth rate and low death rate. The expansion of the population slows down.

- Lower birth rates are the result of changing socio-economic conditions. Greater numbers of women in the workplace reduce fertility rates, family planning enables couples to choose how many children to have, a higher cost of living makes rearing children more expensive and changing cultures and fashions create a preference for smaller families.
- Death rates continue to fall.

Stage 4: Low stationary

This stage has low birth and death rates. Population levels are stable but high.

Stage 5: Decline

This stage is characterised by birth rates that fall lower than death rates. This causes population decline.

- Birth rates fall even lower as a result of higher aspirations, the financial independence of women and a social acceptance of childless couples.
- Death rates remain the same or may even increase slightly due to an ageing population.

The validity of the DTM

The DTM has provided a useful insight into the way that the population of a country changes over time. The timescales are not fixed and so there is no set time that a country is expected to take in order to pass through a stage. It is easy to understand and it allows comparisons to be made between countries. There are, however, some limitations to the DTM:

- The fifth stage is a new addition. The original model was created at a time when no country was experiencing population decline. Many countries such as Japan, France and Germany now fit into stage 5.
- Countries pass through the stages at different speeds and this is not reflected in the model. Some countries have taken political decisions to manage their population, for example the 'one-child policy' reduced birth rates in China from 33.43 to 18.21 births per 1000 in just ten years.
- Knowledge about vaccinations and disease prevention can be passed on, which speeds up the reduction in death rates in some countries. It took around 200 years for death rates in Sweden to fall, whereas those in Mexico have fallen in around 70 years (Figure 10.34).
- The model assumes that countries will only pass through the DTM in one direction. However, it is possible for countries to regress. In 2014 the population of Syria decreased by about 9.73% compared with the previous year. Conflict in the country led to an estimated death toll in excess of 220 000

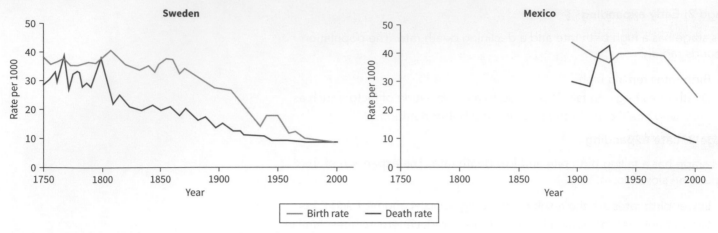

Figure 10.34 Demographic transition: Sweden and Mexico.

people, with an estimated 64.7% of people pushed into extreme poverty, unable to access sufficient food. The prevalence of diseases such as HIV/AIDS has also increased death rates and reduced birth rates in some countries.

- The model only includes natural changes to a population. It does not consider migrational change and so it is not truly representative of a country's population. The UK has experienced significant in-migration as a result of the expansion of EU borders since 2004. This has increased both the total population and birth rates, as migrants have a higher fertility rate than the existing population.

- The model does not consider the physical environment of a country and the availability of resources. The Sahel is an arid region encompassing 22 countries in northern Africa (Figure 10.35). The population of this region grew from 367 million to 471 million people between 2000 and 2010. The Sahel's capacity to produce food is not keeping pace with this rapid population growth. Global warming could also exacerbate this situation and countries could see future rises in death rates.

Figure 10.35 The Sahel may not be able to support the growing number of people who live there.

Physical and human

Climate is one physical factor that limits the use of the DTM. What other physical factors may affect a country's transition through the five stages?

ACTIVITY 10.6

1   Table 10.8 shows birth and death rates for Bangladesh between 1980 and 2020. The 2020 data is based on UN and World Bank estimates.
    a   Calculate the natural increase in Bangladesh for 1980, 2000 and 2020.
    b   State which stages of the DTM Bangladesh fits into in 1980 and in 2020.
    c   Suggest reasons for the changes in birth and death rates in Bangladesh.

	1980	1990	2000	2010	2020 (est.)
Birth rate per 1000	43.09	35.12	27.03	20.93	18.0
Death rate per 1000	13.76	10.07	7.24	5.9	5.4

Table 10.8 Birth and death rates for Bangladesh, 1980–2020.

2   Using Figure 10.33:
    a   Give two ways that the DTM could be useful for governments to plan for future demographic changes.
    b   Explain two limitations of the DTM.

The demographic dividend

The demographic dividend shows how sustainable populations are, in terms of their ability to generate income and develop economically.

As a country passes through Stage 3 of the DTM, fertility rates fall. The dependency ratio falls, as there are more workers in relation to dependents, and so income **per capita** grows. As less money is spent on dependents, more money is available to invest in economic development and welfare, such as education and healthcare. As personal income increases, individuals save and invest money and productivity increases. This positive change is referred to as the first **demographic dividend** and it has been identified as a key reason why many Asian economies grew in the latter part of the 20th century.

During Stage 4 of the DTM, the lower birth rates result in a smaller workforce. Improved economic development and welfare has led to a longer life expectancy. There are now more elderly dependants and so income per capita slows down. This is a negative change.

A second dividend is then possible. An ageing population demands that people work later in life and then still have extended retirements. During their long working life, they may have accumulated assets, such as property, pensions or investments (Figure 10.36). They use these assets to support their retirement, which increases the national income of that country.

In summary, the first dividend creates greater national wealth, and the second transforms that wealth into personal assets and therefore sustainable development. The theory of demographic dividend also depends on the system

Key terms

per capita: per person

demographic dividend: the economic benefit created by the population of a country

Figure 10.36 Older people spending their assets creates a second demographic dividend.

of governance and the ability to implement effective policies. For example, in 2012 the UK government introduced a new 'workplace pension'. Every employer with at least one member of staff must now provide a private pension to top up the state pension that pensioners receive. Employees are automatically enrolled onto the workplace pension scheme. The government hopes that it will encourage people to save more for their retirement, thus increasing the size of the second dividend.

Migration change

The relationship between birth and death rates is not the only factor that affects population: migration, or the movement of people, must also be considered. People are motivated to move for different reasons. **Economic migrants** travel to improve their economic prospects. **Asylum seekers** leave their country or place of origin through fear of conflict or persecution. Asylum seekers become **refugees** once they have residency in another country, e.g. In the UK, an asylum seeker becomes a refugee when the government officially accepts their claim for residency. Immigration and emigration occur as a result of push factors and pull factors:

* Environmental factors: the **carrying capacity** of an environment refers to the availability of food, water and resources. This determines the number of people who can live in a particular location. Climate change is impacting on carrying capacities. The Intergovernmental Panel on Climate Change (IPCC) suggests that the greatest impact on food security will be felt by the middle of this century. When this point is reached, people will move to access new resources. Natural disasters can lead to migration. In 2012, 32.4 million people worldwide were displaced as a result of natural disasters (Figure 10.37). Hurricane Sandy led to 343 000 people moving away from Cuba to find safer places. Some migrants will return to their country of origin, but others remain at their destination.

Key terms

economic migrant: someone moving to find work and earn money

asylum seeker: someone applying for permission to settle in another country through fear for their safety in their own country

refugee: someone who has settled in another country through fear for their safety in their own country

carrying capacity: the number of people that a region or country can sustainably support

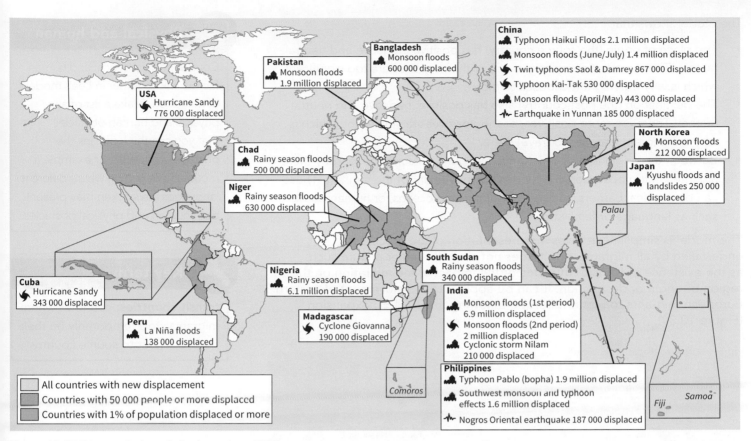

Figure 10.37 Disaster-induced displacement, 2012.

- Socio-economic factors: human causes of migration are usually socio-economic in nature. People move to find employment, education, a better quality of life or to escape political persecution or war. In 2015 hundreds of thousands of Rohingya people from Myanmar (Burma) fled the country to escape violence and political persecution. The government failed to recognise the ethnic group as legal citizens of the country and so many moved to countries such as Thailand, Indonesia and Malaysia.

Processes of migration

Push and pull factors are not the only consideration for migrants. **Intervening obstacles** are the physical and human barriers that make it more difficult for migrants to move. There are many models that exist that attempt to make sense of the migration process. A good example is Lee's model of migration (Figure 10.38).

Key term

intervening obstacles: physical or human barriers that hinder the movement of migrants

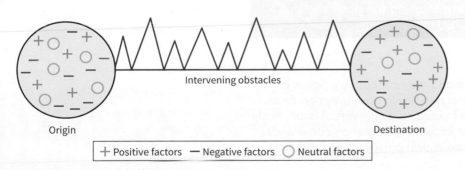

Figure 10.38 Lee's model of migration.

The model shows that:

- The place of origin (the source country) has positive, negative and neutral factors. There are too many negatives, or the negatives are too significant, which is why the migrant chooses to move.
- The destination (the host country) also has positive, negative and neutral factors. There are more positives, or the positives are significant, which is why the migrant chooses to travel there.
- Between the origin and destination is the journey. Along the journey there are intervening obstacles that hinder the movement of the migrant. These can be physical barriers, such as mountains and oceans, or human barriers, such as language or family ties.

The model is simplistic; it gives a representation of the process undertaken by all migrants, but it does not show the wider picture such as the existence of **transit countries** or the impact of the migration on the region of origin or destination. It can be applied to the movement of eastern European migrants to western Europe following the 2004 EU expansion (Figure 10.39).

Consider how physical and human factors link together in Lee's model of migration. Make a list of any physical and human obstacles that you can think of. Link the obstacles together, for example a mountainous region where different languages are spoken may present both human and physical obstacles.

Key term

transit countries: countries where migrants stop temporarily on their way from host to source country

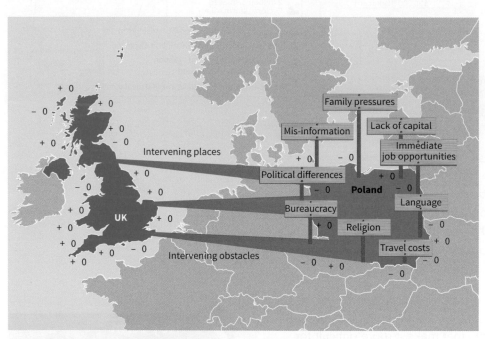

Figure 10.39 Lee's model of migration applied to EU migration.

 Watch a video on **Cambridge Elevate** showing the push and pull factors and intervening obstacles to EU migration.

The implications of migration

Migration always has an impact on the source and the host country. Some of these impacts are positive, some negative, and people do not always agree on which is which. In recent years, migration has become a controversial issue, hotly debated within the news and parliament. The impacts of migration come under several broad headings. Table 10.9 offers some critical perspectives on these impacts.

	Impacts on origin or source country	Impacts on destination or host country
Demographic	Population density and birth rates fall as young, economically active migrants move to improve their quality of life. Issues associated with overpopulation are resolved, although the potential for an ageing population is increased.	An influx of young, economically active migrants increases birth rates and decreases the potential for an ageing population. Retirement migration increases the proportion of elderly residents in some places.
Social	**Remittance payments** help to fund education and improvements to living standards. Returning migrants bring new ideas and generate social change. Family structures can break down and the **dependency ratio** can increase as elderly people become left behind. A loss of culture can be experienced and returning migrants may struggle to resettle and bring unwanted changes home with them.	Multicultural societies can encourage tolerance, add to the vibrancy of urban life, create a fusion of ideas and extend cultural experiences (e.g. the introduction of new languages helps people learn new skills). Local cultures can become diluted as new migrants bring their own cultures with them. Ghettoised ethnic areas encourage segregation and intolerance. Local services may struggle to deal with the influx of people or new languages. Pressure over jobs and social housing can create friction.
Economic	Remittances are sent home and migrants learn new skills for the workplace. Pressure on resources, such as food, is reduced. The loss of workers and the **'brain drain'** reduces the capacity for economic development. Fewer private companies are attracted to the country, increasing the dependency on government and leading to higher taxation.	Migrants fill gaps in the workplace and take up less desirable jobs. This keeps agriculture and food processing prices low, but as a result migrants have low wages and often live in poor conditions. An abundance of labour leads to economic development. New services and housing requirements create jobs and wealth. An overdependence on migrant labour may drive down wages and lead to unemployment for local people. Remittance payments allow money to leak out of the country. Extra pressure on schools, hospitals and other public services costs money.
Environmental	Environmental pressure is reduced as fewer people take resources from the environment. Reduced economic development may put the environment at risk as new initiatives focus on generating income.	Environmental pressure is increased as more people take resources from the environment and new houses are built on greenfield sites. Additional money generated through private companies and taxation is available to fund environmental projects.

Key terms

remittance payments: money that migrants send back home to support their families

dependency ratio: a measure showing the number of people who are too young (aged 0–14) or too old (over the age of 65) to work in comparison to the working population (aged 15–64)

brain drain: the emigration of well-educated or qualified people from a country

	Impacts on origin or source country	Impacts on destination or host country
Health	Migrants are often young and relatively healthy, leaving older or less healthy relatives and friends behind. An exception to this is retirement migration, where older people with a higher potential for degenerative illnesses move away from an area.	New illnesses and diseases can be introduced by a migrant community. Some migrants have difficult journeys and may arrive with health issues associated with this journey, e.g. malnutrition, dehydration and exhaustion. Migrants may find it hard to access healthcare facilities as a result of language barriers. They may struggle to adjust to their new life, which could lead to anxiety and depression.
Political	Policies to discourage migration and encourage natural increase may be developed to counter the impacts of migrants leaving. The mass migration of young people may lead to economic decline, which would necessitate political intervention and potentially require international support.	Controls on immigration may be required to maintain economic standards and public order. Extremist views can often surface as a result of the influx of migrants.

Table 10.9 Critical perspectives on the impacts of migration.

The extract below is adapted from a news article about migration from Ethiopia in 2015.

Despite border crackdown in Ethiopia, migrants still risk lives to leave

Getachew from Ethiopia wants to cross into Sudan. His father died and his mother lives in extreme poverty. In Ethiopia he can't earn enough so he hopes to earn money in Libya to send home.

Three times before, Sudanese police arrested him and sent him back to Ethiopia. Each time, he didn't have enough money to bribe the police.

'I know Libya can be dangerous, especially with Isis,' said Getachew 'but I must try my luck.'

Poverty in Ethiopia has fallen but the country remains one of the world's poorest and is ruled by an authoritarian government.

Thinking like a geographer

Why do urban planners need to consider migration flows? Do migrants always settle in cities or should rural planners also consider their arrival?

Making connections

The depletion of energy resources leads to the exploration, exploitation and development of new resources. This creates flows of people between places. See section 11.5 Energy security.

To read the *Guardian* article in full, look on **Cambridge Elevate** (www.cambridge.org/links/gase6111).

ACTIVITY 10.7

1 Read the news article. Identify the push and pull factors and the intervening obstacles identified in the extract.

For more questions, download Worksheet 10.5 from **Cambridge Elevate**.

10.6 Population growth in Tanzania

Tanzania is an LIC in East Africa (Figure 10.40). In 2012 the population was 44.9 million people and by 2015 the estimated population was 53.8 million. This is an annual growth rate of 5.5%. Table 10.10 shows demographic information for Tanzania in 2015.

Figure 10.40 Tanzania is an LIC in East Africa.

Demographic measure	Rate
Birth rate	37/1000
Fertility rate	5 children/woman
Death rate	9/1000
Maternal mortality rate	410/100 000 live births
Infant mortality rate	43/1000 live births
Under 5 mortality rate	61.5/1000

Table 10.10 Demographic data for Tanzania, 2015.

Fertility rates in Tanzania vary greatly by region, education levels and wealth. Rural fertility levels are higher than urban areas because of differences in education and the use of contraception. The north-east of the country also has lower fertility levels and lower rates of infant and child mortality.

Causes

There are several environmental and socio-economic causes of population change:

- Environmental conditions in Tanzania encourage the spread of malaria. Pregnant women are more susceptible and malaria leads to stillbirths and maternal deaths. Infant mortality rates are lower in northern regions, where the use of indoor residual spraying and insecticide-treated malaria nets reduces infection rates.
- Recent droughts have led to crop failures and lower fertility rates in some areas. Loss of income, loss of time (as women are needed to work on the land) and the likelihood of malnourishment encourages the use of contraceptives.
- Over 5% of Tanzanians have HIV/AIDS and 1.3 million children have been orphaned as a result of HIV-related deaths. The infection has lowered life expectancy and increased infant mortality. It is slowing the population growth and changing the population structure.
- The improved social status of women and better access to basic education has halved infant mortality and decreased maternal mortality in Tanzania over the last 25 years. Children born to mothers with no education are 55% more likely to die before the age of 1.
- The desired number of children for Tanzanian families remains high at 5.3. The peak age group for childbearing is very young (20–24 years), with 44% of Tanzanian women becoming pregnant by the age of 19. Four in ten women are married by the age of 18 and only 27.4% of married women use modern methods of contraception. Urban areas with good access to education and higher levels of wealth have seen the biggest decline in fertility.
- Tanzania has a small net out-migration, which has a minimal impact on population change.

Impacts

If population growth continues, Tanzania could have 138 million people by 2050, making it the 13th most populous country in the world, which will have major implications for Tanzania. Food and resources will be needed to support the growing population. Improvements to maternal and child healthcare will be needed and more school places will be required. Employment opportunities will need to be provided for the growing number of people of working age.

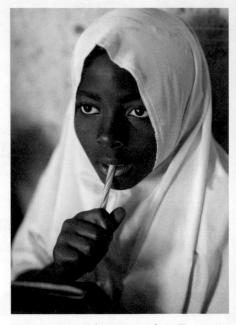

Figure 10.41 Educating girls in Tanzania can reduce fertility, maternal mortality and infant mortality rates.

Slowing down population growth may be possible through economic development and urbanisation. The government may have to intervene with improved maternity services, better infant care and family planning programmes. Improving education and the status of women (Figure 10.41), along with changing perceptions on contraception and family size, would reduce fertility rates and HIV prevalence.

ACTIVITY 10.8

1. Use the data in Table 10.10 to discuss mortality rates in Tanzania.
2. Make a list of environmental and socio-economic factors that lead to population growth and decline in Tanzania.
3. The Maasai (Figure 10.42) are one of an estimated 120 ethnic groups in Tanzania. Fertility rates among Maasai families are higher than many other ethnic groups in Tanzania. This is because families with more children have greater social and political power within the Maasai community.
   a. What are the challenges of reducing fertility rates among different social groupings?
   b. To what extent do you think the Tanzanian government can influence tribal groups such as the Maasai?
   c. How desirable would this level of state control be?

Figure 10.42 A Maasai family in Tanzania.

10.7 Principles of population ecology and their application to human populations

Population ecology looks at the dynamics of species numbers and also of how species interact with their environment. In terms of human populations, ecology looks at how the numbers of people change over time and space.

Population growth dynamics

Section 10.5 Population change looked at how several factors interrelate to bring about natural changes in population levels. This is about birth and death rates, natural increase and natural decrease. Health, education, social provision, cultural preferences, political factors and environmental factors can all bring about changes in birth and death rates.

The **net replacement rate** is a measure of population growth based on how many female offspring are produced by each female member of the population. A net replacement rate of 1 shows a stable population. Rates above or below this show population growth or decline. Changes in population growth rates can lead to one of three scenarios:

- Overpopulation: when there are too many people for the resources available such as food, water and energy. Overpopulation can result from an increase in births, a decrease in deaths, an increase in immigration, or the depletion or destruction of essential resources. Positive effects of overpopulation include the capacity for strong national defences, a potential increase in the labour market to meet the supply of workers and a greater likelihood of foreign investment. Negative effects of overpopulation include food shortages, the potential for high unemployment and a high dependency ratio.
- Underpopulation: when there are too few people to fully utilise the resources available. A much larger, and therefore more productive, population could be supported without experiencing a loss of living standards. Underpopulation can result from a decrease in births, an increase in deaths, an increase in emigration or the emergence or development of new resources. Positive effects of underpopulation include more jobs, less overcrowding and congestion and an abundance of resources. Negative effects of underpopulation include a lack of available labour, reduced national security and lower living standards, as fewer resources are being utilised.
- Optimum population: when the size of population enables high productivity and high living standards. It lies between overpopulation and underpopulation, although the exact size of the optimum population is not easy to define. Optimum population enables all individuals to live in an area to the maximum advantage of each individual, i.e. the highest quality of life with adequate access to food, water and energy.

Balancing population and resources

The ways in which people use or abuse the environment could determine future population levels and living standards, i.e. it could mean the difference between underpopulation and overpopulation. Sustainable development is required to strike a balance between population and resources. Some key ideas surrounding the sustainability of population and resources are as follows.

Key term

net replacement rate: the number of female offspring produced by female members of the population

Carrying capacity

Population is often measured in terms of land area, which is not accurate as it does not take into account how that land is used. Carrying capacity is a more accurate measure. It refers to the maximum number of people that can exist in a given environment, within the limits of the natural resources found there. There have been various estimates for the carrying capacity of the Earth, ranging from half a billion to 800 billion people. Carrying capacities are more difficult to calculate for humans than for animal species because of people's consumption habits. The **IPAT equation** (Figure 10.43) shows how the carrying capacity of humans is a complex calculation determined by population numbers, levels of affluence and technology. Where levels of affluence and technology are higher, more resources are used and fewer people can be supported. Technology can also reduce resource use and increase carrying capacities. The basic idea is that the carrying capacity of a given area is not a fixed number and can be altered.

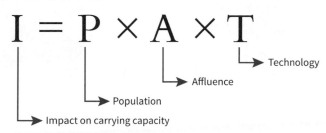

Figure 10.43 The IPAT equation.

If the carrying capacity of an environment is exceeded, the population can no longer be supported and it will decline. This can happen slowly if resources have been stored, although no population can survive beyond the carrying capacity indefinitely. It can also happen quickly and with catastrophic effects such as during famine. More affluent countries tend to have a greater carrying capacity than less affluent countries as they import goods and export waste products. This utilises the environments of poorer nations; although less affluent countries use fewer resources, their productive land area is sometimes used to support the demands of more affluent countries.

Ecological footprints

As global populations increase, humans consume more resources and produce more waste. It is important to measure the Earth's capacity to meet these needs. Ecological footprints calculate the impact that individuals and societies have on the Earth's resources. They determine whether the planet is large enough to cope with the number of people living on it. Ecological footprints are higher in more developed countries, where resource use and waste production are high.

Ecological footprints look at the balance between assets and demands. In terms of assets, biocapacity shows the planet's productive land areas – its forests, cropland and fisheries. Biocapacity levels vary globally (Figure 10.44). As well as producing goods, these productive land areas can also act as sinks for waste and emissions. In terms of demands, the ecological footprint looks at how much of the productive land area is used to provide our resources and accommodate our cities. Ecological footprints vary globally (Figure 10.45).

The ability of a country to sustain its population depends on this balance between assets and demands. Where demands are higher than assets, the population is not sustainable. This situation has already been reached in many

Key term

IPAT equation: a calculation that shows how population (P), affluence (A) and technology (T) have an impact on carrying capacity (I)

ACTIVITY 10.9

1   Using Figure 10.43, list **two** changes that could influence the carrying capacity of an area for each of the following:
    a   population
    b   affluence
    c   technology.
2   Which of your suggested changes would lead to an increase in carrying capacity and which would result in a decrease?

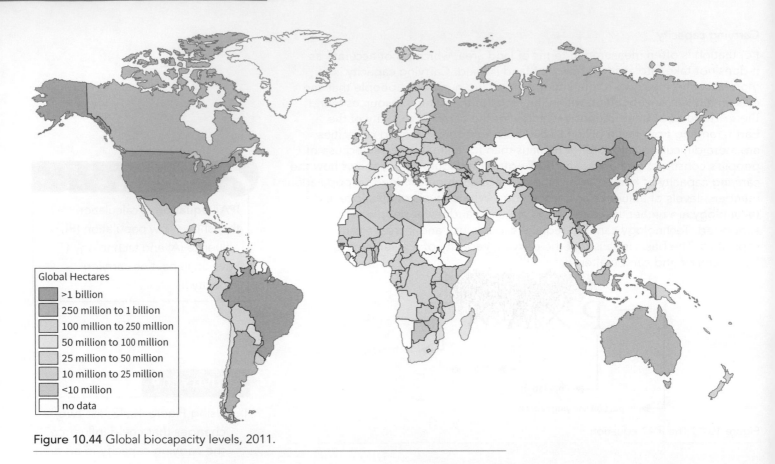

Figure 10.44 Global biocapacity levels, 2011.

Global Hectares
- >1 billion
- 250 million to 1 billion
- 100 million to 250 million
- 50 million to 100 million
- 25 million to 50 million
- 10 million to 25 million
- <10 million
- no data

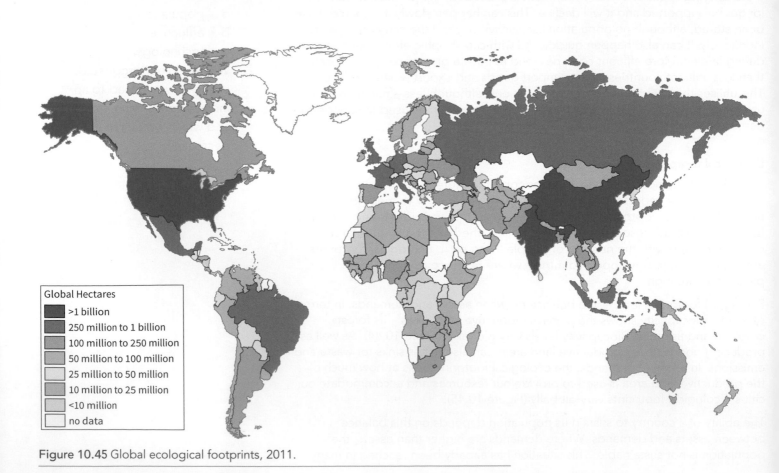

Figure 10.45 Global ecological footprints, 2011.

Global Hectares
- >1 billion
- 250 million to 1 billion
- 100 million to 250 million
- 50 million to 100 million
- 25 million to 50 million
- 10 million to 25 million
- <10 million
- no data

countries and, in these cases, assets are imported from parts of the world where demands are low. As more countries develop, the planet may not have enough resources to sustain everyone in this way.

The Population, Resources and Pollution model

The Population, Resources and Pollution (PRP) model (Figure 10.46) shows how people interact with the environment. Humans take resources from the environment, such as growing crops. In doing so, they disrupt biotic and abiotic processes. In the case of crops, the environment may be affected through loss of habitats or pollution through agrochemical use. The food that is produced from the crop is then transported, which leads to further pollution through the use of transportation vehicles.

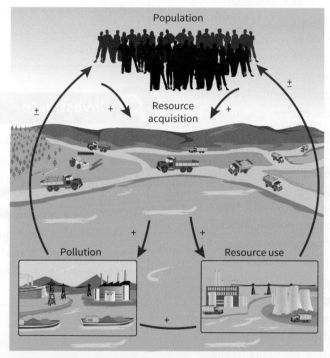

+ Places where one activity enhances the other
− Places where one activity adversely affects the other

Figure 10.46 The population, resources and pollution model.

The negative impacts of human interaction create negative feedback loops. These are where one factor leads to a decrease in another factor. An example of this could be soil erosion from poor agricultural practices, which limits the capacity to grow more food. Negative feedback loops could therefore limit human population existence and growth.

The model also includes positive feedback loops. These are positive in the way that they bring about change; the nature of that change is positive in terms of growth, but rarely positive in terms of outcome. An example of this could be the burning of fossil fuels, which brings about an increase in the amount of air pollution.

Negative and positive feedback loops work together to regulate human and environmental systems. Changing one variable will have an impact on all other variables. The fragile nature of population ecology forces humans to be aware of feedback loops and take steps to manage their impacts. There are several feedback loops that are currently limiting population growth:

- Climate change: the enhanced greenhouse effect is causing the Earth's climate to become warmer and, in some places, harsher. Higher temperatures are leading to sea level rise. Droughts, flooding, warmer temperatures and a greater frequency of extreme weather events disrupt agriculture and therefore limit population growth. Sudan, a country in the Sahel region of Africa, is experiencing frequent droughts. Food and water shortages have fuelled civil wars in the region.

- Water: the supply of freshwater is finite. Clean, safe supplies of water are needed to sustain a healthy population. In developing countries, unclean water and poor sanitation kills over 12 million people each year. Water shortages also impact on a country's ability to grow food. It is estimated that by 2025 the world population will be 8 billion and that 3 billion of those people (across 48 countries) will be facing water shortages.

- Energy: the availability of energy resources such as coal, oil or wood allows populations to expand. Energy consumption makes energy resources scarcer and more difficult to extract. The exploitation of new energy sources alleviates the situation, but non-renewable resources are finite and will eventually run out. The USA makes up 4.5% of the global population, yet the country consumes nearly 20% of global energy supplies. Imported fuel supplies allow this imbalance to exist, but the depletion of global energy resources would limit the population of all countries, particularly those that are net importers of energy.

- Ecosystems: the Earth's biodiversity enables us to grow food and develop new medicines. Human activities are threatening many ecosystems; two out of every three species on the planet are thought to be in decline. Almost half of the world's **primary forest** cover has been removed, with losses of 16 million hectares a year still taking place. Forests are vital to maintaining healthy ecosystems and the global climate.

- Pollution: air and water pollution damage ecosystems and harm human health. Air pollution already contributes to the deaths of nearly 3 million people every year (Figure 10.47). Higher levels of carbon dioxide are reducing the pH level of the oceans. **Ocean acidification** prevents healthy shell growth in marine animals and may cause reproductive difficulties in fish.

- Land: world population has been growing at a faster rate than food supply. The amount of land available is finite, which therefore limits population growth. Overcultivation and overgrazing leads to soil exhaustion and erosion; this has already led to the degradation of around 2 billion hectares of arable land. Future population growth will depend on the ability of the soil to produce enough food.

ACTIVITY 10.10

1. Read the list of feedback loops. Which of these are examples of negative loops and which are examples of positive loops?
2. Using a piece of A4 paper:
   a. Write the headings of the six feedback loops.
   b. Draw arrows between any headings that link together such as climate and water.
   c. Beneath the arrows, explain how environmental constraints are linked to one another.

Key terms

primary forest: areas of native tree species, where no deforestation has taken place

ocean acidification: a reduction in the pH level of the oceans, caused by the absorption of carbon dioxide

Investigate

The Maldives is a group of islands in the Indian Ocean. It is the 11th most densely populated country in the world, with around 400 000 people living on just 298 km² of land. Find out how climate change is threatening the existence of the population of the Maldives.

Figure 10.47 Air pollution causes 1.6 million deaths a year (17% of all deaths) in China.

Perspectives on population growth

Environmental factors can limit population growth. The Malthusian theory, written by Thomas Malthus in 1798, suggests that population grows exponentially whereas food supply grows only arithmetically. Population levels therefore reach a ceiling beyond which food supply is limited and numbers cannot grow any further. In order to avoid extreme poverty and mass starvation, checks limit population growth. The preventive, or negative, checks are voluntary measures such as individuals making rational family planning decisions based on their expected income. The positive checks come into place when preventive checks have not been taken. Disease, famine and war reduce the number of people and re-establish the balance between population and resources.

The neo-Malthusian theory is an extension of the original theory and it was first used around 1877. Neo-Malthusians look at the ideas of Malthus in a post-industrial society, where immigration and the deterioration of farmland have an impact on carrying capacities. Some neo-Malthusians think that fertility, rather than mortality, is the main determinant of population growth. Neo-Malthusians focus more on contraception to prevent overpopulation and environmental degradation as a consequence of overpopulation. Research in support of neo-Malthusian theories was published in 2014. It shows how the inhabitants of Easter Island, a 163 km² Polynesian island in the Pacific, were wiped out through environmental degradation from the 1700s (Figure 10.48). The Rapa Nui people lived on the island from around ad 1200, but evidence suggests that they overcultivated the soil, which led to a loss of fertility, and they depleted the natural resources on the island. With neighbouring islands over 2000 km away, the population began to decline.

Figure 10.48 The Rapa Nui people of Easter Island may have been wiped out as a result of environmental degradation.

The Club of Rome is an independent, non-profit making organisation that focuses on global challenges. Based on Malthusian ideas, in 1972 the organisation commissioned a study called 'The Limits to Growth'. This model of population looked at five variables and how they would be most likely to change over time. The variables were global population, industry, pollution, food production and resource depletion. The book arising from the study suggested that, given current trends, the limits to global population growth will be reached within 100 years.

Malthusian views have also been challenged. In 1965 Esther Boserup wrote that 'necessity is the mother of invention'. She suggested that as population increases and food resources begin to run out, we will find new ways to survive. She believed that agricultural intensification would enable populations to continue to grow. Evidence to support Boserup's ideas come from modern farming techniques such as the use of agrochemicals, irrigation, high-yield crop varieties, the genetic modification of crops and the selective breeding of cattle. As more countries adopt these techniques, Boserup's theory, whereby we will continuously invent new strategies, will be tested.

Julian Simon wrote about the sustainability of population growth. In 1981 he published *The Ultimate Resource*, which suggested that the supply of natural resources is infinite and that the human brain is the ultimate resource. He therefore supported the views of Boserup in terms of human innovation. As natural resources become low, prices will increase, which will encourage people to think about alternative ways of doing things.

10.8 Global population futures

Population predictions are carried out by national governments and international organisations such as the UN, the EU and the World Bank. Predictions exist for the world, regionally and most countries. Each government or organisation uses slightly different calculations, based on their own estimates of current population size and their own ideas about demographic trends. The accuracy of population predictions depends on future demographic trends. The impact of diseases such as HIV/AIDS and potential cures for diseases such as cancer will affect life expectancy levels. Most population predictions made for 2050 are in some agreement.

The UN issues updated global projections regularly through the Population Division of its Department of Economic and Social Affairs (DESA). These are the most widely used and accepted projections worldwide. The UN has predicted that the global population will be just under 9 billion by 2030. It estimates that world population will rise, reach a peak of 9.22 billion people by around 2075 and then decline slightly. The greatest increase by 2100 will be seen in Eastern, Middle and Western Africa, where life expectancies will continue to rise. China, India and the USA will continue to have high numbers of people. The population of Europe will see growth to the west, with lower rates of growth to the east. Many other parts of the world are likely to remain the same or decline.

Health impacts of global environmental change

Calculations surrounding future population levels will need to consider existing and emerging threats, such as ozone depletion and climate change. These environmental changes have the potential to change both the amount and distribution of people on the planet.

Ozone or O^3 is a naturally occurring layer of gas 15 to 30 kilometres above Earth. It protects the planet from the Sun's harmful ultraviolet B radiation.The depletion of the ozone layer has been studied since the mid-1980s. Atmospheric pollution has led to large holes in ozone occurring above the Arctic and Antarctic. Chlorine and bromine, produced through the use of aerosol sprays and heavy industry, are responsible for most of this destruction. The Montreal Protocol on

Substances that deplete the Ozone Layer, originally agreed in 1987, has now been signed by 196 states and the EU. It phases out the production of many of the chemicals that destroy ozone, e.g. CFCs. Estimates suggest that it will still take another 50 years for the ozone layer to recover.

Without the protection of the ozone layer, there is likely to be an increase in the prevalence of skin cancers and **cataracts** (Figure 10.49). Skin cancers are most common at higher latitudes, with Australia and New Zealand seeing the highest prevalence. Skin cancers currently only account for 0.7% of all deaths from cancer, but this figure could increase as a result of ozone depletion. Cataracts cause blindness in around 20 million people per year. Whilst blindness is not a life-threatening condition and will not impact upon mortality rates, an increase in cataracts will affect the global health burden in terms of DALYs.

Climate change is a naturally occurring phenomena, which many believe is currently being exacerbated by human actions. Global temperatures have increased by 1.4°C since 1880, which is having significant impacts upon global morbidity and mortality levels.

- Thermal stress refers to the impact that temperature has upon the human body. Heat waves and cold spells are associated with an increase in death rates. It is thought that climate change will cause more deaths during summer months, but fewer during the winter. The net change could be an overall reduction in deaths.
- Vector borne diseases, like Malaria, are also affected by temperatures. New threats could emerge as climate belts shift towards higher latitudes, creating additional breeding grounds for vectors. The change in distribution of vector-borne diseases may lead to an increase in mortality as newly affected countries are unprepared for the threat and lack immunity.
- Agricultural productivity will be affected by the changes in temperature and rainfall. In mid and high latitudes, crop productivity could increase by as much as 30% by 2050 and **cultivable land** could extend northwards, e.g. maize and soya beans could be grown further north and at higher altitudes. An increase in CO_2 will allow plants to grow larger and at a faster rate. However, in lower latitudes where some farmland is already **marginal**, productivity is likely to decrease. Any changes to agricultural productivity will have the potential to affect nutritional standards and therefore have health implications.

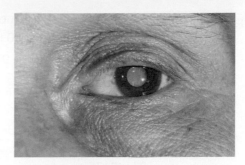

Figure 10.49 UV radiation can cause cataracts, which are the leading cause of blindness globally.

Key terms

cataracts: a health condition which causes the lens of the eye to become opaque, resulting in poor vision

cultivable land: ground that has suitable conditions for the growing of crops or rearing of livestock

marginal: poor quality agricultural land that has unsuitable conditions for farming

Predictions of global population change

Short-term (50-year) predictions for population change are based on current and predicted future demographic trends. Many estimates agree on what the global population will look like by 2050. To extend these predictions to 2300, the UN makes assumptions about what will happen after 2050. In 2004 it put forward three scenarios for the future global population. These are called the high, low and medium scenarios and each is based on fertility and replacement rates. Each scenario results in a shift of age structure towards older ages. They also all result in changes to the global distribution of population.

- High scenario: based on the assumption that long-term fertility rates will be 2.35 children per woman. By 2050 fertility will be 0.5 children above the medium scenario. After 2050 this gap will be more like 0.25 or 0.3 children above the medium scenario.

- Low scenario: based on the assumption that long-term fertility rates will be 1.85 children per woman. By 2050 fertility will be 0.5 children below the medium scenario. After 2050 this gap is more like 0.2 or 0.25 children below the medium scenario.
- Medium scenario: the basis for the other two scenarios. The medium scenario is based on the assumption that fertility rates by 2050 will be 1.85 children per woman. The UN predicts that these fertility rates will increase to replacement level (which, given lower mortality rates, will be 2.05 children per woman) by 2175.

In 2015 the UN published its revised 'World Population Prospects'. This was its 24th set of estimates and projections for global population. The report updated population estimates for 2100 (Table 10.11). It found that population growth had been slower between 2005 and 2015 than was first thought; growth in 2005 was 1.24% per year but in 2015 this had slowed to 1.18% per year.

Major area	Population (millions)			
	2015	2030	2050	2100
World	7349	8501	9725	11213
Africa	1186	1679	2478	4387
Asia	4393	4923	5267	4889
Europe	738	734	707	646
Latin America and the Caribbean	634	721	784	721
Northern America	358	396	433	500
Oceania	39	47	57	71

Table 10.11 Medium scenario predictions of world population.

Maths for geographers

Using Table 10.11, calculate the percentage increases in population for each continent between 2015 and 2100.

'World Population Prospects' predicts that world population will reach 8.5 billion people by 2030 (an increase of over a billion people within 15 years), 9.7 billion people by 2050 and 11.2 billion people by 2100. Figure 10.50 shows these projections as the medium scenario. The graph also gives 80 and 95% confidence levels above and below the medium estimates. The graph shows that the UN have 95% degree of confidence of global population being between 8.4 and 8.6 billion by 2030 and between 9.5 and 13.3 billion by 2100. Global population is almost certainly set to increase, but there is around a 23% chance that it could even out or even fall slightly before 2100.

In terms of future population, it is likely that the following will occur:

- Africa will see the biggest growth rates. Over half of the population growth by 2050 will take place on the African continent. By 2100 the populations of Angola, Burundi, DR Congo, Malawi, Mali, Niger, Somalia, Uganda, Tanzania and Zambia could be five times higher than they are now.

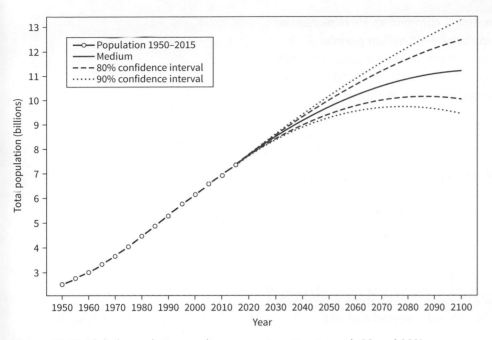

Figure 10.50 Global population medium scenario estimates with 80 and 90% confidence intervals.

- The population of Europe is likely to decrease. Fertility in all European countries fell below the replacement level (of 2.1 children per woman) by 2015 and is not likely to reach replacement level by 2050. Many countries such as Bulgaria, Croatia, Latvia and Lithuania could see a population decline of more than 15% by 2050.
- Future population growth is dependent on fertility rates. Relatively small differences in fertility rates can generate large changes to a population. By 2015 only around 34% of women in relationships within the least developed countries used modern methods of contraception. An additional 22% had unmet needs for family planning. Large variations in fertility rates remain between countries.
- Increased levels of longevity continue. Global life expectancy at birth increased from 67 years in 2010 to 70 years in 2015. Life expectancy is still lowest in Africa, although the continent has seen the greatest increase and now averages 60 years.
- International migration levels remain high. Migration has a lesser impact on population change than birth and death rates, but it is more significant in some countries. Between 1950 and 2015 Africa, Asia and Latin America and the Caribbean have been net senders of migrants. At the same time, Europe, North America and Oceania have been net receivers of international migrants. International in-migration will account for 82% of the population growth in many high income countries, where birth rates remain low.
- Many parts of the world still have youthful populations with the opportunity to benefit from the demographic dividend. In 2015 in Africa, 41% of the population were children under the age 15 and an additional 19% were young people aged 15 to 24.

- Ageing populations are becoming increasingly common as life expectancies increase. In 2015, 12% of the global population (901 million people) were aged 60 or over. Europe has the greatest proportion of elderly people; 24% of its population was already over the age of 60 by 2015. By 2050 nearly a quarter of all populations (except Africa) will be aged 60 or over.

ACTIVITY 10.11

1 Make a list of factors that affect population change, such as war and disease.
2 Why is it difficult to provide accurate population projections for 2300?

Possible implications of future population totals

Table 10.12 shows UN estimates for population growth for the three scenarios. The data is then divided to show world totals, more developed and less developed regions.

Year	World population (millions)			More developed regions population (millions)			Less developed regions population (millions)		
	Medium	High	Low	Medium	High	Low	Medium	High	Low
1950	2519	–	–	813	–	–	1706	–	–
1975	4068	–	–	1047	–	–	3021	–	–
2000	6071	6071	6071	1194	1194	1194	4877	4877	4877
2025	7851	8365	7334	1241	1282	1199	6010	7082	6135
2050	8919	10633	7409	1220	1370	1084	7699	9263	6325
2075	9221	12494	6601	1153	1467	904	8068	11027	5696
2100	9064	14018	5491	1131	1651	766	7933	12367	4726
2125	8734	15296	4556	1137	1885	679	7597	13411	3877
2150	8494	16722	3921	1161	2152	633	7333	14571	3288
2175	8434	18696	3481	1185	2454	593	7249	16242	2889
2200	8499	21236	3165	1207	2795	554	7291	18441	2612
2225	8622	24301	2920	1228	3179	517	7395	21122	2403
2250	8752	27842	2704	1246	3612	482	7506	24230	2223
2275	8868	31868	2501	2363	4100	448	7605	27768	2053
2300	8972	36444	2310	1278	4650	416	7694	31793	1894

Table 10.12 Population change estimates for the three UN scenarios.

- Under the medium scenario, world population will peak in 2075, dip slightly by 2175 and then rise steadily by 2300. By 2050 the population growth for the following 250 years is likely to be minimal. More developed countries will see smaller increases in population (7% between 2000 and 2300) than less developed countries (57.7% between 2000 and 2300).

- Under the high scenario, population will increase from 10.63 billion in 2050 to 36.44 billion in 2300. More developed countries will see their populations almost triple (289% increase between 2000 and 2300) whereas less developed countries will see an increase of more than fivefold (552% increase between 2000 and 2300).

- Under the low scenario, world population will decrease from 7.41 billion in 2050 to 2.31 billion in 2300. More developed countries will see larger decreases in population (65% decrease between 2000 and 2300) than less developed countries (61% decrease between 2000 and 2300).

The estimates between the high, medium and low scenarios vary greatly. Each scenario will change the population–environment relationships for each type of country.

Making connections

An increase in globalisation is likely to lead to an increase in urbanisation. What do you think the implications of this are for urban planning? See Chapter 9 Contemporary urban environments.

Look on **Cambridge Elevate** for more information on future population change from the following websites:

- World Population to 2030 report (www.cambridge.org/links/gase6112)

- World Population Prospects report (www.cambridge.org/links/gase6113)

- The Democratic Challenges in Europe report (www.cambridge.org/links/gase6114)

- ONS (www.cambridge.org/links/gase6115).

Approaches to managing future population change

Globally, there are many challenges that lie ahead in terms of managing future populations and environments. There is no single global strategy; while some countries are currently tackling the issues associated with youthful populations, it is clear that all countries will have to plan for ageing populations in the future. Some parts of the world have greater demographic issues to deal with and some parts of the world have a better capacity to deal with such issues. When managing populations, most countries focus on similar areas:

- Youthful populations with the potential for high rates of growth: reducing fertility and increasing the use of contraception are a priority in this instance. Governments may provide or allow direct or indirect support for family planning. This is when the government (direct) or private companies (indirect) provide family planning information, guidance, supplies and services. Relaxing national laws regarding abortion may also be considered. Although many countries allow abortions to take place under any circumstances, in 2015 other nations allowed abortions only under specific circumstances such as to save a woman's life (Nicaragua), to preserve her physical or mental health (Papua New Guinea) or in the case of rape or foetal impairment (Iraq).

- Ageing populations with the potential for low or negative rates of growth: care for the elderly, pro-natal policies and encouraging in-migration are often considered in this case. Some countries may choose to increase the statutory retirement age to decrease the dependency ratio. Other reforms to the pension system, such as changes to pension contributions, are also a possibility.

- Internal migration and the sustainability of cities: both youthful and ageing populations can increase the need for housing stock. As the world becomes more urban, managing cities is becoming a greater priority. Governments can implement policies to raise, maintain or lower rates of rural-to-urban migration. Incentives to keep people in the countryside are a possibility if funding exists.

- International migration: the movement of people from one location to another can either resolve or intensify population issues. Governments can choose to raise, lower or maintain immigration. They can also implement policies that give easier access to migrants with certain skills or attributes. Some governments put procedures in place that help migrants to return to their home countries, whereas others try to stem losses through focusing on emigration.

In 2013 DESA compiled a report detailing all of the population policies that are in place globally. It found that 37% of governments were attempting to reduce population growth and 43% were attempting to increase it. The figures below show some other findings from the report.

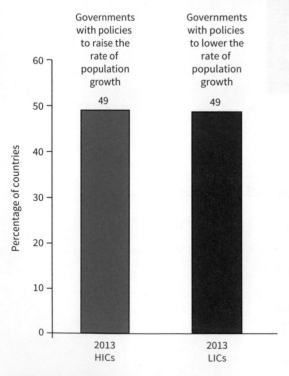

Figure 10.51 Government policies aimed at influencing population growth.

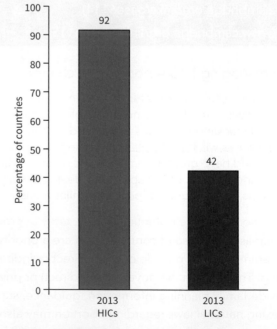

Figure 10.52 Governments that are concerned with ageing populations.

In LICs and HICs, nearly half of all governments had policies aimed at influencing rates of population growth.

In LICs, 42% of governments were concerned with ageing, compared to 92% in HICs.

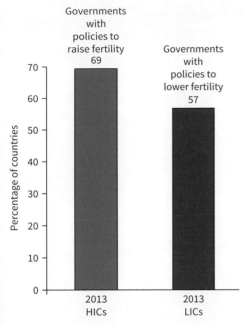

Figure 10.53 Governments with policies to influence fertility levels.

In LICs, 57% of governments were attempting to reduce fertility (anti-natal policies), whereas in HICs 69% were attempting to increase it (pro-natal policies).

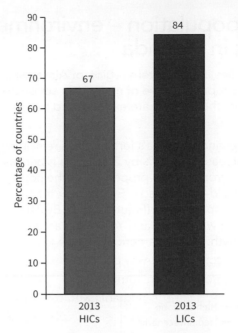

Figure 10.54 Governments with policies to reduce rural-to-urban migration.

In LICs, 84% of governments had policies to reduce rural-to-urban migration, compared with 67% in HICs.

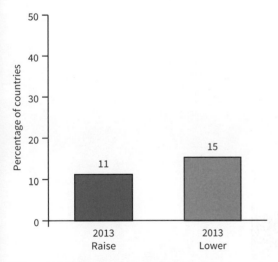

Figure 10.55 Governments with policies to change levels of immigration.

Globally, 11% of governments had policies to raise immigration and 15% had policies to lower it.

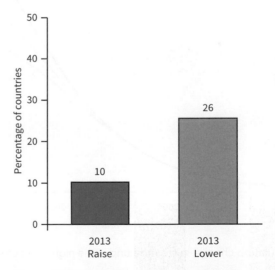

Figure 10.56 Governments with policies to change levels of emigration.

Globally, 10% of governments had policies to raise emigration and 26% had policies to lower it.

ACTIVITY 10.12

1 Explain two alternative approaches to managing populations.
2 Using examples, summarise the key differences between the population policies of countries at different levels of development.

Look on **Cambridge Elevate** for more details on ageing populations from the WHO Ageing and Life-Course website (www.cambridge.org/links/gase6116).

10.9 Future population – environment relationships in Uganda

Uganda is an LIC that lies in the eastern region of Africa, where population increases are high. It is representative of many LICs across the globe; the changes that may affect the country are experienced to a greater or lesser degree in all LICs.

Under the medium scenario, Uganda's fertility rates remain high and its population is set to increase by 206% by 2050. This is because of the momentum that results from a large proportion of the population being young and not yet attaining child-bearing age. Even under the low scenario, Uganda's population will continue to increase (Figure 10.57). By 2100 Uganda will be one of three countries (along with Niger and Yemen) to account for over half of the world's population growth.

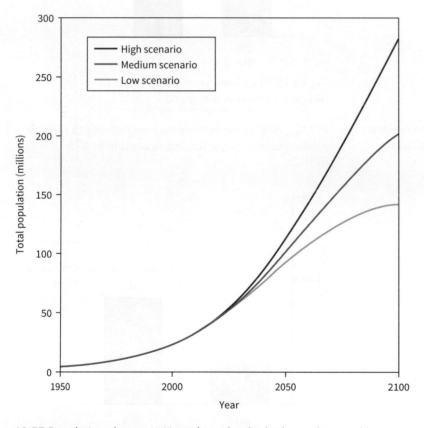

Figure 10.57 Population change in Uganda under the high, medium and low scenarios.

Youthful populations, found in countries like Uganda, have a direct impact on the environment. Increased numbers of people in Uganda means that population densities will increase to 441 people per m². This puts greater pressure on resources and land. More than 80% of people rely directly on land, agriculture and fishing for an income. An increased population density could lead to the degradation of agricultural land, soil erosion, deforestation and increased pollution. The low scenario would see more moderate impacts, but the high scenario would exacerbate this situation.

In urban areas, problems of poverty, overcrowding and disease could increase. Increased urbanisation will require improved infrastructures and additional jobs. Under the high scenario, high fertility rates could increase new job requirements from around 700 000 in 2017 to 1 521 000 by 2037. Under the low scenario, lower fertility rates would increase new job requirements to only 854 000 by 2037. Increased industrialisation and an improved infrastructure will have environmental impacts.

Under all three scenarios, dependency rates in Uganda should decrease (Figure 10.58) and the population pyramid will be narrower at the base and wider in the middle (Figure 10.59). The decrease in dependency may be inhibited by unemployment; in Uganda unemployment rates have risen from 2% in 2006 to 3.75% in 2013, with youth unemployment being much higher. Under the low scenario, Uganda would reduce its population growth rate and increase the country's annual growth of GDP per capita by between 0.5 and 0.6%.

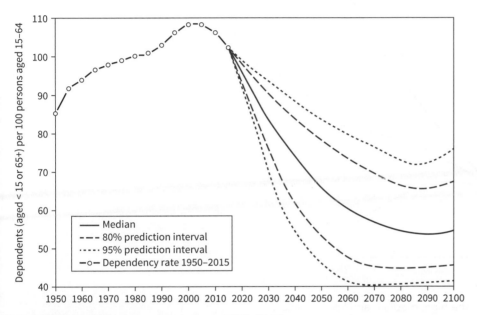

Figure 10.58 Uganda dependency rates, 1950–2100.

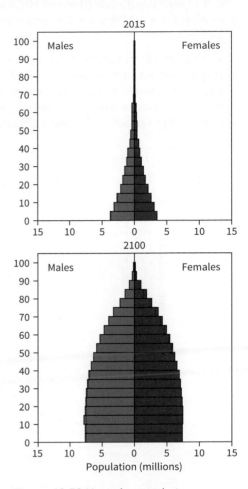

Figure 10.59 Uganda population pyramids, 2015 and 2100.

ACTIVITY 10.13

1. Create **two** flow diagrams to show how future population changes in Uganda will affect rural and urban areas.
2. How could a decrease in young dependents be seen as both positive and negative?

10.10 Future population – environment relationships in the UK

Predictions show that Europe will experience slower growth and lower fertility rates than other major regions. These patterns will occur throughout the whole of the continent, but will be more pronounced in western Europe. Before the 1960s, western Europe had slow population growth of between 0.5 and 1% per year. Since the 1960s, declining fertility has caused the growth rate to fall to zero. The region has managed to maintain population levels through immigration and because incoming migrants have higher fertility rates than the original population. However, evidence suggests that fertility rates are now falling among migrant populations too.

The UK is a HIC in western Europe where population growth is less than 1%. It is representative of many HICs across the globe; the changes that may affect the country will be experienced to a greater or lesser degree in all HICs.

Under the medium scenario, the UK's fertility rates continue to fall and its population is set to increase by 15% (from 65 to 75 million) by 2050. This is because of natural increase, leading to increasingly long lifespans, and in-migration. Under the low scenario, the UK's population will peak around 2040 and then fall to around 68 million (Figure 10.60).

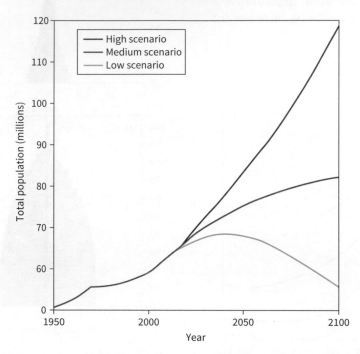

Figure 10.60 Population change in the UK under the high, medium and low scenarios.

As with many other HICs, the UK's population will continue to age. The number of people claiming the state pension is projected to increase by 28% by 2035. As a direct result, people may have to work longer into their old age. Taxes for the working population will also have to increase to fund the cost. Older people also require more healthcare and are more likely to live alone, increasing the pressure on housing stock. The high scenario means higher fertility rates, which would alleviate issues of ageing to some degree. The low scenario would exacerbate the impacts of ageing significantly.

A slow-growing population with an increasing level of dependency will require higher levels of immigration. Immigration should increase fertility rates and push the UK towards the high scenario. However, immigration can also have issues associated with cultural and language differences, segregation and social unrest. Immigrants reduce levels of dependency by paying taxes, but their presence in the country also requires funding as more school and hospital places are required. Estimates of the net economic benefit of immigration vary considerably; some groups claim migrants bring a net loss whereas other studies show a net benefit of around £20 billion a year. Immigrants have close ties with other countries and so are more likely to travel, which has environmental costs.

Ageing populations have direct impacts on the environment. Research has shown that older people use more resources and therefore they have higher ecological footprints and contribute more to carbon emissions than younger people. They consume more energy for heating and are often more mobile, taking more holidays on average than younger people. Greater use of medication among older people can also lead to the bioaccumulation of pharmaceutical products within water sources. Attitudinal studies have shown that older people are also more sceptical about environmental concerns.

Under all three scenarios, dependency rates in the UK will increase (Figure 10.61) and the population pyramid will be narrower at the base and wider at the top (Figure 10.62).

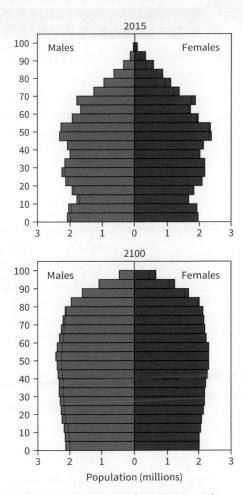

Figure 10.62 UK population pyramids, 2015 and 2100.

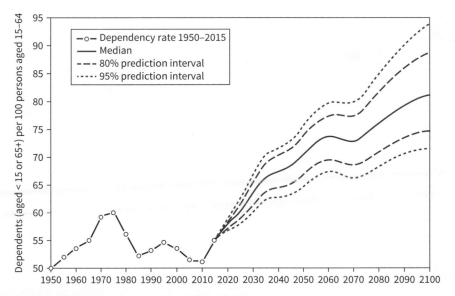

Figure 10.61 UK dependency rates, 1950–2100.

ACTIVITY 10.14

1   Using examples, summarise the different population challenges for HICs and LICs.

 For more questions on global population futures, download Worksheet 10.6 from **Cambridge Elevate**.

Assess to progress

1   Suggest why DALYs are more useful than other development indicators.

6 MARKS [A LEVEL]

2   Using Figure 10.63, describe the burden of disease in Malawi and suggest how the causes of morbidity and mortality are likely to change with economic development.

9 MARKS [A LEVEL]

Burden of disease, 2012

Disability-adjusted life years (DALYs) are the sum of years of life lost due to premature mortality (YLL) and years of healthy life lost due to disability (YLD).

DALYs, YLL and YLD (thousands) by broad cause group

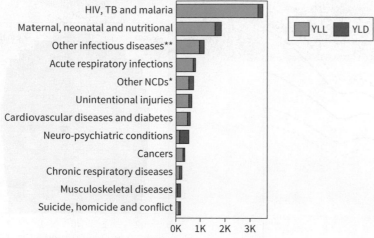

* Other noncommunicable diseases (NCDs) including non-malignant neoplasms; endocrine, blood and immune disorders; sense organ, digestive, genitourinary, and skin diseases; oral conditions; and congenital anomalies.

** Infectious diseases other than acute respiratory diseases, HIV, TB and malaria.

Figure 10.63 The burden of disease in Malawi, 2012.

3   According to a UN report of July 2014:

- 12.4% (1 200 000) of people in Zambia have contracted HIV
- 380 000 children have been orphaned as a result of the disease
- the government is increasing the amount that it spends on HIV/AIDS, but 92% of funding still comes from external organisations
- 45% of the population are under the age of 15 years
- over one-third of people live in urban areas along major transportation corridors.

Assess the social and economic implications of these findings.

20 MARKS [A LEVEL]

Resource security

Figure 11.1 Achieving energy security may be seen as posing issues for the security of uncontaminated water resources.

By the end of this chapter you should know:

- how and why key resources, energy, freshwater and ore minerals are in growing global demand
- where key resources are located, obtained from and how they are used
- how countries attempt to ensure 'security' of supplies
- how attempts to achieve resource security lead to international trade in resources
- how resource trade can result in both international cooperation and conflict
- the environmental implications of resource use and misuse
- attempts to avoid an energy gap, water scarcity and mineral shortage as demand grows while supplies diminish
- strategies to develop sustainable uses of key resources
- how future resource needs are being planned for on a planet of finite resources.

Before you start...

You should know:

- resources may be finite (non-renewable) or renewable
- resource management involves balancing resource demand with resource supply
- resources are traded internationally

- the environmental impact of some resource extraction, distribution and use can be negative
- a lack of access to key resources (such as clean water) can have detrimental impacts on health, welfare and quality of life
- there are ways to use resources more sustainably.

11.1 Resource development

We live in a time of unprecedented resource exploitation, consumption and dependency. When demand is so huge, and with the global population increasing not just in number but in wealth and appetite, the issues of resource access, ownership and affordability pose very real challenges. This chapter explores many of these issues, along with the likely factors that influence decisions with particular reference to energy, mineral and water resources – three categories that most fundamentally influence our quality of life.

A resource is that which carries value and is made use of by people (Figure 11.3). It can be both a tangible item, such as coal, and an abstract quality, such as engineering skill. For something to become a resource, it needs to be:

- recognised as being of value
- exploitable/obtainable
- capable of being processed/transformed into a usable state
- within the physical, economic and ethical reach of people.

Resource classification

Resources can take many forms, but these can be categorised according to common characteristics, as shown in Figure 11.4.

Stock and flow resources

Stock resources consist of finite quantities of non-renewable resources, such as metal ores and mineral deposits.

The difference between a **resource** and a **reserve** is largely one of economic profitability; a resource may exist, but unless the obtaining of it is economically viable it does not become a reserve. A significant resource may be estimated *in situ* for quantity and quality, but the reserve element is likely to be a smaller proportion, representing that which is extractable at a profit. Clearly, if extraction techniques become less expensive, or the value rises, the reserve may become larger.

The process of transformation of a resource into an exploited reserve is shown in Table 11.1 and is largely a consequence of obtaining more detailed and reliable information about the resource and increasing the confidence that it can be extracted profitably.

Stocks may be further classified as:

- potential stocks (evidenced but not yet fully quantified or exploited)
- known stocks (quantified and accessible)
- estimated stocks (when quantification is difficult)
- depleting stocks (when the rate of exploitation is faster than the rate of new discovery)
- exhausted stocks (when the economically recoverable resource has been fully exploited).

These states are not absolutes and may alter with economies of production and technological development. For example, the estimated stocks of North Sea oil

Figure 11.2 A planet of finite resources but with renewable systems within it powered by the Sun.

Figure 11.3 An early 'gusher' on a Texas oilfield at the turn of the 20th century.

 Key terms

stock resources: finite quantities of resources that may be depleted to the point of exhaustion or extinction

resource: an estimate of the quantity of a valued mineral or energy source that is physically contained in the source material

reserve: an estimate of the amount of valued mineral or energy source that can, with realistic expectations, be technically extracted and economically exploited

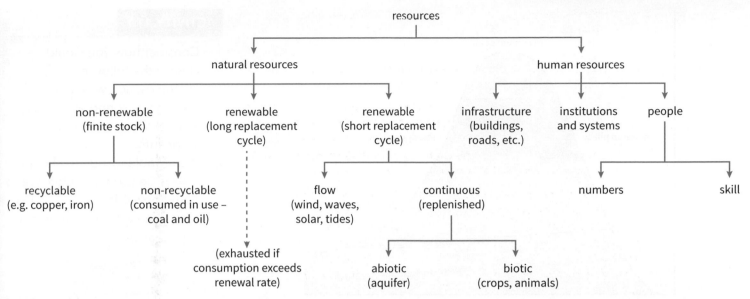

Figure 11.4 Resource categories.

	Possible resource	Inferred resource	Indicated reserve	Measured reserve
Quantity and quality of resource	Indicative in situ information but without sampling	Estimated on the basis of limited sampling into the geology	Estimated with a level of confidence through more extensive sampling	Well established and measured with confidence
Investment stage	Insufficient reliable data to justify an exploration phase	Insufficient data to justify expenditure on planning an exploitation sequence	Mine/quarry/bore planning. Evaluation of economic viability of deposits	Mine/quarry/bore production planning. Evaluation of the economic viability of deposits
Deposit viability information	Unquantified	Limited information and sampling gathered	Sufficient sample tests allow geological and grade (quality) consistency to be reasonably assumed	Sufficient sample tests allow geological and grade consistency to be confirmed
Degree of mineral sampling confidence	Insignificant	Chance of 10% or greater that mineralisation is there	Chance of 50% or greater that mineralisation occurs	Chance of 90% or greater that mineralisation occurs

Table 11.1 Stages in the consideration of a resource to an exploited reserve.

have grown substantially since their initial exploitation in the 1970s due to new finds in deeper waters than it had been technically possible to exploit 20 years earlier and to using 'enhanced recovery' methods. This means that oilfields that were originally estimated to yield 40% of recoverable oil have been obtaining 60% and more.

Flow resources may be thought of as an ongoing stream of renewable potential that does not diminish despite it being exploited. The Sun's energy drives these, such as wind, wave, sunlight and the hydrological cycle replenishing freshwater.

Stock resources life cycle

Stock resources have a recognisable life cycle, as shown in Figure 11.5:

1   Demand: a recognised use and viable need for the resource arising.
2   Exploration: searching for and locating economic quantities.

Key term

flow resources: resources that are renewable, replenished irrespective of how much they are exploited

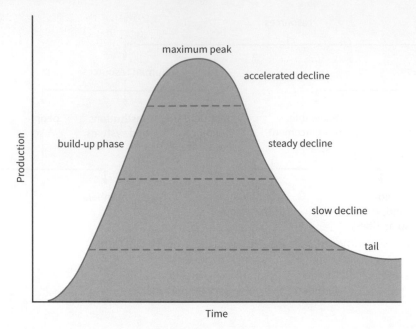

Figure 11.5 The life cycle of a stock resource.

3 Exploitation: extracting and transporting the resource.
4 Development: integrating support infrastructure and maximising production efficiency.
5 Depletion: declining returns as extraction costs increase with declining yields.
6 Exhaustion: further extraction is no longer economically viable or stocks are fully depleted.

The point of economic exhaustion is usually encountered well before physical exhaustion of a finite stock. There will usually be a proportion of the resource remaining, but it is no longer profitable to extract it as the cost of further exploitation increases and/or demand declines.

The Arctic Ocean as a resource frontier

As long-established and possibly low cost reserves become depleted, the exploitation margin is pushed into increasingly difficult locations. These become a new **resource frontier** where resources are often harder to locate, extract and convey to the main markets. The effect is often to raise the price of the resource, which helps to justify the extra costs associated with extracting the resource under difficult conditions. As the world's demand for oil increases, oil companies have pushed the resource frontier into deeper oceans, more diluted sources such as oil shales and more hazardous environments such as Arctic waters (Figure 11.6).

 Key term

resource frontier: a peripheral environment that attracts the latest exploration and subsequent development of resources

 New developments at a resource frontier can provoke reactions both in favour, and against. Look on **Cambridge Elevate** at this article from Business Insider UK (www.cambridge.org/links/gase6117).

 Making connections

Read more about the issues of human activities in cold environments in section 4.5 Human occupation and the development of cold environments.

Figure 11.6 Drilling for oil in the Arctic Ocean at a politically and environmentally controversial resource frontier.

Resource peak

In the mid-20th century, geologist M. King Hubbert proposed the concept of the **resource peak** – the point after which new discoveries of a resource decline as production has exploited the most easily accessible reserves. He argued that most finite resources would follow a bell-shaped curve. The time lag between maximum discoveries and maximum production would lag by, possibly, a few decades as it takes time to get production facilities up to full efficiency. The implications of the downward limb of productivity decline include rising resource prices, potential shortages and, ultimately, a fall in demand.

Sustainable resource development

A variation to the resource peak model shows how a resource may be exploited less intensively and demand reduced or supplied with sustainable alternatives with a view to a slower depletion rate. This is seen in the move from curve A to curve C in Figure 11.7.

Key term

resource peak: the phase of maximum production from a resource deposit before depletion exceeds new discoveries

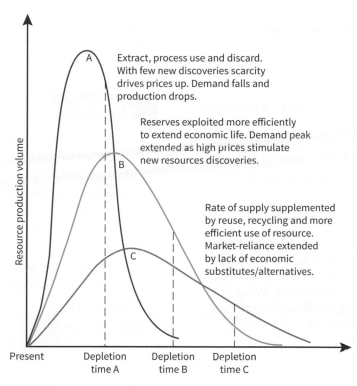

Extract, process use and discard. With few new discoveries scarcity drives prices up. Demand falls and production drops.

Reserves exploited more efficiently to extend economic life. Demand peak extended as high prices stimulate new resources discoveries.

Rate of supply supplemented by reuse, recycling and more efficient use of resource. Market-reliance extended by lack of economic substitutes/alternatives.

Figure 11.7 Depletion curves.

It is renewable resources that provide functional sustainability. Even here, there are restrictions on the rate of exploitation that can be sustainably undertaken.

- Continuous flow resources such as freshwater can be exploited sustainably only at the rate of replenishment. Extracting underground water supplies faster than they are recharged through more rainfall or percolation from rivers and lakes leads to a falling water table. Many deep aquifers in arid areas, such as the Murzuk-Djado basin in North Africa, contain water that fell under more moist conditions thousands of years ago and are subject to unsustainable water abstraction.

- Flow resources can be considered sustainable as far as their exploitation is concerned, but may be subject to disrupted provision. The lack of solar power at night, wind power under high pressure conditions, wave power

For an activity on Norway's physical characteristics and resource development download Worksheet 11.1 from **Cambridge Elevate**.

when the sea is calm and river potential for hydroelectric power (**HEP**) under drought conditions means their sustainable use is conditional upon dependability of flow.

Major resource exploitation proposals within the EU have, since 1999, had to undergo an Environmental Impact Assessment (EIA). This is a requirement for the planning authorities to obtain objective, factual and far-reaching information on the likely impacts on the environment of any major resource developer. It is an attempt to ensure that justifiable projects meeting certain needs do not have unacceptable negative consequences affecting the environment in both the short and long term.

There are seven key elements to an EIA:

1   A description of the project (including the proposed site and the key processes involved in the operation).

2   Alternatives that have been considered (justifying why this project is necessary at this location).

3   A description of the environment that may be affected by the development (both human and natural).

4   A description of the significant effects on the environment (the definition of significant is crucial, often using the **Leopold matrix**).

5   Mitigation (identifying how it is intended that potentially negative effects will be avoided or limited).

6   Non-technical summary (using clear, unambiguous language that is understandable to the general public).

7   Lack of know-how and/or technical difficulties (a recognition that some sources of information within the assessment are weak, unreliable or need strengthening through further research and data collection).

An EIA does not mean a resource development project will have no impact on the environment, but provides a framework in which the potential consequences are considered, planned for and reduced to acceptable dimensions. While an EIA provides a legal planning process for ensuring a degree of sustainability, a political question often surrounds what is deemed acceptable.

11.2 Natural resource issues

Global patterns of energy production, consumption and trade flows

Sources of fuel that became prized in the 20th century, such as oil, gas and uranium ore, are not necessarily matched to where concentrations of people are located. As a result, they form key energy movements which, when crossing national borders, create **trade flows**.

Factors that influence the size and direction of trade flows include:

- the location of the energy resource and the size of its reserves
- costs of extraction and transportation
- the location and size of the energy market(s)
- the ability of an area to secure its own internal energy sources
- the nature of the energy demand – whether for transport, domestic use or electricity generation
- political choices on preferred forms of energy supply

Key terms

HEP: hydro-electric power is generated when flowing water is used to turn a turbine to create electricity

Leopold matrix: a tool for quantifying the likely environmental consequences of a project. Developed in 1971, one axis considers the magnitude of the project consequences, and the other – the significance/importance of environmental impact

ACTIVITY 11.2

1   In 1975 it was thought that global crude oil reserves would last another 25 years before they were exhausted. Why were the predictions so wrong?

2   Look up a map of current mineral exploitation around the world. Where do you observe other resource frontiers occurring?

Key term

trade flows: movements of goods, services or resources across boundaries, involving exports from one place and imports to another

- political restrictions on trade by certain countries (**embargoes**) or energy sources (e.g. uranium)
- environmental considerations of the impact of extraction, transportation and use
- investment decisions by global energy transnational corporations (TNCs).

The global coal trade

Coal is a flexible energy resource contributing, historically, to domestic heating, transport (steam trains and ships), industrial manufacturing processes and the production of town gas. Although most of these uses have faded, coal is still a dominant fuel in the generation of electricity in coal-fired power stations in many parts of the world. China is currently opening a new coal-fired plant every seven to ten days in a bid to meet its growing demand for electricity. Although it supplies much of its coal needs itself, it still relies on significant imports from Australia (Figure 11.8).

Globally, coal demand is expected to increase by 15% up to 2040, with the greatest rate of increase in the next ten years before slowing down (Figure 11.9). India is likely to surpass the USA as the world's second largest

Key term

embargoes: official resolutions by one or more countries to ban trade in a resource or by an organisation or nation by putting in place trade restrictions

Look at this article from the BBC on **Cambridge Elevate** to find out how exploiting a new resource frontier for coal needs to consider not just technological needs, but socio-cultural and environmental consequences (www.cambridge.org/links/gase6118).

Figure 11.8 Coal imports have increased as the cost of bulk coal shipments has fallen.

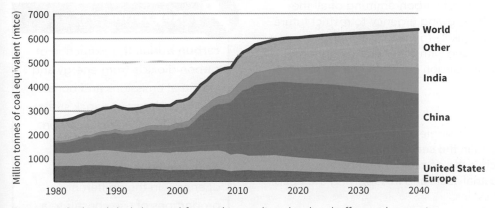

Figure 11.9 The global demand for coal is predicted to level off over the coming decades.

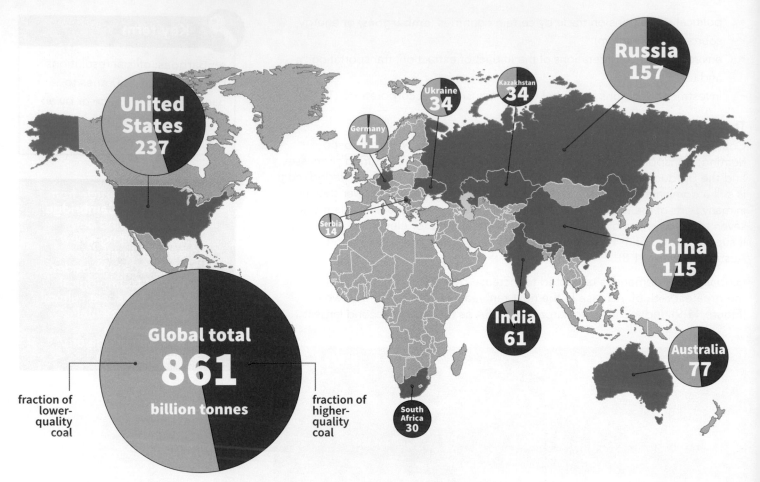

Figure 11.10 The world's coal reserves (proven recoverable coal reserves reported to the World Energy Council by the top ten coal-producing countries at the end of 2008).

consumer of coal by 2020 and is expected to exceed the coal imports of China, despite the top two coal consumers having their own large coal reserves (Figure 11.10). The biggest coal producers of the next two decades are likely to be China, India, Indonesia and Australia contributing 70% of the world's output, with Indonesia and Australia becoming the most significant exporters of coal.

Global coal production is likely to be constrained by continuing concerns about the environmental impacts of burning it – the most carbon-emitting of all the fossil fuels. It is an abundant resource, but the growing urgency to restrict future global temperature increase to 2.0°C or less is likely to mean that without clean-coal technology (such as **carbon burial**) and with other energy options available, governments will look towards lower carbon emission energy sources to constitute their **energy mix**.

The global oil trade

A case can be made that oil (Figure 11.11) is the single most significant global resource to influence the politics of the world in the second half of the 20th century and the beginning of the 21st. Such is the demand for oil by the petrochemical industry, domestic and industrial users and in supplying the needs of transport that it affects entire economic cycles.

The rise in influence of the Organization of the Petroleum Exporting Countries (OPEC) during the 1970s and 1980s gave a huge increase in revenues to many

 Key terms

carbon burial: the extraction of carbon dioxide from energy and industrial emissions and burial in sealed underground rock strata; also known as 'artificial carbon sequestration'

energy mix: the sources of energy in their different proportions of use constitute a country's energy mix

oil producers, particularly those with large reserves in the Middle East. But the increase in oil prices that followed it also stimulated the global search for oil elsewhere as revenue levels rose and exploration in more hostile physical environments meant that exploitable finds became potentially profitable for the first time.

The pattern of global oil production (Figure 11.12) reflects the ease of extraction, the economic cost of exploitation, decisions about rates of production and supply and political preferences (or constraints) in international trade. Patterns of oil imports are affected by reliability of supply, trade embargoes, diversity of supplier options and the nature of the oil (light or heavy). The interests of governments combine with the economic decisions of transnational oil companies in influencing how the international trade in oil evolves.

Figure 11.11 Barrels of oil awaiting export.

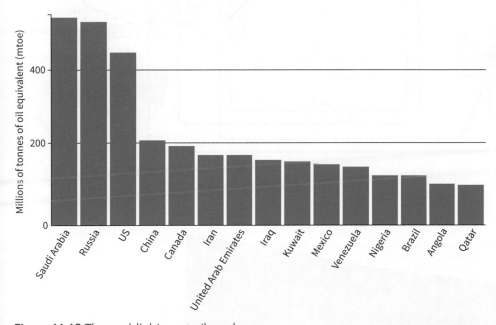

Figure 11.12 The world's biggest oil producers.

The shift in global trade of oil (Figure 11.13) from Europe and North America towards Asia is likely to mirror that of coal. It is expected that by 2040 two out of every three barrels of oil traded on the international market will be going to Asian countries. It will be supplying the growth in energy needs of transport as well as industrial processes and domestic heating as these economies grow rapidly and consumer affluence increases.

Maths for geographers

The USA, India and China all import as well as export oil. Using Figure 11.13, calculate the gross imports and exports for each country (total the arrows in and out) and then work out the net imports (total imports minus total exports). Rank the countries in order of their largest oil trade deficit.

Maths for geographers

Using the graph in Figure 11.14:

a   Create a table of oil demand by region by reading off the scale for 2005 and 2025.

b   Calculate the percentage demand of the total for each region in 2005 and in 2025.

c   Calculate the percentage change for each region over the 20-year period.

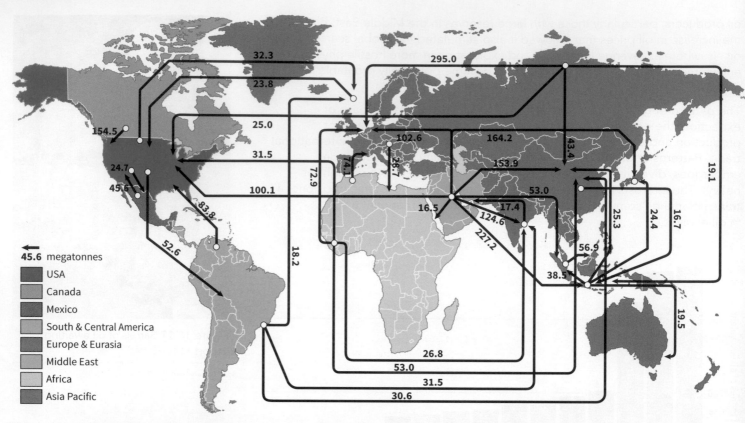

Figure 11.13 Global oil trade flows, 2013.

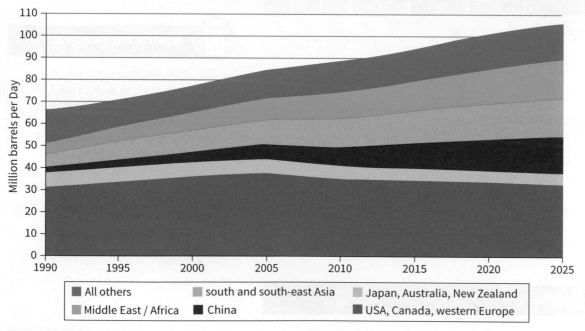

Figure 11.14 World oil demand, 1990–2025.

The global gas trade

Although gas has a long history (since the 1870s) of being transported within countries by pipeline, the international trade in gas with pipelines crossing national borders is more recent. Similarly, bulk shipments of liquefied natural gas (LNG) have a considerably shorter history than oil shipments. The first gas tanker was built in 1959 and only in more recent decades has the development of

Figure 11.15 Engineering developments in LNG carriers have expanded the global trade in this energy source in recent decades.

Look on **Cambridge Elevate** at this article from the *Guardian*, which considers the geopolitical factors influencing the European gas trade (www.cambridge.org/links/gase6119).

Key term

energy gap: where the available supply of energy is no longer able to meet the size and nature of the demand

large-scale cryogenic tankers capable of safely transporting bulk liquid methane at temperatures of −162 °C made the international trade economically viable (Figure 11.15).

The trade in natural gas is increasing at a faster rate than any other fossil fuel and is due to continue over the coming decades for two reasons:

- Gas combustion releases less carbon dioxide (CO_2) than either coal or oil, making it a favoured energy source for companies and nations trying to meet tightening emissions targets.
- The greater trade flexibility offered by LNG shipments over fixed pipeline infrastructure offers consumers a rapidly responsive energy source. After the 2011 Fukushima nuclear disaster and the subsequent (temporary) closure of all its nuclear power stations, Japan relied on switching to imports of LNG to meet its **energy gap**.

It is forecast that the energy demands of India and China will increase the market for LNG in Asia, with Australia anticipated to overtake Qatar as the world's largest producer of natural gas by 2020 and LNG overtaking coal as the country's second largest export after iron ore.

Natural gas is probably the most flexible and convenient of all fuels to transport considerable distances by pipeline. Since the disintegration of the former Soviet Union in 1989, Russia – holding the world's largest natural gas reserves – has become a major supplier to the rest of Europe via a network of cross-border pipelines (Figure 11.16). Following the divesting of state monopolies in the 1990s, Gazprom has become one of the world's largest companies supplying gas in a mutually beneficial trade that has seen the Russian economy underpinned by sales from its gas reserves and European nations meet their growing energy needs for domestic, industrial and power-generation uses.

In the winters of 2006 and 2008–9, disputes over appropriate payments for gas caused Gazprom to suspend gas supplies into Ukraine. The knock-on interruption of supply had severe repercussions for a number of eastern European countries that depended on gas transit through Ukraine (Figure 11.17), resulting in a lack of domestic heating and reduced industrial production. A similar suspension in supplies in June 2014, ostensibly over the failure of Ukraine to pay upfront gas costs, permitted the through-transit of gas to downstream customers as long as Ukraine did not access the supply.

ACTIVITY 11.3

1. List the advantages and disadvantages for a country such as Qatar that has an economy dominated by the export of a single energy commodity such as oil or gas.
2. Consider the pros and cons for a country such as the USA that imports oil from many different sources around the world.

Figure 11.16 A gas pipeline near Kiev, Ukraine supplying gas from Russia.

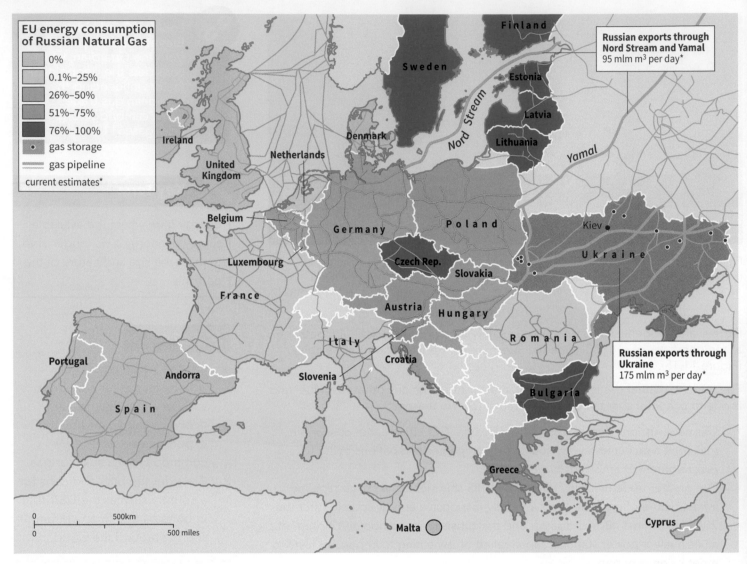

Figure 11.17 EU imports of Russian gas.

The energy of international gas trading arrangements is, as far as Europe is concerned, inextricably entangled with political considerations.

Global patterns of ore mineral production, consumption and trade flows

The global distribution of **ore minerals** relates largely to geological conditions that have enabled concentrations of minerals to infiltrate rocks in particular locations. Within regions of historic tectonic activity the key conditions for ore formation are often found:

- the release of substantial quantities of a mineral from a more diffuse source
- the transport of the mineral from source to a new location in a fluid or semi-fluid state
- the entrapment and further accumulation of the mineral.

However, mineral deposits may form as a result of deposition on ancient ocean floors (banded iron ore) or the effects of gravity on sedimentation of coastal deposits (titanium). Many minerals, such as copper, have more than one formation process.

 Key terms

ore: a rock containing an increased concentration of extractable proportions of a mineral

mineral: a naturally occurring inorganic (non-hydrocarbon based) substance in solid form with a definite chemical composition. It may be metallic (iron oxide) or non-metallic (calcium phosphate) and often formed as a result of geological processes

Ore mineral extraction and processing have historically taken place in close proximity, as the cost of transporting bulky ore that contains both the desired mineral and rock waste has been uneconomic. In Western Australia iron ore mines and coastal processing plants put low-grade ore through a process of **beneficiation**, this not only removes shale waste but transforms fine, powdery concentrate into pellets that are easier to transport and load into a blast furnace at their global market destination.

The distribution of ore mineral resources is uneven as well as unequal in actual and potential value. The significance to a country of its ore mineral wealth is influenced by the:

* size and volume of deposits (vertical as well as horizontal)
* ease of extraction and processing (surface quarries are less expensive than deep mining)
* ubiquity versus rarity of the ore minerals (iron ore is very common; rare-earth minerals are not)
* quality of the mineral reserves (contamination by waste and level of mineral concentration)
* market demand for the ore minerals
* viable exploitation lifetime of reserves
* strategic significance of the ore mineral(s)
* environmental, social and political impact of resource extraction and processing.

Some of the most mineral-rich countries of the world are highly dependent on the global trade in ore minerals and derive a significant proportion of their national income from their exploitation.

Global patterns of consumption of ore minerals are largely a measure of industrial and manufacturing diversity and financial strength. While gold is utilised largely as a financial reserve by national banks, other dominant ore minerals are used in an industrial manufacturing process/product or, in the case of phosphate rocks, in creating agricultural fertilisers. Ranking highest in the import of ore minerals are those countries which have an extensive chemical, agricultural and industrial base and which have limited home supplies on which to draw.

The ore mineral trade is dominated by transnational corporations with a global portfolio of operations from extraction and processing to shipping, rail and production. There are relatively few state-run nationalised ore mineral operations, limited to Namibia and Zimbabwe in Africa, and Bolivia, Venezuela and Ecuador in South America. The situation is unclear in China with layers of state ownership being divested to private ownership on a piecemeal or gradual basis.

The key global corporations involved in ore minerals include Glencore Xstrata (Swiss), which is arguably the world's largest mining company operating over 150 mines and **metallurgical sites** around the world and extracting from the Zanaga iron ore mine in the Republic of Congo, the Collahuasi copper mine in Chile and the Antamina copper-zinc mine in Peru.

The geopolitics of resource use

If sound politics is about negotiating disagreement through to a resolution acceptable to all, then **geopolitics** is the process by which nations and regions attempt to manage the issues that geography deals them. In the case of energy, minerals and water, countries may feel constrained by lack of access to the resources they feel they require. Those constraints may exist because of:

* lack of physical access to the specific regions where the resources exist
* lack of trade access due to insufficient wealth

Making connections

To what extent do mineral resource locations formed in Earth's geological past correspond to current areas of tectonic activity? See Chapter 5 Hazards.

Key terms

beneficiation: processes after mining a metallurgical ore that concentrate the mineral-containing material and separate it from waste rock (tailings). Often involves significant water-use in froth-flotation or gravity separation

metallurgical: technological and scientific processes designed to obtain, purify and modify metal from mineral ores

geopolitics: a study of the issues that arise as a result of the unequal distribution of geographical phenomena and the imbalanced power relationships attempting to access, influence and control them

Making connections

Read how international trade and access to markets operates in Chapter 7 Global systems and global governance.

- lack of trade access due to the difficulty of entering established markets and structures
- excluded access due to restrictive trade agreements, trade embargoes or political isolationism.

Even when access to a resource has been acquired, its use and the consequences of that use may affect neighbouring regions and countries in negative ways that raise serious concerns.

When a nation or a region within a country is short of the resources it needs, it is usually reliant on supplies from elsewhere. That may not be an issue if it has the wealth to purchase positive trade relations with potential suppliers. But conditions arise when that does not happen and options for action become more limited. Obtaining a state of **resource security** is one in which you are as self-reliant as you need to be to meet demand, or you are cushioned against fluctuations in price and availability so that you do not subside into a state of potential crisis.

11.3 Water security

'Water security is defined as the capacity of a population to safeguard sustainable access to adequate quantities of acceptable quality water for sustaining livelihoods, human well-being, and socio-economic development, for ensuring protection against water-borne pollution and water-related disasters, and for preserving ecosystems in a climate of peace and political stability.'

Source: UN-Water, 2013.

Global patterns of water availability and demand

Clearly, climate plays a major role in the global availability of water (Figure 11.18) in both precipitation and evaporation rates. But the presence of historic aquifers, the availability of glacier and snowmelt, and wealth to pay for seawater distillation plants all add further to potential sources of **potable water**. The regions of 'no appreciable flow' tend to be sparsely populated. The regions of most significant **water stress** are those with significant populations but variable or unreliable sources of freshwater.

Water availability – particularly of clean, uncontaminated water – is a fundamental requirement for a satisfactory quality of life (Figure 11.19). The main demands for freshwater include:

- domestic uses – largely involving drinking, cleanliness and hygiene (including sanitation systems) and food preparation (Figure 11.20)
- industrial processes and manufacturing
- energy production (thermal power stations and HEP)
- agricultural needs, such as irrigation of crops.

These vary in proportion according to the environmental, economic and social context of a country.

Rising global population is not the only factor behind the increasing consumption of water (Figure 11.21). As standards of living rise, so expectations of sanitation systems, domestic appliance use (such as washing machines and dishwashers), industrial demands and agricultural needs increase (Figure 11.22). The trend is likely to be intensified as global climate change creates water stress in previously moist regions, leading to demands for more irrigation. In California (Figure 11.23), the percentage of irrigated farmland increased from

Key terms

resource security: the capacity of a population to access sufficient resources for present and ongoing needs to sustain a desired level of consumption or use

potable water: water of a quality that can be safely drunk and used in food preparation without compromising health

water stress: the first level of water scarcity, when available water supplies fall below 1700 m³ per person per year; below 1000 m³ per year, it becomes 'water scarcity' and less than 500 m³ per year it is 'absolute scarcity'

Look on **Cambridge Elevate** for a video discussion with transcript from the Stratfor website, outlining how water supply is affected by geopolitics (www.cambridge.org/links/gase6120)

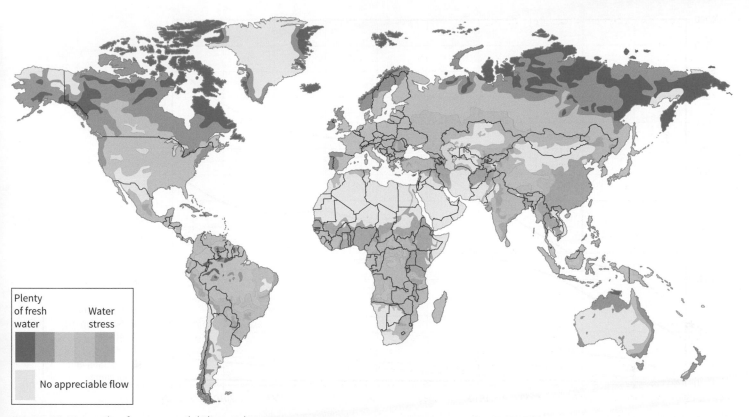

Figure 11.18 Levels of water availability and regions experiencing water stress.

Figure 11.19 Access to safe, clean water is a fundamental human requirement.

Figure 11.20 Water is vital for hygiene and sanitation.

16% in 1980 to 26% by 2011. The water requirements of more high-value crops alongside increasingly frequent drought conditions have resulted in increased consumption.

Strategies to attain a state of water security as demand increases include:

- development of additional water provision within regional/national borders
- increasing storage capacity and reducing the rate of through-flow
- managing existing water supplies more efficiently
- reducing waste and loss.

Making connections

Read more about issues of water provision in arid and semi-arid regions in Chapter 2 Hot desert systems and landscapes.

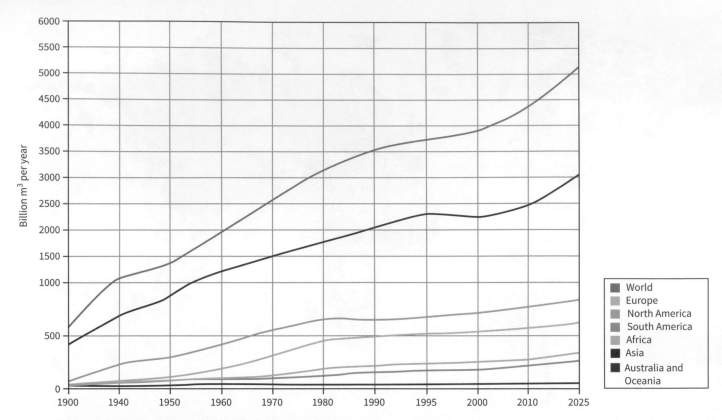

Figure 11.21 Global water consumption, 1900–2025.

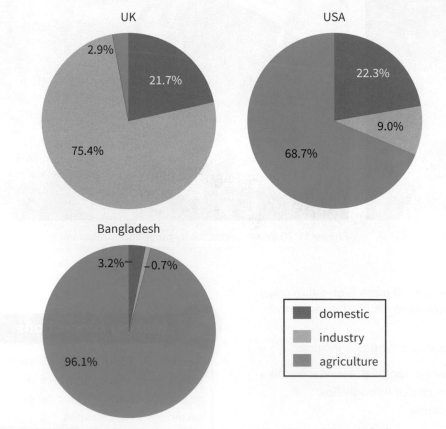

Figure 11.22 Water consumption patterns in the UK, USA and Bangladesh.

Figure 11.23 Irrigating crops in California, where most of the fruit and vegetables for the USA are grown.

Making connections

For more information on the world's water, see section 1.2 The water cycle.

Sources of water

Water is sourced from surface or underground supplies. Surface supplies may make direct use of freshwater from historic stores (glaciers), continuous flow (rivers, rain) or the result of processing of non-potable water (seawater, greywater). Underground sources may be historic (confined aquifers) or recent/current infiltration (groundwater), as shown in Figure 11.24.

River abstraction: probably the oldest way in which humans have obtained water – going down to the river and collecting it. Thames Water, which serves London and south-east England, obtains 70% of its water from rivers.

Reservoirs: storage lakes, sometimes natural but often constructed, that hold quantities of river flow such that it is subject to less short-term fluctuations than

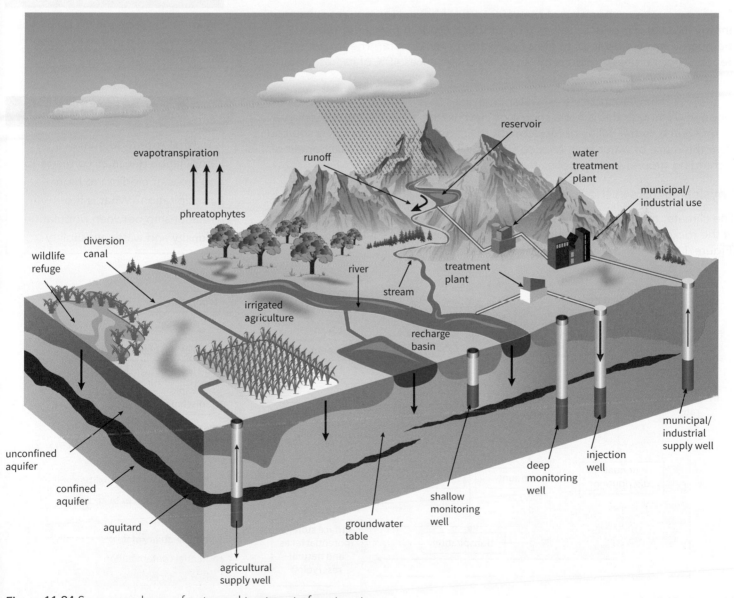

Figure 11.24 Sources and uses of water and treatment of wastewater.

a river level. Welsh Water obtains 95% of its water from river abstraction or reservoirs thanks to high rainfall and impermeable rock predominating.

Boreholes into the water table: traditional wells are sunk through permeable surface layers to penetrate the water table contained in rock structures with water-holding capacity. Thames Water obtains 30% of its water in this way.

Pumping from aquifers: an aquifer is a confined layer of saturated rock, usually deeper than that which forms a water table, and capped top and bottom by impermeable rock such that when it is bored into the substantial pressure it is under forces water to rise. The Ogallala aquifer of the American Midwest stores as much water as Lake Huron in the Great Lakes.

Snow and glacier melt: around 60% of Iran's freshwater for urban industrial uses and agricultural irrigation is sourced from its melting glaciers. Climate change poses serious issues about the medium-term sustainability of this water source for the country. The meltwater from glaciers in the Hindu Kush Himalayan region (Figure 11.25), which covers eight countries across Asia, supplements several great river systems such as the Indus, Ganges and Brahmaputra.

Desalination: the evaporation of seawater to distil freshwater requires substantial energy input and produces salt as a by-product. Modern plants use dual-membrane reverse osmosis to filter freshwater from seawater. The largest dependency on desalination is by Israel, which produces 40% of its freshwater using this method.

Water reuse: as demand for freshwater intensifies, it is increasingly being recycled. Although this is not a source of 'new' water, it can still be classed as a water source. In the Valley of Mexico, approximately 90% of irrigation is sourced from the reuse of water from Mexico City. This has had the additional benefit of recharging groundwater supplies through percolation.

Physical factors in the quantity and quality of water availability

The climate, the nature of the ground surface and the structure and organisation of the rocks all contribute to the availability and quality of freshwater in a region (Figure 11.26).

Figure 11.25 Glaciers in the Himalayas provide meltwater and source major river systems.

 Physical and human

To what extent do human population densities correspond to areas of medium to high precipitation? What is the relationship between population density and water availability?

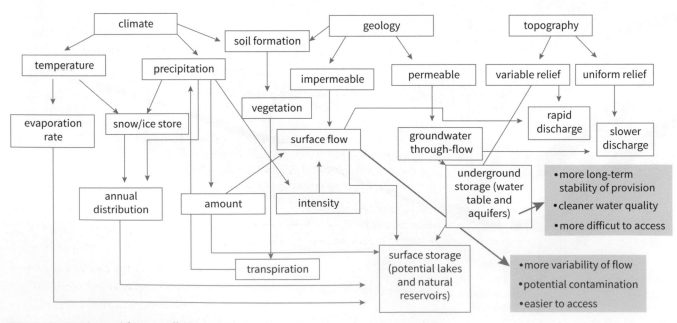

Figure 11.26 Physical factors affecting the quantity and quality of water availability.

Human interventions in water supply

Human interventions in the water system can influence the rate of flow, storage capacity, whether it takes the form of surface or underground flow, and the quality of water moving downstream. Users downstream are affected both in terms of the quantity and quality of water that they receive. A range of these interventions is summarised in Table 11.2.

Human intervention	Usage and consequences
Reservoirs	Increase water storage, reduce flow rate and can increase water loss due to evaporation.
Borewells	Extract groundwater and lower the water table (Figure 11.27), although the groundwater may be returned if it is used for irrigation systems.
River abstraction	Reduces river volume and may return it as wastewater, resulting in a change in water quality.
Channel straightening	Increases the rate of river discharge, but may reduce flooding and subsequent infiltration to resupply groundwater.
Urban growth	Increases the demand for water, but also increases the rate of surface runoff into channels under conditions of heavy rain.
Industrial developments	Much industry has heavy water demand for key processes, washing and thermal power. Industrial effluent can leach into groundwater or contaminate surface flow.
Power generation	Thermal power stations require vast quantities of water to convert to steam. Too much abstraction lowers river levels. Some river water is lost as water vapour. Water contaminated with heat or radioactivity from nuclear power stations may be returned to the river system.
Agricultural development	Heavy machinery may compact soil, reducing permeability and increasing surface runoff. Heavy use of chemicals (nitrate/phosphate fertilisers and pesticide chemicals) (Figure 11.28) may leach into rivers and contaminate downstream supplies.

Table 11.2 Human intervention in water systems.

Water scarcity

Water stress and **water scarcity** are likely to be intensified in coming decades as a result of:

- rising population numbers
- increasing population concentrations in urban areas
- rising living standards accompanied by greater water use per household
- industrialisation of former agricultural societies
- intensification and commercialisation of agriculture
- climate change disrupting historic patterns of precipitation.

Thinking like a geographer

Consider the range of variables influencing a geographical issue. How is global climate change likely to affect supplies of water in different parts of the world? Will the impacts be similar or different? Will they increase or decrease water availability?

Key term

water scarcity: the lack of sufficient freshwater of an acceptable quality for the human needs of a region; it has degrees of severity ranging through water stress, water scarcity and, ultimately, water crisis

Figure 11.27 Drilling a village borewell in an arid part of India.

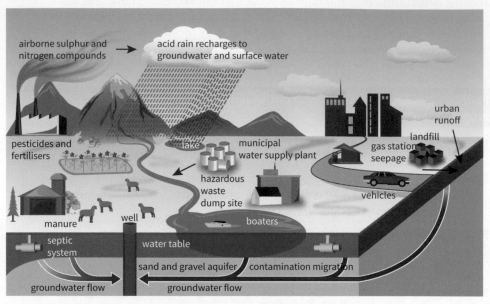

Figure 11.28 Sources of pollution in the water cycle.

The issues encompass both the quantity of freshwater available to satisfy needs (Figure 11.29), as well as water quality.

Water stress can be attributed to physical water stress (caused by declining levels of precipitation, groundwater or glacier melt) and economic water stress (when there is sufficient water but it is poorly managed, distributed and maintained to satisfy needs). The United Nations Development Programme estimates that economic stress is the most widely experienced cause of water issues across nations; most have sufficient supplies, but there is mismanagement in getting it to where it is required in acceptable quantities and quality (Figure 11.30).

The negative consequences of water stress include:

- health issues from using contaminated water or insufficient water for sanitation systems to operate effectively
- nutrition issues from insufficient water to irrigate crops or water animals
- economic issues from lower yields from commercial farms, reduced industrial output or tourism revenue
- environmental issues as biomes adapted to a historic level of moisture experience rapid change to drier conditions. Groundwater may increase in salinity as a consequence
- social issues as more time is devoted to water collection or having to purchase from private water sellers
- infrastructure issues if energy providers are unable to generate electricity due to reduced reservoir capacity (HEP) or river flow (thermal power stations)
- political issues if there is a widely held sense that certain groups within society have unfair access to reasonable water provision to the detriment of other, less powerful, groups.

Making connections

Read more on the issues of polluted water supplies in urban areas in section 9.4 Urban climate.

For an activity on water stress affecting different countries download Worksheet 11.2 from **Cambridge Elevate**.

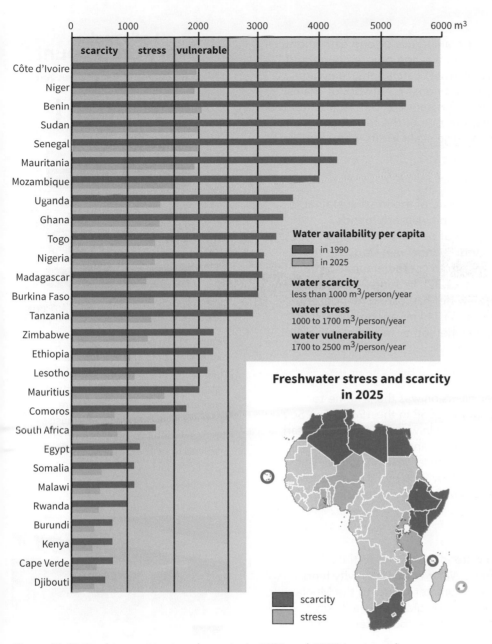

Water availability per capita

- in 1990
- in 2025

water scarcity
less than 1000 m³/person/year

water stress
1000 to 1700 m³/person/year

water vulnerability
1700 to 2500 m³/person/year

Freshwater stress and scarcity in 2025

- scarcity
- stress

Figure 11.29 Freshwater stress and scarcity in 1990 and 2025 (projected).

Figure 11.30 Water collection can take up valuable hours each day and limits the quantity available to families.

Strategies to increase water supply

Capturing and storing additional water so it is more readily available is one way in which water scarcity can be avoided. Clearly, any attempt to interrupt and slow the flow of water through any one region will have consequences for neighbouring areas downstream. In this sense, increasing water supply through **catchment** strategies is a **zero-sum game**: one region benefits to another's detriment.

Large-scale catchment schemes

These involve the construction of a number of dams to create reservoirs along the course of one or more rivers. In 2014 Australia announced plans for a major extension of reservoir storage through the increase in capacity of existing dams and new dam construction. Twenty-six projects were being considered from Queensland in the north-east to Tasmania in the south.

Key terms

catchment: the total surface area from which water drains into a particular river system

zero-sum game: when an initiative benefits one group, but at the expense of another

493

Regional catchment schemes

Operating for the benefit of a specific city or making use of one catchment basin, these are smaller in scale but may involve a range of interconnected programmes. With two-thirds of Singapore as water catchment, rainwater that falls in these areas is collected through an extensive network of drains, rivers, canals, storm water collection ponds and reservoirs, before it is treated for drinking water supply. This makes Singapore one of the few countries in the world to harvest urban storm water on a large scale for its water supply (Figure 11.31).

Small-scale catchment schemes

Rainwater harvesting via individual buildings is one of the most sustainable and accessible ways for households to reduce their water demands on city-wide provision, secure their own supply of potable water and replenish groundwater reserves. Plastic gutters channel rain from the roof through a simple charcoal and sand filter system to containers that protect the water from subsequent contamination (Figure 11.32). In June 2001 the Indian state of Tamil Nadu was the first to make rainwater harvesting mandatory in all new buildings with a roof area of more than 111 m² and in all existing plots with an area of more than 223 m², since when other Indian states have followed.

Drainage diversion programmes

Perhaps the most notorious example of river diversion was the scheme to increase water supply in relatively arid parts of the USSR in the 1960s. The Soviet government's plan for large-scale cotton production in what is now Uzbekistan was achieved by diverting the flow of the Amu Darya and Syr Darya rivers at the expense of the Aral Sea, the world's (once) fourth largest inland sea. With drastically reduced input, the Aral Sea had shrunk by 90% by 2014 as its losses continued (Figure 11.33). It is a study in successful drainage diversion resulting in incalculable devastation.

Water transfer programmes

In southern Africa, water is transferred from water-rich Lesotho to the water-scarce Gauteng province in South Africa. Water flows by gravity feed from the Katse dam through a 47 km long, 5 m diameter tunnel to the Muela Tailpond dam. The water is then transferred, again by gravity, via a 38 km tunnel into South Africa. In this way, water is one of Lesotho's international exports.

Desalination

The two main ways of obtaining freshwater from salt water are vacuum evaporation and reverse osmosis. Neither method is cheap, but the risk of water shortage is making this water source increasingly attractive.

Research point

Research the Soviet policies that led to the eventual decline of the Aral Sea. What have been the economic, social and environmental consequences of this drainage diversion scheme on human populations in the region? Has the local climate been affected as a consequence?

Figure 11.31 Water demand management is just as important in securing an adequate supply of water; Singapore's public information programme from the Singapore National Water Agency, emphasises the need for all to be committed and involved in water conservation.

Figure 11.32 A household rainwater harvesting storage tank.

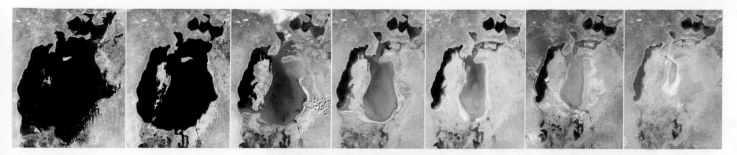

Figure 11.33 The disappearing Aral Sea – a consequence of drainage diversion.

Environmental impacts of water supply schemes

A lot of dam construction is for multi-purpose schemes, that not only offer more consistent provision of freshwater for regions adjacent to the reservoir (both for domestic uses and irrigation of crops), but also control potential flooding downstream and generate hydro-electric power. However, most dams are single-purpose and according to the World Register of Dams irrigation is still the most common purpose (48%), 17% are for hydropower, 13% for water supply, 10% for flood control, 5% for recreation and 1% to aid river navigation. Whatever the justification, while the benefits are social, economic and/or political, the environmental implications can quickly become negative.

Upstream

- Reduction in fish stocks as breeding fish cannot make their way up to headwaters.
- Less steep long profile causes upstream rivers to reduce velocity increasing flood risk.

Within dam/reservoir zone

- Flooding of significant areas of low-lying land, reducing biodiversity.
- Methane generation as submerged biomass decomposes in anaerobic conditions.
- Displacement of communities occupying and making use of flooded zone.
- Increase in malaria as mosquitos breed in brackish water of low-energy reservoir shorelines and brackish canal distribution networks.
- Nutrient-rich reservoirs encourage toxic algal blooms.
- Evaporation of moisture from reservoir can affect microclimate of the area and alter the local ecosystem.
- Saline deposits accumulate on irrigated land with intense evaporation of water content.
- Pressure of reservoir water may create seismic pressure and instigate earth tremors.

Downstream

- Reduction in maximum flow levels of river so sediment is not flushed from channels.
- Lower river level causes groundwater level to fall increasing water borehole failure.
- Increased salinity of river water makes it less suitable for some fish species and irrigation

- Reduced flow of nutrients limits aquatic species.
- Reduced flow of nutrients and flood occasions prevents replenishment of flood plain soil fertility.

A study in the *Malaria Journal* in 2015 estimated that one million Africans caught malaria that year because they live near a large dam and reservoir.

Making connections

Read more on the impact of dams with the case study on the Three Gorges Dam in Chapter 6 Ecosystems under stress.

The Koka Reservoir in Ethiopia was completed in 1961 and is the oldest large dam in the country. Initially constructed for hydropower it is now multipurpose and its functions include provision of irrigation water for the 6000 hectares. A study collecting data between 1994 and 2002 and published in 2007 found that malaria cases were 1.47 times higher for people living within 3 km of the reservoir than for those living 3.6 km away, and 2.31 times as great compared with those living 6–9 km away. The findings were consistent with those of other dams in malaria-prolific regions. In the case of the Koka Reservoir it stimulated higher rates of mosquito breeding for several reasons:

- The reservoir raises the groundwater level in adjacent sites encouraging the development of stagnant puddles that provide the breeding grounds for malaria-carrying mosquitos.
- The gentle gradient of the reservoir shoreline also encourages puddle-formation as the reservoir level recedes during dry periods and after heavy rain.
- Water seepage below the dam creates a swampy habitat that supports the life cycle of larvae into fully adult mosquitos.

Making connections

Read more about the global distribution of malaria and the infection process in Chapter 10 Population and the environment.

The recommendations urge that dam construction and reservoir creation include mitigation strategies that reduce the breeding opportunities of mosquitos at source, rather than having to deal with the increased rates of malaria that are a frequent consequence.

Strategies to manage water consumption

Attempts to more closely match water provision against demand focus on four main areas:

- improving storage as water passes through a regional system
- recycling water within the regional system
- using water more efficiently
- reducing demand.

Improving storage

Capturing and holding water within a regional system is usually achieved using surface reservoirs. However, the construction of a dam or increasing the height of a natural barrier at the mouth of lake is not without issue:

- Considerable low-lying land is likely to be submerged and populations will require relocation.
- The construction of dams requires vast amounts of concrete, the production of which is one of the most significant industrial contributors of carbon dioxide in global emissions.

- Reservoirs have to be sited on impermeable rock. If, however, that is a relatively thin layer, the huge pressure of water can fracture the underlying rock.
- Water loss due to evaporation can be substantial with a standing body of water with a large surface area (Figure 11.34).
- Tectonic activity and active faults can endanger the internal coherence of dam structures and lead to catastrophic collapse, releasing millions of litres of water down a valley.
- The silt that is brought down by rivers feeding into a reservoir, together with that washed off adjacent slopes gradually accumulates a layer of sediment on the reservoir floor. Difficult to dredge, the consequence is that from the moment it is opened each reservoir is losing capacity to store water.

Many of the world's reservoirs are built in historically high rainfall areas with relief favourable for damming. These conditions often mean they are some distance from areas of dense population, so their water needs to be pumped to where it is required. This is both an expensive transfer and subject to water loss through leakage. Where climate change is reducing precipitation amounts, a reservoir is a fixed asset that is not subject to relocation. It is arguable whether reservoir storage is a sustainable option in terms of construction impacts, storage loss, energy requirements and operational lifespan.

Recycling water

Israel became the world's foremost water recycling country in 2010, treating 80% of sewage and reclaiming water for landscape and irrigation needs (Figure 11.35). For the highest-quality water needs, after the usual chemical and biological treatment some sewage water is fed into gravitational filtering ponds whereby water is allowed to percolate through successive sand layers into the aquifer below. After 400 days it is in a suitable condition to be pumped to the surface again as high-quality purified water.

Figure 11.34 Lake Nasser's large surface area in a hot desert results in considerable water loss by evaporation.

Figure 11.35 The Ashkelon wastewater treatment facility in Israel.

Using water more efficiently

Grading water quality

One of the criticisms of much high-quality water provision is that water of potable quality is used to wash clothes and cars, spray on gardens and flush toilets: it is over-engineered for many of the uses to which it is put. In Australia domestic water is classified as blackwater (from toilets) and greywater (from baths and showers, basins and laundry). Greywater may be reused indoors for flushing toilets and in washing machines (two of the largest domestic uses of water) once it has been filtered and disinfected, and outdoors for garden irrigation and car washing with very little treatment (Figure 11.36).

Step 1 Collect | The **Aqua2use®** GWDD diverts water from the laundry, bath and shower

Step 2 Filter | **Aqua2use®** GWDD's state of art filter mats offer the best filtration available for greywater.

Step 3 Flourish | The filtered water is immediately and automaticaly pumped via subsurface dripper irrigation to keep your garden green.

Figure 11.36 A Taiwanese greywater recycling company advertises its filter products.

Appropriate provision

In agriculture, the choice of irrigation method can affect water efficiency. Flood irrigation and sprinkler systems both deploy water where it is not necessarily needed, making it liable to losses through evaporation and percolation. Drip irrigation, however, supplies water much more precisely to both the location and needs of certain crops and brings much higher efficiency in the use of water (Figure 11.37).

Reducing losses

It is estimated that many of Britain's water networks lose up to 25% of the water that enters ageing pipe systems from reservoirs versus that which comes out of taps in homes. Locating leaks can be more expensive than repairing them. Privatised water companies are limited in how much they can invest in repairs to leaking pipes by the water regulation body Ofwat. Although Ofwat sets targets for water companies to reduce leaks, it regulates water bills such that companies argue they do not have the financial reserves to carry out necessary repairs.

Reducing demand

In the case of many resources, one way of reducing demand is to find substitutes or alternatives. However, water is such a unique resource that it has no appreciable substitutes. However, wastefulness can be managed through the use of cost incentives and disincentives – the 'carrot and stick' approach.

- Incentives: all new homes built in Britain since 1990 have required a household water meter. This allows occupiers to see exactly how much

Figure 11.37 Drip irrigation delivers water directly to the area of the plant's root system.

water they are using and, if they want lower water bills, to reduce it. In 2013 government ministers ordered 9 of the 24 water companies in England and Wales to consider compulsory metering in order to prevent forecast water shortages from becoming critical.

- Disincentives: in Bangalore, India, property owners are threatened with having their water supply cut off if they fail to install rainwater-harvesting facilities. This follows successful initiatives in Chennai whereby all three-storey buildings are required to have functioning rainwater-harvesting facilities in order to be connected to water and sanitation systems.

Reducing the virtual water trade and water footprint

The concept of **virtual water** trade was coined by Professor Tony Allan in the 1990s and refers to the total requirement of water for a commodity or manufactured product that is subsequently exported. The production water is lost to the origin as it has been removed from alternative uses to create a product that is utilised elsewhere. As a consequence, the producers become exporters of virtual water and the destination of the good becomes an importer of virtual water. An example is the growing of flowers for UK supermarkets through irrigated glasshouse floriculture in Kenya, when areas of the country are experiencing drought. Allan suggests that water-scarce nations can release water for more essential needs by avoiding the production and export of water-intense products and importing these from more water-rich countries if they are a desired commodity.

In a development of this, Arjen Hoekstra developed the concept of the **water footprint** in 2002. This accounts for not only the water in the preceding processes, but the associated contamination of freshwater with pollutants rendering it beyond use. Many would consider that a cup of coffee requires just the water in the cup, but 140 litres of water is 'virtually traded' when Brazil exports coffee to Europe – this being the volume used to grow, produce, package and ship the coffee beans. The electricity required to boil the water and washing up the used cup adds to the water footprint of the consumer of that one cup of coffee. Similar to the quantification of a nation's carbon footprint, knowledge of a nation's water footprint compared with others can encourage countries to implement water-saving and effluent-reduction programmes.

Water conflicts

The nature of this resource in flowing from one region to another and frequently between nations means there is a dependence upon upstream neighbours in what they do with it and the condition in which they release it to flow downstream. Similarly, if water is abstracted from underground reserves so that the water table falls substantially, some groups may find their wells drying up if they do not have capacity to extend their borewells.

Local water conflicts

As a global brand, Coca-Cola is one of the most successful companies in the world. Its soft drink is exported from its Atlanta base in the USA in concentrated syrup form. The franchised drink is constituted and bottled in countries with significant markets, which requires access to large quantities of filtered water. In the state of Uttar Pradesh in northern India, this has been sourced from an underground aquifer through company borewells since a plant was first built at Mehdiganj in 1999. Not only is filtered water required to make up the drink, it is also needed to wash bottles and equipment. Conflict has simmered for over a decade as local farmers claim their wells have dried up as a direct result of the company's rate of aquifer abstraction. The water table has fallen to such an extent that their borewells no longer penetrate the water table (Figure 11.38). They also claim that effluent from the plant has polluted fields and groundwater.

Key terms

virtual water: the water volume involved in the full production process of a commodity or manufacture destined for export, representing water lost to the origin of the item

water footprint: an indicator of the volume of freshwater involved in producing goods and services at any scale from the individual, the community, a business or a nation. It includes the totality of water used plus contamination of related water supplies

Look on **Cambridge Elevate** for an online water footprint calculator from National Geographic, which encourages American consumers to check how much water they use and suggestions on how to reduce it (www.cambridge.org/links/gase6121).

Research point

Look up the countries with the largest and smallest water footprints. To what extent do the patterns reflect economic factors (wealth) or water availability (precipitation)?

Look on **Cambridge Elevate** to read an article from the *Guardian*, about why water conflicts may occur at the local scale but can reflect the impacts of globalisation of production (www.cambridge.org/links/gase6122).

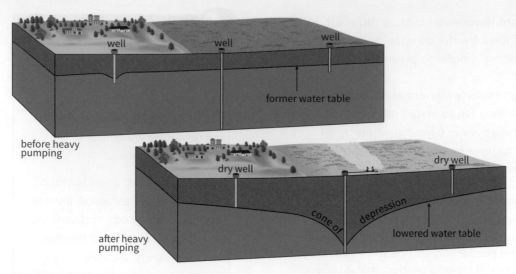

before heavy pumping

after heavy pumping

Figure 11.38 Heavy pumping can lead to shallow borewells drying as the water table falls.

However, the company argues the fall in water table is due to long-term drought and a reduction in precipitation totals. Nevertheless, the plant was ordered to close by state officials in June 2014, giving breaches in the operation licence as the reason. Coca-Cola operates a further 57 plants throughout India in what is one of its most rapidly expanding markets in the world.

Inter-regional water conflicts

Water shortages in Spain have seen both regional conflict as well as economic sector divisions over who should get access to an increasingly stressed resource. In 2008, during a particularly severe drought, the Catalan government in north-east Spain proposed diverting water from the Segre River (a tributary of the Ebro) to help meet Catalonia's needs. However, this was resisted by the national government in Madrid as it would exacerbate the water crisis in neighbouring Aragon through which the Segre flows for a short section of its route. The Spanish constitution states that where rivers flow through more than one of the country's 17 autonomous communities, decisions on water diversion must be taken at the national level.

Catalonia has long demanded independence for this part of Spain and the conflict further inflamed divisions with both its neighbouring region and the national government. Eventually, Catalonia imported water by tanker from France and accelerated work on a desalination plant. Since then, the EU has helped fund two more desalination plants to supply part of Barcelona and the Catalan region's needs.

International water conflicts

There are estimated to be 263 **transboundary rivers** in the world where flows cross international borders. Transboundary aquifers require particular cooperation, such as the shared aquifer underlying Jordan and Saudi Arabia. One of the most sensitive regions that will put the issue of international cooperation to the test focuses on the Himalayas and the many rivers that flow from them.

Between India and its eastern neighbour Bangladesh flow 54 rivers, including the River Ganges (Padma River in Bangladesh), with most originating in the Himalayas. The significantly smaller country has accused India of reducing the Padma's flow with the construction of the Farakka barrage. Possibly more controversial yet, India has commenced a mega-engineering scheme of redirecting river flow throughout the sub continent with the India Rivers Interlinking Project, the first stage of which was completed in September 2015. Parts of this scheme could have substantial implications for Bangladesh if the proposed transfer of waters from rivers in north-east India to more water-stressed states in the south goes ahead.

Key term

transboundary rivers: rivers that extend either side of at least one political boundary, either a border within a nation or an international boundary

ACTIVITY 11.4

1 Use an atlas to find five major world rivers and list the countries they flow through. Which river flows through most? Are there any that flow through only one?

11.4 Securing sufficient clean water in Peru

Peru is among the top 20 countries in the world for water availability per capita, but is in the top 30 countries experiencing water scarcity and stress. This apparent contradiction lies in the geography of the country: most of the freshwater capacity is in the eastern part covering the Amazon Basin, while 70% of the population lives in the arid/semi-arid central Andes and western coastal zone (Figure 11.39). The capital Lima, with a population of 8 million, is the world's second driest capital city (after Cairo).

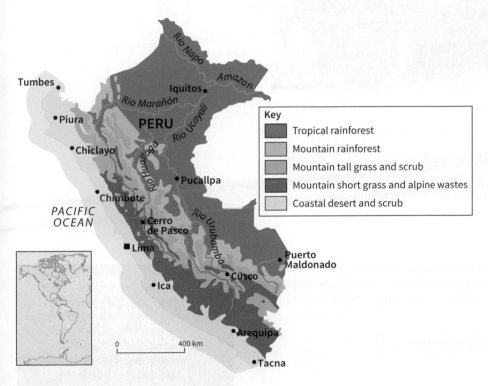

Key
- Tropical rainforest
- Mountain rainforest
- Mountain tall grass and scrub
- Mountain short grass and alpine wastes
- Coastal desert and scrub

Figure 11.39 Peru's vegetation zones.

A number of additional geographical issues intensify the problems surrounding clean water supply and access in Peru:

- A growing population that is increasingly urban: Peru's population is expected to reach 36 million by 2025 (30.5 million in 2015)
- Water conflict between industry and rural communities: mining dominates Peru's economy, generating 39% of its export earnings (Figure 11.40).
- The unreliability of rainfall: this is compounded by the periodic impact of El Niño/Southern Oscillation events.
- Climate change is resulting in the rapid melting of Peruvian glaciers: short-term intense flows are expected to be followed by future long-term flow decline.
- Water network mismanagement: in heavily populated and industrial areas, groundwater is increasingly subject to contamination from mismanaged sewage and industrial effluent.

501

Figure 11.40 Protestors from local communities protest against a proposed new mine in southern Peru.

- Ineffective national coordination: until 2009, an inefficient water-management structure in the country based upon political departments was ill-equipped to coordinate effective water distribution. Since 2009 it has been based on river systems allowing for a more coordinated approach to water management.

Managing need

In 2010 the National System for Water Resources Management was established, which finally provided an organisational arm of government to coordinate the management of water resources in Peru. The current water plan, which runs from 2009 to 2020, places an emphasis on:

- efficient use of water, as well as sustainable water use
- wastewater treatment and reuse
- improving both water availability and quality.

Additional water supplies are being provided via coastal desalination plants, largely financed by and for use by the mining industry. These plants do, however, help reduce conflict with local communities about appropriation of surface and groundwater sources.

In Lima especially, the problem of improving the water supply is intensified by the 2% urban population growth it experiences each year – largely poor rural–urban migrants. In 2007, 18% of Lima's population was living in 'severe poverty' including over 19% without access to clean drinking water and nearly a quarter lacking connection to a public sewer network. All this in a city with, on average, only 9 mm of rainfall each year.

For many of those not on the city water system, municipal water lorries drive into neighbourhoods to fill up residents' water butts every few days at a nominal or free rate. This means water has to be carefully managed and there is insufficient for fully flushed sanitation systems. As a result, health is compromised for those too poor to afford additional supplies.

A target for urban areas is, by 2021, to treat 100% of waste domestic water and to reuse 50% of it. This is being accomplished in Lima by the construction

Look on **Cambridge Elevate** at this article from Circle of Blue, which considers the problems of supplying water and dealing with the waste in Lima, the capital of Peru (www.cambridge.org/links/gase6123).

of water treatment facilities. In 2013 the Taboada wastewater plant was begun, which will become the largest water treatment facility in South America, processing 1.8 million m³/day of wastewater. A further plant, La Atarjea 2, was commissioned in 2014 to the north of Lima to produce potable water.

Rural Peru has been handicapped by historically low water tariffs. The profits of water supply companies are not sufficient to maintain and repair existing water networks and there is little incentive for private water companies to make the necessary investment when the likelihood of them recouping the outlay is remote.

External funding has come from global organisations such as the World Bank as well as non-governmental organisations (NGOs) carrying out small-scale projects with specific communities. The World Bank operates the National Rural Water Supply and Sanitation Project (PRONASAR) in Peru, which seeks to upgrade water provision in rural areas and towns of fewer than 30 000 people. There are four elements to their work, all based on increasingly larger scales of responsibility:

1 Implementing sustainable basic water provision and sanitation services according to local need. This may involve constructing systems from new or upgrading existing pipelines.
2 Strengthening community involvement in the project by **building human capacity** in leadership and group responsibility, particularly in terms of the financial and economic sustainability of the scheme.
3 Developing regional management capacity – in effect, building up a higher tier of water management oversight across geographical provinces to coordinate and sustain the individual local provision.
4 Strengthening central government capacity to monitor and collect relevant data, enforce legislation concerning water and sanitation standards, and generate new policies.

A number of NGOs work with individual communities in stand-alone, local **appropriate technology** projects. One example is Just a Drop, a water charity whose project in Peru focuses on Misminay – a community of 1500 people high in the Andes. Just a Drop is working with two other organisations to construct a horizontal tunnel dug into a hillside to intercept the water table of the local aquifer. Water will then be gravity-fed to the village below. Villagers should be able to access 80 litres of water per person each day – a sevenfold increase – and have access for longer each day. It is hoped this, along with other benefits, will reduce the incidence of stomach and kidney conditions, particularly among children.

Key terms

building human capacity: developing self-confidence and the technical abilities required to oversee a local project and ensure its continuation

appropriate technology: engineering improvements that use, as far as possible, local resources, skills and community involvement not only in the initial construction but to oversee long-term maintenance, repair and operation

ACTIVITY 11.5

1 'Industrial needs for water should be a priority in Peru because the country's economy is so reliant on export earnings from its mineral wealth.' Do you agree?
2 'It is not the lack of rain; it is where the people choose to live that is the cause of water issues in Peru.' In your view, to what extent is this the case?
3 What lessons can be extended to other countries encountering water stress from Peru's experience?
4 Discussion: The principal factors responsible for Peru's water scarcity are the inadequacy of human systems rather than physical ones.

For an activity on Peru's water situation download Worksheet 11.3 from **Cambridge Elevate**.

11.5 Energy security

A state of **energy security** is having ongoing access to a reliable supply of energy sources that a country requires for its needs now and into the foreseeable future. The opposite condition – **energy insecurity** – means you are liable to:

- exhaustion of your own nation's reserves of energy stocks or suspension of renewable flows
- external suppliers unwilling to make their energy resources available to you for political reasons
- being incapable of paying the price demanded by external energy suppliers
- being reliant on one or two providers who, for one reason or another, stop supplying you.

In attempting to create a state of energy security, countries have to look at the nature of energy demand within their borders and the types of energy required, and forecast how demand is likely to change and match that to economic, environmental and political considerations.

Key terms

energy security: having access to reliable supplies of energy to meet a country's needs in the short and medium term

energy insecurity: lack of control over energy provision due to factors beyond a country's influence

primary energy: energy that, upon release, is used directly

secondary energy: energy that is released from one or more sources in order to generate a second form of energy – most commonly, electricity

Research point

Research more than one water charity and NGO, such as WaterAid, Thirst Relief International or Water.org to compare their focus, operations and areas of activity. What features do they have in common and what distinguishes them? Aim to evaluate their impact.

Sources of energy

Energy takes various forms, but is essentially the capacity to change a stable condition through the input of power. That may take the form of raising the temperature in a domestic setting, moving vehicles or generating electrical power.

Primary energy is energy that upon release is used directly. A water-wheel powered by a river, gas fuelling a gas cooker, wood in a log-burning stove for heat – these all release energy that is used directly.

Secondary energy this is the release of one type of energy in order to transform it into another type of energy. The most common occurrence of this is in the generation of electricity by thermal means: burning coal, gas and oil in power stations, or releasing radiation from uranium to convert water to steam, to create pressure, turn a turbine and generate electricity. Sources of energy do not form neat classifications; a lump of coal can be used as both a primary and a secondary source of energy.

Energy demand takes various forms, often within the same building (Table 11.3). Figure 11.41 shows energy consumption in the UK by sector.

The energy mix

The energy mix is the various energy sources and their proportional contributions that meet a nation's energy needs. The UK's energy mix (see Figure 11.51) is dominated by the big three: oil (mainly transport uses), gas (domestic uses and electricity generation) and coal (electricity generation).

Norway has a very different energy mix. Its physical landscape and climate mean that HEP is relatively cheap to produce and it dominates electricity generation.

Energy demand	Primary energy uses	Secondary energy uses
Domestic	Oil, gas and coal for central heating	Electrical circuits and lights
Industry	Oil, gas and coal for processes	Electrical power and circuits
Transport	Oil fuel for road, rail, ship and air transport	Electric trains, electric cars
Agriculture	Oil fuel for farm machinery; oil and gas for heating	Electrical pumps and circuits

Table 11.3 Energy demand.

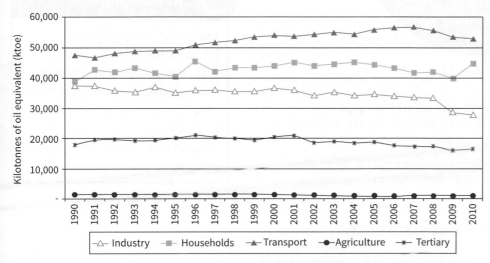

Figure 11.41 UK energy consumption by sector, 1990–2010.

Primary source	%
Hydropower	39.5%
Oil	32.0%
Gas	18.0%
Biomass	7.0%
Coal	3.5%

Table 11.4 Norway's energy mix, 2009.

Norway also has extensive oil and gas reserves in its North Sea sector, so it has sufficient energy to be able to export most of its fossil fuels. In terms of primary energy consumption, in 2009 Norway's energy mix was dominated by **hydropower** (Table 11.4).

In contrast, the energy mix of Angola in south-west Africa is largely dominated by fuelwood (Figure 11.42), which is collected for use as wood among rural communities and converted into charcoal for many less affluent urban residents.

Global energy trade

The 20th century saw a huge growth in the international energy trade as fuels were moved from continent to continent, a trend that has continued into this

For an activity on the UK's energy mix download Worksheet 11.3 from **Cambridge Elevate**.

Key term

hydropower: sourcing energy from the power of flowing water

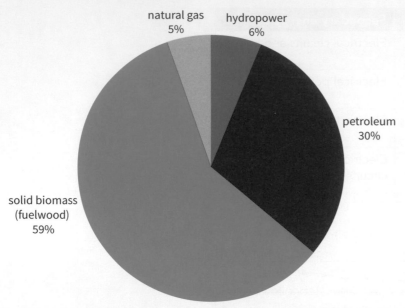

Figure 11.42 Angola's primary energy consumption, 2011.

century with the further construction of international oil and gas pipelines (Figure 11.43), the bulk carrying of liquid gas under pressure by sea and large coal-carrying vessels reducing the cost of transportation further still.

The ways in which the global energy trade evolves is shaped by a range of factors, some operating individually and others in combination.

Economic factors

- The price of an energy source influences the size and demand of potential markets.
- The ability of a population to pay energy bills and purchase items that require energy determines the size and location of energy markets.
- The size and ease of access to energy reserves determines the price at which it is economic to exploit them.

Figure 11.43 The Trans-Alaskan Pipeline taking oil from the northern to the southern coast of Alaska and then by oil tanker to Los Angeles.

- The number of competing producers has an effect on the price any one provider can set.
- The price affects whether purchasers look to alternative providers or different energy sources.

Political factors

- International cooperation: the Langeled gas pipeline (at one time the world's largest undersea gas pipeline) runs from the Nyhamna facility on the Norwegian coast, receiving gas from the Ormen Lange North Sea gasfield and pumping it 1166 km to the East Yorkshire coast at Easington (Figure 11.44). This provides around 20% of Britain's annual gas imports.
- International conflict: disputes between nations can see trade agreements broken and energy supply reduced by producers or embargoed by potential customers. Oil exports from Iran have been subject to a decade-long UN, US and EU trade ban since tension in the region escalated following Iran's development of nuclear power without full access by international nuclear inspection teams. In July 2015 agreement was reached that allowed inspectors proper access to Iran's nuclear facilities in exchange for lifting the trade bans. As a result, Iran expects to double its annual oil exports to 2.3 million barrels a day.

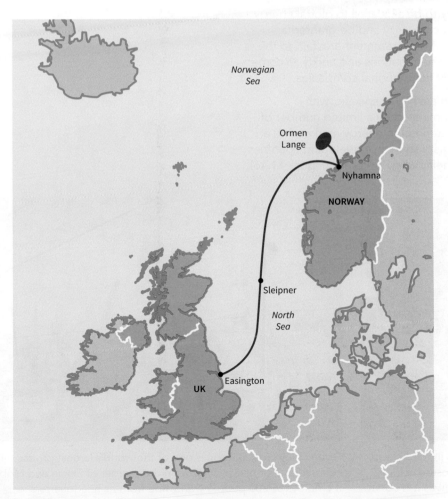

Figure 11.44 The route of the Langeled gas pipeline between Norway and the UK.

- International regulation: the trade in uranium is closely monitored and partially regulated by the International Atomic Energy Agency (IAEA). As part of the nuclear weapons non-proliferation treaty of 1970, states that have signed up commit to using enriched uranium for solely peaceful purposes if they were non-nuclear weapon states before 1967.
- Strategic considerations: in order to sustain energy security, countries may offer economic inducements for developing supplies of an energy source from within their own borders in order to avoid dependency on foreign suppliers or to expose import movements to disruption in times of international crisis. To avoid dependency on OPEC oil supplies coming largely from the Middle East, the US government has supported the development of home exploitation of its large oil-shale reserves.

Making connections

Read more about world governance and international trade agreements in Chapter 7 Global systems and global governance.

Environmental factors

The Madrid Protocol, signed into law for 50 years from 1998, bans mineral exploitation in Antarctica. However, no such restriction covers the Arctic Ocean. In September 2015, the Anglo-Dutch oil multinational Shell announced it was withdrawing from oil exploration off the Alaskan coast, partly as a result of the strength of public protest about possible environmental devastation following potential oil leaks.

Structural factors

Even if a low income country (LIC) has reserves of coal, oil, gas or HEP potential, the capital costs of developing an energy industry are often beyond the means of a country with limited wealth. Licences are likely to be allocated to global energy corporations to explore and, if successful, produce energy and be granted a proportion of the revenues. Whether the terms of the agreement are 'fair' to the host country often depends on the nature of the negotiations and ability to come to a mutually acceptable agreement with energy transnational companies.

The technology and skills of energy exploitation are highly specific, with processing, distribution, marketing and sales dominated by a limited number of the world's largest companies (Figure 11.45). Entering the energy market with a home-grown, indigenous industry is financially risky so many developing countries resort to transnational companies to develop their energy potential (Figure 11.46).

Figure 11.45 Traders buying and selling oil futures in the New York Mercantile Exchange. The development or closure of oilfields is as much to do with the global price of oil as it is about the ability to extract it.

Figure 11.46 ExxonMobil is one of the world's largest private oil companies. Formed in 1999 from the merger of Exxon and Mobil, it employs 82 000 people worldwide from its headquarters in Irving, Texas.

The role of transnational corporations in the energy trade

In some parts of the world, the state runs the main energy concerns. This may be through the overnight nationalisation of once private-industry operations or by increment. Saudi Aramco (Arabian-American Oil Company) is still the operational name of the company that was fully nationalised in 1980 (a process started in 1973) by the Saudi government to become the Saudi Arabian Oil Company, fully responsible for oil and gas exploitation within the country.

On the other hand, once state-owned energy companies may be privatised. With the collapse of the USSR in 1989, the vast state gas organisation Soviet Ministry of Gas Industry became the commercial and privatised company Gazprom, with the selling of shares to the Russian public in 1994. The Russian state maintains ownership of 38% of the company's shares. Gazprom is now one of the largest companies in the world.

The following operational stages of a major multinational energy company such as BP (Figure 11.47), Britain's largest individual company, fall into a functional as well as geographical pattern:

1 Exploration: the search for new reserves, often in hostile environments.
2 Development: bringing new oil and gasfields into a state ready to be exploited by developing the infrastructure network.
3 Production: accessing the oil and gas reserves in commercial quantities.
4 Transportation: moving oil from where it is produced to where it will be processed.
5 Refining: converting crude oil and raw gas into commercial variants.
6 Marketing: finding a range of customers for the products and distributing products to markets.
7 Research and development (R&D): identifying new extraction procedures, more efficient processing, alternative products and new areas of commercial activity to expand into.

ACTIVITY 11.6

1 With reference to Figure 11.47, is there a pattern to the countries where BP doesn't have an operational interest?
2 Draw up a list of benefits and issues that having an energy TNC such as BP operating in your country may bring.

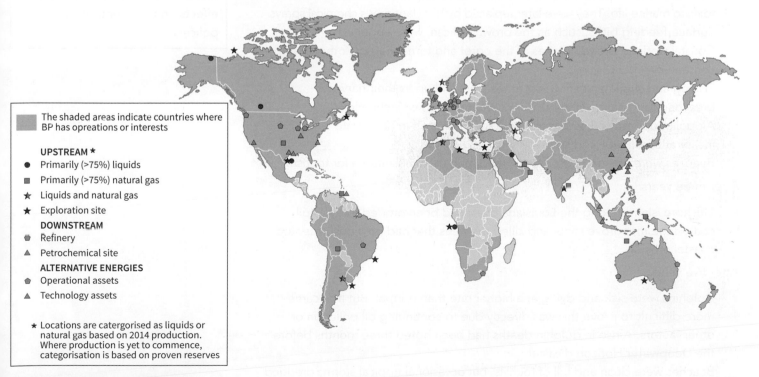

Figure 11.47 BP's global operations.

Exploration and production can take place in almost every environment on Earth. However, BP's oil-refining operations tend to take place closer to the major markets, particularly in western Europe and North America, requiring the vast movement of crude oil by tanker and pipeline. R&D also occurs in centres of academic prestige, recruiting the most highly qualified scientists and engineers.

Environmental impacts of a major energy resource development

As well as concerns about their use and the management of their residues and waste, there is increasing environmental sensitivity concerning the preceding stages: their extraction and distribution.

Issues of extraction

Super-regional scale: the explosion on the Deepwater Horizon drilling rig in the Gulf of Mexico on 20 April 2010 created oil giant BP's biggest ever environmental disaster (Figure 11.48). Operating 84 km south of the Louisiana coast, the rig was drilling through the seabed at a depth of 1525 m when an explosion killed 11 oil workers and resulted in oil pollution that extended along nearly 2000 km of the Gulf coast of the USA. Over 87 days, the leaking sea-floor well discharged approximately 3.2 m barrels of crude oil until it was finally capped. BP spent $44 billion in legal and clean-up operations and finally settled a $18.7 billion compensation claim in July 2015.

The Gulf of Mexico is a rich, natural environment for marine and coastal flora and fauna. The habitats of oyster reefs, mangroves, deltas and marshes in tropical waters support over 17 500 species in a widely diverse, yet ecologically sensitive, environment.

The immediate environmental impact of the oil leak included the following:

* The damage to several cold-water coral reefs from the crude oil.
* Oil entering the food chain as it was taken in by marine creatures in feeding.
* Initial chemical dispersants sprayed on the crude-affected areas of sea were too toxic to marine life. They were later replaced by less dangerous chemical sprays.
* Surface-feeding birds, such as the brown pelican, were engulfed in sticky oil.
* Coastal wetland breeding sites of the egret and tern, amongst others, were contaminated.
* Fishing and shell-harvesting industries were laid up as their harvests breached food-safety standards for contamination with chemicals.
* Air pollution resulted as surface crude was burnt off in deliberate incineration of captured spill.
* Beaches were affected by tar balls, rendering them unsuitable for tourism.

After three years:

* Offshore islands along the Louisiana coast had been eroded away as oil coated the mangrove roots and killed the trees that had previously resisted coastal erosion.

After five years:

* Dolphins were sick and dying at a higher rate than normal. But if became more difficult to prove this was directly due to continuing oil pollution or other factors. A rise in dolphin deaths had been noted three months before the Deepwater Horizon disaster.
* Beaches were clean and full of tourists, but occasional tropical storms dredged tar balls from the sea floor offshore and deposited them along the coast.

Figure 11.48 Fire ships attempt to control the blaze on the Deepwater Horizon oil platform in the Gulf of Mexico.

 Investigate

Examine the impact of the Great Sendai (or Tohoku) earthquake of 2011 on the Fukushima nuclear power station in Japan and the effects on the country's energy policies.

Since the largest accidental oil disaster in the world, the Gulf of Mexico has regenerated far more strongly after the Deepwater Horizon crisis than many environmental scientists had anticipated. Natural systems have shown themselves to be surprisingly resilient. Five years after the event, fish and oyster industries were operating again, shrimp, crab and bird populations were expanding and coral reefs were in recovery. But the psychological environmental impact has been, arguably, longer-lasting as visitor numbers continued to fall short of pre-disaster numbers and the perception of an oil-tainted coastline may be the longest persisting environmental impact.

Issues of distribution

Regional scale: oil leaks and the devastation of agricultural land in the Ogoni region of south-east Nigeria (Figure 11.49) have triggered significant compensation payments by Anglo-Dutch Shell for the impacts of its activities in the region. Long controversial, Shell's operations in one of the world's largest oil producing countries outside the Middle East have had a history of friction with regional groups representing the Ogoni people and the Nigerian government.

Peaceful demonstrations in the 1990s concerning Shell's alleged pollution of farms and fishing grounds on the Niger delta through which its pipelines ran swiftly deteriorated into mutual violence between armed groups claiming they represented the Ogoni people's interests and the Nigerian military. In 2011 the United Nations Environmental Programme judged that the alluvial soils of the delta lands would no longer support agriculture after 50 years of oil leaks, spills, flaring and waste discharge (Figure 11.50). The people of Ogoniland claimed

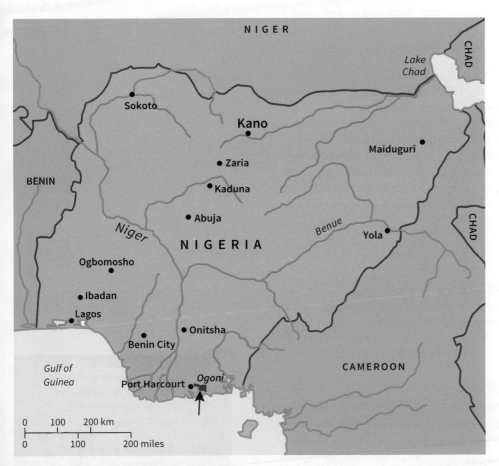

Figure 11.49 The Ogoni region of Nigeria.

Figure 11.50 Oil-contaminated land in the Ogoni region of southern Nigeria.

that Shell has been irresponsible in its lack of maintenance of oil pipelines, allowing them to deteriorate and leak. In the meantime, Shell claimed that the leaks were often due to illegal theft of oil from the pipelines and threats to damage pipes by militant armed groups who have, in the past, kidnapped company employees to gain ransom payments. Despite the disagreement about the cause of the major leaks, in July 2015 Shell agreed to pay £55m to 15 600 Ogoni farmers and fishermen whose livelihoods were affected by two major oil spills in 2008 and 2009, for which Shell accepted responsibility.

A study of the environmental impact of oil exploitation and distribution in the Ogoni region was undertaken by the United Nations Environmental Programme and published in 2011. Surveying over 200 locations, 5000 medical records and meeting with over 23 000 people in local community meetings it concluded as follows:

- Serious threats to human health arise from hydrocarbon-contaminated drinking water, some of which has benzene levels (a carcinogen) over 900 times the World Health Organization guidelines.
- The high rainfall of the region means any oil spill, if not quickly cleaned up, is rapidly washed across farmland, ends up in creeks and causes vegetation to die when it reaches the root zone.
- Heavy contamination is long-lasting; at one site pollution was still having an impact 40 years after the original oil spill, despite repeated clean-up attempts.
- Considerable soil contamination by hydrocarbons has occurred, which penetrate through to groundwater supplies.
- Root crops, such as cassava, become unusable and farmland shows signs of stress with reduced productivity.
- Loss of fish species from contaminated creeks with consequent decline in catch for fishermen.

Oil production commenced in Ogoniland in the 1950s and the last production wells were closed in 1993. But these facilities were never effectively decommissioned and numerous pipelines still pass through the region distributing oil from one part of Nigeria to another. The poor maintenance of both, as well as deliberate sabotage and pilfering, has resulted in long-lasting and on going pollution of the region. In contrast with the massive but comparatively very short oil pollution emission from Deepwater Horizon, the Ogoni region has experienced over half a century of continuous oil seepage into a land-based environment in which the contaminants have resided and accumulated.

The energy gap

Attempts to prepare for a potential energy gap

In a world of increasing energy demand, the consequence of not meeting that growth with an increase in supply is likely to be an energy gap. This is the point at which demand exceeds supply. The UK is already in this situation, having been in a state of energy surplus for much of the period between 1980 and 2004 (Figure 11.51).

Reasons for the current energy gap

- Energy demand is continuing to rise, especially for transport (more cars, more flights) and domestic electrical demand (more electrical appliances per home).
- North Sea oil and gas reserves passed their peak production phase in the 1990s and are now in a declining phase of output. They are likely to be economically depleted by 2025.

Look on **Cambridge Elevate** at this article from the *Guardian*, which summarises the UK's energy mix, both in terms of demand and supply (www.cambridge.org/links/gase6124).

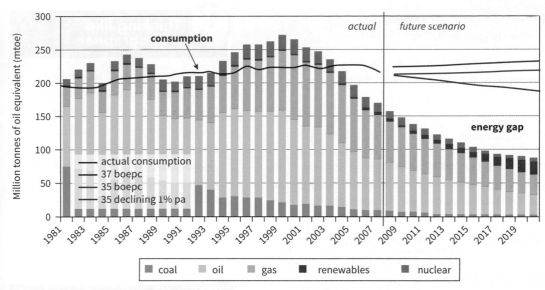

Boepc: barrels of oil equivalent per capita (so 37 boepc = consumption line if annual demand continues at current 37 barrels of oil per person in equivalent energy per year).

Figure 11.51 UK energy consumption vs production.

- Britain's 16 nuclear reactors at 9 power sites are now ageing and coming to the end of their operational life. They are starting to be shut down and decommissioned, with only two still due to be operating by 2025.
- The Chernobyl nuclear disaster of 1986 (Figure 11.52) brought a halt to any new nuclear power stations being commissioned because of public and government concerns over safety.
- While coal stocks are still available, the need to reduce Britain's carbon footprint (and limit its contribution to acid rain and climate change) has seen this fuel fall out of favour for energy generation. Plans are going ahead for the closure of the least efficient coal-fired power plants.

Figure 11.52 The abandoned town of Chernobyl following the nuclear fire of 1986 is evidence of the risks of nuclear energy. The disaster led to many countries abandoning plans for replacement nuclear power stations for at least two decades.

What is Britain's response to the prospect of an energy gap?

The range of strategies to close an energy gap includes:

- increasing energy production from existing domestic supplies
- increasing energy from new, alternative domestic supplies (both non-renewable and renewable)
- importing energy from external suppliers
- reducing energy consumption and demand.

Increasing energy production from existing domestic supplies

In 2010 the Labour government gave the go-ahead for eight new nuclear power stations to be constructed. Unlike Britain's original nuclear power stations, these will be financed and operated by private energy companies. After showing early interest, E.ON and RWE npower pulled out of bidding for contracts, citing escalating costs and reduced potential for profitability. French electricity company EDF Energy is going ahead with plans to build four reactors at two existing sites in a partnership with Chinese nuclear construction companies.

Increasing energy from new, alternative domestic supplies

Non-renewables: the Conservative government elected in 2015 committed itself to encouraging the development of onshore low carbon-emission fossil fuel supplies through **hydraulic fracturing** or 'fracking' of shale rocks containing natural gas (Figure 11.53). Known as the 'shale revolution' in the USA, where domestic production of oil and gas through similar measures has led to a sharp reduction in American reliance on oil and gas imports over last 15 years, the technology is not without its critics and there has been much public opposition to the prospect of licences being awarded for exploratory drilling in parts of the country (Figure 11.54).

Thinking like a geographer

Geographers need to be able to forecast from current trends. Consider the implications of the UK not managing to bridge its energy gap. Classify the likely consequences and rank their relative significance.

Key term

hydraulic fracturing: popularly referred to as 'fracking', this is an engineering technique that drills boreholes into gas-bearing strata of dispersed concentrations and fractures the rock using hydraulic pressure

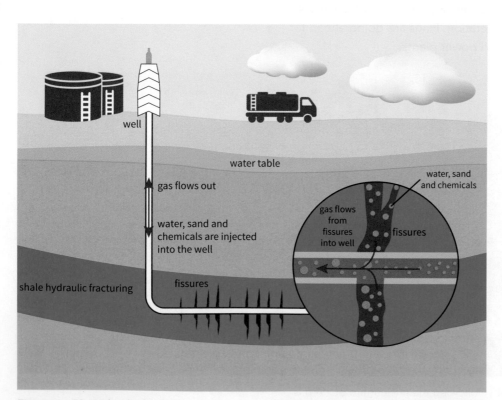

Figure 11.53 Hydraulic fracturing involves vertical, then horizontal boring so that natural gas may be released by fracturing gas-bearing rock.

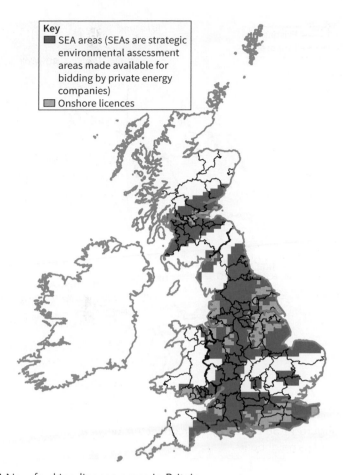

Key
- ■ SEA areas (SEAs are strategic environmental assessment areas made available for bidding by private energy companies)
- ▢ Onshore licences

Figure 11.54 New fracking licence areas in Britain.

Renewables: the EU target of '20-20 by 2020' refers to the goals of member states achieving a 20% cut in emission of greenhouse gases (based on the 1990 baseline) and 20% of electricity generation sourced from renewables. These targets were set in 2008.

The UK has determined that the first of these should be secured by replacing coal with up to 20% energy-equivalent in biomass at coal-fired power stations. Drax power station in Yorkshire is undergoing conversion to see it shift from one of Europe's largest carbon emitters to the world's largest green-fuelled power station.

The second EU target is best achieved, in Britain's circumstances, from an expansion of wind-generation capacity, particularly offshore wind farms (Figure 11.55). With British waters holding considerable potential for wind-generated electricity, the world's largest offshore wind farm has been given the go-ahead for construction in the shallow waters of the North Sea on Dogger Bank.

Importing energy from external suppliers

The most critical times for electricity-generating capacity matching requirements is when there is a temporary surge in demand. These peaks may be quite short lived, for half an hour or so in the evening. International interconnectors have been established – undersea cables capable of transferring electrical current between countries – for mutual transfer and benefit. The UK electricity grid is connected to Ireland, the Netherlands and France, so that when one country experiences a surge in demand, neighbouring countries can supply the shortfall. There are plans to increase interconnectors with Spain (solar power) and Iceland (geothermal power) to further diversify the source of possible suppliers (Figure 11.56).

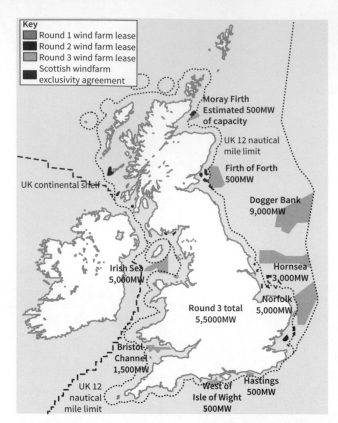

Figure 11.55 Planned offshore wind farms off the coast of Britain.

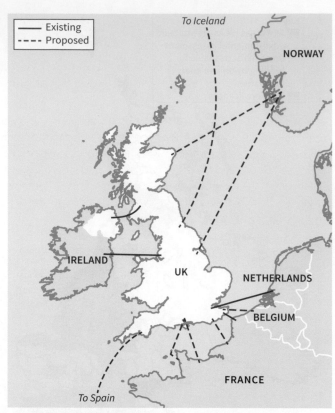

Figure 11.56 Electricity interconnectors between the UK and its neighbours.

Gas supplies are increasingly being supplemented by imports from abroad. Natural gas is pumped from Norway via the Langeled pipeline (Figure 11.44), with liquefied natural gas (LNG) imported by specialised tanker from Qatar to supplement declining North Sea reserves. In 2012 foreign gas imports met 43% of the UK's gas requirement, the highest contribution since 1976.

Reducing energy consumption and demand

The energy gap is not just about plugging falling supply; it is also about reducing demand and using energy more efficiently. The British government has used a mix of persuasion and legislative enforcement to bring about greater efficiency in use of energy in homes, industry and transport.

Domestic energy conservation: building regulation codes from 2006 tightened up the required home insulation on all new constructions. Seemingly to meet its Carbon Emission Reduction Target set by the EU, the measures require major gas and electricity supply companies to assist their customers in putting energy-efficiency measures into place in their homes.

Business energy conservation: to meet the government target of reducing carbon emission levels by 80% by 2050 (on 1990 levels), the Carbon Reduction Commitment Energy Efficiency Scheme was introduced in 2008 for non-domestic energy use. It involves three stages: ensuring energy users monitor and record their energy use; producing a league table of users' performance; and an allowance-trading scheme giving some flexibility to users based on exchange of allocation. The Energy Saving Opportunity Scheme (ESOS) requires all large UK firms to conduct an energy use audit and assessment of energy-saving opportunities once every four years. Failure to conduct an audit by an energy lead assessor can bring fines of up to £50000 charged by the UK Environment Agency.

ACTIVITY 11.7

1   Prepare a presentation on how you think the UK should meet its anticipated energy gap. Identify your strongest and weakest arguments and the evidence you will use to support your case.

Transport energy conservation: in terms of transport, the energy savings from conversion to more modern and energy-efficient vehicles is an indirect effect rather than a direct objective of the attempts to reduce damaging vehicle pollution. Through the use of variable car-tax rates – banded since 2001 according to emission levels – car drivers are encouraged to consider more fuel-efficient engines when purchasing a new car.

Energy recovery: increasingly, local authorities are looking to manage waste in a way that reduces landfill and provides recoverable energy to help meet local needs. In Sheffield the Veolia Energy Recovery Facility incinerates waste collected by its refuse teams and the heat produced is used to create steam that generates electricity that then feeds into the National Grid. In addition, the hot water created is piped to over 140 buildings in the centre of Sheffield as part of the District Energy Network (Figure 11.57).

Figure 11.57 Sheffield's Veolia energy recovery plant in the heart of Sheffield, transforming the city's waste into hot water and electricity.

Sustainable energy issues

If a renewable energy source is exploited but its impact is unsustainable, that influences its interpretation as a sustainable form of energy generation.

Fuelwood

The use of fuelwood, either in its original state or as charcoal, is essentially a renewable form of energy. However, not only is the rate of forest exploitation beyond natural replacement rates in many parts of the developing world, the environmental and social impacts of wood collection are potentially negative. In rural Nepal over 80% of domestic energy is sourced from fuelwood (Figure 11.58). Not only does the burning of this smoky material affect the health of families in confined homes, with women and children in particular suffering from respiratory and eye conditions, the collection of wood can also take considerable amounts of time each day – usually a female chore (Figure 11.59). It can lead to girls dropping out of education to devote time to wood collection and can cause deformation of young bone development. The environmental impact is equally unsustainable, with large areas of once-forested slope cleared of vegetation and subject to rapid soil erosion and subsequent landslides.

Wind energy

Wind energy is subject to interruption when wind speeds fall, which is more likely under high pressure systems. Public opinion over wind turbines is an increasing social factor in whether their onshore development goes ahead, with public protests occurring over their impact in rural areas. Offshore developments can go some way to moderating the opposition. The decision of the Conservative

517

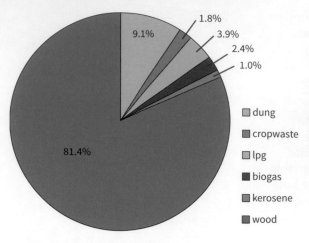

Figure 11.58 Energy sources in rural Nepal.

Figure 11.59 Children collecting essential fuelwood near Chitwan, Nepal.

government to substantially reduce subsidies for onshore wind from April 2016 is likely to see plans for up to 240 wind farms abandoned on economic grounds.

Solar energy

Global photovoltaic (PV) cell production has increased sixfold in the five years up to 2014. However, their fabrication involves the use of caustic chemicals such as hydrofluoric acid and sodium hydroxide and one Chinese manufacturer of solar panels in Zhejiang province has been taken to court accused of releasing toxic waste into a nearby river. Increasingly, the energy budget of renewable energy generation is taking into account the energy costs of their manufacture, distribution, operation and maintenance.

Biomass

The ethics of devoting high-quality agricultural land to the production of crops destined for energy use in a world where malnourishment is an ever-present feature poses challenging moral questions. In the case of biofuel production, the crops best suited to its use are sugar cane and palm oil – plants adapted to tropical conditions. There are concerns that in order to supply the EU's 2020 target of 10% of transport fuel coming from renewable sources – probably biofuel – the primary rainforests of Brazil, Malaysia and Indonesia may be put under pressure to capture this lucrative market (Figure 11.60).

Figure 11.60 Tropical rainforest is prevented from regenerating when removed for oil palm plantations to produce biofuel.

Nuclear energy

The question of whether nuclear energy should be classified as renewable or non-renewable has exercised academics and politicians in recent years. (The Arizona State committee on Water and Energy passed a vote in 2015 to declare it is renewable.) Uranium-235, which is used in conventional fission reactors, is estimated to have 100+ years' reserve life, but when fast-breeder reactors are considered (which produce further fuel during their process operation) the lifespan of uranium-238 runs from tens of thousands of years to millions of years. Breeder reactors and possible fusion reactors are considered renewable by the World Commission on Environment and Development.

As a low carbon-emission energy source capable of generating large quantities of uninterrupted electricity, nuclear power is a favoured way to meet future energy needs by some. However, the issues of safety of operation have been brought into stark perspective by the events at Chernobyl in 1986 (Figure 11.52) and Fukushima in 2011. The issue of whether it produces unacceptable waste in the form of plutonium – a lethal substance with a **radioactive half-life** of 24 100 years – or whether plutonium is considered a resource that can give virtually unlimited years of energy generation depends on the availability of technology that is affordable and the environmental risks that countries perceive as acceptable.

Issues of use

Urban scale: the concentration of petrol and diesel engines in vehicle-heavy urban areas can have significant health implications for resident populations. Exhaust emission of nitrogen oxide (NO_x) and volatile organic compounds (VOCs) produce ground-level ozone. This can irritate bronchial passages and intensify problems for those with asthma. During cold weather temperature inversions may trap primary pollutants such as nitrogen dioxide (NO_2), carbon monoxide (CO) and particulate matter – the latter particularly from diesel engines. The elderly and the young are especially vulnerable to these emissions, which can lead to increased rates of cancer, cardiovascular problems, asthma and premature birth. Southern California has the worst air quality in the USA according to the American Lung Association and experiences around 21 000 early deaths each year, largely due to vehicle emissions and commercial and domestic heating and cooking.

Continental scale: the burning of fossil fuels releases contaminants that can generate significant environmental deterioration over a continent-wide scale. The emission of sulphur dioxide (SO_2) and nitrogen oxide from the combustion of fossil fuels – largely by industry, power stations and vehicle exhausts from the direction of the prevailing winds – leads to a mixing with water droplets in clouds and the production of sulphuric acid (H_2SO_4) and nitric acid (HNO_3) that falls as acid rain (wet deposition). Although rain is naturally acidic as a result of combining with atmospheric carbon dioxide, the acidity may increase with the addition of these reactions to a pH of below 5. In the absence of moist conditions, contaminants may cling to dust and carbon particulates and fall as dry deposition (Figure 11.61).

Forests in Canada, eastern USA, Scandinavia, Poland and much of eastern Europe including the Czech Republic have all been severely affected by acid rain – often generated in urban areas many hundreds of kilometres away. Acid rain can destroy the fine nutrient-absorbing rootlets of plants and cause trees to weaken and become susceptible to disease and stress, resulting in decline and death. Streams, rivers and lakes may become more acidic, particularly in spring after heavy snowmelt and increased winter emissions from coal-fired power stations. In addition, buildings and water pipes suffer faster corrosion and require more frequent replacement. Fisheries may suffer extensive economic loss as young fish cannot tolerate the more acidic water and salmon

Key term

radioactive half-life: the time it takes for half the neutrons of a radioactive mass to disintegrate, known as radioactive decay

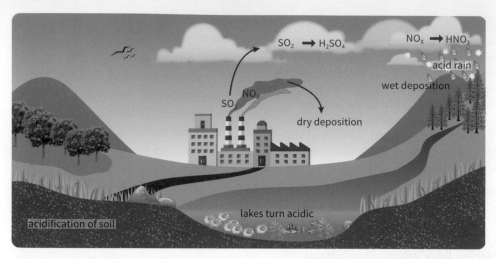

Figure 11.61 Chemical processes triggered by contaminants lead to acid rain.

and trout farms have seen their stocks suffer. In 2006 it was estimated that 13 000 km² of lakes in Norway were experiencing damage to fish stocks, although this was down 38% on the figure for 1990. The negative impact has been improved to a certain extent in Norway by adding lime to rivers and lakes in order to neutralise their acidity, at a cost of around £6.5 m annually.

Global scale: the addition of significant volumes of carbon dioxide (Figure 11.62) through the combustion of fossil fuels since the 19th century has led to the 'enhanced' greenhouse effect in which human activity raises the insulating capacity of the atmosphere, leading to rising global temperatures (see Chapter 1, Water and carbon cycles).

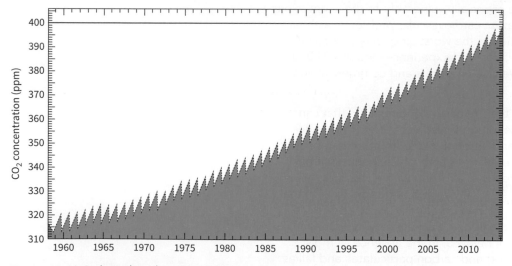

Figure 11.62 Carbon dioxide concentration at Mauna Loa Observatory, Hawaii.

The Kyoto international conference in 1997 witnessed the first formal agreement by most industrialised nations establishing legally binding carbon emission reduction targets, aimed to start in 2005 (known as the Kyoto Protocol). This was followed by the COP21 conference held in Paris in November 2015 to tighten up agreements and ensure all nations made binding commitments to limit emissions to ensure the 2 °C target is achievable. Many countries are now adopting low-carbon or carbon-reduction policies to bring about the desired change.

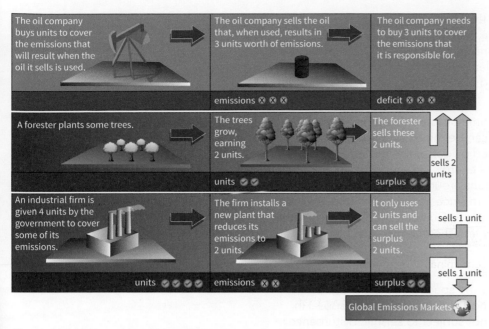

Figure 11.63 How emissions trading operates.

One of the strategies adopted by all EU member states is the EU Emissions Trading System (EU ETS), which sets a legally binding cap on greenhouse emissions by industry, power plants and air transport. The cap operates on a declining scale, such that by 2020 emissions per sector are destined to be 21% lower than the 2005 baseline, and by 2030 43% lower. A company is granted an annual emission allocation which it must monitor and match if it is to avoid substantial fines. To permit expansion and growth, companies can 'trade' their allowances with each other and buy additional, or sell surplus, credits (Figure 11.63). They also have the opportunity to buy additional credits for investing in low-carbon technology. If a company achieves a surplus at the end of the year, they can be banked and added to future years' activity. In this scheme, carbon emissions have been 'marketised' and the use of a financial carrot and stick is encouraging divestment of dependence on fossil fuels. These costs have led to the closure of uneconomic coal-fired power stations such as Longannet – Scotland's largest coal-fired power station.

Issues of residual waste

In the case of fossil-fuel thermal power stations, coal ash is the main solid waste to be disposed of. The material resulting from coal combustion is a viable material in demand by the construction industry for the manufacture of concrete blocks, cement products, grouting and road surfacing. What remains unmarketable is used in landfill and disused mine filling material.

For many countries without access to large-scale HEP, the nuclear industry is the only one that can reliably generate large quantities of electricity without emitting greenhouse gases. However, apart from operational safety concerns, the issues of managing nuclear waste dominate the safety consideration of the industry. Low- and medium-level waste is stored or buried in near-surface containment. It is the nuclear **high-level waste (HLW)** that results from the operation of the uranium rods inside the reactor which poses the biggest safety risk.

As the uranium rods undergo a fission process, waste radioactive material is produced which dampens down the fission reaction over time. It takes three or four years for the rods to lose sufficient efficiency to warrant removal and reprocessing or replacement.

Key term

high-level waste (HLW): this is very hot, highly radioactive and dangerous waste that is produced as a result of nuclear fission in a reactor

521

Most of the rod (96%) is reusable uranium that can be separated to manufacture new rods and 1% is plutonium. Plutonium has been used by some countries to produce nuclear weapons and it is a key consideration whenever a nation starts to develop a nuclear industry what their plans are for the plutonium produced. The remaining 3% comprises end waste with no further use.

If no military use is intended for the plutonium, it is considered highly toxic radioactive waste. Alternatively, plutonium can be mixed with uranium to produce a nuclear fuel known as MOX (mixed oxide), which further lengthens the life of uranium reserves by yielding yet more energy. However, a combination of reduced construction of nuclear power stations around the world in the last two decades together with a low price for uranium since 2007 has led to plans to close the Thorp reprocessing plant at Sellafield in Cumbria by 2018, ending the UK's only facility for feeding plutonium back into the energy cycle.

At present, countries store HLW at existing nuclear facilities – in the case of the USA, this extends to 121 sites. The bulk of Britain's most dangerous nuclear waste from 60 years of activity could occupy the space equivalent to two suburban houses, so there is a search for long-term underground disposal in secure deposits where the local geology is not subject to seismic disturbance and where possible water contamination is reduced to virtually zero. However, local opposition to hosting such a facility has meant that a number of countries, including the USA (Nevada) and the UK (Cumbria), have had difficulty in turning proposals into construction projects. France has committed to a facility in the Champagne province that will see the waste from 50 years of nuclear activity stored deep underground in steel and concrete-sealed chambers. The long half-life of radioactive waste means the storage term is measured in tens of thousands of years before the material can be considered anything like 'safe'. It is for this reason that the French plans have stated that the storage chambers have to be accessible and not permanently sealed, in case a better way of dealing with nuclear waste emerges in the future.

Look on **Cambridge Elevate** to read more about the issues of what to do with long-lived nuclear waste and why it is a daunting one for all nuclear energy countries. This article from the BBC explains how France is choosing to deal with it (www.cambridge.org/links/gase6125).

11.6 Mineral security

Ore mineral security

Unlike water or energy resources, ore minerals may be desirable, but it is arguable whether they are 'essential' to a national interest. In early 2016 concerns were focused on the threatened closure of Britain's steel-making capacity and on the profitability of the Port Talbot and Scunthorpe steel-making works. While some argued the UK needed its own steel industry for strategic reasons, there was no discussion on the need to source the component iron ore from home sources; it was assumed iron ore would be freely available on the international ore market. (Two-thirds of the UK's iron ore is imported from three countries: Brazil, Canada and Sweden. There is no home production.)

There are several categories of ore mineral:

- Industrial ore minerals: iron, copper, tin, zinc, manganese, chromium, etc.
- Energy ore minerals: uranium.

- Precious ore minerals: gold, silver, platinum.
- Rare earths: zirconium, niobium, thorium, etc.

Estimated reserve lifetimes are often on shaky ground because so many factors can alter:

- Technological development in mining and processing can identify new resource deposits and extract from low-grade ores that did not previously figure in reserves.
- Economic factors may stimulate the search for more sources if the price is high and make low-grade ores viable.
- Political factors may open up trade restrictions and barriers and allow the easier flow of ore minerals.
- Social factors can encourage recycling and reduce the need for fresh supplies.
- Innovation may replace or substitute a once essential use (such as fibre optics for copper cable).

The international copper trade

Copper is one of the earliest worked minerals in the history of metallurgy. It was the first metal to be smelted from its ore around 5000 BCE and the first to mixed with another (tin) to create an alloy (bronze) around 3500 BCE. There is estimated to be a vast amount of copper in the Earth's crust, with 10^{14} tons in the top kilometre alone. However, not all of that is in concentrated quantities sufficient enough to consider it viable reserves. To be commercial, ore needs to contain from 0.5 to 6% copper, which is between 100 and 1000 times the crustal average. Consequently, copper is a relatively scarce geochemical element (Figure 10.64).

There are three main sources of copper ore as shown in Table 11.5.

Key term

intracratonic basin: a large depression within a stable continental mass containing sedimentary rocks from marine and/or continental deposits in shallow inland seas, formed millions of years ago

Ore mineral source	Description	Geological formation	Location
Porphyry deposits	The most common occurrence accounting for about 45% of the world's copper reserves. The richest reserves are found in Chile and Peru containing 1–2% copper.	Igneous intrusions with copper sulphide minerals. Located in ancient subduction zones and now feature in island arcs and convergent/destructive margins.	Discontinuous belts. Western Canada through south west USA, Mexico, Central America, Peru, Chile and west Argentina. Another through Papua New Guinea, Indonesia, Philippines, into China and east Siberia.
Strata-bound deposits	Less common and extensive than porphyry deposits. The richest reserves are found in the Democratic Republic of Congo, DRC (formerly known as Zaire) with 4–6% copper.	Old marine sediments such as shales and sandstones deposited in **intracratonic basins**	Zambia and the DRC
Massive sulphide deposits	Large concentrations of mixed sulphide minerals (copper, nickel, lead and zinc) (1–5% copper)	Igneous intrusions in volcanic rocks, appearing as veins and as massive replacement in limestone associated with metamorphic processes	Namibia, South Africa, Australia, Japan, Cyprus, eastern Canada and Great Lakes region of the USA

Table 11.5 Three main sources of copper ore.

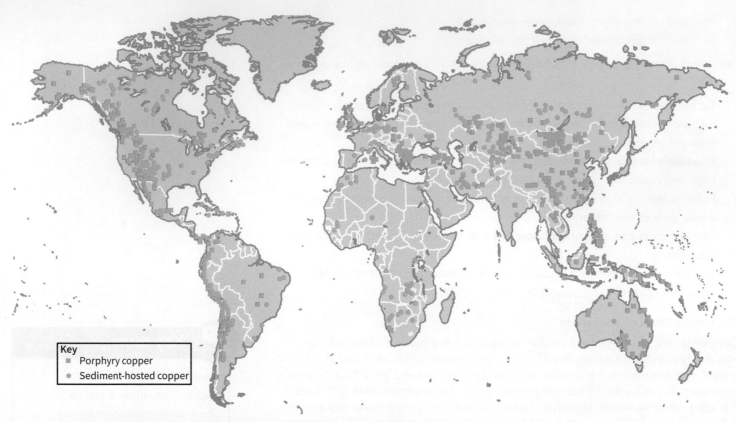

Figure 11.64 Global distribution of copper ore in massive igneous intrusions (porphyry) and contained in sedimentary rocks.

The physical geography of copper ore deposits

Because copper is relatively reactive, it is often formed in a variety of ways, features in a range of mineral forms and is often found in deposits that also contain nickel, cobalt, lead, zinc, gold and/or silver.

Porphyry deposits: these had an igneous origin, forming in active tectonic zones, particularly subduction zones, from large masses of molten rock that cooled and solidified inside the Earth's crust. The slow cooling allowed large crystals to grow which were then surround by smaller crystals – a feature known as porphyries. As the crystals developed, copper was contained in a separate fluid mineral soup in a relatively dilute form, but as crystallisation continued and the fluid reduced, the concentration of copper within it increased. Once the intrusion was almost entirely solid it contracted and cracked. The remaining copper-rich fluid infiltrated fissures where it, too, solidified to form veins of copper sulphide.

Strata-bound deposits: mature sedimentary beds in large continental (intracratonic) basins also contain significant copper, such as in the central African 'copper belt'. The origins of the deposits are still being debated, but it has been proposed that hydrothermal fluids (hot, mineral-rich water) suffused into carbon-rich deposits and were capped by overlying shales within a massive evolving basin in central Africa. The impermeable layer trapped copper-rich fluids which precipitated into solidified mineral deposits during a metamorphic period associated with mountain-building earth movements.

Massive sulphide deposits: these are associated with volcanic activity (so a more surface manifestation of tectonic activity than porphyry deposits) and formed as a result of hydrothermal infusions in submarine environments. Sometimes referred to as volcanic-hosted massive sulphide (VMS) deposits, they often include copper and zinc sulphides that precipitate out from hydrothermal fluids on or below the sea floor, erupting from submarine vents, hot springs and 'black smokers' on the seabed. VMS deposits occur today surrounding submarine volcanoes and along mid-ocean ridges. Currently exploited reserves are a result of very ancient submarine volcanic activity that has been uplifted and deformed by subsequent tectonic activity to surface formations. The copper-zinc-lead-silver ore of Parys Mountain on the isle of Anglesey originated from this source to create Britain's largest deposit of this type.

The pattern of copper ore extraction is a function of both the richness of the ore, the size of reserves, the ease of extraction and the investment stability of the region. While Chile does not possess the richest reserves, they are by far the largest (Figure 11.65) accounting for over a third of all global copper reserves.

Physical and human

How does the geological origin of different copper reserves affect the way they are exploited, their profitability and environmental impact of extraction?

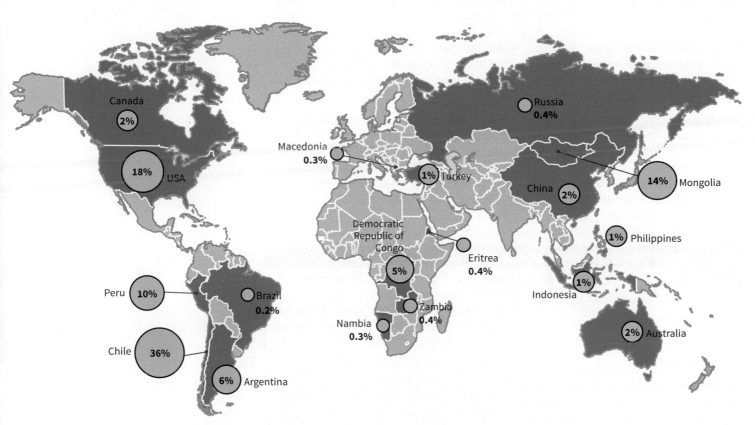

Figure 11.65 Global distribution of copper ore reserves.

Most copper ore (2% copper on average) is extracted via open-cast quarrying although it may be obtained by underground mining or by leaching in a soluble form. Once extracted the ore is processed according to its mineral origin, but most is crushed finely and concentrated by a flotation process upon water (30% copper). This may be followed by roasting (60% copper). Heat and chemical conversion further refines the metal (99%) and it may be re-fired or cast into anodes (cathodes in a variant of the process) for electrolysis (99.99%). Copper obtained directly from mineral ore is referred to as primary copper (Figure 11.66), but increasingly recycling of used copper products has raised the contribution of this secondary copper to 18–30% of total copper production in 2013.

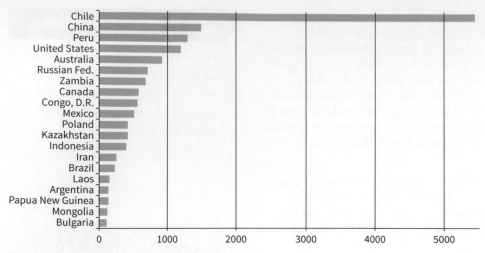

Figure 11.66 Copper mine production by top 20 countries, 2012 (thousands of tonnes).

The uses of refined copper are many; some familiar – others less so. As a very low-resistance, malleable, corrosion-resistant metal, copper has long been the dominant choice of electrical conductor, accounting for its most widespread use (Table 11.6).

The key manufacturing and construction end-users of copper are located in established and rapidly industrialising countries that are the setting for much globalised industrial production. Dominated by China, copper is used in volume in the construction industry of a rapidly urbanising nation and in the manufacture of consumer products, transport fabrication and the electrical and electronics industry. Global copper consumption doubled between 1990 and 2015 with the trend likely to continue.

Functional category	Proportion	Specific uses
Electrical	65%	Circuitry wiring, electrical connectors, printed circuit boards, micro-chips, semi-conductors, internet lines, electromagnets, renewable energy technology (solar, wind, geothermal, fuel cells), etc.
Construction	25%	Copper tubing for water and heating systems, heat exchangers in power stations, irrigation and sprinkler systems, tubes for petroleum distribution and seawater feed lines, light fittings, hinges, locks, door handles, fire sprinkler systems
Transport	7%	Car radiators and oil coolers, heated seats, hydraulic lines, high-speed electric trains, electric cars, overhead contact wires for trams, aircraft control systems, ship propellers and hulls
Other products	3%	Cookware, clocks and watches, coins, scientific and musical instruments, brass items (copper is the major constituent alongside zinc) such as ammunition cases)

Table 11.6 Uses of copper.

Environmental impacts of mineral extraction and distribution

The extraction of a mineral contained in an ore, 98% of which is unwanted, is likely to lead to issues of waste disposal. But the environmental impacts of copper mining revolve around more than the extraction. The processing of the ore at site to render it economically viable to transport to where it will ultimately be smelted can have significant impacts on air, water, soil and people.

The world's largest open-pit copper mine in the world (by excavated volume) is the Chuquicamata mine in Chile's Atacama Desert (Figure 11.67). Nearly 3000 m above sea level the air is thin, and the atmosphere very dry.

The employees of state-owned CODELCO, Chile's largest company which produces high-quality copper from porphyry deposits, largely for the Chinese market, used to live next to the mine. In 2008 the town, of the same name as the mine, with a population of 25 000 people was closed and the inhabitants moved to the oasis town of Calama, 17 km away. The reason was largely the contamination of the settlement by the environmental consequences of the mine. Specifically:

Figure 11.67 Chuquicamata copper mine in Chile, one of the world's largest.

- Fugitive dust: airborne particles dispersed by winds from waste tips are particularly prevalent in the arid conditions surrounding the location of this mine. Not just rock dust, but dust containing toxic mineral compounds.

- Water extraction: huge volumes of freshwater are required in processing copper ore and this, in one of the most arid regions of Earth, puts significant pressure on surface and groundwater supplies. What is used by the copper processing is unavailable for alternative uses.

- Contamination of water supplies: dust, effluent and seepage from the million litres of sulphuric acid produced annually as a by-product of the processing system contaminated the original town's water supplies. Tailing dams that contain toxic effluent and discharge of mine waters are the main sources of water contamination. (Though a government ruling in 1997 stated that contamination of the local River Loa was from natural sources of contaminants rather than the mine, a ruling challenged by the Ministry of Agriculture.)

- Smelting, electric furnace and electrolytic refinery processes: sulphur dioxide, arsenic and copper particles were part of the airborne emissions from these copper concentration stages. Sulphur dioxide, in particular, is harmful to the flora of the region. Arsenic, however, is harmful to human populations and the mine was emitting 30–35 metric tons per day in the late 1980s.

- Soil contamination: dry deposition of airborne particles coats the surface of soil, building accumulations that can be taken up by food crops.

- Dust from ore-carrying lorries: trucks carrying 400 tonnes of ore operating seven days a week generate dust and each consumes three litres of diesel every minute. Each day, 400 000 tonnes of waste are removed by the trucks.

- Sea contamination: heavy metal compounds eventually reach the sea and affect the coastal water of Chile together with hydrocarbons from ore-carrying tankers. Contamination is largely in the estuaries fed by rivers that flow past mining operation, such as Chañaral Bay, and have been known to kill shellfish, fish and algae by the high concentration of heavy metals, which has affected fishermen's livelihoods.

Steps have been taken to clean up the Chuquicamata mine operations and the town of Calama has now grown to over 150 000 inhabitants. It is partly through the insistence of copper customers demanding more environmentally responsible sources for their copper, that improvements have been made, alongside green policy pressure groups within Chile that campaigned for a cleaner, healthier environment, resulting in falls in arsenic and sulphur dioxide emissions from the mid-1990s at the plant.

Sustainability issues associated with ore minerals

It is improbable that the world will run out of copper in the foreseeable future; since forecasts commenced in the 1950s there has always been, on average, 40 years of copper reserves and 200 years of resource remaining (Figure 11.68). Technological developments in mining and processing have continuously extended the window. In addition to new crustal deposits being discovered, previously unexploited copper sources are being contemplated, such as seabed copper nodules and submarine massive sulphides.

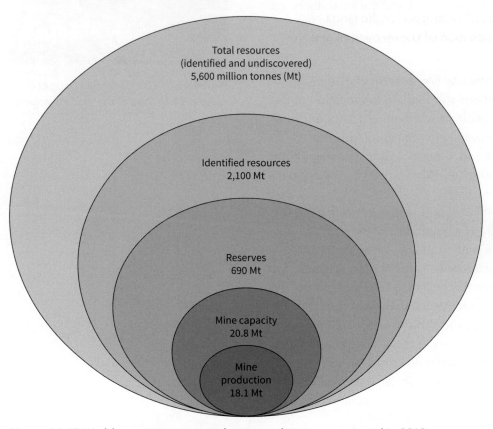

Figure 11.68 World copper reserves and estimated resource potential in 2013.

Unlike iron, copper is far less reactive in air and remains viable for recycling many years after its original use and can fetch high prices (hence the illegal stripping of copper piping from buildings and trackside cables from railways in the UK, and industrial-scale recycling of electrical goods in India and China). Annual global copper use is now approaching 35% sourced from recycled copper.

Many of the sustainability issues that illustrate the challenge of meeting future demand for ore minerals are exemplified in those facing the copper industry:

- Increasing waste per ton of copper obtained: declining quality of ore grades as the richest are consumed first. This is becoming a significant issue in Chile and the USA, two major producers.
- Price fluctuations affecting investment finance: the sharp decline in commodities markets in early 2016 following the reduced rate of economic growth in China saw the price of many metals fall substantially.

Obtaining investment to explore new reserves and improve existing capacity is harder to achieve when the anticipated profitability of ventures declines.

- Water supply constraints: many regions are facing uncertain water supplies due to increasing domestic and agricultural water demand and fluctuating rainfall regimes as a result of climate change. Water availability is a critical input into mining, quarrying and processing the ore.
- Energy input: fuel costs and carbon taxes are increasing the energy costs that are integral to mineral processing.
- Environmental restrictions: tighter environmental checks and pollution regulation are increasing the costs of cleaning up throughout the extraction and processing cycle to limit effluent, waste and pollutants.
- Social incursion: maintaining a higher level of respect for the lands of indigenous people can restrict the exploitation of known mineral reserves, such as in Peru and the Philippines.

Taking steps to reduce the environmental impact of ore extraction and processing proceeds most rapidly when there is a legislative framework of enforced environmental regulation in the extracting country, a desire by producers to limit their impact on the environment for social and marketing purposes and a customer preference for products derived from environmentally responsible producers. Measures include:

- Water: water conservation practices can reduce demand. In Canada, mining has one the highest rates of water recycling amongst all industrial sectors and reduced its total water intake by 33% in the decade up to 2005.
- Energy: Kennecott Utah Copper mine's haul truck idle management system has won awards in the USA for pollution reduction from ore extraction vehicles. Cutting the idle time on its 68 haul trucks has significantly reduced diesel fuel use. Solar power plants have been built in Chile to cut fossil-fuel energy imports required by the copper smelting industry.
- Mine waste: reprocessing of waste can reduce its toxicity and volume. Waste management plans help reduce dust release, soluble runoff and contamination of adjacent water courses.
- Land reclamation: once mine sites have been exhausted site reclamation plans can restore the area to a state acceptable for reuse by ecosystems and people. The Island Copper Mine on the northern part of Vancouver Island, Canada, which closed in 1995, saw 480 hectares of mine operations converted into productive woodland, wildlife habitat and waste rock transported to Rupert Inlet to construct six bays to create marine habitat.

11.7 Resources futures: water, energy and ore minerals

Water futures

Key future challenges in providing sufficient water include the following:

- Climate change: not only making precipitation less reliable, but also affecting glacier melt rates, evaporation, biomass cover and demand.
- Global population growth: the world's current population approaching 7.5 billion is forecast to grow by another 1.5 billion by 2050, putting

extra demands on water provision. The greatest growth areas are already experiencing water stress.

- Increasing global affluence: it is not only the number of people, it is also their consumption habits that will impact most upon water demand.
- Depletion of historic reserves: it is estimated that over half the world's population lives in 18 countries that are depleting aquifers faster than they are being replenished.
- Contamination from cities, agriculture and industry: water quality deteriorates as urban growth continues, agriculture relies increasingly on chemical pesticides and fertilisers and industry grows to meet higher material aspirations. The effluent and residues of these processes are likely to increasingly contaminate surface and groundwater supplies – particularly for downflow users.

However, there are developments that make the future of water provision look more positive:

- Urban efficiency: as a greater proportion of the world's population move to cities, it is more efficient to construct effective urban water supply provision and recycle used water for reuse.
- Agricultural efficiency: not only do appropriate irrigation techniques make more effective use of the available water, genetic modification of crops is enabling them to be grown in more saline conditions than would traditionally have been possible. Monsanto has been trialling genetically modified maize in the USA that is more drought tolerant by reducing transpiration rates.
- Industrial efficiency: if there are environmental requirements in place, enforced and pursued with carrot and stick policies, industry can be steered into being more efficient in its use of water and environmentally responsible for the effluent it discharges. The UK government encourages businesses to invest in water-efficient plant and machinery by allowing them to claim expenditure against tax payments through the Enhanced Capital Allowance (ECA) scheme.
- Structural frameworks: the UN draws suggestions for improving water provision to member nations that are largely structural. It advises:
  - Establish effective legal frameworks of laws and regulation to balance water supply with demand, protect water supplies from contamination and ensure sustainable use of water sources so that future generations are not compromised.
  - Reduce inequality between social and sectoral groups and establish the basis for economic progress through investing in effective water, sanitation and hygiene (WASH) provision.
  - Increase investment in water storage, distribution and supply as a key spending area.
  - Intervene to manage the use and quality of water among the different users, some of whom may be more powerful and influential and need to operate within a managed framework if others are not to be disadvantaged.

Energy futures

The fastest growth in demand for energy in the next 50 years is likely to come from newly industrialising countries (NICs) and low income countries (LICs). It is among these communities that low cost, appropriate technology developments may have the most dramatic benefit.

Appropriate technology strategies

Fuel-efficient stoves

Each year, around 4 million hectares of woodland are chopped down in Africa, mostly to supply fuelwood. The World Food Programme warns that this rate of destruction could see the end of the continent's forests in 50 years' time. However, fuel-efficient stoves that require minimal fuel and use it far more effectively could do more than protect woodland. The reduced consumption of fuel could see girls and women have far more time in their day to devote to education, paid employment or cash-generating activities. DARE, the Nigerian Development Association for Renewable Energies, subsidises the cost of fuel-efficient stoves to rural communities so that the outlay can be recouped from reduced fuel bills in 6–14 months. A stove can burn 80% less fuel than the traditional three-rock open fire and emits far less health-compromising smoke.

However, social attitudes can sometimes be a barrier to the acceptance of the new product. Some women claim food tastes better with swirling wood-smoke and the traditional hearth can play an important role in family network and community interaction. To overcome reservations, DARE has a programme of village demonstrations of the use of the stove, providing information about its health benefits and raising awareness about the environmental issues of local deforestation.

Barefoot College solar engineers

The Barefoot College was established in Tilonia, 360 km from Delhi in India by Sanjit 'Bunker' Roy in 1972. It recruits two grandmothers nominated by a committee of village representatives from villages throughout India and other Asian and African countries. For six months they are taught the basics of electronics and solar engineering, irrespective of their native language. They then return to their villages equipped with the skills to install, maintain and repair a solar lighting system purchased by funds raised by the village committee from contributing households (Figure 11.69).

The benefits include the environmental, economic and social. The use of kerosene and fuelwood has declined substantially, villagers can arrange their work beyond the hours of natural daylight and conduct income-generating activities well into the evening if they so wish, and children can attend evening school after working with parents during the day. Perhaps the biggest impact is in the reappraisal of the identity of women within the community. The choice of grandmothers is deliberate: they are less likely to migrate to a city once trained, unlike young men; they have a vested interest in the improvement of their community through their children and grandchildren; and their success inspires other women of whatever age to challenge traditional stereotype assumptions of their roles and capacities. Since 2008 the Barefoot College claims 'Solar Mamas' have brought light to over 40 000 households in 1000 villages and improved the lives of 450 000 people.

High-technology strategies

The moves away from a carbon-based economy in high income countries (HICs) hold significant challenges. Renewable energy alternatives are not always consistent in supply, close to main areas of demand or easily scaled up to equivalent power generation of that which has gone before. Even transitions to electric cars, which many manufacturers are introducing into their ranges, raises the issue of how and where the electricity will be generated.

Carbon capture and storage (CCS)

The concept behind carbon capture and burial is a natural development of the principle of enhanced oil recovery by which water and sand is pumped under pressure into oil and gas reserves to extract additional stocks (Figure 11.70). In an extension of the practice, carbon dioxide is extracted during the process

Watch a video clip of an example of appropriate energy technology through the use of biogas in rural India on **Cambridge Elevate**.

Figure 11.69 A solar cooker used by the community.

For an activity on the use of appropriate technology such as rural solar power download Worksheet 11.5 from **Cambridge Elevate**.

For an activity on carbon capture and storage download Worksheet 11.6 from **Cambridge Elevate**.

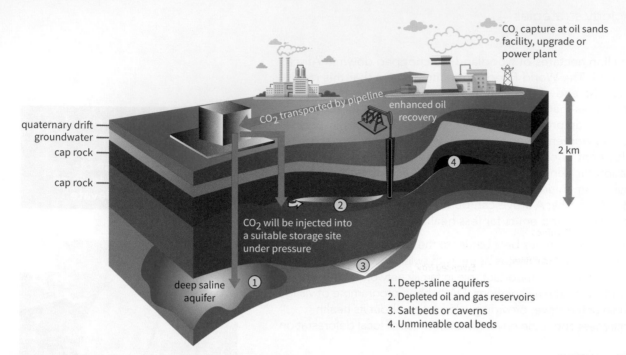

Figure 11.70 Carbon capture and storage processes.

of coal combustion, piped to exhausted oil- and gas-bearing strata or saline aquifers and locked into rock strata by permanently capping, in a process known as human carbon sequestration. (Natural carbon sequestration occurs when marine creatures decompose and accumulate on the seabed – see Chapter 1, Water and carbon cycles.)

The Boundary Dam power plant in Saskatchewan (Figure 11.71) will capture up to 1 million tonnes of carbon dioxide per year, transporting it to nearby oilfields for EOR. Globally, there are over 24 CCS schemes in advanced planning and construction stages.

Tidal barrages

There is one renewable energy source that is regular, predictable and can generate significant quantities of electricity: the hydraulic effect of the rise and fall of tides every 6½ hours or so. With the construction of a barrage to hold the higher level of the tide either side, then releasing water through to the lower tidal side, a reliable supply of HEP can be generated at both high and low tide via turbines set within the barrage.

The plan for a tidal barrage in Swansea Bay (Figure 11.72) was given the go-ahead in 2015 by the UK government. The £1 billion scheme could operate for 120 years and, as part of five similar tidal barrages the company behind the plan wants to see built, could generate 8% of the UK electricity requirement. Critics argue that the production of cement for the 22.5 km barrage would generate so much carbon dioxide that calling the scheme carbon-free would be inaccurate.

Future social scenarios

Whether energy is sourced from existing fuels or from new technology, it is likely that the long-term price for consumers will rise. Existing finite resources will see escalating costs of exploration and production as reserves are depleted. For capital-heavy schemes such as CCS and tidal barrages, power companies and finance providers need to be assured there will be a high rate of return to validate their investment. The UK government has

Look on **Cambridge Elevate** for this Special Report on Energy in sub-Saharan Africa, from the International Energy Agency. I considers the key uses and potential developments in supply that could see the region develop its energy infrastructure (www.cambridge.org/links/gase6126).

Figure 11.71 The Boundary Dam power plant in Saskatchewan, Canada.

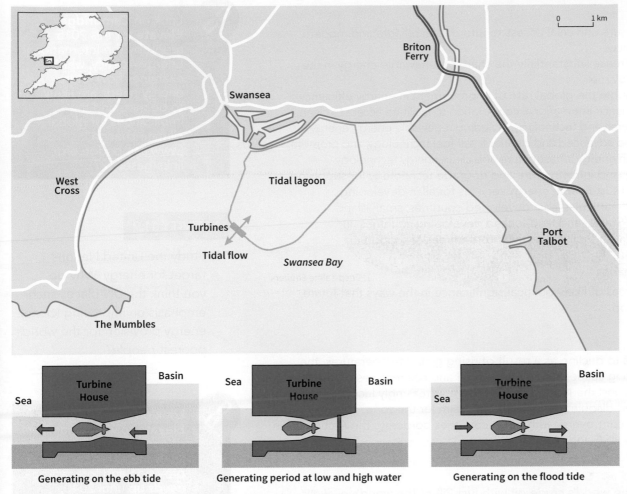

Generating on the ebb tide
Generating period at low and high water
Generating on the flood tide

Figure 11.72 The tidal barrage planned for Swansea Bay, Wales.

stated that the cost of the Swansea tidal barrage project must come from private investors, with the costs ultimately borne by energy consumers through their electricity bills.

As a result, there are likely to be social questions about whether energy costs will intensify **fuel poverty**. This is a feature of not only LICs but also among increasing sections of society in HICs. Defined in the UK as the threshold where expenditure on essential fuel for a household is greater than the national median level, and where – in the spending – the residual household income remaining drops it below the official poverty line, fuel poverty affected 10.4% of households in England in 2013. Highest among the unemployed, those in privately rented accommodation, low income lone-parent households and low pension elderly, fuel poverty can affect health and life expectancy as well as quality of life.

Access to affordable energy is goal 7 of the UN's 17 Sustainable Development Goals. Due to follow on from the eight Millennium Development Goals, this new global target started in 2015.

Goal 7: Affordable and clean energy

Energy is central to nearly every major challenge and opportunity the world faces today. Be it for jobs, security, climate change, food production or increasing incomes, access to energy for all is essential.

Sustainable energy is opportunity – it transforms lives, economies and the planet.

Key term

fuel poverty: there are different definitions of this term, but it refers to essential fuel costs being so high for an individual or family that their well-being is compromised in terms of quality of life and health

Physical and human

Read more on using the potential of tidal energy of existing tidal barrage schemes, such as La Rance on the Brittany coast of France and the Sihwa Lake and Incheon tidal barrage constructions in South Korea.

Goal 7 targets:

- By 2030, ensure universal access to affordable, reliable and modern energy services.
- By 2030, increase substantially the share of renewable energy in the global energy mix.
- By 2030, double the global rate of improvement in energy efficiency.
- By 2030, enhance international cooperation to facilitate access to clean energy research and technology, including renewable energy, energy efficiency and advanced and cleaner fossil-fuel technology, and promote investment in energy infrastructure and clean energy technology.
- By 2030, expand infrastructure and upgrade technology for supplying modern and sustainable energy services for all in developing countries, in particular least developed countries, small island developing States, and land-locked developing countries, in accordance with their respective programmes of support.

Future political scenarios

The following are areas of likely political significance in the ways that future energy issues develop.

The Arctic

As sea-ice continues to decline as a result of rising global temperatures, the prospects of exploiting suspected and known oil and gas reserves on the floor of the Arctic Ocean around the North Pole will seem increasingly lucrative. Russia has already provoked disquiet by its territorial claim for the zone. This may become a region of controversy with other countries bordering the Arctic Ocean, notably Canada, the USA and Norway.

The Middle East

Producing 30% of the world's crude oil with just 2% of the world's oil wells, the oil reserves of this region are highly productive, which affects the global price per barrel. Political instability may cause the loss of production, as in Libya. Political trade embargoes may be lifted or put in place again in Iran. Competition with alternative higher-cost producers may cause Middle East producers to increase production to flood the market, drive down the price and put competitors out of business – a key factor behind the oil price dropping by over 50% from $110 per barrel in July 2014 to $40 per barrel in July 2015.

Russia and western and southern Europe

By far the biggest holder of gas reserves, along with Iran, Russia has positioned itself over the last 20 years as a major supplier of gas to central, southern and western Europe. However, conflict in Ukraine and a steep cooling in international relations with its potential customers has caused some countries to look for alternative supplies to ensure their energy security. In October 2015, Turkey announced it was planning to double its coal production and quadruple its number of coal-fired power stations from 22 to over 80, citing energy security as its priority.

China and India

China and India are the two most populous countries in the world and, with economies that are among the fastest growing, their appetite for more energy will undoubtedly increase for the foreseeable future (Figure 11.73). The energy demands of what constitute over a quarter of the Earth's population are heavily dependent on coal at the moment (Figure 11.74), with the two countries consuming 60% of the world's coal production.

Look on **Cambridge Elevate** for this 2015 report by the International Energy Agency, which examines how future energy needs are likely to be met, and the implications for global climate change (www.cambridge.org/links/gase6127).

ACTIVITY 11.9

1   Study the United Nations target for energy. Why do you think the UN places such emphasis on improving (clean) energy provision for the world's poorest people?

Look on **Cambridge Elevate** to view a number of graphics illustrating likely future global energy provision and forecast needs up until 2040, from The International Energy Agency (www.cambridge.org/links/gase6128).

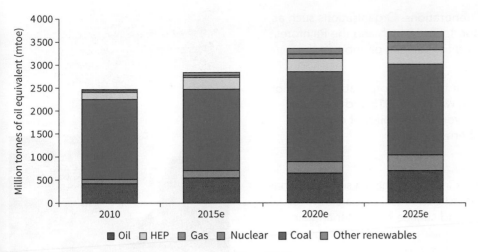

Figure 11.73 Energy sources in China, 2010 to 2025.

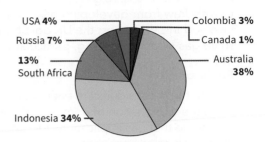

Figure 11.74 China's sources of steam coal imports, 2012.

The only likely restrictions on further use of coal are concerns about air quality, which is notoriously poor in urban areas, and signing up to international agreements to reduce carbon emissions to combat climate change.

Africa

The limiting factor in many sub-Saharan countries is not lack of energy resources, both renewable and non-renewable, but lack of distribution and supply infrastructure. Electricity tariffs are among the highest in the world and, outside South Africa, there are significant losses in poorly maintained transmission networks. HEP offers considerable potential, with only 10% of possible utilisation yet harnessed. These schemes, however, require considerable capital investment and distribution infrastructure. That investment will be forthcoming only if potential lenders have confidence that loans will generate profitable returns over the medium to long term.

A further uncertainty in exploiting HEP is the impact of climate change. The world's largest man-made reservoir, Lake Kariba in Zambia, suffered significant falls in water level in 2015 following reduced flow of the River Zambezi. Power cuts affected agricultural and industrial production as the reservoir level fell to 40% full. In a previous severe drought in 1995, it took four years before the lake started to refill.

South America

There is considerable potential for countries in and around the Amazon Basin to exploit HEP potential further. However, three key constraints may limit exploitation: climate change leading to unreliable rainfall; the remoteness of many energy locations from the key urban markets; and international concern over the impact of reservoirs flooding primary rainforest and the consequences for indigenous forest-dwellers.

Brazil has one of the least carbon-intensive energy profiles in the world with not only significant HEP but, increasingly, solar power, onshore wind and bioenergy – 43% of the country's domestic energy mix comes from renewables. The country is the world's second largest producer of biofuels, mainly bioethanol produced from sugar cane. The government insists it has strict controls on conserving equatorial forest and that enhanced use of existing farmland will enable it to contribute 40% of the world's biofuel trade by 2035 and contribute almost one-third to its domestic transport fuel needs.

Pressure groups

Active groups seek to put pressure on governments, corporations, international organisations and the financial markets to change, amend or strengthen policies

Investigate

Investigate the arguments for and against fracking. Do you think it has the potential to fill the UK's energy gap as it has transformed US energy provision, or do you think it should not be pursued due to economic or environmental arguments?

that will conserve the natural world for future generations. Organisations such as Greenpeace, WWF (World Wide Fund for Nature), Earthwatch and the Rainforest Alliance engage in a range of activities designed to maintain or improve the environment.

A number of pressure groups claimed success for the Shell corporation's decision to withdraw from developing oilfields in Alaskan waters in 2015 and some are involved in persuading the UK government to overturn its policy of exploiting shale gas through fracking, particularly in northern England.

Public opinion

One of the most significant energy developments in North America since 2000 has been the exploitation of domestic shales for oil and gas. Fracking is a controversial technique that has implications for groundwater and surface soil, water and air conditions as contaminants can compromise their quality.

The procedure is increasingly dividing town, city and state authorities. In June 2015 the state governor of Texas outlawed the option for municipal councils to impose bans on local fracking activities. The ruling established the rights of shale gas companies to unrestricted access being a higher priority for state and national needs than the concerns of towns and cities. In the UK, soon after the 2015 general election, the government announced a similar move to fast-track planning applications to frack and ensure that if local authorities do not act quickly enough on coming to a decision, the judgement will revert to the government. It is a move that may be seen as prioritising national policy over local public opinion. The strength of public opposition (Figure 11.75) has led the SNP devolved government in Scotland to impose an indefinite ban on fracking, a declaration that has also been seen in Ireland, Germany, France and Bulgaria.

Ore mineral futures

There are some concerns over the medium-term provision of major ore minerals over the next half century as known reserves are exploited and demand rises. But there is also confidence in the capacity of technology, forthcoming investment finance and increasing demand to drive the discovery of new reserves. Where there is a degree of doubt over long-term sustainability is in the group of minerals known as **rare earth** chemicals. They are typically used in new-technology produces, often in very small but essential quantities and which are found in few places on the Earth, in low concentrations and difficult to separate from each other (Figure 11.76).

Once processed they offer unique magnetic, luminescent and electrochemical properties that make them crucial for many advanced-technology products, including mobile phones, touch-sensitive tablet screens and medical imaging machines (Table 11.7). Despite their name, rare earth elements are not particularly rare, but they are difficult to separate and process.

Much of the focus on rare earths has been on the dominance of China in their production and its control over their global availability. Until 2005 China exported rare earths cheaply to be processed overseas, mainly in Japan, where they went into high-technology products. China then imposed export quotas limiting the amount of REE it was prepared to release, raising strategic concerns in the USA and Japan over rapidly rising prices and a potential shortage. Partially as a result of geopolitical trade pressure, in 2015 China suspended the quotas and replaced them with a resource tax, using pricing to control demand and supply rather than export limits.

Other elements exist outside this group and are much rarer, such as tellurium. This metal is used in the production of the most efficient photo-voltaic cells for solar panels and is produced exclusively as a by-product of other mineral

Figure 11.75 Caroline Lucas, MP for the Green Party, being arrested in August 2013 at Balcombe, West Sussex while protesting against fracking.

 Key term

rare earths: 17 elements with chemical properties that make them vital to cutting-edge technologies and advanced engineering. REE (rare earth element) / REM (rare earth metal)

 Investigate

Find out the contribution of rare earths to your mobile devices – phone and tablet. What are the implications of increasing global demand for these products?

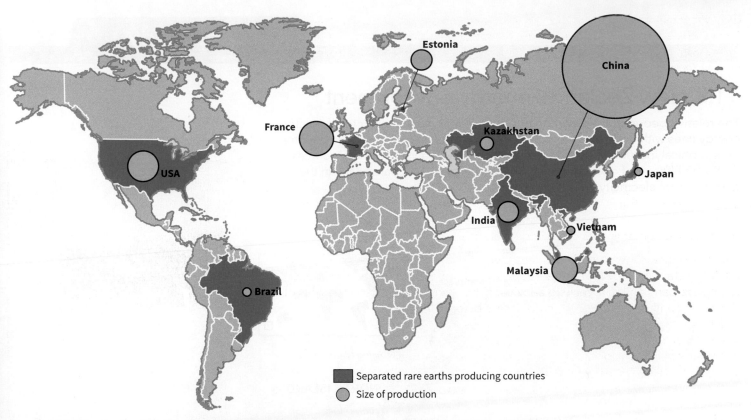

Figure 11.76 Production volumes of rare earth elements around the world.

Rare earth element examples	Uses
Samarium	Permanent magnets, cancer treatments, nuclear reactor rods
Gadolinium	Medical imaging/radiography
Holmium	Lasers, microwave equipment
Thulium	Lasers, portable X-ray machines
Yttrium	Capacitors, superconductors, pulsed lasers, cancer drugs
Cerium	Catalytic converters in exhaust systems
Praseodymium	Jet engines

Table 11.7 The uses of some rare earth elements

processing, often as a by-product of copper mining and processing. While its price is high, only 0.5 kg of tellurium is obtained from the processing of 500 tons of copper ore so its production depends on continued copper processing; such small quantities cannot justify production costs alone. In addition, more modern methods of copper production use a different process that can operate on lower-grade ores, but do not permit the recovery of tellurium.

Future concerns over ore mineral exploitation, processing and trade are likely to focus less on physical resource constraints of a particular ore and increasingly on the environmental and geopolitical context influencing the availability of economically viable reserves.

11.8 New Zealand's energy environment

The relative geographical isolation of New Zealand means that interconnector energy lines with neighbouring countries is not feasible. However, the country's geographical location (Figure 11.77) provides it with a variety of fuel sources that offer a range of options in meeting its energy needs, particularly in the generation of electricity.

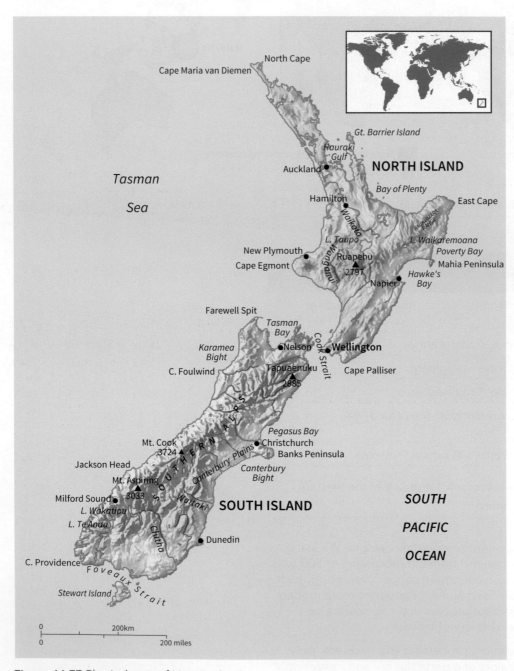

Figure 11.77 Physical map of New Zealand.

In 2014, 40% of New Zealand's total energy needs came from renewable sources – primarily HEP, geothermal and increasingly, wind (Figure 11.78). This puts New Zealand in third place of all OECD countries (behind only Iceland and Norway) in meeting its energy demand from renewable sources. The physical geography of the country is closely linked to the energy mix New Zealand exhibits and helped enable it, in 2014, to produce nearly 80% of its electricity generation from renewable sources and able to pursue a target of 90% by 2025.

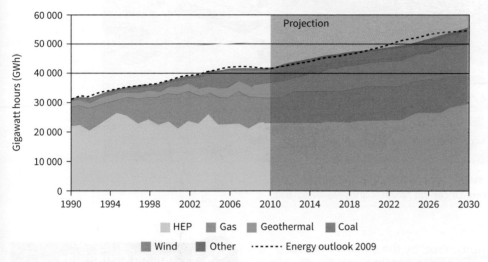

Figure 11.78 Electricity generation by fuel in New Zealand.

Fuel sources

HEP

HEP has been the dominant source of electricity in New Zealand for decades, and it is forecast to continue to be, providing 57% of New Zealand's electricity. Three major schemes with multiple plants lie on South Island: the high rainfall and deep, glaciated valleys of the Southern Alps giving rise to many lakes and high discharge rivers that, along with snow and glacier melt, make this an area rich in HEP potential. North Island has two large-scale schemes: Tongariro, involving two power plants, and Waikato, with nine. Climate change may restrict further development of HEP potential and any further increase in capacity is likely to require the flooding of valued land. In the 1970s public protests brought a halt to plans to raise Lake Manapouri for increased HEP generation and further schemes have provoked a similar response.

Geothermal energy

New Zealand's location on the convergent tectonic boundary of the western Pacific and eastern Australian plates has provided it with significant geothermal energy potential. Mostly concentrated around the Taupo Volcanic Zone in central North Island (Figure 11.79), geothermal energy is exploited by boring wells into sub-surface hot rocks, pumping down cold water and extracting both steam to power turbines and hot water to be used directly in horticulture and domestic heating. First tapped in 1958, geothermal energy has grown to provide 16% of New Zealand's electricity production from six main fields. Expansion is taking place, with new developments such as the Nga Awa Purua power plant that started operating in 2010 and has the world's largest geothermal steam turbine.

Although geothermal energy is considered the most consistent of renewable energy sources in New Zealand – avoiding the interruptions that both wind and HEP may periodically encounter – there is recent evidence that long-term

Figure 11.79 The Ngatamariki geothermal power station, opened in 2013, has seven geothermal wells and lies in the Taupo Volcanic Zone of central North Island, New Zealand.

exploitation of sub-surface heat may be compromised by the constant pumped infusion of cold water. Some plants are, therefore, capped in the volume of steam extraction they can exploit, giving time for heat regeneration to take place. This, along with exploitation of most near-surface geothermal potential, may limit its expansion capacity.

Wind power

The fastest-growing renewable energy source in New Zealand is wind power. Contributing 5% of electricity generation in 2014, the sector is due for substantial expansion as more onshore wind farms are developed. Located in the path of the 'Roaring Forties' (particularly strong westerly winds operating in the southern hemisphere between 40° and 50°), North Island is particularly well placed to exploit them, accounting for 70% of wind turbines. The New Zealand Wind Energy Association suggests this source could provide 20% of the country's electricity generation by 2030. But this would require considerable acceptance from a population deeply protective of their national landscape environment.

Coal

Although New Zealand has reserves of coal, imports of cheaper coal from Australia and Indonesia increased dramatically between 2000 and 2006 to supply the country's coal-fired power stations. They fell, equally rapidly, to virtually zero by 2012. In 2010 New Zealand was one of the early OECD countries to commit to the Copenhagen Accord on climate change. In order to reduce carbon emissions by 10–20% by 2020 (on 1990 levels), a comprehensive carbon trading scheme called New Zealand Emissions Trading Scheme (NZ ETS) was introduced to cover all sectors by 2015. As a result, coal use in electricity production is due to cease by 2018. Although coal-fired power stations contributed barely 5% to New Zealand's electricity production at their peak in 2006, they provided a reliable reserve in times of low river and reservoir levels when HEP generation dropped. In August 2015, Genesis Energy – the country's largest producer of electricity – announced it was to close the last of its two coal-fired boilers at the Huntly plant (the country's largest power station, south of Auckland) by December 2018. This will mark the end of coal-fired electricity generation in New Zealand.

 Look on **Cambridge Elevate** for this comprehensive report: New Zealand Energy 2015 from the New Zealand Ministry of Business, Innovation and Employment, which identifies the key energy needs, sources and factors affecting energy prices in New Zealand (www.cambridge.org/ links/gase6129).

Gas

New Zealand is self-sufficient in natural gas from the coastal Taranaki Basin. These reserves are depleting rapidly, however, and the era of cheap gas is likely to end soon. The government is encouraging the search for new reserves. In 2014 geothermal energy (16.2%) overtook gas (15.7%) for the first time as the country's second largest electricity generation source after HEP. It is likely that some gas-fired plants will be mothballed so they can be put back into energy generation rapidly should the need arise.

Oil

The largest single energy demand by New Zealand is oil. Domestic production supplies 47% of its needs from reserves adjacent to its gasfield. Imports are likely to increase substantially as domestic oilfields are being rapidly depleted. Oil is required for transport, the petrochemical industry, agriculture, domestic heating and industry, but it is no longer used for electricity generation other than in small-scale generators in remote regions.

Nuclear

New Zealand declared itself a nuclear-free zone in 1987. Although the legislation did not specifically prevent the construction of nuclear power stations, the persisting commitment to a non-nuclear outlook has meant New Zealand has rarely considered a nuclear energy option. Currently there are no plans to construct a nuclear power station.

Reducing demand by tackling energy inefficiency

After decades of relatively cheap, abundant energy New Zealanders have relatively inefficient homes when it comes to energy consumption, falling below the efficiency of North American or European domestic property. As a result, the government rolled out the Warm Up New Zealand programme in 2009. This provided advice and subsidies for insulating homes and fitting clean energy systems in properties built before 2000.

The energy potential of Waikato region

To the east of North Island the Pacific plate is subducted beneath the Australian plate giving rise to the Central Plateau and the Taupo Volcanic Zone. Magma intrusions into the fractured crustal rocks raises temperatures to over 350°C within 5 km of the surface.

The Taupo district in the centre of North Island can be considered the renewable energy heart of New Zealand. Located in the south-east of the Waikato region around Lake Taupo – New Zealand's largest lake in the caldera of an ancient supervolcano – the folding of the crust and volcanic activity associated with being adjacent to an active convergent margin has provided the area with considerable geothermal potential. Additionally, the raised relief in the path of the Roaring Forties ensures high levels of precipitation, giving rise to New Zealand's longest river, the Waikato, and yielding significant hydroelectric potential.

The Wairakei geothermal field, 8 km north-east of Taupo, is one of the largest and long-established sources of geothermal energy in the country:

- It has over 50 production wells boring to depths of between 0.3 and 2.4 km. and producing fluid at temperatures between 209 °C and 261 °C.
- There are four separate power plants, all owned by Contact Energy, generating 333 MWe (2014).
- Geothermal fluid is a naturally occurring mix of pressurised water and steam. The high-pressure hot water is separated and the remaining dry steam is used to spin turbines, generating electricity.

For an activity on New Zealand's energy environment download Worksheet 11.6 from **Cambridge Elevate**.

- Secondary turbines make use of low-pressure exhaust steam to heat pentane, a liquid with a low boiling point of 34 °C; the evaporated gas then drives a further turbine.
- Approximately 43% of the hot water is re-injected via injection wells into the ground. This is to prevent a cooling of groundwater temperatures as cooler groundwater is naturally drawn in to replace that abstracted. It also reduces the amount of contaminated discharge water that is released containing chemicals such as arsenic that is drawn up in the geothermal fluids.
- Most of the remaining water is discharged into the Waikato River once it has cooled to an acceptable temperature where it helps maintain river discharge volume. Some heat is utilised in heat-exchangers to provide warm water for a nearby commercial freshwater prawn farm and a small proportion provides a heat source for offices.

ACTIVITY 11.10

1. To what extent has physical geography provided New Zealand with advantages in meeting its energy needs and to what extent has it limited its energy capacity?
2. A country's geographical isolation matters less in meeting its energy needs in these days of mass shipments of fuel within a global trade network. Thinking of New Zealand, do you agree?

 Physical and human

'New Zealand needs to consider nuclear energy as the most reliable carbon emission-free back-up for when renewable energy sources inevitably encounter interruptions in supply.' Do you agree?

 Assess to progress

1. With reference to **either** energy supplies **or** water supplies, explain why a region or country may change from being energy/water secure to a condition of energy/water insecurity.　9 MARKS [A LEVEL]
2. Select **one** resource from: energy, mineral ore, or water supplies, and explain the problems that a region or country may encounter in attempting to meet increasing demand for the resource.　9 MARKS [A LEVEL]
3. Explain the factors responsible for **one** of the following: an energy conflict, a mineral ore conflict, **or** a water conflict you have studied. What were the consequences of the conflict?　9 MARKS [A LEVEL]
4. 'Local, community-based projects are the most effective way to meet increasing water and energy needs rather than large, capital-intensive schemes.' To what extent do you agree with this statement?　20 MARKS [A LEVEL]
5. 'Increasing supplies of key metals will always lead to an increase in environmental issues.' With reference to one or more ferrous or non-ferrous minerals you have studied, to what extent do you agree with this statement?　20 MARKS [A LEVEL]

Fieldwork

Figure 12.1 A weather monitoring station in Tenerife. The instruments are (from the left): a Stevenson screen for sheltering meteorological instruments while allowing air to circulate freely, an anemometer for measuring wind speed and a rain gauge to measure rainfall. You could use these instruments in your own investigations.

By the end of this chapter you should know:

- how to plan and carry out your own geographical fieldwork investigation
- the requirements of the fieldwork section of the AS Level Component 2 exam
- how you could write and structure your individual geographical investigation (A Level).

Before you start…

You should know:

- how to conduct a geographical enquiry
- geographical enquiries can be used to investigate both human and physical geography
- what quantitative and qualitative data are, and how to collect and evaluate primary and secondary data
- about drawing evidenced conclusions in relation to the original aims of your enquiry, and considering the extent to which these conclusions are reliable

 Tip

This chapter provides various suggestions as to how you could approach your geographical fieldwork investigation. These should not be taken as definitive though, and you must devise your own approach.

12.1 Conducting a fieldwork investigation

Fieldwork is a fundamental part of any geography course and your understanding of the fieldwork process is assessed both at AS and A Level.

- At AS Level you must complete at least two days of fieldwork, but you do *not* submit an enquiry. Your fieldwork knowledge is assessed in Section B of the Component 2 exam paper.
- At A Level you must plan and carry out your own individual investigation and submit a fieldwork report; this is Component 3 of your A Level and comprises 20% of your final mark.

At AS Level, it is likely that you will work with your classmates to carry out fieldwork, with direction from your teachers. It is, however, still important that you understand the fieldwork process and can write confidently about your investigation independently.

There are five main stages to a fieldwork investigation (Figure 12.2).

In practice you will be evaluating at all stages of the fieldwork process, which may lead to you going back to a previous stage and changing methods of data presentation or collection, or even your hypotheses or research questions. Although it might not feel like it at the time, this is a good thing. You are likely to learn much more from an investigation that is a bit 'messy' at times!

Stage 1: Planning your investigation

Aims

Getting the planning right is key to a successful investigation; you need be clear about what you are trying to find out and where and how you are going to do it. At both AS and A Level you are required to undertake fieldwork relating to both physical and human geography; these can be investigated separately or through an integrated approach. Your investigation topic may therefore be physical or human or both. Once you have chosen the topic area that you want to concentrate on, you need to identify an overall **aim**. This is a broad but focused statement of what you are planning to do. Here are a couple of examples:

1   To investigate the effectiveness of the coastal defences at Withernsea, East Yorkshire.
2   To compare the socio-economic characteristics of two wards in Leeds.

It can be helpful to write your aim as an overarching question, so the two examples above could become:

1   How effective are the coastal defences at Withernsea, East Yorkshire?
2   What are the similarities and differences in the socio-economic characteristics of the Gipton/Harehills and Alwoodley wards of Leeds?

When you are choosing your aim or overarching question, you should aim to ensure that it is broad enough to allow you to carry out a detailed, A-Level standard investigation, but small enough to be realistic and manageable.

Once you have decided on an overall aim or question, you should aim to create a number of more specific **research questions** to help you address it. It is important to spend time thinking through your research questions as these indicate what you want to find out in your investigation and, therefore, underpin the rest of your research.

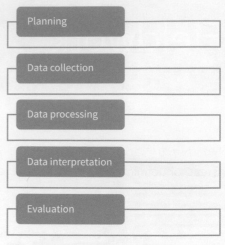

Planning

Data collection

Data processing

Data interpretation

Evaluation

Figure 12.2 The five stages of a fieldwork investigation.

 Making connections

See section 3.9 Case Study: The Holderness coast for a coastal fieldwork investigation.

 Key terms

aim: a clear statement of the purpose of your investigation

research question: an answerable inquiry into a specific concern or issue; it is the central element of both qualitative and quantitative research, and indicates what you want to find out in your investigation

For example, for question 1) How effective are the coastal defences at Withernsea, East Yorkshire?, some possible research questions could be:

a   Why is the coastline at Withernsea susceptible to coastal erosion?
b   What are coastal erosion rates at Withernsea? How do these vary from unmanaged areas north and south of Withernsea?
c   What is the environmental impact of coastal defences at Withernsea?
d   What is the social and economic impact of coastal defences at Withernsea?

Hypotheses

Instead of defining a set of individual research questions, you could also choose to identify a series of **hypotheses** from your overarching aim or research question. A hypothesis is a clear, directional statement that can be tested or measured. As is the case with research questions, your hypotheses will help you to decide on appropriate data collection methods.

Looking again at the first aim, there are several different aspects to consider when judging the effectiveness of the coastal defences. Here are some possible hypotheses:

i   *Local residents in Withernsea believe that the coastal defences have had a positive impact.*
ii   *Accumulation of sand is greater on the northern side of the groynes.*
iii   *The rate of coastal erosion at Withernsea has been reduced by the coastal defences.*

As with research questions, you are likely to want to consider more than one hypothesis in order to achieve a more holistic ('big picture') view of the situation, especially with a management-related study such as the one on coastal defences. If you have more than three hypotheses though, your investigation is likely to become unmanageable, so stick to two or three hypotheses that are clear and focused.

If you are using statistical tests, such as Spearman's rank (see Chapter 13 Geographical skills and techniques), you will also need to have **null hypotheses**. Although you will usually start an investigation with an expectation of what you will find, you actually try to find evidence to reject your null hypothesis (which then allows you to accept your alternative hypothesis) rather than trying to find evidence to support your alternative hypothesis. This idea often confuses students at first, but think of it as 'innocent until proven guilty'.

The null hypotheses for the alternative hypotheses above could be:

i   *Local residents have no particular opinion about the coastal defences in Withernsea.*
ii   *There is no difference between the accumulation of sand on the north and south sides of the groynes.*
iii   *The rate of coastal erosion at Withernsea has not been reduced by the coastal defences.*

Methodology

Once you have written your research questions or hypotheses, you can then use these to plan your **methodology**. You will have to think carefully about the data you will need to address each research question or hypothesis, and then how you can collect that data. It might be useful to create a table during this planning process to show how your methodology is related to your overall research question or aim. Examples for how you might do this for two different projects are given in Tables 12.1 and 12.2 or you could devise your own method.

 Key terms

hypothesis: a specific, focused, directional statement of what you expect to find

null hypothesis: a statement that there is no relationship between the two variables being considered, or no significant difference between two groups being compared

methodology: the general research strategy that outlines the way your field investigation will be undertaken; it includes an outline of what data you will need and how you will collect it

Overall aim: To explore the impact of the King Power Football Stadium in Leicester on the local area	
Research questions	**Examples of data collection methods**
1 What is the effect of the football club on the local economy?	Interview owners of local stores and garages, asking about impact of match days on trade. Footfall survey outside local stores and garages on match and non-match days. Obtain employment figures for local people at the club.
2 To what extent does the football stadium impact the local environment?	Visual impact survey of the ground from a variety of distances and angles. Impact of floodlights survey in transect away from stadium for an evening match to assess light pollution. Traffic flow surveys before, during and after the match. Decibel recorder before, during and after the match at selected distances from the ground.
3 What are the social impacts of the football club on the local area?	Interview member of the club's administration, the secretary of the supporters' club and the local police unit to assess policing issues. Questionnaires to local households. Vandalism and graffiti surveys around the stadium and on main routes used by supporters (e.g. between the train station and the stadium). Interview community development officer at the club to record the club's involvement with local schemes. Housing condition and Environmental Quality Assessment (EQA) surveys in the local area. House price surveys for area around the stadium and other local areas. Crime data for the local area (e.g. from police.uk).

Table 12.1 Examples of research questions and methods of data collection for an investigation exploring the impact of a football stadium on the local area. What other secondary data could you use?

Overall research question: To what extent is Stoke-on-Trent an urban heat island?		
Hypotheses	**Null hypotheses**	**Examples of data collection methods**
1 Temperature decreases with distance from the city centre.	There is no relationship between temperature and distance from the city centre.	Weather data, including temperature, cloud cover and type, visibility, wind speed and direction, relative humidity, recorded along three contrasting transects from Central Business District (CBD) to rural fringe. Data collection repeated on three separate days, ideally with contrasting weather conditions (at least one bright sunny day and one cloudy, overcast day).
2 Temperature increases with height of buildings.	There is no relationship between temperature and height of buildings.	In addition to data collected for hypothesis 1, street exposure (sky view angle) collected at each site. This assumes that the taller the buildings, the greater the retention of heat at ground/street level.
3 Areas of parkland reduce the local temperatures.	There is no relationship between temperatures and areas of parkland.	In addition to data collected for hypothesis 1, land use and level of construction recorded at each site.

Table 12.2 Examples of hypotheses and methods of data collection for an urban heat island investigation. What other secondary data could you use?

Choosing your location

Choosing the location for your investigation goes hand in hand with identifying your aims and research questions. In some cases, your location might be dependent on your aim. For example, you might be interested in investigating the impact that the new Westfield shopping centre has had on the centre of Derby, so your location is predetermined. If you wanted to study factors affecting infiltration rates, however, your choice of locations may be much greater. If this is the case, then it is important to consider carefully *where* you choose to go. Collecting data from field locations close to where you live, for example, means you can go back if you need to collect more data. If you do choose to go further afield, such as combining your fieldwork with a family holiday, make sure you build in sufficient time to return to particular locations to collect additional data, for example in different weather conditions or at different times of the day. You will also need to think carefully about access to particular fieldwork sites. You may be particularly interested in undertaking an ice investigation, but are you able to travel to a glacial environment? For some protected environments, such as dunes, access may be restricted. You will need to seek permission from landowners or organisations who manage the area to enter them before you begin. Even if you choose to undertake fieldwork in a more accessible urban area, such as a town centre or theme park, you may need to seek permission from the local council or landowner before you begin.

At AS Level, your teachers are likely to make the decision about where you carry out your fieldwork, but you will still need to be able to justify this choice if you are asked. A good location needs to be safe and accessible. Having a fieldwork location you can easily return to is helpful because it allows you to go back and collect additional data, but this is not a requirement. You might be asked to draw an annotated sketch map showing the characteristics of your study site – make sure you can do this! Figure 12.3 is an example of a sketch map; notice that much of the detail that you would see in an OS map has been omitted so that the features that are most important for the investigation are clearer. The sketch map also has a title, a scale and a North arrow.

Making connections

The urban heat island effect is explored in section 9.4 Urban climate.

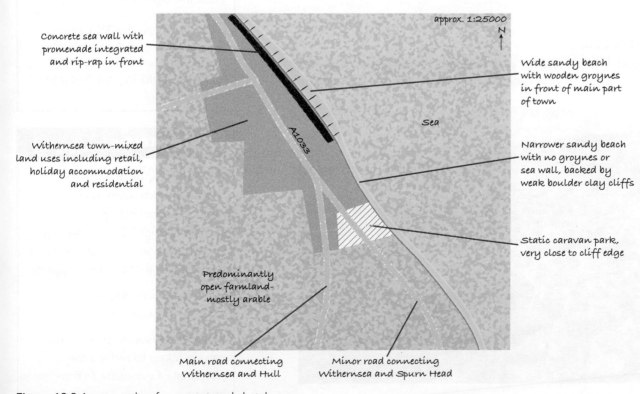

Figure 12.3 An example of an annotated sketch map.

For some fieldwork investigations, it may be helpful to use secondary data to identify specific fieldwork locations. For example, if you are investigating people's perceptions of flood risk on a flood plain in Shrewsbury, you could use data from the Environment Agency to locate sites at which to undertake questionnaires with local residents. Alternatively, if you want to examine incidence of bicycle theft in central Cambridge, you could use crime statistics from the police.uk website to identify areas in which to undertake fieldwork surveys. There are a number of online **GIS** packages, such as ArcGIS Online, that you could use to combine datasets from different sources. Remember that you can use this information to explain and justify your choice of location in your final report.

Risk assessment

Any fieldwork activity involves an element of **risk**. You will need to be able to explain how you assessed and minimised the risks associated with your fieldwork. The risks you face will vary depending on the type of fieldwork you are doing, and where. For many physical geography investigations, you will be walking over rough terrain in the countryside and this brings risks such as spraining an ankle or encountering ticks which can carry Lyme disease. Taking care with your footing, wearing sturdy footwear such as walking boots and wearing long trousers can all help to minimise these risks (these are **control measures**).

ACTIVITY 12.1

1   Figure 12.4 shows Malham Cove, a popular location for geography fieldwork. Make a list of the risks you might encounter if you were carrying out fieldwork here, and suggest how you could minimise each one.
2   Discuss how the risks here would compare to those in an urban fieldwork location.

Stage 2: Data collection

Primary and secondary data

When collecting geographical data for your fieldwork investigation, you will have to give careful thought to your data sources. These may be in the form

Figure 12.4 Malham Cove, North Yorkshire.

Look on **Cambridge Elevate** to find crime statistics for England, Wales and Northern Ireland on the police.uk website. (www.cambridge.org/ links/gase6130).

Look on **Cambridge Elevate** to access the following websites:
*   ArcGIS Online (www.cambridge.org/ links/gase6131)
*   ArcGIS Online Getting Started presentation (www.cambridge.org/ links/gase6132).

Research point

You can use online GIS packages to support your fieldwork investigation as they can be used very effectively throughout the planning, data collection, data presentation and data analysis stages of your investigation. Work through the Getting Started presentation to familiarise yourself with how to use ArcGIS Online. For one example, then look at ArcGIS Online and list how it might be useful in your fieldwork investigation.

Key terms

GIS (Geographical Information Systems): computer-based methods of collecting, storing, sorting, manipulating, analysing and presenting spatial information (information that can be mapped)

risk: a situation involving exposure to danger

control measures: actions that can be taken to reduce the potential of exposure to the hazard

of **quantitative data** (numerical data) or **qualitative data** (non-numerical, descriptive data). Neither is 'better' than the other, but they provide various classes of data that will be analysed and used in different ways.

The two main types of data that you will use in your investigation are **primary** and **secondary**; these can both be quantitative or qualitative data. Secondary data is additional data obtained from other sources and is particularly important for putting your investigation into a wider context. It can be derived from a number of sources, including:

- Previous researchers (e.g. combined datasets of students from previous years in your school/college)
- Web sources (e.g. census data, National Statistics or government bodies)
- Written evidence (e.g. newspaper articles, academic papers or blogs)
- Photographs and video (from numerous websites)

For your A Level investigation you will need to carefully consider, and discuss in your final report, issues of data sourcing (see the later section on Data-sourcing considerations).

There are many different methods that you can use to collect primary data, and the ones you choose will be dependent on what you are trying to find out. You are likely to need to carry out some measurements, for example you might want to conduct traffic or pedestrian counts. For investigations with a predominantly human geography focus, such as the earlier coastal example, which looks at management and potential conflicts, you will need to consider whether a **questionnaire** or **interview** survey best serves your data collection needs (see Table 12.3). Photographs and field sketches can also be valuable primary data.

Geographical data sources

Your choice of data source(s) should be related to its appropriateness for answering the geographical question or aim you have posed. Your choice will also be influenced by accessibility, time and cost to obtain the data, safety considerations and potential risk, and ethical and socio-political implications of attempting to capture certain types of data. What you collect, how you collect it and from what range of sources will influence the quality of analysis that you can conduct on your accumulated data.

Much secondary data is not obtained for specifically geographical purposes; it may be for health organisations, economic or political groups, or for journalistic purposes, among others. You can make use of it for a geographical enquiry if:

- it clarifies knowledge and understanding of place
- it facilitates comparison of places
- it helps identify geographical patterns, flows, distributions, networks – and possible anomalies
- it relates to geographical concepts, theories, models, processes, systems and issues
- you cast a geographical eye over the data to question its appropriateness, accuracy, reliability and avoidance of bias, using the skills you have learnt through study of the subject.

Please note that this list is not exhaustive.

Possible sources of geographical data include, but are not limited to:

- Measurements in the field (primary) and secondary data sources (results from previous studies)
- Surveys – both primary (see above) and secondary

Key terms

quantitative data: numerical data, often obtained through measurement, questionnaires or from public secondary databases

qualitative data: non-numerical, descriptive data which may be obtained from personal observation (noting behaviour, field-sketching, photographs, etc.), analysing printed/audio-visual material or investigating people's opinion, attitudes and beliefs

primary data: the data that you and your group collect 'in the field'

secondary data: data obtained from other sources, for example OS maps, census data, historical land use maps or newspaper articles

questionnaire: a predetermined and piloted set of structured questions, most of which require coded responses in order to tabulate and calculate frequency

interview: an in-depth discussion with someone, usually following a predetermined set of questions but following up responses with supplementary lines of enquiry

	Questionnaire survey (quantitative)	Interview survey (qualitative)
Description	Asking a valid sample of people a set of standardised questions and coding their responses into predetermined options. May be carried out face to face, via telephone, online or posted through letterboxes with a date for collection.	A series of questions that initiate a discussion with an individual or small group of people. Follow-up questions may be posed as a result of the responses. The initial area of investigation may be broadened as a result of the responses received.
Data processing	Coded responses lend themselves to tabulation on a spreadsheet and totalled, ranked, cross-referenced and graphed. Subsets can be analysed (e.g. attitudes to a new road by 'people over 55' compared with 'people between 20 and 35'). Some responses may indicate the need for more in-depth follow-up and provoke an interview with a few people.	Patterns among the responses may be identified as well as the breadth of diversity of response. Pursuing lines of enquiry may indicate the choices and reasons behind certain attitudes or decisions. Findings may be used as 'quotes' to support arguments or open up potential new enquiry routes that may lead to a questionnaire being conducted.
Strengths	An objective way to gather quantitative data from a sample of the population. Can accumulate the number responding relatively easily by using multiple surveyors. Can include qualitative responses to some questions with open-ended options.	The discussion may open up lines of information (and further enquiry) that had not previously been considered by the researcher. Topics may be investigated in further depth through supplementary questioning than questionnaires permit.
Weaknesses	Cannot ask supplemental questions. The quality of the questionnaire design determines the value and reliability of the responses. More difficult to obtain personal data as interviewees may refuse to answer. Data reliability affected by the accuracy of the sampling.	Heavy time-costs in conducting interviews. Respondents may be less willing to be subject to an interview than a more rapid and less intrusive questionnaire. Different interviewers may affect the type of response obtained. Coding responses is difficult and more subjective.

Table 12.3 Characteristics of questionnaire and interview surveys.

- Photographs – digital images taken yourself (primary) and secondary images
- Video and secondary film sequences – primary and secondary
- Annotated field sketches – primary
- Sketch maps, self-constructed maps (primary) and secondary maps (OS, commercial, digital)
- Journalism (print, digital or film) – secondary
- Texts (factual books, magazines, websites) – secondary
- Historical sources (as long as they are compared with contemporary data) – secondary
- Experimentation – primary and/or secondary
- Real-time geo-located information (websites, apps, data recorders) – primary and/or secondary

Data-sourcing considerations

When collecting data for your geography investigation you will need to consider your sources for their suitability, appropriateness and accuracy.

Images: the use of photographs and digital images can help justify the selection of your data collection sites. Images may also form data in their own right. They could, for example, be used to compare changes in a scene from one time period to another.

Some key considerations:

- Does the image represent the location faithfully, or is it 'selective' and gives a false impression?

- Have you avoided taking images of people's faces, vehicle registrations or house numbers, or have you anonymised them?
- Are you actively 'risk assessing' in trying to get the 'perfect shot'? Ensure your safety and that of others when obtaining an image.
- If using someone else's images, have you checked they are free to use or available under Creative Commons or some similar image-sharing agreement?

Different types of text: quoting or referring to secondary text sources can provide much useful information. However, be aware of the author's purpose, audience and objectivity.

- Is the text factual material, creative, discursive or deliberate rhetoric (arguing a particular case)? Some journalism may strive to be objective and balanced but some writers may be deliberately (or unconsciously) deploying a political bias and/or writing for an audience with a particular attitudinal preference.
- How current is the material? Have things moved on since the text was first published?
- Is there a sense that the author is providing appropriate evidence to support their points?
- Is supporting evidence balanced and being accurately presented and interpreted, or is there a sense it has been deliberately misused to support a particular argument or attitude?

Different types of data: most data transmission is now digital, although analogue data (some radio broadcasting) should still be considered a potential geographical information source.

- Numeric digital data: this may be, for example, census data obtained from various websites. Be aware that some datasets are in the form of percentages while others may be actual totals. You may need to convert percentages to a decimal equivalent for some calculations. When comparing numeric totals, ensure the area units you are comparing are of comparable size.
- Geospatial data: you need to consider the most appropriate map scale to display data that can be mapped. If you are using digital map layers to overlay data, consider the most suitable base map that provides useful information without being over-complicated.
- 'Big data': this is the growth in high-volume, rapidly changing data-rich environments. For example, the widespread use of digital devices with geo-located features (or the ability to encode locations of individual web users) provides huge amounts of data to organisations that manage digital information flows. Popular browser organisations may develop maps of a pandemic influenza outbreak by mapping the number and location of people carrying out searches on 'flu'. However, the accuracy of forecasts based on this information has not always been reliable; it may be the case that the sheer wealth of information creates obscurity in identifying clear patterns among the information being sought. If you access this data, you need to be careful that you 'see the wood for the trees' and isolate the key data that is useful to your study.
- Crowdsourced data: this is volunteered data generated from a range of willing participants. It enables an enquiry to collect a wider range of primary

information than you may obtain on your own. An example might be to ask a group of people in a city centre to take a digital image of the street where they are at an agreed time. A geo-located map could be created of footfall of pedestrians showing areas of high to low pedestrian flow.

- GIS: these are methods of collecting, storing, sorting, manipulating, analysing and presenting information that can be mapped – geographical information. Data may be collected as a result of remote data-logging (river levels in real-time hydrographs) or going into the field to collect first-hand data.

Data safeguards

In all data collection, whether primary or secondary, first-hand or remotely, there are four key safeguards that should be maintained:

1   Safety: the safety of those carrying out the data collection, those providing it and those who are in the same vicinity should be your prime consideration. In addition to compiling and sharing a risk assessment prior to your fieldwork, you should be actively assessing the situation throughout your data-collecting phase. Be prepared to extend and modify your risk assessment as and when necessary to ensure the highest standards of safety are constantly maintained.

2   **Ethical dimension** and socio-political impacts: you should demonstrate a sensitive awareness and concern for the attitudes and emotions of groups involved in data collection. This will guide a study throughout, from the initial hypothesis or investigation question to the implications of findings and conclusions. All major academic studies follow an ethical code to avoid (or minimise) stress, anxiety or harm for participants. You will want to ensure all are treated with courtesy, consideration and respect for their beliefs, their way of life and their circumstances. Consider drawing up a set of ethical guidelines when you do a risk assessment.

3   Legality: there is the potential for infringement of laws in certain elements of an investigation, from photocopying copyright material without permission, to trespassing when conducting surveys in the field. Ensure you know what you intend to do and to use, and check that it is all above board.

4   Academic rigour: be prepared to explain how you have tried to be as accurate as possible while carrying out your study. In a survey, the questions you ask and the way they are phrased can affect the responses you obtain; your choices in how you code answers in questionnaires can emphasise certain responses or under-represent others. Often data doesn't 'fit', is apparently conflicting and results may be 'messy'. You should make it clear at every stage of your investigation how you have tried to be accurate, and that your choices and decisions in the ways you collected data, processed, presented, analysed and concluded from it have all been completed with this in mind.

Accuracy and reliability

In order to ensure that your results are as **accurate** and **reliable** as possible, you will need to be organised. It is a good idea to make recording sheets with tables in which to record your results before you go out into the field – this will help you to make sure that you collect all the data you need, and if they are used properly, will ensure that you understand the results when you come to process them.

Key terms

ethical dimension: paying due regard to the ethics of your enquiry by taking steps in the upkeep of respect and in reducing stress, anxiety or avoidable discomfort for participants

accuracy: the degree to which a measurement determines the correct (or accurate) value

reliability: the extent to which a method of data collection will give the same results if repeated more than once

For an example of a weather observation recording sheet, download Worksheet 12.1 from **Cambridge Elevate**.

Human error can affect the reliability of fieldwork data; this might be through inconsistencies in the use of equipment, or through results being recorded inaccurately.

You will also encounter natural variability in your fieldwork; taking several readings at each site and calculating a mean helps to reduce the impact of this variability.

Pilot studies

Although it is not always possible to do, carrying out a **pilot study** is good practice in research. This means conducting a small-scale version of your fieldwork and it allows you to identify any potential issues with your data collection methods. It is particularly helpful to pilot questionnaires so that you can ensure that your respondents are interpreting questions in the way that you had intended, and any confusing questions can be eliminated.

Sampling

Sampling is the process by which you select individuals within the 'population' you are studying. It might be where you put a quadrat to look at vegetation in a sand dune system, which buildings you look at in a land-use study, which pebbles you measure on a beach or whom you ask to respond to your questionnaire. Sampling is used because it is not possible to measure the whole population.

The bigger your sample, the more likely it is that your results will be representative of the population you are studying. Certain statistical tests require a minimum sample size (often ten or more sites). However, the practicalities of time and access are likely to limit your sample size.

There are four main sampling strategies:

- Random: each member of the population has an equal chance of being selected. There are various ways to do this but random number tables are often used.
- Systematic: a rule or system is used to determine which members of the population are selected. For example, a quadrat is placed every 10 metres, or every 5th person is interviewed.
- Stratified: to ensure that the sample is representative of the whole population, subsets such as tourists/residents or different age groups are identified; if 60% of a population is aged over 65, 60% of the questionnaire respondents should be over 65. Within the subsets, random or systematic samples can be used.
- Pragmatic: modifies one of the above sampling strategies for practical purposes, for example, if you are placing quadrats every 10 metres to measure vegetation in a sand dune system, but a stream runs through the dune slack at 30 metres.

Using technology to support your fieldwork

You might also wish to use technology to support your fieldwork. This can increase the efficiency and speed of data collection, and it allows you to analyse your data instantly, minimising data processing back in school/college. Using GIS is one method and combined with a smartphone or tablet, can support data collection for a wide range of fieldwork investigations. For example, you could collect primary field data on pedestrian flow across a city using a data collection app on a smartphone. At the most basic level, you could then plot this data

ACTIVITY 12.2

1 Working in groups and using your own fieldwork plans (or one of the examples given earlier in this chapter), make a list of errors that could occur in your data collection. What could you do to minimise the risk of these errors occurring?

Key terms

pilot study: a small-scale version of a fieldwork investigation, carried out to identify any problems with the plans and modify the research design accordingly

sampling: the process of selecting a small number of units from a broader population you are studying to measure

ACTIVITY 12.3

1 What advantages and disadvantages might there be to each of the sampling strategies outlined?

onto an online image or map, such as Google Earth. At a more sophisticated level, you could use simple GIS software to create maps or perform analyses using the same data, such as creating isolines (see the section on Cartographic skills section in Chapter 13 Geographical skills and techniques) or undertaking hotspot analyses to support your investigation.

Stage 3: Data processing

Always present primary and secondary data so that it's easy for you to analyse the results and identify patterns, relationships and **anomalies**. In addition, make sure that it's easy for your readers to understand your data.

Tables of data can be useful, but it is often more beneficial to use graphs or maps. There are many different types of graph and map, and these are covered in detail in Chapter 13 Geographical skills and techniques. Make sure you use the appropriate type of graph or map for the data that you have collected.

Processing of your data may also involve statistical analysis. This could be through the use of descriptive statistics (e.g. mean, range) or **inferential statistics** (e.g. Spearman's rank). Again, these are covered in Chapter 13.

Stage 4: Data interpretation

The most important, and perhaps most challenging, part of your investigation is the interpretation; you need to make sense of your results and use them to draw conclusions in relation to your hypotheses and your overall research question or aim.

When describing a map or graph, you could:

- Look at the 'big picture' – what is the overall trend and why is it like this?
- Then focus in on the results – is there a period where change is slower or more rapid, or a dividing line (north/south, core/periphery) on a map?
- Finally look for anomalies – are there results that do not 'fit' or that were not what you expected to find? Remember that an anomaly is not (necessarily) a result that is 'wrong' – you need to try to find a geographical explanation for an unusual result.

Once you have discussed each graph, map or statistical test, write a clear, concise conclusion. One method of concluding your investigation is to take each research question or hypothesis in turn and write a simple statement about whether you can accept it or not, followed by a short paragraph answering your overarching question. Remember that there should not be anything in your conclusion that you have not mentioned before.

Stage 5: Evaluation

The final stage in the fieldwork process is to evaluate your investigation. You could examine what the limitations of your investigation were, suggest ways in which you might address these limitations and consider what the implications of your fieldwork are – are there other issues that need to be investigated further, or could your findings influence future planning or local authority policies?

The limitations that you identify need to be specific and geographical. For example, the demographics of your city centre questionnaire sample are likely to be quite different depending on whether you carry out the questionnaire on a week day or at the weekend.

Key terms

anomaly: something in the data that is unusual or does not fit in; it often deviates from what is standard, normal or expected

inferential statistic: an inferential statistical technique studies a sample taken from a larger population and 'infers' that the findings from it represent the rest of the population that was not sampled. Spearman's rank correlation and the Chi-square test are both inferential statistical techniques. A significance test estimates the likelihood that the sample 'reliably' represents the larger population

12.2 Writing your report

For A Level, your independent fieldwork investigation must be written up and submitted as a report for Component 3 of the assessment. Carefully plan the structure of your report before you begin writing it. For example, what section headings are you going to include within your report? How are you going to present your data analysis and findings? How will you evaluate your investigation? Taking the time to think about this at the beginning of your writing may save you the time and effort of having to redraft work later on.

It is also useful to read through the assessment criteria for the report and have these in mind when you are structuring and writing it. Your teacher will be able to give these to you, but Table 12.4 contains a summary.

Assessment area	Description	Marks available
Area 1: Introduction and preliminary research	This area assesses your ability to: • define the research questions on which your field investigation is built • research relevant literature sources and understand and write up the theoretical or comparative context for your study.	10
Area 2: Methods of field investigation	This area assesses your ability to: • plan and justify the practical approach you take to data collection in the field, including frequency/timing of observation, sampling and data collection approaches • show that you have a practical knowledge and understanding of field methodologies appropriate to your investigation • put into practice your chosen methodologies to collect good quality data/information which is relevant to the topic you are investigating.	15
Area 3: Methods of critical analysis	This area assesses your ability to: • show that you understand and can use a range of appropriate quantitative or qualitative techniques for analysing and presenting your primary and secondary data • show that you can question and critically examine field data in order to comment on its accuracy and/or how representative it is. You then need to use the experience of having interrogated your data to extend your geographical understanding • apply your existing knowledge of geographical theory and concepts to understand your field observations.	20
Area 4: Conclusions, evaluation and presentation	This area assesses your ability to: • write up your field results clearly and logically, using a range of presentation methods • evaluate and reflect on your fieldwork investigations, explaining how the results relate to the wider context of your topic • show an understanding of the ethical dimensions of field research.	15

Table 12.4 Summary of the assessment areas for your final report

Structuring your report

There are several ways you can structure your final report – as long as you include all the required elements it is up to you which way you choose. Table 12.5 shows two possible examples or you could devise your own. You can see that the key sections are the same within each – it is only the layout that varies between them.

Example 1	Example 2
Introduction	Introduction
Methodology	Methodology
Results and analysis	Presentation of results
Conclusions	Analysis and discussion
Evaluation	Conclusions and evaluation
Appendices	

Table 12.5 Two possible structures you might consider for your fieldwork report.

The key content for each section is summarised below.

Introduction

You should aim to begin by clearly introducing your individual investigation:

- On what geographical topic area is your investigation based? Is there a particular theory or model which you plan to test? You should aim to draw on (and reference) relevant literature sources and show that you understand the geography on which your investigation is based. Reference to literature should extend beyond your A Level textbooks and there are a number of resources you could use for this purpose, such as journal articles or websites.
- What is the locational context of your investigation? Provide an outline as to why you selected this location and how it is of use for exploring your particular topic. You might wish to include one or more maps (at a variety of scales) to support this section.
- What are the aims of your investigation? What research questions and/or hypotheses have you defined to consider or test throughout your report?

Methodology

Within the methodology you could usefully explain how you designed your research programme to support your overall investigation:

- What overall strategy did you employ to plan your data collection? How did you ensure that all the data you collected was relevant to the topic under investigation? Did you undertake a pilot study to test some of your methods, for example questionnaires, before your main data collection (if so, explain the impact it had on your final methodology)?
- What risk assessment did you undertake? What did you do to mitigate any risks you identified?
- Which methods of primary data collection did you use and when/how often did you use them? What sampling strategy did you use and why? How did you ensure that data collected in the field was reliable and accurate?
- What methods of secondary data collection did you use? How did you ensure this data was from a reliable source?
- What were your methods of data analysis? For example, you should make reference to any statistical tests that you have undertaken and state to which significance level the test has been completed to.
- What were the ethical dimensions of your field research?

Results and analysis

It is important to think carefully about how to structure this section. For example, if you have a number of research questions, structure the analysis of your results around these so that all the data relating to each question is considered together. Alternatively, you could analyse data from each method separately and then consider them together within a separate 'discussion' section before your final conclusions. You could, for example, consider:

- Have you used a range of presentation methods to display your data, for example different graphs (such as line, bar or triangular graphs), annotated field sketches or photographs, and maps (including those created electronically, e.g. within a GIS)?
- Have you clearly, logically and coherently described your data, referring in the text to any figures you have included?
- Have you identified any anomalies or uncontrolled variables within your data, and given an explanation of any reasons you can identify for these?

Conclusions

Towards the end of your report, it is important to summarise the main findings of your investigation. This allows you to draw all of the strands of your investigation together, for example primary and secondary data, literature sources and theoretical ideas. You should refer back to your original research questions or hypotheses, drawing on evidence from both your data and from your reading of the literature to address them. You could, for example, consider:

- If you have a series of research questions, how do your results answer these? Alternatively, if you have designed your investigation around a series of hypotheses, can you accept these? What is the specific evidence to support this (can you quote specific figures or refer to tables and graphs)?
- For investigations into *spatial distributions*, refer to patterns, trends and relationships (with the support of maps to illustrate your points).
- For investigations into a *temporal change*, there should be some reference to conditions *before* and *after* and conclusions drawn as to how those changes occurred and why.
- Does your data support or contradict ideas from other sources (such as models or theories within the literature)? Why/Why not?
- Reflect on how your findings provide opportunities for further research in this field of study. For example, if you investigated the effectiveness of coastal defences at Overstrand, what do you think would be useful to study in future research in this field? Could you suggest a similar investigation at a different location to compare and contrast findings, or might you suggest the carrying out of similar research at Overstrand over a longer timescale to explore sea defence effectiveness over a period of a year or more?

Evaluation

It is important to evaluate and reflect on the process of undertaking your investigation. You should aim to consider not only your methods (of data collection and analysis), but also the limitations of your conclusions; a good evaluative comment might show how limitations in the method affect the validity of the conclusions. You should aim to include:

- A specific evaluation of the individual methods of data collection and analysis you used for your investigation (although this could also be included within your methodology section). What were the difficulties or issues with your specific methodology? Were your methods valid (did they measure what they were meant to measure)? Were they reliable (or consistent)? How accurate was your data? To what extent do you think this data is representative? For example, if you collected river transect data, how representative is that data of that river at a different time of day? That river at a different time of year? That river at a different location along the river long profile? Or even other rivers in that area/the UK/the world?

- An overall evaluation of the limitations of your investigation. What problems did you encounter throughout the process? What might you do differently were you to do it again, and why? Include information about what did not go well during the process; often reflecting on the problems you have had throughout your fieldwork investigation is a good way of showing what you have learnt.

Appendices

An **appendix** is a section at the back of your report in which you can include additional information or data from your investigation. When attaching appendices, you should include examples of raw data, such as data collection sheets and questionnaires, rather than every questionnaire used. You need to ensure that you refer to all appendices within the main body of your report.

Presenting your report

Your report should be 3000–4000 words in length; this includes all the text, text boxes and supplementary material such as photographs, graphs and other figures. However, it does not include appendices. You must stick to this word limit; if you exceed it then it is likely that your report lacks precision and focus and you will be penalised under assessment area 4 (Conclusions, evaluation and presentation). Conversely, if your report is significantly below the suggested word count, it is likely that it does not sufficiently cover the assessment objectives.

Your report should be well presented throughout, using subheadings to structure it and including a range of carefully named and numbered figures and tables (Figure 1, Figure 2, Figure 3, and so on). Include a contents page at the beginning, as well as a list of figures and tables. You should remember that you are writing a formal report which means that you should avoid informal language, abbreviations and colloquialisms. You should write in the past tense (explaining what you did). Using the first person can help you to be more reflective throughout your report (e.g. 'I used systematic sampling, taking measurements of pebble size every 1 m along my beach transect, to ensure even coverage of the beach profile').

Key term

appendix: a section of additional material at the end of a report

Tip

- For question 1 it is important to refer to the specific location where you undertook your fieldwork to answer this question *and* then explain how and why you chose to go there. Think about this in practical terms (such as its accessibility), as well as how it was appropriate for your geographical enquiry.

- Question 2 is asking you to explain why *and* how you obtained secondary data so you should consider both.

- Remember the command phrase 'to what extent' requires you to consider both sides of an argument. For question 3, you should consider how your conclusions match the geographical theory, how they do not *and why*.

Assess to progress

1. With reference to your own investigation, explain how and why you selected your fieldwork location. `6 MARKS [AS LEVEL]`

2. Outline why you used and how you obtained secondary data in your fieldwork enquiry. `6 MARKS [AS LEVEL]`

3. To what extent did your fieldwork conclusions match the geographical theory or idea on which your investigation was based? `9 MARKS [AS LEVEL]`

Geographical skills and techniques

By the end of this chapter you should know:
- how best to present a variety of data
- how to carry out a number of statistical analysis techniques.

Figure 13.1 By the end of the AS and A Level courses, you need to be confident at using a range of maps.

Before you start…

You should know:

- what qualitative and quantitative data are
- different cartographic, graphical and statistical skills
- that some techniques are more appropriate than others for presenting/analysing data.

In your fieldwork investigation you will need to present the results of your data collection as accurately as you can. This means selecting the most appropriate data presentation technique that describes the information clearly and from which deductions and inferences can be made, leading to valid conclusions being reached.

You may choose to show data results in tables, but a visual representation of your findings often carries additional meaning. You will want to consider various forms of graphs, charts and maps (cartography), and make use of statistical techniques to objectively describe aspects of your results as well as verify the validity of your data before basing conclusions upon it. This chapter considers the options you have available when presenting and analysing the results of your investigations, and develops many skills which you may find helpful.

13.1 Data presentation and extraction skills

Making sense of visually presented data is a skill that is worthy of practice. The selection of a particular type of graph or chart should be justifiable on the basis of it being the most appropriate for the data you have collected and intend to present. In cases where there is a spatial component to your data, you will wish to consider an appropriate cartographic method of presentation.

It is important to understand the strengths and limitations of various methods of presentation. You also need to be able to extract information and pose further questions about the data, and develop your critical reasoning in more depth. This section considers how data is presented as graphical information and cartographic information.

Graphical data techniques

Raw data does not become useful information until it has been processed, analysed and interpreted. This is true of both data you have accumulated yourself and secondary material you are studying to extract the key information. Interpreting the principal messages of a graph or chart requires you to ask some key questions of the specific graphical tool selected. When displaying data in your own fieldwork investigation, your choice of presentation technique should be based on that which conveys accurately and clearly the messages you have identified.

Table 13.1 shows a range of graphical techniques for representing geographical data. All the charts are exemplars.

Type of graph	Useful for...	Watch out!
Line graph This can be: • simple (one set of data) • comparative (two sets of data) • compound (multiple sets of data); see Figure 13.2. 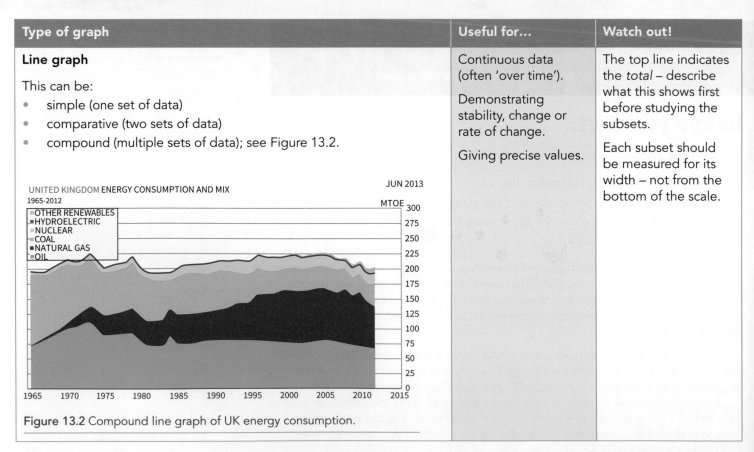 **Figure 13.2** Compound line graph of UK energy consumption.	Continuous data (often 'over time'). Demonstrating stability, change or rate of change. Giving precise values.	The top line indicates the *total* – describe what this shows first before studying the subsets. Each subset should be measured for its width – not from the bottom of the scale.

Table 13.1 Graphical techniques for representing geographical data.

Type of graph	Useful for...	Watch out!
Bar graph This can be: • simple (one set of data) • comparative (two sets of data) • compound (multiple sets of data) • divergent (bipolar divergence from a central measure); see Figure 13.3. 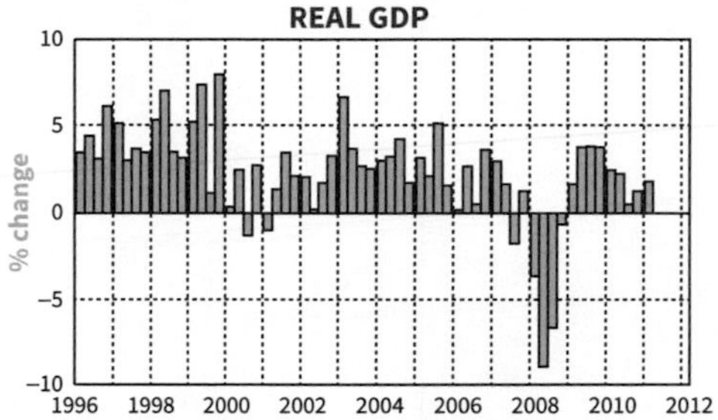 Figure 13.3 A divergent bar graph showing percentage change in real GDP.	Discrete data (in categories). Demonstrating stability, change or rate of change. Giving precise values.	Describe the overall trend before identifying subsets or anomalies. Consider the intensity/size as well as the frequency of divergence.
Pie charts These can be: • comparative proportions/share • proportional divided circles (size indicates quantity); see Figure 13.4. 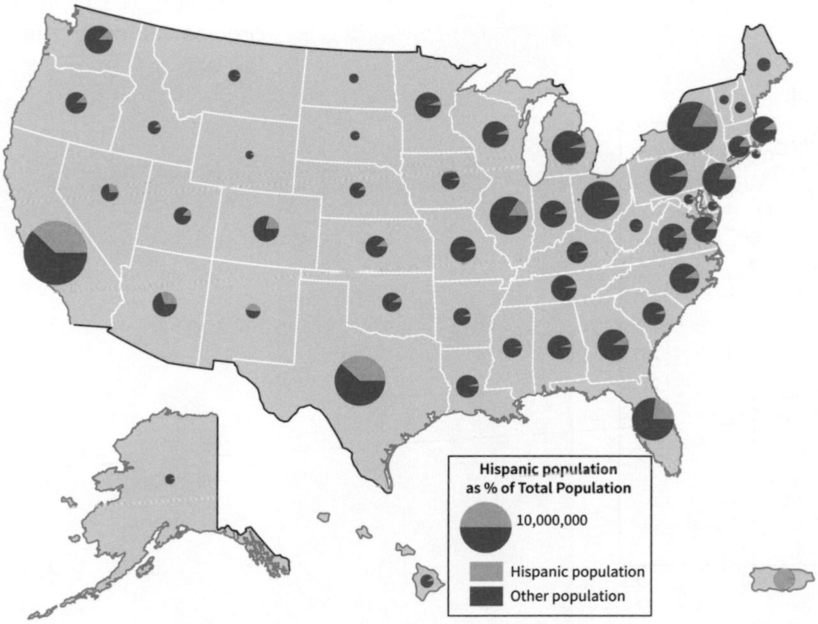 Figure 13.4 A proportional divided circles map of Hispanic population as a percentage of total population.	Indicating percentage share of subsets. Demonstrating significant subsets. Showing geographical distribution if used with base map.	May not provide actual values – just a percentage. Unwieldy with multiple subsets.

Table 13.1 (*continued*)

561

Type of graph	Useful for...	Watch out!
Triangular graph 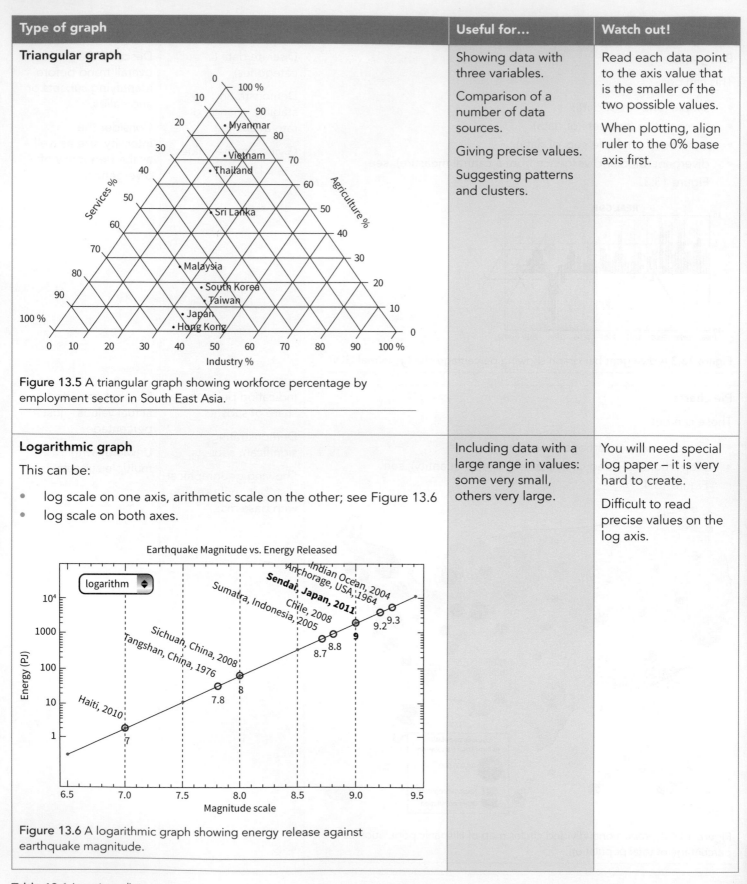 **Figure 13.5** A triangular graph showing workforce percentage by employment sector in South East Asia.	Showing data with three variables. Comparison of a number of data sources. Giving precise values. Suggesting patterns and clusters.	Read each data point to the axis value that is the smaller of the two possible values. When plotting, align ruler to the 0% base axis first.
Logarithmic graph This can be: • log scale on one axis, arithmetic scale on the other; see Figure 13.6 • log scale on both axes. **Figure 13.6** A logarithmic graph showing energy release against earthquake magnitude.	Including data with a large range in values: some very small, others very large.	You will need special log paper – it is very hard to create. Difficult to read precise values on the log axis.

Table 13.1 (*continued*)

ACTIVITY 13.1

1 Beach material has been noted from five sample quadrats (A–E) along a beach transect from shore to upper beach, and the results plotted on a triangular graph (Figure 13.7)

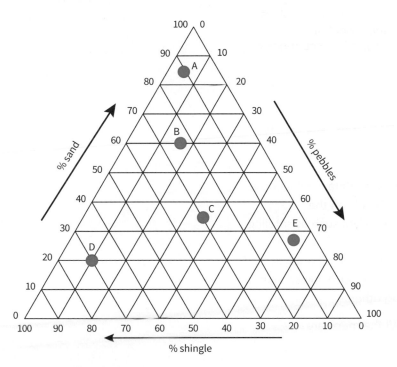

Figure 13.7 Survey results of beach material along a beach transect.

a Complete Table 13.2 using information from Figure 13.7.

Quadrat	% sand	% shingle	% pebbles
A	85	11	
B			16
C			
D			
E			

Table 13.2 The percentage of different beach material in each quadrat.

b Describe what the data indicates about the distribution of beach material along the beach transect.

c Suggest a possible explanation that is consistent with the data.

For another activity using a triangular graph, download Worksheet 13.1 from **Cambridge Elevate**.

Cartographic skills

If geography's initial enquiry is always 'what – and where?', then the map is the obvious tool of choice to represent this visually. Cartography – the use of maps – requires particular skills to both construct and extract meaningful information, and interpret accurately.

You may be required to interpret and create or modify a range of geographical mapping formats. As with graphs, a map should convey the essential information as clearly as possible while also describing the spatial occurrence of geographical phenomena.

Be aware of the appropriate skills for:

- annotating maps
- using base maps, overlays (GIS digital and physical), OS maps at a variety of scales, atlas maps
- using weather maps and synoptic charts
- using data collected from remote sensors and automated data recording devices such as those that record live river levels on the Environment Agency website, as well as other mapped data such as satellite and vertical air images
- using electronic databases such as census details presented at different scales: national, local authority, middle layer super output area (MSOA), lower layer super output area (LSOA) and individual ward, among others.

Table 13.3 shows a range of cartographic techniques. All the maps are exemplars.

Type of map	Useful for...	Watch out!
Atlas maps These can: - offer a wide range of information on specific areas - offer a global perspective; see Figure 13.8 - make use of latitude and longitude co-ordinates. 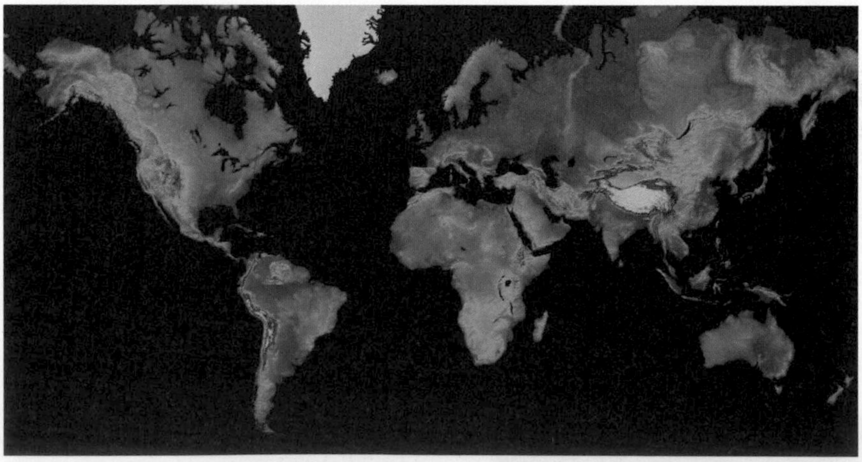 **Figure 13.8** An atlas world physical map.	Giving a global perspective from small- to large-scale. Permitting visual correlations between, for example, climate and population distribution.	No flat map can fully accurately represent a sphere. There are different map projections; be aware of the one being used. Map projection can seriously distort apparent surface area.

Table 13.3 Different types of cartographic representation.

Type of map	Useful for...	Watch out!
Weather maps and synoptic charts These can: • display pressure isolines (isobars of air pressure) • indicate areas of low and high pressure and weather fronts; see Figure 13.9 • indicate weather features such as wind strength and direction and infer likely temperature shifts. 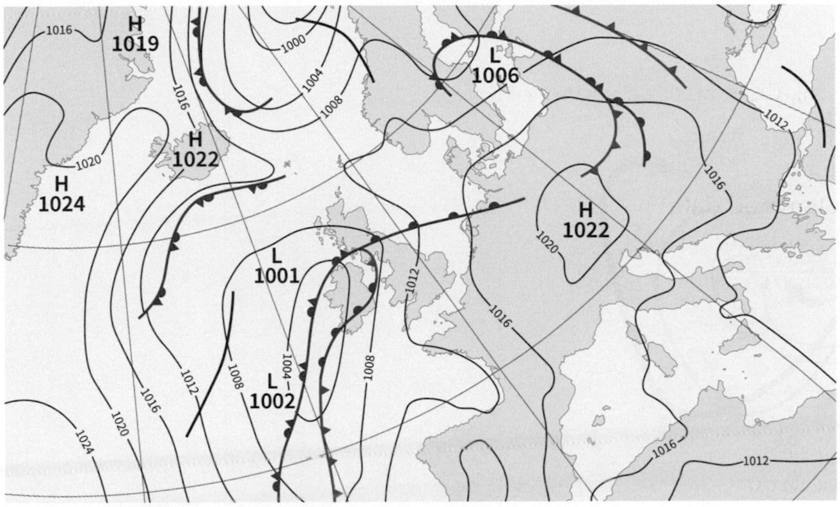 **Figure 13.9** Surface pressure chart showing pressure and weather fronts for Europe and the North East Atlantic.	Indicating spatial variations in weather conditions. Using air pressure conditions to infer wind direction, cloud cover and precipitation conditions.	A synoptic chart may be confused with a weather forecast chart. The synoptic chart denotes measures of temperature, humidity, air pressure and wind direction from which the likely weather conditions have to be inferred. A synoptic chart shows conditions at one level of the atmosphere. But the atmosphere is multi-layered.
Map with located proportional symbols This can: • display quantitative distribution • quantify via reference to a scale • have symbols, bars or circles that represent the actual feature; see Figure 13.10. 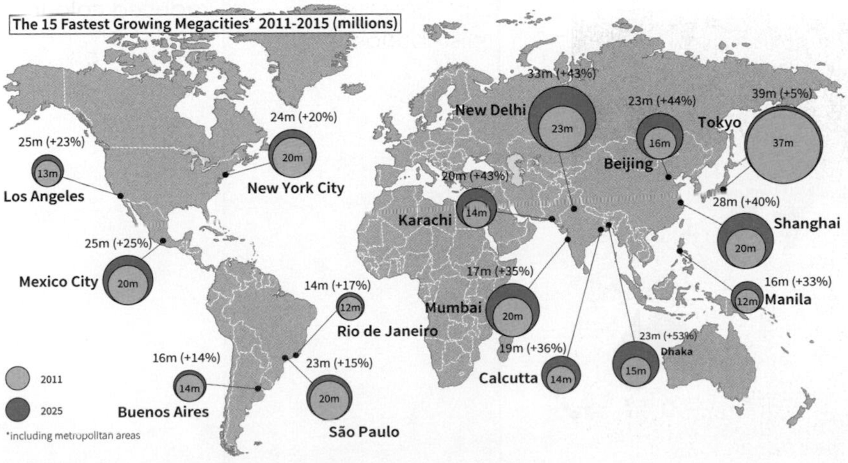 **Figure 13.10** The 15 fastest growing megacities.	Showing distribution and quantity. Allowing patterns of distribution to be described.	It is not easy to identify precise values of size. Symbols may overlap and become difficult to identify individually. Symbols may obscure other base-map information.

Table 13.3 (*continued*)

Type of map	Useful for...	Watch out!
Maps showing movement The lines used on these maps can: • indicate both size and direction of a movement or flow; see Figure 13.11 • often show quantity via width of flow arrow or density of lines • take the form of flow lines, desire lines and trip lines. 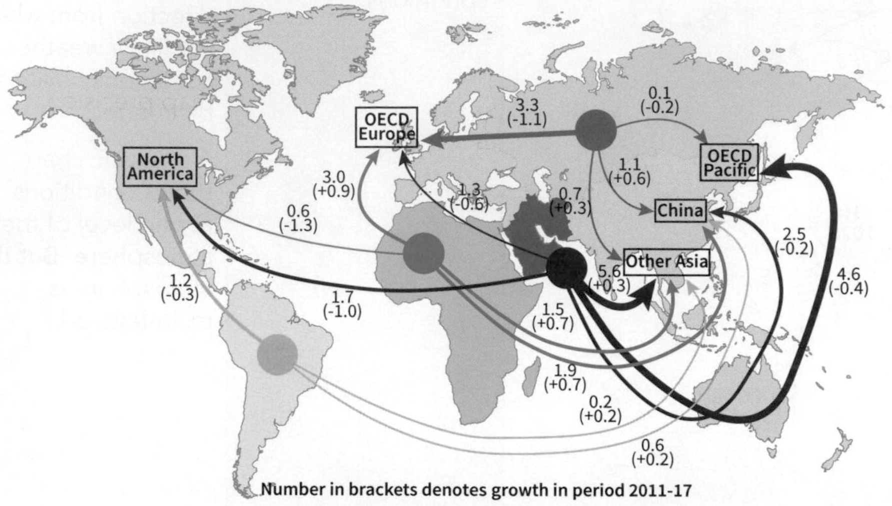 **Number in brackets denotes growth in period 2011-17** Figure 13.11 Crude exports in 2015 and growth in 2009–15 for key trade routes.	Indicating origin and destination. Displaying major and minor flows or moves.	Too many lines may be confusing to follow. Flows can change quite rapidly; a map suggests they are fixed.
Spatial maps: Choropleth maps These maps can: • indicate variation or similarity by colour/shading use • represent intensity by colour/shading choice • suggest patterns and anomalies visually; see Figure 13.12. 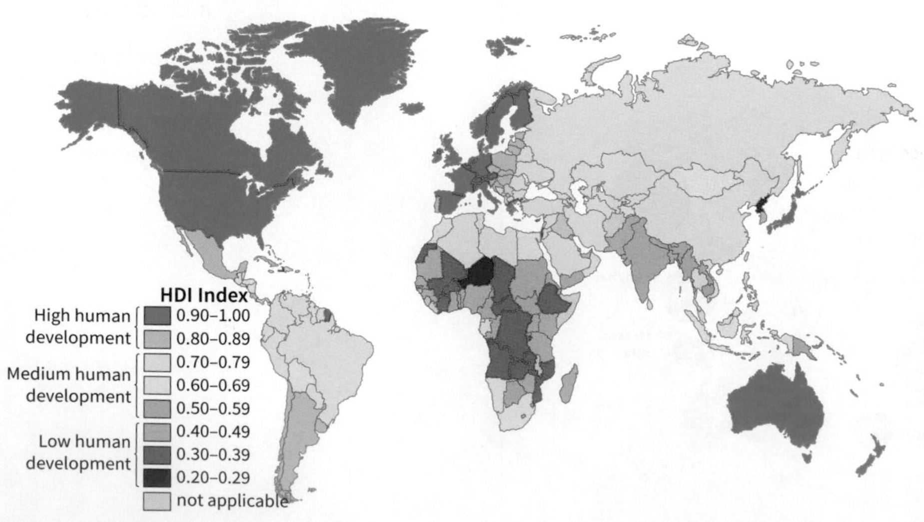 Figure 13.12 Human Development Index.	Showing discrete data ranges. Use of colour or shading to represent scale in a visually accessible way.	Limited to a few (7–8) categories before confusion arises. Can mask variations within regions or countries. Some people have reduced colour vision.

Table 13.3 (continued)

Type of map	Useful for...	Watch out!
Spatial maps: Isoline maps These maps can: • indicate a similar value along each specific line; see Figure 13.13 • show fine gradation • represent a wide range of data values. 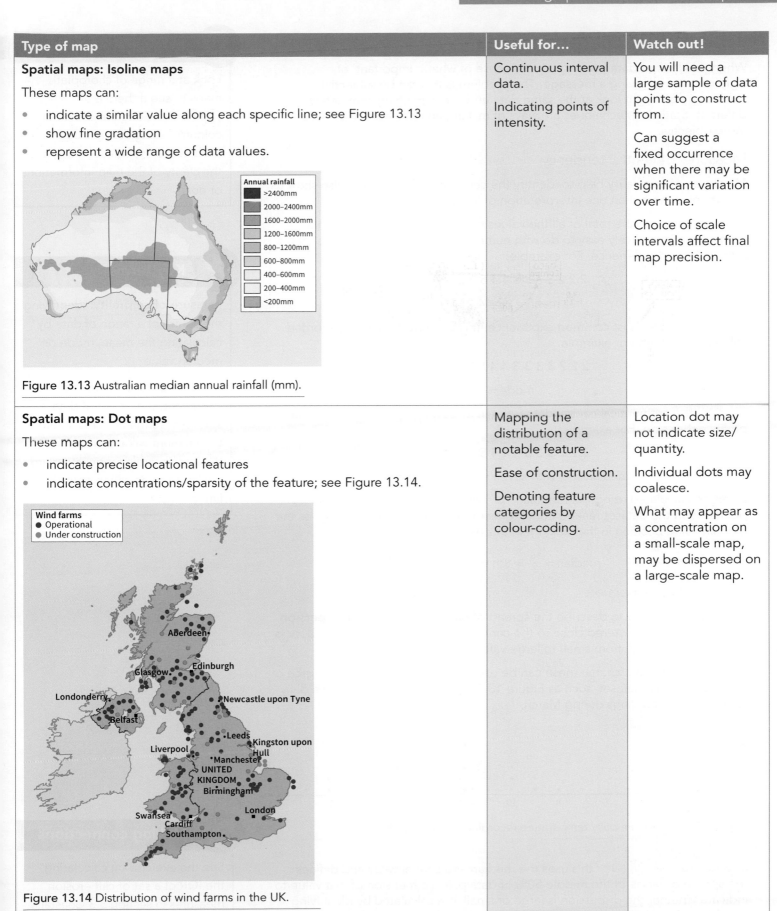 **Figure 13.13** Australian median annual rainfall (mm).	Continuous interval data. Indicating points of intensity.	You will need a large sample of data points to construct from. Can suggest a fixed occurrence when there may be significant variation over time. Choice of scale intervals affect final map precision.
Spatial maps: Dot maps These maps can: • indicate precise locational features • indicate concentrations/sparsity of the feature; see Figure 13.14. **Figure 13.14** Distribution of wind farms in the UK.	Mapping the distribution of a notable feature. Ease of construction. Denoting feature categories by colour-coding.	Location dot may not indicate size/quantity. Individual dots may coalesce. What may appear as a concentration on a small-scale map, may be dispersed on a large-scale map.

Table 13.3 (continued)

13.2 Statistical techniques

When you look at data you might get a sense of what is important, of significance and giving a message. The problem is this can be subjective; someone else might look at the same data and see something completely different. Statistical techniques are ways of making analysis less subjective and more objective.

Measures of central tendency

Measures of centrality help to identify the centre of a data set, but also show us that there is more than one interpretation of 'centre'.

Mean (arithmetic): the total of all the values divided by the number of data points. This is relatively easy to do with numerical data but can misrepresent the most common experience. For example:

$$2\ 2\ 2\ 3\ 3\ 3\ 3\ 4\ 4\ 5\ 5\ 5\ 6\ 7\ 7$$

$$\text{mean} = \frac{61}{15} = 4.067$$

Mode: this is the most common experience. It is the most frequently recorded value in a dataset. For example:

$$2\ 2\ 2\ 3\ 3\ 3\ 3\ 4\ 4\ 5\ 5\ 5\ 6\ 7\ 7$$

$$\text{mode} = 3$$

Median: the arithmetical central data point in a set with equal numbers of data points either side. For example:

$$2\ 2\ 2\ 3\ 3\ 3\ 3\ 4\ 4\ 5\ 5\ 5\ 6\ 7\ 7$$

median = 4, with seven values either side.

It can be calculated using the formula: $\frac{(n+1)}{2}$ where n is the number of data points. With the dataset ranked from highest to lowest, the calculation gives the median value position in the ranking. In this example:

$$\text{median} = \frac{16}{2} = \text{8th rank position}$$

Measures of dispersion

Often it is necessary to describe the spread of data, the **measure of dispersion**. Are all the values clustered close to the central measure we have identified, or is there much variation from small to large values in our dataset?

Dispersion diagrams/charts: these can be used to visually describe the degree of variation within a dataset, such as Figure 13.15 which charts the maximum daily temperature recordings during March.

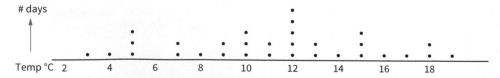

Figure 13.15 Maximum daily temperature recordings during March.

Inter-quartile range (IQR): this uses the median as a central value and defines the spread or range of the middle 50% of data points either side of that value to indicate whether the dispersion is large or small. It is calculated by identifying the data values that correspond to the quarter and three-quarters positions in the dataset.

Investigate

Look at a range of choropleth maps to see if there is an apparent logic to the choice of colour/shading that has been used. Does the selection assist in the clarity of the map information, or not?

Key terms

measure of centrality: identifying the centre of a range of data by calculating the mean, mode or median value

measure of dispersion: calculating the extent of data spread or range from maximum to minimum value by means of the inter-quartile range, standard deviation or deviation from the line of best fit

Making connections

See the exercise on calculating the IQR of a set of cliff erosion measures in section 3.3 Coastal geomorphology: Processes.

- The upper quartile (UQ) is the value that distinguishes the highest 25% of values and is identified using the formula:

$$UQ = \frac{(n+1)}{4}$$

This gives the ranking of the data point marking the highest quarter of values.

- The lower quartile (LQ) is the value that distinguishes the lowest 25% of values and is identified using the formula:

$$LQ = \frac{3(n+1)}{4}$$

Again, counting down from the largest value gives us the data point at the 75% position in the ranked dataset.

The IQR is the difference between the UQ and the LQ (IQR = UQ − LQ). On its own it gives a certain indication of spread, but is more useful when compared with the IQR of a contrasting dataset.

Look at this worked example:

Consider two rivers in which the depth of the water is measured. Sometimes the river levels are low (after dry summers), sometimes the river levels are high (after floods). They will both vary throughout the year. The ranked monthly results for 15 months are:

- River Ay (river depth in m) 3 3 4 4 4 5 5 5 6 6 6 6 7 7 7
- River Bee (river depth in m) 1 1 2 3 3 4 5 5 5 6 7 8 8 8 9 9

Both rivers have the same median level but River Bee is much lower in the dry times and much higher in the wet times compared to River Ay.

To compare the **degree of variation**, calculate the IQR, which shows the extent of spread in the datasets either side of the median:

- River Ay (river depth in m) 3 3 4 4 4 5 5 5 6 6 6 6 7 7 7
- River Bee (river depth in m) 1 1 2 3 3 4 5 5 5 6 7 8 8 8 9 9

The IQR of River Ay is UQ − LQ = 6 − 4 = 2

The IQR of River Bee is UQ − LQ = 8 − 3 = 5

The larger IQR for River Bee provides a statistical description of how much more variation it has in its river level than River Ay.

Standard deviation: this measure makes use of the mean as a central point from which to calculate the average divergence of each data value from that central value. It is used when you can expect a **normal distribution** of data values either side of the mean.

$$\text{Standard deviation} = \sqrt{\frac{\sum(x-\bar{x})^2}{n}}$$

where:

x = each score

$\bar{x}$ = the mean

n = the number of values

$\sum$ = summate the values

Tip

You may come across an IQR formula that uses numerical quartiles of:

Q0: the minimum value

Q1: 25% of the values are below

Q2: 50% of the values are below

Q3: 75% of the values are below

Q4: the highest value

In this case the Upper Quartile is represented by Q3 and the Lower Quartile by Q1. The IQR is calculated as Q3-Q1. As the values are counted from lowest to highest using this notation, the formula is reversed:

$$Q1 = \frac{(n+1)}{4}$$

$$Q3 = \frac{3(n+1)}{4}$$

Key term

normal distribution: when there is symmetry in the distribution of quantitative data either side of the mean, but clustering around it

Tip

When the data represents the whole population under study, n alone is used in the lower part of the equation. When the data represents a sample of a whole population for which the SD is required, then $n-1$ is used. This is known as Bessel's correction.

Look at this worked example:

Imagine you are conducting a beach study of deposited material and want to give a statistical description to the range of pebble sizes on a particular stretch of beach. You have measured the long axis of 15 pebbles and these are recorded in Table 13.4.

Size of pebble (mm) x	$\bar{x}$	$x - \bar{x}$	$(x - \bar{x})^2$
14	29.87	−15.87	251.86
18	29.87	−11.87	140.90
26	29.87	−3.87	14.98
11	29.87	−18.87	356.08
38	29.87	8.13	66.10
22	29.87	−7.87	61.94
19	29.87	−10.87	118.16
47	29.87	17.13	293.44
44	29.87	14.13	199.66
37	29.87	7.13	50.84
19	29.87	−10.87	118.16
26	29.87	−3.87	14.98
39	29.87	9.13	83.36
27	29.87	−2.87	8.24
61	29.87	31.13	969.08
		Σ	2747.78

Table 13.4 Long axis length for 15 beach pebbles.

$$\text{Standard deviation} = \sqrt{\frac{2747.78}{15}} = 13.53$$

In this example, the sampled pebbles deviate from the mean pebble size by an average of 13.53 mm. Given that the data range is from 11 to 61 mm, this is quite a substantial standard deviation. It is likely to have greater meaning if compared with the range of pebble sizes on another stretch of beach.

Download Worksheet 13.2 from **Cambridge Elevate**, for an activity on calculating the standard deviation for precipitation amounts over a 12-month period, for two different regions.

Maths for geographers

Look at the standard deviation worked example again. Imagine that the sample size was only 14 and the last pebble (61 mm) had *not* been collected.

a   Recalculate the standard deviation for the sample of 14 pebbles.

b   How different is the resultant standard deviation? What does this suggest about the importance of your sample size?

Thinking like a geographer

Consider why different statistical techniques are used. would the 61 mm pebble not have affected an IQR calculation to the same extent? Why might the IQR sometimes be used instead of the standard deviation?

Scatter graphs: these go beyond simple frequency descriptions and permit the possibility of noticing a relationship between two discrete datasets (Figure 13.16). Plotting data that contains two variables holds the potential to:

* construct a line of best fit (trend line) that can establish the mean vector of the two variables
* assess the degree of spread (deviation) of the data from the mean
* identify any anomalies (outliers) that deviate more than may be expected – always interesting to investigate
* propose whether the data pattern suggests a correlation may be evident.

A line of best fit is drawn so that it lies on as many data points as possible, with 50% of any variance above the line and 50% below. If most of the data points lie close to the trend line it can indicate a correlation.

There may be data points that lie far from the trend line. You will have to decide if these are exceptions that suggest something else is happening to cause them (anomalies), or whether there are sufficient of them to make a correlation doubtful and the pattern is tending towards random.

Scatter graphs may indicate particular characteristics of the correlation (Figure 13.17):

* Strong v weak correlations: depending on how much the data points deviate from the trend line.
* Positive v negative correlations: depending on the direction (vector) of the trend line.
* Linear v non-linear correlations: a straight trend line (consistent ratio) or curving (varying ratio).

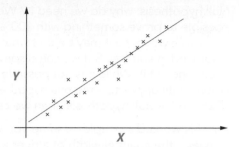

Figure 13.16 A scatter graph showing the line of best fit.

Making connections

Consider the evidence in section 1.3 The carbon cycle, whether there is a strong, weak, or no correlation between rising carbon emissions and global temperature changes.

Tip

Make sure you know the difference between 'correlation' and 'causation'. While there may be a clear relationship between two variables, there may be a third unknown variable that is influencing them both to give a false impression of direct causation.

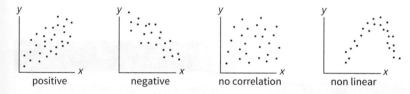

Figure 13.17 Types of correlation.

Inferential relational techniques: Spearman's rank correlation test

A relational statistical technique is one that provides an objective description of the strength (or otherwise) of an association between two variables. A significance test then considers the likelihood of any apparent relationship being due to chance. A technique often used in geography is the Spearman's rank correlation test:

* This test uses pairs of numeric data of two variables.
* The data should be capable of being ranked.
* It is more reliable with between 10 and 30 data pairs.
* The result will be between +1.0 (a 'perfect' positive correlation) and −1.0 (a perfect negative correlation); 0 represents a completely random relationship between the datasets.
* A **significance test** is used to determine the extent to which the result may be due to chance.

Procedure

Establish your hypothesis (H_1) before your initial examination of the data. Convert this into a null hypothesis (H_0). For more information on hypotheses, see Chapter 12 Fieldwork.

Key term

significance test: a statistical check to establish the likelihood of a result being due to random associations; it establishes whether the null hypothesis may be rejected or not

Null hypothesis: why do we need it? Well, in the investigative process it's not possible to prove something with 100% certainty – we never get to sample the whole world, so it may be that what we think we've proved in one place is disproved in another. But we can disprove assumptions by finding a contradictory occurrence of it. While it is not possible to *prove* a hypothesis fully, we can fully *disprove* its opposite – the null hypothesis. If our statistical tests allow us to disprove the null hypothesis, then we can accept that our hypothesis has validity.

For this worked example, assume you wish to know if there is a correlation between the channel width of a river and its surface velocity, with your hypothesis assuming there is. So the null hypothesis is: there is no relationship between channel width and river velocity.

- Enter the data for 'channel width' and 'surface velocity' for the 12 sites where you took measurements (Table 13.5).
- Rank the data in each column with the largest value being 1.
- Any equal values will take the rank average of their combined positions, and the subsequent rank value will acknowledge those rank positions as having been used.
- Subtract the Rank 2 number from the Rank 1 number for each pair to give value *d*.
- Square each *d* value to provide the d^2 entry (that is, multiply it by itself; this gets rid of minus numbers).
- Add up all the d^2 values in the column to give you $\sum d^2$.
- Enter the values in the Spearman's rank equation:

$$R_s = 1 - \frac{6(\sum d^2)}{n^3 - n}$$

Where:

      n = number of data pairs

      $\sum$ = summate the values

Tip

In the Spearman's rank equation, it is 1 minus the equation value, not the equation value minus 1 (an easy error to make on a calculator).

Site	Channel width (m)	Rank 1	Velocity (ms⁻¹)	Rank 2	d (R1 – R2)	d²
1	3.2	12	0.24	12	0	0
2	3.9	11	0.26	11	0	0
3	4.8	10	0.31	10	0	0
4	5.3	9	0.38	7.5	1.5	2.25
5	7.7	4.5	0.39	6	−1.5	2.25
6	6.4	7	0.47	3	4	16
7	7.7	4.5	0.36	9	−4.5	20.25
8	8.5	3	0.42	5	−2	4
9	8.7	2	0.44	4	−2	4
10	6.2	8	0.49	2	6	36
11	6.8	6	0.38	7.5	−1.5	2.25
12	8.8	1	0.51	1	0	0
					$\sum$	87

Table 13.5 Data for channel width and surface velocity at 12 river locations.

$$R_s = 1 - \frac{6 \times 87}{1728 - 12}$$

$$R_s = 1 - \frac{522}{1716}$$

$$R_s = 1 - 0.304$$

$$R_s = 0.696$$

The result is a positive number, which suggests a positive correlation (as one value gets larger, so does the other; in this case, the wider the river channel, the faster the velocity). It is close to 0.7, which suggests a reasonably strong correlation but with some weakness.

You now need to test the significance of the result to ensure that your sample has validity. This leads on to the concepts of **confidence levels** and **critical values**.

Significance test

To establish whether the result has significance, it needs to be checked against a set of statistical significance values (Table 13.6). Given that you only sampled a very small part of a whole geographical dataset, you may just have happened upon an unrepresentative river or set of recordings on that river. Geographers tend to work to the 95% (0.05) probability, meaning only 5 in 100 samples are irregular or 'random'. For even more rigour, they may use a 99% level of confidence (0.01), or a 1 in 100 chance that the sample set is rogue. These are known as 'confidence levels'. Ignore a minus sign in a correlation result when testing for significance.

Key terms

confidence level: how certain we wish to be that our survey results are not due to chance; usually the 95% (0.05) confidence level is used, and 99% (0.01) if greater rigour is required

critical value: the value in a statistical table for the selected confidence level (interval), against which the statistical calculation value is compared

Download Worksheet 13.3 from **Cambridge Elevate** for another Spearman's rank correlation activity.

Confidence	95%	99%		95%	99%
n	0.05	0.01	n	0.05	0.01
5	1.000	–	18	0.472	0.600
6	0.886	1.000	19	0.460	0.584
7	0.786	0.929	20	0.447	0.570
8	0.738	0.881	21	0.436	0.556
9	0.700	0.833	22	0.425	0.544
10	0.648	0.794	23	0.416	0.532
11	0.618	0.755	24	0.407	0.521
12	0.587	0.727	25	0.398	0.511
13	0.560	0.703	26	0.390	0.501
14	0.538	0.679	27	0.383	0.492
15	0.521	0.654	28	0.375	0.483
16	0.503	0.635	29	0.368	0.475
17	0.488	0.618	30	0.362	0.467

Table 13.6 Selected values of Spearman's rank correlation test (R_s); the result is significant if the calculated value of R_s is higher than the table value.

Your study had 12 datasets (n). Using Table 13.6, look at the appropriate row and read down the column for a confidence level of 95% (0.05) probability that your result was due to chance. You will find the critical value is 0.587. If your R_s value is larger than this, you have a statistically significant result at the 95% confidence level. Clearly 0.696 is larger, so you can reject the null hypothesis and accept your hypothesis that there is a positive correlation between the width of a river channel and its surface velocity.

If you want even tighter rigour, you may decide to select a confidence level of 99% (0.01) – read down the column in Table 13.6 to check the critical value. In this case, your R_s value is smaller than 0.727 (value in the table), so you cannot have this level of confidence that your result is not due to chance data.

Inferential relational techniques: Chi-square test

The Chi-square test is used to make an objective judgement on whether an observed association between two variables is dependable, or whether it may be due to chance.

This test may be carried out at the start of an intended geographical investigation. It helps to identify whether an observed pattern between two variables in the human or physical landscape is statistically valid. It assists in convincing us there is a valid relationship worth further study, or in persuading us to move on to consider something else: 'nothing to see here'.

The equation compares what has been measured (observed) in the distribution of the two features with what may be anticipated (expected) 'if' the feature was randomly distributed.

Procedure

For the feature under investigation, establish a hypothesis and then convert it to a null hypothesis. In this worked example, assume you are studying the number of food retailers in an urban area. You have collected data for seven wards extending to the suburbs from the inner city and get the sense that more food retailers are located in the wards further away from the centre (Table 13.7).

Hypothesis (H_1): there is a statistically significant variation in the number of food retailers with increasing distance from the city centre.

Null hypothesis (H_0): there is no statistically valid variation in the number of food retailers in different wards of the city.

- Enter the recorded values in the observed column (O) of Table 13.7.
- Calculate the mean value for O (add up the column and divide by number of datasets).
- Transcribe the mean into the expected column (E).
- Calculate $O - E$ for each row.
- Calculate $(O - E)^2$ for each row and total up the column.
- Enter the values in the Chi-square equation:

$$X^2 = \frac{\Sigma(O - E)^2}{E}$$

Where:

Σ = summate the values

O = observed frequency

E = expected frequency (if random in theory)

Tip

A correlation is not the same as 'causation'; we cannot be sure that a change in one variable is causing the change in the other – there could be a third (or fourth) factor influencing them both. Even if there is causation, we need to be careful to analyse which is causing which – which is the dependent and which the independent variable. Is the faster river causing the wider channel, or vice versa?

Making connections

Consider how a Chi-square test could test observed vegetation variations in a local environment described in Chapter 6 Ecosystems under stress.

Urban ward	Observed (food retailers)	Expected (food retailers)	$O - E$	$(O - E)^2$
1	12	23	−11	121
2	18	23	−5	25
3	14	23	−9	81
4	28	23	5	25
5	23	23	0	0
6	30	23	7	49
7	36	23	13	169
Mean	23		Σ	470

Table 13.7 Data for the number of food retailers in seven wards in an urban area.

$$X^2 = \frac{470}{23} = 20.43$$

On its own, the Chi-square statistic has little meaning – it needs validating against critical values. These are found in tables or on graphs that have been calculated by statistical experts (an example is shown in Table 13.8).

Download Worksheet 13.4 from **Cambridge Elevate** for another Chi-square activity.

Critical values of the chi-square (x^2) distribution		
df	0.05	0.01
1	3.841	6.635
2	5.991	9.210
3	7.815	11.345
4	9.488	13.277
5	11.070	15.086
6	12.592	16.812
7	14.067	18.475
8	15.507	20.090
9	16.919	21.666
10	18.307	23.209
11	19.675	24.725
12	21.026	26.217
13	22.362	27.688
14	23.685	29.141
15	24.996	30.578

Table 13.8 Critical values for χ^2.

Decide which confidence level you wish to use: 95% (0.05) or 99% (0.01). Then define the degrees of freedom (df) to use. This is usually calculated as $n - 1$ (where n is the number of datasets), which in this example is $7 - 1 = 6$. Therefore use the df 6 row in Table 13.8 to look up your critical value.

If your result is larger than the critical value, it is valid, which means you can reject the null hypothesis and accept your original hypothesis. If your result is smaller than the critical value, you have to accept the null hypothesis – there is no statistically valid association between the two datasets.

The Chi-square value you obtained (20.43) is larger than the critical value of 12.59 (0.05) and also 16.81 (0.01) in Table 13.8, so the null hypothesis can be rejected and the hypothesis accepted. It will not indicate what the association between the datasets actually is – that needs investigating further. But you now know there is something going on geographically concerning where food retailers are located. It gives further study legitimacy by confirming that a geographical factor(s) is at work in the distribution of food retailers.

Assess to progress

1   Explain what you understand by the importance of scale when presenting geographical data. **4 MARKS [AS LEVEL]**

2   How would you ensure that the appropriate scale has been selected for data you are presenting in a visual form? **6 MARKS [AS LEVEL]**

Glossary

1002 area: a 6070 km² coastal plain area lying between the Brooks Range and the Beaufort Range; it is the only area of the ANWR that does not have protected wilderness status

abiotic: the non-living or physical components of an ecosystem (e.g. the climate, soil and drainage)

ablation: the natural removal of snow or ice in a glacier

ablation zone: the area of net loss in a glacier or ice mass

acid rain: volcanoes erupt sulphurous gases which can result in acidic rainwater

accumulation: the addition of snow or ice in a glacier

accumulation zone: the area of net gain in a glacier

accuracy: the degree to which a measurement determines the correct (or accurate) value

adaption: the action of changing or adapting behaviour in order to reduce the severity of a volcanic eruption

aeolian processes: the action of the wind on the landscape, involving the movement of fine sediment, which can be used to erode the landscape and eventually be deposited in a new form or location

aeroponics: growing plants in air that contains a mist of water and nutrients

aggregates: particles that bind together

agrochemicals: artificial pesticides and fertilisers that are used in farming

aim: a clear statement of the purpose of your investigation

albedo: the reflectivity of surfaces that redirects shortwave solar radiation back into space with limited heat absorption; ice sheets and sea ice have a high albedo

alluvial soils: fertile soils deposited when a river floods

altitude: the height of land in relation to sea level

anomaly: something in the data that is unusual or does not fit in; it often deviates from what is standard, normal or expected

anthropogenic: impacts as a consequence of human activity

appendix: a section of additional material at the end of a report

appropriate technology: engineering improvements that use, as far as possible, local resources, skills and community involvement not only in the initial construction but to oversee long-term maintenance, repair and operation

aquaculture: farming the seas

arboreal: relating to trees and usually an animal's habitat

aridisols: desert soils; they are often lacking in organic material, and can also be baked hard on the surface by the heat, forming a duricrust

aridity index: an index which determines the aridity of a region, based on the actual precipitation that falls, combined with water losses through evapotranspiration

arresting factors: natural or human events that interfere with succession, leading to the establishment of a sub-climax vegetation

asymptomatic infections: when an infection is present but there are no symptoms

backwash: the return flow of water due to gravity as the energy of the swash subsides)

basal sliding: large-scale movement of ice as a result of subglacial meltwater

basaltic eruption: a gentle (effusive) eruption, which is characterised by fluid lava and is relatively predictable

base flow: the normal day-to-day flow of a river

Benioff zone: the zone where earthquakes tend to occur as the oceanic crust is being subducted underneath the continental crust at a destructive plate boundary

beneficiation: processes after mining a metallurgical ore that concentrate the mineral-containing material and separate it from waste rock (tailings). Often involves significant water-use in froth-flotation or gravity separation

bergschrund: a crevasse that forms where a moving glacier ice separates from the back wall of a corrie or stagnant ice above the crevasse

biodiversity: the variety of species of flora and fauna that are found within an area, and which influence the productivity of an ecosystem

biodiversity hotspots: biogeographic regions with significant reservoirs of biodiversity that are under threat from humans

biogeochemical systems: systems in which chemicals are transferred between living organisms and the environment

biological age: the age of someone's body, regardless of their chronological age

biomass: the total amount of living matter in an ecosystem; it is highest in tropical rainforests

biota: the distinctive animal and plant life of a particular habitat or environmental zone

biotechnology: the science behind genetic modification

biotic: the living components of an ecosystem (e.g. the plants, animals, people and soil microorganisms)

block disintegration: the breakdown of large rocks into smaller ones of varying sizes through the expansion of small cracks in the rock

brown earth soils: the relatively fertile soils found beneath deciduous woodlands

boreal zone: a cold region to the south of the Arctic

brain drain: the emigration of well-educated or qualified people from a country

brownfield site: land that has previously been used, suffered decline and is now available for redevelopment

building human capacity: developing self-confidence and the technical abilities required to oversee a local project and ensure its continuation

buttress roots: very large roots of trees in the tropical rainforests, which allow the rapid and massive uptake of water and nutrients by the tree; they may also have a support function

caldera: a large volcanic crater, often formed following a highly explosive eruption where the summit of the volcano is removed

canalise: straighten a section of a river

capital investment: funds invested in a firm or enterprise for the purposes of furthering its business objectives

carbonation: the chemical conversion of solid carbonate compounds to soluble bicarbonate compounds

carbon budget: the surplus or deficit of carbon once carbon output is subtracted from carbon input

carbon burial: the extraction of carbon dioxide from energy and industrial emissions and burial in sealed underground rock strata; also known as 'artificial carbon sequestration'

carbon offsetting: a deliberate scheme to reduce atmospheric CO_2 through absorption (tree planting) or reduced emissions (moving to green energy use)

carbon pump: a natural energy force resulting in a carbon flux; both gravity and descending cold currents

transfer plankton remains from ocean surfaces to seafloors in the ocean pump

carbon sequestration: the removal of carbon from active cycles by natural or artificial transfer and burial in a long-term store

carbon sink: a store in which the absorption of carbon occurs at a faster rate than it is released

carbon source: a store in which the release of carbon occurs at a faster rate than it is absorbed

carrying capacity: the number of people that a region or country can sustainably support

cash crops: a crop produced to sell rather than for the farmer to consume

caste system: traditionally a Hindu social division system; each caste is afforded different privileges and limitations

cataracts: a health condition which causes the lens of the eye to become opaque, resulting in poor vision

catchment: the total surface area from which water drains into a particular river system

cauliflory: the production of flowers and fruits from the trunks of tropical trees

cavitation: the opening up of cavities within cliffs as a result of stresses imposed by the breaking of waves due to pressure variations as waves crash into and then recede from joints

CBD: central business district

chemotherapy: a treatment for cancer that uses chemicals or drugs that destroy malignant cells

channel flow: water held in the channel as it moves through the drainage basin. This will also act as temporary storage

clasts: rock fragments resulting from the breakdown of larger rocks

climatic climax vegetation: this is the final point in a succession when no further changes will take place; the vegetation is in equilibrium with the environment

climax vegetation: the dominant mix of vegetation species that characterise an environment within a particular climate region given sufficient time for conditions to suit colonisation and attain stability

closed sediment system: a coastal system that receives no additional sediment inputs and has no losses of sediment to areas external to the system

closed system: a system that has no inputs or outputs, but which cycles energy or resources around a closed loop in state from water vapour to liquid as a result of cooling

coastal adaptation strategies: investment in measures to negate the impacts of sea level rise

coastal mitigation strategies: investment in measures to reduce the factors responsible for sea level rise

coastal system: a series of linked elements affecting the coastal zone through which energy and material circulate

communicable (infectious) diseases: illnesses that can be passed on to others

compressional flow: ice in front is moving slower than the ice behind, so a build-up of ice occurs

confidence level: how certain we wish to be that our survey results are not due to chance; usually the 95% (0.05) confidence level is used, and 99% (0.01) if greater rigour is required

conservation cropping: the practice of minimising soil disturbance, planting crops early and retaining stubble (stems left over after harvesting)

continentality: the effect of distance from the sea on the aridity of the air in a region; this tends to create a more extreme climate with higher temperatures in summer

continental crust: the Earth's crust which is found under the continents (although the fit is not exact); it is relatively thick (10–70 km) and not as dense as oceanic crust

control measures: actions that can be taken to reduce the potential of exposure to the hazard

convection column: a vertical, rising column of smoke, ashes and particulates caused by a fire

cooperative: a group that works together to share costs and maximise profits

Coriolis force: the rotation of the Earth which deflects objects and air (usually to the right in the northern hemisphere) moving along the Earth's surface

counter-urbanisation: the movement away from large urban settlements to smaller urban settlements and rural settlements

crevasses: a deep fissure or fracture in the glacier

critical value: the value in a statistical table for the selected confidence level (interval), against which the statistical calculation value is compared

crowdsourcing: a way of obtaining information by enlisting the services of a number of people usually through the internet or mobile-phone technology

cultivable land: ground that has suitable conditions for the growing of crops or rearing of livestock

culvert: a tunnel carrying a river underground; the River Fleet in London is largely found underground in culverts

deindustrialisation: fall in the percentage contribution of secondary industry to an economy in terms of value of input to GDP and importance as an employment sector

demographic dividend: the economic benefit created by the population of a country

denuded mountains: mountains that have been stripped of their vegetation cover

dependency ratio: a measure showing the number of people who are too young (aged 0–14) or too old (over the age of 65) to work in comparison to the working population (aged 15–64)

depth of the food deficit: a measure of the difference between average food consumption and average food requirements (in kilocalories per person per day)

dereliction: an area that has become abandoned or dilapidated

desertification: land degradation in arid and semi-arid areas due to climatic variations and human activities, which threatens the livelihoods of vulnerable populations

disaster hotspot: a location which is at risk of experiencing two or more hazards; Haiti is a good example of a disaster hotspot as it is vulnerable to both tropical storms and earthquakes

discharge: water flowing through a river channel at any given point and is measured in cubic metres per second (cumecs)

diurnal: daily; a pattern that occurs every day

drainage basin (catchment area): the area of land that provides water to a river system

drip tips: the pointed ends of the leaves on many tropical rainforest trees to encourage the shedding of water in order to avoid blocking stomata and the development of bacteria and fungus

dominants: the tallest plants/trees that will grow in an environment (e.g. oak trees in deciduous forests)

duricrust: the hard-baked surface that forms on desert soils

dynamic: a state of constant change

dynamic equilibrium: relative stability in a cycle when key components have reached a state of balance. A change in a component can induce change in the rest of system so that equilibrium is lost

dynamism: the degree of change taking place within a system in terms of scale and/or rate

eco-city: a city that aims to provide a healthy environment for its inhabitants without using more resources than it replaces

ecological footprints: measures the area required to supply the ecological services used by the population, measured in global hectares (gha)

ecology of fantasy: a term associated with Margaret Crawford (1988), in which she described theme parks as public spaces that have become a commodity – the underlying theme is consumption – a kind of disguised shopping centre

economically inactive population: those not in work and not seeking work nor available for work

economic inequality: the gulf between rich and poor

ecosystem: a complex set of relationships among the living resources, habitat and flora and fauna in an area

edge cities: a concentration of business, shopping, and entertainment outside the traditional central business district

edgelands: places where the borders between urban and rural are difficult to define/classify

effusive eruption: an eruption where lava flows on the ground rather than being expelled in an explosive manner

eluviation: the movement of soil material from upper to lower horizons by the downward movement of water

embargoes: official resolutions by one or more countries to ban trade in a resource or by an organisation or nation by putting in place trade restrictions

enabling technologies: inventions or innovations that allow a user or business to significantly impact the way they operate, such as the internet or barcode scanners

endorheic drainage basins: drainage basins that do not have an outlet to the ocean; the rivers usually flow into an inland lake or sea

endogenous: factors within a place that help shape its character (e.g. location and topography)

energy gap: where the available supply of energy is no longer able to meet the size and nature of the demand

energy insecurity: lack of control over energy provision due to factors beyond a country's influence

energy mix: the sources of energy in their different proportions of use constitute a country's energy mix

energy security: having access to reliable supplies of energy to meet a country's needs in the short- and medium term

environmental degradation: the deterioration of the natural environment

ephemeral: referring to a plant which flowers occasionally, when the conditions are right, and not every year

epiphytes: plants such as lianas that grow on other plants, using them to reach the sunlight or as a source of nutrients

equilibrium: a state of balance between outputs and inputs

equilibrium budget: the sediment inputs and outputs are in equilibrium

erosion: the degradation of rock and its removal to expose a fresh rock face

ethical dimension: paying due regard to the ethics of your enquiry by taking steps in the upkeep of respect and in reducing stress, anxiety or avoidable discomfort for participants

eustatic change: a change in the relative level of land and sea due to rises and falls in the global seal level

evaporation: a change in state from liquid water to water vapour, as a result of heating

evapotranspiration: the loss of water by evaporation and transpiration combined – a term sometimes used in equations representing water balance

exfoliation: a type of weathering which leads to the surface of rocks breaking down (also known as onion-skin weathering)

exogenous: factors from outside a place that force a change in a place's character (e.g. its relationships with other places)

exponential growth: when the rate of increase becomes ever more rapid in proportion to the size of the population

extensional flow: ice is moving faster in front than the ice behind, resulting in the development of crevasses

externality: a factor that cannot be changed by an individual but has a bearing on their quality of life (e.g. access to open space, presence of good schools)

falling limb: the part of a hydrograph that records the decrease in a river's flow

fast carbon cycle: relatively rapid transfers of carbon compounds over years, decades and centuries

fauna: the animal life in an ecosystem

feedback loop: where an output may become an input into another part of the same system, instigating a further change in the output

fertility rate: sometimes called total fertility rate (TFR), this is the average number of children that are born to a woman during her lifetime

fetch: the length of ocean over which winds blow from a consistent direction

firstspace: the quantitative analysis of a place (e.g. demographic data and socio-economic data)

flora: the plants and trees in an ecosystem

flow resources: resources that are renewable, replenished irrespective of how much they are exploited

flux: a flow of a gas, liquid or solid matter resulting in a transfer between two locations

food chain: energy transfer in the form of food from plants to herbivores to carnivores

food security: when people have enough affordable and nutritious food to eat

food insecurity: when people do not have reliable access to a sufficient quantity of affordable, nutritious food

food web: a series of interconnected food chains showing how energy is transferred in an ecosystem

freehold: a type of tenure (ownership) in which the owner has outright ownership of the property and the land on which it stands

fortress developments: city developments that integrate greater security into the design of the building or landscaping

frictional effect of distance: the theory that areas that are closer together are more likely to interact, whereas those that are further apart are less likely to do so

fuel poverty: there are different definitions of this term, but it refers to essential fuel costs being so high for an individual or family that their well-being is compromised in terms of quality of life and health

gemeinschaft: the rural extreme – a peasant society which is inward looking, an idyllic community, based on kinship and supported by subsistence agriculture

gentrification: the renewal of an area leading to an influx of affluent people

geoglyph: large motifs or designs carved into rocks or drawn on the ground such as the White Horses of southern England or the Nazca art in Peru

geomorphology: the study of processes that change the shape of the Earth; they include weathering and erosion, and may result from the action of waves, glaciers and rivers

geopolitics: a study of the issues that arise as a result of the unequal distribution of geographical phenomena and the imbalanced power relationships attempting to access, influence and control them

gesellschaft: the urban extreme – the ever changing nature of large, cosmopolitan commercial cities

GIS (Geographical Information Systems): computer-based methods of collecting, storing, sorting, manipulating, analysing and presenting spatial information (information that can be mapped)

glacial period: a time period when ice masses develop and advance into lower altitudes; they are characterised by a sustained decline in temperature and the formation of continental ice sheets

glaciomarine sediments: inorganic and organic material deposited in a marine setting by a combination of glacier- and marine-related processes

global commons: the Earth's shared and unowned natural resources, such as the oceans, the atmosphere and outer space

global village: the world (globe) has been transformed into a 'village' by the almost instantaneous transmission of information, facilitated by improvements in ICT

glocalisation: the production of a global good that is adapted to a local market

granular disintegration: the breakdown of rocks into fine particles, the most common being sand

greenfield sites: undeveloped countryside areas

greenhouse gas: a gas that absorbs infrared radiation and contributes to the warming of the atmosphere, such as methane and carbon dioxide

green infrastructure: a network of green spaces, both rural and urban, that are essential to the well-being and quality of life of communities

green roof: a roof of a building that is partially or completely covered with vegetation such as grass to promote wildlife and reduce insulation costs

grey water: used water from bathroom sinks, showers and washing machines

ground deformation: the change in shape of the ground before or after a volcanic eruption; often it is due to the movement of magma below the surface

groundwater aquifers: rocks beneath the ground that store water

groundwater flow: water moving through the soil

growing season: the length of time in a year when the temperature is above about 5 °C to allow plant growth; the rainforest growing season is all year, but it is only a couple of months in the tundra

gullies: deep channels cut into the soil by running water

haboob: a desert storm, with wind-blown sand, which can build up quickly and last for a relatively short time but can create hazardous conditions for human activity

Hadley cell: a tropical atmospheric circulation pattern in which air rises at or near the equator, flows toward the poles, returns to the Earth's surface in the subtropics and flows back towards the equator

halophytic: characteristic of plants which have adopted strategies to increase their tolerance to salt, including excretion of salt on the surface of leave

hard engineering: strategies that are designed to intercept and impede natural marine and coastal processes so that they are less likely to produce undesirable consequences

hazard perception: the way in which someone understands or interprets a hazard

Hazard Management Cycle: a cycle showing phases of response, recovery, mitigation and preparedness in the management of a hazard

health: mentally or physically free from illness or injury

HEP: hydro-electric power is generated when flowing water is used to turn a turbine to create electricity

high-energy coast: a coastline subject to maximum inputs; it is likely to be dynamic

high-level waste (HLW): this is very hot, highly radioactive and dangerous waste that is produced as a result of nuclear fission in a reactor

homogenisation: the process whereby places and social characteristics become more similar to each other so that they eventually become indistinguishable

hotspots: sites where mantle plumes rise up through areas of thin crust, causing volcanic activity in areas away from plate boundaries

Human Development Index (HDI): a composite index combining life expectancy at birth, mean and expected years of schooling and gross national income (GNI) per capita (calculated at purchasing power parity or PPP US $) to measure and rank countries

humus: the dead organic matter incorporated into the soil

hybrid green energy: producing energy using two renewable energy sources

hydration: in geology, when water molecules combine with a mineral leading to a change in structure and a swelling of the rocks

hydraulic fracturing: popularly referred to as 'fracking', this is an engineering technique that drills boreholes into gas-bearing strata of dispersed concentrations and fractures the rock using hydraulic pressure

hydrocarbon: a wide range of chemical compounds based on carbon and hydrogen

hydrograph: a graph of the water level or base flow in a river over a period of time, such as a year, and the response of the river to a precipitation event

hydrology: the study of water on the surface of the Earth

hydroponics: growing plants in material other than soil, such as pebbles and sand

hydrosere: plant succession in a freshwater environment

hydropower: sourcing energy from the power of flowing water

hyper-reality: a condition where what is real and what is fiction is blurred so that no clear distinction between the two can be made

hypothesis: a specific, focused, directional statement of what you expect to find

ice lenses: formed when moisture, diffused within soil or rock, accumulates

impermeable: a surface that does not allow water to pass through it

inferential statistic: an inferential statistical technique studies a sample taken from a larger population and 'infers' that the findings from it represent the rest of the population that was not sampled. Spearman's rank correlation and the Chi-square test are both inferential statistical techniques. A significance test estimates the likelihood that the sample 'reliably' represents the larger population

infiltration capacity: the rate at which water is able to pass through a soil (measured in mm/hr) – this will be high for a sandy soil; lower for a clay soil

informal settlement: a settlement where housing has been built on land to which the occupants have no legal right

insider: the perspective of someone who knows a place well and is familiar with not only its topography but also its daily rhythms and events

in situ: material that has not been transported during or after its formation; this is in contrast to *ex situ*, where material has been moved by transportation processes and deposited a distance from its original location

insolation: incoming solar radiation received at a point on the Earth's surface; values are high in hot desert regions due to the lack of cloud cover

Integrated Coastal Zone Management (ICZM): a process for the management of the coast using an integrated approach to achieve sustainability

interglacial period: a time period when ice cover retreats to the polar regions; we are currently experiencing an interglacial period

internal deformation: small-scale movement and deformation of ice crystals because of the effect of gravity and ice mass

intertidal zone: the shoreline between the highest and lowest spring tides; it is where the predominant wave activity occurs so is subject to most marine erosion, transfer and deposition

intervening obstacles: physical or human barriers that hinder the movement of migrants

interview: an in-depth discussion with someone, usually following a predetermined set of questions but following up responses with supplementary lines of enquiry

intracratonic basin: a large depression within a stable continental mass containing sedimentary rocks from marine and/or continental deposits in shallow inland seas, formed millions of years ago

intraplate: in the middle of a plate, away from the plate margins

IPAT equation: a calculation that shows how population (P), affluence (A) and technology (T) have an impact on carrying capacity (I)

isostatic change: the rise or fall of land in relation to a given sea level

keyhole surgery: operations carried out through small incisions, using special fibre optic instruments

lag time: the time difference between the peak rainfall and the peak discharge that occurs as a result

lahar: a destructive mudflow which occurs as a result of a volcanic eruption

latent heat: the heat required to turn a solid into a liquid or liquid into gas without a change in temperature

latitude: the distance north or south of the equator, often measured in degrees and minutes

latosol soils: the typical soil type below tropical rainforest; it has a very deep, red colour because of iron and aluminium in A horizon

leaching: the loss of soluble nutrients from the soil by the movement of water

Leopold matrix: a tool for quantifying the likely environmental consequences of a project. Developed in 1971, one axis considers the magnitude of the project consequences, and the other – the significance/importance of environmental impact

liminal: in between

line source/sink: an extended zone of coastal where sediment is removed from (source) or deposited (sink)

lithification: the process by which sediments become compressed into solid rock (lithology) due to pressure

(e.g. mud into shale, calcium carbonate into chalk and limestone)

lithosere: plant succession on a dry, bare rock surface

litter layer: the layer of dead organic matter lying on the soil

Living Wage: an hourly rate set independently and updated annually based on the cost of living in the UK

low-energy coast: a coastline that has key inputs, transfers and outputs in balance and is more likely to be in a state of stable equilibrium

malnutrition: consuming an unsuitable amount of energy, protein and nutrients

marginal: poor quality agricultural land that is unsuitable for farming

marine: applying to seas and oceans

marine calcification: the uptake of soluble carbon compounds by marine creatures and conversion into solid carbonate compounds

measure of centrality: identifying the centre of a range of data by calculating the mean, mode or median value

measure of dispersion: calculating the extent of data spread or range from maximum to minimum value by means of the inter-quartile range, standard deviation or deviation from the line of best fit

megacity: metropolitan area with a total population in excess of 10 million people

metallurgical: technological and scientific processes designed to obtain, purify and modify metal from mineral ores

methane hydrates: crystalline structures within sediment deposits of continental shelves and polar seas consisting of methane locked within an ice framework

methodology: the general research strategy that outlines the way your field investigation will be undertaken; it includes an outline of what data you will need and how you will collect it

millionaire city: a city with over 1 million inhabitants

mineral: a naturally-occurring inorganic (non-hydrocarbon based) substance in solid form with a definite chemical composition. It may be metallic (iron oxide) or non-metallic (calcium phosphate) and often formed as a result of geological processes

mitigation: the action of reducing the severity or seriousness of a volcanic eruption

mobility: the ability to move freely

monoculture: the repeated growth of a single crop, often with the aid of large quantities of artificial fertilisers and irrigation

moraine: rocks and sediments carried and then deposited by the glacier

morbidity: how often a disease and poor health occurs in a specific area; co-morbidity is when people have two or more medical conditions

morphological: relating to the form or structure of an animal or plant

natural decrease: when deaths are higher than births and the population gets smaller

natural increase: when births are higher than deaths and the population grows

natural population change: the difference between birth rate and death rate; it illustrates how much the population will increase or decrease per thousand per years of the population

negative feedback cycle (loop): where changes within the system slow down or reduce the causes of further disruption, dampening down the impetus for change

negative multiplier effect: a downward spiral of events that follow the decline of investment in a region such as decreased spending, the loss of other jobs and out-migration

Neoliberalism: an approach that favours privatisation, deregulation, free trade and a reduction in government spending

net primary production (NPP): the growth rate of vegetation in an ecosystem, usually measured by the increase in biomass in a year; high in rainforests and low in deserts

net replacement rate: the number of female offspring produced by female members of the population

névé: granular snow consisting of low-density ice crystals; also called firn

nivation: the erosion of the ground and sides of a hollow as a result of continued freezing and thawing

nomadic cultivation: when a farmer moves from one place to another to find water supplies and better pasture land

non-communicable illnesses: medical conditions or diseases that are not infectious or transmissible from person to person

non-governmental organisation (NGO): an organisation that is not part of a government or for profit businesses; charities, such as Oxfam, are good examples of NGOs

non-organic: compounds that derive from non-living matter

normal distribution: when there is symmetry in the distribution of quantitative data either side of the mean, but clustering around it

nuée ardente: a dense, rapidly moving cloud of hot gases, ashes and lava fragments from a volcanic eruption; a type of pyroclastic flow

null hypothesis: a statement that there is no relationship between the two variables being considered, or no significant difference between two groups being compared

nutrient cycling: the movement of nutrients from the soil to the biomass to the litter in an ecosystem

occupational: related to a person's job

ocean acidification: a reduction in the pH level of the oceans, caused by the absorption of carbon dioxide

ocean–atmosphere exchange: the ability of the ocean to both absorb CO_2 from, and release it to, the atmosphere, depending on ocean and atmospheric conditions

oceanic crust: the crust which is found under the oceans (although the fit is not exact); it is relatively thin (5–7 km) and more dense than continental crust

open system: a system that has both inputs and outputs of energy or other material, and which involves a flow or exchange of material

ore: a rock containing an increased concentration of extractable proportions of a mineral

organic: matter derived from living things; both plant and animal residues

oscillatory wave: a wave in open sea with full circular motion of particles

outsider: the perspective of someone who does not know a place well (e.g. a visitor) or someone who is marginalised in a community, such as the homeless or people from minority groups

outsource: the employment of other people, for example from overseas to do jobs previously done by people in the home country

over-abstraction: taking too much of something, such as too much water from groundwater supplies

overland flow (surface runoff): water flowing over the ground surface; this may be a result of impermeable surfaces, including frozen ground, or infiltration excess during heavy rainfall

oxidation: the reaction of a substance with oxygen; in the case of rocks containing iron, it forms iron oxide which is rust-coloured

Paleoclimatic: climatic conditions in the geological past reconstructed from a direct or indirect data source

parent material: the rock underlying a soil

Park response model: a model to show the changing quality of life through different phases of a disaster

per capita: per person

perceive: to consider/view/regard

perception: how something is viewed, regarded or considered

permafrost: permanently frozen ground in arctic and alpine environments

permeable: a surface that allows water to pass through it

phreatic: steam-driven explosions which occur when water beneath the ground is superheated by magma

phreatophytes: plants which have long taproots so that they can exploit water lying in the phreatic zone (below the water table) that other plants can't reach

phytoplankton: the 'plant' form of plankton using sunlight in surface waters to photosynthesize carbon dioxide into sugars

pilot study: a small-scale version of a fieldwork investigation, carried out to identify any problems with the plans and modify the research design accordingly

pioneers: the first vegetation to colonise in a prisere; usually mosses and lichens

placeless: a place that is indistinguishable from other such places in appearance or character

plagioclimax community: a subclimax community formed as a result of human activity in an area

Pleistocene era: the first epoch of the Quaternary period

podsol: a relatively infertile and acid soil mostly found below coniferous forests

point source/sink: a specific coastal location where sediment is removed from (source) or deposited (sink)

population density: the number of people living in an area, usually given as the number of people per km²

population distribution: the pattern of where people live

positive feedback cycle (loop): where the effect of change is to amplify the original causes so that additional further change occurs

potable water: water of a quality that can be safely drunk and used in food preparation without compromising health

precipitation: the movement of water from the atmosphere to the ground surface. It can take several forms, including rain, snow, sleet, hail and fog

prediction: suggesting what might happen in the future

preparedness: the state of readiness for a volcanic eruption

pressure melting point: the temperature at which ice under pressure melts; this can occur at temperatures below freezing

prevention: the action of stopping something from happening

primary data: the data that you and your group collect 'in the field'

primary energy: energy that, upon release, is used directly

primary forest: areas of native tree species, where no deforestation has taken place

primary hazard: hazards that are directly related to the volcano and its eruption (e.g. lava flows, ash falls and gas clouds)

primary producers: mostly the green plants that are able to produce nutrients or biomass using chemicals in the presence of sunlight

primary succession: succession from a bare rock surface where there has been no previous soil formation or vegetation, such as bare rock, a volcanic eruption, a mudslide or a sand dune

prisere: primary succession on a bare inorganic surface where there has not been any soil formation or vegetation

private space: a space that is privately owned and public access may be prevented or limited

profile: a cross-section of soil

public space: space that is open and accessible to the public

pyroclastic flow: a mixture of hot rock, lava, ash and gases arising from a volcanic eruption that moves at a rapid speed along the ground

qualitative data: non-numerical, descriptive data which may be obtained from personal observation (noting behaviour, field-sketching, photographs, etc.), analysing printed/audiovisual material or investigating people's opinion, attitudes and beliefs

quantitative data: numerical data, often obtained through measurement, questionnaires or from public secondary databases

questionnaire: a predetermined and piloted set of structured questions, most of which require coded responses in order to tabulate and calculate frequency

radioactive half-life: the time it takes for half the neutrons of a radioactive mass to disintegrate, known as radioactive decay

radiotherapy: a treatment for cancer that uses X-rays or similar forms of radiation

rainfed: using water that originates from rainfall

rain shadow: the dry area on the lee side of a mountain or mountain range, away from the (rain-bearing) wind

rainwater harvesting: a system to collect the rainfall and use it in buildings and gardens

rare earths: 17 elements with chemical properties that make them vital to cutting-edge technologies and advanced engineering. REE (rare earth element)/REM (rare earth metal)

rebranding: a form of marketing in which a new development or redevelopment uses a new name, image, symbol, design or combination thereof for an established feature with the intention of developing a new, differentiated identity in the minds of consumers, the public, investors, competitors and other stakeholders

regeneration: a form of renewal and redevelopment of a rundown area; regeneration aims to improve the conditions of an area and the quality of life experienced by those who live there

regime: the pattern of flow of a river, influenced by its catchment characteristics and the climate

regolith: a layer of loose rock and dust, usually thin, that sits on bedrock

reliability: the extent to which a method of data collection will give the same results if repeated more than once

relict feature: a feature in the landscape, which was formed under previous climatic conditions

remittance payments: money that migrants send back home to support their families

research question: an answerable inquiry into a specific concern or issue; it is the central element of both qualitative and quantitative research, and indicates what you want to find out in your investigation

reserve: an estimate of the amount of valued mineral or energy source that can, with realistic expectations, be technically extracted and economically exploited

resource: am estimate of the quantity of a valued mineral or energy source that is physically contained in the source material

resource frontier: a peripheral environment that attracts the latest exploration and subsequent development of resources

resource security: the capacity of a population to access sufficient resources for present and ongoing needs to sustain a desired level of consumption or use

resource peak: the phase of maximum production from a resource deposit before depletion exceeds new discoveries

response: the way that a river responds following the input of precipitation: some rivers rise quickly and are said to be 'flashy'; others rise and fall more slowly

rills: shallow channels cut into the soil by running water

riparian: habitats associated with the land alongside flowing water

rising limb: the part of a hydrograph that records the increase in a river's flow

risk: a situation involving exposure to danger

rock flour: very fine rock particles caused when rocks are ground down by glacial erosion

runoff: water and sediment being moved down the river channel, and out of the catchment area

rural-to-urban migration: the movement of people from the countryside to the city

sabkhas: flat areas, often between a desert and an ocean, with crusts of salt and other minerals resulting from evaporation

salinisation: the process whereby land becomes increasingly salty, ultimately becoming desertified

saltwater intrusion: the movement of saline water (e.g. seawater) into freshwater supplies

sampling: the process of selecting a small number of units from a broader population you are studying to measure

sandur: a glacial meltwater outwash plain

saturated: all the available spaces between the soil particles are filled with water

scree: a mass of small loose stones covering a slope

secondary data: data obtained from other sources, for example OS maps, census data, historical land use maps or newspaper articles

secondary energy: energy that is released from one or more sources in order to generate a second form of energy – most commonly, electricity

secondary hazard: hazards that occur due to the occurrence of another, primary hazard; they are indirectly related to the volcanic event and, by definition, tend to occur after primary hazards

secondary succession: succession where there is some pre-existing soil and vegetation

secondspace: qualitative data for how people feel about a place

sedentary cultivation: farming that occurs in one place

sediment: fine particles of soil or weathered rock, which can form regolith (a thin layer of loose rock and dust) or soil when mixed with organic material and water over a long period of time

sediment budget: the net sum value between quantities of input and output of sediment in a system. Excess is a positive budget, deficit is a negative budget and no overall difference is a neutral budget

sedimentary rocks: rocks resulting from heat and pressure compressing and consolidating depositional material; they most often form on seafloors (e.g. limestone, chalk and shale)

sediment (littoral) cells: a section of coastline in which sediment is recycled but not added to or lost

sediment sink: when sediment is lost to the system by transfer to a location beyond further access. Different to a 'sediment store' where additions and removal of sediment are possible

seismometer: an instrument that measures the seismic waves generated by an earthquake

sensible heat: the amount of heat energy that occurs when an object is heated; when heat is removed from an object and its temperature falls, the heat removed is also called sensible heat

seracs: steep faults on the surface of a glacier

seral community: plants that occur together in a seral stage such as the lichens or the shrubs

seral stage: each stage in a succession with a different type of vegetation is called a seral stage

sheet flooding: flooding where water flows evenly over the surface after heavy rainfall rather than running along a channel

shield volcano: a volcano with gently sloping sides, characteristic of fluid, basaltic lava

Shoreline Management Plans (SMPs): documents describing and addressing the risks associated with coastal evolution; SMPs form an important part of the UK government's strategy for flood and coastal defence

significance test: a statistical check to establish the likelihood of a result being due to random associations; it establishes whether the null hypothesis may be rejected or not

silting: where grains of sand or silt accumulate

sink: site of sediment deposition

slow carbon cycle: transfers of carbon compounds over extensive timescales (possibly millions of years)

social cleansing: the removal from the area of members of a social class considered 'undesirable'

socio-economic disruption: disruption to social (lifestyle) or economic (money or jobs) aspects of society

soft engineering: low-incursion, sustainable coastal protection strategies that work with nature to manage the coast

soil horizon: the different layers in a soil, usually a layer of litter at the surface, then horizons A, B and C, then the bedrock or parent material

soil erosion: the loss of soil through natural forces such as wind or rain

source: contributes sediment

spatial proximity: the development of innovation due to the close geographical locations of universities and industry

Special Economic Zone (SEZ): a designated area within a country that has favourable economic regulations to encourage investment

stock resources: finite quantities of resources that may be depleted to the point of exhaustion or extinction

storm surge: sea level raised to an abnormal height beyond the usual tidal range as a result of particular short-term weather conditions

stratovolcano: a steep-sided volcano made up of alternate layers of lava and ash

subaerial weathering: involves processes at the base of the atmosphere that cause solid rock to lose integrity, internal coherence and to fragment

sub-climax vegetation: the vegetation that results when arresting factors interfere and stop the succession towards the climatic climax vegetation

sublimation: the transition of ice to water vapour without a liquid stage

subduction zones: zones where thin, dense oceanic crust is forced beneath thicker, less dense continental crust at a destructive plate boundary

subsere: secondary succession on a surface where there has been prior soil formation and vegetation

suburb: an outlying district of a city

suburbanisation: the growth of areas on the fringes of cities

succession: the stages vegetation goes through from colonising a bare surface to reaching the climatic climax vegetation

suburbanised village: a small settlement in which most of the workers commute to work, and are said to have 'urban values', and so they are not primarily interested in the rural economy

sustainable: that which is capable of being maintained into the foreseeable future without prejudice to its own continuation or damage to the environment

sustainable development goals (SDGs): UN goals that came into force at the end of 2015; they are international development targets to be achieved by 2030

swash: the forward movement of a breaking translatory wave as it surges up the shore

tarn: a small mountain lake

temperate zone: a region with mild climate found at midlatitudes

tephra: rock fragments ejected during volcanic eruptions

terrestrial: applying to the land rather than air or water

thermohaline system: part of the ocean circulation, caused by differences in water density; differences in density occur due to water temperature and salinity

the tragedy of the commons: the decline of common resources, such as ocean fish stocks, when the rate of use exceeds the rate of natural replacement and regeneration

thirdspace: a combination of both quantitative and qualitative data for a place

throughflow (or interflow): water moving through the rocks beneath the soil at a very slow rate

tidal range: the vertical difference in height of sea level between high and low tide; it varies with the monthly lunar cycle and is at its maximum with spring tide conditions

tillage: land used for cultivation

time–space convergence: the time it takes to travel between places is getting shorter, so distant places are brought closer together in terms of the time taken to travel (and send messages) between them

topography: the shape of the land

topophibia: a fear or dread of certain places

topophilia: a strong sense of place or love of particular places

trade flows: movements of goods, services or resources across boundaries, involving exports from one place and imports to another

trading bloc: a group of countries who agree a range of measures to facilitate trade between themselves

transboundary rivers: rivers that extend either side of at least one political boundary, either a border within a nation or an international boundary

transit countries: countries where migrants stop temporarily on their way from host to source country

translatory wave: a breaking wave in which the circular motion is broken by basal friction

transnational corporations (TNCs): large companies that operate across national boundaries

transpiration: the process by which plants lose water through stomata (pores) in their leaves into the atmosphere

trophic level: the level at which energy, in the form of food, is transferred from one group to another (e.g. from plants to herbivores in a food chain, sometimes called a feeding level)

tsunami: a large wave triggered by seismic activity

tundra: the word means 'barren land'; located in arctic or alpine regions where no trees grow because of severe environmental conditions

turbidity: the cloudiness of a fluid caused by large numbers of suspended particles

unconsolidated sediment: loosely arranged particles of sediment that are not joined together

under-nutrition: consuming too little food, leading to loss of body weight

unemployed population: those not in employment but actively seeking and available for work

urban and peri-urban horticulture (UPH): subsistence farming that takes place on small plots of land within and around the edge of cities

urban canyon winds: wind created by narrow urban streets and high office blocks funneling the wind between them

urban heat island (UHI) effect: the increased temperature in urban areas compared to surrounding rural areas

urbanisation: the growth in the proportion of a country's population that live in an urban environment compared to a rural environment

urban resurgence: the development of an area after a period of decline

urban–rural continuum: the range of settlement types from extremely urban to extremely rural

virga: wisps, streaks or shafts of precipitation that fall from clouds but evaporate before they reach the ground

viticulture: the cultivation of grapevines for wine-making

Volcanic Explosivity Index (VEI): an index that measures the explosivity of volcanic eruptions; volcanoes with a VEI of 0–1 are effusive, while Plinian eruptions tend to have a VEI of between 4 and 6; there have been 42 eruptions of VEI 8 or above in the last 36 million years, including the eruption of Yellowstone in 640 000 BCE

virtual water: the water volume involved in the full production process of a commodity or manufacture destined for export, representing water lost to the origin of the item

walkable urbanism: an urban design movement which encourages planners to design urban spaces that encourage walking and exploring

water budget: the overall balance of inputs and outputs in a drainage basin over time

water footprint: an indicator of the volume of freshwater involved in producing goods and services at any scale from the individual, the community, a business or a nation. It includes the totality of water used plus contamination of related water supplies

water scarcity: the lack of suffiient freshwater of an acceptable quality for the human needs of a region; it has degrees of severity ranging through water stress, water scarcity and, ultimately, water crisis

watershed: the edge of a drainage basin

water stress: the first level of water scarcity, when available water supplies fall below $1700\,m^3$ per person per year; below $1000\,m^3$ per year, it becomes 'water scarcity' and less than $500\,m^3$ per year it is 'absolute scarcity'

water table: the level of the top of the saturated soil beneath the ground

wave-cut notch: a horizontal indentation at the base of cliffs where wave action is most focused and erosional processes are concentrated; it results in the undercutting of cliffs

wave refraction: the changes in wave orientation and frequency as they encounter a non-uniform coastline; waves may be refracted (bent) towards a feature (convergence) or away (divergence) as water depth varies

weathering: the disintegration of rock in situ

world city: a city that acts as a major hub or centre for finance, trade, business, politics, culture, serving not just the country or region but the world

xerophytic: characteristic of plants which can cope with low levels of water availability and high temperatures

zero-sum game: when an initiative benefits one group, but at the expense of another

zonal soils: the global soil types

zooplankton: the 'animal' form of plankton that can be found at a range of depths and feeds on phytoplankton and its remains

Index

Acknowledgements

The authors and publishers acknowledge the following sources of copyright material and are grateful for the permissions granted. While every effort has been made, it has not always been possible to identify the sources of all the material used, or to trace all copyright holders. If any omissions are brought to our notice, we will be happy to include the appropriate acknowledgements on reprinting.

Text

Extract on page 63 from © Holkham Estate; Extract on page 203 adapted from Market Business News, 31 October 2015; Extract on page 313 Table 7.7 from Murray, W. and Overton, J., 2006. *Geographies of globalization*, London, UK. Routledge, Table 2.1, p. 41. 1st ED ISBN 978 0415 318006 and 2nd ED ISBN 978 0415 567626; Extract on page 399 Table 9.9 Reproduced by kind permission of The Economist Intelligence Unit Limited; Extract on page 400 Table 9.10 Reproduced by kind permission of The Economist Intelligence Unit Limited; Extract on page 440 Table 10.7 from *Green Spaces: Benefits for London* by BOP Consulting, © City of London Corporation; Quote on page 441 from http://www.bost.org.uk/; Extract on page 410 Table 10.3 from the Food and Agriculture Organization of the United Nations, 2002, Joint WHO/FAO Expert Consultation on Diet, Nutrition and the Prevention of Chronic Diseases, World agriculture: towards 2015/2030. Summary report., http://www.fao.org/docrep/004/Y3557E/y3557e00.htm#TopOfPage. Reproduced with permission; Extract on page 432 Table 10.5, reprinted from WHO Media Centre, News Release (16 June 2006), "Almost a quarter of all disease caused by environmental exposure"; Extract on page 462 Table 10.11 from United Nations, Department of Economic and Social Affairs, Population Division (2015). World Population Prospects: The 2015 Revision, Key Findings and Advance Tables. Working Paper No. ESA/P/WP.241; Extract on page 464 Table 10.12 United Nations, Department of Economic and Social Affairs, Population Division (2015). World Population Prospects: The 2015 Revision, Key Findings and Advance Tables. Working Paper No. ESA/P/WP.241.

Images

Fig. 1.1 © VitalyEdush/Thinkstock; Fig. 1.2 Igor Shildermanov's chapter "World fresh water resources" in Peter H. Gleck (editor) 1993, Water in Crisis: A Guide to the World's fresh Water Resources. (Numbers are rounded); Fig. 1.4 © Woods Hole Oceanographic Institution; Fig. 1.8 © Construction Photography/Alamy Stock Photo; Fig. 1.9 © Image Source/Alamy Stock Photo; Fig 1.12 imageBROKER/Alamy Stock Photo; Fig. 1.13 From data generated by the following studies http://www.nature.com/nature/journal/v453/n7193/full/nature06949.html http://science.sciencemag.org/content/317/5839/793; Fig 1.14. © Stocktrek Images, Inc./Alamy Stock Photo; Fig. 1.16 © Vaara/iStockphoto; Fig. 1.17 © Bettmann/Contributor/Getty Images; Fig 1.19 © Dhoxax/iStockphoto; Fig. 1.22 © Morley Read/Alamy Stock Photo; Fig. 1.24 © Scenics and Science/Getty Images; Fig. 1.27 © Mark Boulton/Alamy Stock Photo; Fig. 1.31 © Martin Shields/Alamy Stock Photo; Fig. 1.33 © Photo_Concepts/iStockphoto; Fig. 1.34 © Alan Parkinson; Fig. 2.1 © theskaman306/Shutterstock; Fig. 2.5 © Victor Englebert/Science Photo Library; Fig. 2.6 © Mlenny/iStockphoto; Fig. 2.9 © Timothy Messick/iStockphoto; Fig. 2.10 © imageBROKER /imageBROKER/SuperStock: Fig. 2.11 © Planet Observer/Getty Images; Fig. 2.12 © belfasteileen/Thinkstock; Fig. 2.13 © Travel Pictures / Alamy Stock Photo; Fig. 2.14 © Mlenny/iStockphoto; Fig. 2.18 © STR/Stringer/Getty Images; 2.19 © STR/Stringer/Getty Images; Fig. 2.20 © Pavliha/iStockphoto; Fig. 2.21 © KamilloK/iStockphoto; Fig. 2.22 © Simon Hathaway; Fig. 2.24 © Lucky-photographer/Shutterstock; Fig. 2.25 © Simon Hathaway; Fig 2.26 © Sonja_bkm/iStockphoto; Fig. 2.26 © Alan Parkinson; Fig. 3.1 © keithmorris news/Alamy Stock Photo; Fig. 3.2 © Pichugin Dmitry/Shutterstock; Fig. 3.7 © Andy Day; Fig. 3.11 © Andy Day; Fig. 3.12 © Andy Day; Fig. 3.15 © Eye Ubiquitous/Alamy Stock Photo; Fig. 3.20 © Andy Day; Fig. 3.23 © Josh McCulloch/All Canada Photos/Alamy Stock Photo; Fig. 3.25 © Dan Burton Photo/Alamy Stock Photo; Fig. 3.26 © Jack Sullivan/Alamy Stock Photo; Fig. 3.27 © Marli Miller/Visuals Unlimited, Inc./Getty Images; Fig. 3.32 © Colin Weston/Getty Images; Fig. 3.33 © Dan Burton /robertharding/SuperStock; Fig. 3.34 © Lumi Images/Romulic-Stojcic/Getty Images; Fig. 3.35 © pjmalsbury/iStockphoto; Fig. 3.39 © Andy Day; Fig. 3.40 Fig. 3.41This work was produced by the Center for Remote Sensing of Ice Sheets (CReSIS) with funding provided by the U.S. National Science Foundation (Project ANT-0424589); ©keithmorris news/Alamy Stock Photo; Fig. 3.43 © John Eccles/Alamy Stock Photo; Fig. 3.44 © Michael Reinhard/Getty Images; Fig. 3.45 © chillingworths/iStockphoto; Fig. 3.50 incamerastock/Alamy Stock Photo; Fig. 3.51 © University of Cambridge Collection of Air Photographs/Science Photo Library; Fig. 3.54 © Eco Images/Getty Images; Fig. 3.55 © David Weyand/imageBROKER/Alamy Stock Photo; 3.56 © drpnncpp/iStockphoto; Fig. 4.1 © © Daniel Prudek/Shutterstock; Fig. 4.5 © Mlenny/iStockphoto; Fig. 4.6 © robertharding/Alamy Stock Photo; Fig. 4.13; Fig. 4.15 © robertharrison/Alamy Stock Photo; Fig. 4.16 © Grasstrax/Alamy Stock Photo; Fig. 4.18 © Bob-McCraight/Thinkstock; Fig. 4.19 © Chris Craggs/Alamy Stock Photo; Fig. 4.22 © Robert_Ford/Thinkstock; Fig. 4.24 © jarcosa/Getty Images; Fig. 4.25 Image Copyright Ron Thomson. This work is licensed under the Creative Commons Attribution-Share Alike 2.0 Generic Licence. To view a copy of this licence, visit http://creativecommons.org/licenses/by-sa/2.0/ or send a letter to Creative Commons, 171 Second Street, Suite 300, San Francisco, California, 94105, USA; Fig. 4.26 mage Copyright Ian Capper. This work is licensed under the Creative Commons Attribution-Share Alike 2.0 Generic Licence. To view a copy of this licence, visit http://creativecommons.org/licenses/by-sa/2.0/ or send a letter to Creative Commons, 171 Second Street, Suite 300, San Francisco, California, 94105, USA; Fig. 4.30 © Sebastian Wasek/Alamy Stock Photo; Fig. 4.31 Used with permission and courtesy of the Northern Alaska Environmental Center, Fairbanks, Alaska; Fig. 4.32 © Paul Davey/Alamy Stock Photo; Fig. 4.33 © YvaMomatiuk/John Eastcott/Getty Images; Fig. 4.35a© Bygone Collection/Alamy Stock Photo; Fig. 4.35b © John Bentley/Alamy Stock Photo; Fig. 4.36 © GertjanHooijer/Shutterstock; Fig. 4.37a © Alfonso de Tomas/Alamy Stock Photo; Fig. 4.37b ; Fig. © Roberto Cornacchia/Alamy Stock Photo4.37c © leaf/iStockphoto; Fig. 4.38 © EvgenySergeev/

Fig. 9.17 © wlablack/Shutterstock; Fig. 9.18 © dade72/ Shutterstock; Fig. 9.21 © Huw Jones/Getty Images; Fig. 9.23 © Arup/UK Space Agency; Fig. 9.24 Reproduced with permission from City of London Corporation, designed by Bonfire Creative Intelligence; Fig. 9.26 © Sean Gallagher/Getty Images; Fig. 9.27 © Bloomberg/Contributor/Getty Images; Fig. © 9.28 Zhang et al (2014). Historic and future trends of vehicle emissions in Beijing, 1998–2020: a policy assessment for the most stringent vehicle emission control program in china. atmospheric environment, 89, 216–29; Fig. 9.31 © By JJ Harrison (jjharrison89@facebook.com) (Own work) [CC BY-SA 3.0 (http:// creativecommons.org/licenses/by-sa/3.0)], via Wikimedia Commons; Fig. 9.33 © wda cache/Alamy Stock Photo; Fig. 9.34 © Glyn Baker [CC BY-SA 2.0 (http://creativecommons.org/ licenses/by-sa/2.0)], via Wikimedia Commons; Fig. 9.36 © Andrey Bayda/Shutterstock; Fig. 9.37 © 2014 WWF. All rights reserved. WWF. 2014. Living Planet Report 2014: species and spaces, people and places. [McLellan, R., Iyengar, L., Jeffries, B. and N. Oerlemans (Eds)]. WWF, Gland, Switzerland; Fig. 9.39 © Ashley Cooper/Visuals Unlimited, Inc./Getty Images; Fig. 10.1 © Byelikova_Oksana/Shutterstock; Fig. 10.2 © TukaramKarve/ Shutterstock; Fig. 10.4 © i-Stockr/iStockphoto; Fig. 10.6 © HildaWeges Photography/Shutterstock; Fig. 10.7 © McGraw-Hill Education; Fig. 10.9 © Gil.K/Shutterstock; Fig. 10.11 © Zack Frank/Shutterstock; Fig. 10.12 © National Oceanic and Atmospheric Administration (NOAA); Fig. 10.14 © FAO 2001, Lecture notes on the Major Soils of the World, Set #6, http:// www.fao.org/docrep/003/y1899e/y1899e08a.htm#TopOfPage. This is an adaptation of an original work by FAO. Views and opinions expressed in the adaptation are the sole responsibility of the author or authors of the adaptation and are not endorsed by FAO.; Fig. 10.17 © Yuri Kravchenko/Shutterstock; Fig. 10.18 © gopixgo/Shutterstock; Fig. 10.19 © sharps/Shutterstock; Fig. 10.20 Reprinted from Health Statistics and Information Systems (HSI), World Health Organization, Copyright 2014. http://gamapserver.who.int/mapLibrary/Files/Maps/Global_ HALE_BothSexes_2012.png; Fig. 10.21 Reprinted from Health Statistics and Information Systems (HSI), World Health Organization, Copyright 2014. http://gamapserver.who.int/ mapLibrary/Files/Maps/Global_GHE_Dalys_2012.png; Fig. 10.22 Reprinted from Health Statistics and Information Systems (HSI), World Health Organization, Copyright 2014. http://gamapserver.who.int/mapLibrary/Files/Maps/Global_ NCD_deaths_2012.png; Fig. 10.24 The World Factbook 2013–14. Washington, DC: Central Intelligence Agency, 2013. https://www.cia.gov/library/publications/the-world-factbook/ index.html; Fig. 10.25 The World Factbook 2013–14. Washington, DC: Central Intelligence Agency, 2013. https:// www.cia.gov/library/publications/the-world-factbook/index.html; Fig. 10.28 © Sandra van der Steen/Shutterstock; Fig. 10.29 Credit: Cancer Research UK, http://www.cancerresearchuk.org/ health-professional/cancer-statistics/worldwide-cancer/ incidence#heading-Zero, Accessed May 2016. Statistics from Ferlay J, Soerjomataram I, Ervik M, Dikshit R, Eser S, Mathers C, Rebelo M, Parkin DM, Forman D, Bray, F. GLOBOCAN 2012 v1.0, Cancer Incidence and Mortality Worldwide: IARC CancerBase No. 11 [Internet]. Lyon, France: International Agency for Research on Cancer; 2013. Available from: http:// globocan.iarc.fr, accessed on 11 May 2016; Fig. 10.30 © ssuaphotos/Shutterstock; Fig. 10.35 © giulionapolitano/ Shutterstock; Fig. 10.36 © Monkey Business Images/ Shutterstock; Fig. 10.37 Reproduced with permission of the International Displacement Monitoring Centre (IDMC); Fig. 10.41 © Dietmar Temps/Shutterstock; Fig. 10.42 © Avatar_023/Shutterstock; Fig. 10.44 © 2016 Global Footprint Network. www.footprintnetwork.org; Fig. 10.45 © 2016 Global Footprint Network. www.footprintnetwork.org; Fig. 10.47 © TonyV3112/Shutterstock; Fig. 10.48 © Filipe Frazao/ Shutterstock; Fig. 10.49 © ARZTSAMUI/Shutterstock; Fig. 10.50 United Nations, Department of Economic and Social Affairs, Population Division (2015). World Population Prospects: The 2015 Revision, Key Findings and Advance Tables. Working Paper No. ESA/P/WP.241; Fig. 10.63 Reprinted from "Malawi: WHO statistical profile", Country statistics and global health estimates by WHO and UN partners, Graph showing Burden of disease, Page 3, Copyright January 2015; Fig. 11.1 © A Katz/ Shutterstock; Fig. 11.2 © Alexey Repka/Shutterstock; Fig. 11.3 © Bettmann/Contributor/Getty Images; Fig. 11.6 © Steve Morgan/Alamy Stock Photo; Fig. 11.8 © Moises Fernandez Acosta/Shutterstock; Fig. 11.9 © OECD/IEA 2014 World Energy Outlook: Presentation to London, 12 November 2014, IEA Publishing. Licence: www.iea.org/t&c/termsandconditions; Fig. 11.10 © The World Energy Council, London, UK; Fig. 11.11 © gemenacom/iStockphoto; Fig. 11.15 © Stephane Jaquemet/ Alamy Stock Photo; Fig. 11.16 © Jakub Sukup/Getty Images; Fig. 11.19 © ChinaFotoPress/Getty Images; Fig. 11.20 © Jake Lyell/Alamy Stock Photo; Fig. 11.23 © National Geographic Creative/Alamy Stock Photo; Fig. 11.24 Source: The California Department of Water Resources; Fig. 11.25 © Vanzyst/ Shutterstock; Fig. 11.27 © The India Today Group/Getty Images; Fig. 11.29 © 2008, United Nations Environment Programme; Fig. 11.30 © Alain Lauga/Shutterstock; Fig. 11.31 © PUB, Singapore's national water agency; Fig. 11.32 © Steven Frame/Alamy Stock Photo; Fig. 11.33 © NASA/Science Photo Library; Fig. 11.34 © pandapaw/Shutterstock; Fig. 11.35 Photo credit: IDE Technologies; Fig. 11.36 © Copyright Aqua2use®: "The Answer for Greywater Reuse"; Fig. 11.37 © TortoonThodsapol/Shutterstock; Fig. 11.40 © epa european pressphoto agency b.v./Alamy Stock Photo; Fig. 11.41 Source: ODYSSEE-MURE project; Fig. 11.43 © Ruth Peterkin/ Shutterstock; Fig. 11.45 © EdStock/iStockphoto; Fig. 11.46 © Ian Dagnall/Alamy Stock Photo; Fig. 11.47 Source: BP Annual Report and Accounts 2014; Fig. 11.48 © US Coast Guard Photo/ Alamy Stock Photo; Fig. 11.50 © LIONEL HEALING/AFP/Getty Images; Fig. 11.52 © Lutique/Thinkstock; Fig. 11.55 © The Crown Estate 2016; Fig. 11.57 © Veolia; Fig. 11.59 © AgencjaFotograficzna Caro/Alamy Stock Photo; Fig. 11.60 © Vaara/iStockphoto; Fig. 11.62 © Scripps Institution of Oceanography, UC San Diego; Fig. 11.65 as featured in CIM Magazine, August 2011; Fig. 11.67 © bohemia8/iStockphoto; Fig. 11.69 © Universal Images Group/Getty Images; Fig. 11.71 © Lloyd Sutton/Alamy Stock Photo; Fig. 11.72 Reproduced with permission from Tidal Lagoon Swansea Bay Plc; Fig. 11.75 © David McHugh/REX Shutterstock; Fig. 11.79 © Mighty River Power; Fig. 12.1 © Radharc Images/Alamy Stock Photo; Fig. 12.4 © George Green/Shutterstock; Fig. 13.1 © omersukrugoksu/Getty Images; Fig. 13.8 © Map Resources/ Shutterstock.